Lecture Notes in Computer Science   10912

Commenced Publication in 1973
Founding and Former Series Editors:
Gerhard Goos, Juris Hartmanis, and Jan van Leeuwen

More information about this series at http://www.springer.com/series/7409

Pei-Luen Patrick Rau (Ed.)

Cross-Cultural Design

Applications in Cultural Heritage, Creativity and Social Development

10th International Conference, CCD 2018
Held as Part of HCI International 2018
Las Vegas, NV, USA, July 15–20, 2018
Proceedings, Part II

 Springer

Editor
Pei-Luen Patrick Rau
Tsinghua University
Beijing
China

ISSN 0302-9743   ISSN 1611-3349   (electronic)
Lecture Notes in Computer Science
ISBN 978-3-319-92251-5   ISBN 978-3-319-92252-2   (eBook)
https://doi.org/10.1007/978-3-319-92252-2

Library of Congress Control Number: 2018944396

LNCS Sublibrary: SL3 – Information Systems and Applications, incl. Internet/Web, and HCI

Printed on acid-free paper

This Springer imprint is published by the registered company Springer International Publishing AG
part of Springer Nature
The registered company address is: Gewerbestrasse 11, 6330 Cham, Switzerland

Foreword

The 20th International Conference on Human-Computer Interaction, HCI International 2018, was held in Las Vegas, NV, USA, during July 15–20, 2018. The event incorporated the 14 conferences/thematic areas listed on the following page.

A total of 4,373 individuals from academia, research institutes, industry, and governmental agencies from 76 countries submitted contributions, and 1,170 papers and 195 posters have been included in the proceedings. These contributions address the latest research and development efforts and highlight the human aspects of design and use of computing systems. The contributions thoroughly cover the entire field of human-computer interaction, addressing major advances in knowledge and effective use of computers in a variety of application areas. The volumes constituting the full set of the conference proceedings are listed in the following pages.

I would like to thank the program board chairs and the members of the program boards of all thematic areas and affiliated conferences for their contribution to the highest scientific quality and the overall success of the HCI International 2018 conference.

This conference would not have been possible without the continuous and unwavering support and advice of the founder, Conference General Chair Emeritus and Conference Scientific Advisor Prof. Gavriel Salvendy. For his outstanding efforts, I would like to express my appreciation to the communications chair and editor of *HCI International News*, Dr. Abbas Moallem.

July 2018   Constantine Stephanidis

HCI International 2018 Thematic Areas and Affiliated Conferences

Thematic areas:

- Human-Computer Interaction (HCI 2018)
- Human Interface and the Management of Information (HIMI 2018)

Affiliated conferences:

- 15th International Conference on Engineering Psychology and Cognitive Ergonomics (EPCE 2018)
- 12th International Conference on Universal Access in Human-Computer Interaction (UAHCI 2018)
- 10th International Conference on Virtual, Augmented, and Mixed Reality (VAMR 2018)
- 10th International Conference on Cross-Cultural Design (CCD 2018)
- 10th International Conference on Social Computing and Social Media (SCSM 2018)
- 12th International Conference on Augmented Cognition (AC 2018)
- 9th International Conference on Digital Human Modeling and Applications in Health, Safety, Ergonomics, and Risk Management (DHM 2018)
- 7th International Conference on Design, User Experience, and Usability (DUXU 2018)
- 6th International Conference on Distributed, Ambient, and Pervasive Interactions (DAPI 2018)
- 5th International Conference on HCI in Business, Government, and Organizations (HCIBGO)
- 5th International Conference on Learning and Collaboration Technologies (LCT 2018)
- 4th International Conference on Human Aspects of IT for the Aged Population (ITAP 2018)

Conference Proceedings Volumes Full List

1. LNCS 10901, Human-Computer Interaction: Theories, Methods, and Human Issues (Part I), edited by Masaaki Kurosu
2. LNCS 10902, Human-Computer Interaction: Interaction in Context (Part II), edited by Masaaki Kurosu
3. LNCS 10903, Human-Computer Interaction: Interaction Technologies (Part III), edited by Masaaki Kurosu
4. LNCS 10904, Human Interface and the Management of Information: Interaction, Visualization, and Analytics (Part I), edited by Sakae Yamamoto and Hirohiko Mori
5. LNCS 10905, Human Interface and the Management of Information: Information in Applications and Services (Part II), edited by Sakae Yamamoto and Hirohiko Mori
6. LNAI 10906, Engineering Psychology and Cognitive Ergonomics, edited by Don Harris
7. LNCS 10907, Universal Access in Human-Computer Interaction: Methods, Technologies, and Users (Part I), edited by Margherita Antona and Constantine Stephanidis
8. LNCS 10908, Universal Access in Human-Computer Interaction: Virtual, Augmented, and Intelligent Environments (Part II), edited by Margherita Antona and Constantine Stephanidis
9. LNCS 10909, Virtual, Augmented and Mixed Reality: Interaction, Navigation, Visualization, Embodiment, and Simulation (Part I), edited by Jessie Y. C. Chen and Gino Fragomeni
10. LNCS 10910, Virtual, Augmented and Mixed Reality: Applications in Health, Cultural Heritage, and Industry (Part II), edited by Jessie Y. C. Chen and Gino Fragomeni
11. LNCS 10911, Cross-Cultural Design: Methods, Tools, and Users (Part I), edited by Pei-Luen Patrick Rau
12. LNCS 10912, Cross-Cultural Design: Applications in Cultural Heritage, Creativity, and Social Development (Part II), edited by Pei-Luen Patrick Rau
13. LNCS 10913, Social Computing and Social Media: User Experience and Behavior (Part I), edited by Gabriele Meiselwitz
14. LNCS 10914, Social Computing and Social Media: Technologies and Analytics (Part II), edited by Gabriele Meiselwitz
15. LNAI 10915, Augmented Cognition: Intelligent Technologies (Part I), edited by Dylan D. Schmorrow and Cali M. Fidopiastis
16. LNAI 10916, Augmented Cognition: Users and Contexts (Part II), edited by Dylan D. Schmorrow and Cali M. Fidopiastis
17. LNCS 10917, Digital Human Modeling and Applications in Health, Safety, Ergonomics, and Risk Management, edited by Vincent G. Duffy
18. LNCS 10918, Design, User Experience, and Usability: Theory and Practice (Part I), edited by Aaron Marcus and Wentao Wang

19. LNCS 10919, Design, User Experience, and Usability: Designing Interactions (Part II), edited by Aaron Marcus and Wentao Wang
20. LNCS 10920, Design, User Experience, and Usability: Users, Contexts, and Case Studies (Part III), edited by Aaron Marcus and Wentao Wang
21. LNCS 10921, Distributed, Ambient, and Pervasive Interactions: Understanding Humans (Part I), edited by Norbert Streitz and Shin'ichi Konomi
22. LNCS 10922, Distributed, Ambient, and Pervasive Interactions: Technologies and Contexts (Part II), edited by Norbert Streitz and Shin'ichi Konomi
23. LNCS 10923, HCI in Business, Government, and Organizations, edited by Fiona Fui-Hoon Nah and Bo Sophia Xiao
24. LNCS 10924, Learning and Collaboration Technologies: Design, Development and Technological Innovation (Part I), edited by Panayiotis Zaphiris and Andri Ioannou
25. LNCS 10925, Learning and Collaboration Technologies: Learning and Teaching (Part II), edited by Panayiotis Zaphiris and Andri Ioannou
26. LNCS 10926, Human Aspects of IT for the Aged Population: Acceptance, Communication, and Participation (Part I), edited by Jia Zhou and Gavriel Salvendy
27. LNCS 10927, Human Aspects of IT for the Aged Population: Applications in Health, Assistance, and Entertainment (Part II), edited by Jia Zhou and Gavriel Salvendy
28. CCIS 850, HCI International 2018 Posters Extended Abstracts (Part I), edited by Constantine Stephanidis
29. CCIS 851, HCI International 2018 Posters Extended Abstracts (Part II), edited by Constantine Stephanidis
30. CCIS 852, HCI International 2018 Posters Extended Abstracts (Part III), edited by Constantine Stephanidis

http://2018.hci.international/proceedings

10th International Conference on Cross-Cultural Design

Program Board Chair(s): Pei-Luen Patrick Rau, *P.R. China*

- Na Chen, P.R. China
- Zhe Chen, P.R. China
- Kuohsiang Chen, Taiwan
- Zhiyong Fu, P.R. China
- Toshikazu Kato, Japan
- Sheau-Farn Max Liang, Taiwan
- Dyi-Yih Michael Lin, Taiwan
- Juifeng Lin, Taiwan
- Rungtai Lin, Taiwan
- Cheng-Hung Lo, P.R. China
- Yongqi Lou, P.R. China
- Liang Ma, P.R. China
- Alexander Mädche, Germany
- Katsuhiko Ogawa, Japan
- Chun-Yi (Danny) Shen, Taiwan
- Hao Tan, P.R. China
- P.L. Teh, Malaysia
- Yuan-Chi Tseng, Taiwan
- Lin Wang, South Korea
- Hsiu-Ping Yueh, Taiwan

The full list with the Program Board Chairs and the members of the Program Boards of all thematic areas and affiliated conferences is available online at:

http://www.hci.international/board-members-2018.php

HCI International 2019

The 21st International Conference on Human-Computer Interaction, HCI International 2019, will be held jointly with the affiliated conferences in Orlando, FL, USA, at Walt Disney World Swan and Dolphin Resort, July 26–31, 2019. It will cover a broad spectrum of themes related to Human-Computer Interaction, including theoretical issues, methods, tools, processes, and case studies in HCI design, as well as novel interaction techniques, interfaces, and applications. The proceedings will be published by Springer. More information will be available on the conference website: http://2019.hci.international/.

General Chair
Prof. Constantine Stephanidis
University of Crete and ICS-FORTH
Heraklion, Crete, Greece
E-mail: general_chair@hcii2019.org

http://2019.hci.international/

Contents – Part II

Culture and Creativity

Cross-Cultural Design for Social Change and Development

Contents – Part I

Cultural Differences

Culture, Learning and Games

Assessing the Effectiveness of an Augmented Reality Application for the Literacy Development of Arabic Children with Hearing Impairments

Shiroq Al-Megren[✉] and Aziza Almutairi

Information Technology Department, King Saud University,
Riyadh 12371, Saudi Arabia
salmegren@ksu.edu.sa, aziza.m.m@hotmail.com

Abstract. Word and Sign is a mobile AR application that was developed to support the literacy development of Arabic children who are deaf or hard of hearing. The utilization of AR is intended to support reading, particularly the process of mapping a printed word to its corresponding ArSL. In this paper, the performances of elementary grade children who are deaf or hard of hearing are assessed after they are taught thirteen new words using two methods: AR using Word and Sign and a traditional teaching approach using ArSL, fingerspelling and pictures. The assessment is conducted as a series of tasks in which participants are asked to associate a printed word with its corresponding picture and ArSL. The findings show that participants who were taught via the AR application completed significantly more tasks successfully and with significantly fewer errors compared to participants who were taught the new words via a traditional approach. These findings encourage the utilization of AR inside and outside the classroom to support the literacy development of children with hearing impairments.

Keywords: Augmented reality (AR) · Deaf · Hard of hearing
Mobile augmented reality · Reading · Literacy

1 Introduction

Recent statistics from the General Authority for Statistics in Saudi Arabia reported that approximately 3% of the population was registered as being hearing impaired in 2017 [17]. This segment of the population shares a common native language, i.e., Arabic sign language (ArSL), with Arabic (the official language in Saudi Arabia) being considered a second language. The prevalence of hearing disabilities varies geographically in Saudi Arabia, with almost two thirds of the people with hearing disabilities found residing in rural areas [4]. A study carried out in Saudi Arabia before 2010 showed that a majority of people with disabilities did not have access to psychological and educational services from an

© Springer International Publishing AG, part of Springer Nature 2018
P.-L. P. Rau (Ed.): CCD 2018, LNCS 10912, pp. 3–18, 2018.
https://doi.org/10.1007/978-3-319-92252-2_1

early age. This isolation resulted in below-average literacy skills when entering schools, hence negatively impacting academic progression and achievements [13].

Children are exposed to language early in their development, which leads to the acquisition of the literacy skills necessary for their growth [9]. As a child learns to read, language familiarity is one of the two factors that impact reading. The other factor is the process of cognitively mapping printed text into a familiar language, i.e., decoding, by recognizing the patterns that make letters and words [12,27]. While children who can hear grow familiar with spoken language, children who are deaf are disadvantaged by a limited or non-existent exposure to language at a young age. This late acquisition of language delays the development of literacy skills, which greatly impacts educational, social, and vocational development [22].

Augmented reality (AR) is a user interface paradigm that involves the direct superimposition of virtual objects onto a real environment. This supports the primacy of the physical world while still supplementing the user experience and enhancing the interaction with virtual components. AR was principally introduced in 1993 [28] and has since rapidly expanded, considering the technological advances of the past few decades and the continuously growing amount of information exposed to the user. AR supports users' actions within the current context as they navigate a new enhanced reality using reality sensors [18]. In recent years, mobile or phone-based AR systems have become more prevalent, as they layer information onto any environment without constraining users' locations [24]. Mobile AR has the potential to support users' interactions with a plethora of computer-supported information without distracting them from the real world [10].

The value of AR as an educational tool has increasingly been recognized by researchers, as the enhanced reality can allow for the visualization of abstract concepts, the experience of phenomena, and interaction with computer-supported synthetic objects [29]. The benefits of AR adoption for educational purposes, i.e., increased motivation, attention, concentration, and satisfaction, have regularly been documented [11]. AR has also been found to support active and collaborative learning, interactivity, and information accessibility, which encourage exploration. The value of AR as an educational tool has also been revealed in various studies considering children with varied disabilities, such as autism [8,20,25], intellectual deficiency [25], and hearing impairment [23].

Current teaching techniques in Saudi Arabian schools rely heavily on sound-based approaches that disadvantage the literacy development of students who are hearing impaired. To address this issue, Word and Sign, a mobile AR application, was developed to support the reading comprehension and literacy of Arabic children who are deaf. In this paper, this AR application is evaluated via a comparative user study. The purpose of the study is to determine the effectiveness of the mobile AR application at supporting the acquisition of new printed vocabulary and the necessary decoding onto their visual representations. The results show that the use of AR has the potential to support the decoding process and thus improve the reading comprehension and literacy of Arabic children who are hearing impaired.

The remainder of this paper is organized as follows. Section 2 reviews existing works that adopted AR for the educational development of individuals who are hearing impaired. The section particularly considers children's literacy development and reading comprehension. Next, in Sect. 3, a mobile AR application that supports the decoding of printed Arabic vocabulary from fingerspelling and ArSL, i.e., Word and Sign, is briefly described. The experimental setup and procedure for evaluating Word and Sign are presented in Sect. 4. This section also reports the results of the experiment. These results are then discussed in Sect. 5. Finally, Sect. 6 summarizes and concludes the paper. It also briefly discusses future work.

2   Related Work

Several research efforts have been devoted towards supporting the educational development of children who have hearing impairments. This section reviews a variety of AR applications (mobile and otherwise) that aim to advance the educational progress of hearing-impaired children in various subject areas, including science, religion, reading comprehension and literacy. The review also considers AR applications developed for various sign languages, such as Malaysian, Arabic, American, and Slovenian sign languages.

A sign language teaching model (SLTM) was proposed to support preschool and primary education for children who are deaf [5, 6]. The proposed model, i.e., multi-language cycle for sign language understanding (MuCy), was developed to improve the communication skills of children who are deaf by utilizing AR as a complementary tool for teaching sign language. The MuCy model is a continuous psycho-motor cycle with two levels of education. The first level addresses the learning of the correct use of a sign in conjunction with their visual and written representations. The second level verbalizes these words via imitation of face, mouth, and tongue movements. The model utilizes a sign language book and an AR desktop application. Two pilot lessons involving four children were carried out using the MuCy model, and additional feedback was collected from parents and teachers. Data were collected via observation of the children and interviews with parents and teachers. The findings showed that the model can easily be adapted by teachers and can improve sign language communication skills in children who are deaf.

A mobile AR application was developed to augment pictures that represent word signs performed by an interpreter with sign language interpretation videos that are played on a mobile phone [19]. The application is intended for signers who are deaf or hard of hearing and also those interested in learning Slovenian sign language. A comparative user study was conducted to evaluate the efficiency of using AR when learning sign language and users? perception of augmented content. The study compared the success rate of signing words when using (a) a picture, (b) the mobile AR application, and (c) a physically present sign language interpreter. The study recruited 25 participants with a mean age of approximately 30 years old, 11 of which were deaf or hard of hearing and 14 of which were hearing non-signers. The results from a between-within subjects analysis showed a significant success rate when utilizing the AR application or an interpreter compared to using a picture. Of these two, the latter showed an increment in success rate of 9% compared to the AR application. The findings also showed that there was no significant difference between participants who are deaf or hard of hearing and hearing non-signers. These results suggest the potential of AR for learning sign language; nevertheless, the study did not objectively measure sign language skills prior to the study.

A communication board was developed to support the communication skills of children who are deaf as a means to supplement speech [7]. The communication board is based on the Fitzgerald Keys teaching method, which involves a linguistic code of visual representation that utilizes color codes in the form of questions in which a word sequence is put together. The proposed communication board was designed based on findings from an observational study involving children in secondary education who are deaf and do not have a grasp of the American sign language. In the study, five mobile applications that each function as a communication board and a newly developed application called Literacy with Fitzgerald were comparatively observed. The results revealed that the digital application can potentially produce more favorable results when allowing for interaction with a real environment. This led to the development of a physical communication board that consists of physical cards that correspond to virtual content of visual information via an augmented 3D model.

The visual needs of children who are deaf were elicited from a preliminary study that was conducted on three groups of respondents: education officers, teachers, and learners who are deaf [21]. The purpose of the study was to identify the visual needs that can support scientific acquisition when learning about science. The findings from the interview with the education officers highlight the lack of material that supports the science education of children who are deaf. Science teachers were similarly interviewed, and the results underline several difficulties faced by students who are deaf: difficulty understanding abstract concepts and a lack of visual materials. While observing three students who are deaf, several difficulties were identified as they attempted to recognize text compared to pictures, understand abstract concepts, and grasp complex words. These findings enabled the development of a Malaysian secondary (fifth year) science courseware, PekAR-Mikroorganisma, that utilizes AR in a web-based environment to augment a physical notebook with 3D objects [30]. The new system was heuristically evaluated by seven usability experts to identify design problems, who provided positive feedback highlighting the potential of AR in enhancing learning for science courseware.

Najeeb is a mobile AR application that was developed to educate children who are deaf or hard of hearing on religious traditions [3]. Prior to development, a review was conducted to explore current ArSL mobile AR applications and explore parameters that impact their effectiveness as educational tools. The review considered signing avatars, analyzing texts, and dictionaries. The findings signify the importance of using 3D imagery to allow for realistic and fluid movements between fingers and hands. Several of the reviewed applications support text analysis, which can provide assistance to individuals who either are deaf or can hear during the learning process. Due to their different functionalities, the applications maintained words that differ from one application to another. More importantly, the findings show an unavailability of educational resources for individuals who are deaf or hard of hearing. Najeeb is an educational Islamic tool that teaches basic tenets of Islam to children who are deaf or hard of hearing. The application uses images, video, and 3D animations to motivate and support the learning process. The design of Najeeb was grounded in a theoretical framework of the information processing theory that promotes engagement and learning in an e-learning environment. Tenets are presented in the application as multimode tutorials that take into account the presentation of information that can impact comprehension and memorization.

The use of Google glass as a head-mounted display for an AR application was proposed to improve the reading process of children who are deaf or hard of hearing [16]. Using the prototype, a child would point to a word in an augmented book to request its representative American sign language. The user's finger is detected by Google glass, which determines the word location above the fingertip, after which a blob detection algorithm is used to detect the edge of the image. Once the word boundaries are recognized the image is cropped and passed on to an optical character recognition algorithm, which converts the cropped image into text and finally to a corresponding sign video. Several limitations were identified when it comes to displaying the correct sign. The meaning of the word also varies based on its context; thus, the accuracy of the sign is affected when the word is extracted regardless of its contextual meaning.

The purpose of this review was to introduce several efforts made towards the adoption of AR with various sign languages to supplement and enhance communication and learning. The review focuses on AR applications that are intended for educating children or adults who are deaf or hard of hearing. The majority of the articles reviewed address the visual communication needs of individuals who are deaf or the development of supportive information. Nevertheless, only a few of these studies conducted user studies to assess their effectiveness as educational tools in real contextual settings. This underlines the value of this work's contribution, as evaluations were conducted in a class against a control group to asses the effectiveness of a mobile AR application for the literacy development of children who are deaf or hard of hearing.

3 Word and Sign

A series of user studies was previously conducted to elicit requirements that highlight the visual needs of children who are deaf or hard of hearing as they learn new printed Arabic vocabulary [2]. These needs were determined from various perspectives, i.e., teachers and interpreters, parents, and children who are deaf or hard of hearing, via interviews, surveys, and observations, respectively. The visual preferences determined based on the user studies are summarized and presented in Table 1.

Table 1. The visual needs of children who are deaf or hard of hearing as elicited from teachers and interpreters, parents, and children [2]. The order of preference is shown in the table.

Media	Interview	Survey	Observation
Picture	$\checkmark^2$	$\checkmark^1$	$\checkmark^2$
Video	$\checkmark^2$	$\checkmark^1$	$\checkmark^3$
Sign language	$\checkmark^1$	$\checkmark^2$	$\checkmark^4$
Fingerspelling	-	-	$\checkmark^1$

According to interviews conducted, teachers of children who are deaf or hard of hearing advocated for the use of sign language to represent printed text. They also recommended the use of pictures and/or videos to further supplement the mapping of printed text with its sign. Survey results collected from parents of children who are deaf revealed higher precedence for picture and videos than for sign language. Observations of first-grade elementary school children who are hard of hearing were made as they completed tasks that required linking printed text with pictures, videos, fingerspelling using signs of individual letters, and sign language. These findings showed that students performed the tasks best when mapping a printed text with fingerspelling. The observations showed that children's performances were better when the signer face and body were shown, i.e., not limited to showing the hands. Intriguingly, children also performed better when the interpreter was an actual person and not an avatar. The children fared the worst with sign language, which clearly indicates a weakness when decoding signs into printed text.

Fingerspelling has been utilized for reading by educators of children who are deaf and hard of hearing in a systematic way by using sequences called "chaining" and "sandwiching". Both techniques comprise a series of steps used to create links between signs, printed text, and fingerspelling. The chaining technique begins with the educator pointing to a printed word, followed by the fingerspelling of each of the letters in that word, and finally signing of the word. In sandwiching, the educator essentially 'sandwiches' the fingerspelling of a printed word with its corresponding sign, or vice versa. The utility of such techniques has previously been documented for American sign language [1,14,26]; however, this was not reported in the interviews, with no systematic technique reportedly being utilized when learning new vocabulary and reading [2].

These findings led to the development of Word and Sign, a mobile AR application for the literacy development of Arabic children who are deaf or hard of hearing. Unity and Vuforia were used to develop the application for Android smartphones. The application is supported by an electronic book that shows a series of Arabic words along with picture representations. These words were collected from the original first-grade courseware to support educators in the classroom, acting as a supplement to existing teaching methods. When a phone's camera detects a word, the picture is superimposed with a video depicting the

(a) The application's main functionalities: ArSL chaining or sandwiching video (middle), sound (right), and representative video (left).

(b) The application's settings options, from top to bottom: about, tutorial, e-book, and exit.

Fig. 1. Word and Sign mobile AR application.

word using either the chaining or sandwiching techniques. This is to guarantee that the text is always evident to encourage decoding. Due to the lack of video resources for ArSL, a female child interpreter aged 10 years old was video recorded. These videos are maintained in the video-based dictionary. A sound option is included to encourage the participation of hearing friends or family in learning ArSL. The user is also presented with a video option to display video representing the detected word. Figure 1 shows the Word and Sign application with the three main options: ArSL chaining or sandwiching video (middle), sound (right), and representative video (left). The figure also shows the settings menu, which provides access to the electronic book.

4   Assessing the Efficacy of Word and Sign

The efficacy of utilizing a mobile AR application for the literacy development of children who are deaf or hard of hearing was assessed by conducting a user experiment. The goal of the experiment was to comparatively assess the performance of children who are deaf when taught new vocabulary using the traditional method of teaching (control group) and with the aid of the mobile AR application. The experiment adopted a between-participants design. In the experiment, we studied the similarities and differences between these two groups as they completed a series of association tasks that link the new taught words with representative pictures and ArSL based on three measures: completion rate, number of errors, and time on task. Based on these measures, the following hypotheses are proposed:

– H1: Compared to the traditional method of learning new printed vocabulary, utilizing Word and Sign increases the completion rate and reduces the error rate in an association task between a new learned word and a representative picture or ArSL.
– H2: The time needed to complete the association tasks is reduced when the participants are taught the new word via Word and Sign compared to the traditional method.

4.1   Participants

Twenty participants who are deaf or hard of hearing were recruited from Al-Amal Institute (six students) and public elementary school 300 (fourteen students). Al-Amal Institute is an exclusive deaf institute, while public elementary school 300 is a public school with exclusive classes for students who are deaf or hard of hearing. Both schools utilize the elementary curriculum provided by the Ministry of Education in Saudi Arabia. All participants were female first-grade students with mild (four students) or moderate (5 participants) to severe (11 participants) hearing loss. None of the students suffered from any additional disabilities. Students' ages ranged from 7 to 12 years old, with a mean of 8.5 years and a standard deviation (SD) of 1.28 years. All students were familiar with tablets and/or smartphones.

The reading levels of the students, prior to recruitment, were determined with the assistance of the educators using two scales: students ability to understand a word and link it with its corresponding sign and the ability to fingerspell the word. The teachers were asked to assess the reading level of a student as either poor, good (i.e., average), or excellent based on these scales. The recruited participants were then divided equally into two experimental groups based on this assessment (10 students for each group). Each group consisted of two poor students, three average students, and five excellent students.

4.2   Materials

An Android smartphone with the Word and Sign application was utilized for the experiment. The electronic book provided with the application was printed to produce a physical book, as recommended by the educators, to support the learning process. Morae, a usability software tool, was used to record the users' interaction with the application and log test results, which were then analyzed and visualized.

Experimental Word Set. Twenty six words were originally selected from the current first-grade reading and comprehension curriculum. A knowledge test was performed a week prior to the experiment to exclude already known vocabulary. The knowledge test was carried out by asking the participant to associate a printed word with its corresponding pictures and ArSL. Of the twenty six words, thirteen words were excluded. This leaves thirteen words that were taught to the students.

Experimental Task. To assess the effectiveness of utilizing Word and Sign when learning new printed vocabulary and thus its effectiveness in aiding reading, a series of association tasks were used to determine the acquisition of the new words by the participants. The tasks were divided into two groups to determine two levels of possible new vocabulary acquisition via pictures or decoding to ArSL. Children who are deaf or hard of hearing are arguably known as visual learners [15]. When associating printed text with its corresponding pictures, a child maintains the image as a memory and recalls it when presented with the text. In the case of decoding into ArSL, a child who is deaf maps the sign to the corresponding text, therefore bilingually linking the Arabic (second language) written word with its corresponding sign from their native language, i.e., ArSL. These two levels of acquisition were represented by two tasks:

– Associate printed word with corresponding picture: in this task, participants are presented with one of the taught words and four pictures, only one of which corresponds to the printed word.
– Associate printed word with corresponding ArSL: this task asks the participants to link the printed word with one of four videos of a human interpreter performing the word's corresponding sign.

Each of the tasks consisted of ten subtasks, which were selected from thirteen words not known to the students. The main goal of the tasks was to determine if there are any learning differences when using the traditional method of vocabulary teaching and when using AR with Word and Sign.

4.3   Procedure

The twenty participants were divided into two equal groups. The first group was taught the thirteen new words using a traditional method of teaching. This involved the teacher presenting the printed word and then using pictures, fingerspelling, and ArSL to convey its meaning. The second group was taught the new words using Word and Sign. In this case, the teacher presented the written word and used the application in groups of students to convey the word's meaning. Prior to evaluation, the AR group and the educator were introduced to the AR application using the words already known by the students. The size of the phone often required the educator to group a smaller number of students together to show them the application. To assure the attentiveness of the educator while teaching, the first group was similarly instructed in subgroups of

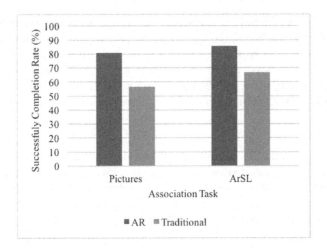

Fig. 2. Average successful completion rate for participants between groups (AR versus traditional) and association tasks (pictures versus ArSL).

students after an initial traditional approach was used. Each group was taught the thirteen words over three days. The same collection of words was taught in the same order over the three days for each group.

On the final day of the evaluation, the tasks were presented to the participants individually. This session was held in the classroom and lasted approximately five hours for each experimental group, i.e., half an hour for each participant. Teaching was, of course, held in the classroom as well. For each task, the participant was asked to form the correct association between the printed word and picture or ArSL. The participants were allowed two trials to obtain the correct answer. If by the second trial they did not give the right answer, the participant was shown the correct association. The association tasks were counterbalanced across participants for pictures and ArSL. All sessions were video recorded via a video recorder, and the task answers were recorded via Morae.

4.4 Results

The results were analyzed using a mixed factorial analysis of variance (ANOVA) that treated the teaching methods, i.e., groups, as a between-participant factor (AR versus traditional) and the association tasks as a within-participant repeated measure (picture versus ArSL).

The completion rate measures the ability of the participants to complete each of the association tasks successfully. Figure 2 shows average successful completion rate for participants between groups and association tasks. An ANOVA showed that participants taught via AR using Word and Sign ($mean = 83.33\%, SD = 12.09\%$) completed significantly more tasks successfully ($F_{1,18} = 18.78, p < 0.01$) compared to the group in which the participants were taught the new words via the traditional teaching approach ($mean = 61.67\%, SD = 19.19\%$). The

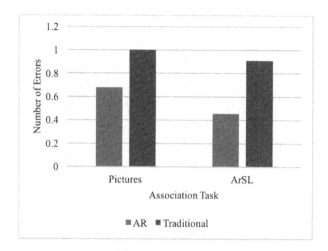

Fig. 3. Average number of errors for participants between groups (AR versus traditional) and association tasks (pictures versus ArSL).

analysis showed that there was no significant difference ($F_{1,18} = 2.18, p = 0.16$) in completion rate for the same participants on the two association tasks: link printed word with picture and with ArSL. There was also no significant group × task interaction ($F_{1,18} = 0.24, p = 0.63$).

The number of errors was also logged and analyzed. Each participant can have zero, one, or two errors. Participants with zero or one error were considered to have completed the task successfully; however, those with two errors did not complete the task successfully. Figure 3 shows the average number of errors for participants between groups and association tasks. An ANOVA showed that the number of errors was significantly higher ($F_{1,18} = 11.27, p < 0.01$) for the traditional group ($mean = 0.57\%, SD = 0.32\%$) than for the AR group ($mean = 0.95\%, SD = 0.36\%$). No significant difference in number of errors ($F_{1,18} = 2.72, p = 0.12$) was found between the two association tasks. There was also no significant group × task interaction ($F_{1,18} = 0.49, p = 0.49$).

Time on task refers to the time required by a participant to associate a printed word with its corresponding picture or ArSL. Figure 4 shows the average time on task for participants between groups and association tasks. An ANOVA showed that participants taught the new words via AR ($mean = 0.18$ min, $SD = 0.04$ min) took significantly less time to perform the tasks ($F_{1,18} = 9.12, p < 0.01$) than those that were taught via the traditional method ($mean = 0.23$ min, $SD = 0.06$ min). The analysis showed that there was no significant difference ($F_{1,18} = 2.79, p = 0.11$) in time on task between the two association tasks. However, there was a significant group × task interaction ($F_{1,18} = 8.17, p = 0.01$), with the time difference between the two groups significantly widening when participants associated the printed text with ArSL ($mean = 0.22$ min, $SD = 0.02$ min) compared to associating the words with pictures ($mean = 0.19$ min, $SD = 0.07$ min).

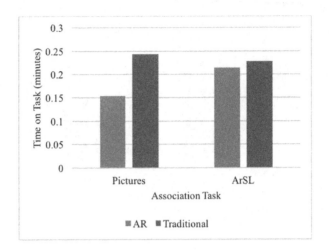

Fig. 4. Average time on task for participants between groups (AR versus traditional) and association tasks (pictures versus ArSL).

5   Discussion

This section discusses the results in view of our hypotheses, which argue for better performances (completion rate, number of errors, and time on task) when completing the association task after being taught thirteen new vocabulary words.

The completion rates of participants on the association tasks were significantly higher after being taught the new printed vocabulary using Word and Sign, a mobile AR application. This significance was noted for the two evaluated tasks, i.e., associating printed text with either pictures or ArSL, with no observed interaction between the groups and tasks. This evidence partly supports our hypothesis (H1), which states that, compared to the traditional method of learning new printed vocabulary, utilizing Word and Sign will increase the completion rate and reduce the number of errors for participants as they complete the evaluation tasks. The second part of the hypothesis (H1) regarding the number of errors was similarly supported. The participants were given two chances to complete the tasks successfully, and errors were logged. The results showed that participants made fewer mistakes when having learned the words via AR compared to the traditional method.

The second hypothesis (H2) states that the time needed to complete the association tasks will be significantly reduced for participants who are taught the new words via the mobile AR application compared to those taught using the traditional approach. The results support this hypothesis, with the participants requiring significantly less time to associate printed words with a picture or ArSL when having learned the words via AR compared to the traditional approach. The analysis also showed that there was an interaction between the type of group and association task, with participants taking significantly longer when

(a) A child fingerspelling (along with the interpreter) the first letter of the Arabic alphabet while spelling the word "turtle".

(b) Another child fingerspelling the third letter of the Arabic alphabet while spelling the word "fox".

Fig. 5. Screen grabs from the video recorded observations.

associating the printed words with ArSL. This was to be expected, as the struggle with ArSL was previously observed for the same participants [2].

Several observations were noted as the children interacted with the mobile AR application. The children took to the application easily after an initial introduction to its features. This is understandable since previous findings have shown that a majority of parents of deaf children encourage their children to use technology for educational and entertainment purposes [2]. While using Word and Sign, the majority of the children signed along with the child interpreter, as can be seen in Fig. 5. The use of a child interpreter for the ArSL videos was not previously considered in the literature, where the majority of studies either utilized avatars or videos of adult interpreters (see Sect. 2). It was said by the teacher that this might have encouraged the children's participation with the interpreter.

These findings highlight the value of incorporating visually enhancing technologies, such as AR, to aid literacy when teaching children who are deaf or hard of hearing. The reception of the technology by educators and the children was greatly encouraging, signifying the considerable need of this societal niche in Saudi Arabia. The mobility of the AR application can also support access outside the classroom, thus encouraging parental participation as well. The tool can also be used by hearing non-signers to learn ArSL.

6   Conclusions and Future Work

This paper evaluated the use of Word and Sign, an AR application created for the literacy development of children who are deaf or hard of hearing. The performance of the AR application was compared against that of traditional teaching methods that utilize pictures, fingerspelling, and ArSL. Twenty students who were deaf or hard of hearing were recruited for the evaluation and divided into two groups: one that was taught via AR and the other via a traditional approach. Through a series of association tasks (linking printed words with pictures and ArSL), the students' performances were logged to determine the completion rate, number of errors, and time on task. The AR group was found to have performed significantly better, with a greater completion rate and fewer errors, compared to the traditional group. This group also took significantly less time to associate printed words with pictures and ArSL. These results highlight the effectiveness of AR for the literacy development of Arabic children who are hearing impaired.

In future work, we intend to improve and extend the AR application and examine various factors in the following ways:

- Expand the number of words to incorporate vocabulary from other elementary grades.
- Thematically divide the presentation of words to mimic current elementary curricula and thus better support learning.
- Provide support for Android-based tablets and consider further expansion to other mobile operating systems, e.g., iOS.
- Conduct evaluations to assess the performances of children who are deaf or hard of hearing over time.

Acknowledgments. This work was supported by the Deanship of Scientific Research at King Saud University. We thank the students, educators, and directors of Al-Amal Institute and public elementary school 300 for their encouragement and cooperation throughout the assessment.

References

1. Allen, T.E.: ASL skills, fingerspelling ability, home communication context and early alphabetic knowledge of preschool-aged deaf children. Sign Lang. Stud. **15**(3), 233–265 (2015)
2. Almutairi, A., Al-Megren, S.: Preliminary investigations on augmented reality for the literacy development of deaf children. In: Badioze Zaman, H., et al. (eds.) IVIC 2017. LNCS, vol. 10645, pp. 412–422. Springer, Cham (2017). https://doi.org/10.1007/978-3-319-70010-6_38
3. Alnafjan, A., Aljumaah, A., Alaskar, H., Alshraihi, R.: Designing 'Najeeb': technology-enhanced learning for children with impaired hearing using Arabic sign-language ArSL applications. In: 2017 International Conference on Computer and Applications, ICCA 2017, pp. 238–273. IEEE (2017)
4. Alyami, H., Soer, M., Swanepoel, A., Pottas, L.: Deaf or hard of hearing children in Saudi Arabia: status of early intervention services. Int. J. Pediatr. Otorhinolaryngol. **86**, 142–149 (2016)

5. Cadeñanes, J., Arrieta, A.G.: Development of sign language communication skill on children through augmented reality and the MuCy model. In: Mascio, T.D., Gennari, R., Vitorini, P., Vicari, R., de la Prieta, F. (eds.) Methodologies and Intelligent Systems for Technology Enhanced Learning. AISC, vol. 292, pp. 45–52. Springer, Cham (2014). https://doi.org/10.1007/978-3-319-07698-0_6
6. Cadeñanes, J., González Arrieta, M.A.: Augmented reality: an observational study considering the MuCy model to develop communication skills on deaf children. In: Polycarpou, M., de Carvalho, A.C.P.L.F., Pan, J.-S., Woźniak, M., Quintian, H., Corchado, E. (eds.) HAIS 2014. LNCS (LNAI), vol. 8480, pp. 233–240. Springer, Cham (2014). https://doi.org/10.1007/978-3-319-07617-1_21
7. Cano, S., Collazos, C.A., Flórez Aristizábal, L., Moreira, F.: Augmentative and alternative communication in the literacy teaching for deaf children. In: Zaphiris, P., Ioannou, A. (eds.) LCT 2017. LNCS, vol. 10296, pp. 123–133. Springer, Cham (2017). https://doi.org/10.1007/978-3-319-58515-4_10
8. Cihak, D.F., Moore, E.J., Wright, R.E., McMahon, D.D., Gibbons, M.M., Smith, C.: Evaluating augmented reality to complete a chain task for elementary students with autism. J. Spec. Educ. Technol. **31**(2), 99–108 (2016)
9. Clark, M.D., Hauser, P.C., Miller, P., Kargin, T., Rathmann, C., Guldenoglu, B., Kubus, O., Spurgeon, E., Israel, E.: The importance of early sign language acquisition for deaf readers. Read. Writ. Q. **32**(2), 127–151 (2016)
10. Craig, A.B.: Mobile augmented reality (Chap. 7). In: Understanding Augmented Reality (2013)
11. Diegmann, P., Schmidt-Kraepelin, M., Eynden, S.V.D., Basten, D.: Benefits of augmented reality in educational environments - a systematic literature review. Wirtschaftsinformatik **3**(6), 1542–1556 (2015)
12. Goldin-Meadow, S., Mayberry, R.I., Read, T.O.: How do profoundly deaf children learn to read? Learn. Disabil. Res. Pract. **16**(4), 222–229 (2001)
13. Hanafi, A.: The reality of support services for students with disabilities and their families audio and satisfaction in the light of some of the variables from the viewpoint of teachers and parents. In: Conference of Special Education, pp. 189–260 (2007)
14. Haptonstall-Nykaza, T.S., Schick, B.: The transition from fingerspelling to english print: facilitating english decoding. J. Deaf Stud. Deaf Educ. **12**(2), 172–183 (2007)
15. Herrera-Fernández, V., Puente-Ferreras, A., Alvarado-Izquierdo, J.: Visual learning strategies to promote literacy skills in prelingually deaf readers. Revista Mexicana de Psicologia **31**(1), 1–10 (2014)
16. Jones, M., Bench, N., Ferons, S.: Vocabulary acquisition for deaf readers using augmented technology. In: 2014 2nd Workshop on Virtual and Augmented Assistive Technology, VAAT 2014; Co-located with the 2014 Virtual Reality Conference - Proceedings, pp. 13–15. IEEE (2014)
17. Kingdom of Saudi Arabia General Authority of Statistic: Demographic Survey (2016). https://www.stats.gov.sa/en/852
18. Kipper, G., Rampolla, J.: Augmented Reality. Elsevier, New York (2013)
19. Kožuh, I., Hauptman, S., Kosec, P., Debevc, M.: Assessing the efficiency of using augmented reality for learning sign language. In: Antona, M., Stephanidis, C. (eds.) UAHCI 2015. LNCS, vol. 9176, pp. 404–415. Springer, Cham (2015). https://doi.org/10.1007/978-3-319-20681-3_38
20. McMahon, D.D., Cihak, D.F., Wright, R.E., Bell, S.M.: Augmented reality for teaching science vocabulary to postsecondary education students with intellectual disabilities and autism. J. Res. Technol. Educ. **48**(1), 38–56 (2016)

21. Zainuddin, N.M.M., Badioze Zaman, H., Ahmad, A.: Learning science using AR book: a preliminary study on visual needs of deaf learners. In: Badioze Zaman, H., Robinson, P., Petrou, M., Olivier, P., Schröder, H., Shih, T.K. (eds.) IVIC 2009. LNCS, vol. 5857, pp. 844–855. Springer, Heidelberg (2009). https://doi.org/10.1007/978-3-642-05036-7_80

22. Mellon, N.K., Niparko, J.K., Rathmann, C., Mathur, G., Humphries, T., Jo Napoli, D., Handley, T., Scambler, S., Lantos, J.D.: Should all deaf children learn sign language? Pediatrics **136**(1), 170–176 (2015)

23. Oka Sudana, A.A.K., Aristamy, I.G.A.A.M., Wirdiani, N.K.A.: Augmented reality application of sign language for deaf people in Android based on smartphone. Int. J. Softw. Eng. Appl. **10**(8), 139–150 (2016)

24. Singh, M., Singh, M.P.: Augmented reality interfaces. In: IEEE Internet Computing (2013)

25. Smith, C.C., Cihak, D.F., Kim, B., McMahon, D.D., Wright, R.: Examining augmented reality to improve navigation skills in postsecondary students with intellectual disability. J. Spec. Educ. Technol. **32**(1), 3–11 (2017)

26. Stone, A., Kartheiser, G., Hauser, P.C., Petitto, L.A., Allen, T.E.: Fingerspelling as a novel gateway into reading fluency in deaf bilinguals. PLoS ONE **10**(10), e0139610 (2015)

27. Torgesen, J.K., Hudson, R.F.: Reading fluency: critical issues for struggling readers. In: What Research Has to Say About Fluency Instruction, pp. 130–158 (2006)

28. Wellner, P., Mackay, W., Gold, R.: Computer-augmented environments: back to the real world. Commun. ACM **36**(7), 24–27 (1993)

29. Wu, H.K., Lee, S.W.Y., Chang, H.Y., Liang, J.C.: Current status, opportunities and challenges of augmented reality in education. Comput. Educ. **62**, 41–49 (2013)

30. Zainuddin, N.M.M., Zaman, H.B., Ahmad, A.: Heuristic evaluation on augmented reality courseware for the deaf. In: International Conference on User Science and Engineering, pp. 183–188 (2011)

Research Model for Traditional Board Game Renaissance

Erik Armayuda[1(✉)], Po-Hsien Lin[2], and Rungtai Lin[2]

[1] Visual Communication Design, Faculty of Creative Industries and Telematics,
Trilogi University, Kalibata, South Jakarta, Indonesia
armayuda@trilogi.ac.id
[2] Graduate School of Creative Industry Design,
National Taiwan University of Arts, New Taipei City, Taiwan
{t0131, rtlin}@mail.ntua.edu.tw

Abstract. Cross-Cultural communication in the field of Science, Art, and Design is a part of aspect that influence the growth of creative industrial product. In the context of product design in creative industry, a research related to cross-cultural communication, cultural wealth is a potential source of inspiration in creating global design products. The exploration can also make the culture more adaptive in globalization era with the transformation. There was a lot of studies to exploit cultural products objects into new design products, but not all of the studies using a relevant methods. One of the cultural product that has wide potential is traditional board games. Traditional board game has different character from artefacts because besides its physical form factor, it has an invisible aspect in the form of game rules. In traditional board game design products require special treatment to be able to research and understand it properly. In-depth research an appropriate approach method is required considering the transformation process of traditional game, not only limited to the conventional media shift into new media. This research tries to find the better method in processing the potential of traditional board games, which will later become a map in the research development. This studies aims to find the research stage by applying the model "From SAD to CHEER" in the context of traditional board games studies.

Keywords: Traditional board game · Cultural transformation
From SAD to CHEER

1 Introduction

The globalization is a chance to promote and introduce the nation by a representative product. To be success full, innovative product must have a clear and significant difference feature that is related to market need [5]. Indonesia is the country rich of tribe and culture which is a potency for exploration in cultural studies. In the context of creative industries, the culture could be a resource for product design idea. One of the cultural wealth is traditional board game. According to Misbah, the definition of traditional games is the act of entertaining the hearts of both using tools or not using tools. While the meaning of "traditional" refers to the origin of the word "tradition" which means, "the habit of descending descent is still executed". So the word "traditional" means attitude and way of thinking, and acting that always cling to the norms and customs that existed from generation to generation". Or it can also be interpreted as everything that is spoken and passed down from generation to generation from parents or ancestors [12]. Culture plays an important role in the field of design and cross cultural design will become a key point in design evaluation in the future [7]. This studies will only focus on the traditional game which is using "board" or traditionally using ground as the board or place to play the game.

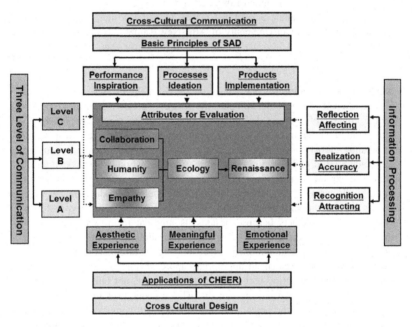

Fig. 1. Cross-cultural communication in design collaboration: from SAD to CHEER. In International Conference on Cross-Cultural Design. Springer, Cham (to be publish in 2018)

To explore the potency of the traditional board game, the right method is required. Because the process of transforming the potency of traditional board game into new design product is not as easy as replacing the old material or shapes into new modern material. For design strategy, cultural value-adding creates the core of value adding [5]. Deep studies will help to determine the element of the game which should be maintain and which can be replace. The studies will begin by apply "From SAD to CHEER" method to find research model for traditional board game (Fig. 1).

2   Research Framework

Based on "SAD to CHEER" it revealed 3 level of communication, design process, audience response, and also product impact. The approach to applied the method in case study of traditional board game, is to use descriptive analysis of traditional board game. The description will be a key to get a better understanding to the value of the culture manifest in the game. The value of the game will be a key in design evaluation point. "Culture" plays an important role in the design field, "and cross cultural design" will be a key design evaluation point in the future. Designing "culture" into modern product will be a design trend in the global market (Gao et al. 2016).

The Breakdown of design process at basic principle of SAD; 1. Performance Inspiration (which is traditional board game as the inspiration), 2. Process Ideation (the idea is creating cross cultural board game product), 3. Product Implementation (board game product design) and product implementation as application of CHEER; 1. Aesthetic Experience (transforming the form of the game), 2. Meaningful Experience (exploring game play), 3. Emotional Experience (elaborate context) (Fig. 2).

Fig. 2. Implementation SAD to CHEER in traditional board game Renaissance

The context of SAD of this topic is about SAD in Traditional board game. By using the model, there is a process of exploring traditional board game and transform it into 3 level of transformation, which is in each level, there is an assessment measurement to evaluate the process. Than define it by aesthetic experience, meaningful experience that will be a Renaissance of traditional board game, into global product board game.

The process to apply SAD to CHEER in traditional board game, will use the level of communication as the level of transformation the potency of traditional board game. There will be 3 level of transformation; (level A) The lower level which is only about tangible transformation will be a matter of turning physical aspect from the game so the game could visually attractive. (level B) Including Intangible transformation such as game play, so the transformation will define, does the product easily understand or not by the original game player user and also explainable to the new user. (level C) the higher level contain the context value which combine with the original concept of game which touch the emotion of the user.

The other side of the information processing will be the assessment measurement; (level C) Recognition Attracting: how much the product attract the user visually. (level B) Realization Accuracy: how easy user will understand the game play of the product. (level A) Reflection Affection: how much the product affect the user emotion. This break down will help the designer to assess how much the product give impact to the user from inside to the outside. Its because "the outer level can be a very direct experience to present its tangible element. It is a direct manifestation of visual and morphological aspects combine with the conversion mode for colour, texture, pattern conversion…" (Gao et al. 2016).

3   Methodology

The research based on SAD to CHEER model to break down the traditional board game and translate it into the model for board game product context. The method to applying from SAD to CHEER model for transforming traditional board game into modern product with cultural attribute as the adding value of the product. Finally, for global market, adding cultural dimension to ergonomic has become an important issue for exploring interaction and experience in product design [10] (Fig. 3).

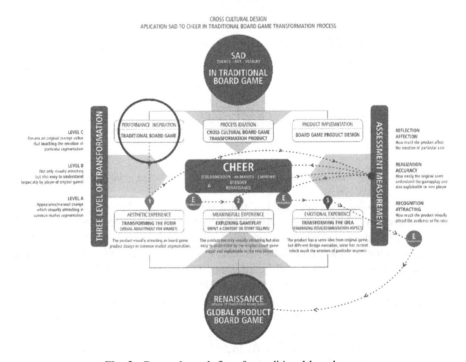

Fig. 3. Research work flow for traditional board game

The research method to exploration traditional board game studies using SAD to CHEER will be done in 3 level of research and design process;

(1) Transforming the form

In this research level, the designing process will be only in the matter of transforming the tangible aspect. The process of design could be called as 'Redesigning' or 'Repackaging' the traditional form into new design product for particular market segmentation using visual matter. The media exchange include from traditional into printing media, or even from traditional into digital media, as long there is no change in the game play aspect and only adding visual aspect into new design is also in this category.

(2) Exploring the game play

In this level, the research focus on game studies. Breakdown the value, meaning, and the purpose of the game play which can be explore and improve, so the game could be relevant into particular segment. The result of the studies will be a new suitable game play, or the theme of the game that will be a content of the game, improve from the game mechanic. The result will be a 'modification' of original game.

(3) Elaborating the context

In this level the design process already touch the marketing strategy matter, especially in the segmentation aspect. Design strategy is considered to be one of the pivotal component in cultural and creative design industries, and this will have a significant impact on consumer perception of innovation [5]. By inputting a context or adding a story telling in design process, the result of product design process will affect the emotion of the audience. So the idea of the original game may still include in the new product, but with a different look and different game play.

To applied the perfect method of SAD to CHEER, all of three level should be done in the design process with an evaluation in every design process level. After all of the level is done, the assessment measurement process should be applied to assess the impact of the product.

4 A Case Study of Evaluating Traditional Board Game

One of the famous oldest board game is a chess. To get better understanding of applying SAD to CHEER in traditional board game transformation, the studies will take the famous board game chess as case study. To evaluate the model for traditional board game method, the studies will put chess in all of three level of transformation (Fig. 4).

The precursors of chess originated in India during the Gupta Empire, where its early form in the 6th century was known as chaturaṅga, which translates as "Four divisions (of the military)": infantry, cavalry, elephantry, and chariotry, represented by the pieces that would evolve into the modern pawn, knight, bishop, and rook, respectively [16]. Chess board game from the history already has a lot of improvement

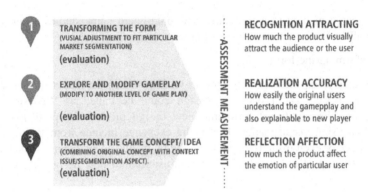

Fig. 4. Evaluating of design process in traditional board game

and adaptation in every country and century. From Chess.com we know that there is so many transformation and evolution of chess board game (Fig. 5).

Fig. 5. Fragment of a chessboard and chess pieces from the 17th century (left) & chess today (right)

4.1   Transforming the Form

The process of design transformation of this stage as mention before, is about the tangible aspect including visual style. In the case study of chess board, the game could be redesign into different variation of product. From the ordinary chess board, there is a potency to modify the form and the visual of the chess. At first picture (below) the form and the visual is manipulate to imitate Mario Bross character concept. And the second picture is Umbra Wobble Chess, a modification of the chess form which has a round shape in every pawn's bottom (Fig. 6).

At this level, the key of transforming is there is no need to deep study about the game, all that need to do is creating a new looks of all game equipment. The key point of this level is if there is an increasing value of the product appearance (Aesthetic, Colour, Form, texture, material, icon, shape, and also the content) and the product will be visually attracting. The achievement of the design process should be assess by putting a key factor about the visual comparison of before and after product.

Fig. 6. Chess board redesign form and visually; 1. Mario bross chess, 2. Umbra wobble chess

4.2   Exploring the Game Play

The next step of previous level is about intangible aspect studies. In this level, the transformation design process need a deeper studies, especially in the matter of game play, the mechanic of the game, also the game studies which purpose to explore and improve the game play of the game. So the result of the process will be a new game with different level of play that still be understand by the original user and explainable to the new user (Fig. 7).

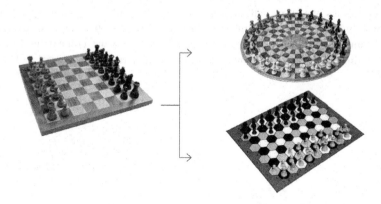

Fig. 7. Chess board game adaptation; 1. 3 Man chess, 2. Hexagonal chess

The picture above explain, from the ordinary chess could be transform into a new game adaptation from the original chess. The first picture (above) is 3 Man Chess, the chess which can be played by three player. The second picture called Hexagonal Chess, the chess which has an improvement shape and rule (by adding more pawns and different game play).

The process of exploring the game play could be support by doing a deep research in the game studies, and also doing some experiment to improvise the original game into a new form of game. The key word of this transforming process called adaptation of the original game, it because the result of the design process will be a similar game from the original one, but contain different rule or equipment which can define that the game is different from the original one, with some of similar aspect such the form of the board, the number of the equipment, or event the rule.

The evaluation of this level is by using assessment measurement which is include a key factor of the game play and the level of understanding the game play by the original user. The visual aspect could be change and improve, but the main different of this level and the previous level is the intangible aspect of the game which is about the game play improvement.

4.3   Elaborating the Original Idea with the Context

This level will takes deep studies covers, game studies, product design, market segmentation, and also the studies of story telling which can help to build the context of the game, such educational issue, campaign, intelligence and soon. So the result of the game should be really new and different from the original. The original game will be only the source of inspiration. The key factor of this design process is the novelty gained from a traditional board game exploration. At the other hand the design process could be an innovation of exploring the original game. In the global market - local design era, connection among local culture, global market, and innovative products in design strategy becomes increasingly close (Lin 2012).

From the ordinary chess board game, the process has to catch the idea of the original game as the inspiration to create a new kind of board game. As the context of chess case studies, we know that the game is about the battle of two kingdom involve a group of kingdom element. By this context there is a lot of possibility to explore the original game into a new different product by exploring the context, replacing the content, adding the rule of the game, and also modify the whole aspect of the game (Fig. 8).

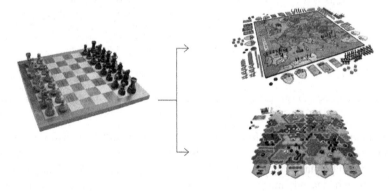

Fig. 8. Chess board game adaptation; 1. Kingdom builder (Vaccarino 2011), 2. Risk (Parker Brothers/Hasbro 1957)

5 Resume

From the case studies above, it can be resume that there is 3 level of board game transformation based on SAD to CHEER method application. The level contain the lower level into higher level of transformation design process (Fig. 9).

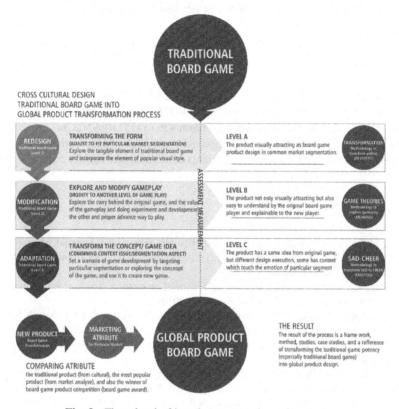

Fig. 9. Three level of board game transformation design

As the result three level of board game transformation process as an approach to create new board game product design which can be a global product is; (1) Redesign level, which explore the tangible aspect and redesign it into a product which visually attractive. (2) Modification level, which explore the intangible aspect and modify the game play, so the game has some improvement of game play, but still can be recognize as original game in some element. The assessment is still require to know how much the product will be understand by the original game player and also explainable to the new user. (3) the other level of traditional board game transformation process is the Adaptation, which is the original board game is used as the inspiration aspect to create a new board game. And the result of this design process is a new board game which is totally different with the original one. The idea may the same with the original game but has different design and game play execution. This level of processing the potency of traditional board game may become an innovation.

By using all of three level above, the research will come closer to explore traditional board game as one of the cultural richness. For the next research, the process will use the real case of traditional board game which transform by applying al of three level of transformation process. So there will be a better understanding and method to explore the potency of traditional board game, into modern global product.

Image Source

Ancient chess:	https://en.wikipedia.org/wiki/List_of_chess_variants
Chess nowdays:	https://goo.gl/sC84Ne
Chess before:	https://goo.gl/eCuAZA
Modern set chess:	https://id.pinterest.com/pin/211035932508487669/
Chess lamp:	https://id.pinterest.com/pin/526639750154233230/
Round chess:	https://id.pinterest.com/pin/439734351106950876/
3 playerchess:	http://tvtropes.org/pmwiki/pmwiki.php/Main/VariantChess
Hexagonal chess:	http://www.chessvariants.com/hexagonal.dir/rex.html

References

1. Alif, M.Z.: Perubahan dan Pengembangan Bentuk, Fungsi dan Material Mainan Dalam Permainan Anak di Masyarakat Sunda. Tesis Program Magister Desain FSRD. Institute Teknologi Bandung, Bandung (2006)
2. Browan, T., Jocelyn, W.: Design thinking for social innovation. Stanford Social Innovation Review Winter. Graduate School of Business (2010)
3. Dharmamulya, S., Dkk: Transformasi Nilai Melalui Permainan Rakyat Daerah Istimewa Yogyakarta. Departemen Pendidikan dan Kebudayaan, Yogyakarta (1993)
4. Dharmamulya, S., Dkk: Permainan Tradisional Jawa. Kepel Press Puri Arsita A-6, Yogyakarta (2008)
5. Hsu, C.H., Chang, S.H., Lin, R.: A design strategy for turning local culture into global market. Int. J. Affect. Eng. **12**(2), 275–283 (2012). Japan Society of Kansain Engineering
6. Khamadi, K., Sihombing, R.M., Ahmad, H.A.: Perancangan Konsep Adaptasi Permainan Tradisional Bas-Basan Sepur dalam Permainan Digital "Amukti Palapa". Wimba: Jurnal komunikasi dan multimedia **5**(2) (2013)
7. Lin, R.: Transforming Taiwan aboriginal cultural features into modern product design: a case study of a cross-cultural product design model. Int. J. Des. **1**(2), 45–53 (2007)
8. Lin, R., Chen. C.T.: A discourse on the construction of a service innovation model: focus on the cultural and creative industry park. In: Ifinedo, P. (ed.) EBUSINESS-Application and Global Acceptance, pp. 119–136. InTech, Rijeka (2012)
9. Lin, R., Kreifeldt, J., Hung, P.-H., Chen, J.-L.: From dechnology to humart – a case study of Taiwan design development. In: Rau, P.L.P. (ed.) CCD 2015. LNCS, vol. 9181, pp. 263–273. Springer, Cham (2015). https://doi.org/10.1007/978-3-319-20934-0_25
10. Lin, R., Hsieh, H.-Y., Sun, M.-X., Gao, Y.-J.: From ideality to reality- a case study of Mondrian style. In: Rau, P.-L.P. (ed.) CCD 2016. LNCS, vol. 9741, pp. 365–376. Springer, Cham (2016). https://doi.org/10.1007/978-3-319-40093-8_37

11. Lin, R., Li, H.L., Wu, J.: Cross-cultural communication in design collaboration: from SAD to CHEER. In: International Conference on Cross-Cultural Design. Springer, Cham (2018, to be publish)
12. Misbah, I.H.: Peran Permainan Tradisional Yang Bermuatan Edukatif Dalam Menyumbang Pembentukan dan Identitas Bangsa. IPI, Bandung (2007)
13. Nugraha, A.: Transforming Tradition: A Method for Maintaining Tradition in a Craft and Design Context. Aalto University, School of Arts, Design and Architecture, Helsinki (2012)
14. Purwaningsih, E.: Permainan Tradisional Anak: Salah Satu Khasanah Budaya Yang Perlu Dilestarikan. Jantra History And Culture Jurnal $1(1)$, 40–46 (2006). Departemen Kebudayaan dan Pariwisata, Yogyakarta
15. Sachari, A.: Budaya Visual Indonesia. Erlangga, Jakarta (2007)
16. Ostler, J.: History of Chess, 2 May 2012. https://goo.gl/HB47jR

What Makes for Successful Game Storytelling? A Model for Evaluating Game-Adaptability of Stories in China

Yun Gong[1], Bingcheng Wang[1], Pei-Luen Patrick Rau[1(✉)], and Dinglong Huang[2]

[1] Department of Industrial Engineering, Tsinghua University, Beijing, China
rpl@mail.tsinghua.edu.cn
[2] Shenzhen Malong Artificial Intelligence Research Center, Shenzhen, China

Abstract. Storytelling is important for game flow experience, yet there is no accepted model or theory for game developers or investors to use for evaluating the composition, purchase and adaption of game stories. This paper proposes a concise model, the Game Story model, integrating 12 existing models from the fields of scriptwriting, game playability, and game motivation studies, with empirical findings based on content analysis of over 100 replies from Zhihu on topics related to game storytelling and interviews of 6 experienced game players. Factor extraction conducted afterwards through a survey (N = 516) and exploratory factor analysis (EFA) results in a model of 11 factors, with each factor containing a set of detailed criteria. A validation of the model on stories indicates that GameStory is able to explain the high game-adaptability of stories of many popular video games. This interpretation can be applied to the evaluation, understanding and improvement the game-adaptability of stories.

Keywords: Storytelling · Digital game · Game-adaptability

1 Introduction

The video game industry, as a fast-growing and expanding industry worldwide, has produced spectacular global revenue of 100 billion dollars each year, amounting to approximately three times the revenue of the movie industry. Storytelling in games, meanwhile, is drawing much attention worldwide, not only because of its fundamental role in communicating emotion, conveying values and enhancing immersion but also due to the growing awareness throughout the global game industry to the strategic reservation of IPs (intellectual property). One can take the recent battle for the adaption right of a Chinese online novel as an example. This novel, titled Wu Xing Tian, with only 1% written, was finally sold to a local game company for 8 million RMB (approximately 1.2 million dollars). Another notable trend is the increasing prevalence of gamification projects in companies outside the game industry, where story creation is also of great significance to the project leaders and developers.

However, no comprehensive model has been found to evaluate the quality of stories for the game adaption, which we refer to as the game-adaptability of stories. Some

© Springer International Publishing AG, part of Springer Nature 2018
P.-L. P. Rau (Ed.): CCD 2018, LNCS 10912, pp. 30–45, 2018.
https://doi.org/10.1007/978-3-319-92252-2_3

existing works, which may contribute to such evaluation, lie in three main areas: scriptwriting in the traditional movie industry [1–3], game immersion and playability [4–8], and game motivation studies [16, 17, 21]. However, none of these models are specific to the creation, selection and adaption of game stories. A game story, more specifically, is different from a movie script in terms of interactivity and non-linear characteristics [9], and other game features (e.g., mechanism design, difficulty design). It is also different with regard to spiritual impact – the way in which it conveys values, communicates emotion and influences the understanding of life and humanity.

This paper aims to explore the factors of the stories that influence game adaptability. Three steps were taken in this study: (1) Determine variables based on literature and empirical studies, including content analysis and interviews; (2) Survey construction and distribution to collect players' ratings of the importance of each variable to game playability; and (3) exploratory factor analysis to extract a concise model from the variables. The potential implementation of the study is to provide guidance for game story writing, selection and adaption, not only for game designers but also for the leads of gamification projects in a wider domain.

2   Related Work

2.1   Game Storytelling

The definition of game storytelling is always confused with that of game narrative. Some researchers have referred to game narrative in discussions that are actually about storytelling [10]. To clarify, the core of the story is the description of the process of a character confronting a series of obstacles on the way to obtaining the goal [3]. There is a structure to most stories, which often consists of a beginning, a middle and an ending, according to Aristotle. And the main elements of a story include events (actions and happenings) and existents (characters and setting) [1]. However, narrative is the method and style used to tell the story of the game [9, 11]. The story can be created either by game designers or by players themselves. Therefore, not all games tell stories, but many games do have narratives [12]. For example, fighting games usually do not have storytelling, but may have some narratives. Majewski [10] observed that not all genres of games tell stories, but some genres are mainly dependent on stories, such as first-person shooter games, role-play games and adventure games.

Although previous research regarding screen scriptwriting exists in the film industry [2], these works are not adequate for the analysis of game story writing or selection for two main reasons [9]: film scripts lack interactivity and have a linear structure. According to the famous game designer Chris Crawford, what a computer game really sells is interactivity. A traditional story is entirely created by the author, and the audience rarely interacts with the story. A game story, however, involves users in the story's creation. Actions performed by players may be "listened to" and "considered" by the game engine and may influence the outcome [13]. Non-linearity is another characteristic of a game story. While the structure of a traditional story is completely fixed the moment when the author finishes the story, game stories have a myriad of possibilities for their structure. Meadows [14] summarized three plot structures in game storytelling. According to these plot structures, each game story may include several main storylines and crossover between the storylines. The elements of storytelling are summarized in Table 1.

Table 1. Variables derived from storytelling models

Source	Variables derived from storytelling models
Glassner [3]	Character
	Goal
	Obstacle
Chatman [1]	Actions
	Happenings
	Character
	Setting
Aristotle	Starting
	Middle
	End
Mckee [2]	Plot
	Character
	Structure
	Goal
	Logic
	Value
	Profound insight

2.2   Models of Motivation for Game Engagement

A simple and intuitive reason for game play is "because games are fun". However, fun is such an ambiguous expression that it can also be used to describe many other activities, such as watching a movie, singing, or dancing. However, almost none of these forms of entertainment are comparable to games with regard to their appeal, sustained engagement and effect on well-being [15].

Both empirical literature [16, 17] and theoretical research from a psychological perspective [15, 18] noted that games can provide experiences that satisfy universal human needs. In 1996, Bartle first proposed a Player Type model based on an online debate regarding the question, "What do people want out of a multi-user dungeon (MUD)?" Answers from experienced players of MUDs were summarized, and the players were categorized into four main types: Achievers, Explorers, Socializers and Killers. The main motivation for achievers is to accomplish game-related goals, advance to higher levels and gather treasures and points. Explorers are motivated by the quest for knowledge of the internal machinations of the game. They enjoy exploring the out-of-the-way places and have fun discovering interesting features. Socializers are motivated by a desire to maintain inter-player relationships. Killers are fulfilled when they cause massive distress to other players [16]. Based on Bartle's model, Yee conducted a factor analysis study on the motivation for game play. The importance of 39 items (such as "level up as fast as possible") were rated by 3200 respondents. A principal component analysis revealed 10 factors, which fit into 3 categories: Achievement, Social and Immersion. Achievement players seek advancement, want to learn mechanics, and enjoy competition. Social players like to socialize with other players, establish in-game relationships and have fun with teamwork. Immersion players enjoy exploring the virtual world, being immersed in the new world, customizing their characters and escaping from the real world [17].

Other theoretical works [15, 18] on the motivations for game playing are mainly rooted in self-determination theory [18, 19]. According to self-determination theory, both intrinsic motivation (i.e., the fundamental needs of human beings: competence, autonomy and relatedness) and extrinsic motivation (e.g., reward, punishment or self-esteem pressure) are important for understanding what people want out of a game. Intrinsic motivation is especially significant. Competence needs refer to the necessity of challenge and feelings of reflectance. Autonomy needs refer to feelings that the decision making will impact results. Relatedness needs refer to the needs for social interaction. Table 2 lists the variables derived from the motivational models.

Table 2. Variables derived from game motivational models

Source	Variables derived from motivational models
Bartle [16]	Achievement within the game context
	Exploration of the game
	Socialize with others
	Imposition upon others
Yee [17]	Advancement
	Mechanics
	Competition
	Socializing
	Relationship
	Teamwork
	Discovery
	Role-play
	Customization
	Escapism
Deci and Ryan [19]	Competency
	Autotomy
	Relatedness

2.3 Game Design Heuristics

In the last three decades, several video game design and evaluation heuristics for enhancing the immersion, playability, enjoyment, or generally speaking fun of game play have been published [4–8].

The earliest heuristics concerning video games were proposed by Malone [4], in which three features were observed to make the system enjoyable: Challenge, Fantasy and Curiosity. Several sub-features such as clear goal, uncertain outcome, emotionally appealing fantasies, and metaphors were also mentioned. Clanton [15] developed a list of usability guidelines for computer games based on hundreds of hours of observation, mainly from three perspectives: game interface, game mechanics and game play. Federoff [6] reviewed the existing heuristics and enriched the list of guidelines based on a case study of a game design team. Desurvire et al. [7] introduced a Heuristic Evaluation for Playability (HEP) model which included game story as an evaluation category in the model. Sweetser and Wyeth [8] developed a new evaluation model, GameFlow, which concentrated on player enjoyment in games rather than usability and validated the model with two games. Eight elements were included in the model: Concentration, challenge, skills, control, clear goals, feedback, immersion, and social interaction. The related variables are listed in Table 3.

Table 3. Variables derived from game design heuristics

Source	Variables
Malone [4]	Challenge
	Goal
	Uncertain outcome
	Fantasy
	Emotions
	Metaphor
	Curiosity
Clanton [5]	Establish goals quickly discovered and easily stated
	Gentle on-ramp
	Spread clues, tolls, obstacles out but not too much
	Pressure can be fun
	Avoid linear, monotonous pacing
Federoff [6]	Immediate feedback
	Quickly and easily involved
	Clear overriding goal presented early
	Variable difficult level
	Multiple goals
	Easy to learn
	Challenge
	Unexpected outcome
	No definite way to win
	Illusion of win-ability
	Fairness
	Allow players to build content
	Create great storyline

(*continued*)

Table 3. (*continued*)

Source	Variables
Desurvire et al. (HEP model) [7]	Consistency
	Clear goals
	Interesting storyline
	Uncertain outcome
	Fairness of outcome
	Transport the player into a level of personal involvement emotionally
	Character
	Shorten the learning curve
Sweetser and Wyeth (GameFlow model) [8]	Concentration
	Challenge
	Player skills
	Control
	Clear goals
	Feedback
	Immersion
	Social interaction

3 Methodology

This research adopts a three-step methodology: variable derivation, questionnaire construction and exploratory factor analysis. The goal of the first step is to derive related variables from both theories and empirical findings, while the next two steps

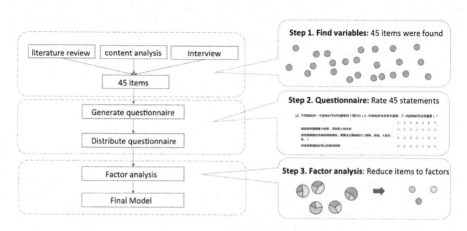

Fig. 1. Research framework

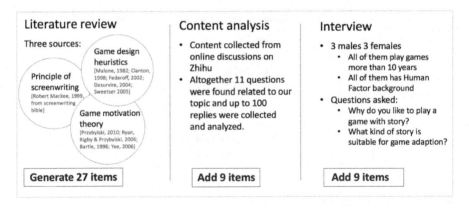

Fig. 2. Procedure for finding variables

aim to reduce the dimension of the model. The research framework is shown in Figs. 1 and 2.

3.1 Variable Derivation

Originally, 27 variables were derived from a literature review with the following principles: (1) items that do not change with stories were removed (e.g., the "reward" item from Clanton [5] and the "Use visual and audio effects to arouse interest" item from Federoff [6]); (2) similar items were combined into a single item (e.g., "uncertain outcomes", "no definite way to win", and "ending" were combined into "Ending" - "The ending of the story can be changed"); and (3) keep as many variables as possible when ambiguity occurs.

To include the opinions of game experts or professionals, we chose to conduct a content analysis based on online discussions on Zhihu, a Chinese community question answering system known for professional answers, over interviews after evaluating the content quantity as well as quality and time efficiency. Altogether 11 questions were found related to our topic and up to 83 replies and 18,538 Chinese characters were collected and analyzed. The conventional approach to content analysis was employed without making pre-assumptions on the category of results. The purpose of this is to allow the categories to flow from the data. Following the process described in Hsieh and Shannon [20], 9 clusters were found and added to the item pool.

Finally, 6 students from the HCI laboratory of Tsinghua University with experience in questionnaire design and more than 10 years of game-playing experience were invited to the pretest. The interview has three purposes: (1) further explore potential factors; (2) check if they can understand the statements of each variable (The statements were carefully phrased to describe the factors. They are composed of original sentences from the literature, which are translated into Chinese, and brief quotes from the interview and answers from zhihu.com; and (3) minimize redundant questions. Nine items were added, of which 5 items were expanded from the original 27 items. The final 45 variables are listed in Table 4.

Table 4. Items list

Storytelling	Game design	Game motivation	Others
Main plot	Comprehension	Advancement	Power (i)
Subplot (c)	Challenge & skills	Competition	Heroism (i)
Character personality	Curiosity	Discover	Rival camp (c)
Character preference (i)	Concentration	Role-play	Counter strike (i)
Structure	Control	Socializing	Strategy (c)
Logic	Empathy	Teamwork	Romance (i)
Ending	Empathy 2 (i)	Customization	Attractive female
World conception (c)	Familiar events	Escape	character (c)
Goal	Familiar conception of world (i)	Autonomy	Attractive male character
Profound insight	Familiar character (i)	Relatedness	(c)
Values	Adapt from famous history (c)	Relatedness 2 (i)	
	Adapt from famous literature, films, TV (c)	Competency	
	Adapted into films, literature, films, TV (c)	Violence	

(c): Items added based on content analysis; (i): Items added based on the interview

3.2 Construct Questionnaire

The questionnaire contained the following parts: demographic information (age, gender, and education), game preference (type), game experience (maximum game-playing frequency, current game-playing frequency, subjective ratings on expertise), overall rating on the importance of storytelling in game play, and ratings on the importance of each variable with a statement. All of the statements were checked by interviewees to ensure correct understanding and minimal redundancy. For each question requiring a rating of attitude, a 7-point Likert scale was adopted in which 7 represented strongly agree and 1 represented strongly disagree.

3.3 Procedure

The questionnaire was posted on websites in December 2014. The links were spread over social media platforms (WeChat and Renren.com) and a game forum (Baidu Tieba "Steam" - the forum of a large game distribution platform). Approximately four-fifths of the participants were from the game forum. Experienced game players were targeted as participants. To prevent inexperienced game players from participating, the following pre-screening question was added: Do you satisfy the following conditions: Love games; Spend much time playing games; Have played at least one game with a story. Participants who failed to meet the requirements were filtered out. The questionnaire was introduced as an "investigation of game preferences in China", without informing participants of the actual purpose of the study. We rewarded each participant with a 10-yuan mobile phone bill credit.

3.4 Participants

Overall, 516 questionnaires were collected. 84% of the participants were male. The ages of over 90% participants ranged from 15 to 3. Additionally, 74% of the participants had a bachelor's degree or higher. 94% had no working experience in the game industry. On average, the participants had played computer games for 9.48 years (SD = 4.11). The maximum duration of their game-playing career is on average 1.22 h per day (SD = 5.127). However, currently, over 80% of them play games for less than 5 h per day. The top five game types preferred by the participants were shooting games (51.68%), action games (40%), role-playing games (39.6%), strategy games (29.31%) and adventure games (2.99%). Finally, 72% of the participants claimed that they played many types of games, and 56% of the participants regarded themselves as experts in game playing.

4   Results

Among the 516 answers, 11 unqualified participants (who did not satisfy the pre-screen conditions) and 51 invalid answers (answers with nulls, all-7 answers, 1 vs 7 in highly correlated questions) were eliminated, resulting in 454 valid answers.

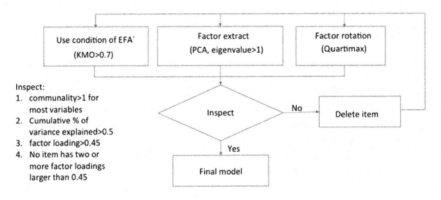

Fig. 3. EFA procedure

An exploratory factor analysis (EFA) was conducted to find the structural characteristics of the questionnaire. The Kaiser-Meyer-Olkin test (KMO = .876) revealed significant correlation between items, which means that the items have enough common information. The EFA enabled the reduction of the items into factors that are comparatively less correlated.

The procedure of EFA is shown in Fig. 3. First, factors with an eigenvalue larger than 1 were extracted. A component matrix was calculated and rotated relative to orthogonal rotation for further interpretation. Quartimax rotation was adopted in this study to get factors with lower correlation. After the calculation, the following conditions were imposed: (1) the communality should be larger than 1 for most variables; (2) the total variance should be larger than .5; (3) The factor loading of each item should be larger than .45; and (4) there should be no items with two factor loadings larger than .45. If these conditions were not satisfied, the items violating the conditions were deleted one by one until all of the conditions were met.

Following the procedure, 2 items were eliminated: Teamwork and Concentration. The communality of these items was less than .5, indicating that less than half of the variance in measured variables is reproduced by the latent constructs. All of the conditions were met after the elimination. As a result, 11 factors were extracted from 43 items, explaining 63.24% of the total variance. The results of EFA were shown in Tables 5 and 6.

Table 5. Total variance explained

Compo-nent	Initial eigenvalues			Extraction sums of squared loadings			Rotation sums of squared loadings		
	Total	% of Var	Cumu-lative %	Total	% of Var	Cumulative %	Total	% of Var	Cumulative %
1	1.049	23.37	23.370	1.049	23.37	23.37	4.73	11.001	11.001
2	3.57	8.303	31.673	3.57	8.303	31.673	3.759	8.743	19.744
3	2.185	5.081	36.754	2.185	5.081	36.754	2.789	6.485	26.229
4	2.06	4.791	41.545	2.06	4.791	41.545	2.579	5.997	32.226
5	1.878	4.368	45.913	1.878	4.368	45.913	2.514	5.847	38.073
6	1.732	4.028	49.941	1.732	4.028	49.941	2.247	5.227	43.3
7	1.299	3.021	52.962	1.299	3.021	52.962	2.223	5.17	48.47
8	1.228	2.857	55.819	1.228	2.857	55.819	1.655	3.849	52.319
9	1.119	2.601	58.421	1.119	2.601	58.421	1.605	3.732	56.051
10	1.041	2.421	6.842	1.041	2.421	6.842	1.59	3.697	59.748
11	1.032	2.400	63.241	1.032	2.400	63.241	1.502	3.493	63.241
12	.949	2.207	65.449						
13	.900	2.094	67.542						
14	.844	1.964	69.506						
15	.78	1.814	71.320						
16	.748	1.739	73.059						
17	.73	1.697	74.756						
18	.703	1.635	76.391						
19	.685	1.593	77.984						
20	.649	1.508	79.492						
21	.610	1.418	8.910						
22	.597	1.389	82.299						
23	.573	1.332	83.631						
24	.556	1.294	84.925						
25	.514	1.196	86.121						
26	.507	1.18	87.301						
27	.481	1.118	88.419						
28	.470	1.093	89.511						
29	.446	1.038	9.550						
30	.428	.995	91.545						
31	.399	.927	92.472						
32	.383	.891	93.362						
33	.369	.859	94.221						
34	.360	.838	95.059						
35	.347	.807	95.866						
36	.317	.737	96.603						
37	.282	.657	97.259						
38	.270	.628	97.887						
39	.254	.591	98.478						
40	.218	.508	98.986						
41	.180	.419	99.405						
42	.134	.313	99.717						
43	.122	.283	100						

Table 6. Rotation matrix

	Component										
	1	2	3	4	5	6	7	8	9	10	11
Familiar event	.852										
Familiar world conception	.849										
Adapted from famous history	.823										
Adapted into films, literature, TVs	.820										
Adapted from films, literature, TVs	.795										
Familiar character	.790										
Relatedness 2		.75									
Relatedness		.71									
Empathy		.679									
Romance		.581									
Empathy 2		.546									
Profound insight		.509									
Structure			.703								
Character personality			.691								
Main plot			.678								
Logic			.576								
Counter attack				.652							
Violence				.641							
Competition				.638							
Rival camp				.572							
Strategy				.493							
Advancement				.454							
Autonomy					.694						
Control					.663						
Customization					.631						
Escape					.542						
Ending					.486						
Discover						.720					
Role-play						.626					
Socializing						.554					
Power							.857				
Heroism							.824				
Competence							.581				
Comprehension								.586			
Goal								.566			
Curiosity								.505			
Conception of world								.452			

(*continued*)

Table 6. (*continued*)

	Component										
	1	2	3	4	5	6	7	8	9	10	11
Attractive female character									.68		
Attractive male character									.515		
Values										.754	
Character preference										.482	
Challenge & skill											.612
Subplot											.483

5   Discussion

To measure the game-adaptability of stories, this study proposes an evaluation model with 11 factors (as shown in Fig. 4) based on players' ratings: engage & explore, scriptwriting, distance from reality, autonomy, empathy, values, competition, power, multi-challenge, physical attractiveness, and familiarity. Here is the further explanation of these factors: (Detailed items see Table 7).

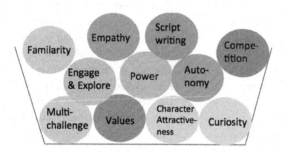

Fig. 4. Final model of game-adaptability evaluation

Engage and explore refer to the attraction on the players that arouses their desire to explore the world in games. Game design is not just about the design of the gameplay and stories. Game design is also about the creation of a lively world, a world that contains many interesting places and stories. Scriptwriting is about how to tell a story in a game, which includes design of a main plot, design of the story structure, depiction of characters and logical correctness. Most of the games are very far from reality, which calls into full play the players' imagination. Dungeons & Dragons, a famous game category originating from a tabletop role-playing game, is a good example of distance from reality. This type of game creates a world with history and culture which is quite different from the real world. The species in this world are quite different and have their own unique abilities. And the world is mysterious for the player, which arouses their curiosity. Power is one of the most important concepts in most games. Players solve problems and accomplish tasks in the game to improve their abilities. And the more power they acquire, the more tasks they are able to fulfill. This positive feedback will motivate players to move forward in the games. Many games require players to accomplish various challenges and achievements. Attractive characters contribute a great deal to the story telling of a game.

Table 7. Important factors for creating, choosing and adapting high game-adaptable stories

Factor	Item	Statement: is it important to the playability of games if …
Engage & explore	Discover	There is a lot for me to discover in the game world
	Role-play	After reading the story, I want to be personally on the scene and experience what happens to the character
	Socializing	I can talk with other players about the plot and character
Scriptwriting	Main plot	The main plot is attractive
	Structure	The structure is delicate
	Character personality	The characters are distinctive
	Logic	The story is logically correct
Distance from reality	World conception	The conception of the world (including ages, domain, history etc.) is attractive
	Curiosity	I am curious about the world in the story
	Comprehension	I can quickly understand the whole story, the relationship of the characters and their goals
	Goal	The goal of the main character is attractive to me
Autonomy	Autonomy	I can explore how my operation leads to different endings
	Escape	I can accomplish what I cannot do in the real world
	Customization	I can customize characters/choose from different characters
	Ending	The ending of the story can be changed
	Control	I can control the progress of the story
Values	Character preference	I like the character of the story
	Values	I agree with the personal values and attitudes possessed by the character
Empathy	Relatedness 2	How the characters are related is touching
	Relatedness	I feel warmth of the world after reading the story
	Profound insight	The story has profound insights to humanity and society
	Romance	There is romance between characters
	Empathy 2	After reading the story, I wish to help the character to achieve his/her goal
	Empathy	I am always influenced by the emotion of the characters

(continued)

Table 7. (*continued*)

Factor	Item	Statement: is it important to the playability of games if …
Competition	Strategy	Strategy, tactics, scheme should be used to achieve the goal in the story
	Rival camp	There are several rival camps entangling with each other, but we cannot determine right and wrong, good or evil
	Competition	In the story, the character needs to compete with others
	Advancement	The character grows with my operation
	Violence	There are fight scenes in the story
	Counter strike	The character comes back with a fantastic counter strike
Multi-challenge	Challenge & skills	Many types of talents are needed for the challenge in the story (strategy, quick reaction, socializing…)
	Subplot	The subplot is attractive (conversation with non-player characters, subtasks…)
Power	Competence	I feel I can exploit my talents in this virtual world
	Heroism	I can become a hero in the game
	Power	I can experience the sense of power in the game
Physical attractiveness	Attractive female character	There are many attractive female characters in the story
	Attractive male character	There are many attractive male characters in the story
Familiarity	Familiar event	I can experience events which I am familiar with in the game (e.g., famous events in the history, in other games, novels, or films
	Familiar world conception	The conception of the world in the game is familiar to me
	Familiar character	I can encounter familiar characters in the game (e.g., eminent person in the history, in other games, novels, or films)
	Adapted from famous history	This game is adapted from famous history
	Adapted from famous films, literature, TV	This game is adapted from famous films, novels or TV series
	Adapted into films, literature, films, TV	This game is adapted from famous films, novels or TV series

The Witcher 3, the winner of The Game Awards 2015, provides players with great autonomy. It adapted from a famous Polish novel, which promises high quality and high completion of the game story. The plot is well organized, and the characters are well portrayed. Those who have read the story are likely to be familiar with the plot and characters when playing this game. Players can slaughter monsters, collect materials and make their own armor and sword. Additionally, the storyline has various choices. Players are able to change the fate of some other characters by choosing some action or conversations. And due to the different choice, the ending will be different. The main character of The Witcher, Geralt of Rivia, has many friends and enemies. The relationships between characters are complex and touching, which offer profound insights. The presence of many difficult choices in The Witcher 3 arouses players' empathy. No decision is easy for players because they have to consider morals and interests. Players sometimes have to judge what is right and what is wrong. Sometimes, helping some people in the game means you have to damage interests of other people. Most of these choices are ambiguous, depending on players' own values, which is a reflection of the real world.

6   Conclusion

In this research, a model for measuring the game-adaptability of stories was established with 11 factors (sorted by significance): engage & explore, scriptwriting, distance from reality, autonomy, empathy, values, competition, power, multi-challenge, physical attractiveness, and familiarity. Among these factors, engage & explore and scriptwriting are the most important factors in a game storytelling. A story with higher potential in these factors is more likely to be welcomed by players when adapted to a game. If a story was extraordinary in some respects, it is also likely to succeed when adapted to a game.

There are three main limitations of this study. Firstly, the study was based on the views of players. And players tend to focus on their own experience of the games. They are not concerned about commercial prospects and technological difficulty, which also play important parts in game development for developers or investors. Secondly, most of the participants of the survey were steam players, which is different from the players who play console games. Thirdly, the survey was conducted in China, and the results of this study might be influenced by culture differences. In addition, the game industry in China is quite different from the game industries in other countries, which might also have some influence on the result. Thus, it will be very interesting to explore the cultural differences in game storytelling in future work.

Acknowledgement. This research was supported by Shenzhen Malong Artificial Intelligence Research Center.

References

1. Chatman, S.B.: Story and Discourse: Narrative Structure in Fiction and Film. Cornell University Press, New York (1980)
2. McKee, R.: Substance, Structure, Style, and the Principles of Screenwriting. HarperCollins, New York (1997)

3. Glassner, A.: Interactive storytelling: people, stories, and games. In: Balet, O., Subsol, G., Torguet, P. (eds.) ICVS 2001. LNCS, vol. 2197, pp. 51–60. Springer, Heidelberg (2001). https://doi.org/10.1007/3-540-45420-9_7

4. Malone, T.W.: Heuristics for designing enjoyable user interfaces: lessons from computer games. In: Proceedings of the 1982 Conference on Human Factors in Computing Systems. ACM (1982)

5. Clanton, C.: An interpreted demonstration of computer game design. In: CHI 1998 Conference Summary on Human Factors in Computing Systems. ACM (1998)

6. Federoff, M.A.: Heuristics and Usability Guidelines for the Creation and Evaluation of Fun in Video Games. Citeseer (2002)

7. Desurvire, H., Caplan, M., Toth, J.A.: Using heuristics to evaluate the playability of games. In: CHI'04 Extended Abstracts on Human Factors in Computing Systems, pp. 1509–1512. ACM April 2004

8. Sweetser, P., Wyeth, P.: GameFlow: a model for evaluating player enjoyment in games. Comput. Entertain. (CIE) 3(3), 3 (2005)

9. Qin, H., Patrick Rau, P.L., Salvendy, G.: Measuring player immersion in the computer game narrative. Int. J. Hum.-Comput. Interact. 25(2), 107–133 (2009)

10. Majewski, J.: Theorising Video Game Narrative. Bond University (2003)

11. Dansky, R.: Introduction to game narrative. In: Game Writing Narrative Skills for Videogames, pp. 1–24 (2007)

12. Jenkins, H.: Game design as narrative. Computer 44, 53 (2004)

13. Crawford, C.: Chris Crawford on Game Design. New Riders, Indianapolis (2003)

14. Meadows, D.H.: Thinking in Systems. A Primer. Chelsea Green Publishing, White River Junction (2008)

15. Przybylski, A.K., Rigby, C.S., Ryan, R.M.: A motivational model of video game engagement. Rev. Gen. Psychol. 14(2), 154 (2010)

16. Bartle, R.: Hearts, clubs, diamonds, spades: players who suit MUDs. J. MUD Res. 1(1), 19 (1996)

17. Yee, N.: Motivations for play in online games. CyberPsychol. Behav. 9(6), 772–775 (2006)

18. Ryan, R.M., Rigby, C.S., Przybylski, A.: The motivational pull of video games: a self-determination theory approach. Motiv. Emot. 30(4), 344–360 (2006)

19. Deci, E.L., Ryan, R.M.: The "what" and "why" of goal pursuits: human needs and the self-determination of behavior. Psychol. Inq. 11(4), 227–268 (2000)

20. Hsieh, H.F., Shannon, S.E.: Three approaches to qualitative content analysis. Qual. Health Res. 15(9), 1277–1288 (2005)

21. Ryan, R.M., Deci, E.L.: Intrinsic and extrinsic motivations: classic definitions and new directions. Contemp. Educ. Psychol. 25(1), 54–67 (2000)

Integrated Strategies of Participatory Design and PBL Towards Collaboration Quality

Chenhan Jiang[(✉)] and Yongqi Lou

Tongji University, Shanghai, China
chenhan0713@126.com, louyongqi@tongji.edu.cn

Abstract. PBL (Problem-Based Learning) as a self-directed learning approach had been widely used in the K12 education area. However, researchers and practitioners still face confusion and challenges on collaboration quality. We defined the problems for such quality through observation at Tongji-Huangpu School of Design and Innovation (THDI). Then the hypothesis that participatory design could improve the quality of collaboration and involvement has been put forward based on related work analysis of integration PD in PBL. The enhancement orientation includes using inclusive and interactive PD approach to improve valuable inquiry clues and group attendance towards high collaboration quality. To analyze the collaboration quality degree and performance based on PD approaches, we took the method of user research for participants who are involved in the PD-driven PBL module at THDI. The research focus factors, effectiveness implementation of integration the participatory design approaches in PBL. We further explored the accessible and efficient strategies for applying such methods in PBL scenario as research findings. This study proposed a theoretical framework which takes the advantages of participatory design towards smooth and efficient collaboration quality in PBL progression, and the research at THDI also has also provided an action paradigm and feasible guideline for similar context.

Keywords: Problem Based Learning (PBL) · Participatory design
Collaboration quality · K12 education
Tongji-Huangpu School of Design and Innovation

1 Introduction

Problem-based learning (PBL) has been a heatedly discussed topic in the cross-disciplinary education area for decades, the practicality and effectiveness of this learning methodology have been validated in various ways. The definition of PBL could be divided into three categories generally: the theory of 'curriculum,' 'instructional strategy' and 'a total approach' (Boud and Felleti 1997; Barrows and Tamblyn 1980). This learning mode begins with a well-designed problem that empowers

This paper is supported by National Centre of Schooling Development Programme's Key Research Project: "Design Driven STEAM and PBL Curriculum Development - the Case of Tongji-Huangpu School of Design and Innovation" (CSDP17FS1108).

P.-L. P. Rau (Ed.): CCD 2018, LNCS 10912, pp. 46–59, 2018.
https://doi.org/10.1007/978-3-319-92252-2_4

students to construct structured knowledge, critical thinking, problem-solving skills, self-directed learning strategies and collaboration; Such PBL curriculum requires instructors and teachers to have a deep understanding for learning content and scenario. For developers, creating a learning project should contain a variety of background knowledge and possible solutions. The inquiry meditation and driven force could not only turn students from passive recipients into active explorers, but also foster mentors being facilitators and co-learners. As an innovative curriculum, the PBL objective is enabling learners to acquire relevant knowledge, reprocess information and improve their abilities solving similar problems in the living environment or the future work (Barrows and Tamblyn 1980). Compared with a passive knowledge generation method in traditional learning, PBL begins with a complicated inquiry problem which is driven by learners. Depending on this active starting point, knowledge integration and acquisition process could be highly motivational and impressive. The learning objective is to define issues which could represent an incongruity of the phenomenon in real living context. Under this scenario, the self-directed learning topic and framework could enable participants developing solutions with constructive knowledge, the habits of thinking and reflection could also be cultivated spontaneously. Such continuous cycle is a so-called inquiry process (Audet and Jordan 2005). It could not only facilitate a sustainable mode of knowledge generation but also realize a cross-disciplinary knowledge flow among all roles of participants in co-creation context. In one word, PBL is a relevant and sustainable knowledge generation and redefinition process (As Fig. 1). In this cycle, appropriate and effective inquiry problems have to represent students' actual needs, and also enable them to internalize the self-constructed experience into the reproducible and expanding knowledge (Neame 1981).

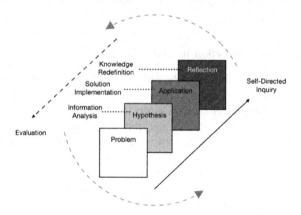

Fig. 1. Problem-based learning cycle

Although PBL has such positive effects on capability building, the collaboration quality is still a research area that not been discussed sufficiently. Participatory design (PD), as an interactive and inclusive approach, has the advantage for different roles involvement and sharing thinking, comments, knowledge, and skills based on the mutual context-understanding (Spinuzzi 2005). Suitable design task could trigger collaborative learning behaviors for bottom-up knowledge redefinition (Knudstrup 2004). Therefore, some practitioners had tried to take such approaches into PBL to improve individual participation and knowledge diversity in some cases, but there still some confusion about the useful guides for developing such PD curriculums, especially for teenagers in the stage of K12. And there is still a gap between the PD implementation methods and the intervention orientation of collaboration quality. Based on above discussion, the purpose of this study is to clarify such quality and how to use the participatory design approaches to improve this.

2   Challenges and Problems of PBL Collaboration Quality

2.1   PBL Collaboration Quality

In the theoretical area, experts used the California Critical Thinking Disposition Inventory (CCTDI) as measuring criteria for PBL collaboration. Seven qualities are involved in this standard: Truthseeking, Open-mindedness, Analyticity, Systematicity, Critical Thinking Self-confidence, Inquisitiveness, and Cognitive maturity (Margeston 1994; Maudley and Strivens 2000). To achieve this, there are five widely-accepted steps which are: forming a new learning group and creating an acquisition problem, starting the acquisition problem, implementing a problem solving, outcome presentation, and reflection on the learning outcome (Barrows and Tamblyn 1980; Schmidt and Moust 2000; Christensen 2004). However, there is little practice-based research for PBL collaboration quality, especially for the challenges analysis or inspiration methods. Thus, we took the emerging practice of Tongji-Huangpu School of Design and Innovation (THDI), Shanghai China as observation object to define the challenges of PBL collaboration quality.

2.2   Observation and Reflection in THDI Practice

THDI is the first design thinking school founded by Prof. Yongqi LOU in 2016. It was the joint-effort of the College of Design and Innovation at Tongji University (Tongji D&I) and the Educational Bureau of Huangpu District of Shanghai. The aim of this school is to educate the future leaders who can change the world through implementing design thinking across the contexts. In THDI, 60% of the learning in THDI is subject-based, all related to today's Real World Challenges, while the rest of 40% is PBL. These two parts are integrated and interacted closely based on the principles of "design thinking." The key idea is to encourage the students to use the knowledge across the contexts (As Fig. 2) Prof. Yongqi LOU established a team led by Prof. Tiina Laurila of Tongji D&I to develop the curriculum and instructional strategies of the PBL teaching. One of their key agendas is to collaborate and interact with subject-based teaching group closely.

Now, the THDI has been operating for half a year. From the feedback analysis on multiple roles of participants based on the previous two modules, we found the PBL collaboration quality is one of the key challenges of the success. There are two aspects, which limit the integration of the contents with the contexts and then, further limit maximizing the potential of PBL.

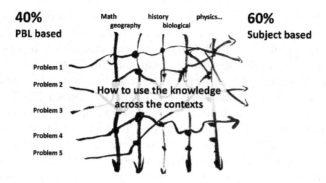

Fig. 2. The framework of curriculums at THDI designed by Prof. Yongqi Lou (Source: hand drawing of Prof. Yongqi Lou)

On the one hand, through the participatory observation, we found students encountered difficulties in defining the suitable line for probing into the underlying problems and generation systematic solutions. Students expected to follow an intended learning guide like filling in blanks in examinations, rather than to design an exploratory framework by teamwork based on problem scenario. Parts of such factors are due to the internal capabilities of group members, but the underlying cause is the attractive clue and common group goal that could arouse sustainable motivation for incremental learning.

On the other hand, we found students were lack of the strong sense of self-driven problem probing and adjustment based on real-time learning progression. Once the ideas or concepts failed to get recognition or agreement in the process of brainstorming, they would lose the strong motivation contributing to the group collaboration and then turned to the negative auxiliary. On the one hand, through the self-evaluation questionnaire after on curriculum module, most students defined their roles as 'concept supporter,' 'follower' and 'modelling maker'. Only a small number of students had the strong self-identity and confidence as crucial participants to foster group collaboration towards a right direction. The less of group belonging and cohesion would directly affect teamwork experience and effectiveness when they meet new members. Some inner-harmonious groups also faced limits that there was lack of control on discussion boundary and concepts depth. For example, group chatting sometimes were instead of effective arguing for knowledge generation. Thus, above objective and subjective factors that affect the ideal collaboration quality.

3　Related Works

3.1　Participatory Design Approaches in Education

Under the background of globalization and knowledge-based economy, how to use integrated design methods to involve existing theories and practices actively is becoming an emerging research issue (Lou 2017). Participatory design (PD) is a set of theories, practices, and studies related to end-users as full participants in design activities (Schuler and Namioka 1993). The technical solution is not a given in PD process, design decisions that shape the solutions should be shared with those who will use it (Bratteteig and Wagner 2012). For users, it allows users to share information and know the whole process; For designers, it helps them understand the unfamiliar scenario and requirements, and develop prototypical solutions with interdisciplinary knowledge and co-defined frameworks (Wilkinson and Angeli 2014). Some PBL practices have introduced design-driven approaches into class to empower participants cooperating with consensus and common targets. Take the case of 'Mission D' case at College of Design and Innovation of Tongji University as an example. It aims at cultivating students who are "deep problem solvers in their home discipline but also capable of interacting with and understanding specialists from a wide range of disciplines and functional areas" (Yongqi et al. 2016). The comparison of traditional learning, PBL learning and the PD-driven PBL is as following figure (As Fig. 3).

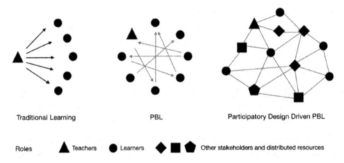

Fig. 3. PD key advantages for enhancing PBL collaboration quality

3.2   Projects Analysis of Integration PD into PBL

Through literature review and the case analysis of the Design Tech High School and NuVu school, we found the common approaches towards smooth and deep collaboration is using PD as an inclusive learning framework and motivation of joint efforts. Take the 'Design Advisory' course at Design Tech High School as an example. Students would be encouraged to identify and address real issues in communities nearby. PD acts the key role in cultivating students' empathy the learning target and framework like users who would benefit from the design solutions. The participatory design task has provided an attractive line of group inquiry with a deep motivation. In this open system, students have involved in entrepreneurship skills cultivation unintentionally and naturally. Another case at the NuVu School represents the PD contributions on multidirectional knowledge flow and participant full contribution with the prototype co-creation and design iteration with users. That means the shared, mutual-help and complementary learning between students with different personalities and capabilities could be realized through the PD-driven PBL courses. Based on above analysis, the collaboration quality enhancement orientation with PD approaches could be summarized as following two aspects:

Inquiry Clues. In the theoretical and practical area, experts and practitioners face difficulties that are how to develop meaning problems to trigger self-motivated learning with inquiry and reflection value (Barrows 2000). As the core of such collaborative behaviors in education, an appropriate clue which is from real lives could illustrate learning target and stimulate curiosity nature with a continuous probing. With this standard goal at the beginning of exploration process, participants would recognize the feasibility and possibility for solution-making in the teamwork (Torp and Sage 2002). It could also be presented as learning needs and sustainable driven force throughout whole learning cycle. Thus, how to design this clue is the most vital part of curriculum development because it directly affects the information gathering among students and restricts the collaborative behaviors among students and mentors.

Group Attendance. Group attendance as another factor including the collaborative motivation and joint efforts on learning participation affect the PBL collaboration quality directly (Van Berkel and Schmidt 2000). Only within well-functioning PBL groups, new knowledge will be constructed and tested through negotiation, leading to true constructivist learning (Savery and Duffy 1996). In this context, students have to achieve common cognitive for the learning task, to experience a sense of interdependence, feel comfortable and encouraged to express their ideas that their group can work in an effective way (Van den Bossche et al. 2006). When they share common goals, they are dependent on and accountable to each other (Johnson et al. 2007; Van der Linden et al. 2000). Such performance of group attendance relates to the knowledge sharing and mechanism to inspire individual's contribution. However, the factors affecting group attendance are quite complicated that could not be solved with a simple approach.

Based on above discussion, researchers and developers need to rethink this tricky problem and develop participatory strategies to empower all stakeholders for knowledge contribution and capabilities complement. Thus, a hypothesis is put forward: the participatory design driven learning task as the intervention into PBL could enhance learning collaboration actively and comprehensively. Firstly, PD as an open system could involve more stakeholders' contribution and relationship reconstruction in a controllable group scope. In this collaboration networks, learners could empathize target users' demands and define the context-based learning frameworks; Secondly, PD as the hands-on activity with interest-orientation and teamwork could provide fruitful inquiry lines to facilitate learners following, defining and exploring learning content. Thirdly, for the new knowledge itself, PD as a dynamic mechanism could foster the pattern transition from one-way flow to peer-to-peer sharing towards an active group collaboration.

4   User Research

To analyze the effectiveness and feasibilities of integration the participatory design into PBL towards high collaboration quality, we designed a PBL course module called 'Creative Communities' at THDI after the previous reflection. The purpose of this module is using PD methods to improve previous collaboration quality challenges like attractive inquiry clues and group attendance performance (As Fig. 4).

Fig. 4. Learning scenarios of 'Creative Communities' module at THDI (Source: THDI Teaching Group led by Prof. Tiina Laurila)

4.1   Participants

Analysis results come from the qualitative user research methods of expert interview, students feedback analysis and participatory observation for the collaboration quality insights and evaluation for this module. The course period is 3-weeks which involved forty-eight students, two PBL teachers, two subject-based teachers and one teaching assistant with design background. The roles and responsible work of the interviewees in this module are as following table (As Table 1).

Table 1.   Interviewees information

Interviewee	Role and responsibility
Mrs. Xu	The teacher in charge of the class. She manages the learning quality and students real-time feedback and problems in the collaborative learning process
Mrs. Qian	Politics teacher. She is in charge of the integration of subject-based knowledge (i.e. basic financial knowledge and consumer psychology) into the PD design tasks (i.e. business model innovation for a service)
Mr. Ma	PBL teacher. He is in charge of the technical part including using interactive tools for the surrounding environment investigation and prototypes making
Mr. Huang	PBL teacher. He as the facilitator is in charge of leading students to probe user underlying demands and visualization for design concepts
Miss. Zhao	Teaching assistant. She is in charge of supporting the collaborative quality improvement like grouping, task description, team work problems collection and concepts development

4.2 Procedure

We set up a framework of participatory design in this one-month of design course. The first week was to understand design scenario, through the lectures of managers and co-founders of several community innovation projects students got the basic cognitive of the problem of this context and potential design-driven solutions. Then they started the design framework co-creation and brainstorming based on research of surrounding communities to formulate the specific problem to be solved and preliminary concept. In the second week, we facilitated students using model making tools to define and visualize the problems scenario and related users they need to involve in the design process. This tool helped students get insights for people flow, business forms and capital flows in the community around the school during model construction and interaction process. Based on each group's concept they used the user research and participatory tools to observe, interview and co-create design points with residents in the communities. The third week was the development of design works. Each group used visualization and prototyping methods to realize their concepts, such as rescue service design for community pets, tourism information interactive design in old streets, design for sharing leisure space in communities, redesign for telephone booth and the intelligent parking system design. In the final report, teachers and part of target users were invited to sharing ideas, comments and suggestions (Fig. 5).

	CREATIVE COMMUNITIES														
FOCUS	*YOU* focus on interaction and collaboration qualities in design process to foster the community creativity WEEKS 8,9,11 (WEEK 10, Mon 6/11, Tue 7/11 sports, Wed, Thu, Fri Exams)														
Week	8. Cultural Heritage and Urbanism					9. City Scope workshop					11. Entrepreneurial Service and Creative Communities				
date time If more time needed Mon-Thu can be extende d to 5:15	Mon 23/10 2:55-4:25 Lectures: Cases Sharing of Creative Communiti es and Approaches to Foster Old Community Creativity	Tue 24/10 2:55-4:25 Lectures: Urbanizat ion and Cultural Heritage Urban Develop ment, case Red Town	Wed 25/10 2:55-4:25 Lecture: Design Harvest Project on Chongmi ng Island	Thu 26/10 2:55-4:25 Lecture: Basic knowledg e of Open communi ties and Service Design	Fri 27/10 1:10-4:15 Visit to Shanghai Urban Planning and exhibition Centre	Mon 30/10 2:55-4:25 City Scope: Map that matters-introductio n of the task and mapping of experience s around the school	Tue 31/10 2:55-4:25 City Scope: Using City Scope to illustrate the values, spatial properties of the environme nt	Wed 1/11 2:55-4:25 City Scope: Presenting CityScope and starting to make design prototypes	Thu 2/11 2:55-4:25 City Scope: Prototypes improveme nt	Fri 3/11 1:10-4:10 Presentations for Design Issues to Foster the Community Creativity with the City Scope	Mon 13/11 2:55-4:25 Tutorial: Problems to trigger an entreprene rial service, Business modelling	Tue 14/11 2:55-4:25 Tutorial: Concept generation, Service Blueprint Drawing	Wed 15/11 2:55-4:25 Tutorial. Group Collaborati on, Touchpoint s Visualizatio n	Thu 16/11 2:55-4:25 Prototype Making (skethces, collague, models , performance)	Fri 17/11 1:10-4:10 Exhibition of the students' design processes and results in High School
	Cultural Heritage, Urbanization, Open Communities Lectures and small Exercises					City Scope workshop Lectures and Tutorials					Entrepreneurial service generation and Presentations Exercises and Tutorials				
WHAT?	Learning of the development of the urban-rural environment, systems and creative open communities					Experiencing the City Scope tool for designing the urban environment					Learning to develop the business concept based on the learnings and experience in the previous weeks and presenting the work in an exhibition				

Fig. 5. 'Creative Communities' module at THDI (Source: THDI teaching group led by Prof. Tiina Laurila)

We listed the interview framework to collect participants' feedback after this course. To study the feasibility, effectiveness, and weakness of PD approaches towards

PBL collaboration quality, the interview questions for teachers focus on following aspects, and the feedback of interview is shown as Fig. 6.

– Compared with general PBL, what are the contributions of PD courses to students' collaboration motivation, enthusiasm, and effect?
– Compared with the previous PBL courses, does the PD task give students better learning guide and research clue to define solutions and construct context-based knowledge? How does PD achieve this?
– In collaborative learning, does every team member has sufficient knowledge or skill contribution to the group work through integration PD methods into PBL? Any complaints or problems?
– In the process of PD, what design topic is the most enthusiastic to trigger the group collaboration and idea sharing? What type of issue has negative effects on group discussion and concept development? What are the causes of such problems?

The interview questions for students focus on the following aspects:

– What is the self-definition of your role in the group collaboration?
– What is the performance and development of your team members in this design process?
– What is the crucial point motivating you and your team members to engage in the collaboration? And what is the barrier to sharing ideas and developing concepts in the teamwork?
– What is the improvement or iteration orientation of your group design work?

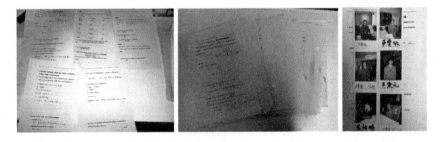

Fig. 6. Interview feedbacks (Source: photography by the authors)

4.3   Results

Through the card sorting and summarization for interview information, we classified the feedback data into four main aspects including the users' points of view, affecting aspects of the collaboration quality, attributes of this quality and the PD contributions in this process (As Table 2).

Table 2. Effectiveness and feasibilities of PD approaches towards PBL collaboration quality

Users' points of view	Affecting aspect of collaboration quality	Attribute	PD contributions
Attractive and well-designed grouping in this PD course has greatly improved students' motivation of teamwork. Collaboration with new partners has inspired the complementary skills cultivation	Group attendance	Capability and personalities matching	Random grouping game based on students' participation like self-cognitive and self-evaluation
Instead of the top-down assignments in traditional PBL, the integration the subject knowledge into the design task has triggered student context-based knowledge acquisition in specific learning progression impressively	Inquiry clue	Context understanding with inquiry lines	Offering a divers and complex inquiry line for learning and solution making in collaboration with other disciplinary teachers
Compared with the traditional PBL, the fewer technical requirements and professional restrictions of PD tasks allow everyone to touch the methods and imagine potential outputs. Thus, it has inspired all participants' joint efforts for developing final works. Especially for some marginalized members of the weak participation, they are also divided into reasonable tasks and encouraged to input ideas collaboration actively	Group attendance	Capability division; Teamwork congruence (encouragement & motivation)	The depth and scope of PD concept development is flexible that different students with diverse personalities and learning habits can get the rational capacity matching
A good PD task has facilitated the sustainable and continuous learning beyond the course and school, students have inspired to search further information to improve their dissatisfied concepts and find resources like NGO, social activities or organizations for implementation and iteration	Inquiry clue	A degree of complexity, diverse and iteration of inquiry clues	PD could foster the knowledge into action, knowledge flow and the relationship reconstruction. As an interactive inquiry clue, it has been proved in this process and has profound effects on learners

5 Findings

5.1   PD Characters Affecting Collaboration Quality

Contextualization and Complexity of Inquiry Clues. Firstly, at the start point of a PBL inquiry process, a PD task could give a clear description of the research content which has inner-linked problems and potential approaches to solve the problem at the same time. It illustrates the content related to a realistic context that could trigger common understanding and deep empathy sense. For instance, such context-based understanding could include the incongruence, which means contradictions and conflicts in a situation or phenomenon. Like the relationship reconstruction issues in immigrant communities, if students face to this learning topic, they need to inquire cultural, economic and psychological reasons for the involvement and self-identity of the excluded groups. Behind this scenario, they could learn complicated social problems and build collaboration behaviors from bottom up. Moreover, a suitable and interactive inquiry clue under the PD task also have a degree of complexity which means diversity, difficulty, and tolerance for potential solutions and design methods. It emphasizes to activate every participant's contribution towards a strong passion and exploration willing with a common using scenario for design outputs. For instance, PD could foster complex clues with accessibility include a problem to be solved, a topic of the design output, the channels and methods, the technical and cultural conditions required, the resources and partners, the job division of team members, and the alternative concepts. The complexity also should consider the active communicating environment for brain-storming to avoid too weak or too straightforward topic.

Capability Matching Towards Group Attendance. To empower and activate the individual knowledge and skills construction, the attractiveness, participation and feasibility mechanism for capabilities matching has to be taken into account. PD as self-driven creative activities allow diverse forms for gamification grouping, task division and collaboration scope. On the one hand, through self-cognitive and existed knowing for students, multiple design tasks could attractive students with differentiated personal abilities and knowledge reserves into suitable groups, they would search partners with complementary skills to achieve high learning experience and quality, such skills like illustration concepts, technology for prototypes making, presentation, leadership for efficient work or knowledge in particular subject could be divided reasonably. On the other hand, the high participation could enable the random and interactive grouping methods to ensure the collaboration scope and depth. From the THDI, mentors used ice-breaking activities and grouping games based on tangible products co-creation or student mutual evaluation to divide optimists, introverts, cooperator or mavericks into suitable teams had achieved positive effects on teamwork.

5.2   Implementation Strategy

PD implementation strategies which are integrated into PBL to enhance the collaboration quality are abstracted as three inner-liked and continuous steps based on above factors. They include empathy for inquiry context understanding, capability-based grouping towards group attendance, and relationship reconstruction towards further collaboration.

Empathy for Context Understanding. With the goal to achieve context understanding for inquiry clues, mentors have to use PD empathy approaches to guide students where is an inquiry problem comes from, what is the cultural or physical factors or limitations, and who are target users relating to this context. This strategy needs mentors guide students to apply empathy design methods like the participatory observation, focus group interview and user profiles on simulating pain points, demands, and benefits that users would face too. The aim of this strategy is turning students' roles from objective observers into stakeholders, from spectators to the people who will be spontaneously involved in this matter based on empathy stage of PD. For instance, students could draw user profiles to understand strange or professional scenario visually following three questions: (1) What is the context that users will choose your products? (2) What is the situation without using such products? (3) What is the thinking pattern, emotional factors and using behaviors of your target users?

Capability-Based Grouping. With the self-defined clue and iteration feature of PD, bottom-up concepts creation is instead of the top-down education. A suitable grouping mechanism in this particular specific design task could ensure the smooth and efficient teamwork of different skills and personalities. It aims at using interactive grouping methods without obvious mentor-interference but under well-designed to trigger the contribution of every group member. An important part of grouping is capability-based mode to train students adaptability and leadership for challenging missions. This requires mentors design grouping games to encourage students jumping from their comfortable zone or familiar friends to apply their proficient skills into a designated group collaboration. An interactive and self-directed grouping game through PD clues attributes is shown below (As Fig. 7). Other potential grouping index like engineering, programming, perception thinking or deep insights also could be taken into consideration.

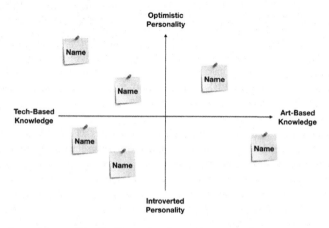

Fig. 7. Example of grouping method

Relationship Reconstruction. This strategy is using PD activities to build sustainable learning communities for teacher role transformation and teacher-student relationship reconstruction. In this context, 'Reconstruction' refers to the flat teacher-student relationship instead of the leader-receipt relationship. It requires teachers turn the role into the active collaborators, experienced participants, and academic guides from the one-way information communicators. The self-cultivate probing skill is necessary for this context which is discovering the weakness in group collaboration and making intervention solution instantly. This also requires mentors have a full understanding of students' existing knowledge and ability reserve based on collaboration performance. During the learning progression, mentors have to give promotion suggestions, counseling guides and constraints according to specific design task, and also guide students to contact related stakeholders to define solutions. Besides, teachers also could renew learner profiles and self-improvement during quality tracking with real-time assessment tools to further learning after the courses. With PD methods to create, develop and improve concepts with target users, the hierarchy of collaborative relationship between students and other stakeholders like residents, managers or other partners need to be break. This strategy needs teachers facilitate peer-to-peer learning communities beyond the school and turn their roles from simple leadership role into co-creators.

6   Conclusion

Through the critical literature review and the observation of practice at DHDI, we defined the PBL collaboration quality problems. Through related work analysis for practice of integration PD into PBL, this research put forward the quality enhancement orientation including inquiry clues and group attendance. Then the research hypothesis which is participatory design could solve problems of attractive inquiry clues and the group attendance towards high PBL collaboration quality. With such concern, we collected THDI as the user research object to analysis PD feasibilities and approaches based on the redesigned PBL module with PD approaches. Based on participatory observation, interview for participants and feedback collection from students and teachers, the feasible PD implementation strategies for integration of PD advantages into PBL methodology as the core research findings are put forward. It is the theoretical and experiment response to previous research questions including participatory design factors affecting PBL collaboration quality and the accessible application guidelines. This study provides a context-based action paradigm for researchers and developers who face related problems in PBL practice, and it also extends the application PD diversity and depth for other similar scenarios.

Acknowledgments. We would like to thank all the participants who are dedicated for the PBL practice at the THDI. We also express gratitude for the students, subject-based teachers and PBL experts who are involved in the research process.

References

Audet, R.H., Jordan, L.K.: Integrating Inquiry Across the Curriculum (2005)

Barrows, H.S., Tamblyn, R.M.: Problem-Based Learning: An Approach to Medical Education. Springer, Heidelberg (1980)

Barrows, H.S.: Problem-Based Learning Applied to Medical Education. Southern Illinois University Press, Springfield (2000)

Van Berkel, H.J.M., Schmidt, H.G.: Motivation to commit oneself as a determinant of achievement in problem-based learning. High. Educ. **40**(2), 231–242 (2000)

Boud, D.E., Feletti, G.I.E.: The Challenge of Problem-Based Learning, 2nd edn, 344 p. (1997)

Van den Bossche, P., Segers, M., Kirschner, P.A.: Social and cognitive factors driving teamwork in collaborative learning environments: team learning beliefs and behaviors. Small Group Res. **37**(5), 490–521 (2006)

Bratteteig, T., Wagner, I.: Disentangling power and decision-making in participatory design. In: Participatory Design Conference: Research Papers, pp. 41–50. ACM (2012)

Christensen, H.P.: Seven-step problem-based learning in an interaction design course. Eur. J. Eng. Educ. **29**(4), 533–541 (2004)

Johnson, D.W., Johnson, R.T., Smith, K.: The state of cooperative learning in postsecondary and professional settings. Educ. Psychol. Rev. **19**, 15–29 (2007)

Knudstrup, M.A.: Integrated design process in PBL. In: Action for Sustainability - The 2005 World Sustainable Building Conference (2004)

Yongqi, L., Fei, F., Jin, M.A.: Mission D, an interdisciplinary innovation and venture program at Tongji University. In: Banerjee, B., Ceri, S. (eds.) Creating Innovation Leaders. UI, pp. 201–213. Springer, Cham (2016). https://doi.org/10.1007/978-3-319-20520-5_12

Lou, Y.: New environmental design in the global knowledge internet time. J. Nanjing Arts Inst. (Fine Arts Des.) (2017)

Margeston, D.: Current educational reform and the significance of problem-based learning. Stud. High. Educ. **19**(1), 5–19 (1994)

Maudsley, G., Strivens, J.: Promoting professional knowledge, experiential learning and critical thinking for medical students. Med. Educ. **34**(7), 535–544 (2000)

Neame, R.L.B.: Construct a problem-based course. Med. Teach. **3**(3), 94–99 (1981)

Savery, J.R., Duffy, T.M.: Problem based learning: an instructional model and its constructivist framework. In: Wilson, B.G. (ed.) Constructivist Learning Environments: Case Studies in Instructional Design, pp. 135–148. Educational Technology Publications, Englewood Cliffs (1996)

Schmidt, H.G., Moust, J.H.C.: Factors affecting small-group tutorial learning: a review of research (2000)

Schuler, D., Namioka, A.: Participatory Design: Principles and Practices. L. Erlbaum Associates Inc., Hillsdale (1993)

Spinuzzi, C.: The methodology of participatory design. Tech. Commun. **52**(2), 163–174 (2005)

Torp, L., Sage, S.: Problems as Possibilities: Problem-Based Learning for K-12 Education, 2nd edn. ASCD, Alexandria (2002)

Wilkinson, C.R., Angeli, A.D.: Applying user centred and participatory design approaches to commercial product development. Des. Stud. **35**(6), 614–631 (2014)

Van der Linden, J., Erkens, G., Schmidt, H., Renshaw, P.: Collaborative learning. In: Simons, P.R.J., Van der Linden, J.L., Duffy, T.M. (eds.) New learning, pp. 37–55. Kluwer, Dordrecht (2000)

Can Virtual Reality Help Children Learn Mathematics Better? The Application of VR Headset in Children's Discipline Education

Xin Lei, Andong Zhang, Bingcheng Wang,
and Pei-Luen Patrick Rau[✉]

Department of Industrial Engineering, Tsinghua University, Beijing, China
rpl@mail.tsinghua.edu.cn

Abstract. It is difficult for children to learn scientific disciplines like mathematics, but virtual reality (VR) headsets offer more direct and effective learning methods for children. This paper represents an exploratory study of the application of VR in children's education. We observed ten children as they played with four educational VR applications. Fourteen experts, including six teachers, were interviewed to explore whether and how VR can help children to overcome learning difficulties in different subjects. Based on the insights from the user study and expert interviews, we propose a series of design guidelines for educational VR applications. For example, children seek a sense of achievement when learning mathematics; therefore, applications should have a hierarchy of different difficulty levels with which the children can practice, make progress, and experience success.

Keywords: Virtual reality · Children · Education · Scientific studies
Social studies · Creativity

1 Introduction

Problems in mathematics, especially those related to three-dimensional (3D) geometry and motion, are difficult for children. When they learn 3D geometry, children must continually convert between a 2D figure in the book and a 3D model in their mind. When they solve motion problems, for example, the 'catching-up' problem, children have to imagine the whole moving process in their minds, then establish the relevant abstract equation. However, a difficulty arises, one with two principal aspects. First, these problems require children's spatial ability, their transfer ability, and abstract thinking ability, yet these are precisely their weaknesses. Second, the limitations of traditional teaching methods increase the learning challenges. It takes additional mental costs not only to learn 3D knowledge from 2D materials but to learning dynamic processes from static materials.

Virtual reality (VR) offers potent new possibilities for children's learning in mathematics. For example, children can directly observe 3D models from all angles, and no longer need to convert between 2D figures and 3D models. Additionally, children can watch the movement of targets directly, reducing the demands on

© Springer International Publishing AG, part of Springer Nature 2018
P.-L. P. Rau (Ed.): CCD 2018, LNCS 10912, pp. 60–69, 2018.
https://doi.org/10.1007/978-3-319-92252-2_5

children's spatial and imaginative abilities. VR offers a more direct and effective learning method for children, one that reduces learning difficulties and improves learning performance. In addition to scientific studies like mathematics, VR also offers opportunities in social studies, such as history and art. The ruins of historical sites can be reconstructed with VR; thus, children can visit sites that previously had only existed in pictures. With respect to art education, while traditional painting is limited to pen and paper, VR breaks out of the 2D-space boundaries and offers a 3D painting environment instead.

The present paper explores whether and how VR can improve children's abilities to learn science and social studies. We observed ten children as they played with educational VR applications. Typical behaviors were recorded and analyzed. Next, we interviewed fourteen experts about their experiences in children's education and about their opinions on applying VR to children's education. These experts included six teachers, four parents and four experts in psychology, creativity training, user research and human computer interaction. We discovered that the advantages and potentials of VR for children's academic education should be emphasized at the application design stage. Ultimately, we propose a series of instructional guidelines for the design of superior educational VR applications for children. The following sections describe the related work, user study, expert interviews, and design guidelines.

2 Related Work

2.1 The Role and Potential of VR in Education

Previous studies indicated some of the advantages and potentials of VR in educating children:

First, it is important to arouse children's interests and stimulate their intrinsic motivation for learning [1]. VR performs better than traditional education in generating learning interests; moreover, it is the children's intrinsic motivations that ultimately lead them to change their behavior [2]. In addition, VR can help children to go outside of their comfort zones, challenging the boundaries of the self, which is an important part of education [2].

Second, VR can create fantastic situations that demand serious attention in education. These situations help feasibly teach concepts in unique and often creative ways [3]. They also induce children's imagination, which is critical to creative work [4]. In addition, these simulated situations can enhance children's attention, essentially guaranteeing a high-quality educational experience. The first person aspect, the 3D panoramic animation, and the speaking voice associated with VR situations all help to enhance children' attention [5].

Finally, VR permits experiential learning. Children learn the knowledge necessary within the situation and then apply the knowledge learned to that situation. This can also train children's comprehension as VR activities entail observation, communication and self-clarification [2]. Moreover, VR provides a safe environment for children to act vicariously and practice [5]. Furthermore, VR offers a cost-effective means of implementing and optimizing almost all conventional creativity enhancement techniques [6].

2.2 Educational VR Applications for Children

Several studies have designed educational VR applications or created virtual reality environments (VREs) for children.

Specifically, there are VREs designed to introduce abstract concepts to children. For example, the "Round Earth Project" transforms children's mental model of the Earth's shape, helping to teach them that the Earth is spherical [7]. Second, some VREs allow children to freely create new virtual objects. For example, an immersive multiuser learning environment called NICE allows children to create their own virtual garden wherein they control the weather conditions as well as the time, allowing the children to explore complex ecological interrelationships [8]. Third, VR is also closely associated with cultural education. Historical sites that no longer exist can be reconstructed using VRE [9]. As a result, students can visit and experience these sites, which previously could only be experienced in pictures of the past. Indeed, VR also offers many useful applications for tourism [10].

3 User Study

The purpose of this user study was to observe children's behaviors and evaluate their performances while playing with educational VR applications. We observed ten children as they played with VR applications while wearing a VR headset. Their behaviors were also video recorded.

3.1 Materials and Tasks

Four educational VR applications were selected: a story-telling application, a physics learning application, a 3D painting application, and an engineering application.

The first application children played was Allumette, a story-telling application inspired by The Little Match Girl. Children were asked to retell the story and to answer several open-ended questions after having watched the VR film. This process helps to train children's language ability as well as shape their values. The task took approximately 20 min.

The second application was Galileo's Ideal Lab, a physics learning application that uses a virtual image of Galileo to teach children about the force of friction. Children were first asked to read written learning materials about friction and then answer five questions on paper before watching the VR class. Next, after watching the VR class, children re-answered the five questions. Finally, the children were asked to talk about their learning from the written materials, the traditional class, and the VR class. This task took approximately 20 min.

The third application was Tilt Brush, a 3D painting application that provided a 3D environment for painting with different virtual paintbrushes and special effects. Children had five minutes to practice and fifteen minutes to paint a future city. They were also asked to think aloud while painting. The experimenter asked questions like "what are you painting?" or "what is it used for?" to help the children think aloud. This task took approximately 20 min.

The fourth application was called Water Bears and is an engineering application that provides a 3D environment for connecting pipes that guide water to its destination, which trains children's comprehensive abilities. Children could use only a limited number of pipes of different types to solve a puzzle, and they were encouraged to use as few pipes as possible. This task took approximately 30 min (Figs. 1 and 2).

| Allumette | Galileo's Ideal Lab | Tilt Brush | Water Bears |
| Story-telling | Physics learning | 3D painting | Engineering |

Fig. 1. Materials: four educational VR applications

Fig. 2. A child is playing the VR application

3.2   Results

Trial-and-Error. The children followed an iterative trial-and-error process until a satisfactory result was achieved. In Tilt Brush, the children frequently used the eraser to erase their unsatisfactory drawings at the beginning because they were unfamiliar with the paintbrush. In Water Bears, children continued using trial and error until they figured out a feasible solution. Ultimately, this process of trial and error helped the children to work out a correct solution more quickly when they encountered a similar problem later.

Empathy. Children showed empathy behaviors when they played with these applications. In particular, six children re-told stories using emotional words to describe the mental states of the virtual character while retelling the story, and two children in Allumette patted the virtual character to comfort it when it was sad.

Interaction. Children interacted with the virtual characters even though they received no feedback. In Allumette, a boy waved his hand to a leaving ship, and a girl talked to a virtual character. In Galileo's Ideal Lab, children instinctively nodded when the virtual teacher asked a yes-no question. Meanwhile, in Water Bears, children tried to catch the flying water bears with their hands.

Creativity. Children exhibited their creativity while playing Tilt Brush. In the absence of an experimenter's instructions, the children tried different paintbrushes, as well as a rich selection of materials for their drawings. One child used the flame paintbrush to draw a river in blue and a flame in red. Another child used a metallic paintbrush to draw the rail. One child drew a smart city teeming with high technology. Examples from other children included the drawing of an ice-cream house, a lotus house, and a letter house.

4   Expert Interviews

4.1   Method

A total of fourteen experts with diverse backgrounds were interviewed. The experts included: six primary and junior high school teachers, who taught science, technology, mathematics, arts, and language. Next were four parents who attached great importance to their children's education and development. Additionally, the group included a doctor of psychology, who was insightful with respect to the fostering of children's creativity; an entrepreneur, who had worked for several years on children's creativity training programs; an interaction designer; and a user researcher with a rich background in human computer interactions.

Due to the diverse nature of the expert backgrounds, their interviews were conducted in a semi-structured format. In the interviews, the expert introduced his or her background, then shared their experiences and insights regarding the education of children. Ultimately, they expressed their opinions about applying virtual reality to children's academic/disciplinary education and creativity enhancement.

4.2   Results

VR Makes Abstract Knowledge Easier to Learn. Scientific studies involve abstract knowledge, which is difficult for children to learn. Four experts stipulated that *"they took great efforts to solve this difficulty by making abstract knowledge concrete, visual and realistic" (P1, P3, P5, P6).* VR helps facilitate these goals.

First, VR supports a 3D visual representation. For example, it can rapidly generate a specific geometric model, allowing children to observe the model from all angles, and can even help children establish geometric equations. When talking about the application of VR to mathematics teaching P3, a mathematics teacher noted.

"If children can observe a model from all angles or make a model by themselves, the learning outcomes will be much better. In addition, some mathematical thinking modes can be taught using a virtual reality environment. Four important math thinking modes include symbolic-graphic combination, classified discussion, transformation, and equation." (P3)

Second, VR helps make abstract knowledge concrete. It can simulate natural phenomena and allow children to learn from observation.

"VR can simulate phenomena which cannot be simulated in the real world, thereby diminishing the learning difficulty for children. In addition, VR can solve the limitations of experimental equipment as it can provide countless pieces of equipment while reducing their operational difficulty." (P5)

Third, VR can create situations that are realistic, mimicking real life situations, and enabling children to acquire knowledge from concrete examples. Additionally, VR can teach children how to apply the same knowledge in different situations, which is an important transferring ability. Three experts mentioned knowledge transfer or transfer ability in their interviews.

"Children are more likely to face difficulties in situation transferring." (P1)
"Transforming is a comprehensive ability. For example, transforming an engineering problem into a math problem. The greatest success in education is a student's ability to apply what they learn in class to solve real problems in life." (P3)
"VR enables children to receive more external stimulus, which in turn, will provide useful memories to be recalled to solve problems in the future." (P12)

VR Enhances the Achievability in Scientific Studies. Children care about whether or not they can do well in scientific studies, and they seek a sense of achievement in learning. A good learning experience is related to solving a difficult problem, while small breakthroughs lead them to try more challenging problems and gain even more knowledge. There is also a vicious cycle in which children give up scientific studies they find too difficult. VR can provide the necessary guidance and the timely feedback in the problem-solving process, breaking a complex problem into several simpler ones. The provision of continuous feedback not only reduces a problem's difficulty but also allows children to accumulate a sense of accomplishment instead of frustration.

"Children are likely to be confused or even lost in a virtual environment without guidance; however, too many instructions may also hinder children's creativity. Heuristic-based tasks can help children to explore a virtual environment step by step. A small cue may give children an aha experience, which is critical in creativity education." (P13, P14)

VR Makes Social Studies More Interesting. Children care more about their own interests than about their performance in social studies. VR has many elements to make social studies more interesting, such as verisimilar situations, virtual characters, and even special visual and sound effects. VR can create fancy and aesthetically pleasing situations that not only attract children's interests but also excite their imagination. Indeed, virtual characters and their images can refer to animals, plants, even cartoon figures. They can stimulate children's interests and act as children's mentors. Three experts spoke highly of applying VR in education.

"Experiencing is the best way to learn. Experiencing virtual reality is much better than learning from pictures or videos. VR allows children to see the desert and gobi from a first-person perspective, which makes it easier to feel its drought and desolation." (P1)

"An English context is required for listening and speaking practices, and virtual reality is able to provide a more vivid and flexible context for children to practice English listening and speaking." (P2)

"VR offers more space for children to create. Traditional paintings are limited to two dimensions, but VR allows three-dimension drawing. Children are no longer limited to pen and paper; their possibilities are dramatically extended." (P4)

VR Allows More Active Activities for Children. It is in the nature of children to be active. Children prefer active tasks, such as crafts, sports and performances. In contrast, they do not like purely mental activities, such as playing piano, learning English and reading. For example:

"As long as they are allowed to move, children have a higher degree of enthusiasm and will be more active." (P1)

"A hands-on experience enables children to learn easier and better." (P6)

"Children prefer construction activities rather than mental activities for two reasons: First, construction activities give children hands-on experiences. Second, there is a real product of their own work, which gives them a sense of achievement." (P11)

VR makes active activities more convenient. The materials, tools, even the instructors become digital in a VR environment, and as such, they are all continuously available. Moreover, VR environments are safe environments. For example, *"some operations, like cutting and sawing, are dangerous in a traditional environment but are safe in a virtual one" (P11)*. Finally, VR provides more context for active activities. For example, *"children who like taekwondo can fight with virtual taekwondo players to promote their skills" (P4)*.

5   Design Guidelines

5.1   Guideline 1: Make Full Use of VR's Advantages in Education: 3D Environments and Abundant Situations

The advantages of VR in children's academic/disciplinary educations lie mainly in the 3D environments and the abundant situations. VR is an effective method for teaching children knowledge that requires spatial abilities, such as 3D geometry, architecture, and space motion. VR can construct a 3D model and allow children to observe, operate, and calculate with this space. This more "tangible" model reduces learning difficulties. VR is also able to construct numerous and lifelike simulations which enable children to learn on their own from the experience itself. Additionally, these abundant situations help children to realize that knowledge learned in one situation can be used in another, thus cultivating their knowledge transfer ability.

5.2 Guideline 2: Stimulate Children's Intrinsic Motivation for Scientific Studies

Children seek a sense of achievement in scientific studies. Therefore, applications related to scientific learning should make efforts to stimulate children's intrinsic motivations. The application should have a hierarchy of different difficulty levels. Children could then practice, make progress and experience successes. For the tasks to be appropriate, they must seem challenging but actually remain within the children's abilities. Children must expend considerable effort to complete the task, but they gain a sense of accomplishment upon completing it. Next, there should be clear goals for children. Different types of applications have different appropriate goals, such as finishing a specific task, reaching a higher level, or creating a satisfactory product. Finally, extrinsic motivation can also enhance intrinsic motivation. For example, virtual bonuses, material rewards, and even encouraging words can motivate children to make efforts.

5.3 Guideline 3: Balance Social Studies with Children's Interests

Children are driven more by their personal interests than by an interest in excelling in social studies. Therefore, it is necessary to balance social studies with children's interests. Again, children like active activities but dislike purely mental ones; as a result, rich interaction approaches should be offered. VR allows for multimodal interactions, which are effective for enhancing children's attention and their enthusiasm for learning. Additionally, the application can combine the following interaction forms: story-telling, scene-exploring, task-executing, and creating freely.

5.4 Guideline 4: Trial and Error Is an Important Way of Learning for Children

Trial and error is the typical learning style of children, and is itself an important form of learning. Therefore, educational applications should emphasize error-tolerance instead of error-prevention. Children should be encouraged to make different attempts and be allowed to make mistakes. As a result, what they learned in the application leaves a profound impression on them. In addition, heuristic guidance should be provided as part of the problem-solving process. Without guidance, children are likely to be confused, even lost, in a virtual environment; however, too many instructions may also hinder the children's creativity. Thus, heuristic guidance is appropriate. A small hint can help children to organize their thoughts and take an additional step forward. Finally, informative feedback is also necessary if children are to successfully complete the task or create a work.

5.5 Guideline 5: Social Needs of Children Should Be Satisfied

Children value social activities. Consequently, including them in educational VR applications is a sound pedagogical principle. In addition, these interactions are critical to developing children's capacity for collaboration as well as their ability to work with others, to have social-emotional control and to form social communities. As a result, multiplayer applications are good choices for children. It is also a good idea to offer a social platform to children. A platform not only breaks spatial and temporal boundaries, but enhances communication among innumerable users while increasing children's interests and their dedication to the application. Lastly, a platform for exhibiting one's work is attractive for children. They tend to like all kinds of galleries in which they can present themselves and display their creations. VR essentially offers children a much larger platform, even a worldwide platform, for the exhibition of their works.

5.6 Guideline 6: Children Should Always Be Clear About Answers to Who Am I? Where Am I? and What Should I Do?

Self-role and self-perception are essential to the VR environment. When children are immersed in a VR environment, from their perspective, three questions emerge: Who am I? Where am I? What should I do? (the 3W's for short). A good VR application makes sure that children know their self-roles and can accurately perceive themselves. This helps them to understand both what is going on, and be fully immersed in the virtual situation. Otherwise, children are likely to feel confused and to perceive chaos. In terms of the 3W's, the first improves empathy and the immersion experience, while the other two prevent children from losing themselves in the virtual environment.

6 Conclusions

This paper examines the use of a VR headset for children's subject matter-specific education. First, we selected four representative educational VR applications and observed ten children as they wore their VR headsets while playing with these applications. Second, fourteen experts with diverse backgrounds shared their experiences and insights with respect to children's learning and education. As a result, a series of design guidelines emerged and are summarized below.

First, the advantages of VR in children's discipline education chiefly emerge via two aspects: the 3D environment and abundant situations. Second, applications related to scientific studies should make efforts to stimulate children's intrinsic motivations, while applications related to social studies should balance the factual knowledge with children's interests. Third, applications should emphasize error-tolerance rather than error-prevention. Fourth, applications should support a social function to satisfy children's social needs. Finally, answers to the following questions should be clear to the children: "who am I", "where am I", and "what should I do".

Acknowledgements. This study was funded by National Key Research and Development Plan grant 2016YFF0202605 and 2016YFF0202600.

References

1. Amabile, T.M.: Within you, without you: the social psychology of creativity and beyond In: Runco, M.A., Albert, R.S. (eds.) Theories of Creativity, pp. 61–91. Sage, Newbury Park (1990)
2. Lin, M.T., Wang, J.S., Kuo, H.M., Luo, Y.: A study on the effect of virtual reality 3D exploratory education on students' creativity and leadership. EURASIA J. Math. Sci. Technol. Educ. **13**(7), 3151–3161 (2017)
3. Hu, R., Wu, Y.Y., Shieh, C.J.: Effects of virtual reality integrated creative thinking instruction on students' creative thinking abilities. EURASIA J. Math. Sci. Technol. **12**(2), 477–486 (2016)
4. Patera, M., Draper, S., Naef, M.: Exploring magic cottage: a virtual reality environment for stimulating children's imaginative writing. Interact. Learn. Environ. **16**(3), 245–263 (2008)
5. Van Wyk, M.M.: The use of cartoons as a teaching tool to enhance student learning in economics education. J. Soc. Sci. **26**(2), 117–130 (2011)
6. Thornhill-Miller, B., Dupont, J.M.: Virtual reality and the enhancement of creativity and innovation: under recognized potential among converging technologies? J. Cogn. Educ. Psychol. **15**(1), 102 (2016)
7. Johnson, A., Moher, T., Ohlsson, S.: The round earth project - collaborative VR for elementary school kids. In: SIGGRAPH 1999 Conference Abstracts and Applications, Los Angeles, California, pp. 90–93 (1999)
8. Roussos, M., Gillingham, M., Moher, T.: Evaluation of an immersive collaborative virtual learning environment for K-12 education. In: American Educational Research Association Annual Meeting. University of Illinois, Chicago (1998)
9. Mosaker, L.: Visualising historical knowledge using virtual reality technology. Digital Creativity **12**(1), 15–25 (2001)
10. Guttentag, D.A.: Virtual reality: applications and implications for tourism. Tour. Manag. **31**(5), 637–651 (2010)

An Innovated Design of Escape Room Game Box Through Integrating STEAM Education and PBL Principle

Jui-Ping Ma[1(✉)], Miao-Hsien Chuang[2], and Rungtai Lin[3]

[1] Center for Humanities and Arts Education, Kaohsiung Medical University,
Kaohsiung City, Taiwan
jpma@kmu.edu.tw
[2] Department of Visual Communication Design,
Ming Chi University of Technology, New Taipei City, Taiwan
joyceblog@gmail.com
[3] Graduate School of Creative Industry Design,
National Taiwan University of Arts, New Taipei City, Taiwan
rtlin@mail.ntua.edu.tw

Abstract. The aim of this study is to explore a design project of "escape room game box" through integrating STEAM education and PBL principles in a series activities within a creative course. To analyze, the STEAM education and PBL principles are applied to inspire the problem-solving potential of students. The findings show: (1) that there is no direct correlation between time and space factors with regard to the subjects' access to the Citizen Cloud service; (2) that because of its convenience, subjects consider contacting others and sharing should be a standard feature in the Citizen Cloud; (3) that while comparing subjects' use of Citizen Cloud, "command" is more popular than other online features; (4) In their overall experience subjects prefer higher interaction with cloud computing service.

Keywords: STEAM education · PBL · Makerspace · Escape room game

1 Introduction

To face the complex problems of the world, the current trend and challenges are towards to train learners owning multiple abilities constructed by interdisciplinary experience. Since 2000, in the US, the importance of STEM-related teaching has been proved by some educational organizations through teaching and studies. Some attaching organizations of the US government, for instance, the NASA, or NSF aimed at STEM innovation and assisted to fund the development of STEM education in succession through some community projects [18]. For the past several years, the STEM teaching not only has been taking root but also is surging forward as the active style of movement. However, in order to match the demand of the economy in the 21st century, the original STEM movement is integrated with "art" to evolve into STEAM education [2]. While [12] proposes that educators should have a duty to inspire students

© Springer International Publishing AG, part of Springer Nature 2018
P.-L. P. Rau (Ed.): CCD 2018, LNCS 10912, pp. 70–79, 2018.
https://doi.org/10.1007/978-3-319-92252-2_6

to spread better talents in courses of STEM or STEAM and in their later career, it will be "part of the solution to a major national problem".

Obviously, today's learners need an innovated vision and skill to overcome any difficulty in their life. Until now, there are some researchers find that children those who perform well on academic tests for creativity may correlate positively with playing video games [14, 21]. While a new style game named "escape rooms" may create a Connection between individual and problem-solving. The "escape rooms" is a live-action team-based game where players discover clues, solve puzzles, and accomplish tasks in one or more rooms in order to accomplish a specific goal (usually escaping from the room) in a limited amount of time [24]. This study is shaped from a series of "escape rooms" table game design with PBL principle in a creative design class.

2 Literature Review

This section firstly reviews related literatures of STEM and STEAM education, principle of maker and makerspace; then, introduces the features of the problem-based learning (PBL) that will be exploded on game design of "escape room" to arrange for later experiment design.

2.1 STEM/STEAM Education

The term "STEM" was married from science, technology, engineering, and math by the National Science Foundation (NSF), the US in 1996. It's an assembled educational tactic, which is guided students to learn science, technology, engineering, and mathematics, obtaining the ability of inquiry, dialogue, and critical thinking. While, the STEM is gradually transformed to STEAM, according to Julian and Parrott [22] states that to inject art into STEAM is for resulting from some art projects based on science and mathematics.

Also, STEAM is an interdisciplinary approach as students apply science, technology, engineering, arts, and mathematics to coupled with real-world issues and learn to make connections between rigorous academic concepts of school, community, work and the global enterprise in context [32]. The concept of STEM/STEAM is to encourage student attempting to hands-on do something with plural knowledge, skills, as well as to encourage higher-order reasoning and problem-solving skills. The final target is to offer students thinking risks, engage in experiential learning, persist in problem-solving, embrace collaboration, and work through the creative process (educationcloset.com), then, to be the whole new innovators, leaders, and learners of the 21st century. Due to the society that is in transition can enable the development of STEM/STEAM connotation. More and more styles of STEM/STEAM courses are popular, especially, Julian and Parrott argue that one current successful direction to develop STEM/STEAM education is to establish some makerspaces.

2.2 Maker and Makerspace

The "maker" means some people who like to do something by himself, especially concrete objects; while the maker movement, promoted by maker groups with an artisan spirit will form a social, cultural movement. The maker culture is a contemporary subculture representing a technology-based extension of trendsetting DIY that intersects with hacker culture [35]. According to Dougherty [6] proposed, some features of maker are - 1. The general engineer focuses on a single technical field, and the maker is interested in the technology in each field; 2. They would like to know the operation principle of things and make some devices to verify it; 3. They have a "play" quality; 4. Be willing to share with the open source community; 5. They can think the world can be improved, problems can be solved, things can be changed.

The "Make magazine" is the initial publication of maker by Dale Dougherty, as well as the one who gave the maker movement its name in 2005 [20]. Through "Make magazine", Dougherty wants to help people starting a hobby, learning new skills, and help the new hobbyist find a community of like-minded tinkerers to talk with about it [6]. In 2006, a year after the Make magazine, Dale Dougherty held her first makerspace in San Mateo, California, the Bay Area named "Maker Faire". The Makerspace is a place can let makers expand their idea of learning and continue the conversation with members of the community. Although the first Makerspace first appeared around 2005 as part of the popular DIY (Do it Yourself) movement [13], however, the purpose of a new pattern of makerspace is to create a comfortable environment for users to experiment, create and learn within a controlled setting. These places enable makers (educators and students included) to apply scientific principles and meet curricular science through the design, creation, and building of products [22], as Rivas [27] is an electrical engineer and educator, she created a makerspace for young women being able to create real products, like toys, video games, and electronic garments in the community.

2.3 Problem-Based Learning (PBL)

PBL means problem-based learning, began in the 1960s at McMaster Medical School in Canada [31] has been applied in health professions education for a long time. Nowadays, PBL methods have been adopted across several institutions, medical curricular and also been introduced in many different disciplines such as social work, science, engineering, business, management etc. [1], and especially, is extensively promoted in science education [8, 25].

In PBL situation, the learning task is addressed by the students in a real naturalistic context [32]. On one hand, PBL has been located as a transformative instructional strategy in existing literature, and one of the vital key component of PBL for its success is the provision of feedback to learners [19]; on another hand, PBL is a learning strategy that students in a small social group adopt it to solve problems and reflect upon to regard their group activity as learning processes collaboratively [17].

During a learning task, students co-work in small groups (called tutorial groups) brainstorm the problem and identify what they need to learn [9] trying to solve the problem, guided by facilitators. However, the facilitators won't teach them, but just guide the students on the way to discovering new knowledge on their own [28]. Therefore, the feedback of course shaped from the facilitator will be a very influential strategy for elevating learning, PBL facilitators also need to emphasize it [10]. Hence, the main characteristic of PBL is contextualized learning through a problem solved by students within a tutorial group without formal lectures or prior preparatory study [33]. In general, there are some important reasons for the implementation of PBL: training professionals with competencies such as critical thinking, problem solving, reflection, collaborative, self-directed as well as life-long learning [29, 34].

3   Methods

This pilot study was one arm of a major creative design course study. In this study, a qualitative method was applied to consist of an analysis of the contents of both creative concept maps in the design procedure and interviews with students. The objective was to present an all-inclusive of the contextual process of learning in a PBL class [5, 15]. Due to the process of drawing the creative concept maps let the participants express their perspectives in a more innovative, active, and autonomous manner than usual, the study will survey the creative concept maps produced by the students [3, 4, 11].

3.1   Phase and Flowchart of Executing

The study is separated into four steps to explore the design procedure of "escape room game box" design and evaluation of players' experience. The flowchart of executing refers to the 4D method developed by the UK design council. This study modifies the 4D method as well as integrate PBL principles and a part of knowledge from STEAM courses into the design procedure, a whole research flowchart through PBL model is shown in Fig. 1.

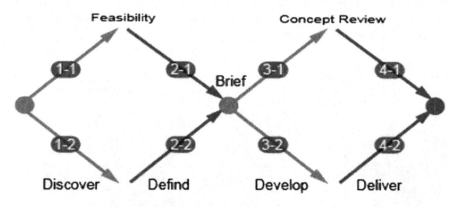

Fig. 1. Research flowchart

The phases of the study are shown as followed:

Phase 1.   To conduct a literature review on PBL, maker, game design of escape room etc. In this step, the work of "1-1 Read and analyze the scenario of situation in every gate" and "1-2 List your personal understanding, ideas, or hunches" are included.

Phase 2.   The data from a series of creative maker courses are recorded through participant observation. In this step, the work of "2-1 List what is known" and "2-2 List what is unknown" are included.

Phase 3.   To conduct content analysis to classify the recording data. In this step, the work of "3-1 List what needs to be done" and "3-2 Develop a problem statement" are included.

Phase 4.   To integrate different kind data. Write a research full paper that combines the relevant theory and data analysis results. In this step, the work of "4-1 Gather information" and "4-2 Present findings" are included.

3.2   Participants

The participants were twenty-four undergraduate students from various departments of a medical university were recruited by selecting randomly out of volunteer on a social media website in Taiwan. They consisted of ten males and fourteen females ranging from 19 to 22 years old ($M = 20.17$, $SD = 1.31$). In terms of experience with creative thinking and design, eleven of the participants were realizable with something else. Eight of them had ever planned one table game at least, seven stated to be experts of table games, and the rest of them had interested in the table game but were not well-versed in design the game. Only one of them had never played any table games, near half played some table games less than one hour a week, and others spent more than one hour every day on table game. They were randomly distributed into four groups in a classroom, each containing six students, to participate in cooperated one concept maps during the creative design class, as shown in Fig. 2. When the study The ethical of body approval was obtained prior to collect the data with the consent forms were collected from the participants.

Fig. 2. The design procedure of "escape rooms" games

3.3   Estimative Material – Escape Room Game

The estimative material of this study is a table game named "escape room". This table game is modified from real-life escape rooms, represented a new type of game. In real-life escape room game, people to be players are locked in a room or series of inclosed spaces, so they must deal with some tasks for solving puzzles or riddles in order to escape these airtight spaces. Therefore, through considering the holistic, essential, and functional constraining of escape room rules, the students learn to find answer of problem-based by some creative thinking skills can lead them to finish the tasks. Moreover, the real-life escape room games not only are represented to train a collaborative experience where players work on team building, communication, and coordination, but also based on live-action role playing games, treasure hunts. Most of such a game often ask players try to escape within a set time limit, typically 45–60 min [16].

3.4   Design Contents and Standard

To consider the integrity of escape room game, the researcher and teacher formulate standard contents of this game in the design and plan procedure are - A. story/role cards (human or non-human) as shown in Fig. 3; B. boxes (scenes of game) as shown in Fig. 4; C. game accessories (break the cue card, password card for each gate are included) as shown in Fig. 5.

The play rules of the escape room game are - (1) three scenes with individual riddle or puzzle; (2) coded lock on the door of the scene. The players must unlock the coded locks step by step with a right password through the story, roles, game accessories, and break the cue card.

Fig. 3. The design of multiple story card in "escape rooms" games

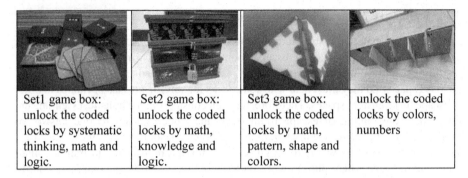

Set1 game box: unlock the coded locks by systematic thinking, math and logic.	Set2 game box: unlock the coded locks by math, knowledge and logic.	Set3 game box: unlock the coded locks by math, pattern, shape and colors.	unlock the coded locks by colors, numbers

Fig. 4. All of 4 sets "escape rooms" game boxes

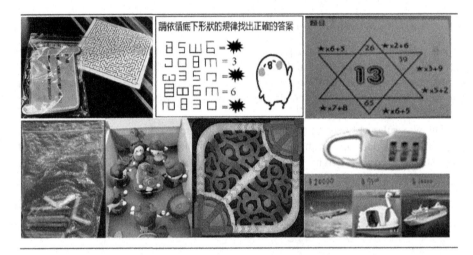

Fig. 5. The design of Game accessories in "escape rooms" games

3.5 Data Collection

In the creative design class, students are asked to collaboratively do an escape room box with multi-materials. They tended to start discussing the concept and mode of escape room game by analyzing the key points of the story-telling and logical context of the patient's situation. Then, they share and present their own experience and make some sketches. Finally, they build the concept model and write down the key point of it. After they are satisfied with the final set of the game they developed, they take photographs of the concept model and other accessories of game. Ultimately, a total of 4 sets of a concept model of the game box were collected.

4 Result and Discussion

4.1 Escape Room Game Box

The groups of students in the creative design class design the concept models of escape room game box with PBL principle shown in Fig. 3. There are 4 sets of escape room game boxes developed by students. All design of game box is used by students to combine the systematic thinking, math, logic, color, numbers, pattern, shape, and knowledge etc.

5 Conclusion

Although in this pilot study we adopt simple samples from a creative course, the findings are usefully shown as follows:

(1) Most of the concept model of escape room game boxes had a balance of informative and artistic elements. The students demonstrated creative skills by concreting the design processes of PBL application using simple shapes.
(2) However, since the composition of these game boxes is restricted by the PBL procedure, storytelling, etc. the theoretical connection among the concepts was not fully spread out.
(3) The students can show more of their artistic ability by building a game box on the faces of the STEAM positions.
(4) Even if students' not enough experience in PBL content, they can share or contact others through cooperation to apply STEAM knowledge, moreover, the students can have employed more critical thinking on the contents of escape room game.

References

1. Anderson, W.L., Glew, R.H.: Support of a problem-based learning curriculum by basic science faculty. Med. Educ. Online **7**(10), 4537 (2002)
2. Arts Integration and STEAM. http://educationcloset.com
3. Clayton, L.H.: Concept mapping: an effective, active teaching-learning method. Nurs. Educ. Perspect **27**(4), 197–203 (2006)
4. Conceiçao, S.C.O., Taylor, L.D.: Using a constructivist approach with online concept maps: relationship between theory and nursing education. Nurs. Educ. Perspect **28**(5), 268–275 (2007)
5. Dempsey, P.A., Dempsey, A.D.: Using Nursing Research: Process, Critical Evaluation, and Utilization, 5th edn. Lippincott, Philadelphia (2000)
6. Dougherty, D.: Makerspaces in Education and DARPA (2012a). http://blog.makezine.com/2012/04/04/makerspaces-ineducation-and-darpa
7. Dougherty, D.: The maker movement. Innov.: Technol. Gov. Glob. **7**(3), 11–14 (2012b)
8. Duschl, R.: Science education in three-part harmony: balancing conceptual, epistemic, and social learning goals. Rev. Res. Educ. **32**, 268–291 (2008)

9. Dutch, B.: Writing problems for deeper understanding. In: Duch, B., Groh, S., Allen, D. (eds.) The Power of Problem-Based Learning. Stylus, Sterling (2001)

10. Dysthe, O.: What is the purpose of feedback when revision is not expected? A case study of feedback quality and study design in a First Year Master's Programme. J. Acad. Writ. **1**(1), 135–142 (2010)

11. Edwards, S., Cooper, N.: Mind mapping as a teaching resource. Clin. Teach. **7**(4), 236–239 (2010)

12. Farkas, M.: Making for STEM success. Am. Libr. **46**(5), 27 (2015)

13. Fisher, E.: Makerspaces Move into Academic Libraries. ACRL TechConnect is a Site of the Association of College and Research Libraries, a Division of the American Library Association (2012)

14. Granic, I., Lobel, A., Engels, R.C.: The benefits of playing video games. Am. Psychol. **69**(1), 66 (2014)

15. Hansen, E.C.: Successful Qualitative Health Research: A Practical Introduction. Open University Press, Maidenhead (2006)

16. Lo, H., Pan, R., Neustaedter, C.: Communication, collaboration, and coupling: what happens when friends try to escape the room? Connections Lab Technical report 2015-1109-01, Simon Fraser University, Canada (2015)

17. Harden, R.M., Sowden, S., Dunn, W.R.: Educational strategies in curriculum development, the SPICES model. Assoc. Med. Educ. Eur. **2**, 7–16 (1999)

18. Hmelo-Silver, C.E., Barrows, H.S.: Goals and strategies of a problem-based learning facilitator. Interdiscip. J. Probl.-Based Learn. **1**(1), 21–39 (2006)

19. Hopwood, J.: Initiating STEM learning in libraries. Child. Libr. **10**, 53–55 (2012)

20. Jeffries, A.: At Maker Faire New York, the DIY Movement Pushes into the Mainstream (2013). https://www.theverge.com/2013/9/23/4760212/makerfaire-new-york-diy-movement-pushes-into-themainstream

21. Jackson, L.A., Witt, E.A., Games, A.I., Fitzgerald, H.E., von Eye, A., Zhao, Y.: Information technology use and creativity: findings from the children and technology project. Comput. Hum. Behav. **28**, 370–376 (2012). https://doi.org/10.1016/j.chb.2011.10.006

22. Julian, K.D., Parrott, D.J.: Makerspaces in the library: science in a student's hands. J. Learn. Spaces **6**(2), 10–18 (2017)

23. Koester, A.: Full STEAM ahead: inject art into STEM with hands-on learning. Sch. Libr. J. **59**(10), 22 (2013)

24. Lehrer, R., Schauble, L.: Scientific thinking and scientific literacy. In: Handbook of Child Psychology. Wiley, Hoboken (2006)

25. Nicholson, S.: Peeking behind the locked door: a survey of escape room facilities. In: White Paper. http://scottnicholson.com/pubs/erfacwhite.pdf

26. Preddy, L.: School library makerspaces: grades 6–12. Libraries Unlimited (2013)

27. Rivas, L.: The Maker Mom: Helping Parents Raise STEM-Loving, Maker-Friendly Kids (2014)

28. Savery, J.R.: Overview of problem-based learning: definitions and distinctions. Interdiscip. J. Probl. Based Learn. **1**(1), 9–20 (2006)

29. Schimdt, H.G.: Problem-based learning: does it prepare medical students to become better doctors? Med. J. Aust. **168**, 429–430 (1998)

30. Sheridan, K., Halverson, E.R., Litts, B., Brahms, L., Jacobs-Priebe, L., Owens, T.: Learning in the making: a comparative case study of three makerspaces. Harv. Educ. Rev. **84**(4), 505–531 (2014)

31. Schwartz, P., Mennin, S., Webb, G.: Problem-Based Learning: Case Studies, Experience and Practice. Kogan Page, London (2001)

32. Torp, L., Sage, S.: Problems as Possibilities. Problem-Based Learning for K-16 Education. Association for Supervision and Curriculum, Alexandria (2002)
33. Tsupros, N., Kohler, R., Hallinen, J.: STEM education: a project to identify the missing components. Intermediate Unit 1: Center for STEM Education and Leonard Gelfand Center for Service Learning and Outreach, Carnegie Mellon University (2009)
34. Ward, J.D., Lee, C.L.: A review of problem-based learning. J. Fam. Consum. Sci. Educ. **20** (1), 16–26 (2002)
35. Maker Culture. https://en.wikipedia.org/wiki/Maker_culture

Designing an Application for Learning Chinese

Vu Thu Thi Hien[1], Ganta Murali[1], Nguyen Khanh Linh[1],
Nguyen Hai Yen[1], Nguyen Thi Thu Hien[1], Aymen Saleh Abuzied[1],
Zhe Chen[1], Lin Ma[1], and Lin Wang[2(✉)]

[1] Beihang University, Xueyuan Road No. 37, Haidian District,
Beijing 100191, China
[2] Incheon National University, 119 Academy-ro, Songdo 1-dong, Yeonsu-gu,
Incheon, South Korea
`linwang0@gmail.com`

Abstract. The Chinese language is considered as an extremely difficult language to learn for non-native speakers. Mostly foreigner learners and even Chinese students feel writing part is the biggest challenge in learning Chinese process. This paper presents a mobile learning Chinese application, with consists of the combination of features like character writing, reading, listening, speaking with images, stories, and audios. The application will enhance the memory and make the process of learning Chinese easy and effective for user.

Keywords: Learning Chinese · Chinese character · Heuristic methodology
Application to learning Chinese characters

1 Introduction

Chinese writing is hieroglyphic, different from Latin word system. Chinese characters have more than 80,000, but the most commonly used Chinese characters are about only 3,500. It is easier to remember a Chinese character following certain steps. First, be familiar with the basic radicals of a Chinese character and its innate sense. It help you distinguish 王 (king) 壬 (ancient burden) and 玉 (jade) or 土 (ground) and 士 (knight). The majority of Chinese characters include two or more basic radicals. Radicals build a link to its meaning, a little story to help learner to memorize a character or even a best explanation. For example, the character 明 (i.e. bright) consists of sun (i.e. 日) and moon (i.e. 月). The character 休 (i.e. to rest) consists of a person (i.e. 人) and a tree (i.e. 木) - mentally fix the idea of an exhausted hiker resting against a tree. This rule applies to complex characters as well.

Besides, there are multiple ways to decompose a Chinese character into radicals. For example, 偷 (i.e. thief) can be decomposed as person (i.e. 人) + making a canoe (i.e. 俞) or as person (i.e. 人) + roof (i.e. 人) + moon(i.e. 月) + knife (i.e. 刂). In this case, it makes more sense in a story involving a thief on the roof of a house in moonlight, knife in hand, in order to climb into one of the windows and steal stuff. Stories can be colorful, absurd, racy, and non-sensual even, as long as learner personally find them memorable.

© Springer International Publishing AG, part of Springer Nature 2018
P.-L. P. Rau (Ed.): CCD 2018, LNCS 10912, pp. 80–94, 2018.
https://doi.org/10.1007/978-3-319-92252-2_7

Information and communication technology applications have become an integral part of learning Chinese characters [1]. Smart phone and tablet devices as well as mobile apps for learning language have changed and enhanced foreign language studying in many aspects [2, 3]. These changes can be seen in the avenues in which foreign languages are studied (in the traditional classrooms vs. online). More importantly, these changes can be seen in how foreign languages are studied with integrating technology, which has been found to facilitate learning foreign languages' in many efficient and effective ways. This is particularly true about the learning of Chinese characters. Chinese characters are writing scripts that are considered extremely difficult language elements for Chinese characters learners, especially for whose native language does not have Chinese characters or something similar. What has made Chinese characters difficult to learn? How can technology help? This paper tries to address these two questions through a substantial review of related literatures, beginning with identifying the difficulties that exist in learning Chinese characters, following with a discussion of the role that technology can play in learning Chinese characters based on theoretical frameworks. Furthermore, this paper introduces a technology-enhanced character learning model. Lastly, it mentions some popular websites and apps that can be used to help provide daily learning activities for learning Chinese characters, followed by suggestions for new practical application by our design.

2 Our Basic Application

2.1 Survey

In recent years, the number of people learning Chinese language has been increasing quickly. But we can have denied the reality Chinese still is one of the hardest language to learn in the world, both for people whose native language is alphabet-based and people whose native language is character-based.

In order to know the difficulty in learning Chinese process of foreigners, especially Chinese character and find the solution make it simply and easily, we do a small survey for international students in Beihang University, Beijing, China.

Firstly, we randomly select 10 students in class and ask them: "Do you think learning Chinese characters is difficult?" Then we make survey 200 foreigners with the questions "how difficult to learning Chinese characters?" "Which functions do you want for a Chinese learning application?" After collecting data and literature review we begin to establish our application.

2.2 Our Basic Application

Application Description
Our product is "Chinese Panda", shown in Fig. 1, an application to learn Chinese characters easily with English and multi-languages you can choose. Our app's logo use image of Panda, because Panda is the most famous animal in China, representing "Friendly". The size of app is a 65 MB, compatible with IOS and Android.

Fig. 1. Application logo

Features of Application
Chinese Dictionary (Fig. 2)

- User can choose which languages they use.
- User can input Chinese character or pinyin also to get the meaning of the word.
- User can find example to a word and each word is with a HSK level (HSK -汉语水平考试 is the standardized test of Standard Chinese language proficiency for non-native speakers. The higher level of HSK, the more difficulty, so depend on user's level, they should focus more on which words suit for their level.

Fig. 2. Chinese dictionary

Lesson (Table 1)

Table 1. Lesson

Lesson 1	Greeting
Lesson 2	Foods
Lesson 3	Animals
Lesson 4	Games
Lesson 5	Education
Lesson 6	Transportation

- 20 lessons with 500+ characters about different topic, each lesson consists of an average 20 characters. The characters learned in previous lessons are used to build new words in later lessons.

Writing: Animation Demo (Fig. 3)

- Writing system guide how to write a word step by step

Fig. 3. Writing

Listening and Speaking (Fig. 4)

- User can hear chosen words or phrases. After listening the words or phrases user can practice and repeat and compare with original sound

Fig. 4. Listening and speaking

Gaming Features (Fig. 5)

- Use their fingers to draw a line horizontally or vertically over the characters that form the correct word/phrase. Or Matches the word/phrase along with the pictures.

Fig. 5. Game

3   Heuristic Evaluation Method

Evaluation is criteria of Application or Website developing process of design. An evaluation examines usability problems of the application by users or experts. A heuristic evaluation is a usability examination manner, particularly involves evaluators testing user interface and judging its acquiescence with recognized usability rules (the "heuristics").

3.1   User Design (UD) and Future Implementation

We have taken our application for three users to evaluate. Table 2 is the list of evaluator of mobile application.

Table 2. Evaluators

	Sunil Mishra Country: Bangalore, India Language: English, Hindu
	David Logan Country: Warsaw, Masovian District, Poland Language: English, Polish
	Nisarg Shah Country: Ahmedabad Area, India Language: Hindu, English

User evaluate the functions and features of the Application:

- **Visibility of Application:** The App system always giving information to users about running action, by exclusive feedback within reasonable time.
- **User control:** Users want to leave the function at middle, after it will start when the user leaves the function.
- **Help to users, recognize errors, solutions to correct errors:** Application system should be expressed Error messages in simple language mainly shows the problem, and productive methods for problems solving.
- **Consistency and standards:** Obey the Application platform arrangements, Users wish to do different type of words, situations, or actions the reaction same as per function standards.

3.2　User Interface

- **Images:** attractive colors.
- **Layout:** simple.
- **Sound:** high quality.
- **Reaction time:** 145 ms.

4　The Results of the Heuristic Evaluation

After Heuristic Evaluation of the Application, we sum up recommendations from the evaluators: improve writing system, colorful pictures with characters to memory, more interesting games, more interaction among learners. Evaluation results are shown in Tables 3, 4 and 5.

5　Modified the Learning Chinese Application

Throughout the above recommendations from the experts, we have realized that modifying the application plays essential role to improve memory's learners effectively, and to learn Chinese easily.

Table 3. Sunil Mishra's evaluation

Functions of the application	Very bad	Bad	Good	Very good	Excellent
Writing	✓				
Reading			✓		
Listening		✓			
Game		✓			
Memory		✓			

Table 4. David Logan's evaluation

Functions of the application	Very bad	Bad	Good	Very good	Excellent
Writing	✓				
Reading			✓		
Listening		✓			
Game	✓				
Memory		✓			

The application needs be diverse, intuitive, beautiful, and easier to use which will cause learning Chinese effective, and stimulate their interest in studying.

Table 5. Nisarg Shah's evaluation

Functions of the application	Very bad	Bad	Good	Very good	Excellent
Writing		✓			
Reading		✓			
Listening			✓		
Game		✓			
Memory	✓				

From the advantages and disadvantages of the specialist, we have still remained the process and solved the cons such as upgrading more lessons along with four skills (reading, listening, writing, speaking), the memory and more interesting games, additionally social functions.

We will describe in detail as follows:

5.1   Function 1: Dictionary

With varying frequency, participants used all functions of the application. Specifically, they used the dictionary functions heavily because translation feature plays very important role for beginners to understand meanings and remember words. We have used flashcard with each character, pinyin, audio native speakers of pronunciation, and meanings by multi- languages instead of the traditional way of having a text book, dictionary, audio CD player and a notebook to write characters.

And dictionary will be divided into the different subjects such as: fruits, animals, transportations, clothes etc... in order that learners find the easiest. For example, when you want to buy fruits, you are able to open the fruits subject of the dictionary to find a kind of fruit you need to buy such as 苹果–Píngguǒ – apple, or 西瓜–Xīguā – watermelon. Moreover, dictionary will be added functions about taking pictures and scanning images of characters. While you are shopping, and running into a new character you don't know, you could scan its image, the app will take the right character with pinyin and meanings (Figs. 6 and 7).

In additional, many researchers expressed that the human brain is sensitive to the images and sounds, therefore learning Chinese characters with colorful pictures will be

Fig. 6. Dictionary-1

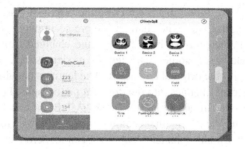

Fig. 7. Dictionary-2

attractive and help to remember more. Three examples are reported by Joseph et al., Hasegawa et al. and Looi et al., who showed that to create vocabulary learning contents in the form of vocabulary-captioned photos or videos to illustrate individual words will help learners remember fast. Also, Chinese scholars have found that identifying the origin of character configurations helps students to recognize and write characters more accurately. Therefore, we have designed Chinese characters related to the colorful images of themselves so that learners are able to reminiscent easily, and besides stories of characters have been brought out by flash or videos to affect their brain deeply. Each word has historical views related the image of characters in order that the students have understood why the Chinese characters have their existing sharpness as now. The below picture shows the process of characters from the beginning period of the Chinese words to the official writing system. For instant, the sun is a round with small inside point at first, after it was changed into a rectangle with an inside straight (Figs. 8 and 9).

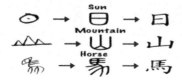

Fig. 8. Dictionary-3

Fig. 9. Dictionary-4

Chinese scholars have found that identifying the origin of character configurations helps students to recognize and write characters more accurately. The application show their students how characters have been formed and changed from their original pictograph over time. However, some characters in modern simplified format may not completely connect with the original characters. The learners are able to study phonetic radicals and remember the changes into the different pictographs. For example, with the "person" word, it has two strokes in one character "人". But if this "person" character is double into the characters "从" with the meanings "follow". If the "following" characters is added a above roof, which is changed "众" by meaning "crowd" (Figs. 10 and 11).

Fig. 10. Dictionary-5

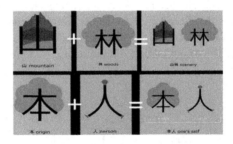

Fig. 11. Dictionary-6

5.2   Function 2: Lessons

In the start-up application, the programmers had established the lessons system with +1000 characters in 20 lessons. After examining, we decided to upgrade +2500 words with more than 40 lessons. In addition, the lessons will be divided into new words following HSK test from low level to high level at 6. This expressed that students have a chance to practice gradually to take part in the HSK exams and receive Chinese certifications.

5.3   Function 3: Listening Skill

With the developing application, it is not only feature that learners can hear chosen words or phrases in the basic app, but people also hear Chinese words, see the meaning of the words, then choose the suitable picture with characters of the words.

Beyond, in the life, students of noncharacter-writing systems feel that the tone of Chinese is very difficult to pick up which makes them met difficulties and misunderstands when hearing conversations with Chinese people. We have built more conversation audios and videos about the daily life such as introduction yourself, going shopping, going to restaurant, etc... which makes learners, especially foreigners feel convenient to communicate to others. Additionally, music the system has various famous Chinese songs participants can practice the listening skill of themselves by hearing, seeing lyrics and singing (Fig. 12).

Fig. 12. Listening

5.4 Function 4: Speaking and Reading Skill

These functions have been evaluated well by the professional experts. However, we have still taken some solutions to complete the reading and speaking skill the best. About speaking skills, beside to the high-quality sound, the programmers have also taken the recording in the application in order to improve the learner's pronunciation. In the start-up, the speakers will record their reading voice after the system will compare to their voice and the native sound in order to check their pronunciations effectively.

About reading skills, the developers have added some small paragraphs or stories by Chinese characters and pinyin so that readers find easy to remind the handwritings and train this skill fluently (Fig. 13).

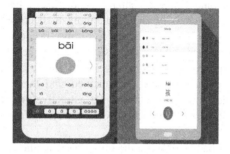

Fig. 13. Speaking and reading

5.5   Function 5: Writing Skill

The issue increasing difficulties in learning Chinese characters is the under-emphasis of writing characters when teaching in the beginning stages of Chinese language learning. Huo found that stroke order is still relevant when learning Chinese with the use of technology, and claimed that stroke order helped memories characters. Based on the research she carried out with learners of Chinese at a our university, Chung claimed that practicing Chinese characters with a mobile phone had led to the students learning basic stroke order, familiarizing themselves with structural components of the characters, and gaining knowledge of the history and culture behind the words. Therefore, the developer has built a function in order that people know the correct positions of the strokes. The writers will use their fingers to draw again the step-by step strokes indicated on the screen after they can also hear how to their pronunciation. The application has also given ten characters which the writers will practice every day. We create some writing games is mentioned in the below paragraph, the younger can join to practice and entertainment (Fig. 14).

Fig. 14. Writing

5.6   Function 6: Games

A multimodal mobile learning game that aims to help children and young adults remember and increase their Chinese Hanzi vocabularies by engaging them in a collaborative game-like group activity and challenging their creativity and imagination through drawing, taking pictures, and audio recording. Feedback from the experts of the mobile softwares have realized that the basic app's designers had known the uses of the game to make learning and remembering Hanzi characters easier, more fun, and more interesting. However, they have commented that there is a lack of exciting multiform games which makes itself not be attractive to youngers, hence, the researchers should built the high applicability games system and competitive network among joiners.

Beside to the games had been set in the initial basic applications we mentioned the above, the designers have built more three new games with a default list for the three difficulty levels, namely "Easy", "Medium", and "Hard", will be created to help remember characters easier and funnier.

Furthermore, the players can send their challenge to their friends or the other joiners in the social networking. The system will count the scores of each competitor and show the results which help them competitive and practice more to have high scores.

- Game 1:
  Identify the character along pictures. This game show has three stages.

In the first stage, as the below image, the system will take the meaning of word and four pictures with character and pinyin. The players would have to choose the right picture and character which is suitable for the starting means.

In the second stage, based on the crossword puzzle game, the screen has a picture being described with few blank square and Chinese characters. Then, the players will find the right characters to fill the blank.

In the third stage, In Multimedia Word, the players write the correct Chinese character based on hints such as a sketch, a photo, or an audio recording of the pronunciation. The game is said to have been primarily inspired by two popular Chinese games, specifically the String game and Pictionary (Figs. 15, 16 and 17).

Fig. 15. Game 1

- Game 2:
  The players will see 6 strokes of a word, and then they would have to match the strokes of this word together. If they are right, they will take score and hear again.

Fig. 16. Game 2

- Game 3:
  Drumming Strokes was based on a famous traditional game where the children form a circle and pass a flower to each other as the drum beats. When the drum beat stops, the person holding the flower is chosen. In the mobile game adaptation, instead of using a flower, a mobile device is used and is passed around. However, before passing the device, the player has to hear the voice of the characters and correctly kick the right characters being flight in the screen, then write one stroke of a given Chinese character. The stroke order also has to be correct; otherwise, the voice of the character sound stops and on the contrary, the person is asked to correct the stroke and must receive a penalty. For the penalty, the player has to again write another character in the correct stroke order. This is done until the joiner writes the correct answer. In the case where the player has difficulty providing the correct answer, the game offers a highlighted clue of the stroke. After successful completion, the sound restarts and everyone passes the device again.

Fig. 17.   Game 3

5.7   Function 7: Another Feature

Based on the remind feature in the mobile phone, the designer have created the systems which the users are able to install five characters each day in time you have chosen. Every day in the time, the system will choose five characters randomly with pinyin and the meanings to appear in order that you practice and remember deeply.

5.8   Function 8: Social Networking

The participant has created their accounts in the app to practice and make scores after learning, then evaluate your learning and skills every day. The system connects to the social networking site, Facebook, Twitters, etc… Posting results motivates students to do their best in the different components because parents, teachers, and fellow classmates can view what they have done and evaluate their skills.

Additionally, the environment is shared there are common visual points of reference for everyone. The members of groups can easily collaborate, communicate, and work on group projects. The joiners could connect chat group with the other learners, Chinese teachers, and Chinese friends to discuss each other (Fig. 18).

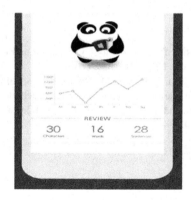

Fig. 18. Social networking

6   Conclusion

With the purpose to support foreigners learning Chinese characters more easily, this report discussed the design, development and use of a mobile application, called Chinese Panda.

Chinese is in the system of hieroglyphs with more than 8000+ characters, so it is difficult for learners to remember them. Therefore, in this application we describe the life history of characters, create the games with images and vivid colors, created miniature social network for exchanging spatial learning, share experiences ... to arouse excitement for learners, helping them to learn and remember better.

Preliminary results from research using the survey from learners and assessment of expert shows that Chinese learning with this application help learners feel funny and enjoyable. From there, they learn more effective.

However, the research study time is quite short, so it has a few limitations. Example: The number of participants this research was small, so it would be better to assess the effectiveness of this activity with a delayed test and number of participants larger.

In the future work, we will precise and add measurements should be introduced to explore the effects of Chinese seamless learning activity.

Besides, nowadays modern mobile technologies with new system versions (phone, tablet, PC...) have been developing. We have upgraded suitable reproductions of the application to the technological devices. This will help learners updated the improvement, progress and create attractive for application.

We hope Chinese Panda application would help foreigners easy to learn Chinese, especially Chinese characters.

Acknowledgement. This study was supported by the National Research Foundation of Korea (NRF) grant funded by the Korea government (MSIP) (NRF-2017R1C1B5076718), the National Nature Foundation of China grant 71401018, the Social Science Foundation Beijing grant 16YYC04, and China Scholarship Council.

References

1. Zhan, H., Cheng, H.-J.: The role of technology in teaching and learning Chinese characters. Int. J. Technol. Teach. Learn. **10**(2), 147–162 (2014)
2. Wong, L.-H., Chin, C.-K., Tan, C.-L., Liu, M.: Students' personal and social meaning making in a Chinese idiom mobile learning environment. Educ. Technol. Soc. **13**(4), 15–26 (2010)
3. Rosell-aguilar, F.: Design and user evaluation of a mobile application to teach Chinese characters. Jaltcall J. **11**(1), 19–40 (2015)

Mobile VR Game Design for Stroke Rehabilitation

Jia Yu, Rong Jiang, Yuan Feng, Meng Yuan, Yong Il Kang,
and Zhenyu Gu[✉]

School of Design, Shanghai Jiao Tong University, Shanghai, China
zygu@sjtu.edu.cn

Abstract. This essay studies the combination of virtual reality (VR) technology and conventional stroke rehabilitation physiotherapy. Specifically, we propose a novel therapeutic device coupled with an immersive VR software environment to foster hand rehabilitation. We first study the current state of the art in VR technology use in medical rehabilitation. Next, we investigate the conventional stroke rehabilitation process to integrate accepted methods of physical therapy into mobile games. The game system's input device (V-rehab) is an improvement on existing rehabilitation equipment, designed to maximize interaction between user and game. We feature a prototype game system based on sensor hardware and a custom environment running on the Unity3D software platform. Finally, we show results of system testing and discuss the application of VR in stroke rehabilitation.

Keywords: HCI · Virtual reality · Stroke rehabilitation · Useful games

1 Introduction

1.1 Research Background and Goals

Stroke is a medical condition in which poor blood flow to the brain results in cell death [1]. China has the highest incidence of stroke in the world. In recent years, the number of stroke survivors has increased with the development and progress of medical technology. However, about 75% of patients still suffer from varying degrees of motor dysfunction, especially hand motor dysfunction, with up to 10% of patients living with severe disability. The primary stroke hand dysfunction defects are buckling contracture, weakened grip, side clips, and other functional loss to palm and fingers [2]. Hemiplegic hand dyskinesia significantly reduces quality of life and increases the economic and psychological burden of patients as well as their families [3].

Prior research has demonstrated that exercise rehabilitation training can not only promote spontaneous nerve function recovery in patients with hemiplegia and help patients to restore central nervous system control and control of limb movement, but it can also prevent atrophy from muscle disuse and improve the recovery of motor function [4]. Physical therapy has become one of the most commonly used methods for rehabilitating motor function in clinical practice. At present, motor-function

P.-L. P. Rau (Ed.): CCD 2018, LNCS 10912, pp. 95–116, 2018.
https://doi.org/10.1007/978-3-319-92252-2_8

rehabilitation in patients with hemiplegia is still carried out under the guidance of a therapist, who assists patients with passive or auxiliary exercise training. However, these methods have obvious shortcomings:

(1) Waste of manpower and material resources. Rehabilitation therapists cannot simultaneously guide more than a small number of hemiplegia patients in technique, and this costly and specialized field is impractical in a huge developing country like China;
(2) Rehabilitation training is mechanically tedious: hemiplegic patients rarely participate enthusiastically, which leads to lapses in treatment;
(3) It is very difficult to obtain feedback to gauge the intensity and effectiveness of rehabilitation training [5].

Existing research shows that the introduction of virtual reality technology and games into rehabilitation training is helpful for the rehabilitation of patients with motor dysfunction [6]. This method can provide a variety of feedback during training and reasonable rehabilitation recommendations according to the patient's specific condition. A virtual environment can greatly increase patients' initiative to participate in therapy, so as to effectuate rehabilitation [7]. With its three primary characteristics of interaction, imagination, and immersion, VR technology uses a synergistic merger of virtual and real environments to give patients strong sensory stimulation [8], which can greatly improve their enthusiasm for training.

1.2   Research Status

Since late in the twentieth century, researchers have extensively studied virtual reality technology and its application in rehabilitation medicine. In 2001, U.S. researchers developed a five-finger rehabilitation robot. Each fingertip is fixed with a prosthetic which can allow the entire finger to flex and extend [9]. In 2003, researchers at the University of Manchester in the U.K. designed an exoskeleton-based system for physical and occupational hand therapy, which uses a modular design for a four-finger rehabilitation exercise in an interactive VR environment [10]. The American company Rolyan developed and successfully marketed a CPM (Continuous Passive Motion) machine for the rehabilitation of small joints such as those of the wrist and fingers. Kagawa University in Japan developed a rehabilitation device that restores the flexibility of the finger, which allows patients to control the movement of a virtual object by a pre-designed trajectory [11]. Ljubljana University in Slovenia has developed a finger-rehabilitation game system based on a virtual maze, the patient controlling the movement of a ball in the virtual environment by changing the position of the hand [12]. New Jersey Institute of Technology developed a VR-based hand-rehabilitation system for individual motion of the finger and coordinated movement between the fingers. A sensor reads the articulation angle of the finger and shows it in a virtual environment, where different degrees of bending play different piano sounds [13]. Purdue University in the U.S. has also developed rehabilitation equipment to restore patients' writing ability and guide patients in English writing [14].

There is a gap between China and foreign countries in the field of VR rehabilitation research. At present, several universities and the Rehabilitation Research Center in China have researched robots for rehabilitation, but the main focus is on joint rehabilitation and single-function rehabilitation robots. Harbin Institute of Technology has developed a new type of rehabilitation training manipulator for hand movement dysfunction that uses gearing, integrated mechanical sensors and angle sensors to achieve exercise, but at present only a single finger can be trained at a time [15]. Southeast University developed a training device for finger rehabilitation, with both active and passive assistance. Its disadvantage is the lack of real-time feedback and accurate evaluation of technique and progress [16]. In 2007, Harbin Engineering University developed an automatic finger rehabilitation trainer using a micro-DC motor to drive a special curved rod, allowing a patient's finger to perform mechanical movements according to various preset modes [17]. Hua Zhong University of Science and Technology designed a rehabilitation training robot for improving the ability of patients with joint activities using pneumatic muscle assistance, conducting preliminary experiments in the hospital. Although the immersive quality of its virtual environment was found to be deficient, the system still demonstrated some beneficial effect [18].

1.3   Research Purposes

To summarize, the use of VR technology to help patients in physical rehabilitation is feasible and effective. In the course of this research, we evaluated several VR environments; although each had certain positive qualities in game form and rehabilitation effectiveness, an almost universal problem was that the equipment was too precise and too expensive, not suitable for the general public to use. In addition, despite the era of mobile Internet, there has still been very little research on VR technology to help the rehabilitation of stroke patients on mobile platforms such as smart phones. Smartphones, however, have already reached 57% penetration in China [19]. Mobile games are a potentially convenient and easy-to-use rehabilitation training medium. The purpose of this project was to design a VR game system for hand rehabilitation of stroke patients. Interactive input devices improve existing hand rehabilitation solutions, and virtual reality mobile games offer an innovative immersive healing environment not possible with static mechanical tools. In combination with the scientific principles and methods of hand rehabilitation in stroke patients, this project is devoted to allowing patients to perform hand rehabilitation in easy-to-use and useful games.

There are three main parts to this study: (1) Build a prototype device, (2) Develop and implement the games on mobile platform, and (3) Test the prototype.

The object of this study is to design mobile games based on mobile virtual reality that can help stroke patients recover from hand rehabilitation. According to the prior art, hand movement data of the patient is acquired by using existing hand rehabilitation equipment (for example, the data of the movement direction, the movement distance and the hand grip force are mainly obtained by the three-dimensional motion sensor with a G-sensor). These data are imported into the game system as the input data and the game interface gives the corresponding feedback, so as to complete the interactive process of the game. The specific research contents are as follows:

First, investigate the existing virtual reality technology and products for physical rehabilitation, to evaluate their advantages and limitations.
Second, study the mechanical aspects of hand rehabilitation therapy to help determine appropriate game motifs to foster hand exercise;
Third, research the specific types of target users to understand their pain points in the rehabilitation process;
Fourth, select a suitable hand rehabilitation device, optimize its shape, and install sensors to collect movement data of users' hands;
Fifth, develop a mobile application specifically to suit the target users' behavior.

2   Design Research

2.1   Stroke and Rehabilitation Training

Stroke, also known as cerebrovascular event (CVE), cerebrovascular accident (CVA), cerebrovascular incident (CVI), or brain attack, refers to brain cell death caused by cerebral ischemia. Stroke is divided into two types: one is ischemic stroke caused by vascular obstruction; another is hemorrhagic stroke caused by bleeding. Either ischemic or hemorrhagic stroke can cause brain dysfunction [1]. Common symptoms of stroke include but are not limited to: an inability to move unilateral limbs or the partial paralysis of one side of the body; an inability to understand language or to speak; dizziness; an inability to see one side of the visual field. [20, 21] The symptoms of a stroke can become permanent sequelae.

In 2010, there were about 17 million stroke incidents and 330 million survivors had a history of stroke. Between 1990 and 2010, the incidence of stroke in developed countries dropped by about 10%, while in developing countries it increased by 10%. [22] Stroke was the second most common cause of death in 2013, accounting for 12% of the total (6,400,000 cases) [23], of whom about 3.3 million were due to ischemia stroke deaths and 3.2 million due to hemorrhagic stroke [23]. About half of those who have had a stroke have an average remaining life of no more than one year [4]. Overall, two-thirds of strokes occurred in people over 65 years of age [22].

Most patients with cerebrovascular disease have different levels of hand dysfunction in the process of functional recovery, which affects their ability to take care of themselves in normal life and their professional ability to return to society. The functional recovery process is begun a few days after onset of cerebrovascular disease. Recovery was most rapid in the first 3 months and was slowed down after 3 months due to disuse syndrome and misapply syndrome. Function recovery of the lower extremity is better than that of upper extremity, while the upper extremity is dominated by flexible, coordinated and skilled exercise. Recovery is not easily achieved, especially the function of the hand. The recovery is usually divided into the following stages:

Flaccid paralysis period: Hand, fingers included, is weak and feeble.

Fretting period: Fingers have partial active flexion but cannot stretch.

Holistic grasping period: Hand can grasp as a whole without finger-straightening extension action but cannot relax.

Functional recovery period: Patients can grip with the whole palm, such as cylindrical or spherical objects. Although performance is not fully competent, and the function of the hand is limited, the fingers can scratch voluntarily.

Functional period: All grasping patterns are under patient's control.

2.2 User Interview

Our research method was primarily based on a user interview.

Interviewees: Patients with a stroke experience who are recovering or who have recovered.

Interview form: One-to-one interview

Interview purpose: To understand the basic physical condition of patients during rehabilitation, rehabilitation methods, and psychological and physical demands during the rehabilitation process.

Main questions:

- Medical history (including age, stroke time, affected part, duration of rehabilitation)
- Hand rehabilitation training method and auxiliary equipment
- The family's role in healing
- State of mind and emotional state since suffering strokes
- Lifestyle and exercise before strokes
- Views and attitudes towards the combination of virtual reality technology and stroke rehabilitation.

The following is an overview of interview records of two stroke patients:

Mr. Zou: In the summer of 2011, Mr. Zou suffered from a stroke, and is now in the later stages of rehabilitation. He can now take care of himself, but his impaired right arm injury is permanent. Mr. Zou was hospitalized for three months after the stroke onset and completed systematic rehabilitation training in the rehabilitation department of the hospital to restore language ability and swallowing ability. He has insisted on daily rehabilitation exercises in the year after his discharge from the hospital, and with the help of his wife has maintained passive exercise training on the muscular atrophy of the right arm (rehabilitation ball, fingerboard, tractor), which he can now lift slowly. During his recovery, Mr. Zou often felt up and down, but has been supported by his family's tolerance. He has heard of VR technology and showed interest in it,; he expressed willingness to try it if the price is reasonable.

Mr. Zhu: Following a sudden stroke (reversible ischemic neurological deficit) in November 2016, his physical condition has returned to normal with no sequelae now. Hospitalized for a month, he performed daily bed activities and passive exercise with acupuncture and massage under the guidance of doctors' rehabilitation. After discharge from the hospital, it was very difficult for Mr. Zhu to persist in completing a set of movements hundreds of times without supervision from a doctor. He felt very impatient when his progress did not recover, and eventually spent an additional month to fully restore function. Although the current recovery prognosis is optimistic, Mr. Zhu and his family's life have still been greatly affected. Since suffering from stroke, he has become more aware of the importance of health. As to the introduction of new technologies, he said that he would accept any kind of technology that can make him recover faster.

In communicating with stroke patients, we learned that patients must remain at home for an extended period during the rehabilitation process, and they usually cannot meet the standard training requirements without the supervision of a doctor. Furthermore, the lack of positive feedback in the process causes patients to suffer some emotional distress. Patients generally regard feedback and incentives as important during the rehabilitation process; our contacts reported that they would appreciate more reward forms in the game design, so that they can get a sense of accomplishment in the game process, as well as to ensure adequate training exercise. Finally, rehabilitation equipment should ensure safety and comfort, and it should be able to be handled by patients independently.

2.3   Competitive Product Analysis

The hardware used by patients for rehabilitation also serves as the operating handset for the game system. In form, this is essentially an improved version of existing mechanical hand rehabilitation equipment. Among the devices that are already available on the market, this article compares their sensitivity to hand motion and aspects of their operation, operationalized as follows:

Operation: Hand rehabilitation training methods can be divided into active training and passive training. Active training is exercise through patients' own muscle flexion and extension, while passive training is hand movement assisted by the equipment via motors or mechanical force devices.

Flexibility: The degrees of freedom of hand movement and the number of joints involved (Fig. 1).

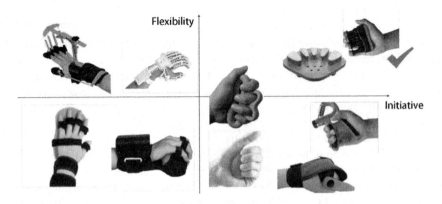

Fig. 1. Comparison chart of hand rehabilitation equipment

In order to ensure the rationality of the rehabilitation equipment, the choice of equipment refers to the existing hand rehabilitation equipment and is evaluated by the scientific program of hand rehabilitation. To offer the user a greater sense of interactivity and fully autonomous exercises during the rehabilitation process, the device should to have higher initiative and sensitivity and should be able to precisely record data for each finger press. Therefore, we chose a device with four pressure elements that users will need to press with the four fingers.

The selection of a virtual reality gaming platform was based on two considerations, one being the cost of purchasing head-mounted devices, and the second being the compatibility of the device for different phone size and system version. In order to allow use of these devices on a variety of mobile phones and to make this stroke rehabilitation system affordable, we chose the cheaper, more compatible Google cardboard and Google Daydream as a basic platform; users may choose a higher-cost platform according to economic situation, but we decided on this as a baseline (Fig. 2).

Fig. 2. Comparison chart of existing virtual reality devices

To operate a VR game, the user opens the virtual reality game application in the smartphone and inserts the phone into a Google Cardboard or Google Daydream visor. The content displayed in front of the user will change via the phone camera and sensing by the phone or visor's built-in gyroscope as the user moves his or her head. Figure 3 shows a user following the game interface training introduction to interact with the game scene.

Fig. 3. Use of Google Daydream

3   System Design

This project used the Unity3D game software development platform with the "Google Cardboard SDK for Unity" plug-in to develop mobile virtual reality games. Our mobile game system structure is shown in Fig. 4.

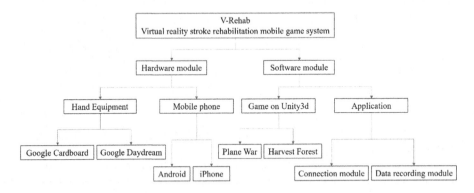

Fig. 4. Game system structure

3.1   Hardware Design

As shown in Fig. 5, the game system is divided into three parts: users, hand equipment, and mobile VR games. The user's finger movement is captured and recorded by the pressure sensor in the handgear, and the data is read by the Bluno module and transmitted to the handset program via Bluetooth. After the mobile program receives the input data, the system responds and changes the corresponding scene in the screen and feedbacks to the user. These form the complete interactive process for our system.

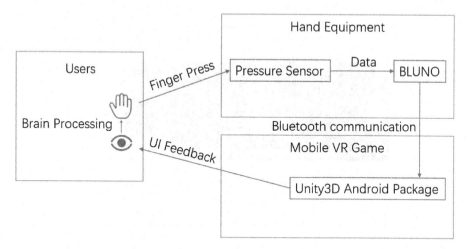

Fig. 5. Technical path diagram

Because pressure is the main action in stroke rehabilitation training, a pressure sensor was deemed as the best choice for input sensing. The pressure sensor we chose was the FSR402 Resistive Film Pressure Sensor, which converts the pressure applied on the FSR sensor film area into a change in resistance to obtain pressure information. The higher the pressure, the lower the resistance, allowing it to be used at 0 g–10 kg pressure to meet our design needs. It is small enough and light enough to be used in equipment with high experience requirements (Fig. 6).

Fig. 6. FSR402 Resistive Film Pressure Sensor

Based on the requirements of our project, we needed a device to communicate with the Arduino microcontroller and mobile phone. The Bluno Bluetooth module suited our requirements as the communication unit between our mobile gaming and hardware device (Fig. 7).

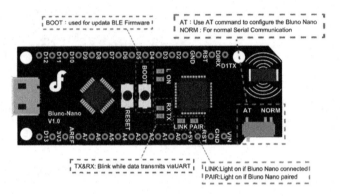

Fig. 7. Bluno Nano

We implemented a hardware device consisting of an Arduino microcontroller, a Bluno Bluetooth module, and pressure sensors. Four pressure sensors serve as the proximal interface for the user; they receive the user's movement information directly. In the game, we defined the meaning of each of the four finger presses, each representing different actions in the user's view. The function of the pressure sensor is to converts finger pressure into an electrical signal through the resistance effect described above, and to send the data to the microcontroller via pins connected to the Arduino.

The Arduino microcontroller program will rapidly poll the four pressure sensors. After acquiring this information in each polling cycle, the microcontroller will know which fingers made a pressing action, and with how much force. Then the microcontroller will package the pressure sensor information and send it to the Bluetooth module for further processing.

Bluno receives the packaged signal from the microcontroller and uses Bluetooth to send the package to the mobile phone. It should be noted that before the first use there is a procedure for pairing the Bluno Bluetooth module with the phone's Bluetooth device; only after this pairing process can data be exchanged.

After the mobile device receives this data packet, it will decode it according to the reverse process of that of the microcontroller and restore it to the original data of the four pressure sensors. By analyzing these data, the mobile game program can know what operations the user has performed and make corresponding modifications to the program interface according to these operations to provide feedback. Because the electronic components used to implement this process are relatively mature products and our products do not require a large data stream, the program is highly responsive (Fig. 8).

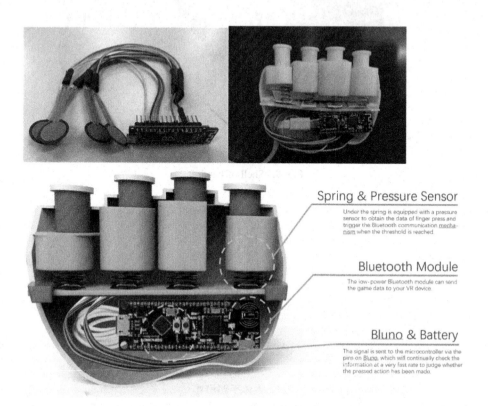

Spring & Pressure Sensor

Under the spring is equipped with a pressure sensor to obtain the data of finger press and trigger the Bluetooth communication mechanism when the threshold is reached.

Bluetooth Module

The low-power Bluetooth module can send the game data to your VR device.

Bluno & Battery

The signal is sent to the microcontroller via the pins on Bluno, which will continually check the information at a very fast rate to judge whether the pressed action has been made.

Fig. 8. Handset hardware combination

3.2 Handset Shape Prototype

Because the handset it is hand-held equipment, we needed to ensure that all electronic components such as hand-pressure devices, sensors, control panels, batteries, switches, and other devices will fit into the product, and that the product can be held by the average-sized hand and comfortably fit the shape of the hand (Fig. 9).

For handset design, we designed hand lines based on ergonomics principles suiting ease and comfort for users (Fig. 10).

Depending on the size of the hand and the features of the product, our design was most concerned with the fit of the thumb muscle to the handset, as this contributes most to the degree of comfort the when users hold the product.

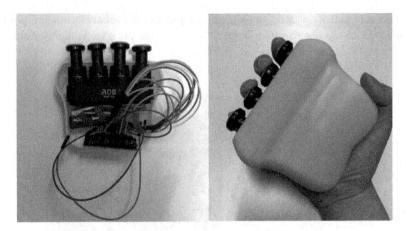

Fig. 9. Shell of handset

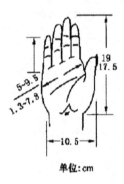

单位：cm

表1　人体手部尺寸

Tab.1 Dimensions of hand

测量项目	18~60岁（男）							18~55岁（女）						
	百分位数													
	1	5	10	50	90	95	99	1	5	10	50	90	95	99
6.2手宽/mm	73	76	77	82	87	89	91	67	70	71	76	80	82	84
6.3食指长/mm	60	63	64	69	74	76	79	57	60	61	66	71	72	76

Fig. 10. Ergonomic dimensions of human hand

The following is the modeling iteration process:

Stage 1:
The initial model (Fig. 11) used an ellipsoid as the main form with the original four finger pressing parts of the same length. Our primary goal was to achieve a good fit between the thumb muscles with the handset.

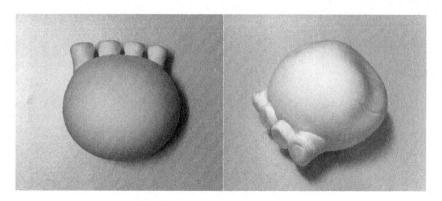

Fig. 11. Preliminary model no. 1

Stage 2:
In the second model (Fig. 12) we made more adjustments in the curve of the arc
which took into account the state of the full finger press given differing heights of
each of the four fingers. Thus, the length of each button is adjusted according to
different height. At the same time, the hand grip has also been changed to a greater
curvature, making an overall shape resembling a bear's paw.

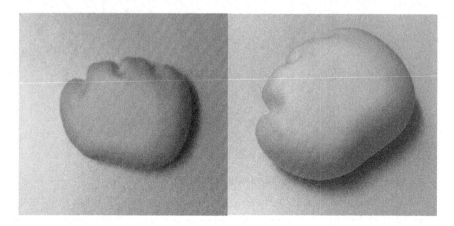

Fig. 12. Preliminary model no. 2

Stage 3:
After confirming the design of the finger portion and the design of the bottom surface,
we made the bottom line clearer on the original model. At the same time, the buttons
were enlarged, resulting in a slightly mellower whole shape. Meanwhile, corresponding concavities and convexities were added to the hand-fitting area, so that the
handset fits the natural contours of the palm.

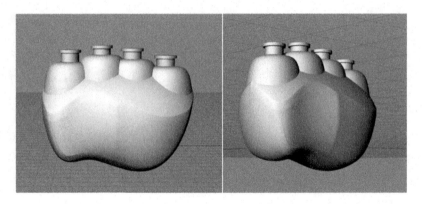

Fig. 13. Digital model no. 1

Stage 4:
The previous model had a rather inelegant appearance, so we made a few further adjustments.

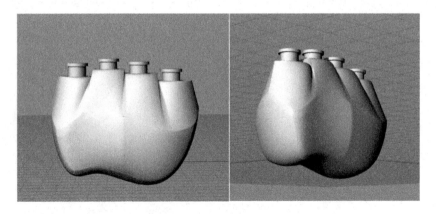

Fig. 14. Digital model no. 2

The shape of the finger areas was improved to make it more abstract and give up the rounded shape; we also performed better blending on the palm-contact surfaces, making the shape more concise and clear. The final model is shown in following figure (Figs. 13, 14 and 15).

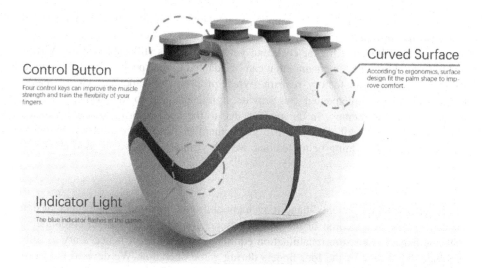

Control Button

Four control keys can improve the muscle strength and train the flexibility of your fingers.

Curved Surface

According to ergonomics, surface design fit the palm shape to improve comfort.

Indicator Light

The blue indicator flashes in the game

Fig. 15. V-rehab model rendering

4   Game Design

4.1   Design Platform

Our plan is to guide and encourage patients to carry out rehabilitation training, through the development of a human-computer interaction device in the form of a mobile game that includes virtual reality, sensing, networking. There are two main reasons for choosing a mobile phone as the platform: (1) As one of the fastest-growing platforms in the past decade, mobile phones have become fully integrated into people's lives and work, so using a cell phone as a rehabilitation device should feel quite natural to many patients. (2) There has been comprehensive recent development of mobile devices and virtual reality technologies. For example, Google Cardboard can display the content in a split-screen in the mobile phone to produce a stereoscopic effect by the parallax of the two eyes. Reference to these relatively mature products allows us to move our product quickly through the technology development phase, to facilitate our human-computer interaction analysis and experiments.

Virtual reality is a new and emerging discipline that communicates and interacts with users through a variety of sensors, and ultimately simulates realistic, real-time three-dimensional environments. There are a number of aspects characterizing virtual reality technology, including: (1) Presence refers to the user's feeling as the protagonist in the simulated environment. The test of the ideal simulation environment measures the extent to which it is difficult for the user to distinguish between reality and fantasy. (2) Autonomy refers to the degree to which objects in the virtual environment act according to the laws of physical movement in the real world. (3) Multi-perception refers to the auditory, tactile, motor perception, and even taste, smell, perception and other senses besides visual perception. (4) Interactivity refers to the extent to which the user may manipulate objects in the simulated environment and receive feedback.

Virtual reality technology was applied to medicine soon after its development and maturity. In the treatment of some patients, a relatively special environment is necessary, often calling for higher cost, and yet the solutions still lack realism. Virtual reality technology offers a channel that can be adapted to the specific needs of users as well as providing satisfactory realism. When properly implemented, virtual reality technology when implemented can provide significant help to the medical field, in particular at-home therapy. In our project, due to the need to provide stroke patients with a environment sufficiently real to guide them in various kinds of rehabilitation training without becoming being tedious, we felt virtual reality was a good choice.

4.2 Game Content

Stroke rehabilitation patients' hand movement ability is impaired, so our game design needed to take full account of the patient's finger movement, in careful combination with the hand acupressure rehabilitation equipment. To do so, it is necessary to fully mobilize the motion of the four fingers during game operation. We devised the game settings in an attempt to achieve optimally effective finger movement according to the sequence and frequency of practical finger rehabilitation exercises. In the game design, we developed two styles of game scenes based on user characteristics of different genders and ages.

Scene 1: "Aircraft War" features explosions and realistic effects, incudes awards or penalty.

Game scene: Simulation of shooting down enemy planes in an actual first-person shooting confrontation. The player's perspective is to drive a tank equipped with a machine gun. An enemy set in the game will send out a low-flying fighter to prevent the player from moving forward and will cast bombs at the right place to injure the player. Players must operate the tanks and use the machine guns to shoot as many enemy planes as possible to crash them, one point for each. The game scene is as shown (Fig. 16).

Fig. 16. Plane war

Game Operation: A total of five operational dimensions; four fingers control the movement (forefinger controls fire, middle finger controls moving to the left, fourth finger controls moving forward, little finger controls moving to the right.), head rotation controls firing direction.

Under such a dynamic and stimulating environment, patients can train the pressing force of the four fingers, and it can also assist in training the hand to grasp the equipment. Through the control of frequency and azimuth of flying planes, we can guide users to press four fingers at a certain frequency and fully exercise their finger joints and muscles.

Scene 2: "Harvest Forest" is a more leisurely game offering players a more relaxed and pleasant experience.

Game scene: Players wander in the forest according to the established route, along the way catching falling fruit from the trees with a basket. The basket must be placed at one of four possible places to catch the fruit, which is controlled by four fingers. Players need to catch as much fruit as possible, each catch earning a gold coin (Fig. 17).

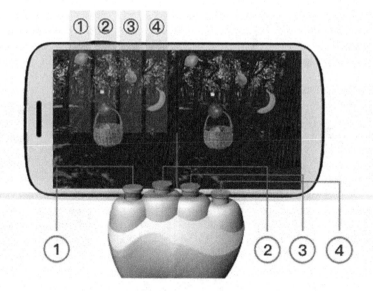

Fig. 17. Harvest forest

Game operation: The four buttons on the handset correspond to the four locations where the fruit falls. Press one button and the basket in the scene will quickly move to the corresponding position to catch the falling fruit.

The patient can fully exercise the joints and muscles on the hand while controlling the basket using four fingers, and at the same time the frequency and location of the fruit drop are programmed to meet the rhythm and frequency of finger rehabilitation exercises, so as to help patients complete the finger exercises per the program of therapy and avoid muscle or joint damage caused by improper exercise during the game.

4.3   Application Design

Aside from the game portion of the application, there are also device connection and data recording modules present in the mobile application. As for the connection module, the mobile application will automatically search for the user's V-rehab equipment via Bluetooth. After matching the equipment, the user may select a game and then follow instructions to put the mobile into a Google Cardboard or Google Daydream headset. The user may now perform rehabilitation training in the panoramic game (Fig. 18).

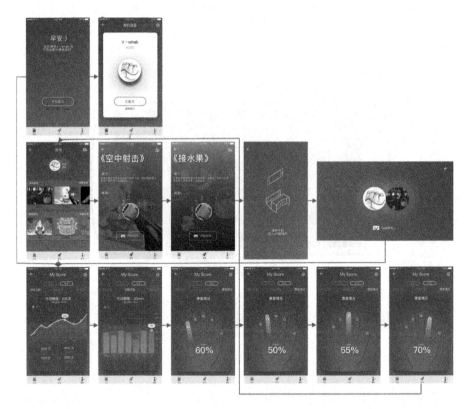

Fig. 18. Application interface

After the user completes the game, the application can record the progress results, including the number of repetitions of the exercise, duration of the exercise, finger flexibility and indicator completion percentage. The condition of rehabilitation can be intuitively displayed in the data recording module, achieving the effect of supervision and providing incentives. At the same time, the user's family members can also familiarize themselves with the patient's training situation through the application and give positive encouragement to the patient's progress.

4.4 Test and Optimization

After developing the basic game system prototype, including the improved hand rehabilitation device prototype and the mobile phone virtual reality game prototype, we tested the game system and used the results to draft a plan for improving the design. The test was divided into two parts, one being the test of comfort level when the user grasps the equipment and presses the buttons; the other being the test of the smoothness of the game scene with the device.

Hardware testing:

Subjects: Subject A, male, 22 years old, completely healthy with no injuries to his hand. Subject B, male, 22 years old, suffered a ligament strain in hand a month previous. Current hand rehabilitation has reached 80%, fingers are not as flexible as they used to be in fine motor function but are able to do simple press and hold.

Test tasks: (1) Grasp the handset, hold one minute; (2) Press the buttons on the handset with the index finger, middle finger, fourth finger and little finger in the order, do ten groups of this movement at a constant speed.

Test Record: Recorded the pressure intensity of the first and the tenth group of the finger press of two volunteers. Asked the two volunteers about the comfort of the handset, and also asked about the softness and smoothness of the equipment surface felt by the hand. Asked the degree of fatigue of the hand after holding the equipment for a long period of time.

Test results: Subject A: The difference of finger press intensity between the first group and the tenth group was within the 0.5F (since the device measures capacitance, F or farads is the unit of pressure in the Arduino), which can be regarded as almost no fatigue; Subject was satisfied with the comfort of the handset and fairly satisfied with the texture of the surface. Subject reported no significant fatigue after an extended period grasping the handset. Subject B: The difference of finger press intensity between the first group and the tenth group was about 1.2F. Subject was satisfied with the comfort of the handset and the texture of the surface. Subject reported feeling as though the equipment was a little heavy after gripping it for an extended period.

Improvement proposals: There is still a difference in muscle endurance between hand-impaired and healthy people. In order to minimize the burden on the user's hand so that the patient does not feel tired after prolonged use, the shell and components of the hand equipment should be made of lighter materials.

Game scene testing:

Subjects: Subject C, male, 50 years old, completely healthy with no injuries to his hand. Subject D, male, 59 years old, suffered a sudden stroke about one year before (reversible ischemic neurological function defect) and current physical condition is basically restored to normal. Since leaving the hospital, Subject D has been insisting on rehabilitation exercises at home, including the use of equipment to restore finger flexibility and arm strength.

Test tasks: (1) start the game "harvest forest" with Google Cardboard; (2) In the harvest forest, hold the equipment and complete the game of about 90 s.

Test Record: Record the number of fruits that two volunteers have caught in the game. Ask two volunteers about the head burden they feel when wearing the device, the clarity of the field of vision, the degree of dizziness when turning the head, the smoothness of the response while operating the equipment, and an appraisal of the game tasks.

Test results: Subject C: Equipment felt slightly heavy. Satisfied with visual clarity of the screen but felt a bit of dizziness when moving head. The screen gives very smooth feedback for the finger press, and the operations conforms to intuition. Subject D: Equipment felt slightly heavy. Felt a sense of dizziness when moving head. The feedback of the scene is adequately smooth during the game. The linkage effect of the other three fingers except the index finger is apparent, and this leads to the misoperation from time to time.

Improvement proposals: 90 s per round of intensive operation may bring heavy burdens to the users, such as causing dizziness and hand fatigue. One way to improve is to shorten the round of time, such as from 90 s to 60 s per round. The second way is to increase the number of frames so as to reduce dizziness.

5   Summary and Improvement

This work combines the emerging virtual reality technology with the hand rehabilitation training of patients needing stroke rehabilitation by studying the existing technology. We developed virtual reality games on the Android platform and focused on the user experience of existing products.

We conducted thorough research on existing VR technologies and games for medical rehabilitation and have reached two conclusions: First of all, the proactiveness of patient training increased by applying VR technology to medical rehabilitation. Secondly, a number of domestic and foreign universities, as well as research companies, have developed prototypes of the relevant products. Thirdly, a personal computer is necessary for the display in existing products, and for treatment users need to purchase expensive equipment, such as Kinect somatosensory equipment. This has increased the cost of rehabilitation to some extent and is not suitable for patients with ordinary conditions to enjoy gamification of rehabilitation. Migrating such therapeutic products to smartphone devices make the product available to a more diverse population.

Subsequently, the article conducted a detailed investigation of stroke conditions, rehabilitation methods and patients undergoing rehabilitation, and interviewed two patients in the later rehabilitation phase to derive basic product positioning and design aims. In the research of the prior art, we make a detailed comparison of current hand-rehabilitation products and existing virtual reality head-mounted devices, finally settling on a finger-pressure device as the hardware improvement target while using Google Cardboard and Google Daydream as the head-mounted device.

In V-rehab's hardware design, sensors and Bluno (a combination of Arduino and Bluetooth module) were used for functional prototypes. Pressure sensors perceive hand-movement and Bluno reads the data and packages and transmits it to the mobile game via Bluetooth communication as a "handle" for the game. As for the shape prototype, applied ergonomic considerations and made it accommodate all electronic equipment. After several iterated improvements, we designed an attractive and comfortable handset which can accommodate intelligent hand rehabilitation equipment. In terms of game design, two game scenarios were designed that considered the characteristics of different patient groups. In combination with the four-finger operation of the hand rehabilitation equipment, corresponding game operation settings were designed so that the four fingers were trained according to standard therapeutic practice.

Finally, after developing the prototype of the game system, we invited several volunteers to conduct user tests. We divided the volunteers into two groups: those whose hands exercise functionally and half-hand-impaired people. The user tests aimed to judge whether the game system is suitable for hand-impaired people to use. The test was divided into two parts, testing the handset and testing the gaming experience. Combined with the user's performance and attitudes, this paper proposes an improvement solution for both components, and this can be further studied in the future.

This article is an attempt to apply virtual reality to stroke rehabilitation training. The rehabilitation target is limited to the hand, specifically the restoration of the gripping and squeezing functions of affected fingers. Stroke rehabilitation requires training of many body functions, especially for the hand in restoring grip, wrist rotation, and other aspects. It can further be improved by exploring the game design for rehabilitation of other body functions of stroke patients. For this experiment, we only developed a simple action game scene with a simple plot. Developers can design more complex scenarios and scenes in order to understand the characteristics of patients with stroke and help them recover. In addition, this study did not establish a complete recovery evaluation mechanism due to time constraints. Thus, comprehensively assessing the recovery effects for patients playing virtual reality games wearing head-mounted equipment is beyond the scope of this paper. Future research can verify the effect of virtual reality technology for rehabilitation of stroke patients with fuller attention to recovery assessment methods. In conclusion, our design is a small attempt to solve the traditional problems with new technologies. With the development of medical technology and virtual reality technology, virtual reality will undoubtedly continue to provide options for medical treatment.

References

1. What is a Stroke? National Heart, Lung, and Blood Institute, 26 March 2014. Accessed 26 Feb 2015
2. Gabriele, W., Renate, S.: Work loss following stroke. Disabil. Rehabil. **31**(18), 1487–1493 (2009)
3. Tierney, N.W., Crouch, J., Garcia, H., et al.: Virtual reality in gait rehabilitation. MODSIM World (2007)

4. Riwu, L., Maoen, L., Shihai, P., et al.: Mandatory exercise therapy in the treatment of stroke hemiplegia clinical application. Cardiovasc. Cerebrovasc. Dis. Prevent. Control 7(2), 97–98 (2007)
5. Dongrui, Z., Geng Yanjuan, X., Lisheng, Z.X., Guanglin, L.: Design and implementation of virtual reality hand rehabilitation training system. Integr. Technol. 2(4), 33–40 (2013)
6. Saposnik, G., Mamdani, M., Bayley, M., et al.: Effectiveness of virtual reality exercises in stroke rehabilitation (EVREST): rationale, design, and protocol of a pilot randomized clinical trial assessing the Wii gaming system. Int. J. Stroke 5(1), 47–51 (2010)
7. Levanon, Y.: The advantages and disadvantages of using high technology in hand rehabilitation. J. Hand Ther. 26(2), 179–183 (2013)
8. Saposnik, G., Levin, M.: Virtual reality in stroke rehabilitation: a meta-analysis and implications for clinicians. Stroke 42(5), 1380–1386 (2011)
9. Uurda, J.P.R., Vroohhoven, R.H.: Robot-assisted surgical systems new era in laparoscopic surgery. Ann. Roy. Coll. Surg. Engl. 84, 223–226 (2003)
10. Sarakoglou, I., Tsagarakis, N.G., Caldwell, D.G.: Occupational and physical therapy using a hand exoskeleton based exerciser. In: IEEE/RSJ International Conference on Intelligent Robots and Systems, pp. 2973–2978 (2004)
11. Guo, S., Song, Z., Song, G.: Development of a self-assisted rehabilitation system for the upper limbs based on virtual reality. In: Proceedings of 2007 IEEE International Conference on Mechatronics and Automation, pp. 1452–1457 (2007)
12. Bardorfer, A., Munih, M., Zupan, A., et al.: Upper limb motion analysis using haptic interface. IEEE/ASME Trans. Mechatron. 6(1), 253–260 (2001)
13. Adamovich, S.V., Fluet, G.G., Mathai, A.: Incorporating hapic effects into three-dimensional virtual environment to train the hemiparetic upper extremity. IEEE Trans. Neural Syst. Rehabil. Eng. 17, 512–519 (2009)
14. Kim, Y.K., Yang, X.: Hand writing rehabilitation in the haptic virtual environment. In: IEEE International Workshop on Haptic Audio Visual Environments and Their Applications, pp. 161–164 (2006)
15. Liu, H.: Hand injury rehabilitation manipulator structure design and analysis. Harbin Institute of Technology Library, Harbin (2007)
16. Zhou, S., Gong, Z.: Discussion on the definition of virtual reality. Comput. Simul. 23(9), 219–222 (2006)
17. Yu, J., Qian, J., Shen, Y., et al.: A finger rehabilitation device mechanism and control experiments. Chin. J. Tissue Eng. Res. Clin. Rehabil. 14(30), 5596–5601 (2010)
18. Zhang, J.: Research on finger rehabilitation system based on virtual reality technology, Huazhong University of Science and Technology, Wuhan (2012)
19. Pew Research Center: Spring 2015 Global Attitudes Survey, Q71&Q72 (2015)
20. Donnan, G.A., Fisher, M., Macleod, M., Davis, S.M.: Stroke. Lancet. 371(9624), 1612–1623 (2008)
21. What are the Signs and Symptoms of a Stroke? National Heart, Lung, and Blood Institute, 26 March 2014. Accessed 27 Feb 2015
22. Cotran, R.S., Kumar, V., Fausto, N., Robbins, S.L., Abbas, A.K.: Robbins and Cotran Pathologic Basis of Disease. Elsevier Saunders, St. Louis (2005). ISBN 0-7216-0187-1
23. Who is at Risk for a Stroke? National Heart, Lung, and Blood Institute, 26 March 2014. Accessed 27 Feb 2015

Designing Craft Learning Experience for Rural Children: A Case Study on Huayao Cross-Stitch in Southwest China

Duoduo Zhang[(✉)], Yuanyuan Yang, Tie Ji, Huiling Xie,
and Yuwei He

School of Design, Hunan University, Changsha, China
zhang_duoduo@hnu.edu.cn

Abstract. Craft is characterized by tacit knowledge, which is featured as embodiment and contextualization. In the circumstances that the rural craft learning socio-cultural context have already changed significantly, this paper tries to probe the issue that how to capture those characteristics of craft knowledge and transfer them successfully into an attractive craft learning experience for rural children.

Taking Huayao cross-stitch–an ethic minority Intangible Cultural Heritage in southwest rural China as a case study, the paper regards digital game as a mediated method to arouse the craft learning interest of rural children and facilitate their understanding of craft knowledge. Focusing the acquisition and presentation of craft "Know-How" knowledge in craft, aiming at promoting the learner's reflective observations in learning experience, this paper proposes a game-based craft learning experience design model and verifies the model with a Huayao Cross-Stitch Game.

Keywords: Craft · Learning experience · Rural children · Digital game
Skills

1 Introduction

As one of the principal modes of self-sufficient production in the pre-industrial age, rural handicrafts carry the socio-culture information of certain regions. In many rural areas of China, based on kinship and geographic, craft knowledge can be passed down from generation to generation. During this process, not only the local knowledge is reproduced, but also the learners' socio-cultural identities are shaped. With the rapid modernization, great changes have taken place on rural craft in China. On the one hand, in order to make living, many young people have to leave their villages and become migrant workers in big cities, which not only break the traditional rural craft inter-generational inheritance, but also turn their children into so called left-behind children. On the other hand, since mass production with increased access to ready-made goods, craft skills now are no longer necessary for rural everyday life. In recent years, with the growing concern about intangible cultural heritage in China, rural crafts which were once neglected, now are back into the spotlight. In some rural areas,

© Springer International Publishing AG, part of Springer Nature 2018
P.-L. P. Rau (Ed.): CCD 2018, LNCS 10912, pp. 117–132, 2018.
https://doi.org/10.1007/978-3-319-92252-2_9

local crafts are integrated into the primary curriculum with the name of "Bringing the Intangible Cultural Heritage into School".

Aiming at this kind of craft courses, usually the primary schools will invite local craft masters to teach the pupils—most of whom are left-behind children. For these young learners, however, the craft learning is neither attractive because of local craft masters' traditional teaching methods, nor is motivational in this new socio-cultural situation. Existing data and researches show that as the "digital natives", today's children are growing up in information age, who are surrounded by computers, cell phones, video games and other digital devices [1]. Even in remote rural China, there is no exception. With the improvement of mobile communication networks and the popularization of smart phones in China, now rural people can get smart phones with affordable price too. As a daily necessity, smart phones are used by left-behind children to communicate with their parents who are migrant workers. With various applications, smart phone have became the favorite toy for rural children. Prensky pointed out that as a new generation of learners, "digital natives" have different learning and cognitive characteristics from the previous generation, and the old teaching methods are no longer adapt to these new learners [2]. Moreover, it is necessary to construct a new learning and education system to deal with changes of these young learners [1].

Thus, based on the interests of these rural "digital natives", this paper tries to probe the issue that how to capture those characteristics of craft knowledge and transfer them successfully into an attractive craft learning experience for rural left-behind children.

2 Theoretical Background

Craft as an activity is based on the intellectual and physical characteristics of the maker. In crafts, a special way of knowing about the world has been formed: Knowing is directed by a vision of doing by hand and shaped by the mental and concrete products of doing [3]. Craft includes a large amount of "Know-How" content, not only so-called procedural knowledge in the cognitive psychology–the execution of single actions and entire chains of actions, or processes [4], but also those informal, difficult to expressed experiences or skills, and even those shared knowledge that must be transmitted through human interaction. In recent years, with the development of embodiment cognition, scholars interpreted characteristics of craft knowledge from the new theoretical perspective–on the one hand, it is embodied and individualized, which implies that people's intellectual cognition of this kind of practical knowledge is based on specific body structures and physical activities in a certain environment; On the other hand, craft knowledge also has the collective attributes which can be shared by a certain community. It is embedded in certain environment and social relations, that can be reproduced through the artisans community, social hierarchy and division of labor assumptions [5–7]. Coherently, so far knowledge in these areas has been transmitted mainly by observation or imitation of craft experts in real contexts—it is so called "learning by doing", or "apprenticeship". In general, the acquisition of handicraft requires long term repetitive practice, which can form the whole cognition of "insight" in the process of touching and using materials and tools [8].

Experiential learning is the process of learning through experience, and is more specifically defined as "learning through reflection on doing". Compared to rote learning or didactic learning that makes learners to learn passively, one of characteristics of experiential learning is initiative. As a "hands-on" learning, craft is undoubtedly "participatory" and "experiential". However, in the changing socio-cultural context, craft learning situation is quite different from that of traditional apprenticeship learning. Some craft education researchers have proposed that "'Hand' should include by the present technology can provide all of the hands and hearts of extensions" [3, 9]. Some scholars also pointed out that for craft education, the main challenge is to recognize current educational patterns. In order to solve the problem of all kinds of complicated situations in the future, now we should put more emphasize on how to stimulate learners' interest, promote their active participation and cooperative learning, and help them to use different tools and techniques to create new knowledge [3, 10].

In the field of digital learning design, Experiential learning theory had inspired many researchers. Prensky pointed out that digital game is not always the enemy, it can also become the effective means to provide the best learning experience for children [11]. Experiential learning theory consists of several models that stress the importance of direct experience and reflective observation. One of them that gave great inspirations to game learning designers is Kolb's four stages experiential learning model [12]. According to Kolb, the experiential learning is a continuous circle which consists four stages of goal-directed actions. The circle begins with a concrete experience; then followed by reflective observations of that experience; after that is the abstract conceptualization stage in which the learner can makes generalization; at the end of the circle, through active experimentation the learner will test these ideas in new circumstances. Based on Kolb's model, a game researcher Kristian Kiili, who comes from Finland, proposed an experiential gaming model with the combination of flow theory and game design. Kiili's model stresses the importance of providing the player with immediate feedback, clear goals and challenges that are matched to his/her skill level [13]. Both of models became the theoretical bases for this research using digital game as a mediated learning method for rural left-behind children.

In recent years, there are some efforts to use serious games to enhance the learner's learning experiences in the field of intangible cultural heritage education, such as i-Treasure project from Italy. Instead of declarative knowledge, one of main concerns of these attempts is the acquisition of procedural knowledge, then transmit these knowledge by game based learning with various cutting-edge technologies, such as AR, VR etc. As a result, the learner's motor skills were trained, together with their learning engagement and motivation are enhanced [14].

Therefore, these previous studies provide theoretical and practical basis for our research. In this paper, digital game is regarded as a mediated method to arouse the craft learning interests of rural left-behind children and facilitate their understanding process of craft knowledge. Further, how to acquisition and presentation of craft "Know-How" knowledge in games becomes the focus of this paper. In this respect, this paper initiates the case study on Huayao Cross-stitch–a national intangible cultural heritage in southwest china.

3   Research Objects and Methodology

Huayao cross-stitch is one of the unique techniques of an ethnic minority Huayao in the poor remote rural regions of southwest China. The earliest Huayao cross-stitch can be traced to Han dynasty, and in the following centuries Huayao cross-stitch technique has made considerable development. In 2006, Huayao cross-stitch was listed in the *China National Intangible Cultural Heritage Catalogue*. Because of without their own national characters, patterns made with cross-stitch on Huayao costumes become records of its ethnic history. Huayao cross-stitch differs a lot from the ordinary cross-stitch which has the same pattern on both sides, although they are both produced on warp and weft fabrics. Under the guidance of its back side up stitching, Huayao cross-stitch can create different patterns on both sides of a cotton fabric at the same time by counted thread: the front side is a pattern composed by countless "X", and the back side is made up of numerous short dash "-" (Fig. 1).

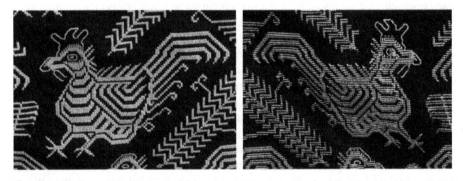

Fig. 1. Huayao cross-stitch can create different patterns on both sides of the fabric at the same time by counting thread: the front side is a pattern composed by countless 'X' (Left), and the back side are made up of numerous short dash '-' (Right).

For a long time, Huayao cross-stitch is an essential skill for local Huayao women. A cross stitch master usually will be regarded as ideal marriage partner with the characteristics of dexterity and intelligence. As a local custom, Huayao women begin to learn cross-stitch at her 8 or 10 years old. Normally, the first teacher of their cross-stitch learning is their female relatives, such as mother, sister, aunt, etc. By kinship, Huayao women can acquire this traditional skill–from the most basic cross stitches such as "X" or "-" to the most complicated patterns consist of numerous these basic units which will be used for their future life (Fig. 2). With the rapid modernization progress in Huayao villages, although the old generation keep wearing traditional Huayao costumes, the way of cross-stitch learning has changed a lot. Owing to the changing lifestyle, most of local young people are not wearing traditional clothes any more. Moreover, for making living, a large number of young people poured into cities, which turned their children into left-behind children, and broke the traditional craft transmission mechanism based on kinship as well. As a consequence, Huayao cross-stitch gradually became an intangible cultural heritage that requires to be protected. Then with the name of

"Bringing the Intangible Cultural Heritage into School", cross-stitch course entered local elementary school since 2016. In order to observe current Huayao cross-stitch teaching and learning patterns in primary school, and redesign the craft learning experience for rural left-behind children with digital games, we chose the pupils in grades 5 and 6 (aged 9–12 years old) in Baishuidong Primary School as the start learner and conducted our research.

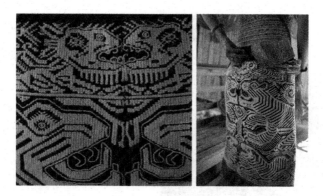

Fig. 2. Traditional Huayao dress with pattern of tigers

The whole research consisted of two stages: the pilot study and the main study. Both stages were aimed at rural children who have not any experience on Huayao cross-stitch, no matter their gender differences. In pilot study, firstly, by interviews and questionnaires, the digital environment of conducting digital game based craft learning experience design for Huayao left-behind children were confirmed. Then, the existing teaching and learning situations in the Huayao cross-stitch course in Baishuidong primary school were observed. In the main study, aimed at the most important and difficult "Know-How" part both for cross-stitch expert and pupils, we designed a digital game as a mediated learning method, afterwards we made a set of comparison tests to observe the craft learning process and evaluate the craft learning effect of left-behind children with digital games.

In both stages, taking into account of the "one-to-many" actual teaching situation in classes, the pupils were divided into several groups which include 5 students each. In each group, for better observation, we arranged an observer to record activities of both teacher and pupils with "multiple-scan" and tabular recording, and besides, a video camera was set up to assistant the observation (Fig. 3). Multiple-scan is a sampling method for social-behavioral research on a group of children [15]. In our research, each observer was responsible for observing 5 children in his/her group. With recording tables corresponding to each child, every half a minute the observer should record the behaviors and activities of each pupil with certain order, then write down the exact time of each activity. The recording form stressed four aspects of children's craft learning–knowledge acquisition and comprehension, interaction with classmates and teachers, concentration and motivation, motor skills and attitudes (Fig. 4) [16]. Video graphic approach is an adequate method for studying craft teaching and learning, especially for making hidden aspects of craft learning visible [17, 18]. Thus, at the end of each stage, the final work of each child (Huayao cross-stitch patch) was photographed to assess the final results in combination with their respective learning in each group [18]. In addition, each child was asked to conduct a learner's self-valuation with 5 stars at both the beginning and the end of each stage. The main concern of this evaluation included three aspects, which was Liking, Challenge, Frustration (Fig. 5).

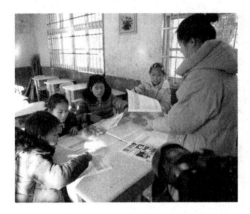

Fig. 3. In each group, there were one observer and a video camera

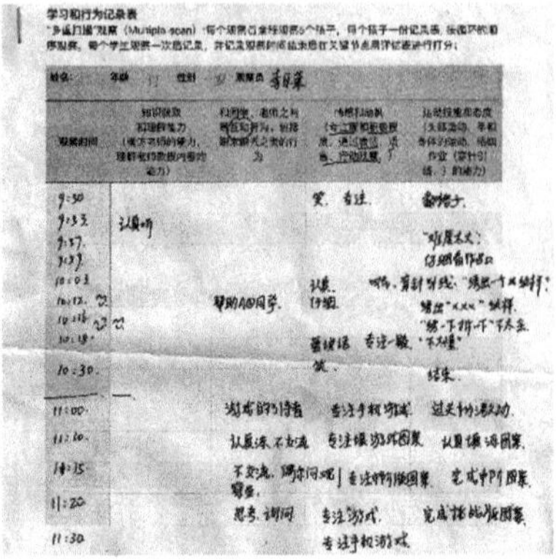

Fig. 4. A recording form stressed four aspects of children's craft learning

4.参与者自我评估：在学习活动之前和之后要求参与者进行自我感觉评估，从喜欢挑花学习的3个变量：参与，挑战和挫折，用5分制记录（儿童采用5颗星星标记）

姓名	喜欢程度	挑战指数	挫折感	备注
课前	★★★★☆	★★★★★	★★★★☆	
课后	★★★☆☆	★★★★★	★★★★★	
结束后	★★★☆☆	★★★★★	★★★★★	

Fig. 5. A recording table of learner's self-evaluation

4 Practical Work

4.1 Pilot Study

At the start of this research, a pilot study was used to confirm the possibility of experiential game-based learning in local left-behind primary school, as well as know ahead of the procedure and the current situation in Huayao cross-stitch learning class. By observing the teaching and learning procedures of craft master and pupils, we extracted the procedural knowledge of cross-stitch skill, and drew the Learner Experience Map which could help us to find out both of the pain points for pupils' cross-stitch learning and opportunities for designing a better craft learning experience for them. Further, we proposed a game-based craft learning experience design model for these left-behind children.

Procedure

In the very beginning of pilot study, a general survey was conducted in Baishuidong primary school. By interviews and questionnaires, we visited more than 30 student's families and received 109 questionnaires from the pupil in Baishuidong primary school. Based on the data we collected, the digital environment of using digital game as a mediated craft learning method for Huayao left-behind children was confirmed. There were about 84.4% pupils had digital electronic equipment (smart phone, computer, etc.), and most of them showed great interests in digital games. In addition, according to these data, there were only 55% pupil interviewees indicated that they were willing to learn cross-stitch if only we could offer the craft learning opportunities. And in those who were unwilling to learn this craft, 75.5% of them were boys. The survey showed that it was gender that had great influence on students' learning willing of cross-stitch.

Then, aimed at pupils around 10–12 years old, a 45 min class of Huayao cross-stitch was organized. A 58 years old craft woman M, who is the Intangible Cultural Inheritor of Huayao cross-stitch acted as the teacher. There were 27 students in this class. They were divided into 5 groups by random (two groups with 6 people, others with 5). The task of this class was to teach students how to count thread, and make "X" in the front and "-" in the back of a fabric with the most basic Huayao stitching skills.

The whole teaching process included 4 stages: (1) Introduction; (2) Distribution of cross-stitch material; (3) Hands-on demonstration of key skills–counting thread and the basic stitches; (4) Practicing time for pupils. With methods of 'multiple-scan', recording forms, video graphics and learner's self-evaluation forms, we collected all the data and drew the Learner Journey Map (LJM) of Huayao cross-stitch learning (Fig. 6).

Results and Analysis

According to the LJM, in M's cross-stitch teaching class, the most unclear and frustrating part was the 3rd stage–demonstration of key skills–which was exactly the most important part of cross-stitch learning. Moreover, the final work (Huayao cross-stitch patch) of each child also showed that no more than 33.3% learners finished the cross-stitch patches correctly. And the learners' self-evaluation form indicated that compared to before class, after hands-on practices, the number of students who showed interests in cross-stitch was increased to 59.3%. Those who still dislike the craft were boys.

As an elderly craft master, M used to teach apprentice with one-by-one hands-on demonstration, and the apprentice could learn by observation or imitation. Both counting thread and doing the basic stitching on a cotton fabric are subtle skills. Although the craft master could finish a set of basic stitches in 1–2 s, actually a set of stitching procedure was complicated, which included a sequence of action: (1) stitching back up to the front side of fabric; (2) counting 5 threads along the weft in the front, (3) stitching from the front to the back side; (4) counting 5 threads along the warp, then counting 5 threads along the weft; (5) stitching back up to the front side of fabric again. What's more, a set of these stitches were happened on an area no more than $5 * 5 \text{ mm}^2$ (Fig. 7). As a result, to acquire these skills, the learners had to observe very closely and

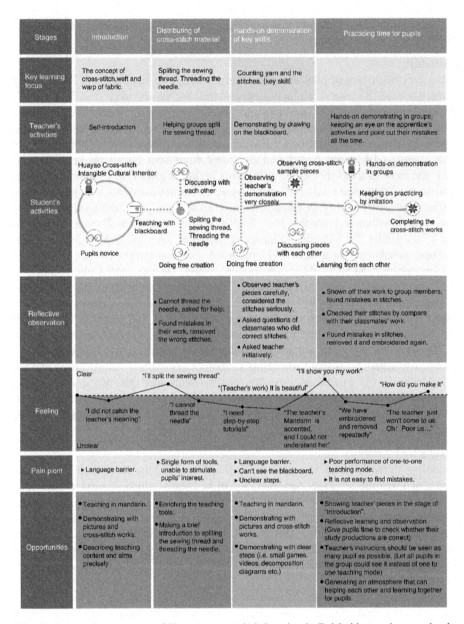

Fig. 6. Learner journey map of Huayao cross-stitch learning in Baishuidong primary school.

keep on practicing. Even though, these stitches were too fine for them to do without make any mistakes, which makes it necessary for the craft master to keep an eye on the apprentice's activities all the time. Thus, this traditional cross-stitch teaching method might work when there were only one or two students, but was not suitable for a craft class. Once the number of student went up to 5 or more, it was a little bit difficult for the learner to capture the key point of the skill knowledge. In addition, because M could use only native Huayao language rather than mandarin, which increased the difficulties to communicate with pupils.

Fig. 7. Surrounded by pupils, M was demonstrating the key skills of counting thread and basic stitches

If we regard the whole process as an experiential learning circle, it is obvious that to get better learning experience and results in a craft class, we can make full use of all kinds of methods to promote the learner's reflective observations, such as improving key skills demonstration with illustrations, or offering immediate feedbacks when the learner do wrong or correct operation with digital games, and adding multi-media effect and reward mechanism to enhance learning interest of the learners etc. Therefore, we proposed a game-based craft learning experience design model (Fig. 8) and designed the Huayao Cross-Stitch Game based on the model.

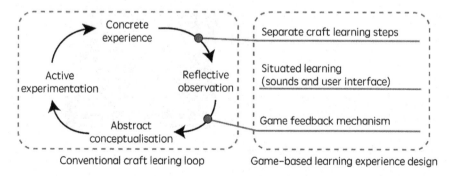

Fig. 8. Game-based craft learning experience design model.

4.2 Main Study

In main study, to verify the impact of digital game on the craft learning experience, we organized a comparative experiment. The task of both Group A and Group B was to teach students how to count thread, and make "X" in the front and "-" in the back of a fabric with the most basic Huayao stitching skill in 45 min, the same with pilot study. And both of groups included 1 teacher, 1 observer, and 5 pupils.

The differences between Group A and Group B lay in the teacher's different teaching methods. In Group A, craft learning was kept in a traditional hands-on demonstration and instructed by a 35 years old craft master H who can speak mandarin fluently and her stitch skill was as good as M. Based on the feedbacks of pilot study, this time H used graphics as teaching aid (Fig. 9). In Group B, craft learning was instructed by a cross-stitch novice 24 years old L, who did know how to stitch, but was not as masterful as H. L used several smart phones and iPad with Huayao Cross-Stitch Game as teaching aid (Fig. 10). Same as pilot study, we used multiple-scan, recording forms, video graphics and learner's self-evaluation forms to collect all the data.

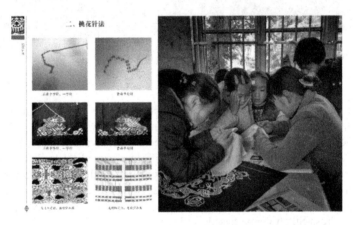

Fig. 9. H and Huayao cross-stitch teaching aid graphics in Group A

Fig. 10. L and Huayao cross-stitch teaching aid digital-game in Group B.

Procedure

Group A

Similar with the pilot study, the whole teaching process of H included 4 stages: (1) Introduction; (2) Distribution of cross-stitch material; (3) Hands-on demonstration of key skills—count thread and the basic stitches (by H); (4) Practicing time for pupils. The pupils learned skills still mainly by close observation or imitation. Moreover, with the assistance of process graphics, pupils can understand the key skills easily. H's fluent mandarin contributed a lot for communication with pupils especially in pupils' practicing time for answering their questions.

Group B

The whole teaching process of L consisted of 5 steps: (1) Introduction; (2) Distribution of cross-stitch material; (3) Hands-on demonstration of key skills—counting thread and the basic stitches; (4) Playing Huayao Cross-Stitch Game in turns (by pupils); (5) Practicing time for pupils. Compared to the teaching process of Group A, Group B added a step of playing digital-game, which attracted pupils to participate actively and promoted their reflective observations in both step 4 and step 5.

Based on the analysis on the key skills of Huayao cross-stitch in pilot study, the newly designed Huayao Cross-Stitch Game had 4 features as follows (Table 1).

(1) Setting clear learning goals. As it mentioned before, a set of basic stitches consisted of procedure knowledge, which was a consequence of actions. In game, we divided all actions into 3 game levels. From easy to difficult, these levels were: 1. counting threads (stitching back up to the front side of fabric, then counting 5 threads along weft in front, to form "-"); 2. 45° stitch (counting 5 threads along the warp, then counting 5 threads along the weft, to form a "/"); 3. Finishing a cross stitch (counting 5 threads along the weft, then counting 5 threads along the warp, to finish a "X"). Once accomplished a level, there was a page of celebration to encourage the learner.

(2) Providing demonstration with simple animation. Cross-stitch skills were subtle, for better demonstration, we magnified the operations and represent them in a simplified, animated way. For example, the length of counting 5 threads along weft was about 5 mm on a cotton fabric, now we used grid which can represent the weft and warp and show the spatial relation of thread as well. Further, each step of the skill was animated in the game.

(3) Offering immediate feedbacks. In traditional cross-stitch learning, the instructor had to keep an eye on the apprentices in case they make mistake. It was common that the apprentice cannot find the mistake until he/she finished all the work. In game, we designed the feedback mechanism, only when learner's operation was correct, they can proceed to the next step. This immediate feedback can facilitate students' reflection behavior and improve their learning efficiency.

(4) Providing situated learning with multimedia. By adding attractive Huayao cross-stitch patterns and local music with happy rhythm, learner's learning interests were aroused.

Table 1. The improvements of game-based Huayao cross-stitch learning experience design

Pain points of traditional Huayao Cross-Stitch teaching	Huayao Cross-Stitch Game	
	Solution	Game Screenshot
Fine and subtle	Zoom in fabric Turn weft and warp of a fabric into grid on screen	
Counting thread	Use animation to show the number of threads.	
Stitches	Use Trace of lines to show different stitches.	
Stitches in the front and the back of a fabric are different	Use the grid to show the spatial relation of thread.	
Setting clear learning goals	Divide all actions into 3 game levels; Use a page of celebration to encourage the learner	

Result and Analysis

The main study data showed that there were great differences between Group A and Group B both in the learners' final works and their learning experiences.

By contrasting their final works finished in 45 min—cross-stitch patches, generally, Group A showed higher level of accuracy and completeness than Group B. There were two students in Group A who were able to complete a complete rectangle with cross-stitches, which were much more than the task required (Fig. 11). In Group B, there were only two students completed two "X" (Fig. 12). Obviously, one more step in Group B took up more time and affected the completeness of pupils' final works. And the two teachers' proficiency in cross-stitch skill effected pupils' accuracy as well.

But it is worth noting the accuracy of pupils' final works is not necessarily in accordance with their learning enthusiasms and their self-evaluation of the cross-stitch learning experience.

In Group A, with the traditional craft demonstration method, on the whole, students' learning experience were passive. In addition, H is a quiet lady and is not good at creating an active atmosphere, which also led to a serious atmosphere in class. As a consequence, after class, most of the students showed lower interests in cross-stitch than before class, and they felt more frustrated than Group B (Fig. 13).

In Group B, L is also a quiet young lady, but with the assistant of digital game, the whole learning and teaching processes were relaxed. All the students in Group B showed greater interests in cross-stitch after class. Two boys in this group even said that they were more interested in making cross-stitch than game because of the former's higher challenges (Fig. 13). Moreover, research data showed that pupils turned back to the game when they have difficulties during the practicing time. With the help of L, students could find the corresponding game levels quickly. More surprising was that instead of remembering the stitching steps, there were two boys kept in mind the patterns of stitching traces in game. They drew it down, once they felt confused in the stitch practicing, they could review these patterns (Fig. 14). Overall, digital game engaged pupils in Group B into an active learning status during the whole learning process.

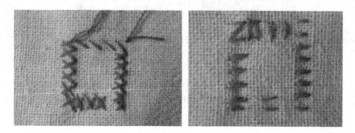

Fig. 11. A complete cross-stitch rectangle made by a pupil in group A, instructed by H.

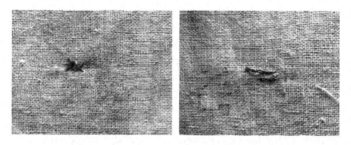

Fig. 12. Few complete cross stitches made by a pupil in group B, instructed by L and game.

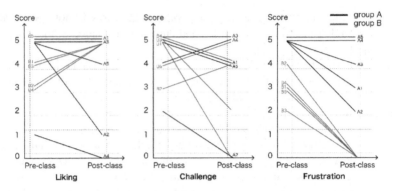

Fig. 13. The contrast analysis chart of pupils in Group A and Group B of "Liking, Challenge, Frustration," before and after the class.

Fig. 14. The left: Pupils turned to the game when they have difficulties during the practicing time. The right: Two boys kept in mind the patterns of stitching traces in game, and draw them down.

5 Conclusion

Taking learning Huayao cross-stitch as a case study, based on the analysis of existing rural digital environment and craft learning experience, this paper regards digital game as mediated method of craft learning for rural children. Then focusing on "Know-How" knowledge in craft, this paper proposes a general model of game-based craft learning experience design. According to the model, a Huayao cross-stitch learning game for rural children was designed. Further, through observation, comparison and evaluation of rural children's digital-game mediated learning, the paper draws conclusion from the following three aspects.

Firstly, by transferring the craft procedure knowledge into digital game and using the game in the reflective observation stage of experience learning circle, it was verified in our research that digital game can significantly enhance the interest and motivation of rural children's craft learning, reduce their learning difficulties, and further facilitate them to grasp craft procedural knowledge as well. In the game-based craft experiential learning, the traditional craft learning methods of observation and imitation can be improved greatly by a series of means normally used in games, such as clarifying the goal of craft learning, separating craft procedural knowledge and turning them into different game tasks, providing immediate trial and error feedbacks and reward mechanisms, designing learning situations with multi-channel(i.e. haptic, visual, aural) experiences that enable children to learn in a participatory manner.

However, although there are so many advantages of game-based craft learning, the paper shows that this kind of digital-games present on smart phone or other mobile devices, can only be a mediated way for craft learning, rather than replacing the learner's real hands-on making process with materials and tools.

Secondly, this paper find that during the gamification process of craft skill, because of the "knowledge gap" between craft master and designer, it is very difficult for the designer to transfer those subtle embodiment knowledges with digital game. Therefore, it is very necessary to invite skilled artisans to participate in the game design process, otherwise, there will be some mistakes that cannot be found from the perspective of designer. For example, before designed Huayao Stitch Game, designers did follow the craft expert and learn how to make Huayao cross-stitch, and represent these subtle stitches successfully in the game (see Table 1, "Counting thread"). Based on the writing habits of average people (right-handed person), the direction of the line that simulates real stitch line was designed from left to right. In fact, this design is wrong. Because in the actual cross-stitch making process, normally the one will take the fabric with her/his left hand, and with the needle in the right hand, which means that the direction of counting thread should be from right to left. Unfortunately, because of lacking embodied experiences, none of designers noticed this mistake during several times of game trial until cross-stitch expert H pointed it out when she accidentally played the game after the main study stage.

Finally, the use of digital games for craft learning can provide some opportunities for local crafts to break barriers of socio-culture tradition and be spread cross-culturally and cross-regionally. As shown in this paper, game-based craft learning attracted several boys who did not want to learn cross-stitch in the very beginning because it was seemed as a female work. In this paper, we present the general theoretical frame of game-based craft experience learning design, for further exploration, some psychology research fields such as flow, situational learning and cognitive schema should be involved in, which will be our next research themes.

Acknowledgements. The project is funded by the Department of Development Planning, Ministry of Education P.R.C, under project No. (2017)304; Qipai Intangible Cultural Heritage Protection and Research Fund, Academy of Arts & Design, Tsinghua University, under project No. (2015)05. We would like to thank Zhang Bo, Hu Yuzhe, Li Yongbin and their students in Baishuidong Primary School for their participation on the study.

References

1. Prensky, M.: Digital natives, digital immigrants. Horizon **9**, 1–6 (2001)
2. Tapscott, D.: Educating the net generation. Educ. Leadersh. **56**(5), 6–11 (1999)

3. Pöllänen, S., Urdziņa-Deruma, M.: Future-oriented reform of craft education. In: Kimonen, E., Nevalainen, R. (eds.) Reforming Teaching and Teacher Education, pp. 117–144. Springer, Rotterdam (2017). https://doi.org/10.1007/978-94-6300-917-1_5
4. Pirttimaa, M., Husu, J., Metsärinne, M.: Uncovering procedural knowledge in craft, design, and technology education. Int. J. Technol. Des. Educ. **27**, 215–231 (2017)
5. Eyferth, J.: The technical locations about Chinese handicraft industry under the anthropologic vision. J. Ethnol. **3**(2), 1–10 (2012)
6. Ingold, T.: The perception of the environment. In: Essays in Live hood, Dwelling and Skill. Routledge, London (2000)
7. Li, H.W., Sheng, X.M.: Embodied cognition. Stud Sci. Sci. **20**(2), 184–190 (2006)
8. Zhang, D.D.: Tacit knowledge: the microscopic perspective of design innovation research on traditional crafts. ZhuangShi **266**, 117–119 (2015)
9. Brey, P.: Theories of technology as extension of human faculties. In: Mitcham, C. (ed.) Metaphysics, Epistemology, and Technology Research in Philosophy and Technology, vol. 19, pp. 59–78. JAI Press, London (2000)
10. Binkley, M., Erstad, O., Herman, J., Raizen, S., Ripley, M., Rumble, M.: Defining 21st century skills. In: Griffin, P., McGaw, B., Care, E. (eds.) Assessment and Teaching of 21st Century Skills, pp. 17–66. Springer, New York (2011). https://doi.org/10.1007/978-94-007-2324-5_2
11. Prensky, M.: Digital game-based learning. ACM Comput. Entertain. **1**(1), 1–4 (2003)
12. Kolb, D.: Experiential Learning: Experience as the Source of Learning and Development. Prentice Hall, Upper Saddle River (1984)
13. Kiili, K.: Digital game-based learning: towards an experiential gaming model. Internet High. Educ. **8**, 13–24 (2005)
14. Dagnino, F., Ott, M., Pozzil, F., Yilmaz, E., Tsalakanidou, F., Dimitropoulos, K., Grammalidis, N.: Serious games to support learning of rare 'intangible' cultural expressions. In: 9th International Technology, Education & Development Conference (2015). https://www.researchgate.net/publication/274063812_Serious_Games_to_Support_Learning_of_Rare_'Intangible'_Cultural_Expressions
15. Li, Y.: Play and Child Development. Zhejiang Education Publishing House, Hangzhou (2008)
16. Connolly, T.C., Boyle, E.A., Hainey, T., McArthur, E., Boyle, J.M.: A systematic literature review of empirical evidence on computer games and serious games. Comput. Educ. **59**(2), 661–686 (2012)
17. Degerbøl, S., Nielsen, C.S.: Researching embodied learning by using video graphic participation for data collection and audiovisual narratives for dissemination – illustrated by the encounter between two acrobats. Ethnogr. Educ. **10**(1), 60–75 (2015)
18. Yliverronen, V., Seitamaa-Hakkarainen, S.P.: Learning craft skills: exploring preschoolers' craft-making process. Techne Ser. A **23**(2), 1–15 (2016)

Culture and Creativity

New Approach to Design in Cultural Society from ABCDE to FGHIJ

Wen-Ko Chiou[1], Erik Armayuda[2(✉)], Yang Gao[3], and Rungtai Lin[3]

[1] Department of Industrial Design, Chang Gung University, Taoyuan, Taiwan
wkchiu@mail.cgu.edu.tw
[2] Visual Communication Design, Faculty of Creative Industries and Telematics,
Trilogi University, Kalibata, South Jakarta, Indonesia
armayuda@trilogi.ac.id
[3] Graduate School of Creative Industry Design,
National Taiwan University of Arts, New Taipei City, Taiwan
lukegaol991@gmail.com, rtlin@mail.ntua.edu.tw

Abstract. Culture and advancement of century is one of the dynamics in the growth of the creative industry. In the context of globalization, local culture can be a source of inspiration in creating creative products. Back in the old days cultural artefact usually use to fulfil the needs of human daily life. Changes in human lifestyle affect the changing needs of their life which impact to market demand. Traditional cultural products are no longer a necessity to meet lifestyles in modern times and tend to change from function into a symbolic products of a particular culture. This is because cultural products is no longer relevant with today's markets, which only cares about the products they need, want, and desire. That's what makes the model ABCDE (Art, Business, Creative, Design, and E-business) of cultural transformation model. The model should be complete by following model to give a better impact on humanity in cultural society especially for the actor of culture as an inspiration itself such as inheritors or its villager. While designers who get inspiration are be able to create a new derivative products that can gives both, financially and non financially benefits, cultural actors are still untouched in the cycle of business models. This studies try to propose additional model to explore culture in context of creative industries. This research aims to offer the alternative model of FGHIJ (Fairness, Gain, Humanity, Impact, and Joy), as a business model that can provide more appropriate cultural exploration that impact cultural society.

Keywords: Social design · Cultural exploration · Business model

1 Introduction

Culture is "The arts and other manifestations of human intellectual achievement regarded collectively" [10]. Koentjaraningrat defines that culture as a "power of mind" in the form of creativity, intention and taste, while culture is the result of creation, intention, and taste [2]. According to Liliweri, culture is the life view of a group of people in the form of behaviours, beliefs, values, and symbols they receive unconsciously that are all inherited through the process of communication from one

© Springer International Publishing AG, part of Springer Nature 2018
P.-L. P. Rau (Ed.): CCD 2018, LNCS 10912, pp. 135–144, 2018.
https://doi.org/10.1007/978-3-319-92252-2_10

generation to the next [3]. By all of those definition, the definition can be simplify as 'manifestation of human thought process that inherited from time to time'.

There are various types of cultural products, from tangible aspect such as artefacts, behavioural aspect that involving cultural tools, to any intangible aspect as cultural norms and values. Koentjaraningrat also distinguishes three forms of culture: (1) The form of culture as a complex of ideas, ideas, values, norms, rules and so on. (2) The form of culture as a complex of activity and the patterned actions of man in a society. (3) The form of culture as objects of human works [2]. Among the types, products that are tangible can be a representative symbol of particular cultural group.

Culture and development of the times is one of the dynamics in the growth of creative industry. In the context of globalization, local culture can be a source of inspiration to develop creative products. The development of the times indirectly changed the lifestyle of society slowly. These lifestyle changes also affects cultural products that are no longer a product that fulfil market needs. Cultural products that used to be functional transformed into symbolic products, where buyers of the products no longer buy because of its function, but rather because of historical and symbolic factors over the identity of a particular culture as an art.

The effort to preserve the cultural product already taken by conducting some studies and experiment. One of the solution is by doing cultural transformation by transferring the values from cultural product into a new product more relevant form that needs by market to face the change of times. According to Lin, changes in consumer perception regarding innovation are also important in cultural product design. In addition, "Culture" plays an important role in the design field, and "cross cultural design" will be a key design evaluation point in the future. [6]. That is why the ABCDE (Art, Business, Creative, Design, and E-business) model of the cultural transformation model becomes a relevant way to explore cultural wealth, both in the context of cultural preservation as well as in the business model context. To turn "Art" into Business, we need "Creativity" and "Design", which allows the creative products to be transformed into "E-business" [7].

Nevertheless, the model is still focused on exploring the cultural richness and adapting into market needs by making design changes to creating new products with the same spirit with the original one. Meanwhile, in the effort to preserve a culture, the focus should not only focus on cultural products as a representation of a particular culture, but also should be explore wider to the cultural actors themselves. Thus, through the ABCDE model, the values contained in cultural products can still be conveyed through new creative products, while the original product can still be found and produced by indigenous cultural actors for specific market segmentation. When designers comes to the cultural society researching the cultural products and get the idea to create a new cultural product that will give them both financial and non-financial benefits, the cultural actors and the village where the culture originated have not changed much and still living in low economic circumstances.

While designers gain profit and economic change, cultural actors are still untouched. That is why a complementary model is needed to provide a holistic view of the process of cultural exploration into a creative product, so that the model not only focuses on how to preserve the cultural product, but also to have a positive impact on original cultural society as an actors. This paper encourage to pay attention to the other

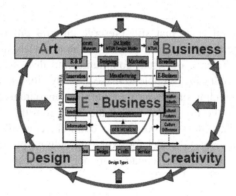

Fig. 1. ABCDE model for E-business model [7]

aspect of cultural preservation. Especially in the case of cultural actor that still preserve the culture and depend their economic life by doing the cultural stuff.

Design must be an innovative, highly creative, cross-disciplinary tool responsive to the needs of men. It must be more research-oriented, and we must stop defiling the earth itself with poorly-designed objects and structures [11]. This study aims to provide a complementary model of ABCDE model as a model in exploring the culture into a better model so that it can provide impact on humanity, society, especially the community of cultural actors themselves. So that the exploration of culture and its use in the design of creative products, but also gives a good impact on the cultural ecosystem itself with due regard to the business model of cultural actors.

2   Research Framework

Culture and design have a close relationship in the development of century. In the era of globalization, people's lifestyles change supported by technological advances becomes more easy. In the context of design and creative industries, culture is a source of inspiration for creating a creative product. Culture plays an important role in the field of design and cross cultural design will become a key point in design evaluation in the future [6]. That because the change of life style impact of product need. Culture could be adapt to create a new product that still relevant to the market, not only for the function adaptation but also in the level of visual, shape, and the other element which could be an inspiration.

Besides its own function and meaning, the cultural product is rich of value from the particular cultural society. As an inspiring idea, culture could be a diversification or identity of particular nation in the global market competition. With all of the potency, the value of culture should be preserve with the proper way to maintain the wealth of cultural value.

The effort to preserve the culture in design field mostly focusing about preserve the cultural product itself such as artefact for its aesthetic, function, shape, and meaning. Just few of the studies gives a concern of the actor itself. The exploration still didn't touch the aspect of humanity which discuss about the ecosystem of the cultural source especially to the cultural actor that still preserve cultural product by create it and depend their life by selling the product. Pirous in an interview about visual communication design said "Science of visual communication design is not just design to fulfill the needs of the industry. But able to make a lonely city into a shining city" [10]. To get a better understanding of preserving culture by encourage designer empathy in cultural society design, the Fig. 1 shows that the flow from the culture as source has two aspect of concern, cultural product and cultural actor, by conducting proper research the flow than create a model for exploring cultural product as inspiration to create new creative product, also create a model for empathy to create a better ecosystem of cultural society (Fig. 2).

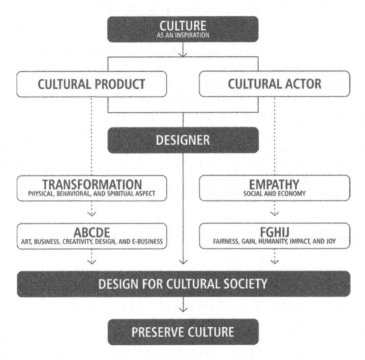

Fig. 2. Framework of design model for cultural society

When the cultural product already switch from functional product into symbolic product of particular area because of the life style change, the cultural product can still be preserve by transforming the spirit into new creative product, and also create a better design model for its own ecosystem by conducting design for cultural society. According to Papanek in his book Design for the real world, in the chapter of design responsibility express his argument about creating "How does the professional stand for this? designer help to wield power to change, modify, eliminate or evolve totally new patterns. Have we educate our clients, our sales force, the public? have the designer attempt to stand for integrity and better way? have we tried to push forward, not only in the market place, but by considering the needs of people?" [11].

3 Methodology

To get a better understanding of exploring culture as source of inspiration in creating new creative product, Lin conduct a model for turning "Art" into "Business" is realized, while the process is combined with "Creativity", "Design", and "E-Business" to transform the aesthetic values into commerce by service innovation [6].

Lin conduct a step to explore culture into a business model by set a scenario from Inspiration by Culture, idea to create a product, implementation in daily life with design process, and the next step is complete the product by brand [5].

Fig. 3. Design thinking to creating business model from culture

The model above help us to get a picture about exploring culture into business model. In context of design for cultural society, to get a better understanding about the business impact to the actor, there will be one element of "monetizing for business" add to the model. So the model will be complete as shown in Fig. 3.

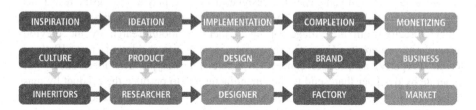

Fig. 4. Design thinking breakdown to creating business model from culture and its actor

From the figure above we can see the correlation from the idea and the actor behind each element. "Inspiration from culture" is operate by Inheritors as the person who still preserve the culture by creating the cultural product and most of them still depend their economic life by doing a cultural stuff. "The process of ideation to create product" mostly doing by researcher, even sometimes designer also does the research. "The implementation stage in daily life" is conduct by designer to create a daily product. "The completion of production by brand" are involving the factory to maintain its quality. The stage of "Monetizing by business" are the element of understanding the market as final purpose of process to get the advantage (Fig. 4).

This study aims to provide a complementary model of ABCDE model as a model in exploring the culture into a better model so that it can provide impact on humanity, society, especially the community of cultural actors themselves. So that the exploration of culture and its use in the design of creative products, but also gives a good impact on the cultural ecosystem itself with due regard to the business model of cultural actors. From the figure above we know the stage to explore the culture into business and also the actor behind each stage. The figure bellow will explain about mutual correlation and the condition of gain distribution equity (Fig. 5).

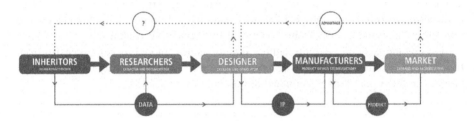

Fig. 5. Mutual correlation and gain distribution

The figure above shows that most of cultural exploration especially in design field area start with the "inheritors" as the cultural actor. Inheritors in this context is not only the terms of individual person who inherit the cultural tradition, but also could be a group of cultural society. Because in some case the place/village where the culture are establish, most villager or the society around also doing the cultural stuff that influence the society. From inheritors the other people that come to the village get the data about the original story or concept of the culture itself, in the academics context we can call it as "researchers" but in some case the designer itself also play a role for the researcher. The next step is about "designer" who can create a concept from the data that they collect directly from the village, or by a documentation/research by the previous researcher as reference. From the data, designer conduct an idea to create IP (Intellectual Property) as product concept to create a prototype. The idea/concept that generate by designer than send to the "manufacturers" to produce the product by mass production by factory. The last step is putting the product that already produce by factory into "market" by setting marketing strategy to focus on particular segmentation, especially global market segmentation.

The process of selling the product in the market gives a feedback to the designer as the creator of concept to create product as advantage feedback, both financially or non-financially. But the problem is While designers gain profit and economic change, cultural actors are still untouched and live with their low economic condition. As mention before, the most reason of this phenomena is because most cultural actor has a limitation of market knowledge. All they know is how to create product by traditional ways as they got from their ancestor. When the market needs already change as the impact of globalization, they still create the same product as they know. Despite a reason of preserving the original idea of culture, the cultural grip of ethic, or the lack of marketing knowledge, the condition put them into the same economic situation.

The designer as the outsider has no boundaries of cultural ethic who get the idea from the culture create a product that inspire from the culture with a relevant function or context to the today's market. It gives designer opportunity to explore more idea and blending the culture with daily product idea that still need, want, desire by market.

The condition give a wide chance for the designer to do more about cultural society especially in the effort of preserve cultural society in economic case. Its time for the designer to get a bigger picture of preserving culture by put a focus not only in the cultural product but also the cultural actor. So the Science of design is not just design to fulfil the needs of the industry. But able to make an industrial design system into a shining humanity design system. Designers do need to know more about science and engineering, but without becoming scientists or engineers. We must not lose the special talents of designers to make our lives more pleasurable [8].

4   FGHIJ Model for Design in Cultural Society

Preserving culture by paying attention in cultural society especially the inheritor who still doing cultural stuff and depend their economic life in the process, for the practician in the design field, basically give a concern about Fairness, Gain, Humanity, Impact, and Joy in the process of design model (Fig. 6).

The model will adapt from the design thinking by Tim brown. Generally Tim introduce encourage the designer to give a better impact in design process using design thinking from Empathy, Define, Ideation, Prototype, and Test. Brown and Wyatt [1], describe that to create a design that is relevant to the user, a comprehensive research process that starts from the empathy process, defines the problem, generates the idea, creates the prototype, and tests the user. In context of design for cultural society especially in case of cultural actor that depending their economic life by doing cultural stuff, the design thinking conduct to get the FGHIJ models. The models stand for Fairness, Gain, Humanity, Impact, and Joy.

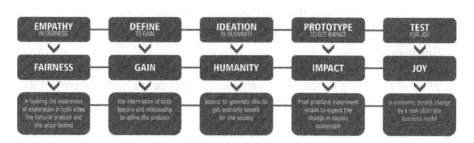

Fig. 6. FGHIJ model fro design thinking in cultural society

"Fairness" is about the 'empathy' of building the awareness of cultural actor by identify cultural feature that should get an focus attention, the cultural product itself and the role of the cultural actor as the user or creator. So the exploration will be fair in both side cultural product and the actor behind the product itself. After build the awareness of exploration focus, the next step is "Gain" the information of both sides, the cultural product feature and the role of the cultural actor which has a mutual correlation. The information of the relationship will 'define' the problem. The "Humanity" stage will focus on generate the 'idea' to give a economy benefit in the cultural society by design. By conducting the research of cultural product relationship with the cultural actor, the design process conduct the idea to give the alternative solution in design field. For the example, the designer could give a better ways, tool, or design to solve the problem of production time or marketing challenge. "Impact" aspect is an experiment to create a 'prototype' or practical action and expect the positive impact that change the cultural society ecosystem. The process will bring a "Joy" in the economic field by establish a new business model with design as the core of the alternate solution (Fig. 7).

Fig. 7. FGHIJ model for design in cultural society

5 Summary

The effort of preserving culture is not only focus to take care the cultural product, but also considering the existence of the cultural actor/practitioner. The cultural actor in this context is the one who depending their economic life by doing cultural stuff. The ABCDE model could be a model to explore the potency of cultural product into business. In the other sides the cultural actor could be explore by setting FGHIJ model to give a positive impact by establish a business model in design context.

Despite the level of each cultural element, Norman in his book Emotional Design, divide a product into three level, Visceral Design, is what nature does. Behavioural Design, is all about use. Reflective Design, its all about message. [9] by break down the feature of the model, the ABCDE model could be a matter of Visceral Design (in the cultural product itself could be break down by three level of design), when the FGHIJ could be a matter of behavioural design, especially in the present business model. The level of reflective design could be gain by combining this two design model from ABCDE to FGHIJ for cultural society (Fig. 8).

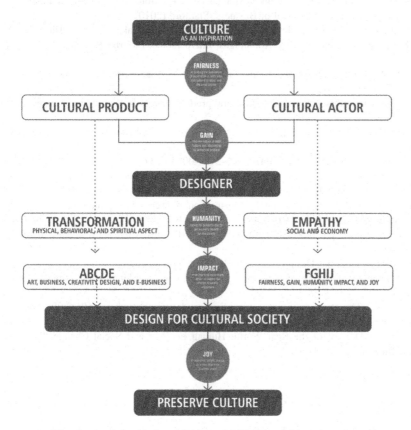

Fig. 8. Applying design thinking of FGHIJ model in preserving culture

From the figure above the FGHIJ model is applied to bring the "Fairness" in building the awareness of focus in cultural exploration, both in cultural product and cultural actor in 'empathy' process. The exploration in the both sides to "Gain" the information or data to 'define' the problem. The next step is focus on "Humanity" aspect to get a better understanding of the problem to do 'ideation'. "Impact" stage is focus to create a 'prototype' of business model by focusing on changing economic ecosystem. The indicator of the process to 'test' the model to bring "Joy" in economic system change. By the model the result of this studies shows that designers do need to know more about business model and economic ecosystem, but without becoming an economist or accountant. Designer should not lose the special talents of designers to make the shining cultural society.

References

1. Brown, T., Wyatt, J.: Design thinking for social innovation. Stanford Social Innovation Review Winter. Graduate School of Business, Stanford (2010)
2. Koentjaraningrat: Pengantar Ilmu Antropologi. Rineka Cipta, Jakarta (2000). Hardjana, A. M.: Komunikasi Intrapersonal & Komunikasi Interpersonal. Penerbit Kanisius, Yogyakarta (2003)
3. Liliweri, A.: Gatra-gatra komunikasi antar budaya. LKiS Pelangi Aksara, Yogyakarta (2002)
4. Lin, R., Sun. M.X., Chang, Y.P., Chan, Y.C., Hsieh, Y.C., Huang, Y.C.: Designing "culture" into modern product – a case study of cultural product design. In: Conference Paper, DBLP (2007). https://doi.org/10.1007/978-3-54-7328-7_19
5. Lin, R., Hsieh, H.-Y., Sun, M.-X., Gao, Y.-J.: From ideality to reality - a case study of Mondrian style. In: Rau, P.-L.P. (ed.) CCD 2016. LNCS, vol. 9741, pp. 365–376. Springer, Cham (2016). https://doi.org/10.1007/978-3-319-40093-8_37
6. Lin, R.: Transforming Taiwan aboriginal cultural features into modern product design: a case study of a cross-cultural product design model. Int. J. Des. **1**(2), 45–53 (2007)
7. Lin, R., Chen. C.T.: A discourse on the construction of a service innovation model: focus on the cultural and creative industry park. In: Ifinedo, P. (ed.) E-Business - Application and Global Acceptance, pp. 119–136. InTech, Rijeka (2012). ISBN 978-953-51-0081-2, https://goo.gl/Jygpwz
8. Norman, D.: Emotional Design. Basic Books, New York (2002)
9. Oxford Dictionary Online, 4 January 2018. https://en.oxforddictionaries.com/definition/culture
10. Pirous, A.D.: The story of visual communication design. Youtube: 8:50/10:00. Amphibi Studio: https://www.youtube.com/watch?v=g4BSUNcn-zw
11. Papanek, V.: Design for the Real World: Human Ecology and Social Change. Pantheon Books, New York (1971)

A Cheerful Journey or a Depressive Process? A Study of the Integrated Cultural and Creative Design Curriculum

Shu Hui Huang[(⊠)], Chun-Liang Chen, and Po-Hsien Lin

National Taiwan University of Arts, New Taipei City 22058, Taiwan
shhuang@textiles.org.tw, jun@ntua.edu.tw,
t0131@mail.ntua.edu.tw

Abstract. The study explores the learning effectiveness of collaborative teaching in a university design course, which uses case planning and service design to present a service design planning model of teaching and industry-university cooperation. The course works with the companies of the incubation centers, forming groups to carry out course experiments on industry-university cooperation. The research methodology includes participant observation, data analysis, and in-depth interviews. Analysis of the results indicate that the students gave positive feedback regarding the level of happiness of the experience. This shows that an integrated teaching plan can trigger motivation to learn and enhance learning effectiveness. The learning effectiveness of depression learning showed negative feedback regarding the learning process. The study found that the benefits and attitudes of collaborative teaching are very much recognized in the curriculum teaching process. Building a new model for industry-university cooperation to be integrated into cultural innovation design course is an advantage in developing a new experiential model for industry-university cooperation and learning in design courses, increasing the learning motivation of the students and enhancing their developmental potential. Whether student learning is a positive or negative process, the study has achieved the goal of resolving the issue of practical learning effectiveness, and, with the emphasis on cooperation between the fields of "research, education, and service," is able to serve as a reference for cultural creative design education and industry-university cooperation.

Keywords: Design curriculum · Cultural and creative industry
Collaborative teaching · Industry-university cooperation · Service design

1 Introduction

The cultural and creative industry provides "design service industry chain" value services, from design needs, creative design, market link-ups to product commercialization. It needs to bring together people from different fields of expertise, which changes the face of design service activities as a whole. In terms of teaching and learning, the Ministry of Education has been encouraging institutions of higher learning to embark on more industry-university cooperation to promote local development, meet real-time industry needs, as well as to nurture students' practical skills and develop enhanced capacity to act, resulting in a win-win for the educational and the industry sector [1]. Industry-university cooperation is a situation which makes use of the different educational resources and environments of the educational institution and the workplace. The workplace provides the venue for actual job training and mentors on the practical aspects, while the school assists in continued innovation, making the relationship mutually beneficial. By carrying out collaborative teaching, instructors are able to ensure that the learning process of both the faculty and student body is more productive. At the same time, the Ministry of Education also emphasizes that learning in any field be carried out through integrated and collaborative teaching in principle, in hopes that teachers would be able to make full use of their professional expertise. Through this combination of courses, it will resolve the inadequacies brought about by the teaching of distinct separate courses, break the trend of course design and instruction centered on theoretical knowledge, develop abilities which the students can apply in real life, and allow for the integration of both teacher and student learning [2].

The learning process of undergraduates stems from the expectations of individuals of themselves, their peers, the number of courses, their workload, and their academic scores as well as the pressures they feel in the face of social opinion and future career developments [3]. An important strategy of course instruction is how to transform the pressure of the learning process into a happy learning experience. In addition, related literature on collaborative teaching and learning effectiveness largely indicate the necessity of experiments and the importance of knowledge application. At the same time, the actual needs of the industry do affect the learning environment as well as the university's teaching orientation to allow educational training to meet the needs of the workplace and those of society. There is actually no relevant empirical study on how to build a teaching plan for an integrated creative design curriculum, create value through industry-university cooperation, or on the learning effectiveness of using collaborative teaching in higher education courses for industry-university cooperation. If the students are learning in a program that combines intrinsic motivation and affective learning, then it can be an internal force that helps inspire them to carry on [4]. The idea behind the study originates from a pragmatic philosophy that students need to be able to use what they have learned. Therefore, the motivation of this study is to build an interdisciplinary teaching curriculum integrating industry-university cooperation to help enhance student learning effectiveness, provide successful transition to employment and practical industry aspects, promote learning preparedness, improve instruction, and develop professional talents.

The study explores curriculum design for professional fields in higher education, conducting research on the empirical learning effectiveness of collaborative teaching courses as well as the industry-university cooperation of the cultural creative incubation center. It uses daytime students taking up a cultural creative design course in graduate school; the course integrates design and business management with two instructors who carry out interdisciplinary collaborative teaching. Experiential learning, the case method, and university-industry cooperation are used as instructional strategies. Through the learning process that includes direct and concrete experiences, with the course targeting design topics as well as the needs of the industry-university cooperation, enabling the teaching of professional courses to meet the needs of the design industry, can the study understand interdisciplinary collaborative teaching and its implementation process? How do students react to the practical aspects of collaborative teaching implementation? How has university-industry cooperation affected the learning area of the students? Consequently, the objectives of the study are first, to understand the collaborative teaching plan and implementation process in the field of interdisciplinary learning and instruction. Second, to explore how students respond to collaborative teaching and the learning effectiveness of conducting industry-university cooperation within the curriculum.

2   Review of Related Literature

The implementation of curriculum teaching and learning is an important way to reach the goal of education. It is necessary for teachers to convey professional knowledge and skills, and for students to participate in a serious and active manner. It is also the process of a two-way interaction between teachers and students [5]; Collaborative teaching focuses on teamwork, consisting of two or more teachers or professionals forming an instructional team. It emphasizes cooperation and participation of teachers, using their individual expertise to jointly plan the curriculum as well as to implement and evaluate its instructional effectiveness [6]. During the process of carrying out coherent teaching activities, the priorities are team cooperation and sharing of responsibilities [7]. All collaborative teaching participants in the team are able to learn by observing others. They all work together, making greater contributions than if they were working separately [8]. The effectiveness of collaborative teaching is significantly better than that of individual instruction. It is believed that teachers can have more opportunities for participation, enhancing the acquisition of new knowledge and improvement of skills, which enables both teachers and students to experience and recognize the importance of cooperation and the division of powers and responsibilities [9, 10].

Diverse instruction provides students with different learning experiences; professional teachers each have their individual strengths. While students absorb the best of those strengths, integrating knowledge into a systematic and complete concept allows for adaptation to the students' individual differences. Collaborative teaching engenders cooperation to complete the teaching activity, ensuring optimum performance of the teaching team [11]. Pan et al. pointed out that collaborative learning is a kind of mutual learning relationship between partners. There are no leaders and consensus is not required; each person is allowed to participate equally in the learning process [12]. It can help with the learning effectiveness of the students regarding professional theories in design theory courses, enabling them to take more initiative in asking questions, which improves learning outcomes [13]. The traditional instructional mode of teaching single courses has been unable to meet the training needs for developing multi-faceted individuals. Interdisciplinary collaborative teaching helps in the promotion of the new instructional mode and aids in developing these multi-faceted individuals in the new era [14].

The Ministry of Education promotes the principle of industry-university cooperation jointly creating value in working together. It endeavors to enable the implementation of the academia's cutting edge and practical research as well as to encourage active participation by the corporate world in nurturing research talents, creating a win-win situation. This is the symbiotic relationship behind industry-university cooperation. Both industry and higher education contribute to the output of new knowledge and technologies through consensus-based systems of operation. Moreover, the value created is in the combination of theory and practice, which can accelerate and improve the learning process and enhance the effectiveness of industrial education [15]. Apart from the educational goal of cultivating talents, higher education can be combined with the needs of industries to enhance the interaction between industries and universities as well as to take advantage of high value added cooperation benefits [16]. Industry-university cooperation from an educational standpoint suggests that the school focuses on specific research issues, establishing working relationships with targeted industries. Through this interaction, faculty members are able to enhance the breadth and depth of their research, while the students are able to acquire solid pre-employment practical experience and applicable technologies. In the principles of interaction and mutual trust, instructors look to practical aspects to modify teaching content and direction, boosting the possibility of increasing the school's resources, exchanging information, or creating a new knowledge economy [17]. As far as the industry sector is concerned, it hopes to use the R&D resource pool and knowledge resources of the academia through the industry-university cooperation to have better business philosophies and help it to upgrade and gain more profits [18]. In the course of the industry-university cooperation, respect and good use of each other's strengths, and through discussion and sharing, enable both parties to strongly benefit from and complement each other's professional capabilities. Through new cooperative experiences which are honest and direct, both parties can reach their goal of creating optimum results [19].

3   Research Methodology

3.1   Cultural Innovation Design Course Overview and Course Design

The study selected a university with a "cultural innovation design course" in its combined master's and PhD program as its case and field. The course runs for 18 weeks, combining theories and practice, integrating instruction in design and business management. The study uses participant observation, data analysis, and in-depth interviews as its methodology. The primary student background is that of being design students, a total of 15, with 5 PhD students and 10 master's degree students from the Graduate School of Creative Industrial Design. Based on the curriculum design of the case university department, these students are professional graduate school students who have taken foundational design courses before signing up for this course. At the same time, the PhD students are on their second year and have already taken relevant professional cultural creative courses. This means that they have the requisite skills, learning, and actual practice necessary to carry out practical design in the course curriculum. Hence, the study has chosen them to be survey subjects. In accordance with their professional learning backgrounds and interests, students chose five companies involved in industry-university cooperation to carry out curriculum experimentation. Each group is led by a PhD student with practical design experience who serves as the learning group leader, leading four master's degree students in learning together and applying the knowledge gained.

3.2 The Use of Cooperative Teaching in Program Planning Design and Service Design Applications

Program planning and design is an important service concept in the field of social services in recent years. The planning process includes situation analysis, project concept creation, target and program objective setting, understanding of needs, learning activities design, program marketing, evaluation, budget control, and process management [20]. The formation of the program, its development and the presentation of the results emphasize the completion of the work from the definition of the scenario and the analysis of the problem, the estimation of the demand, the assumption of the plan, the formulation of the plan's objective, the design of the service, the evaluation of the plan, and the creation of the budget. Based on the cumulative results of empirical research and substantive work experience, measures to implement "program objectives" can then be designed and implemented [21]. The study uses project planning design as contemplation of the system, from integrating interdisciplinary teaching design, teaching implementation, teaching effectiveness evaluation, and the level overall teaching goals are achieved. At the same time, it is anticipated that the learning process of this course would be able to nurture students' ability to learn the planning, design, and execute skills needed for actual industry design projects. The study refers to the essential connotation and process of service design by Song which includes four stages: exploration, design, execution, and evaluation [22]. It focuses on integrating course goals systematically, positioning participants within the interactive process of the teaching service experience, allowing for course transformation from the original lecture learning to industry-university cooperation service design.

4   Case Analysis

The study is different from other literature on service design relating to the design process of cultural creative products in that it explores and categorizes the implementation of appropriate instructional service design processes under the concept of service. This is to truly understand the needs of the design course as well as those of industry-university cooperation, solving the problems and issues of company owners, and achieving the teaching goals of the course. The study also hopes to interpret integrated cultural-creative design courses in the service design context, incorporating empirical information on participants cooperating and jointly creating value during the service design process.

4.1   Building a Service Design Model for Course Instruction and Industry-University Cooperation

Using service design planning absolutely meets the expectations of learning from student-driven teaching activities as well as cultural company innovations developed from industry-university cooperation. Program planning design based on result-based logic as well as the service design of Goldstein et al. gradually transforms the design concept into actual systematic design [23]. Furthermore, the service design model for course instruction and industry-university cooperation is built and presented based on the predicted changes achieved by the students while learning in the course (Fig. 1). With design students as subjects, the study conducts analysis and needs assessment on the issues and difficulties facing commercialization and industrial development. Then, based on the teaching objective's specific timeframe within the semester when tangible results are expected, interdisciplinary teaching courses integrating diverse resources and cooperation are incorporated and core insights are used to help company owners and students in industry-university cooperation ventures to have a common understanding of course design and conduct collaborative teaching for practical research and hands-on output. Finally, the study creates a collaborative teaching assessment measuring the effectiveness of the combination of actual scenarios and hands-on work during the course process to completely reflect the learning results of the students.

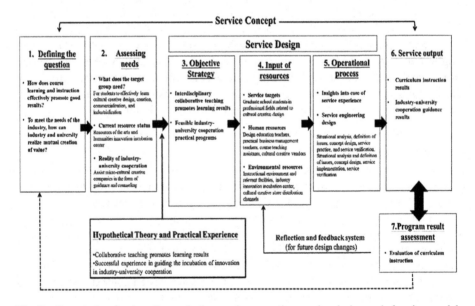

Fig. 1. Case study of university curriculum and cooperative service design and planning model.

4.2   Implementation Results of Collaborative Teaching and Students' Learning Results

Theme-Based Curriculum Design – Inter-disciplinary Collaborative Teaching Plan Page Numbering and Running Heads. The instruction of this study establishes its course orientation, content, and the need to bring in resources through the diagnostic process of discovering the problems and assessing the needs. The two professional teachers of the course conducted interdisciplinary collaborative teaching. To meet the teaching objectives and requirements, the course is divided into two major themes: innovative design and creative business, where interdisciplinary collaborative teaching is planned. Teachers help guide the teaching and discussion process in the classroom, encouraging free questioning, taking control of discussions, helping to integrate students' opinions, and guiding students to ask questions and try to solve problems, as well as giving them timely guidance in major learning points or hidden issues.

Carrying Out the Teaching Plan – Insights into Service Experience. The hands-on case of the course first conducted analysis of group theme and initial insight exploration of the experience. Before each group conducted observation and interviews, students gathered information on the companies involved in the incubation center, which forms the basis for the observation and interview content. Students then go to the second phase which uses the service experience core insight method, to carry out exploration, drafting of the group interview plan and observation analysis after communicating with the companies. Before the formal company visit, which is part of the teaching activity design of the course, the students sought prior consent from the business owner, who also agreed to having the students and the researchers to conduct observation and interviews on the sideline. The researcher continues to visit the company work area, and through individual interaction with the company, observes its cultural innovation concept and product planning. During the interview, an understanding of the work that is being done, as well as company objectives, are obtained. Then, the materials obtained from the observation and interview will be analyzed to record details regarding the projects developed by companies involved in industry-university cooperation. Cultural innovation design courses are introduced into the service design planning model for industry-university cooperation. Both the research student participants divided into groups and manufacturers continuously explore, create and reflect, implementing gradual improvement, to conceptualize cultural design ideas, as well as to revise and plan original plans for new businesses.

Curriculum Transformation and Learning Production. The third phase of the implementation involves service actualization, with the teaching activities and student learning of the course gradually making the transition to a tangible, feasible industry-university cooperation company proposal plan. This includes drafting the cultural creative proposal concept and proposal structure. Building a prototype of an actual project design plan is the students' most difficult learning task. The integration of a proposal plan is centered on the students and industry-university cooperation companies, exploring and focusing on the company providing experience and the students interacting, tracking problems and solutions, and integrating the process. The service design orientation of the entire content of the course is geared towards helping out with the drafting of the cultural creative industry subsidy plan and, using value creation as a starting point, participate in the service design that is company-centered, to actually understand design, motivation, style, culture, product, and marketing promotion status, which can provide insight into the needs of the company and solve problems in the process.

Curriculum Instruction Results and Feedback. The fourth stage is service and business verification, i.e. project planning (revisions, recommendations) testing, (logical deduction) project validation, and (actual results and feedback) project demonstrations and deliverables. In publishing and practicing the teaching results of the course, the inter-disciplinary teachers were able to reinforce the creativity and innovation or uniqueness, core competencies and business management methods (What kind of companies? What size? Etc.), understanding of marketing and distribution, as well as financial and cost planning of cultural creative products and services. The feedback and recommendations the teachers gave each group, which made up for the inadequacies of feasibility of the vendor project planning framework and the lack of student implementation, have enhanced the practical capabilities of design project. The course learning group conducted interaction, communication, and discussion as modes of learning. Through the teachers' lectures and focused themes, the groups are able to achieve awareness and practice of action experience through "learning by doing and doing by learning." The teachers' feedback and recommendations for each group are as follows (Table 1):

Table 1. Teacher feedback and recommendations.

	Teacher feedback and recommendation
A	1. Develop a product series with a theme that is logical, creative, and implementable 2. Increase product line in developing product series; reduce costs 3. Enhance cultural innovation element of local stories and content; how does it merge into the lifestyle 4. Products with exquisite craftsmanship mean higher prices, may use product mix or may be produced partly in modules 5. New product series development or creative extension of old product series; consider the advantages 6. Lock in key partners and major distribution channels 7. Shelving fees should be added to promotional budget 8. Continue participating in international exhibitions to get orders; how will the products be promoted and distributed locally? 9. Establish brand image; explore and develop distribution channels
B	1. Product diversity and brand image must be consistent 2. For role brand endorsement, think about the possibility of developing a "role family" 3. Position as a unique imagery of Taiwan 4. Consider possibility of partners and increased cooperation with different fields 5. Develop diverse distribution channels, like the comic book market, international cultural creative market, the internet, etc. 6. Develop brand licensing guidelines and expand international licensing opportunities 7. Complete business plan and business model

(continued)

Table 1. (*continued*)

	Teacher feedback and recommendation
C	1. Pay attention to cultural context and design behind the meaning, experience, and value of cultural creative products 2. Linked to local tales or local elements? Nostalgic or popular orientation? Product use? 3. Discrepancy between the target market and age bracket positioning and actual situation 4. How can one break through sensory boundaries and commercialized image, in terms of the relationship between pottery and local Taiwanese culture? 5. What is the pressure artists face in terms of product commercialization? In terms of pure art or trial commercialization, bringing the design stage into the creative ideas of end products 6. Consider cost and operational plan in art creation or trial production plan 7. Think of other marketing strategies and distribution markets to sell the products, aside from local and international art exhibitions
D	1. Develop series of products made from various media 2. Continue current online sales channels; add new overseas strategic partners into the emerging marketing team 3. Participation in foreign design competitions and exhibitions can effectively increase visibility and exposure 4. Building of official website content and objectives presented in the planning proposal needs to be carefully assessed 5. There is a significant gap between the distribution channel expansion plan and actual feasibility. Retail distribution costs and revenue estimates need further analysis
E	1. Extending award winning works into a new series of products 2. Relationship between new series and local culture 3. Develop a few products as limited edition products 4. Business model, product theme, and channel image must be focused and consistent 5. Cost and revenue estimates must match feasibility of the plan 6. Promote in local and international exhibitions to enhance reputation and increase exposure; expect corresponding increase in marketing costs

4.3 Evaluation of the Effectiveness of Teaching Courses and Service Design

Thoughts and Feelings About Collaborative Teaching. Collaborative teaching of interdisciplinary fields expands and mixes knowledge of cultural creative design and business operations. It emphasizes guidance and inspiration, rather than pure instruction and answering questions. This gives the students the opportunity to be responsible for their own research and study (i.e. self-directed learning) by completing case proposals to achieve in-depth instruction and build effective systems of interaction in industry-university cooperation as well as students' hands-on learning, maximizing the service value of teaching and learning.

It's been a great help, learning about professional theories and knowledge on cultural creative and innovation industries, about how to transform them into feasible plans and proposals, as well as receiving training on how to combine cultural creativity and business marketing to commercialize creative works and bring them to the market (Student C7).

Cultural creative products that are marketable should be things that the consumers would want to own. They should not only emphasize creative design, but should also have value and unique features to be able to attract attention. These features may not necessarily be functional or physically attractive. What is more important is that there is a market for these products, that they are marketable, and who will be buying them. Design and creation are definitely not enough; experience in creativity and actual market aspects should be gained. A professional teacher who works in a single field of design may be unable to satisfy the real learning needs of students who are entering the industry (Student E13).

The key to interdisciplinary teaching is professional cooperation, with the content enabling students to learn the essence of culture in innovative commercial products through hands-on work (Student D10).

Inadequate insight of design theories and business practices often lead to a gap between creative design and market needs, thus making it necessary to have competency in diverse professional fields (Student B4).

Creative designs that do not consider the consumer market are nothing more than self-appreciation and conceit. The learning done in an integrated design course should combine elements that would satisfy the market. Usually, design students lack ideas about marketing and distribution; they're not very clear about finances and costs. Through the teachers' instruction as well as discussions between peers from different professional fields, everyone goes away learning something different and valuable (Student C7).

Interdisciplinary teachers can use integrated comprehensive viewpoints to help students understand more clearly how design as well as tools and methodology can effectively be employed within the context of cooperation (Student A1).

Experience and Thoughts Regarding Industry-University Cooperation. Although there are both positive and negative reactions to the course design as well as the industry-university cooperation experience, students who have undergone the process achieved the learning outcomes of solving problems and hands-on learning within the semester.

The class incorporating industry-university cooperation is very interesting and beneficial. It's very different from the usual design course, and is a new experience and a new form of learning. However, there was a lot of pressure because students have different areas of expertise, working directly with cultural creative companies (wood, visual art, accessories, metalcraft, pottery), each has different needs and demands. Furthermore, each company has its own issues, needs, and limitations. When students were divided into groups, various activities, discussions, and worksheets were used to arrive at appropriate and effective solutions (Student C7).

The level of willingness for cooperation of the matching companies in the incubation center was not consistent. There were those which were not able to coordinate with the pace of the course in terms of producing output and plans, which made the group lag behind significantly; group members were nervous about this (Student D10).

Companies which have strong design skills and numerous awards, are very hard to talk to. They are usually unable to work with us during the discussion stage of the course; there were many times when meetings would be canceled at short notice and they were not very active during the cooperation process. It was difficult to reach an agreement on the balance between products and cost. Problems were unable to be solved despite numerous discussions, which created a lot of pressure and challenge (Student A1).

We worked very closely with the company we were matched with, which means, we had to do extra work in looking for themes, reference materials, and case plans. Although it was exhausting, we gained so much from the process, there was a strong sense of achievement and everyone was happy (Student C7, E13).

The company has a lot of partner resources and experience in commercializing products, which are a great help in my own career or entrepreneurial goals (Student B4, E13).

The students' professional background is closely matched to that of the cooperating company, which helps in the interaction and discussion. For example, students with a background in industrial design had a higher level of participation in product development. Those with backgrounds in media or graphic design would have unique perspectives on marketing and promotion. Team discussions brought forth the different ideas of many people, leading to exchange of opinions, and brainstorming a lot of interesting new ideas. The recognition and approval gained during the cooperation process inspired a sense of self-achievement (Student A1, B4, C7, E13).

The syllabus calls for completing a cooperative proposal plan within the cooperation period. There was a lot of back and forth discussion going on between the students and the company; coupled with the pressure of final exams, it was inevitable that learning would be accompanied by irritation and helplessness (Student A1, B4, D10).

Feelings and Thoughts Regarding Self-expectations and Learning Outcomes. Discussion of actual cases in class as well as group work not only increased class participation, but also resulted in deeper interaction between teachers and students. This allowed interdisciplinary learning to attain its optimum level.

Thanks to the teachers who patiently guided the discussion and hands-on work and to the companies which were willing to open their doors and work with the students. They have made it possible for us to complete this joint proposal and gain experience in putting together a comprehensive plan; I have also learned how to work within a team (Student C7).

If matching can be done earlier in the course, then the students and companies can set the themes sooner, establishing stronger sense of rapport, and shorten the adjustment period; then the time would be more than enough to help smoothen the cooperation process (Student B4).

The companies expect teachers and industry experts to work together to produce a feasible business proposal plan that would combine design innovation and business model as the actual result of the industry-university cooperation. Joint student discussions and business owners sharing professional and future development plans, identifying needs, forming the plan, and the companies participating in discussions with the students as well as interdisciplinary learning, these are all parts and parcel of the whole new cultural creative design learning experience. Not only is it academically effective, it also achieves the goal of reinforcing professional competencies (Student A1).

We were not very familiar with the actual application of the company for marketing distribution channels as well as the financial plan and we lacked workplace experience. Initially, we felt frustrated, not knowing how to talk to the company. There were a lot of discussions with our teachers and students; many of the problems were solved through the use of the suggestions shared by more experienced classmates. The pace of the course significantly improved, and learning became more effective, so there was more interest on my part (Student D10).

5 Conclusion and Recommendation

The study uses "Cheerful" and "Depressive" as the introduction to its conclusion. The teaching and learning model of the learning and interaction process can be the experiential process of service exchange, which leads to the learning experience of the student curriculum from the teaching service process. In the end, is the service process emotionally positive and pleasant or negative and unpleasant? When the learning experience is positive, the learning process can be joyful, happy, satisfactory, proud, exciting, and hopeful. On the other hand, when the learning process is negative, it results in feeling annoyed, disquieted, anxious, insecure, frustrated, disappointed, fearful, nervous, and tense with the learning. This case study examines the effectiveness of teaching and learning. The learning effectiveness of "Cheerful" experience comes from students participating in course learning responding positively to the collaborative teaching, as well as the learning effectiveness of industry-university cooperation being implemented within the course. On the other hand, the learning effectiveness of "Depressive" experience comes from the negative responses of students towards collaborative teaching as well as the learning effectiveness of industry-university cooperation being implemented within the course. The conclusions of the study are as follows:

1. Building a "Service Design Plan Model for Course Teaching and Industry-University Cooperation," can help in further understanding of the planning and implementation process of interdisciplinary teaching and learning as well as collaborative teaching. This model would include teaching design, teaching implementation, teaching effectiveness assessment as well as incorporating interdisciplinary innovations into the course, and evaluating the effectiveness of teaching projects. Furthermore, future course teaching will be designed and revised based on feedback, reflection, introspection, and criticism.

2. Aside from being able to improve the students' research and practical skills in design and creative work at the same time, interdisciplinary collaborative design courses can reinforce the professional knowledge lacking or neglected in a single course, given that the nurturing of interdisciplinary skills encompasses practical research in industry business development, including managing new businesses as

well as market linking and feasibility. Integrated theme-based course design and experiential teaching effectively motivates learning, determines learning objectives, establishes correct directions, and helps to enhance student's learning effectiveness. By examining and revising the learning actions of the theme, student participation slowly becomes more proactive and positive, enhancing the ability to solve problems, and increasing the motivation to learn.

3. Interaction between teacher and students as well as among peers does improve the learning atmosphere. Student group leaders lead the members to collaborate, divide work, and cooperate, communicating in the spirit of mutual respect. For the teachers, it means mutual growth in teaching; participants in collaborative teaching are able to discover both problem and solution during reflection and criticism. The common goal of all the participants is to clarify and solve the problem. Maybe it is not possible to reach a consensus, but, as long as there is mutual respect in the continuing interaction, making clear thoughts and actions to each other, then the process is of great help in design course teaching and industry-university cooperation jointly creating value.

4. The learning which occurs in the teaching of experiences and practices in industry-university cooperation cases helps students try to solve problems, enabling them to connect to the real-life applications in the workplace. This increases learning motivation, and, since it allows the industry and the academic sectors as well as students to inquire as well as communicate with each other, it enhances the students' learning effectiveness. It was unavoidable that learning effectiveness was compromised at some stages, given that cooperation required much flexibility in meeting company needs, where the limitation in time adversely affected the proposal, breeding pressure and anxiety as well as negative feelings toward the learning in the process. However, through reflection learning, the students were able to translate these negative feelings into positive learning motivation and action, which means these situations still helped generate positive feedback in maintaining balance in learning, allowing it to be more effective.

Through studying teaching practices and implementation, service design not only effectively promotes the cooperation between industry and design courses, but also provides new values of cooperation between schools and industries. Feedback and reflection enhance practical teaching and research results, and actually carry out practical study of industry-university cooperation. It is hoped that the results of this empirical research as well as the integrated cultural creative design course may benefit students, teachers, and the industry, thus creating a winning situation for all parties.

The study recommends that when future industry-university cooperation uses the conceptual structure presented in this study, given appropriate teaching content and allowable timeframe, it should increase the categories of industry-university cooperation as well as screen partners in terms of their level of willingness, which will be beneficial to the implementation of the course. Moreover, the needs of the company have to drive the interdisciplinary action research of the empirical study; teaching design and flexible revisions need to be made on time, place, objectives, or needs. Adjustments in the mode of interaction should be made based on the difference in the participating partners (company, student), which can enhance the student's learning effectiveness and change learning attitudes. The limitation of the study is that it focused solely on design courses. Future research may use similar design concept and apply to EMBA programs or to learning in different fields. However, further understanding of the students' prior knowledge and competencies is required, to tailor and adjust course teaching and industry-university cooperation service design.

References

1. Ministry of Education Industry-University Cooperation Information Network. https://www.iaci.nkfust.edu.tw/Industry/index.aspx. Accessed 31 May 2017
2. Su, Y., Chen, C.: The impact of industry-university cooperation on the development of students' careers: a case study of the industry-university cooperation in Taiwan's semiconductor industry. Minghsin J. **38**(2), 143–156 (2012)
3. Chen, W.: An initial exploration into the learning pressures of industrial design students in university. Ind. Des. **133**, 7–12 (2015)
4. Hong, P.: Results of small group counseling in motivational and affective learning programs. Arch. Guidance Couns. **24** (2003)
5. Wu, K.: Sociology of Classroom Instruction. Wunan Publishing, Taipei (2005)
6. Oja, S.N., Smulyan, L.: Collaborative Action Research: A Developmental Approach. Falmer, London (1989)
7. Flowers, N., Mertens, S.B., Mulhall, P.F.: What makes interdisciplinary teams effective? Middle Sch. J. **31**(4), 53–56 (2000)
8. Buckley, F.J.: Team Teaching: What, Why, and How? Sage, Thousand Oaks (2000)
9. Hoogveld, A.W.M., Paas, F., Jochems, W.M.G.: Application of an instructional systems design approach by teachers in higher education: individual versus team design. Teach. Teach. Educ. **19**(6), 581–590 (2003)
10. Moran, M.J.: Collaborative action research and project work: promising practices for developing collaborative inquiry among early childhood preservice teachers. Teach. Teach. Educ. **23**(4), 418–431 (2007)
11. Chang, C.: How to implement collaborative teaching? Educ. Mon. **387**, 43–47 (1999)
12. Pan, H., Chen, P., Chang, S., Cheng, S.-H., Chen, W.: Discussion and analysis of learning communities from learning leadership. In: International Symposium on Educational Leadership and Learning Communities, Tamkang University, Taipei (2003)
13. Lin, R.: Impact of collaborative teaching on learning effectiveness of design students. J. Univ. Taipei **39**, 1–38 (2008)
14. Lu, C.: Thoughts on collaborative innovation for industrial design talent development. Fujian Light Text. Ind. Holdings **2**, 52–54 (2017)
15. Bektaş, Ç., Tayauova, G.: A model suggestion for improving the efficiency of higher education: university–industry cooperation. Procedia-Soc. Behav. Sci. **116**, 2270–2274 (2014)
16. Hsiao, L.: The role and positioning of talent development in industry-university cooperation. Technol. Vocat. Educ. Bi-monthly **60**, 12–14 (2000)
17. Wen, T., Fan, H.: Theoretical research and policy implementation process of industry-university cooperation in Japan. J. Manag. Syst. **20**(2), 201–226 (2013)
18. Chou, T.: Strategic model for Taiwan's promotion of industry-university cooperation-industry R&D and talent development. Chaoyang Acad. J. **18**, 85–109 (2013)
19. Fang, S.: Five Thinking on Value Creation. http://iconada.tv/profiles/blogs/3600580:BlogPost:509554. Accessed 25 Dec 2016

20. Wei, H.: An action research on the creative teaching design and implementation of project planning. Curriculum Instr. **10**(4), 63–83 (2007)
21. Hsieh, L., Wang, H., Pai, C., Wu, L.: Project Design and Assessment. National Open University Press, Taipei (2015)
22. Song, Z.: Foreword – nature and process tools of service design. J. Des. **19**(2), 1–8 (2014)
23. Goldstein, S.M., Johnston, R., Duffy, J., Rao, J.: The service concept: the missing link in service design research. J. Oper. Manag. **20**(2), 121–134 (2002)

S.A.D in Education and CHEER in Practice: A Case Study of DTIT Program at NTUA

John Kreifeldt[1], Hong-lin Li[2], Ming-Xean Sun[3], Wei Bi[4], and Rungtai Lin[5(✉)]

[1] Tufts University, Medford, MA, USA
john.Kreifeldt@tufts.edu
[2] Department of General Education,
National Taiwan University of Arts, New Taipei City, Taiwan
larryli@ntua.edu.tw
[3] Institute of Applied Arts, National Chiao Tung University, Hsinchu, Taiwan
buddasfox@gmail.com
[4] Graduate School of Creative Industry Design, College of Design,
National Taiwan University of Arts, New Taipei City, Taiwan
beebvv@qq.com
[5] Taiwan Design Center, Taipei, Taiwan
rtlin@tdc.org.tw

Abstract. Recently, the growth of Taiwan's graduate education in design fields has boomed. There are a number of well-established design programs in universities ranging from undergraduate to postgraduate and even doctoral level. In the past, the main concern was about the "capability" of design rather than the "power" of design. Currently, there are projects in Taiwan involving academia, industry and government agencies, which is an encouraging phenomenon. By blending Science, Arts and Design (S.A.D), we can bridge the gap between academia and industry to reach Collaboration, Humanity, Empathy, Ecology and Renaissance (CHEER). Therefore, this study intends to explore the relationship between SAD in education and CHEER in practice through a case study of the DTIT (Design Team In Training) program at National Taiwan University of Arts (NTUA). Results presented herein help us create an approach to examine the manners designers transform S.A.D as well as the interwoven experience of CHEER in design process. In addition, this study presents a paradigm to integrate ergonomic considerations into human performance in "pleasure" for keyboard design. In a word, we suggest that S.A.D in education and CHEER in practice through the DTIT program would be validated through more testing and evaluating in further studies.

Keywords: SAD in education · CHEER in practice · Cross-culture design
Interdisciplinary

1 Introduction

Recently, the prosperous growth of Taiwan's design has attracted international design masters to visit the island to witness the rise of our design industry. Some people like Philippe Starck [1] propose that Taiwan should foster design talents. In the OEM era,

© Springer International Publishing AG, part of Springer Nature 2018
P.-L. P. Rau (Ed.): CCD 2018, LNCS 10912, pp. 160–171, 2018.
https://doi.org/10.1007/978-3-319-92252-2_12

Taiwan manufacturers were busy developing products to meet manufacturing deadlines; there was no time for them to enhance design capabilities, so how could such an environment nurture design talents? [2] Therefore, another voice came out: "Taiwan needs to foster good design teams." Although Taiwan had no international design masters in recent years, the fight for survival in the global market has driven Taiwan enterprises to incubate design teams, design studios, and even design companies to promote the development of Taiwan design [3].

The importance of team-work among designers and those in other disciplines cannot be underestimated. On one hand, each member of the collaboration teams can contribute in his/her own field such that designers can focus on the creation of art forms, usability experts can work on usability assessment and user feedback, marketers can help satisfy the needs of customers for products, etc. In particular, a relatively large and complex product/service often requires a team consisting of industrial designers, usability engineers, marketers, systems engineers, developers, and testers [4]. On the other hand, while the design of products has been the primary focus of training and practice of design education in Taiwan, service design has not been considered as part of the design domain. This is true of Taiwan and is also mostly true of the global design community. As the use of Internet services mushrooms, and governments and companies have increasingly relied on the Internet for their sales and services, the design of services has gained more deserved attention. Even though the design of services is rather different from the design of products, the two share common science principles, art esthetics and design methodologies [4, 5].

To collaborate between design and other disciplines, we would also emphasize the benefits that can be derived from joint projects between industry and academia. Currently, there are projects in Taiwan involving academia, industry and government agencies, which is an encouraging phenomenon [4]. Design education through joint design projects originating from the combination of the real and the virtual worlds is not a new approach. Therefore, it is important that a wider range of experience should be incorporated into the design approach. In this study, we introduce the basic ideas of SAD in education and CHEER in practice to underlie the approach to the DTIT program in NTUA as well as the application of SAD to achieve CHEER.

2   SAD in Design Education – Design Team in Training Program

Over the last few years, we have witnessed the growth of Taiwan's postgraduate education in design fields. There are numerous well-established design programs in universities ranging from undergraduate to postgraduate and even doctoral degrees. In the past, the main concern was about the "capability" of a design rather than the "power" of a design. In view of this, the National Taiwan University of Arts (NTUA) established an art museum, known as "Our Museum" in 2007 in order to achieve the purpose of linking professional teaching with design research, education, and display while presenting cultural and aesthetic ideas about arts and artifacts to the public [6, 7]. Developing craftsmanship and creativity as well as competences related to the arts are of strategic importance to NTUA. In addition, a plan called 'ABCDE' was conducted to transform "Arts" to "Business", to integrate "Creativity" and "Design", and, furthermore, to put the content into 'E-commerce' to build the link with the market [8–10]. Therefore, a design studio, known as "Our Studio", was set up at the College of Design at NTUA following the "Our Museum" to provide innovative products. Due to the challenging nature of cultural and creative industries, NTUA is devoted to developing its regional and international networks by operating a cultural and creative industry park, known as "Our Factory" [11, 12]. NTUA has established the link between "Arts and Business" and combined "Creativity" and "Design" through Our Museum, Our Studio, and Our Factory respectively. It is a new approach that integrates design, culture, artistic craftsmanship, creativities and service innovation design in cultural and creative design industries [6, 7, 13].

Internship programs have multiple potential benefits. First, students gain the experience of working in the real world by developing business-oriented design projects and therefore they could better relate what they learn at school to what they will do after graduation. Second, the internship experience can also lead to future employment which can also be viewed as benefiting companies that provide internship opportunities [4]. Given the importance of internship experience, we need to review critically whether the current design educational programs meet the needs of the society and the professional requirements of designers. In order to satisfy these needs, we should bridge "the last mile" between universities and enterprises for design practice, which is to boost not only the capability but also the power of design [4]. To this end, NTUA established a two year program called "Design Team in Training" (DTIT) at a graduate institute school, which was promoted by recruiting a design team of students and then seeking a supporting enterprise. Shneiderman [14] used three elements S, E, and D to achieve breakthrough collaborations in the new ABCs of research, where S, E, and D designate Science, Engineering, and Design. Similarity, by combining Science, Arts, and Design (SAD), DTIT can produce a higher impact on design education by bridging the gap between academia and enterprise as shown in Fig. 1.

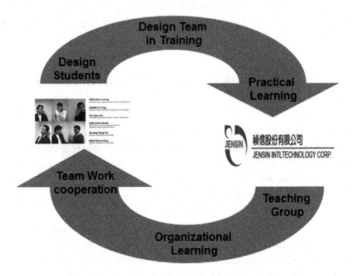

Fig. 1. A framework of design team in training (DTIT)

DTIT integrates the concept of SAD in training and education. In the first year, a design competition is used to help the design team learn how to work together. They will select design contests, both domestic and international, as design problems and then work cooperatively on them. In the second year, the team identifies an internal design problem, and works together to solve it, which helps the team develop new skills, including technology, manufacture, and marketing. At this stage, the team is working on the real-world problems instead of simply receiving instruction in classrooms. Regular meetings between the student design team and the teaching group are conducted for each student's needs to be evaluated and a personalized study plan to be setup or regularly reviewed. Which projects to work on, what courses to take, and which professional internships to consider can all be discussed. This process can not only make students' studies more productive and reassuring but also ensure a more successful career for them in the future [4].

3 CHEER in Design Practice – Designing 'Cheerful' into Keyboard

When a designer starts to design a new product, he or she needs to integrate many demands, wants and desires that prospective users of the product may have. Specifically, not only should technical and objective demands be tackled, but also aesthetic, emotional, and other experiential factors, some of which are hard or impossible to express objectively, should be attended to in design [15–18]. Thus, in the practice of design, the designer has to strike a balance between functional technology and emotional expressiveness to satisfy the requirements of the product. This study proposes that by combining Science, Arts and Design (SAD) we can produce a higher impact on design practice to reach Collaboration, Humanity, Empathy, Ecology, and Renaissance (CHEER).

The property "cheerful", which is pleasure, enjoyment, and fun, is the quale to emotional design [19, 20]. As the Greek philosopher Epicurus wrote in his Letter to Menoeceus, "We recognize pleasure as the first good innate in us, and from pleasure we begin every act of choice and avoidance, and to pleasure we return again, using the feeling as the standard by which we judge every good." [17, 18, 21]. Even given the growing interest of Human-Computer Interaction (HCI) research in how to achieve pleasure and fun as the goal of computer peripheral products [22], designers are far from having a deep understanding of what enjoyment actually is and how it can be designed "cheerfully" into products [23–25]. Let us take computer keyboards as an example: many people want more feedback from the pleasing feel of the keys on many laptop computers as well as keyboards.

Ergonomic considerations are very important to keyboard design, since people undertake a large number of activities and spend most of their time on computers. The most important ergonomic consideration for designing daily-life products is "designing for human use", while a concept emerging as a new human factor is "designing for human feel" [26, 27]. Feel is the most intimately bound up in "pleasure" as well as "pain", and would seem to be a legitimate subject of investigation if one wishes to produce a pleasant product [16, 28, 29]. Jordan [30] noted that usability as a concept does not seem to include positive feelings such as pride, excitement, or surprise. He added that caring about positive emotions is not reflected in traditional human factor practices. In the context of products, "pleasure" can be defined as "pleasure with products" – the emotional, hedonic and practical benefits associated with products [31]. It is important to note that pleasure with products comes from the relationship between users and products. Pleasure, then, is not simply a property of a product but an interaction between a product and a person [32, 33].

A designer might question whether designing for fun, pleasure and enjoyment is a desirable goal and whether the processes and topics involved differ in any significant way from designing for usability [25]. Beyond usability, pleasure would be one of the major feelings from the impression obtained by emotional design. However, when designing products, designers are concerned with not only the visual appearances but also the other properties of the product. Object content as well as context are considered. Designers give their attention to the behaviors of users when they perceive images or products and study how their personal preferences or cultural differences relate to their feelings [34].

Taiwanese people reportedly averaged 42.6 h in using computers and the Internet each week. In other words, people spend a large amount of time using mice, keyboards, or other input devices which provide people with an interface to interact with the computer system. As motioned above, the DTIT program conducted a project of designing a "pleasure keyboard" and a "usability keyboard" by addressing ergonomic considerations. Mings' design team worked on the real-world problem in place of receiving classroom instruction. First, the team identified a focus of internal design, including technology, manufacture, and marketing. In particular the core technology of Jensin International Technology Corp in flexible printed circuit, membrane switch, and plastic injection is taken into the designing process. As the next step, the team worked together to develop new ideas and design for a new keyboard of "pleasure" and "usability" in the designing process, including product analysis, marketing research, concept developing, design evaluation, mock-up, and mass production, as shown in Fig. 2.

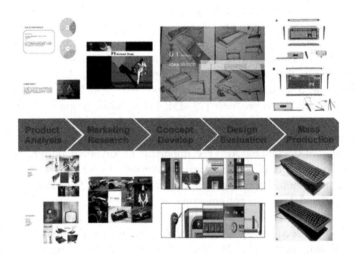

Fig. 2. The process of designing usability and pleasure into a keyboard

In the design process, with the benefit of collaboration from various team members, careful considerations should be given to the design's feasibility, usability, Kansei engineering, and marketability, so that the new design will enhance and enrich user needs of pleasure and usability. We believe that a design concept is more likely to become a successful consumer product if there is collaboration from relevant design consideration throughout the entire product design process – from design concept to final product. Figure 3 shows the final design for usability consideration, and Fig. 4 illustrates the emotional design for infusing pleasure into the keyboard.

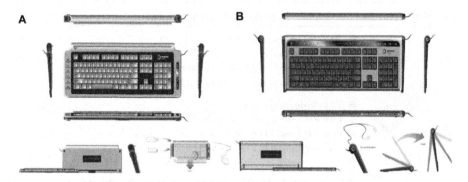

Fig. 3. Keyboard design for usability consideration

Fig. 4. Designing pleasure into the keyboard

4   Validation of CHEER in Design Practice

4.1   A Questionnaire-Based Evaluation Checklist

The use of a questionnaire-based checklist is a convenient evaluation method because it is relatively undemanding of time and facilities. The evaluation checklist provides an effective way of gaining an overview of users' responses to a product [35]. Therefore, an evaluation checklist was used to evaluate the potential reactions that a user may have to the keyboard design. The participants were asked to mark against the reactions that they had or that they anticipated that they would have to a keyboard. Based on the Jordon's research [31], the list of potential reactions could include those in all four pleasure categories: physiological pleasure, psychological pleasure, sociological pleasure, and ideological pleasure, depending on the keyboard design. The evaluation checklist is shown in Fig. 5 where participants can indicate the reactions that they have when experiencing each keyboard design.

Keyboards	Evaluation Checklist
	● Physiological pleasure 1. The keyboard feels good in the hand. 2. The buttons feel good to the touch. 3. The keyboard can be comfortably operated
	● Psychological pleasure 4. The keyboard has useful functions. 5. The keyboard is easy to use. 6. The keyboard is fun to use.
	● Sociological pleasure 7. I feel proud when others see me with the keyboard. 8. Owing and using the keyboard enhances my social image. 9. I enjoy being permanently comfortable by the keyboard.
	● Ideological pleasure 10. Having this keyboard makes me feel better about myself. 11. I find this keyboard to be aesthetically pleasing. 12. I feel the keyboard with a good taste.

Fig. 5. The evaluation checklist for keyboard designs

4.2 Stimuli

The stimuli consisting of 4 keyboard designs were constructed for the DIIT program. One condition presented the design characterizing the infusion of "usability" into the keyboard (Fig. 3), the other demonstrated the design profiling "feeling" for the keyboard (Fig. 4). The 4 keyboards were designed by Mings' Design Team, which were the fruit of the design project of the DTIT program supported by the Jensin International Technology Corp.

4.3 Participants

All participants were university students who volunteered from the northern and southern regions of Taiwan. A total of 179 participants, composed of 77 males (43%) and 102 females (57%) covering the ages of under 30 (65%), 31–50 (27.2%), and above 50 (7.8%), took part in the study. The majority of the participants came from design-related departments (83/46.1%), followed by departments in business and management (63/35%) and others (33/18.9%). Participants were informed of the purpose of the experiment, and were requested to report information including their age, gender, and background. An introduction and product pictures of the keyboard designs were presented and participants were asked to rate each keyboard design according to the degree of association as specified on a five-point Likert scale in the evaluation checklist. The questionnaire was established on the website: https://docs.google.com/forms/d/e/1FAIpQLSdKyvxqmbaixQ-HQNR55elJjjrsQUvXYxqOpkp2l3a4L_ktrQ/viewform.

4.4   Results

Table 1 summarizes the rating data of performance in all four pleasure categories, depending on the four keyboard designs. The paired t-test results show that the average rating of keyboard L is significantly higher than that of keyboards A, B and F. For all the keyboard designs, the average rating of physiological and psychological pleasure is significantly higher than that of sociological and ideological pleasure. Thus, the factors of usability (e.g. physiological pleasure) are more tangible than those of emotion (e.g. ideological pleasure).

Table 1. Experimental subjects

Evaluation Checklist	N	Keyboard A		Keyboard B		Keyboard F		Keyboard L	
		mean	s.d.	mean	s.d.	mean	s.d.	mean	s.d.
Phys. 1	179	3.07	1.02	3.15	1.01	3.35	0.97	3.66	0.83
Phys. 2	179	3.11	0.98	3.04	0.98	3.41	1.00	3.64	0.82
Phys. 3	179	3.09	0.99	3.13	0.98	3.33	1.00	3.65	0.83
Psyc. 4	179	3.42	0.94	3.28	0.99	3.50	0.92	3.60	0.87
Psyc. 5	179	3.18	1.07	3.21	1.04	3.63	1.00	3.73	0.81
Psyc. 6	179	3.06	1.05	3.01	1.00	3.08	1.13	3.24	1.00
Soci. 7	179	2.95	1.08	2.90	1.05	2.78	1.22	3.07	1.14
Soci. 8	179	2.78	1.05	2.81	1.09	2.64	1.22	3.02	1.17
Soci. 9	179	2.89	1.04	2.88	1.07	3.04	1.12	3.24	1.07
Ideo. 10	179	2.76	1.04	2.84	1.11	2.66	1.11	3.09	1.13
Ideo. 11	179	2.80	1.10	2.81	1.15	2.90	1.29	3.27	1.10
Ideo. 12	179	2.78	1.13	2.84	1.12	2.89	1.28	3.23	1.11
AorB-13	179	A:36% / B:64%							
ForL-14	179							L:63% / F:37%	
Most-15	179	A:16% / B:16% / L:45% / F:23%							

Furthermore, three questions were asked as follows. Question (13) asked: "In the comparison of keyboards A and B, which one do you prefer?" Question (14) asked: "In the comparison of keyboards F and L, which one do you prefer?" Question (15) asked: "In the comparison of all the keyboards A, B, F and L, which one do you prefer?"

For the comparison of keyboards A and B, 115 (64%) participants prefered keyboard B to keyboard A (64/36%), while keyboard L (113/63%) was more preferable relative to keyboard F (66/37%). The paired t-test results show that the average rating of keyboard B is significantly higher than that of keyboard A, and that of keyboard L is significantly higher than that of keyboard F. For the comparison of all the keyboard designs, keyboard L gains the highest preference rating by participants (80/45%) in contrast to keyboard F (41/23%), keyboard A (29/16%), and keyboard B (29/16%). The rating results indicate that the effects of "usability" versus "pleasure" keyboards are split in cross-category comparison. Thus, an in-depth study should be executed to explore the distinct impacts of perception between usability and pleasure.

4.5 Discussion

As alluded to above, Mings' Design Team was asked to design keyboards using the difference approach of "usability" and "pleasure". The U1 keyboard was a design based on the definition of "usability" as "the effectiveness, efficiency and satisfaction with which specified users can achieve specified goals in particular environments" (ISO DIS 9241-11). The traditional ergonomic considerations, as tackled in product analysis, marketing research, concept develop, design evaluation, mock-up making, and mass production, were used in the design process as shown in Fig. 6. Beyond the ergonomic consideration, designing "pleasure" into products is a concept of designing for human emotion [16, 36]. "Pleasure", as the Oxford English Dictionary defines, denotes "the condition of consciousness or sensation induced by the enjoyment or anticipation of what is felt or viewed as good or desirable; enjoyment, delight, gratification." Along this line of reasoning, the F1 keyboard design was created based on the emotional, hedonic, and practical benefits associated with the product [30, 31]. That is to say, by using the image of the F1 racing car, the design team was trying to convey the feelings of effectiveness, efficiency, and satisfaction, which are the key factors in usability as shown in Fig. 7.

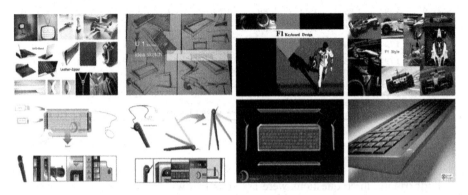

Fig. 6. Usability in keyboard design   **Fig. 7.** Pleasure in keyboard design

Based on Table 1, the design of keyboard L obtained the highest rating score in the checklist and the highest preference value from the subjective rating. This result finds support from the design competition: The design of keyboard L won the 2006 Japan G-mark award, and received the comment from the jury – original, appealing, fresh, and creative life experience's design.

5 Conclusions and Recommendations

Tradition does play a big role in the characteristics of design education. This is true when it comes to design programs in Taiwan. On the other hand, design thinking, design philosophy, material, technology, etc., are also changing over time. All these factors can impact design educational programs [36]. In the traditional education system, students have been required to study sciences and arts at a relatively early age. Recently, educational reformation has been proceeding, and the concept STEM (as the acronym of Science, Technology, Engineering, and Mathematics) has been adopted by numerous programs as an important focus for renewed global competitiveness [15, 37]. As a follow-up on STEM, a theoretical model for education - STEAM has been proposed for science educators and curriculum developers: STEAM being the the acronym for Science, Technology, Engineering, Arts, and Mathematics [38]. In design research, Shneiderman [14] used three elements S, E, and D to "achieve breakthrough collaboration". The A, B, and C in the title of his work stand for "applied and basic combined", whereas the elements of S, E, and D, as he proposed, designate "science, engineering, and design".

Sciences and arts education have already been established in the general education system. However, design in general education has been a missing "third area". Therefore, this study proposes an approach to build an interdisciplinary connection between "SAD" in design education and "CHEER" in design practice. For SAD to be realized in education, we conducted the DTIT program, and we believe that a much broader, different, interdisciplinary training, above and beyond artistic talents, is in order for contemporary designers in Taiwan. In addition, since we recommend collaboration between designers and other professionals, a design project of designing "pleasure" into keyboards was carried out through the DTIT program.

Results presented herein have helped us create an approach to examine the manner in which designers apply and embody the idea of SAD as well as the interwoven experience of CHEER in design process. In addition, this study offers a paradigm to integrate ergonomic considerations into human performance in "pleasure" for keyboard design. Finally, the notions of SAD in education and CHEER in practice manifested through the DTIT program would be validated through more testing and evaluating in further studies.

Acknowledgements. The authors would to thank Mr. Fong-Chi Hsu, the President of Jensiin International Technology Corp. for funding this study. Special thanks should go to Mings' Design Team for joining the DTIT program at NTUA and designing the keyboards for the purpose of this study.

References

1. http://www.starck.com/en (2017)
2. Lin, R., Kreifeldt, J., Hung, P.H., Chen, J.L.: From dechnology to humart – a case study of Taiwan design development. In: Rau, P. (ed.) Cross-Cultural Design Methods, Practice and Impact, vol. 9181, pp. 263–273. Springer, Heidelberg (2015). https://doi.org/10.1007/978-3-319-20934-0_25
3. Hsu, C.H., Chang, S.H., Lin, R.: A design strategy for turning local culture into global market products. Int. J. Affect. Eng. **12**(2), 275–283 (2013)
4. Tsao, Y.C., Lin, R.: Reflections on the training and practice of industrial design in Taiwan. In: Proceedings of 2011 IDA Congress Education Conference, pp. 87–94. Taiwan Design Center, Taipei (2011)
5. Lin, R., Yen, C.-C., Chen, R.: From adaptive design to adaptive city-design in motion for Taipei city. In: Rau, P.L.P. (ed.) CCD 2014. LNCS, vol. 8528, pp. 643–649. Springer, Cham (2014). https://doi.org/10.1007/978-3-319-07308-8_61
6. Lin, R., Chen, C.T.: A discourse on the construction of a service innovation model: focus on the cultural and creative industry park. In: Ifinedo, P. (ed.) EBUSINESS – Application and Global Acceptance, pp. 119–136. InTech, Croatia (2012)
7. Lin, R., Lin, C.L.: From digital archives to E-business: a case study on turning "art" into "business". In: Proceedings of the 2010 International Conference on e-Business (ICE-B), pp. 1–8. IEEE (2010)
8. Hsu, C.H., Fan, C.H., Lin, J.Y., Lin, R.: An investigation on consumer cognition of cultural design products. Bull. Japan. Soc. Sci. Des. **60**(5), 39–48 (2014)
9. Hsu, C.H., Lin, C.C., Lin, R.: A study of framework and process development for cultural product design. In: Rau, P.L.P. (ed.) HCII 2011. LNCS, vol. 6775, pp. 55–64. Springer, Heidelberg (2011). https://doi.org/10.1007/978-3-642-21660-2_7
10. Ko, Y.Y., Lin, P.H., Lin, R.: A study of service innovation design in cultural and creative industry. In: Aykin, N. (ed.) IDGD 2009. LNCS, vol. 5623, pp. 376–385. Springer, Heidelberg (2009). https://doi.org/10.1007/978-3-642-02767-3_42
11. Lin, R.: Transforming Taiwan aboriginal cultural features into modern product design-a case study of cross cultural product design model. Int. J. Des. **1**(2), 45–53 (2007)
12. Lin, R., Lin, P.H., Shiao, W.S., Lin, S.H.: Cultural aspect of interaction design beyond human-computer interaction. In: Aykin, N. (ed.) IDGD 2009. LNCS, vol. 5623, pp. 49–58. Springer, Heidelberg (2009). https://doi.org/10.1007/978-3-642-02767-3_6
13. Lin, R.: Designing friendship into modern products. In: Toller, J.C. (ed.) Friendships: Types, Cultural, Psychological and Social, pp. 1–23. Nova Science Publishers, New York (2009)
14. Shneiderman, B.: The New ABCs of Research: Achieving Breakthrough Collaborations. Oxford University Press, Oxford (2016)
15. Breiner, J.M., Harkness, S.S., Johnson, C.C., Koehler, C.M.: What is STEM? A discussion about conceptions of STEM in education and partnerships. Sch. Sci. Math. **112**(1), 3–11 (2012)
16. Kreifeldt, J., Lin, R., Chuang, M.C.: The importance of "feel" in product design feel, the neglected aesthetic "DO NOT TOUCH". In: Rau, P.L.P. (ed.) HCII 2011. LNCS, vol. 6775, pp. 313–322. Springer, Heidelberg (2011). https://doi.org/10.1007/978-3-642-21660-2_35
17. Monk, A., Hassenzahl, M., Blythe, M., Reed, D.: Funology: designing enjoyment. In: Extended Abstracts on Human Factors in Computing Systems, CHI 2002, pp. 924–925. ACM (2002)

18. Monk, A., Lelos, K.: Changing only the aesthetic features of a product can affect its apparent usability. In: Monk, A., Lelos, K. (eds.) IFIP TC 9, WG 9.3 HOIT 2007. IFIP, vol. 241, pp. 221–233. Springer, Heidelberg (2007). https://doi.org/10.1007/978-0-387-73697-6_17
19. Crilly, N., Moultrie, J., Clarkson, P.J.: Seeing things: consumer response to the visual domain in product design. Des. Stud. **25**(6), 547–577 (2004)
20. Djajadiningrat, J.P., Overbeeke, C.J., Wensveen, S.A.: Augmenting fun and beauty: a pamphlet. In: Proceedings of DARE 2000 on Designing Augmented Reality Environments, pp. 131–134. ACM (2000)
21. Long, A.A.: Hellenistic Philosophy: Stoics, Epicureans, Sceptics. University of California Press, Berkeley (1986)
22. Ma, J.P., Wei, S., Lin, R.: Designing cloud computing into Taipei city: a pilot study of the service design from Taipei cloud. In: Rau, P.L.P. (ed.) CCD/HCII 2014. LNCS, vol. 8528, pp. 688–695. Springer, Heidelberg (2014). https://doi.org/10.1007/978-3-319-07308-8_66
23. Hassenzahl, M., Burmester, M. Beu, A.: Engineering joy. IEEE Softw. **1**(2), 70–76 (2001)
24. Hassenzahl, M., Tractinsky, N.: User experience-a research agenda. Behav. Inf. Technol. **25** (2), 91–97 (2006)
25. Hollnagel, E.: Keep cool: the value of affective computer interfaces in a rational world. In: Proceedings of the HCI International 1999, vol. 2, pp. 676–680 (1999)
26. McGinley, C., Dong, H.: Designing with information and empathy: delivering human information to designers. Des. J. **14**(2), 187–206 (2011)
27. McLoone, H., Jacobson, M., Goonetilleke, R.S., Kleiss, J., Liu, Y., Schütte, S.: Product design and emotion: frameworks, methods, and case studies. In: Proceedings of Human Factors and Ergonomics Society Annual Meeting, vol. 56, no. 1, pp. 1940–1941. SAGE Publications, Thousand Oaks, September 2012
28. Yen, H.Y., Lin, C., Lin, R.: A study of applying Qualia to business model of creative industries. In: Rau, P.L.P. (ed.) CCD 2013. LNCS, vol. 8023, pp. 148–156. Springer, Heidelberg (2013). https://doi.org/10.1007/978-3-642-39143-9_17
29. Yen, H.Y., Lin, P.H., Lin, R.: Emotional product design and perceived brand emotion. Int. J. Adv. Psychol. (IJAP) **3**(2), 59–66 (2014)
30. Jordan, P.W.: Human factors for pleasure in product use. Appl. Ergon. **29**(1), 25–33 (1998)
31. Jordan, P.W.: Designing Pleasurable Products: An Introduction to the New Human Factors. CRC Press, Boca Raton (2002)
32. Lottridge, D., Chignell, M., Jovicic, A.: Affective interaction: understanding, evaluating, and designing for human emotion. Rev. Hum. Factors Ergon. **7**(1), 197–217 (2011)
33. Ma, J.P., Huang, N.L., Chuang, M.H., Lin, R.: From dechnology to humart. In: Rau, P. (ed.) CCD 2015. LNCS, pp. 348–360. Springer, Heidelberg (2015). https://doi.org/10.1007/978-3-319-20934-0_33
34. Lee, S., Harada, A., Stappers, P.J.: Pleasure with products: design based on Kansei. In: Pleasure with Products: Beyond Usability, pp. 219–229 (2002)
35. Ma, J.P., Lin, M.T., Lin, R.: Affective fusion of PAD model-based tactile sense: a case study of teacups. In: CCD 2013. LNCS, vol. 8023, pp. 420–429. Springer, Heidelberg (2013). https://doi.org/10.1007/978-3-642-39143-9_47
36. Norman, D.A.: Emotional Design: Why We Love (or Hate) Everyday Things. Basic Books, New York (2004)
37. Kuenzi, J.J.: Science, technology, engineering, and mathematics (STEM) education: background, federal policy, and legislative action (2008)
38. Yakman, G.: STEAM education: an overview of creating a model of integrative education. In: Pupils' Attitudes Towards Technology (PATT-19) Conference: Research on Technology, Innovation, Design & Engineering Teaching, Salt Lake City, Utah, USA (2008)

Design Method and Application of DNA in the Design of Cultural Creative Products

Yi Li[1(✉)], Jin Li[1], and Qiu Yan[2]

[1] Beijing Institute of Technology, Zhuhai, Zhuhai, China
Jonli0324@163.com, 3834114@qq.com
[2] Zhongshan Torch Polytechnic, Zhongshan, China
roxy_qq@sina.com

Abstract. With integration and regional fusion of global economy, cultural creative industry is also continuously deepening and developing. The Paper aims to analyze DNA evolution and transformation mode in such design from three levels, respectively, instinct, action and reflection for design of cultural creative products through integration and application of cultural design gene DNA in cultural creative design, establish product modeling image model and product modeling design situation model during creative design process of cultural design gene, provide structural rearrangement for design and application demand, complete effective organization and expression oriented at cultural creative design, and verify feasibility of DNA application oriented at cultural creative design through application examples. A cultural gene design method oriented at creative design is proposed from the perspective of cultural creative design, thus providing cultural creative designers with originality, stimulate design inspiration, improve design efficiency, effectively assist in cultural creative design and provide supporting services for development of cultural creative industry.

Keywords: Cultural creative design · Cultural design gene · Design method
Product design DNA

1 Introduction

Cultural creative product belongs to product and is also a kind of unique "creative activity" [1]. Its difference from general product lies in that it mainly relies on culture, takes creative design as development means, analyzes and transforms cultural factors contained in substance to design factors, and seek a new physical state form conforming to modern life and emotional need for cultural factors with design. Seeking cultural heredity is also seeking new technology and drive of new technology arising thereby.

Cultural gene decides cultural system inheritance and change and is core to cultural growth and development as well as inheritance and development [2, 3]. It is an effective approach for design of cultural creative product to extract cultural gene, provide design manifestation, form design gene of such specific culture, and apply it to product design. Hence, designers need to emphasize [uniqueness]. In terms of cultural creative

© Springer International Publishing AG, part of Springer Nature 2018
P.-L. P. Rau (Ed.): CCD 2018, LNCS 10912, pp. 172–185, 2018.
https://doi.org/10.1007/978-3-319-92252-2_13

products, source and foundation of [uniqueness] of design creativity connation are its own cultural characteristics and cultural gene. Therefore, it is another design thought transformation facing designers to extract design inspiration and aided design from heredity of cultural gene.

At present, extraction of cultural design gene is often subject to manual extraction method. Professional designers research related culture, analyze and extract cultural design gene in combination with design knowledge and experience as well as cultural characteristics [5, 6]. Such method is of strong subjectivity and designers will extract cultural design gene according to their own understanding. Hence, design gene extracted by different designers from the same kind of culture may be significantly different. At the same time, there are single extraction methods for cultural design gene at present and they cannot completely reflect cultural characteristics and connotations. For above problems, it is the main research contents of the Paper to control subjective influence of designers on extraction of cultural design gene, keep extraction objectivity with appropriate method, extract cultural design genes from several perspectives on this basis, and make designed products accepted by more people. The basic thought is introduced through examples in this study.

2 Extraction Principle of Cultural Creativity Gene (DNA)

2.1 Cultural Design Gene

In terms of theoretical research of cultural gene, Schipper [4] firstly proposed the concept of cultural gene pool. Cultural gene is basic factor, basic element to decide cultural system inheritance and change and core to cultural growth and development and inheritance and development [6]. Cultural gene is different from biological gene. Biological gene belongs to biological inheritance and cultural gene belongs to non-biological inheritance and needs to be inherited by people, society and various cultural phenomena in specific cultural field, such as implements, buildings, activities and customs in cultural field [7, 8]. Cultural design gene is basic characteristic element and basic manifestation mode to act on design manifestation with cultural core characteristics to be extracted from cultural gene. Cultural design gene is extraction of basic characteristic element and summary of manifestation mode for cultural gene from the perspective of design. It aims to extract cultural connotation characteristics and apply them to design. Hence, design is linkage of culture and creation as well as experience and is a bridge.

From the perspective of psychology and information theory, under the effect of design concept, functions, actions, cultures and emotions are selected and then corresponding modeling elements are extracted to be component elements of design before permutation and combination through design composition rules and reconstructing overall model of product. It is a process of information processing. During the process, successful brand will form a set of design language which can be deemed as product design DNA. under the trend of increasing homogenization of product production technology at present, the trend of appearance modeling to be attached to traditional function is increasingly week! Its main function is not technical any more, but to satisfy people's aesthetic and other implicit spiritual demands [3]. All manufacturers hope to establish their own brands through design. Hence, it requires designers to extract brand connotation, value, cultural characteristics and other implicit DNA, transform them to modeling language, composition rule and other explicit DNA and convey them to consumers.

2.2   Extraction Principles of Cultural Design Gene

"Cultural design gene" has basic characteristics like "biological gene". It is basic unit of cultural "inheritance" and inherits cultural characteristic information unlike cultural factors of other cultures. It plays a decisive role in formation of certain cultural characteristics. On the contrary, it is also decisive factor to identify such cultural characteristics [9]. To determine the design gene of certain culture, we can roughly follow principles as shown in Fig. 1:

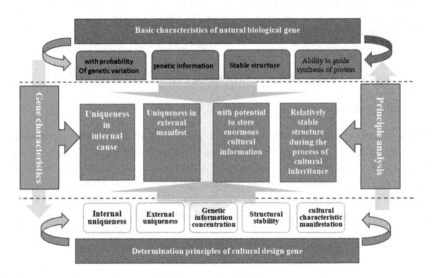

Fig. 1. Principle of cultural design gene

3   Product Design Process Model Based on Cultural Creative Gene

3.1   Research Method for Extraction of Cultural Design Gene

As one of key elements of cultural inheritance, screening of cultural gene lays a solid foundation for creative design. Cultural creative design is a process to review and reflect on cultural characteristics. It re-defines cultural elements and blends them to product design, thus satisfying cultural and aesthetic demands of consumers [10]. Through cultural gene analysis during cultural creative design, we can understand demand in cultural creative design field and improve accuracy of design service.

different from creative design of traditional functional product and design of compli-cated product [11, 12], cultural creative designers need to pay more attention to reflection upon traditional culture, identify essential knowledge in traditional culture. The knowledge runs through the whole cultural creative design process and provides designers with creative inspiration and auxiliary knowledge.

Definition Creative Design Process Model Based on Cultural Gene Can be Expressed as:

$$C\,(culture)\{G, D, O\} \rightarrow P \qquad (1)$$

Where, C indicates the process that cultural creative designer D formulates design scheme P under support of cultural gene G extracted for creative design according to design objective O. D is the designer conducting cultural creative design, O is objective to be satisfied and demand to be met by design, P is produced design [18–20], G is cultural gene supporting cultural creative design (as shown in Fig. 3). ①Design positioning stage: designers cooperate with investigators to analyze cultural image to be expressed by product, user demand and product positioning; ②Knowledge analysis stage: designers cooperate with research experts to collect, analyze and rearrange involved cultural genes and form knowledge table; ③Implementation stage: designers integrate several cultural genes instructive to design with design method, cooperate with engineers by virtue of cultural creative design method, provide design in mod-eling, color, function, texture and structure, creative new design scheme; ④Design evaluation stage: designers cooperate with consumers to provide design test and evaluation for new design schemes produced and see whether it satisfies design task and objective. If not, return to the first three steps for positioning, analysis and design. Next, we will prove with specific research cases that this method can effectively promote designers' design in design analysis stage and design implementation stage.

3.2 Application of Cultural Gene in Design Practice-with Chinese Traditional Lion Dancing as an Example

As shown in Fig. 2, we classify and research elements and characteristics of Chinese lion dancing culture. Lion dancing originates from China Han Dynasty, Lion dancing is

a   b   c

Fig. 2. Traditional Chinese lion dance

a comprehensive art integrating martial art, dancing and gong and drum, representing good luck and force. It is full of oriental cultural characteristics and artistic charms.

3.3   Experiment Mode

Samples of typical cultural characteristics selected in the case of the Paper are mainly manifested in the form of figures and photos and the content and information are characterized with diversification and complexity. We describe indicator meaning and influence factors for eye movement based on photo samples of typical cultural characteristics according to above characteristics in the Paper.

3.4   Experiment Purpose

The main purpose of the experiment is to test and analyze areas and characteristic elements most manifesting cultural characteristics highly noticed by tested objects in cultural characteristic samples, providing reference for extraction of subsequent cultural design gene [13–15].

3.5   Analysis of Experiment Influence Factor

Through analyzing cognitive process of certain number of tested objects for cultural characteristic samples with eye movement analysis experiment, perceptual cognition process of tested objects is quantified through eye movement data. Through comprehensively analyzing watching time, watching track, backlight times and area of interest

Table 1. Analysis of related influence factors in the experiment

Factor classification	Influence factor of eye movement analysis	Scheme
Experiment sample	Size	Uniform size is set up to be 1024 × 680px
	Color distribution	Control group of gray samples
	Demonstration sequence	Determine sequence with Latin square design method
	Playing duration	21 min/person/time
	Switch between samples	Set up with black transition page at interval
Tested object	Number of tested objects	20 tested objects
	Age	21–45 years old
	Gender ratio	The same ratio of the male and the female
	Education background	Above bachelor's degree
	Degree of familiarity with test	Experience to contact or be familiar with cultural creative design. However, all tested

when tested objects observe different area elements of samples, eye movement data are classified, summarized and analyzed to obtain People's common focus area and elements for cultural characteristic samples. With analysis based on experimental psychology used for extraction of cultural design gene, experimental results are influenced by many factors [16] (Table 1).

3.6   Experimental Objects

Tested object of the experiment is 20 people, including 10 girls and 10 boys respectively at the age of 21–45 with education experience above bachelor. Where there are 9 undergraduates, 4 postgraduate students, 4 doctoral students and 3 professors. Naked eye vision of test reaches 1.0 and they do not have color blindness and color weakness. These tests have work experience of cultural characteristics element extraction and cultural creative products design, but it is the first time for all test to see pictures of experiment test samples.

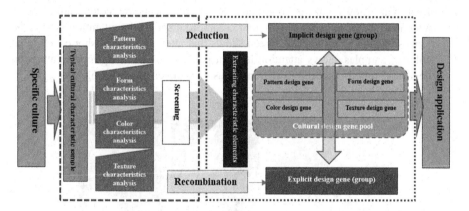

Fig. 3. Flow diagram for extraction analysis experiment of cultural design genes

3.7   Experiment Data Analysis

ASL Results Plus (Eye-trace 6) is used for experiment data analysis [31–33]. Cultural sample characteristics element emphasized by tested objects is mainly analyzed through gaze trail of tested objects, heat map and area of interest these three levels. Sample 1, 2 and 3 are taken as example to be analyzed below.

(1) Gaze trail

Figure 4 is gaze trail diagram of sample 2. In the Figure tested objects gaze at face of dancing lion firstly, and then observe ornamentation in the left side and right side behind lion head successively. Eye leaping activity of tested objects is mainly in lion head and interior of ornamentation area of eyes [30–34]. There are few eye leaping activities in lion head and lion body. Therefore, tested objects mainly pay attention to face of dancing lion and ornamentation on the body.

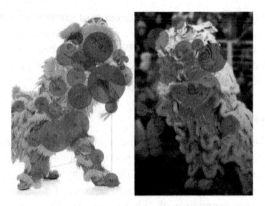

Fig. 4. Gaze trail analysis of sample 2

(2) Heat map

Heat map shows gazing conditions of tested objects by color and displays attention heat of samples by different colors. Red shows that attention time is the longest, followed by yellow. Green shows that attention time is shorter. Original color of samples shows attention has not paid on it. Heat map reflects attention degree of tested objects on different areas of samples directly (Fig. 5).

Fig. 5. Original sample of thermodynamic diagram of visual focus (Color figure online)

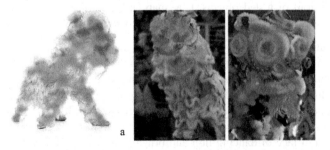

Fig. 6. Gray sample of thermodynamic diagram of visual focus

In general, focus is still mainly in the face of lion head and ornamentation on the body. Screen is captured for area with significant attention. Three general areas with significant attention of tested objects on the figure can be seen: eyes, mouth and mane of neck (Fig. 6).

(3) Area of interest

Area of interest refers to that samples are divided into different areas to study visual rules of tested objects in different area and visual browsing conditions in each area of interest can be contrasted and analyzed. As shown in Fig. 7, sample 2 is divided into ornamentation (AOI 1), head of dancing lion (AOI 2) and the upper body of dancing body (AOI 3) these 3 areas of interest. Attention degree of tested objects on two areas is studied by quantitative contrast.

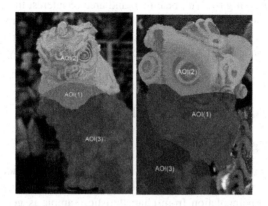

Fig. 7. Area of interest (AOI) analysis of samples

Quantity of fixation point in area of interest reflects importance of the same sample in different area. There will be more gazing frequency for more important area; time proportion of gazing AOI area in the same sample is also an important index to reflect area (namely different cultural characteristics), the longer gaze duration is, more important display area is, and corresponding cultural sample characteristics of the area can reflect the importance more. Analysis on eye movement data of 20 tested objects is shown in Table 2.

Table 2. Data statistics of all areas of interest

Area	Area ratio	Average fixation points	Average fixation time [Ms]	Proportion
AOI1	25%	12.8	5617.8	53.7%
AOI2	13%	9.7	3736.3	37.9%
AOI3	23%	1.5	689.2	6.5%
Outside	29%	0.7	178.5	1.7%

According to percentage of fixation time in all areas of interest, attention degree of heat (proportion is 53.7%) in original sample is more than that of body of dancing lion (the proportion is 31.05%), which shows that tested objects are more interested in cultural characteristics of head of dancing lion generally. Through analysis of control experiment, color can attract tested objects to input more attention. According to experiment data, key focus of tested objects on samples ornamentation and head of dancing lion. [17, 19, 20] Therefore, ornamentation and head of dancing lion, especially characteristics of mouth and mane ornamentation can reflect cultural characteristics of dancing lion mostly. In addition, experiment results present that head of dancing lion, especially mouth and eye positions receive more attention than other positions of the body, therefore, it shall be considered emphatically at the time of extracting cultural design genes.

Through analysis of gaze trail, heat map and area of interest these three levels, key extraction objects of cultural design genes in samples can be determined and they are body ornamentation, mouth and eyes of head position of the dancing lion respectively. Through conclusion, key extraction characteristics pattern as shown in the Figure is determined.

4   Design Application of Cultural Design Gene

4.1   Pattern Design Gene Extraction

Pattern, as typical representative of cultural gene, contains abundant aesthetics and profound cultural connotation. [21–23] Collecting pattern and extracting general core characteristics of ornamentation from characteristics sample is generative process of cultural design gene of explicit pattern. Deducing and recombining general core characteristics of pattern and making expression pattern of pattern ornamentation rich to deduct more pattern ornamentation is generative process of cultural design gene of implicit pattern (as Table 3).

Table 3. Pattern design gene extraction

	Extracting pattern 1	Extracting pattern 2	Extracting pattern 3	Extracting pattern 4	Extracting pattern 5	Extracting pattern
Pattern extraction						...
Pattern deduction and recombination	recombining pattern1	recombining pattern 2	recombining pattern3	recombining pattern 4	recombining pattern5	recombining pattern
						...

4.2   Form Design Gene Extraction

Extraction of form design gene highlights form characteristics of dancing lion at the same time of keeping main face characteristics of dancing lion, which has important significance on highlighting main characteristics of dancing lion in design application.

Traditional dancing lions in China have various forms. As tested objects pay more attention to lion head in the sample, head form is as main extracted original sample. As shown in Fig. 8, external profile of head and tongue characteristics of lion in the face are extracted and extracted form lines are ratified from the angle of design to make it smoother with strengthened expressive force as form design gene of cultural creative gene.

Fig. 8. Characteristics in the mouth extraction of dancing lion

4.3   Color Design Gene Extraction

Dancing lion body and ornamentation these three parts in Tables 4, 5 and 6 to extract color design gene. Extracting color aimed at different characteristics classification helps to study color characteristics [24, 25] of colored drawing and ornamentation of dancing lion with classification. Overall consideration is given to color area, Lab average value and proper threshold value to realize extraction of color design genes in the sample.

Table 4. Color design gene extraction of dancing lion head

Extraction source									
Extraction result									
RGB value	R: 119 G: 139 B: 186	R: 214 G: 121 B: 141	R: 148 G: 101 B: 78	R: 246 G: 216 B: 92	R: 199 G: 56 B: 63	R: 165 G: 132 B: 110	R: 26 G: 28 B: 31	R: 239 G: 238 B: 238	R: 39 G: 50 B: 127

Table 5. Color design gene extraction of dancing lion body

Extraction source								
Extraction result								
RGB value	R: 225 G: 128 B: 86	R: 210 G: 124 B: 106	R: 86 G: 96 B: 99	R: 98 G: 115 B: 165	R: 87 G: 114 B: 84	R: 117 G: 102 B: 58	R: 128 G: 43 B: 47	R: 106 G: 124 B: 135

Table 6. Color design gene extraction of ornamentation of dancing lion

Extraction source							
Extraction result							
RGB value	R: 36 G: 41 B: 38	R: 56 G: 75 B: 69	R: 79 G: 93 B: 94	R: 126 G: 132 B: 136	R: 57 G: 50 B: 48	R: 100 G: 99 B: 88	R: 88 G: 78 B: 66

As shown in Tables 4, 5 and 6, through contrastive analysis, color of three parts of the sample has obvious difference. Color in the head of dancing lion is relatively bright generally, golden (R246, G216, B92) face is matched with creamy white hair and red (R199, G56, B63) lip to highlight bright face characteristics of dancing lion; the color of dancing lion body is slightly dark that is dominated by yellow (R225, G128, B86) and red (R128, G43, B47) and matched with blue (R98, G115, B165), golden yellow (R117.G102, B58) and grayish stripe (R106, G124, B135) for embellishment; dark brown (R57, G50, B48), gray (R126, G132, B136) and dark green (R56, G75, B69) are mainly adopted for color of ornamentation is mainly, which generates comparison with dancing lion with bright color as foreground and highlights sacred and magnificent visual effect of dancing lion.

4.4   Texture Design Gene Extraction

Product material includes organization and texture of material surface and is important carrier to express product design feeling. [26, 27] is painted for silk. Generous and steady dancing lion and lion head surface that is detail of statue are displayed to be finer. Ornamentation of statue is painted out subtly with color taking cork wood and gypsum as adhesive, which highlights sense of depth. Aimed at material utilization characteristics of traditional dancing lion of China, cork wood, plush, silk, painting and other typical materials are extracted respectively. The arrangement is shown in Table 7.

Table 7. Texture design gene extraction

Material name	Cork wood frame	Plush edge	Sequin	Embroidery technology	Metal material
Extraction result					

5   Design Application of Cultural Design Gene

Overall consideration is given to cultural design gene characteristics and modes that are proper to combine with product design. [35, 36] Cultural design gene conforming to design demands is selected to implement cultural creative design. A cultural creative product – lion tongue fan of dancing lion of China is shown in Fig. 11 by extracting test results in the experiment, and purifying scroll design of dancing lion, tongue form in the mouth of dancing lion and color elements these obtained cultural gene elements, thus application of the method in cultural creative design is verified.

As for the lion tongue fan, dancing lion tongue form is adopted for general form, and fan agitation conforms to action language of moving tongues in lion dancing [37] performance. Chinese red, pink green, golden yellow and orange are extracted from dancing lion head as main color. Extracted scroll design, tooth and tongue pattern are matched. Plush texture of headdress of dancing lion is borrowed in texture to create visual quality. Which symbolizes good luck. The fan symbolizes waving lion tongue. Users obtain this lucky implied meaning at the time of stirring up.

狮舌扇
The lion tongye fan

The fan is the wind supplies, the summer requisites. But with the development of The Times, young people have rarely used fans. On a hot summer evening, the old people can be seen taking a fan out for a walk. The fans lack a little bit of flavor for young people, so we use the tongue part as the design element for the lion's lion culture, which can be used in different colors to attract young people to use fans. In this way, while promoting the indigenous culture of foshan, it is also advocated to make life more low-carbon and environmentally friendly.

6   Conclusion

Cultural inheritance is derived from memories in the life. This sediment and memory conveys the same life experiences and spiritual annotation which people have placed on emotions through products. In the challenging modern cultural creation, the problem that cultural creative products need to solve is how to make cultural characteristics mode well code but continue to have its original characteristics, like the biological inheritance. With the combination of modern cultural creative product design self-consistently, they show users their own qualities and traditional values. Subsequently, relevant image models are built. From the two aspects, design methods and development procedure, corresponding research and development are analyzed, and product design gene mapping and deduction methods are proposed in accordance with their forms, characteristics and mapping relations.

By doing so, product image design context models are achieved, which makes the transformation from cultural characteristics element to cultural creative products become available. Such achievement not only provides designers some measures and evaluation models to clearly show the spiritual values of traditional culture but avoids the illogical annotation in the transformation. Through the real case, the feasibility of such method is examined, which offer an effective reference to cultural creative products.

References

1. Lin, R.: Discussion on sensory experience design from service innovation thought. Des. Stud. Spec. Issue 13–31 (2011)
2. Lin, R.: Culture creativity is a way but not technology. Appreciation Arts 7(2), 4–13 (2011)
3. Tseng, Y.C., Howes, A.: The adaptation of visual search to utility, ecology and design. Int. J. Hum.-Comput. Stud. 80, 45–55 (2015)
4. Zhu, W., Wang, Z., Wu, J.: Research on cultural relic management information system based on GIS—taking cultural relic management information system in Zhejiang province as an example. Geo—Inf. Sci. 7(4), 77–80 (2005)
5. Schipper, K.: Chinese Culture Gene Library, pp. 9–28. Peking University Press, Beijing (2002)
6. Luo, S., Dong, Y.: Classifying cultural artifacts knowledge for creative design. J. Zhejiang Univ.: Eng. Sci. 51(1), 113–123 (2017)
7. Eyraud, R., Zibetti, E., Baccino, T.: Allocation of visual attention while driving with simulated augmented reality. Transp. Res. Part F, 32, 46–55 (2015)
8. Khalighy, S., Green, G., Scheepers, C., Whittet, C.: Quantifying the qualities of aesthetics in product design using eye-tracking technology. Int. J. Ind. Ergon. 49, 31–43 (2015)
9. Wang, W., H Y, J X, Yang, X.: Research and application of traditional cultural design element extraction model. Packag. Eng. (06), 73–76+81 (2014)
10. Liu, P.: Establishment and Application Research of Gene Map for Chinese Traditional House Landscape. Peking University, Beijing (2011)
11. Sun, M., Zhou, J.: Historical building protection of ancient towns in the south of China and research on ancient town development mode. J. Anhui Agric. Sci. (31), 12363–12366 (2013)
12. Liu, Q., Xu, C., Falk, H.: Interface availability assessment based on eye movement tracking technology. J. Southeast Univ. (Nat. Sci. Ed.) 02, 331–334 (2010)
13. Wei, P.: Attribute and characteristics of cultural creative products. Cult. Mon. (2010)
14. Xu, H.C.: Design Semiotics, p. 103. Tsinghua University Press, Beijing (2008)
15. Zhang, L.H.: Semiotics Method of Product Design, p. 22. China Architecture & Building Press, Beijing (2011)
16. Zhang, X.: Design Semiotics, p. 188. Chemical Industry Press, Beijing (2004)
17. Li, L.: Design thought of product semiotics. Decoration 4, 4–5 (2002)

18. Shen, W., Tang, R., Liu, Y.: Ontology-based knowledge service modeling for innovation design process of ornament. J. Zhejiang Univ. Eng. Sci. **43**(12), 2268–2273 (2009). Chinese
19. Liu, W., Wu: Cultural creative product made of hyongum and its principle of development design. Packag. Eng. **37**(14), 169–173 (2016). Chinese
20. Xu, J.H., Zhang, M.: Discussion on reconstruction of Chinese traditional cultural symbols in product design. Packag. Eng. 166–167 (2007)
21. Pan, Y.H.: Cultural Composition. Higher Education PressXchange, Beijing (2011)
22. Li, Z.: Image research of cultural symbols in product design. Packag. Eng. **S1**, 16–18 (2010)
23. Li, F., Dong, J.: Interpretation of traditional cultural symbol in product design. Packag. Eng. 132–133+136 (2009)
24. Moalosi, R., Popovic, V., Hickling-hudso, A.: Product analysis based on Botswana's postcolonial socio-cultural perspective. Int. J. Des. **1**(2), 35–43 (2007)
25. Crilly, N., Moultrie, J., Clarkson, P.J.: Seeing things: consumer response to the visual domain in product design. Des. Stud. **25**(6), 547–577 (2004)
26. Monk, A., Lolos, K.: Changing only the aesthetic features of a product can affect its apparent usability. In: Monk, A., Lolos, K. (eds.) IFIP TC 9, WG 9.3 HOIT 2007. IFIP, vol. 241, pp. 221–233. Springer, Heidelberg (2007). https://doi.org/10.1007/978-0-387-73697-6_17
27. Lee, S., Harada, A., Steppers, P.J.: Pleasure with products: design based on Kanski. In: Pleasure with Products: Beyond Usability, pp. 219–229 (2002)
28. Ma, J.P., Huang, N.L., Chuang, M.H., Lin, R.: From Technology to Hamartin Cross-Cultural Design Applications in Mobile Interaction, Education, Health, Transport and Cultural Heritage, pp. 348–360. Springer, Heidelberg (2015). https://doi.org/10.1007/978-3-319-20934-0
29. Moreover, N., Prodan, I.: Absorptive capacity, its determinants, and influence, on innovation output: cross-cultural validation of the structural model. Tec novation **29**, 859–872 (2009)
30. Destem, P., Hecker, P.: Framework of product experience. Int. J. Des. **1**, 57–66 (2007)
31. Hsu, C.-H., Chang, S.-H., Lin, R.: A design strategy for turning local culture into global market products. Int. J. Affect. Eng. **12**, 275–283 (2013)
32. Lee, Y., Connor, C.G.: New product launch strategy for network effects products. Acad. Market. Sci. **31**(3), 241–255 (2003)
33. Swann, G.M.P.: The functional form of network effects. Inf. Econ. Policy **14**, 417–429 (2002)
34. Balakrishnan, A., Shaikh, I., Rangaswami, A.: Small-world markets and their implications for the diffusion of innovations. In: Marketing Science Conference, University of Alberta, Edmonton, Alberta, Canada (2002)
35. Lim, B., Choi, M., Park, M.: The late take-off phenomenon in the diffusion of telecommunication services: network effect and the critical mass. Inf. Econ. Policy **15**, 537–557 (2003)
36. Crossley, L.: Build emotions in design. Des. J. **6**(3), 35–45 (2004)
37. Donald, A.: The Design of Everyday Things. Basic Books Present, Norman (2002)
38. Leo, W.: Managing emotional design in new product development process. Principle Presents (2005)

Teaching Thoughts and Cases Analysis of the Innovative Design of Lacquer Art Products in the Multi-disciplinary and Trans-Boundary Historical Background

Jin Li[✉] and Yonghui Lin

Beijing Institute of Technology, Zhuhai, Zhuhai, China
3834114@qq.com, 53907024@qq.com

Abstract. This paper mainly illustrates how could the design and art major create redesign products featuring various trans-boundary elements, like the art, technology, ecology, humanity and material character, in the multi-disciplinary and trans-boundary historical background. According to the case analysis, it elaborates how to deduce new design products featuring the aesthetic experience, classic succession and spiritual expression in the traditional arts. In this paper, teaching results of the lacquer art design course of Beijing Institute of Technology, Zhuhai are discussed. Brand new design products can be designed through the multi-disciplinary interaction, including arts, design, crafts, high-tech and industrial products, etc. These design products are mainly created and produced by focusing on the theme of eco-environment, arts, diversified cooperation, and renaissance of traditional art. This paper mainly expounds the design of innovative products based on trans-boundary characteristics of the traditional arts, for instance, the aesthetic orientation in the pursuit of humanistic spirit, convenience of high-tech, selectivity of environment and eco-material, and guidance of scientific methods. The trans-boundary and diversified design produces products with new visual effect, and such products conforms to the times, with stronger vitality. Just like the case illustrated in this paper: study the cases of works applying the trans-boundary design, like bamboo materials in eco-environment, lacquer art craft of industrial arts, functions of sports products, etc. among which the relation between bicycles and human life; relation among several materials, like bamboos, paints and metal; relation among the aesthetics of several materials and meaning of innovative design; relation between the reproduction and renaissance of arts and traditional crafts; relation between idea creation and trans-boundary; and relation between conceptual design and product implementation. In addition, the humanistic spirit of scientific design art in the overall frame of traditional Chinese culture is discussed, and combining the present art and design environment, the beauty of lacquer materials and craft is reflected in the newly-designed works through integrating the lacquer art, traditional materials and new expression of traditional crafts under the guidance of classical painting theories. Besides, innovative design of lacquer art products is accomplished, for reflecting the communality pursued by humanistic spirit, aesthetic sentiment, texture pursuit, life performance, intention expression and rhythmic vitality.

© Springer International Publishing AG, part of Springer Nature 2018
P.-L. P. Rau (Ed.): CCD 2018, LNCS 10912, pp. 186–195, 2018.
https://doi.org/10.1007/978-3-319-92252-2_14

Keywords: Traditional craft · Lacquer art · Design · Trans-boundary Modernization

1   Introduction

At first, it analyzes the important craft in the history of industrial arts, namely lacquer art, and its general development context in the Chinese history, and further elaborates the status of lacquer art discipline in Chinese institutions of higher education. Secondly, teaching thoughts and development suggestions are put forward by aiming at the educational problems of lacquer art in the third chapter, for instance, how could traditional culture and art develop in the current society? How could traditional craft "be modernized"? Besides, suggestions and solution to problems are stated: namely artists and designers should cooperate and exchange with each other based on the understanding and grasp of traditional national culture and traditional crafts, and further implement the innovative design by combining new technologies, new thoughts, social topics, pop culture and new aesthetics. Thirdly, with the teaching of lacquer art studio of Beijing Institute of Technology, Zhuhai as a case, examples are cited to prove the feasibility analysis of the above views, and several design products of the teaching practice program are taken to illustrate the views in teaching, namely devoted to the integration of science, art and design and cross-cultural disciplines, and keep cross practicing to create new-craft products. Meanwhile, to encourage students to look for inspirations and stimulate the innovative ideation through the guidance of methods and behavioral inspiration, to carry out the design thinking and multi-dimension reconstruction in the formal expression of lacquer art creation and lacquer culture, and to form the multi-culture trans-boundary product innovation dominated by lacquer art eventually. At last, views proposed in this paper are summarized, the educational view that science, art, and design should be trans-boundary and associate multi-disciplines in the industrial art course of colleges and universities is correct and feasible.

2   Status of Traditional Industrial Art - Lacquer Art

Lacquer art is a category of art with natural lacquer as the main material. The natural lacquer used in traditional technical lacquer art is mainly from the lacquer tree. Restricted by natural environmental factors, like the geographic position, and whether, natural raw lacquer grows in Southeast Asia. According to historical records, Chinese lacquer was used 7000 years ago. It was recorded in *Han Feizi Ten Faults* that "Emperor Yu painted sacrificial utensils black outside and red inside" [1], which was the recorded form of lacquer artwork at that period. Lacquerware reached the peak stage in Ming and Qing Dynasty, and sunk down sharply afterwards. Kou Xiulan stated in the article *Fading of Traditional Lacquerware and Reconstruction of Modern Lacquer Art* that modernism seems to rise again, but actually the struggling modern lacquer art fails to inherit the typicality of the mother language of lacquer ware and abandons the traditional language. Furthermore, the fading of traditional lacquer art and regeneration of modern lacquer art is declared with the modernity symbol of textual deconstruction and cultural criticism, while its parent body is sacrificed with its trans-generational derivatives, and it would be forgotten thoroughly." [2] Lacquer art once made remarkable achievements, which were mainly reflected by the form of lacquer ware. Nowadays, contemporary lacquer artists introduce the lacquer art to the public again, not by recovering the heavy and ancient brilliant state of lacquer ware, but revealing the contemporary understanding of lacquer art in such forms as the lacquer painting and 3D lacquer sculptures. Besides, these lacquer art works aim to reflect the texture of lacquer material and spiritual significance.

Throughout the history of industrial art, art ware occurred to meet the demands of creators for its practical functions. Lacquer ware is the theme of lacquer art, and lacquer ware emerged initially for its functions of use, but when the industrial art developed to a certain stage, it transformed towards art. With the improvement of living standard, transformation of social consciousness, changes of the ruling class in the aesthetic taste, powerful spiritual force of craftsmen, and improvement of aesthetic characters, the aesthetic value of industrial art has been increasingly enhanced, resulting in the gradual segregation of aesthetic functions and practical functions. Lacquer ware is no exception, and it transforms from the practical art ware to the fine-art lacquer painting and 3D lacquer modeling gradually.

"In today's information age, it actually fails to break away from the historical fate, and fades away from the dazzling contemporary life. Despite of several appearances, it just adorns people's memory of history." [3] According to the present situation, problems discussed by critics in the art world and lacquer art world could be roughly known. With clear views and goals, and associating problems in the teaching of lacquer art in colleges and universities, we adjust the teaching mode and improve the teaching direction, and make certain progress in the expansion of lacquer art. The lacquer art relation is shown in Fig. 1.

Figure 1 shows several works of the lacquer art course of the School of Design and Art, Beijing Institute of Technology, Zhuhai, covering the graduation design project and classroom practice program. By focusing on the lacquer art culture and analyzing the development direction of lacquer art, lacquer art experimental projects of our school mainly include the easel lacquer painting, lacquer ware of utensil shape, spatial lacquer device, cooperative and trans-boundary lacquer art jewelry, scientific and innovative 3D lacquer form.

3   Demonstration of Lacquer Art Education – Modernization Development Direction

In the lacquer art teaching and creation, natural Chinese lacquer would of course be applied. Different materials conform to certain fixed number or fulfill certain form of duties. Chinese lacquer material is applied since it has highly individualized and metaphorical connotation, and great attraction in the art form. On the other hand, the constantly developing lacquer art technology changes the attributes of materials slowly.

Contemporary art emerged in the west at the end of 1960s and beginning of 1970s, and was spread to China at the beginning of the 1990s. "Contemporary art" was basically defined by five countries, including America, England, Germany, France and

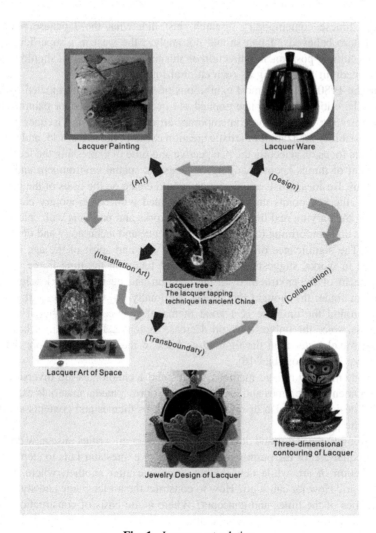

Fig. 1. Lacquer art relation

Italy. Ever since the biennial exhibition in Venice in 1993, the concept of "Chinese contemporary art" has been formed, and it mainly referred to the expression of contents of Chinese themes in the form of western language after the 1970s, or the transformation of traditional Chinese art form with avant-garde western language. After the Cultural Revolution, Chinese contemporary art emerged in the crack of two systems, namely the official art history and western modern art history. With the rise of China, it enters the stage of powerful dominance of nationalism. Currently, Chinese art realized the end of learning from the west, but it is not clear what to do in the future. The proposal of "super-contemporary" is made in such a context. Of course, "super-contemporary" is a starting point of ideology, and more accurately, it should be "mix contemporary" or "pan contemporary" [4]. The cultural orientation should be found in Chinese contemporary research, just like what the Japanese philosopher Nishida Kitaro believed: "Japan should not analyze the west in a superficial level or confirm its cultural position and direction on this basis, and instead, it should regard the west as a medium for seeking its own cultural form" [5].

From the 1980s till now, most exhibitions of lacquer art are dominated by lacquer painting. The critic Peng De once pointed out in 2002 that: "lacquer painting ignores the modernization", while "the contemporary art circle ignores the lacquer painting".

The possibility realization of artistic creation exists in the real world, and artists and art designers focus on selecting the perspective and time of expressing the feelings. The development of things keeps changing, so does the spatial environment and people's mental focus. Besides, artists and designers would create on the basis of the present, by discovering the key points that could be associated with contemporary characteristic elements in the varying real life, thus to design works and products with characteristics of the times and conforming to the humanity, science and technology and the people of the times. The significance of the contemporary age and spirit of the age is of equal importance in works, suggesting that we should focus on the time frame of life and space segment of the environment in the creation and design of works. Just like the view of Yin Jinan: the thought that a man can finally go back to the start point after traveling around the universe is a good theme of science fiction, but it is actually meaningless, since the universe would decrease to zero before a man makes a circle. You must travel faster than the light to go back to the start point before the end of universe, but it is impossible" [6].

The contemporary artistic methods, means and technologies are diversified. With the development of the times and technological progress, media materials expressed by artists and designers are also diversified, and both its themes and contents are directly related to the present.

According to the status and development of lacquer art, critics raise new doubt: "the modern lacquer art for the purpose of contemporary expression fails to step out of the marginalization of art, while new doubts come one after another: where would the lacquer art go? How far can it go? How to construct the art language and style with the characteristics of the times and concepts? Where is the basis of construction? What's the value of utensils? Would it become the expression form of lacquer art?" [2].

By sorting out the conceptual relation between contemporary problems and "civilization and culture" and "technology and art" and the development process, it can be concluded that traditional art must launch the creation and research by combining the contemporary age. Accordingly, "traditional modernization" is mainly defined as: to grasp the essence of traditional art, carry forward the traditional Tao process, analyze the logic used through the ancient and modern times, and form the comprehension of traditional Tao process and innovative ideas, educational and teaching concepts and methodological frame, on the basis of the ancient natural culture. To dialogue with the civilization actively, and associate with the contemporary value of the carrier."

4 Trans-Boundary Teaching Mode of Beijing Institute of Technology, Zhuhai – Trans-Boundary Design Representation of New Technologies, Multi-materials and Lacquer Art

4.1 Teaching Reflection of Lacquer Art and Trans-Boundary Innovation

The reflection on and conclusion of the teaching of lacquer art is shown as below, by associating the above illustrations of the lacquer art status and art modernization and combining Beijing Institute of Technology, Zhuhai. The lacquer ware and 3D lacquer has been formed through dry lacquer and bodiless method. There is such a batch of artists in Japan and South Korea, and most of them are young. Yong lacquer art creation group mainly from Tokyo University of the Arts considers themselves as the modernist school of lacquer, and they would support the modeling with mesh metal materials, also lacquer, paste and ash. In more innovative teaching experiments, materials like hemp rope, transparent plastic film, and foam, are also applied.

Fig. 2. Lacquer art jewelries made of trans-boundary materials: Chinese lacquer, copper, mother-of-pearl inlay, eggshell, etc.

Due to the inspiration, the School of Arts of Beijing Institute of Technology, Zhuhai communicates with and learns from all majors of the School of Computer and School of Chemical Engineering and Materials to enhance the trans-boundary cooperation and give full play to the creativity of lacquer art design, by combining the "craftsmanship spirit" historical background advocated by the country, as well as the practical conditions of economy and culture in Guangdong. Meanwhile, it summarizes the experience, explores to make innovations and inherits the fine connotation of traditional technology during the teaching process, trying to design with high technology, trans-boundary products (Fig. 2), 3D software modeling design, 3D printing technology, etc. Besides, it attempts to give full play to advantages of design talents in the modeling of 3D lacquer art, and handcraft specialty of industrial art majors in the lacquering technology, carries forward and develops all kinds of lacquer art skills, for instance, pineapple lacquer, light-weight materials, variant coating skills.

Henri Focillon mentioned in *Vie DesFormes* that "technology must extract power from materials" [7]. Artists and designers should keep The cultural and spiritual value of lacquer should constantly pay attention to the cultural and spiritual value of lacquer, and know how to transform the natural attributes to works, so as to display the nature of lacquer art work in its inherent modeling and rebirth after the transformation (Fig. 3).

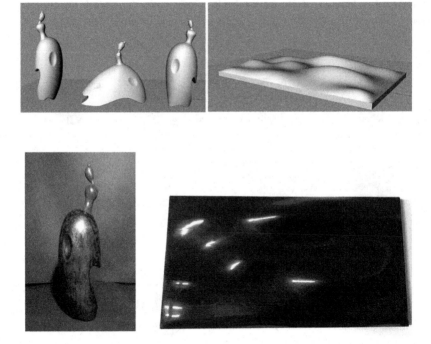

Fig. 3. Trans-boundary lacquer art products: 3D printing and lacquer art

As far as I am concerned, the undergraduate education focusing on the applied talent cultivation model should involve abundant practices and innovation, and be inter-disciplinary, and trans-boundary in teaching. Furthermore, students should be guided to think more, be creative and brave to show in the course setting, so that they could be skillful and flexible. These 3D lacquer shape experiments may not be mature or perfect, but it is reflected that the bold innovative spirit and creative thinking of young people is malleable, and worth encouraging.

4.2 Teaching Project – Case Analysis of "Made in China"

School of Art and Design, Beijing Institute of Technology, case analysis of the lacquer course teaching: Trans-boundary Lacquer Art Design Work of Lacquer Art, Bamboo Art and Functions – "Made in China" (the work was selected in the "Chinese Lacquer World: Time Series – Hubei International Lacquer Art Triennial 2016"):

Relation Between Bicycle and Human. The first problem to be considered in creativity should be the relation, since when there is relation, there would be vitality, and it would be comprehended by analogy. In this case, the start point of design lies in its attempt of integrating human, bicycle, aesthetics, comprehensive materials and lacquer art. Bicycle is familiar to people, and it is environmentally friendly. Besides, it can help with the fitness, so it is available in major cities across the world. The design of this product aims to associate the lacquer art with the industrial design (Figs. 4 and 5).

Fig. 4. Student's work: created in China   **Fig. 5.** Created in China: local image

Relation Between Bamboo, Lacquer Art and Metal Material. The intersecting design of material aesthetics is a basic creative method of trans-boundary design, and it is worthy of practice and creation to observe the relation among all kinds of materials and all forms of beauty, integrate the optimal combination of materials, and produce new esthetic characteristics. The example of this project is *Made in China*, and the creative product is a practical, individualized and decorative bicycle, whose body is made of bamboo and Chinese paint, handle, wheel and seat frame is made of metal material, while the cushion is made of leather.

Material Selection and Extraction. As for the bamboo of this case, Chinese people have always been fond of bamboos, and China is also a country studying, cultivating and making use of bamboos earliest in the world. It has a huge impact on the formation of traditional Chinese culture and spiritual culture. Besides, bamboo has a long-standing relation with the poetries and paintings, and landscape construction in China, and is closely related to the lives of Chinese working people. It is not hard to tell that China is worthy of the reputation, namely the "country of bamboo civilization". Therefore, bamboo has a direct and far-reaching relation with human beings. It is not merely a material, and more importantly, it stands for a spirit.

On the other hand, Chinese art theories are often particular about the "spirit" or "artistic conception", and it is a perception of art. Therefore, "for works taking lacquer as materials, the space where they are placed not just presents the substance, and more importantly, it is the collection of intrinsic spirit" [8]. The implication, Buddhist mood and elegance of lacquer materials is identical with the humble and mild spirit of bamboos. Lacquer art is painted on the wood, ceramic, metal and dry lacquer art in the traditional craft. But it is seldom combined with bamboos. According to the practice, it is found out that lacquer shows good adhesion and expression performance on bamboos, and the two can be closely combined, being consistent in the spirit of materials.

Idea Creation. To look for trans-boundary material, and seek the "hyper text" structure of design. In 1965, Ted Nelson put forward the concept of "hyper text", which changed the single-vision reading form through non-linear logic, and developed the comprehensive perception of perception, touch, vision, hearing, ontology sense and kinesthesia [9]. It reflects the co-existence of the traditional spirit and contemporary value, and takes the bamboo, a material representing the spirit of Chinese culture. There is no plant which can have a such a far-reaching impact on the Chinese civilization as bamboo, and many scholars would use it as a metaphor, and call the impact of bamboo on the material civilization and spiritual civilization on humankind as the bamboo culture. In the long-standing cultural history, plum, bamboo and pine are known as "three cold-weather friends", while plum, orchid, bamboo, and chrysanthemum are known as "four gentlemen". It is evident that bamboo plays a vital role in the mind of Chinese people. Su Shi once said that "he preferred bamboo to meat" in the poem [10]. The material with both spirit and aesthetics really needs attention and exploration in the teaching process.

Premise of the Renaissance of Traditional Lacquering Technology. In this case, the traditional lacquer art is associated with the popular mass culture, namely the bicycle. As for the two forms, one is the ancient classic and the other is the industrial trend. The premise for the renaissance of traditional handicraft is that it should attract the attention in the contemporary age. The reason why the lacquer art experiences a free-fall course in the present industrial age is that users pay les attention, and as a result, it is strange to the public. This project attempts to integrate the form of bicycle and industrial beauty, and make the test and promotion of the lacquer art design in the trans-boundary range.

Implementation of Trans-Boundary Technology. Concerning the intersection of subjects in the teaching, students majoring in the industrial art should make efforts in all kinds of materials and technical skills, since the implementation of trans-boundary technology lies in such accumulation, and grasp of the attributes of all materials, for instance, clipping, adhesion, modeling, polishing, coloring, etc. Furthermore, experiment of the possibility of combining various materials should be conducted frequently in the practice course, and the summary of experience should be carried out in the creative design. Afterwards, materials would be selected for the design according to the textures and technological characteristics of materials, so as to finish the implementation of trans-boundary art ware.

5   Conclusion

In conclusion, the innovative design and implementation of lacquer art products in the multi-discipline and trans-boundary historical background is illustrated, and problems that need attention in the innovative design in the arts of higher education are put forward, for instance, the modernization of traditional art, trans-boundary design of comprehensive material, selection of material, difficulty of trans-boundary technique implementation and solution, spiritual connotation carried by the lacquer material, etc. The triggering of these problems and reflections in the teaching thought, as well as some achievements in the course practice, are analyzed by combining the practical cases. Meanwhile, illustrations are conducted from various aspects, including the start point of creative design, behavioral inspiration, conception process, product implementation, etc. for stating how to resolve the relation among the science and technology, art, design, ecology and vitality of materials, emotional interaction of humanity, and renaissance of traditional technology, etc. Meanwhile, the arguments are combined with the trans-boundary innovative special program of lacquer art products, for guiding the practice.

References

1. Han Feizi, Han Feizi Ten Mistakes
2. Kou, X.: Fading of traditional lacquerware and reconstruction of modern lacquer art. Collected Papers on Era of Lacquer Language. China Renmin University Press (2016)
3. Hu, Z.: Contemporary transformation of traditional lacquer art. Collected Papers on Era of Lacquer Language. China Renmin University Press (2016)
4. Zhu, Q.: Super Contemporary, Mix Contemporary or Pan Contemporary? Fine Arts in China, 11 January 2018
5. Wu, G.: Spiritual Experience of Japanese Intellectuals, Central Compilation & Translation Press (2003)
6. Yin, J.: Knocking at the Door Alone, Sanlian Bookstore (1993)
7. Henri, F.: Vie Des Formes. Peking University Press (2011)
8. Yang, X.: Lacquer – language as a concept. Collected Papers on Era of Lacquer Language. China Renmin University Press (2016)
9. Julian, W.: Critical Keywords in Literary and Cultural Theory. Peking University Press, Beijing (2015)
10. Su Dongpo, Yu Qian Seng Lv Yun Xuan, Song Poe
11. Li, Z.: The Path of Beauty. Tianjin Social Science Institute Press, Tianjin (2008)

Research on the Professional Quality of Product Designers in the Context of the Intelligent Era

Yonghui Lin[(⊠)] and Jin Li

Beijing Institute of Technology, Zhuhai, Zhuhai, China
53907024@qq.com, 3834114@qq.com

Abstract. With the arrival of the intelligent era, people's lifestyles, the industry structure and the needs for talents are undergoing major changes. In the face of the large intelligent era coming in torrents, only updating ideas, innovative thinking and self-transcendence can lead the trend. Industry intelligence is breeding a new era, creating difficult and imaginative scientific myths one after another, subverting people's definitions of many things, and creating an overwhelming amount of new business types, new products and new models. In the context of the intelligent era, what should product designers do to adapt to the development of the times? What professional qualities should they have to reasonably harmonize design and ecology.

In the contemporary design field, plagiarism of designs is a common occurrence, which reflects designers' lack of subjective consciousness of worldwide subjects such as the demand of the times, the natural ecology, the humanistic care and the sustainable development. Designers are of varying quality, some products' life cycles are too short, and flawed products are found in the market from time to time. Under the currently mature operating model of the business environment, problems mentioned above should not have occurred. This phenomenon reflects that designers lack attention to a broader scope in the field and are not comprehensively qualified; designers lack a clear design orientation, and the products they design fall short of a good market prospect; designers' sense of social responsibility and social services is not strong, thus failing to give their product designs any detailed care; and the products designed lack ethical characteristics and local color. In the new era, product designers should have some major qualities as follows: (1) they should give full play to their sensible creative ability and develop their artistic talent; (2) they should seek new development in the multi-dimensional perspective, subject collisions and cross-border experiments; (3) they should design their works on the basis of solving practical problems; (4) they should do a comprehensive research on products from the perspective of the society and services; (5) they should master the ability to harmonize the five major elements, i.e., technology, materials, usage, structure and modeling; (6) they should have a future-oriented (sustainable) learning ability, a comprehensive quality and an innovative design ability; (7) from the design service object, individual per se should be studied rationally and objectively through philosophical theories of anthropology, psychology, phenomenology, etc., and meaningful designs should be made on the basis thereof; (8) they should draw cultural self-confidence, heritage and integration, extension and creation from China's own traditional arts; and (9) since the large

© Springer International Publishing AG, part of Springer Nature 2018
P.-L. P. Rau (Ed.): CCD 2018, LNCS 10912, pp. 196–211, 2018.
https://doi.org/10.1007/978-3-319-92252-2_15

data era required us to solve problems in a more comprehensive, reasonable and accurate manner through resources sharing and joint efforts, it is particularly important to cultivate design teams' sharing, cooperation and innovative collaboration abilities.

Keywords: Intelligent era · Professional quality of product designers
Sharing · Sensible creative ability · Cross-border · Care · Sustainable
Traditional culture

1   Introduction

With the skyrocketing development of high and new technologies, the artificial intelligence (AI) has come to the forefront of the times and constantly subverted human being's imagination in more and more industries. Let's look back on year 2016: Microsoft Tay made outstanding performance in the field of perception. AlphaGo defeated with utmost efforts the great grandmaster in the global Go community. Google, Facebook, Amazon and Twitter rapidly changed their strategic directions, establishing core AI team successively..... Up to the beginning of year 2017, AI system Libratus developed by Carnegie Mellon University won four world top Texas Hold'em Poker players. This is a hot concept promptly igniting various industries. Domestic and overseas magnates of science and technology make arrangement successively. IDC predicts that AI market scale will exceed USD $47 billion in 2020. Moshe Vardi, a professor of Computer Science at Rice University, ever alleged, "AI will take over 50% of the current jobs in the coming 30 years around the globe." In addition to application to some subdivided industries such as finance, medical treatment, transportation and intelligent life, AI starts to be involved into the field of design creativity. For example, Tailor brands releases a special algorithm system that can automatically design logo and raise design suggestion. Voice interaction designer prevails in Silicon Valley. Wix launches AI system ADI that performs automatic web design... It seems that AI triggers a technological revolution in the field of design.

Can AI really replace designers' work in future? The answer is no. AI can replace most repetitive and mechanical work and even participate in design, but it cannot take the place of designers. Technologically, AI can strengthen aesthetic judgment through constant learning and simulation. However, human being's emotion and cognition path are evolved through tens of millions of years, and their inherent creativity and pursuit of aesthetics are what AI is unable to understand. Therefore, what professional qualities should designers have to truly connect with future design and meet new challenges brought about by the intelligent era?

2   Analysis and Argument of the Professional Quality of Product Designers in the Intelligent Era

2.1   Liberation of Sensible Creativity Is Core Competitiveness of Designers in Future

Dancing with shackles on, designers give full play to their own creativity within certain rules and regulations. 70% of designers express that the proportion of their own repetitive work is less than 10%. After AI comes into the field of design, what will happen when sense and sensibility meet? AI can complete repetitive work and simple "creation", liberating designers' brains. In future, the distinctive originality and creativity will be core competitiveness of designers.

On April, 27th, 2017, Design & Artificial Intelligence Report prepared by "Tongji x Tezign Design & Artificial Intelligence Laboratory" was released at Alibaba's user experience design summit UCAN. The report considers that design industry belongs to "co-evolutionary" process of man-machine essentially; in addition, the creativity of human brain is provoked infinitely as machine can help people undertake more repetitive work. Design needs AI to assist co-evolutionary process of "human brain - machine". The report investigated intelligent design cases of advertising industry, clothing industry, high-tech industry in which design is involved deeply and occupies larger proportion and collected back more than 1,000 questionnaires from designers in these industries [1].

This report arrives at the overall brain machine ratio in the design industry in 2017 was 1.55 by collecting a large number of survey samples of the field of design. As displayed in Fig. 1, it's a compound proportion of brain machines of designers on different tasks. Red figure is time distribution proportion (%) of designers on different tasks. Green figure is possibility (%) that different tasks are replaced by intelligentization. During designer's work in next three years, nearly 61% of work is in certain need of human brain and the automated possibility has appeared in 39% of work.

Through investigation and analysis, conclusions are drawn as below:

1. Designers with whatever types and experience all need collecting materials and processing information. "Collecting materials and processing information" occupy nearly 30% of designers' workload. In addition, this proportion will not get reduced with the increase in years of working.
2. Although designers always complain of hardship or fatigue, design is not physical labor. Approximately 70% of designers believe that "repetitive physical labor" in their work is less than 10%, and even nearly 40% of designers think that "repetitive physical labor" in their work accounts for less than 5%.
3. Originality and creation will become the most core competitiveness of designers. From the vertical forecast of Mckinsey model and comparison of horizontal relationship between originality and creation and brain machine ratio, we can see that human designers need such abilities as management, originality and creation, and communication to continue to stay competitive after machines can undertake more work.

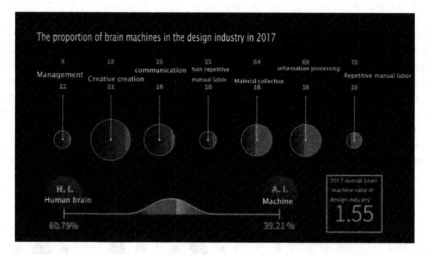

Fig. 1. 2017 overall brain machine ratio in design industry

With the development of science and technology and popularity of in-depth learning, the increasing occupations will be replaced by AI in future. Designers are not exception either. AI can rapidly adapt to various software, output design materials at the fastest response speed and perform design in strict accordance with design specifications without mistakes.

In such a "splendid" era, where is our competitiveness? Sensible creativity cannot be replaced by machines. Only by liberating sensible creativity can designers truly get rid of experience and concept in the design and machine-like duplication and design. Each of us has all kinds of different tags, which are related to our growing environment, people and things we contact, and our likes and dislikes. AI neither undergoes such cultural accumulation and life experience nor feels it. Good at discovering the details in life and summarizing, we exert our advantages to apply cultural factor to design and make design become interesting and connotative. Therefore, sensible creativity is a basic professional quality of designers in the new era.

2.2 Designers Should Seek New Development in the Multi-dimensional Perspectives, Subject Collisions and Cross-Border Experiments

Cross-border design will be a development trend in the future. An aspirant design agency or designer should be brave to be cross-border, attempt breakthrough and use mixed design and cross-border design for the purpose of providing high-quality service for clients instead of confining thoughts and hampering initiative.

Case one: The vintage of red wine is usually indicated on the bottle label. However, how many people can really understand the meaning of the year in which grape is harvested? Actually, the vintage mainly indicates natural conditions of red wine becoming mature, and so to speak, is a biography of red wine. However, in recent years, with the extensive use of insecticide and balance spice, the vintage labeled on the bottle loses its meaning gradually and the taste of red wine becomes ready-made product gradually. It's not related to actual weather conditions in that year.

In order to design label for Piquentum St Vital, Sonda Studio makes an attempt to help people improve awareness to understand the importance of the vintage of red wine. Therefore, Sonda Studio collects weather conditions of the region in which red wine chateau is located and simultaneously records annual precipitation by cooperating with Croatian Meteorological and Hydrological Service (DHMZ). The precipitation has been verified that it is an effective data directly revealing yearly climate variability. Designers use bold dots with different size as a sign of standard precipitation to directly display the precipitation of each particular month in one year. The whole label indicates all-year weather conditions. Therefore, it can be compared easily with different years. See Fig. 2. In this way, red wine as one of the most popular products in history is also a kind of medium displaying the importance of understanding the nature. The cross-border cooperation between designers and the DHMZ make products more humanized.

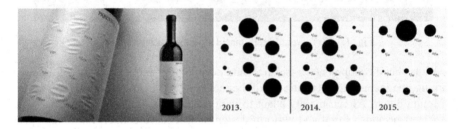

Fig. 2. Design label of Piquentum St Vital

Case two: WANG Boqiao is a founder of normal design and DAC Interactive Technology (Beijing) Co., Ltd., creative design director, council member of CDS, chief planner of China Digital Art (DAC), and also creative consultant of National Museum of China and independent art curator. "Beconer" UVC PLB is a classic cross-border design among many works designed by WANG Boqiao and his team. It's an honor for a designer to work on this because "Beconer" UVC PLB will serve the pilot of home-made carrier-based aircraft. See Fig. 3.

Viewed from a general survey, "cross-border" prevalent in the design community makes the boundary between different fields of design increasingly obscure. Many new

Fig. 3. "Beconer" UVC PLB

interesting collisions are generated and more new possibilities of design are brought about due to "cross-border". It's not only reflected in cross boundary of design industry. Design is allowed to enter into people's life. Such "cross border" arisen from collision reaction between design and society probably make people more excited. Additionally, a deep understanding of China's traditional cultural deposits is also an important reason for those great designers to be able to stand erect in the global design community.

2.3 Designers Should Design Their Works on the Basis of Solving Practical Problems

Design focuses on solving problems and embodying values. Oki Sato, founder of Japanese design powerhouse Nendo Studio, said, "If only conspicuous part is decorated slightly, you can earn design fee without effort as long as clients feel satisfied with it." "Such design does not have any technical content. Its characteristic cannot be manifested. It will only become worse and worse and cannot grow stronger in the long run." In the design process, designers should stand in users' perspective to discover and solve the problems, deeply understanding clients' demand. Design cannot go without life and market, needing to be beautiful, complete and better respectively in form, function and economy. This process reflects designers' value and enhances the value of design products as well. Besides, designers should have a strong awareness of social responsibility instead of only focusing on the promotion and improvement of design towards commercial value. As designers have a sense of social responsibility, they will consider whether it's forward-looking and environment-friendly in the industry in the design process. Under this premise, the most essential design is to make use of the most appropriate technology to solve the problems. Humanistic care and value improvement have a maximized embodiment. As displayed in Fig. 4, people's feelings in the process of using it are fully considered in the design of the coffee pot. By recording preference of different groups of people, palm-print recognition is used to provide personalized service. In Fig. 5, trash can with quadrilateral open design allows usually unused plastic bags to be put in for the purpose of the utilization of waste materials. It's convenient to be stored and used. The protruding parts at both sides in style design can be used as handles and also fasten rubbish bags in use. It's an intelligent design and has practical function.

Fig. 4. Coffee pot uses palm-print recognition

Fig. 5. Discarded plastic bags are to understand personal preferences of making fully used. Such trash can is both coffee easy to use and environment-friendly.

2.4   A Comprehensive Research Is Made on Products from the Perspective of the Society and Services

With the development of human society, value, aesthetics, human concept of modern people have a great change. From the perspective of various benefits, human feelings become more and more indifferent. Such society gives designers more missions. They consider their design constantly from the perspective of humanity, hoping to evoke people's attention to humanity. Design is always in desire for serving more people and satisfying multi-directional demands of the people.

Elie Wiesel noted that "human nature dose not only lie in their desire for truth but also in the sense of mutual assistance and responsibility." An analysis of the vulnerable groups from the perspective of principle of design art is conducive for us to deal with the problems facing design of vulnerable groups in modern design, see clearly design of vulnerable groups, and further find the essence of the problems in multiple contradictions so as to perform design of vulnerable groups better and weed through the old to create the new.

Design is meaningful, especially those made for vulnerable groups.

Great efforts are made for the design of the vulnerable groups from product design to design atmosphere in modern design. The wheelchairs are improved from ordinary ones to the ones controlled by thinking now. Various facilities are designed for the vulnerable groups in public place such as children's amusement park, the seats specially arranged for the vulnerable groups in public bus, sidewalk for the blind, bathroom for the disadvantaged people. In addition, there is camera designed for the blind and the design for the vulnerable groups in immaterial design. For example, as user name is registered, verification code needs to be input. There is a pattern of trumpet nearby verification code. This is a design made for the convenience of the vulnerable groups.

As displayed in Fig. 6, Elevated Bathtub is designed for the elderly, disabled and pregnant people. It comprises two parts: up-and-down movable bathtub and shower with pedestal (simultaneously act as an important role of track). Before Elevated Bathtub is used, its bathtub stays at upper side. As users come to the area of shower, they get it lowered to the bottom by choosing bath mode. After that, water will fill the bathtub gradually. Now users can take a bath. After use, Elevated Bathtub will automatically discharge water through exhaust water pipe as long as bath mode is shut down and then rise to original place. In Fig. 7, designers add a tangent plane with a reasonable angle at the bottom of ceramic lavabo to increase flexibility and multi-functionality of the product and make it more pleasant. As the disadvantaged people and children use it, they can adjust the bathtub to proper angles. This design is full of love.

The era is changing but care remains unchanging. Design is to create more reasonable life-style for human being. The comprehension of such value cognition and judgment as well as practical application to the practice of creating the things about design is to care not only for creating the things but also human civilization. We are living in the world designed by ourselves and, because of our own design, will own an unknown but certain destination corresponding to our design.

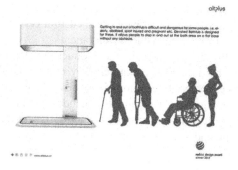

Fig. 6. Elevated Bathtub

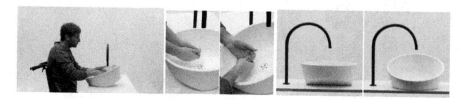

Fig. 7. Un Lavabos

2.5 Designers Need to Have a Future-Oriented (Sustainable) Learning Ability

The environmental issues and energy problems are increasingly prominent today. The sustainable development theory is universally valued. The sustainable development design means that a full use of modern science and technology is made to develop vigorously green resources and cleaner production, and constantly improve and optimize ecological environment so as to facilitate harmonious development between man and nature, and inter-coordination and mutual promotion of population, resources and environment. The sustainable development design is actually to bring the sustainable development theory into the field of design. It can be applied to almost all fields of design from construction and urban planning to production and industrial manufacturing. Such innovative design philosophy requires designers to integrate, analyze and optimize some key elements such as environment, society and economy in every step of design process. For example, designers are required to be able to predict performance of design, compare different schemes, anticipate the influence on the environment, and simulate implementation process and so on in the process of the sustainable development design of construction. Only by realizing these in the development stage of design can the environmental destruction and waste of resources be effectively avoided.

How does this world make sustainable development or connect with the change in life-style of sustainable development? We have to admit that the ability to deal with complexity, ambiguity and uncertainty gets greatly improved after computer appears. Computer system can allow the world to become more transparent and create more collaborative opportunities. Everyone has a good user experience. After a good user experience is created, the world is probably pushed to a certain direction. Hopefully this direction is certain to be sustainable development.

The influence of the design stage in the product development process on final products reaches 70% because many relatively key choices need to be made in this stage: cost, appearance, material selection, innovative point, performance, environmental implication and quality. The quality includes product life, durability, and repair-ability and so on. It can be seen that product designers have an unprecedented opportunity to intervene and affect the impact of products on environment and society (See Fig. 8).

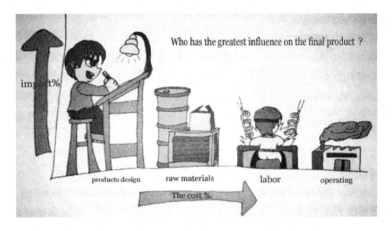

Fig. 8. Influences of product designers on product development

The sustainable design provides a new and broad environment for the field of design. When Birkeland (2002) raised a new version of design concept, she summarized as below:

- Responsibility — The target is re-defined relying on demand. Social/ecological equity and justice are paid attention to.
- Synergy—A positive synergetic mechanism is established. The systematic change is promoted from all kinds of different elements.
- Background—The significance of design convention and concept on social transformation is re-evaluated.
- Entirety—An analysis is made from the perspective of the whole product life cycle to make sure that design results are really low-impact, low cost and multifunctional.
- Authorization—The development of human being's potential and self-sufficient ability as well as understanding of ecological problems are promoted in an appropriate manner.
- Restoration—The integration of civilized society with natural world is made to cultivate an interest and curiosity.

- Ecological benefits—The tenet is actively positioned at the level of increasing energy, materials and economy of cost.
- Originality—Representing a new kind of paradigm, it can transcend traditional boundary of subject ideology to reach a "new realm".
- Vision—Focusing on vision and results, it imagines the appropriate method, tool and process to deliver them [2].

Therefore, every designer should have a future-oriented (sustainable) learning ability, starting with per se, jointly changing our living environment through sustainable design.

2.6 Designers Should Draw Cultural Self-confidence, Heritage and Integration, Extension and Creation from China's Own Traditional Arts

Given its immense influences on the development of modern art design, traditional national culture has become an integral part of the former. It is an indispensable spiritual treasure of Chinese people. Traditional Chinese culture accumulates abundant national cultural materials for our nation in the cultural precipitation process of 5,000 years. It's mainly reflected in such various aspects as Chinese characters, traditional spirit, traditional graph, ink painting and artistic conception, and traditional handicraft art. Although China's native art design has made some brilliant achievements in recent years, its effect is barely satisfactory. Under the circumstances that globalization tendency rapidly predominates in the contemporary society, China's modern art design does not only need a regression of "tradition" and "indigenization" but also keep pace with the times so as to connect with the world and carry it forward simultaneously. This is a kind of reflection of China's designers on traditional national culture, and even a sort of responsibility. What's good is that Chinese people have a deep recognition of traditional culture. In such a modernized society, what we need to do is not to abandon it but to try all means to put Traditional Chinese culture into modern elements and make a good presentation. Although it's seen from the outside that they are only some symbols and forms, these symbols and forms exactly reflect China's cultural spirit of 5,000 years if they are understood truly [4].

Art design constantly goes deep into diversified cultural atmosphere. The abandonment of a shadow, narrow and prejudiced cognition of China's traditional cultural education cannot be made only relying on simple connection and indiscriminate imitation but deeply understanding quintessence and soul of traditional culture. We advocate that high-level works with ethnic flavor are truly designed by integrating traditional culture with modern design, combining aesthetic taste and thinking mode of modern people and retaining art essence and national aesthetic features of China's native design. A broad horizon and creative spirit should be owned to actively absorb all fruits of excellent culture in the world. Only triggering creative inspiration from national culture and art based on profound knowledge of cultural background and unique view can designers create the works belonging to the nation and becoming astonishing masterpieces, more and better art works, and serve China's socialist modernization construction.

Figures 9, 10, 11, 12, 13, 14, 15, 16 and 17 are illustration design works for utensils made by the students majored in visual communication design at Beijing Institute of Technology, Zhuhai. It's inclined to be emphasized in class training that Traditional Chinese culture is taken as elements to make design. While taking tradition for reference, they represent new charm of their works by combining with the elements of times vividly.

Fig. 9. Illustration designs for utensil of robes series in Qing Dynasty

Fig. 10. Traditional dermatoglyphic pattern series

Fig. 11. Dunhuang frescoes series

Fig. 12. Aspiration series

Fig. 13. Facial makeup and cartoon series porcelain series

Fig. 14. Chaozhou-Shantou embedded

Fig. 15. Chinese plants and dermatoglyphic pattern series

Fig. 16. Overseas Chinese hometown "Kaiping"—gourmet and watchtower series

Fig. 17. Chinese zodiac series

Designers should master the ability to harmonize the five major elements, i.e., technology, materials, usage, structure and modeling.

Because product design is a practical subject, the cognition and understanding of materials play an important role in product design. It cannot only remain in the ideas. Designers need to consider the feasibility of implementing the ideas and enable them to be made in mass production, guaranteeing the integrity of original ideas. The relations between materials, craft, structure, usage and style design in the design are interactional. A kind of design promotes the improvement of craft sometimes, and a sort of new craft and new material can react upon the design so as to upgrade the design sometimes. It's a kind of means for designers to master the knowledge of arts and crafts materials. That serves the design. Designers need extensive basic knowledge of materials to guarantee the feasibility of implementing the design. In addition to cognition of basic knowledge of materials such as physical property and chemical attribute, they need to supplement the cognition of place of origin, price, use and surface texture besides material performance for the purpose of arousing desire for use of creation. They need to pay attention to the relation between materials and form in craft, understanding molding law of general materials and limitation of materials technology on the form. Additionally, they can remedy the shortcomings and defects of materials and craft by relying on excellent design.

Fig. 18. Woven bamboo stools by Cheng-Tsung FENG, a Taiwan designer

As displayed in Fig. 18, they are woven bamboo works from Taiwan designer named Cheng-Tsung FENG. Such ancient traditional materials as bamboos are given new vitality and vigor in the hands of younger designers. The perfect combination between traditional craft and modern aesthetics does not only unfold the aesthetic perception of bamboo wood per se but also allow the people to see that it's a spring of inspiration. The modeling and structural design with crossed net rack can completely bear the weight of human body. Five major elements, i.e., technology, materials, usage, structure and modeling are harmonized perfectly in the works.

2.7 The Mode of Sharing, Cooperation and Collaboration Will Become the Working Style for Designers in the New Era

At present, with the dramatic outburst of such technologies as internet, big data, AI and cloud computing and significant breakthrough of cloud technology particularly, an earth-shaking changes occur in the whole industrial design community. The internet brings us the possibility of collective collaboration. The blind design mode with one person or one isolate team will change. The open-mindedness and sharing culture of "Internet + cloud" will make designers' soul crash into each other. Consequently, more intelligent sparkles are generated.

China has implemented the policy of 「Made in China 2025」 actively in recent years. CIIF held currently in Shanghai naturally becomes the focus of attention of global industry. Among it, 「Uni-Orange」 newly established within two years has successfully attracted the attention of industry and media in globally initiative sharing mode of industrial design.

The Internet of Things breaks the fence of various industries that scarcely intervened each other or had less intersection in the past, allowing the industry with the parallel operation to start to ponder in a vertical way. However, it's not easy to make an interdisciplinary development in a short time. Therefore, the enterprises usually assist themselves make development by virtue of external resources or in a way of releasing resources. For example, Advantech makes overall arrangement of cloud service industry focally developed in next stage with 「co-creation」 strategy, becoming a propellent of this industrial development in a form of alliance. For the enterprises with small scale, high R&D cost and deficient technology, the way of sharing resources that is just like a burst of timely rain allows the enterprises to obtain the most appropriate resources under the limited conditions.

Uni-Orange, founded in 2015, has demonstrated to the outside a collaborative R&D design cloud platform CDS (Collaborative Design System), initiating the collaborative industrial design mode of [industry +cloud]. Through the sharing resources platform, Uni-Orange enables customers to solve their problems by outside resources. Using the concept of cloud platform, CDS connects designers, engineers, and technology experts from different areas, and carry out R&D designing works by means of division of labor and collaboration, which can bring holistic industrial design solutions for enterprises with inadequate technology support.

For enterprises with inadequate creative ability, all global elite designer teams may be for their use, satisfying their needs for product creativity, and solving problem such as R&D costs and technology barriers. By the mode of collaboration and cooperation, the R&D designing efficiency of Uni-orange is two to three times higher than that of other counterpart product companies who are using the traditional mode. While the running mode of this platform enables customers to submit the needs waiting to be fulfilled after registering on the official website of Uni-orange. CDS platforms will assign the right human resource to customers, and tailor a feasible solution plan. Even if sometimes customers do not have a understanding of what products they really want, but only a vague requirement, the professional team and instruments on CDS can rapidly assist customers to discern problems, and put forward the outline of designing plan pertinently.

The most heated topic now is "sharing economy". The former phase of sharing economy focuses on labor sharing and idle resources sharing, while the later should focus on intelligence sharing and creativity sharing. The former is like a physical process while the later chemical action, which means a new value is derived from the integration of resources. For example, the chemical action of integrating user, designer and manufacturer is that the user puts forward needs and pain point, the designer figures out solution plan for the pain point, and the manufacturer immediately judges the feasibility of the plan. New commercial mode will be derived from sharing intelligence. For example, if the consumer point out an absolute pain point and the designer puts forward an excellent solution plan, they can totally own the copyright of the product and royalty from sales, since the product belongs to every participant. Even in the future, the genuine brand, even the industry can be shared.

Since 2004 when the enterprise owns over 1,000 staff, LKK has ranked the top in the industry. Looking at the data for the whole industry, there are 160 million people taking the job of designing, which means that a resource of 150 million designers in this industry is available. How to share this resource? Today, our theme is AI. AI can optimally help people to improve working efficiency in some fields, and free some repetitive work. Just as physical sharing and human resource sharing, LKKer is such a platform for "brain sharing", where the ideas of every common user and every designer can generate maxim value.

Back to the innovative design for products, the traditional method is that with their designing experience, designers like to habitually put his experience into the designing works. While in AI era, it is difficult to help an enterprise to carry out industrial upgrade if the designers do not have an understanding of market, technology, or the products are made without the support of big data. Therefore, on the basis of AI and big data, LKKer platform is in assistance of designing for enterprises by a new mode. With all designers on the platform providing product data support, and industrial data support, users can design the product together with designers. For enterprises, instead of enterprises' technology deciding products' definition, it is the combination of users' needs, users' scenes, users' values and innovation power of the designer that push enterprises to do industrial upgrades.

Therefore, the mode of sharing, cooperation and collaboration will be the major working mode for designers in the new era.

3 Conclusions

In conclusion, under the background of intelligent era, what professional qualities should a product designer possess to genuinely go with the future design, and face the new challenges brought by the intelligent era? This essay elaborates on basic requirements for professional qualities of product designers in eight major aspects. First, through the analyses for Design & Artificial Intelligence Report written by "Tongji x Tezign Design & Artificial Intelligence Laboratory", it's ensured that in the future, the originality and creativity of product designer will be designers' core competence; second, through two cases, one of which is the cross-border cooperation between Sonda Studio and the DHMZ to design the label for piquentum st vital with the whole label showing the weather of the whole year, it is certain that cross-border can well satisfy customer's needs. Thus, designers should be equipped with the designing abilities for creativity through the multi-dimensional perspective, subject collisions and cross-border experiments; third, by the case analyses for the designs of coffee pot and trash can, it can be concluded that function is more important than form. Therefore, designers should base their design on solving practical problems; fourth, from the analyses from the perspective of social responsibility and significance of design, designers should care for the vulnerable groups from the perspective of society and services, and design for love; fifth, in order to solve the problems of the environment we live by and energy problems, designers should acquire a future-oriented (sustainable) learning ability; sixth, take the example of the course assignments for the students in Beijing Institute of Technology, Zhuhai, the Chinese culture is broad and profound, therefore, designers should draw cultural self-confidence, heritage and integration, extension and creation from China's own traditional arts; seventh, by the case analyses of works of woven bamboo stools designed by the Taiwan designer Cheng-Tsung FENG, it shows that designers should master the ability to harmonize the five major elements, i.e., technology, materials, usage, structure and modeling; eighth, with the overwhelming explosion of technologies such as Internet, big data, AI, and cloud computing, taking the example of Uni-Orange Design and LKK companies, it is demonstrated that designers should have the consciousness and abilities for sharing, coordination, and cooperation; ninth, through the analysis of third item, the design works of designers should solve practical problems. The foundation to solve practical problems lies in the analysis and comprehension of the designing objects. From the design service object, designers should study individual per se rationally and objectively through philosophical theories of anthropology, psychology, phenomenology, etc. This conclusion can provide theoretical guidance for the cultivation of professional qualities for product designers in the new era.

References

1. Fan, L.: Design & Artificial Intelligence Report 2017, Tongji x Tezign Design & Artificial Intelligence Laboratory (2017)
2. Bhamra, T., Lofthouse, V.: Design for Sustainability—A Practical Approach. China Architecture & Building Press, Beijing (2017)
3. Russ, T.: Sustainability and Design Ethics. Chongqing University Press, Chongqing (2016)
4. Jiao, C., Zhang, X.: A Brief Analysis of Influences of Traditional Chinese Culture on Modern Art Design, Today's Massmedia, August 2014
5. A Research on China's Intelligent Manufacturing and Design Development Strategy. Zhejiang University Press, May 2016
6. Norman: The Design of Everyday Things, China CITIC Press, Beijing (2016)
7. Yu, Y.: Cross-border Thinking: Practices of Interaction Design. Zhejiang University Press, Hangzhou (2016)
8. Sato, O.: Solve Problems with Design. Beijing Times Chinese Press, Beijing (2016). (Japan)

9. Kant: The Practical Anthropology. China Renmin University Press, Beijing (2013). (Germany)
10. He, S., et al.: Materials and Processes of Product Design. Publishing House of Electronic Industry, Beijing (2014)
11. Xun, S.: Source and Stream—Traditional Culture and Modern Design. Jiangxi Fine Arts Publishing House, Nanjing (2007)

The Construction of Cultural Impressions for the Idea of Cultural Products

Po-Hsien Lin[1]([✉]) and Mo-Li Yeh[2]

[1] Graduate School of Creative Industry Design, National Taiwan University of Arts, Daguan Road, Banqiao District, New Taipei City 22058, Taiwan
t0131@ntua.edu.tw
[2] Graduate School of Product and Media Design, Fo Guang University, Taiwan
No. 160, Linwei Road, Jiaosi, Yilan County 26247, Taiwan
110lmoli@gmail.com

Abstract. What determines if a product is perceived as a cultural artefact? What impressions of a product result in consumers' impressions of cultural creativity? David Hume in his book *Treatise of Human Nature* claimed the perceptions of the human mind resolved themselves into two distinct kinds, impressions and ideas. He claimed that simple impressions always take precedence over their corresponding ideas. Hume brought up seven fundamental relations between impressions and ideas, (1) Resemblance, (2) Identity, (3) Space and time, (4) Proportions in quantity, (5) Degrees in quality, (6) Contrariety, and (7) Cause and effect. Based on the perspective of Hume's theory of relation, a questionnaire was developed to obtain information required for style analysis in this study. Through the statistical techniques of Multidimensional Scaling (MDS) and Multiple Regression Analysis, this study explored the cultural impressions of 10 prominent Taiwan cultural products selected from the domestic market. The results of the study suggested that Hume's theory of seven fundamental relations could be applied to interpret the connections between impressions and ideas regarding viewers' perception of the cultural features of a product. Of the seven relations, (5) Degrees in quality contributed significant positive weight to a product's cultural feature. The relation (6) Contrariety demonstrated the diversity within all seven relations.

Keywords: Cultural creativity · Cultural product · Impression
Idea

1 Introduction

In recent years, the Taiwanese government has been aggressively promoting culture creative industries. The goal of this policy is to develop a new economic model and better the living environment through attracting consumers with cultural products and aesthetic experiences. Many studies pointed out that designing products which emphasize local features to increase their cultural value has become a significant facet of the design process [4, 9].

How to define cultural products? How to know that a product is perceived as cultural? What impressions of a product resulted in consumers' idea of cultural

© Springer International Publishing AG, part of Springer Nature 2018
P.-L. P. Rau (Ed.): CCD 2018, LNCS 10912, pp. 212–224, 2018.
https://doi.org/10.1007/978-3-319-92252-2_16

creativity? These questions have become critical in many design competitions, grant-funded projects, and academic arguments. In order to explore how visual experiences were turned into mental ideas, David Hume's theory of connections between impressions and ideas was employed in this study to develop the questionnaire [5]. Based on the perspective of Hume's theory of relation, this study examined the cultural impression of Taiwan modern products. Through an approach of style analysis, 10 prominent Taiwan cultural products were selected from the domestic market as stimuli. The results of the study were expected to reinforce theoretical support for cultural creative design.

2 Research Purpose

Based on the perspective of Hume's theory of relation, this study examined the cultural impression of Taiwan modern products. Through an approach of style analysis, 10 pieces of famous Taiwan cultural products selected from the domestic market as stimuli. The results of the study were expected to reinforce theoretical support for cultural creative design.

3 Literature Review

3.1 An Exploration of the Significance of Culture

In his etymological study, Raymond Williams claimed that the word "culture" is one of the most complicated words in the English language [15]. People usually define culture as "the way of life for an entire society" [3, 7]. This description is simple, easy to understand, and yet ambiguous. In addition to this popular definition, Williams concluded there were another two important aspects of culture. The first is to describe a general process of intellectual, spiritual and aesthetic development. The second is to describe the works and practices of intellectual and especially artistic activity [15]. A more precise depiction of culture is to regard culture as that which deals with the result of the evolutionary process in human civilization based on linguistic, anthropological, and sociological studies [13, 17].

Design scholars have been devoted to researching product semantics since the 80s. Krippendorff and Butter claimed that conventional semantics focused on the interrelationship between sigh, referent and thought, emphasizing linguistic expression; product semantics, on the other hand, regards a product as a symbol system. They suggested that a product designer should investigate the symbolic qualities of a product from the perspectives of its operation and application [6]. To sum up, culture generally refers to styles of human activity and the symbolic structures involving ideologies, languages, customs, religions, arts, and behaviors [16].

3.2 An Exploration of Human Perception of Impressions and Ideas

Over the past decades, many scholars have been devoted to the study of cultural creative design models. Leong and Clark suggest a brief framework for investigating cultural product design, dividing it into three space structures: the external concrete tactile level, middle behavioral level and the inner invisible spiritual level [7].

Norman presents in his book "Emotional Design" three levels of emotional design-visceral, behavioral and reflective. The visceral level involves direct sensations when in touch with a product, including shape, style, tactile impression, material and weight. The behavioral level is non-conscious, including the pleasure after exercise, or the delight after a shower. The reflective level represents conscious behaviors such as the pop culture or style and tastes [12]. Hsu et al. expand the three levels, offering a more detailed explication, and provide a cultural creative design model which could further facilitate comparison, application and thinking for design (Fig. 1) [4].

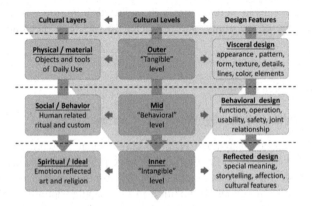

Fig. 1. Three layers of cultural creative design model [4]

This theoretical framework has been put into practice in some projects, for example, in a study entitled *Applying Sakizaya Tribe's Palamal (the Fire God Ritual) into Cultural Creative Products Design*, the design model was employed to create seven pieces of cultural product. The outcome of the study showed that the products were generally appreciated by the reviewers though there were some preference differences between tribal members and the general public [8]. The result of the survey indicated that the reviewers confirmed the application of cultural elements in the product design was successful. However, no further information was revealed on how a product demonstrated its cultural features. To answer this question requires a return to the original inquiry—what makes a product look cultural?

Hill in his book *Meaning, Mind, and Knowledge* discussed the topic of the philosophy of mind. He used the idea of "visual qualia" to explain human visual experience of observing an object [2]. According to Hill, perceptual qualia are the ways that things look, seem, and appear to conscious observers. He further divided visual qualia into two distinctions. The first is "phenomenological sense" expressing how an object looks to an observer. The second is "epistemic sense" which expresses how the observer's current visual experience provides adequate evidential support for the belief that the object looks like [1, 2].

How to turn a sensational experience into conceptual idea is not only the topic for contemporary psychology and Cognitive Science, it is also an important philosophical issue in human history. According to David Hume, a famous Scottish philosopher known for his highly influential philosophical empiricism, all the perceptions of the human mind resolved themselves into two distinct kinds, which were called impressions and ideas [5]. He claimed that the simple impressions always take precedence over their correspondent ideas. In his book *Treatise of Human Nature*, Hume brought up seven fundamental relations between ideas including (1) Resemblance, (2) Cause and effect, (3) Space and time, (4) Identity, (5) Contrariety, (6) Proportions in quantity, and (7) Degrees in quality [5] (Fig. 2).

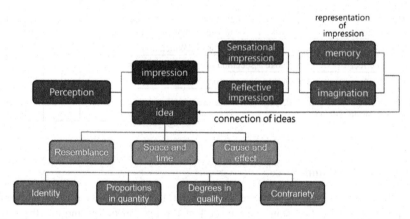

Fig. 2. David Hume's theoretical framework of relations between impressions and ideas

4   Research Methodology

4.1   Research Process

This study intends to explore the cultural impression of Taiwan's modern products. Based on the perspective of Hume's theory of relation. An online questionnaire was developed to examine the 10 pieces of famous Taiwan cultural products selected from the domestic market.

After obtaining the data required for style analysis, this study employed "Multidimensional Scaling" (MDS). MDS is usually used to classify observational values, and is a data analysis method for determining whether a potential structure exists in the data [14]. A statistical technique of Multiple Regression Analysis was employed to explore the significance of these relations in cultural features of the works.

4.2   Research Instrument

Through the five-point scale composing Hume's seven fundamental relations between idea and impression, this study developed a questionnaire to examine participants' reactions to 10 pieces of selected products. Three additional questions were designed to evaluate their opinions about the degree of cultural feature and creativity demonstrated in the product, and the preference of the product (Table 1).

Table 1. The five-point scale of the questionnaire

items	descriptions	5	4	3	2	1
Resemblance	Function or form is similar					
Identity	Function or form is identical					
Space and time	Time sequence or space composition is related					
Proportions in quantity	Evoke association from proportion					
Degrees in quality	Evoke association from style or taste					
Contrariety	Evoke opposite or ironic association					
Cause and effect	Evoke association from causal relationship					
Degree of cultural feature demonstrated in the product						
Degree of creativity demonstrated in the product						
Preference of the product						

4.3   Research Stimuli

As for the selection process of the research object, the products were chosen from two selection stages. The first stage was to collect through an online inquiry the top 20 items recommended by the students and teachers of design departments of the universities in Taiwan. The second stage was to select 10 pieces of representative products from the 20 items in the first stage through the same approach (Table 2).

5   Research Results and Data Analysis

5.1   Analysis of Integrated Impression of the Products

This study analyzed participants' impression towards the products. They evaluated each piece on the degree of cultural feature and creativity demonstrated in the product. The mean scores and the rank of 10 products were shown in Tables 3 and 4. A Preference was designed for evaluating overall impression of the product. The outcome was shown in Table 5.

The Kendall's coefficient of concordance was employed to examine whether the 10 selected products were ranked consistently in three domains of evaluation. The calculated outcome $W = .004$ suggested that there was no significant consistency. However, the ranking of p3, p4, and p7 constantly appeared in the top three.

Table 2. Titles and codes of 10 representative works of the study

p1	p2	p3	p4	p5
Paper Tape by National Palace Museum	*Four Divine Beasts Cups* by National Taiwan University of Arts	*Bamboo Chair* by National Taiwan Craft R&D Institute	*Ceramic Steamer* by JIA Inc.	*Pineapple Cake* by Sunnyhills Inc.

p6	p7	p8	p9	p10
Porcelain Tableware by Franz Inc.	*Ceramic Dumpling Seasoning Set* by Hakka-blue Studio	*Rice Wine* by Sinyi Township Farmers' Association	*Mandarin Lemon Squeezer* by Alessi S. P. A.	*Wooden Toys* by Mufun Design Studio

Table 3. The ranking of the degree of cultural feature

Rank	1	2	3	4	5	6	7	8	9	10
No	p4	p7	p3	p10	p2	p9	p6	p5	p1	p8
Products										
Mean Scores	4.01	3.97	3.89	3.67	3.44	3.43	3.33	3.27	3.22	3.01

5.2   Style Analysis of the Products

A matrix was created from the raw data to illustrate the mean scores of the seven fundamental relations in each of the 10 products as shown in Table 6. The matrix allowed SPSS statistics software to compute MDS and generate a two-dimensional

Table 4. The ranking of the degree of creativity

Rank	1	2	3	4	5	6	7	8	9	10
No	p7	p4	p3	p10	p9	p1	p6	p2	p5	p8
Products										
Mean Scores	4.24	4.16	4.11	3.93	3.83	3.67	3.46	3.34	3.24	2.89

Table 5. The ranking of the preference

Rank	1	2	3	4	5	6	7	7	9	10
No	p4	p3	p7	p10	p1	p5	p6	p9	p2	p8
Products										
Mean Scores	4.19	4.17	4.16	3.84	3.60	3.49	3.36	3.36	3.23	2.79

(2D) spatial plot demonstrating the relationship between two crucial correspondence indices. The Kruskal's stress was .09254, which was less than 0.1 and the determination coefficient (RSQ) was .97650, which was close to 1.0, indicating that the spatial relationships between the 10 products and seven fundamental relations could be appropriately represented in 2D. The stress index indicated that the 2D plot and the original data exhibited a satisfactory fit; the RSQ indicated that the 2D plot was capable of explaining 97.65% of the variance [11].

Another important information is OD distances in a MSD plot. On the coordinate plane, each point of the observed products has an orthogonal projection on the vectors. The formula for calculating OD distance is shown in Fig. 3. The value of b2/b1 is the slope of vector. The vector projection of D onto the origin O demonstrates the characteristic strength, of which the vector contributes to the product (Fig. 4).

Table 7 shows the values of OD distance in the vectors of seven fundamental relations for each of the 10 products. Taking Resemblance (f1) as example, the OD distance of p4 was 1.84, demonstrating the greatest strength in all products. According to the OD distance in each vector of the fundamental relations, the *Ceramic Steamer* (p4) surpassed the other products in f1, f2, f3, f5, and f7. The *Ceramic Dumpling Seasoning Set* (p7) took the lead in f4. The *Paper Tape* (f1) exceeded the other products in f6.

An exploratory factor analysis (EFA) was conducted to search for latent variables within seven fundamental relations. Two factors were extracted with eigenvalues greater than 1.0 and total variance explained 82.641 as shown in Table 8. The first

Table 6. Mean scores of the seven fundamental relations in each of the 10 products

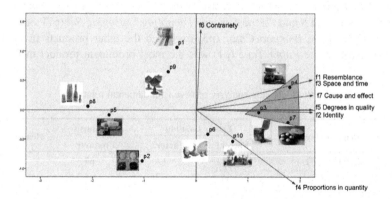

		p1	p2	p3	p4	p5	p6	p7	p8	p9	p10
Resemblance	f1	3.76	3.13	3.91	4.37	3.13	3.77	4.24	3.04	3.63	3.81
Identity	f2	3.14	3.03	3.71	4.11	3.00	3.64	3.97	3.03	3.37	3.61
Space and time	f3	3.21	3.01	3.47	3.41	2.80	3.01	3.34	2.77	3.24	3.27
Proportions in quantity	f4	2.63	3.21	3.30	3.16	2.66	3.10	3.57	2.53	2.79	3.51
Degrees in quality	f5	3.89	3.63	4.24	4.11	3.34	3.81	4.17	3.07	3.40	3.77
Contrariety	f6	2.63	2.09	2.27	2.14	2.13	2.04	2.28	2.20	2.51	2.33
Cause and effect	f7	3.01	2.91	3.23	3.37	3.26	2.97	3.27	2.96	3.14	3.34

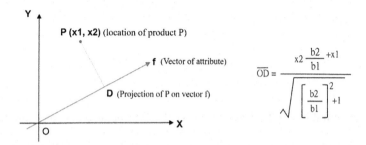

Fig. 3. Cognitive space distribution of the 10 products and seven fundamental relations

$$\overline{OD} = \frac{x2\dfrac{b2}{b1}+x1}{\sqrt{\left[\dfrac{b2}{b1}\right]^2+1}}$$

P (x1, x2) (location of product P)

f (Vector of attribute)

D (Projection of P on vector f)

Fig. 4. Cognitive space distribution of the 10 products and seven fundamental relations

Table 7. OD distances in the vectors of seven relations for each of the 10 products

		p1	p2	p3	p4	p5	p6	p7	p8	p9	p10
Resemblance	f1	-0.10	-1.22	1.16	1.84	-1.65	0.12	1.66	-2.01	-0.36	0.55
Identity	f2	-0.38	-1.03	1.21	1.80	-1.67	0.23	1.77	-2.09	-0.54	0.71
Space and time	f3	-0.09	-1.22	1.16	1.84	-1.64	0.11	1.66	-2.01	-0.36	0.55
Proportions in quantity	f4	-0.92	-0.33	1.00	1.23	-1.30	0.43	1.55	-1.72	-0.82	0.89
Degrees in quality	f5	-0.36	-1.04	1.20	1.80	-1.68	0.22	1.76	-2.09	-0.53	0.70
Contrariety	f6	1.04	-0.92	0.02	0.48	-0.18	-0.40	-0.12	-0.05	0.62	-0.50
Cause and effect	f7	-0.24	-1.13	1.19	1.83	-1.67	0.18	1.73	-2.07	-0.46	0.64

dimension included six items of fundamental relations except Contrariety (f6), which was also the only item in the second dimension.

The most prominent product and its mean score in each fundamental relation was also listed in Table 8. In the first dimension, the *Ceramic Steamer* (p4) surpassed the other products in f1, f2, and f7; the *Ceramic Dumpling Seasoning Set* (p7) took the lead in f4 and f5; and the *Bamboo Chair* (p3) exceeded the other products in f3. In the second dimension, the *Paper Tape* (p1) was the most prominent product in f6.

Table 8. Factor analysis of seven fundamental relations

Fundamental Relations	Factor Loading		Prominent Products	Mean Scores
	Factor1	Factor2		
Resemblance (f1)	.943	.170	p4	4.37
Identity (f2)	.942	-.125	p4	4.11
Degrees in quality (f5)	.904	.031	P7	4.17
Space and time (f3)	.902	.342	P3	3.47
Proportions in quantity (f4)	.798	-.352	p7	3.57
Cause and effect (f7)	.698	.039	p4	3.37
Contrariety (f6)	.041	.982	p1	2.63
Eigenvalues	4.532	1.253		
% of Variance	64.746	17.895		
Cumulative %	64.746	82.641		

5.3   Seven Fundamental Relations to Predict Degree of Cultural Feature

To explore how seven fundamental relations affected the cultural feature when reviewing the products, this study further selected the top three products to conduct multiple regression analyses, taking seven fundamental relations as independent variables and the participant's impression of cultural feature on the product as a dependent variable. The following are the results of the three examined products (Tables 8, 9 and 10).

Table 9. Multiple regression analyses with fundamental relations as the dependent variable (p3)

Products	Predictor Variables	B	r	β	t
	f1	.063	.354**	.072	.516
	f2	.160	.415***	.195	1.298
	f3	.054	.319**	.063	.407
	f4	-.094	.279*	-.137	-.849
	f5	.261	.352**	.229	2.020*
	f6	.211	.439***	.333	2.334*
Bamboo Chair (p3)	f7	.011	.327**	.017	.126
	R=.566		R^2=.320	F=4.177**	

*p <0.05 **p <0.01 ***p <0.001

Table 10. Multiple regression analyses with fundamental relations as the dependent variable (p4)

Products	Predictor Variables	B	r	β	t
	f1	.322	.427***	.302	2.030*
	f2	.021	.388***	.022	.146
	f3	.001	.268*	.001	.009
	f4	.089	.221*	.152	.910
	f5	.246	.412***	.258	2.170*
Ceramic Steamer	f6	-.016	.078	-.025	-.189
(p4)	f7	.085	.289**	.140	.926
	R=.563		R^2=.317	F=4.107**	

*p <0.05 **p <0.01 ***p <0.001

In the product of the *Bamboo Chair*, the multiple regression model with all seven predictors produced R^2 = .320, F = 4.177, suggesting a statistically significant association between independent variables and the dependent variable (p < .01). As can be seen in Table 8, f5 and f6 scales had significant positive regression weights, indicating the product with higher scores on the f5 (Degrees in quality) and f6 (Contrariety) was expected to have the strongest cultural impression.

In the product of the *Ceramic Steamer*, the multiple regression model with all seven predictors produced $R^2 = .317$, $F = 4.107$, suggesting a statistically significant association between independent variables and the dependent variable ($p < .01$). As can be seen in Table 9, f1 and f5 scales had significant positive regression weights, indicating the product with higher scores on the f1 (Resemblance) and f5 (Degrees in quality) was expected to have the strongest cultural impression (Table 11).

Table 11. Multiple regression analyses with fundamental relations as the dependent variable (p7)

Products	Predictor Variables	B	r	β	t
	f1	.069	.277*	.078	.575
	f2	.063	.240*	.079	.607
	f3	.125	.288**	.180	1.165
	f4	.043	.252*	.048	.344
Ceramic Dumpling	f5	.331	.438***	.347	2.621*
Seasoning Set	f6	.055	.089	.086	.682
(p7)	f7	-.095	.117	-.133	-.916
	R=.499		R^2=.249	F=2.933*	

*p <0.05 **p <0.01 ***p <0.001

In the product of the *Ceramic Dumpling Seasoning Set*, the multiple regression model with all seven predictors produced $R^2 = .249$, $F = 2.933$, suggesting a statistically significant association between independent variables and the dependent variable ($p < .05$). As can be seen in Table 10, f5 scales had significant positive regression weight, indicating the product with higher scores on the f5 (Degrees in quality) was expected to have the strongest cultural impression.

6   Conclusion and Recommendations

6.1   Discussion of Findings

This study used the perspective of Hume's theory on the connection between impression and idea to examine the how customers perceived the cultural impression of a cultural product. Discussed below are some important findings:

1. Through an integrated evaluation on cultural feature, creative, and preference of the 10 selected products, though there was no significant correlation of the ranking within, three products including the *Bamboo Chair* (p3), the *Ceramic Steamer* (p4), and the *Ceramic Dumpling Seasoning Set* (p7) were jointly ranked as the top three prominences out of all the products. As shown in the cognitive space illustrated by the MDS plot, these three products spread collectively along the positive side of the

x-axis, the same direction of the vectors of Hume's six relations of Resemblance (f1), Identity (f2), Space and time (f3), Proportions in quantity (p4), Degrees in quality (p5), and Cause and effect (f7). This outcome suggested the perception of cultural feature could be linked to most of Hume's theoretical relations.

2. Through factor analysis, one of Hume's relations of Contrariety (f6) was categorized as a unique factor, separated from another factor wherein the other six relations were grouped together. By checking the MDS plot, the distribution of vector f6 and the other vectors was orthogonal, suggesting the diversity of Contrariety within all seven relations.

3. Through Multiple Regression Analysis, this study employed participants' perception of Hume's seven fundamental relations to predict their cultural impressions when reviewing a cultural product. The results of the study suggested that Hume's theory of seven fundamental relations could be applied to interpret the connections between impressions and ideas regarding viewers' perception of cultural features in a product. Among the seven relations, Degrees in quality (f5) contributed significant positive weight to a product's cultural feature. By checking the MDS plot, the vectors f5 and f6 were at right angles to each other, suggesting that the relation of Contrariety did not correlate with Degrees in quality and was statistically independent of the other relations.

6.2   Conclusion

This study attempted to employ David Hume's theory to explore the possible connection between reviewers' impression and idea, trying to answer how a product was perceived as cultural and what impressions of a product resulted in consumers' idea of cultural features. The theoretical framework of this study was derived from a traditional philosophic conception proposed in the eighteenth century. While conventional theory could be attractive, however, there are plenty of modern theories of cognitive psychology and neuroscience which could support the related investigations. From this point of view, the motif of this study is nostalgic rather than scientific. However, this study manifested humanist concerns for cultural issues by using an empirical approach to reiterate early philosophers' articulation about their achievement on the development of human spiritual civilization.

6.3   Further Research and Recommendations

6.3.1   Extension of Theoretical Sustains

As mentioned in literatures review, Christopher S. Hill used the idea of "visual qualia" to explain human visual experience of observing an object and divided visual qualia into two distinctions of "phenomenological sense" and "epistemic sense". Future research is recommended to apply Hill's theory to expand and deepen the theoretical framework of the study.

6.3.2   Derivation of Interdisciplinary Research

In this study, participants were invited to express their perceptions of the cultural products through subjective visual experience. The application of modern theories of cognitive psychology and neuroscience is suggested for further study.

References

1. Byrne, A.: Hill on mind. Philos. Stud. **173**(3), 831–839 (2016)
2. Hill, C.: Meaning, Mind, and Knowledge. Oxford University Press, Oxford (2014)
3. Ho, M.C., Lin, C.H., Liu, Y.C.: Some speculations on developing cultural commodities. J. Des. **1**(1), 1–15 (1996)
4. Hsu, C.H., Lin, R.T., Chiu, W.K.: Taiwanese aboriginal product design. In: International Innovation Design Symposium Thesis, pp. 157–164 (2004)
5. Hume, D.: A Treatise of Human Nature. Penguin Books, London (1985). Original work published in 1738
6. Krippendorff, K., Butter, R.: Product semantics: exploring the symbolic qualities of form. Innovation, 4–9 (1984)
7. Leong, B.D., Clark, H.: Culture-based knowledge towards new design thinking and practice —a dialogue. Des. Issues **19**(3), 48–58 (2003)
8. Lin, P.H., Tseng, J.H., Tsou, C.Y.: A study of applying Saisait Tribe's Tabaa Sang (buttocks bell) into cultural creative industry from a cross-disciplinary perspective. In: 2012 AHFE International Conference, San Francisco, CA, USA, 21–25 July 2012, pp. 8488–8499. USA Publishing (CD-ROM Format) (2012). ISBN-13: 978-0-9796435-5-2
9. Lin, R.T.: Creative learning model for cross-cultural products. Arts Apprec. **1**(12), 52–59 (2005)
10. Lin, R.T.: Transforming Taiwan aboriginal cultural features into modern product design: a case study of cross-cultural product design model. Int. J. Des. **1**(2), 45–53 (2007)
11. Lin, Z.Y.: Multivariate Analysis. Best-Wise Publishing Co., Ltd., Taipei (2007)
12. Norman, D.A.: Emotional Design: Why We Love (or Hate) Everyday Things. Basic Books, New York (2004)
13. Schoenmakers, H.: The Power of Culture: A Short History of Anthropological Theory About Culture and Power. University of Groningen, Groningen (2012)
14. Wang, P.C.: Multivariate Analysis. Higher Education Publishing Co., Taipei (2003)
15. Williams, R.: Keywords: A Vocabulary of Culture and Society. Oxford University Press, Oxford (1983)
16. Wu, T.Y., Hsu, C.H., Lin, R.T.: A study of Taiwan aboriginal culture on product design. In: Redmond, J., Durling, D., de Bono, A. (eds.) Proceedings of Design Research Society International Conference – Futureground (Paper No. 238). Monash University, Melbourne (2004)
17. Yeh, M.L., Lin, P.H.: Applying local culture features into creative craft products design. In: Rau, P.L.P. (ed.) IDGD 2011. LNCS, vol. 6775, pp. 114–122. Springer, Heidelberg (2011). https://doi.org/10.1007/978-3-642-21660-2_13

Chinese Sociocultural Perspectives and Creativity: Design Practices in the Public Transport Sector

Sara E. Sterling[(✉)] and Bingjian Liu

Xi'an Jiaotong-Liverpool University,
Suzhou 215123, People's Republic of China
sara.sterling@xjtlu.edu.cn

Abstract. Creativity in China in the current era of globalization has become a buzzword for industry, acting as a catalyst for innovative potential and investment. However, while 'Made in China' has long been established, 'Created in China' still requires some legitimization internationally, and alongside creativity comes the need for a more nuanced, cross-cultural perspective in design and manufacturing alike. The 'Belt and Road' initiative is one key national plan in this larger globalization-oriented process and the high speed train, which has been referred to as China's 'national identity card', plays a symbolic role in this initiative. Exporting public transport systems, e.g. high speed trains, to international markets inevitably brings with it the challenge of cross-cultural issues, due to the different cultural background of prospective passengers. The nature of creativity itself bears an intrinsic link with one's worldview, as the act of creating is variable in different perspectives. While a particular social setting in one country or society may be historically aligned with concepts of creativity or idea-generation, that same social setting elsewhere may be viewed as a deterrent or hindrance. The importance of cross-cultural perceptions of creativity in the realm of idea-generation as related to design thus requires a thorough examination. As the conditions and need for growth in innovative thinking grows, the need to understand creativity as it is understood from a Chinese lens becomes a timely area of focus. This paper will examine the relationship between culture and creativity, as evidenced by a study on employees of a publicly owned transportation company in Mainland China.

Keywords: Chinese culture · Creativity · Innovation · Design
Public transportation

1 Introduction

1.1 Overview

China is viewed in the 21st century as one of the world's foremost advocates of globalization and has launched a series of national strategic plan to enhance its identity in the role of a global player, represented most visibly by the 'Belt and Road' initiative. However, alongside the constant increase of labor costs, China, the 'factory of the world', has gradually lost its global advantage in price of products, from small products such as mobile phones, to large systems like the high speed train. With this background at hand, creativity and innovation have become crucial to the development of industry in China and both companies and company cultures need to readjust frameworks of how to achieve competiveness in both current and future global markets.

Creativity was once the defining characteristic of the country's culture in ancient times, evidenced by the 'Four Great Inventions of Ancient China', for instance. However, from the 1990s onwards, products made in China are often labelled as 'lacking innovation' or even 'copies'. The causes of this situation are varied, owing to economic considerations, technological limitations, or cultural factors. Culture encompasses a wide range of meanings, and the part that is connected to creativity within a company relates not only to the social-cultural background of the country or the cultural background of each employee, but also the culture of the company itself.

ATC (a pseudonym that is used to protect employee confidentiality) is a state-owned enterprise in China in the high-speed train industry. Like other state-owned companies, ATC has the dual attributes of enterprise and society [1] and usually has a strict hierarchy and discipline mechanisms, a situation different from both Western and privately-owned companies in China. An examination of the forms of culture within the company could help further the understanding of its positive and negative impact on creativity and innovation and the analysis as well as conclusions can be used as a reference to for the company to improve its performance of creativity and strengthen its competiveness in the global market.

1.2   Literature Review

Culture as a factor in determining or influencing creativity has long been an area of interest and discussion in studies on the topic. Creativity is broadly defined by Amabile [2] as developing novel and useful ideas regarding products, services, work processes and procedures. While many cross-culturally oriented academics from backgrounds ranging from the Social Sciences to Psychology and beyond have been interested in this phenomenon coming from a Western-centric area of interest, the last two decades have also opened the door to studies stemming from both "East" and "West". Authors in studies of culture and cognition (i.e., Nisbett) [3], have found that the way in which one conceptualizes the world has an impact on how he or she determines and identifies a creative action. Researchers such as Rudowicz and Hui, Morris and Leung, and Hempel and Sue-Chan [4–6] have discussed how Chinese culture affects the judgment and practice of creativity, and in particular how the concept is defined and perceived. In comparison to Western countries, the collectivist-orientation in China's culture, combined with the value placed on obedience, and impacting positively upon a larger social group have led to both a lower overall orientation towards creativity, yet a unique understanding of creativity that is linked to the impact of one's contribution to society.

While there are various terms used to discuss the outlook and background of Chinese culture, a form of dichotomization prevails between "East" and "West" in more general terms, with the "East" normally referring to countries such as China, Japan and Korea (with Russia also sometimes included), and "West" meaning predominantly North America and Western Europe. The concepts and terminology most frequently associated with Chinese, and more broadly Eastern cultures are holistic, dialectical [7], and interdependent, in contrast to Western cultures' logic and analytical descriptions. The roots of these constructions, as mentioned by Nisbett, stem from the philosophical foundations within each culture, again, with Western culture arising from the Greek love of logic, order and democracy, and Eastern from Confucian hierarchical social relationships, and an emphasis on harmony within such hierarchy. A great deal of these cross-cultural studies show a correlation between low levels of perceived creativity in Chinese culture compared with levels in the West, particularly with the United States. Scholars such as Liu et al. [8] call for a recognition that the broadness of "Chinese" culture is not the sole identifier of creativity-levels, however, as other factors such as one's job, major in college/university, and individual personality and family life can also lead to divergences even within the seemingly homogeneous "Chinese" categorization. Niu [9] follows a similar recommendation, guarding against "looking at individual characteristics and ignoring the environment" (p. 21) in examinations of creativity across cultures, bringing for the need to examine environmental as well as personality factors in judging creativity and culture.

One particular feature of Chinese culture as it relates to social obligations and hierarchical roles is the concept of "face", or as Miron-Spektor et al. [10] refer to the term, "face logic". They demonstrate the importance of how one presents oneself to the outside with relation to fulfilling the appearance of maintaining social hierarchy presents itself in the case of creativity. Their findings indicate that "face" is not just a cultural peculiarity, but instead, a significant factor in how one is able to make manifest creative ideas within an organization.

While the broad idea of individualism vs. collectivism is oft-cited as a means of categorizing Chinese culture, there simultaneously exist features in Chinese cultural life that are unique to the region, harkening back to ancient philosophy. Markus and Kitayama [11] refer to the "independent-interdependent perspective of the self", stating that the goal of the self in Chinese and other collectivist cultures is not one of individual attainment of perfection or skill-attainment, but of "becoming part of various interpersonal relationships" (quoted in Niu and Sternberg) [12]. A sense of moral obligation that arises from and is central to culture in the Chinese context is also crucial in analyses of creative-thinking and perception. Further, Niu and Sternberg, in a comparative study of Eastern and Western concepts of creativity, find that in analyzing the factors or characteristics that constitute creativity, culture should indeed be taken into consideration, as cognition and overall perceptions of the term 'creativity' are to some extent culturally variable. As Niu and Sternberg reveal, the sense of moralism involved in judgments of creative ideas, thoughts, and actions is a feature that is unique to Chinese culture, and embedded within the deepest levels of societal structure.

Leadership styles and their impact on groups' abilities to be creative is another factor that relates to creativity, as discussed by Zhang et al. [13]. Leadership is particularly important in the case of China, as the characteristics of a leader and authority figure are valued to a higher extent that in more individually-oriented countries such as the United States. Permission to be creative is linked to the style of leadership amongst educators, managers, and other authority figures, as the social environment is always evident. China has a reputation of possessing a paternalistic leadership style within its corporate culture, with leaders representing not just the head of a team or division, but as an almost familial figure, taking care of their subordinates but at the same time demanding their obedience. The structure of an organization is fairly hierarchical within the Chinese workplace, with great emphasis placed on the role and position of the "leader", who often has the sole authority to become a decision-maker. The concept of 'moral leadership' is examined by Gu et al. [14], who point out the significance of both the role of the leader in an organization the fact that many leadership studies are written from a Western-based corporate data-perspective.

The discussion of culture's relationship to creativity and perceptions of individual vs group mentality and work must include reference to the ever-growing body of work on the field of the culture of organizations, or Corporate Culture, discussed in work such as that of Zhao et al. [15]. As China continues to industrialize at a rapidly snowballing pace, it joins countries such as the US and Japan in developing significant literature on corporate culture, and the structures, routines, and rituals involved in the 21st century, as developed in the pioneering work by Deal and Kennedy [16]. Davies [17] provides a thorough ethnography of Walmart's corporate culture in China, in which he provides a succinct analysis and definition of the term as "drawing upon the poetic association and meanings of the larger socio-cultural context to communicate its messages of organization" (p. 5), and points out the gap in understanding between interpretations of culture from an anthropological vs corporate perspective. He rightly warns against the proliferation of the latter's use of the term as a kind of "behavioral software" that management can use to motivate and control staff members, and reminds us of the need to consider culture as a "negotiated symbolic system", as in the anthropological view (p. 4).

Hawes [18] further elaborates on the unique status of corporate culture in China, pointing to the significance of the propagation political and ideological values of Chinese culture through organizational culture, and the emphasis on the perceived necessity to promote "superior" Chinese values in order to connect with industry workers (p. 45). Particular attention to corporate culture with regards to creativity is paid by Hon and Leung [19] in their research on the hospitality and service industry in China, in which they find that a "person-culture fit" is essential in ensuring employee motivation. In other words, if the values and direction of the overall corporate culture and the individual employee are misaligned, creativity and motivation will inevitably suffer as a result.

Culture, creativity, and the context of the workplace in China all play a role in influencing individual and team dynamics within a given task, as will be shown in the case study in the next section.

2   Case Study

2.1   Description of the Company and Participants

The informants in this study consisted of 108 employees of a large, publicly-owned company in the transportation sector in China. ATC railway company is one of the largest of its kind in the world, with employees totaling over 180,000 amongst its various subsidiaries. The participants in the training program hailed from different subsidiaries, and thus held different social roles and expectations. Each one was hand- selected by his or her line manager to participate in a several-months long training program, one of the themes of which was "Creativity and Design-Thinking", as conducted by the facilitators of this study. It should be noted that the range in social roles as well as expected outcome of the training varied amongst the participants as related to their specific employment background, job title, and other assorted reasons. Three groups of 36 participants were organized by the training team, and throughout the entire training process, the unity of each of the 3 groups was maintained through their time both in and out of the classroom, with social events and other team-bonding extracurricular meetings arranged in order to solidify the identity of the three separate groups. These events were arranged either by the participants themselves, or by the organizers of the general corporate training program.

The portion of the training mentioned in this study was conducted by two facilitators who both possess doctoral degrees, with one hailing from a background in Industrial Design, and the other in Social and Cultural Anthropology. All of the participants worked for ATC company, but as mentioned previously, their official job titles ranged from several different types of Engineer, to Marketing Department employees to Managers. Each of these broader categories encompasses a wide range of jobs, ranging for instance to Vice-Chief of the subsidiary to Sales Manager within the overall general category of "Manager". Detailed information on the job titles and educational background of the participants is shown in the Table 1 below.

Table 1. Participants' demographic background

	Total
Gender	
Female	28
Male	80
Education	
Bachelor's degree	70
Masters degree	37
PhD degree	1
Job title	
Engineer	74
Manager	19
Marketing	4
Sales	4
Designer	4
Craftsman	1
Internal auditor	1
Procurement officer	1

The table demonstrates the nature of the participants involved from three aspects: Gender, Education, and Job. As we can see, there are significantly more male than female participants, by a large ratio. Whether or not this is true of within each category of job represented by the data is unknown, but it should be made evident that there is a much larger number of males chosen to participate in external training activities than females, in this particular case study.

At the same time, we can see that the majority of participants have a tertiary-level educational degree, as all of the participants selected for the training possessed at minimum a Bachelors'-level education. A total of 37 out of 108 participants had a Masters'-level education, with one PhD represented. Again, the representativeness of this data in relation to overall averages in Chinese industry is not clear. Similarly, the largest proportion of participants' backgrounds was somehow Engineering-related, as 74 out of 108 in total had a job title that was categorized as "Engineer", ranging from Quality Assurance Engineers to Welding Technicians and beyond. It can be seen that the thinking styles and social roles of the majority of participants involved in this study were primarily thus males, with Engineering backgrounds, and at least a Bachelor's degree. All participants were from mainland China, and the social impact factor of working in a predominantly homogeneous monolithic cultural workplace in China is shared amongst all of the people in this company. At the same time, their direct involvement in an English-language training program strongly reveals the participants' openness towards globalization and communication strategies, regardless of their job titles or backgrounds.

2.2 Design Exercises and Questionnaires

A series of three design tasks were given to the participants for which they were asked to work in individually and then in teams. The nature of the first two tasks required all participants to work in both scenarios, and then to reflect on their experiences via a questionnaire. The third task, given to the participants after training in ethnography and empathic design-thinking, required them to work in teams in order to re-design a train carriage for a specific user group, as assigned by the facilitators. The goal of this practice was to see how these teams were able to identify the needs of a target user group and come up with creative re-designs of standard train carriages. All three tasks required participants to use their imagination, and work with others in order to accomplish a creative goal. While the data from these tasks have elsewhere been analyzed for their creativity levels and the degree of attention paid to the User-Centeredness of their designs, a more critical analysis is required on the results of the questionnaires of the participants, as their own self-reflections on the experience of working both individually and in groups/teams provide a rich set of data that sheds a light on the current state of creative-thinking and social behavior in the workplace in Chinese industry.

The questions as posed in the questionnaire are listed as follows:

1. Have you been inspired by your teammate? Try to elaborate your comments to working in a team.
2. Do you feel it is more efficient to work alone or in a team? Try to elaborate your answers.
3. Do you prefer to design alone or in a team? Try to elaborate your answers.

The results of the questionnaire were analyzed using thematic analysis, with a simple coding scheme developed in order to recognize commonly-held or repeated sentiments into a number of categories, as is common practice in standard qualitative data analysis in the Social Sciences.

2.3 Analysis

Nearly all participants in the study (97%) indicated a positive response to the first question. Some common themes that resulted from the open-ended responses are indicated in the Table 2 below.

Table 2. Content analysis from questionnaires

	Positive	Negative	Neutral/other
Question 1	−Inspire, improve, share, compensate, check −Brainstorm, exchange −Different −More, increase −Energy, confidence, happiness −Easier, faster, more efficient, save time	−Conflict −Feel pressure	
Question 2	−Different or difference background/perspective/opinion −Help −Easier, faster, more efficient, save time −Discuss/together/combine/ −Learn −Complex or difficult problems −Brainstorm	−Lack trust −Not good at communication −Agreement difficult, decisive alone −Save time	−Management of team, leader/leadership −Type of work, depends −May… −Order of time/sequence
Question 3	−Stimulate/inspire −Reduce mistakes/correct −Increase creativity/innovation −Different knowledge/experience/background −Helpful −Easier −Complex/difficult problem-solving	−Convince others	−Alone then team (time/sequence) −Type of team/goal

The column on the left side represents the most commonly-cited words with a positive connotation for each of the three questions, while the middle column represents words that were utilized in a negative connotation. The final column on the right represents words that were neutral in tone, or had a vague or unclear interpretation or meaning. It can be observed that the frequency of words used to describe teamwork in a positive light greatly outnumber that of words with a more negative feeling. While the first question is directly related to the participants' experience in a specific training activity, the second question enquires more broadly about the perception of one's own efficiency in tasks. The third question asks participants to reflect even further, in making an assessment of preference for either individual or team work, with the exercise at hand in mind, but allowing for a broader answer that refers more generally to their own preferred work configuration.

As is consistent with overall theories in the literature on individual vs. group creativity, the majority of those who answered 'it depends', when asked whether they would prefer to work as an individual vs. in a group mentioned that they may prefer firstly to work alone, and then share their individual ideas and thoughts with their team mates in order to reach the optimum result, at least when it comes to design tasks. The timing of the questionnaire reflects the immediate thoughts of the participants after working firstly as individuals and then in teams, and was done so in order for the experience to remain fresh in their minds, so they could accurately express their post-task initial reflections. Although an overwhelming majority expressed a positive sense of inspiration from their teammates, the results of the second question reveal that it is not as simple as being 'inspired', as only 53% perceived that working in teams allowed them to be most efficient in their work.

Those participants who associated negative words or connotations to the notion of team or group work noted issues in communication with team members, as well as time-management, with some citing that they had difficulties coming to an agreement amongst team members, and obtaining timely results. One participant even stated that he "didn't have to convince others" if working alone, with another stating that there was "no need for agreement" in this case.

Overall, a summary of responses can be found in the Fig. 1 below:

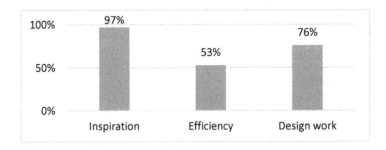

Fig. 1. Answers with positive attitude to teamwork on specific topics

3   Limitations and Further Research

The cultural factors discussed in this paper are predominantly discussed from the perspective of individual and team work, which clearly are not the only determinants of creative perceptions and thought. In addition, the questions posed to the participants may have been too guided, and a more open-ended approach may have heeded different results. However, due to the limited access to participants and nature of the training program, the questionnaire was chosen as a suitable option to get a broad description of perceptions of individual and team work when working together on a design-based task. Further research on this issue would benefit from a deeper ethnographic approach, as well as a more structured analysis based on social role and its position and relationship with various preferences and duties. Another obvious limitation is the selection process and representativeness of the employees selected to participate in these training exercises. 108 high-performing employees in total participated in the study, but from an ethnographic perspective, the authors did not have access to first-hand experience within ATC company itself, or the corporate culture, aside from the accounts given by the informants. Further inquiry into the corporate culture of ATC would hence immensely benefit our understanding of this crucial area of interest.

4 Conclusion

The findings from this paper confirm the evidence from literature that individual and team work are interactional, even in the Chinese cultural context. The characteristic behavioral tendency towards collectivism is clearly demonstrated by the various degrees of compromise that took place among the team members. The lack of effective management in organizing the team creative activities caused complaints regarding the inefficiency of decision making. While an overwhelming majority stated a preference to work in a team when given the choice, the presence of a large number who preferred to work alone and then share their ideas with teammates in order to produce optimal designs cannot be ignored. While the ultimate goal of industry is to produce cutting-edge innovation and design, the relationship between individuals and teams from the perspective of Chinese culture is an embedded component. Alongside the strong performance of creativity of the individuals, the participants' attitude toward team work reveals a mixture of attraction and repulsion, which indicates the awakening of individualism and its conflicts with traditional collectivism. The results from the analysis can be used as reference for Chinese enterprise to further invest into the management and building of teamwork as well as creative company culture, and to transfer the advantages of team work in a productive capacity that can enhance competitiveness in global market.

References

1. Zeng, X.: The dual characteristics of the state-owned enterprises and the reform of the mixed ownership system, 24 December 2015. (in Chinese). http://theory.people.com.cn/n1/2015/1224/c143844-27972599.html
2. Amabile, T.M.: Creativity in Context: Update to "The Social Psychology of Creativity". Westview Press, Boulder (1996)
3. Nisbett, R.E.: The Geography of Thought: How Asians and Westerners Think Differently and Why. Free Press, New York (2003)

4. Rudowicz, E., Hui, A.: The creative personality: Hong Kong perspective. J. Soc. Behav. Pers. **12**(1), 139–157 (1997)
5. Morris, M.W., Leung, K.: Creativity East and West: parallels and perspectives. Manag. Organ. Rev. **6**(3), 313–327 (2010)
6. Hempel, P.S., Sue-Chan, C.: Culture and the assessment of creativity. Manag. Organ. Rev. **6**(3), 415–435 (2010)
7. Apanovich, V.V., et al.: Event-related potentials during individual, cooperative and competitive task performance differ in subjects with analytic vs. holistic thinking. Int. J. Psychol. **123**, 136–142 (2018)
8. Liu, H., Wang, F.X., Yang, X.Y.: More dialectical thinking, less creativity? The relationship between dialectical thinking style and creative personality: the case of China. PLoS One **10**(4), e0122926 (2015)
9. Niu, W.: Individual and environmental influences on chinese student creativity. J. Creative Behav. **41**(3), 151–175 (2007)
10. Miron-Spektor, E., Paletz, S.F., Chun-Chi, L.: To create without losing face: the social effects of face cultural logic and social-image affirmation on creativity. J. Organ. Behav. **36**, 919–943 (2015)
11. Markus, H.R., Kitayama, S.: Culture and the self: implications for cognition. Emot. Motiv. Psychol, Rev. **98**(2), 224–253 (1991)
12. Niu, W., Sternberg, R.: Contemporary studies on the concept of creativity: the East and West. J. Creative Behav. **36**(4), 269–288 (2002)
13. Zhang, A.Y., Tsui, A.S., Wang, D.X.: Leadership behaviors and group creativity in Chinese organizations: the role of group processes. Leadersh. Q. **22**, 851–862 (2011)
14. Gu, Q., Tang, T.L.-P., Jiang, W.: Does moral leadership enhance employee creativity? Employee identification with leader and leader-member exchange (LMX) in the Chinese context. J. Bus. Ethics **126**(3), 513–529 (2013)
15. Zhao, H., Teng, H., Wu, Q.: The effect of corporate culture on firm performance: evidence from China. China J. Account. Res. **11**(1), 1–19 (2018)
16. Deal, T.E., Kennedy, A.A.: Corporate Cultures: The Rites and Rituals of Corporate Life. Addison Wesley Publishing Company, Reading (1982)
17. Davies, D.J.: Wal-Mao: the discipline of corporate culture and studying success at Wal-Mart China. China J. **58**, 1–27 (2007)
18. Hawes, C.: Representing corporate culture in China: official, academic and corporate perspectives. China J. **59**, 33–61 (2008)
19. Hon, A.H.Y., Leung, A.S.M.: Employee creativity and motivation in the Chinese context: the moderating role of organizational culture. Cornell Hosp. Q. **52**(2), 125–134 (2011)

Beijing Opera Cultural Heritage

A Service Design Perspective

Lu Wang[(✉)]

Tongji University, SP 1239, Shanghai, People's Republic of China
seawingwl@qq.com

Abstract. The primary forms of promoting Beijing Opera are stage performances, lectures, and publications. These are one-way conversations, lacking any interaction between different stakeholders. These make Beijing Opera monotonous, unattractive, and lack sustainable cultural heritage.

This study identified the challenges of Beijing Opera development through interview and desk research. It utilizes user research to identify different groups of people's attitudes towards Beijing Opera culture. Costumers analysis illustrates three groups: the public, amateurs and professionals. It insights into the characteristics and needs of different roles and finds opportunities to inherit Beijing Opera culture. It also proposed service called Beijing Opera House.

Beijing Opera House (B.O. House) is a brand-new service combined with people's lifestyle in the future, with the aim of protecting and inheriting the Beijing Opera culture. The service popularizes basic knowledge of Beijing Opera to the public through digital interactive games, promotes different groups communication, organizes amateurs and professionals to perform Beijing Opera together. People could also interact with each other through the Network Platform of B.O. House to upload works, perform, access professional guidance, and manage personal information. It is a service design making three different kinds of people, public, amateur, and professional, communicate with each other and gradually improve their interest's levels of Beijing Opera, and building a benign culture atmosphere to provide a sustainable development of Beijing Opera.

Keywords: Beijing Opera · Cultural heritage · Service design

1 The Problems in Beijing Opera Culture Heritage

1.1 The History of Beijing Opera

Beijing Opera, is a form of Chinese opera which combines music, vocal performance, mime, dance and acrobatics. It is the quintessence of Chinese ancient culture and already has a history of about 200 years.

Beijing Opera arose in the late 18th century and became fully developed and recognized by the mid-19th century. [1] It was born from Hui opera and then combined with Han opera and Kunqu, with its songs mostly coming from Qingqiang. [2] The music of Beijing Opera can be divided into the Xipi (西皮) and Erhuang (二黄) styles.

P.-L. P. Rau (Ed.): CCD 2018, LNCS 10912, pp. 235–244, 2018.
https://doi.org/10.1007/978-3-319-92252-2_18

[3] The form was extremely popular in the Qing dynasty court and has come to be regarded as one of the cultural treasures of China. [4] Beijing Opera has two main changes in its history, which help it become the most popular performance in the country. The first change is ascending, which was developed from the folk to the Capital, and the other one is descending, which was developed from the Capital to the rest of China. [5] Beijing Opera reached its climax in Republic of China (1917), and emerged many wonderful artists, such as Mei Lanfang, Cheng Yanqiu, Shang Xiaoyun and Gou Huisheng.

Beijing Opera features four main types of performance, including songs, speech, dance-acting and combat. [6] There are four major roles on the stage: Sheng, Dan, Jing, and Chou. [7] Sheng refers to men, Dan refers to women, Jing refers to painted-face role, and Chou refers to painted-face role. Mei Lanfang, one of the most famous Beijing Opera artists, was exclusively known for his Dan performance.

Beijing Opera began to see reforms in the 1980s. Such reforms have taken the form of creating a school of performance theory to increase performance quality, employing modern elements to attract new audiences, and performing new plays in addition to traditional canon. During the 1980s, plays with repetitive sequences have been shortened to hold audience interest. [8] Beijing Opera Company even offered an increasing number of free performances in public areas. [9] However, these efforts have not been effective in saving the gradual decline of Beijing Opera culture, especially its market. In 2010, Chinese government declared Intangible Cultural Heritage for Beijing Opera in UNESCO and hoped that, through this measure, Beijing Opera would be valued and protected by the world, not only Chinese people.

1.2   The Challenges in Beijing Opera Cultural Heritage

Since the second half of the 20th century, Beijing Opera has witnessed a steady decline in audience numbers as well as a shrink of the market. In order to identify the challenges Beijing Opera faced, we interviewed three kinds of people: a professor in Beijing Opera Academy, the general public, and some foreigners.

The professor thought Beijing Opera's lyrics and orchestration are becoming far away from people's lives in recent decade, and it is difficult for the general public to understand and accept. (Whereas, the development of Beijing Opera or cultural heritage need young and new students to learn or appreciate Beijing Opera. But many adults) People are reluctant to send their children to study Beijing Opera, (and the students who come to learn are not good enough in learning or don't have high quality of learning spirits. What's more, even the government have given some fund to support the academy development, the funding of the school still couldn't enough and there are no outside ways for them to earn money. When talking about the innovation of Beijing Opera content creation). The professor believed that the new way of Beijing Opera performance must respect tradition, retain classic stories, and combine contemporary lifestyle. In fact, there is a lack of funding, a lack of communication and exchange between Beijing Opera amateurs, ordinary audiences and professionals.

During the street interview, the general public still maintained a positive attitude towards Beijing Opera. They all very interesting in cultural and creative products, such as facial painting and Beijing Opera character dolls, they also mentioned Beijing Opera related films and popular songs. But when ask them if they have watched any Beijing Opera performance or learn any basic knowledge about it, their answers are all surprisingly negative. They also mentioned that the slow rhythm and singing styles are boring that they could not bear them.

For foreigners, they like the costumes of Beijing Opera very much because the colors are bright and beautiful. At the same time Beijing Opera performances and singing styles are very different from those in other countries, which give them unforgettable impression. But they couldn't understand the lyrics' meaning or actions of Beijing Opera performance.

Desk research also helps identify other problems in Beijing Opera cultural heritage. Because of the multicultural impact, fast modern life paces, the younger generations become impatient with the slow pacing of Beijing Opera [10]. What's more, the utilitarian ideas and lower income of Beijing Opera also led them reluctant to study Beijing Opera. [11] The loss of Beijing Opera market, the ageing of actors and actresses, the lack of good new plays and the lack of inheritance of classic plays are other main challenges in Beijing Opera development [12].

The deeper reasons behind are, the conflict between fast life style and slow pacing of Beijing Opera, the conflict between new ways of talking and archaic language, the conflict between new plays and classic contents, the conflict between cultural heritage and old audience as well as old performers, the paradox between modern culture and traditional culture (see Table 1).

Table 1. Paradoxes in Beijing Opera development.

Traditional culture	Modern culture
Slow pacing of Beijing Opera	Fast life style
Archaic language	New ways of talking
Ageing audiences	Young audiences
Old performers	Cultural heritage
Classic contents	New plays

In China, there are three major means to develop or protect Beijing Opera in recent years, one is organizing official competition and programs, such as Channel CCTV-11 (see Fig. 1), with the aim to broadcasting classic Chinese opera productions, including Beijing Opera. [13] The second is cultural and creative products, such as facial painting, movies about famous Beijing Opera stories (see Fig. 2) as well as popular songs featuring Beijing Opera singing methods. The third is allocating fund to support Beijing Opera schools and troupes.

The above three means are one direction to promote Beijing Opera, and it is a descending way from the Government or the professionals to the public, which lacks communication or interaction between different kinds of people. There is a need for ascending ways to attract people and let them be willing to inherit Beijing Opera culture.

Fig. 1. Chinese opera TV quiz

Fig. 2. Beijing Opera movie "Farewell my concubine"

2   Beijing Opera Cultural Heritage by Service Design

2.1   A Brief Introduction to Service Design

In the 1960s, the global industrial structure underwent tremendous changes due to the development of the service industry. The industrial institutions showed a global trend of transition from "industrial" to "service". [14] As Pro. Richard Buchanan said, one of the great strengths of design is that we have not settled on a single definition. [15] The same is true for service design. There is no common definition (or clearly articulated language of) service design. But one of shared description of service design is that it is a cross-disciplinary practice combining numerous skills in design, management and process engineering. Service design is essential in a knowledge-driven economy. There are five principles of service design thinking [16].

1. User-centred: Services should be experienced through the customer's eyes.
2. Co-creative: All stakeholders should be included in the service design process.
3. Sequencing: The service should be visualised as a sequence of interrelated actions.
4. Evidencing: Intangible services should be visualised in terms of physical artefacts.
5. Holistic: The entire environment of a service should be considered.

Service design extends the definition of a user, encompassing all stakeholders, and all individuals affected or interacting with the service system. [17] Service design is a holistic way of thinking that takes into account every part and person in this system.

2.2 Beijing Opera Cultural Heritage as a Service

The cultural heritage of Beijing Opera includes different kinds of people. It involves the Government that provide appropriate protection policies; the media that give publicity for Beijing Opera; investors who provide funding for Beijing Opera inheritance; experts who conduct research on the development and performance of Beijing Opera; the artists who perform in stage and train successors; and the general public who are the potential audience of Beijing Opera. These different groups of people are all stakeholders of Beijing Opera. As Clifford Geertz says: "Scholars, public, artists and the media, etc. will establish a mutual understanding of the relationship between melting in static scripts, costumes, facial painting and the flow of the stage culture" [18], these stakeholders should be included in the development of Beijing Opera culture heritage as far as possible. The protection of cultural heritage should meet the needs of all parties, and be inclusive. In this way Beijing Opera cultural heritage can be seen as a service, which is characterized by user-centeredness and co-creation. The principles of service design thinking also include sequential and evidencing, that is, in promoting for Beijing Opera cultural heritage, there is a need for reasoning and visualization of programs and operations. The two intangible issues, lie culture and heritage, should be turned into tangible solutions.

Through service design, the stakeholders can be divided into two categories: those in the front of the stage system and those in the backstage system. The front of stage system is more about customers operating system which includes how the public interacts with Beijing Opera culture and the professionals. Therefore, the general public, the Beijing Opera culture experts and the performing artists are the major stakeholders of the front of stage. The background system is about service providers and the management system, which includes manufacturers, investors, and the Government.

3 B.O. House Service for Beijing Opera Cultural Inheritance

3.1 The Insight of the Service

We have already explored main challenges in Beijing Opera heritage and identified some opportunities. Here we focus on customers and ascertain the true motivations behind the customer behavior though customer analysis (see Table 2).

Table 2. Customer analysis

Customer		Characteristics attitudes towards life & Beijing Opera	Preferences expectations of Beijing Opera	The conditions of heritage Background and material	Desired effects
Public	Kids & students	May grow interests through education	Interests (games, new technology), easy ways for understanding	Social atmosphere, understanding channels, entry method, knowledge base	Literacy, transforming potential fans
	Young and middle-aged	Fast-paced life, restlessness, strong purchasing power	Sensory stimulation, heart comfort		
Amateur	General lovers (occasional attention)	Art-loving	Prefer classic culture	Access to information	Obtaining the required platform resources
	Fans (self-study)	Spontaneous research (exchange ideas, information sharing, performance)	Respect classic, willing to spread	Platform (resource acquisition, information exchange, performance and skills learning)	Obtaining the required platform resources, exchange opportunities
Professional	Performing artists, teachers	Professional learning, teaching, performing, creating, love Beijing Opera, and eager to spread	Respect classic elements and willing to create and inherit	Platform (new idea gathering, new talent scouting, wide range of art audience)	Knowledge, adding new idea to Beijing Opera, attracting newcomers and providing training

We have illustrated the customer in three groups: the public, the amateur and the professional. The public include kids and students who have not much stress in life and are easily been guided; young and middle-aged who have a lot of stress with fast-paced life but have strong purchasing power. They like interesting things, such as games or new technology. The amateur includes general lovers who would pay attention to Beijing Opera occasionally and fans who would like to learn Beijing Opera. They love art, love exchange ideas and are more like classic culture. They respect traditional culture and even would like to spread it. The professionals include performing artists and teachers who are experts in learning, teaching, performing and creating Beijing Opera. They are trying their best to spread it as well as aiming to inherit it. Besides respecting classic elements of Beijing Opera, such as abstract performing, traditional drama suit, they also want to absorb new culture and create new plays.

We further analyze the customer-related issues relating to service design: How to make the audience enjoy learning the basic knowledge of Beijing Opera? How to make amateurs get the attention they need? How to give their chance to let new plays performed on the stage? How to broaden the opera theme and deepen the impact on the audience? How to explore and cultivate creative talent of Beijing Opera? How to make all people communicate, play, and promote more smoothly?

In Fig. 3, we illustrate some strategies of turning challenges into opportunities. The publics can proactively learn Beijing Opera knowledge through interactive games which trigger interest through a virtual history, and then be willing to and have the ability to disseminate and promote Beijing Opera. Finally, part of them who have a strong interest in Beijing Opera will probably turn to be amateurs. Amateurs can share their ideas and creation, thus obtaining guidance and performance opportunities. They will have a strong desire to create and perform Beijing Opera and be encouraged and progress in their skills. Professionals can discover talents and creative thinkers to enhance the expertise. Through a new service system, it could improve interaction, upgrade transformation, and complete the protection and inheritance of Beijing Opera culture.

3.2   B.O. House Service

We create a B.O. House (Beijing Opera House) service to fulfill Beijing Opera culture heritage (see Fig. 4). As for the front of stage system, the B.O. House service is divided into four parts. First, the Experience Pavilion uses the form of interactive games to convey Beijing Opera knowledge to the public and make them generate interest by enjoyable experience. It adopts a personal customized tutor leading visitors by holographic projection technology and interactive games in computer to help them understand basic knowledge of Beijing Opera, such as creating facial masks, matching costumes with a clear field division, guessing famous figures to learn about metaphors of actions. Second, the Immersion Theater uses Virtual Reality method to reappear traditional Beijing Opera performance in ancient time, in order to let visitors experience classical plays and famous artists' performances. Third, visitors could book B.O. House tickets on the Network Platform. It could also allow general public upload their creative works of facial masks and costumes amateurs to internet and share with others. It also could let amateurs upload their new plays or send questions and get professional

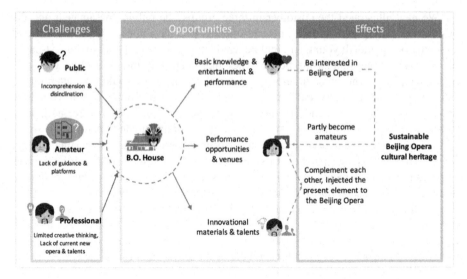

Fig. 3. The strategies of Beijing Opera cultural heritage.

feedback. Professionals could also gain ideas for new plays and search talented people on the internet. Forth, the Boutique Theater is an area where you can watch Beijing Opera live performances. During the process, audience could send real-time comments to the actors. In this way the actors could have an online communication with audience and improve their skills by the comments. What's more, the selected amateurs from the internet could also perform with professionals and raise their level gradually.

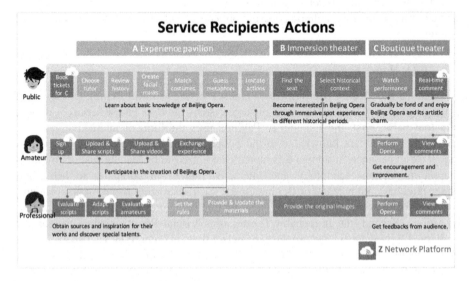

Fig. 4. B.O. House service system map

B.O. House is a public service targeted on promoting Beijing Opera development and cultural heritage facing all kinds of people. As for background system, it needs fund by the Government to create and provide equipment and technology. B.O. House could also attract investment by companies and receive support from the International Intangible Cultural Heritage Protection Organizations. It needs technology company provide big data support and new media to broadcast Beijing Opera culture and cross-disciplines' supports, such as architecture, interior design, etc.

4 Conclusion

B.O. House as a service system, its lifecycle is related with development of technology and lifestyle. When the service concept is replaced by better idea, B.O. House needs to be redesigned or shut down. For example, the contents in Experience pavilion and Immersion Theater need to be updated regularly to keep up with the shifting times to attract visitors. And Boutique theater's operas can be changed with the concerns and interests of society, to meet the audience's enthusiasm for Beijing Opera.

Though B.O. House service, we expand participants, promote communication and innovation of plays, and lower the difficulty of cognitive. Cultural heritage needs cover a wide range of stakeholders, such as the general public, professional performers, governments and markets, and are not problems that can be solved by meeting the interests of one side. Culture need to consider as the whole, to balance the interests of all parties and achieve co-create value to sustain the traditional cultural heritage. Therefore, through overall consideration of the needs of stakeholders to design a specific inheritance program, which create an activeness atmosphere of Beijing Opera cultural heritage, are particularly important.

Whereas, the prototype of the B.O. House also has to be considered how to fulfill it. For instance, the design in interactive games or virtual experience of facial mask and clothing matching have to fit with the norms of Beijing Opera culture. Experience form in B.O. House will apply some new technology, such as front-projected holographic display, big data, Wireless Sensor Network, ThinkGear AM, etc. The entity venues' building also need to be designed by the urban planning and construction program. Let intangible service tangible is our next working step.

References

1. Goldstein, J.S.: Drama Kings: Players and Publics in the Re-creation of Beijing Opera, 1870–1937. University of California Press, San Francisco (2007)
2. Chengbei, X.: Beijing Opera. Cambridge University Press, Cambridgeshire (2012)
3. Jinpei, H.: Xipi and Erhuang of Beijing and Guangdong styles. Asian Music **20**(2), 152–195 (1989)
4. Mackerras, C.P.: Theatre and the taipings. Mod. China **2**(4), 473–501 (1976)
5. WU PROMOTION. http://www.pekingopera.eu/pekingopera-en.html
6. Wichmann, E.: Listening to Theatre: The Aural Dimension of Beijing Opera, p. 2. University of Hawaii Press, Honolulu (1991)
7. Baidu Baike. https://baike.baidu.com/item/京剧/75719

8. Wichmann, E.: Listening to Theatre: The Aural Dimension of Beijing Opera, pp. 149–151. University of Hawaii Press, Honolulu (1990)
9. Wichmann-Walczak, E.: "Reform" at the Shanghai Beijing Opera Company and its impact on creative authority and repertory. TDR **44**(4), 96–119 (2000)
10. Diamond, C.: Kingdom of desire: the three faces of Macbeth (in Report). Asian Theatre J. **11** (1), 114–133 (1994)
11. Li, B.: Heritage of Beijing Opera revitalization of traditional arts culture: a brief talk on the modern inheritance of Beijing Opera arts. Characteristics of Drama (13), 38–39 (2014)
12. Mao, S.: Beijing Opera inheritance and development in the contemporary cultural structure brief description of the fourth China Beijing Opera Festival Symposium. Beijing Opera (02), 76–77 (2005)
13. Goldstein, J.S.: p. 1 (2007)
14. Polaine, A., Lovlie, L., Reason, B.: Service Design: From Insight to Implementation. Rosenfeld Media, Brooklyn (2013)
15. Buchanan, R.: Design research and the new learning. Des. Issues **17**(4), 3–23 (2001)
16. Stickdorn, M., Schneider, J.: This is Service Design Thinking: Basics, Tools, Cases. BIS Publishers, Netherlands (2011)
17. Kimbell, L.: From user-centered design to designing for services. Paper for Presentation to the Design Management Conference 2010, London, pp. 1–9 (2010)
18. Geertz, C.: The Interpretation of Cultures: Selected Essays. Basic Books, New York (1977)

Appearance–Behavior–Culture in Creating Consumer Products with Cultural Meaning Meant to Evoke Emotion

Tyan-Yu Wu$^{(\boxtimes)}$ and Wei-Hsiang Huang

Chang Gung University, Kwei-Shan, Taiwan
tnyuwu@mail.cgu.edu.tw

Abstract. This paper aims to describe an attempt to develop a design process for the enhancement of cultural factors in product design. Appearance–behavior–culture (ABC) theory was applied to construct the six design processes. To test the processes, a collaborative project designing a glass teapot was used, following the six developed design processes step by step, and each step is described. The discussion covers designer and client feedback during the design stages. Designers specifically commented positively on the use of 3-D printing technology as an efficient tool for effectively and quickly checking ideas.

Keywords: Culture · Product design · Development process

1 Introduction

Products with cultural meanings can add emotional value (Desmet et al. 2001) when users perceive the meanings of those products. Most products used in our daily lives are connected with cultural matters, and product semantics are frequently adopted to convey the cultural meaning of a product and embed that meaning into the product's design (Krippendorff and Butter 1984), which evokes consumers' emotions and increases the product's success in the market (Bloch 1995; Creusen and Schoormans 2005; Crilly et al. 2004). Therefore, cultural design is becoming critical in developing new products. However, it is important to understand the types of cultural elements that can be used and the application of these elements into designs to understand how they are integrated into the complete design process. The aim of this study was to develop a design process that can be applied to glass objects by designers to further evoke consumer pleasure.

This research adopted the appearance, behavior, and cultural (ABC) attributes based on Leong's (2003) and Lin's (2007) culture theories (see Fig. 1), while Desmet's (2002) emotional appraisal theory was used to explain how cultural meaning evokes users' positive emotional responses. Leong (2003) organized culture into three special levels: the outer "tangible" level, the mid "behavioral" level, and the inner "intangible" level. Similarly, Norman (2004) argues that there are three levels of product emotions in design: visceral design, behavioral design, and reflective design. In sum, both Leong's and Norman's theories are adopted to support the ABC concept in this study, which applied it for the fulfillment of a complete design process with regard to

© Springer International Publishing AG, part of Springer Nature 2018
P.-L. P. Rau (Ed.): CCD 2018, LNCS 10912, pp. 245–253, 2018.
https://doi.org/10.1007/978-3-319-92252-2_19

materials, behaviors, and the spiritual needs of humans. In other words, the three sides of the cultural triangle address major aspects of human needs, including physiological and psychological needs, and it is expected, according to Desmet's (2002) emotional appraisal theory, that accomplishing this task of integration in product designs will evoke users' emotions because of the fulfillment of their cognitive understanding of cultural elements (e.g., represented meaning).

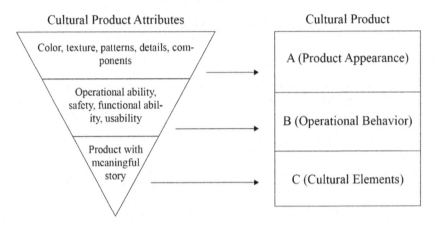

Fig. 1. ABC cultural product (Adopted from Lin's (2007) cultural product attributes)

2   Image Boards as a Vehicle for Enhancing Cultural Content

As mentioned, cultural objects involve three special levels. Among the outer tangible and inner intangible levels, cultural products are frequently interpreted through the cultural appearance that is formed by elements such as patterns, symbols, legends, and ritual information. Thus, users can perceive the typical cultural characteristics when using the item. It is, therefore, the case that products with cultural characteristics are realized by using visual components to enhance those characteristics. For this reason, mood boards and image boards have been broadly used for brainstorming of ideas during product development (McDonagh et al. 2002). Style boards have also been used for this purpose. (McDonagh and Storer 2005). In particular, mood boards and image boards are frequently used for finding and communicating design concepts and creating further valuable ideas. The image board was, likewise, adopted in this study. During a group brainstorming process, an image board can provide a clear and valuable means by which designers can observe images and discuss ideas easily and effectively. These boards allow designers to display images powerfully and communicate concepts easily, particularly those that are hard to describe in text or verbally. The great benefit of using image boards is that they allow participants to obtain personal inspiration, describe their feelings and opinions individually when communicating with team members, and develop valuable ideas quickly and effectively (Wu and Chang 2009). The current study used image boards to explore and identify cultural meanings through patterns, shapes, colors, materials, stories, legends, rituals, and so on.

3 The Development of the ABC Method and Design Processes

In this study, the six design processes were developed based on two categories of research: the product development process (Ulrich and Eppinger 1999) and cultural theories (Leong 2003; Lin 2007). Technically, image boards and 3-D printing technology were used as tools to assist designers in realizing designs that integrate cultural meaning into aspects of the product's appearance and operational behavior, and cultural meaning. In this research, the ABC attributes and six design processes were constructed for the development of products with cultural meanings for the purpose of further enhancing users' emotional responses. Brainstorming and cultural image boards were suggested as design tools for inspiration during the ideation processes. The ABC attributes represent three important dimensions: appearance, behavior, and culture. Appearance represents the product's appearance, emphasizing form development in terms of physical patterns, visual components, and shapes. The behavioral attribute incorporates studies of users' operational behaviors, including ergonomics (i.e., human factors) and usability considerations. Culture brings in the cultural contents, including tales, stories, and meanings behind the patterns or elements that communicate cultural meaning.

To emphasize the ABC attributes in effectively achieving cultural product designs, six processes are developed. These processes include (1) collecting related material, including content and images; (2) analyzing and synthesizing material through display on an image board; (3) the ideation stage, meaning brainstorming and rough sketching of ideas; (4) making sketch models and creating 3-D form models; (5) finalizing ideas and printing a 3-D model; and (6) confirming the final design with the client and making a final prototype. The details of the processes are explained in the following.

The ABC concept was utilized for the enhancement of cultural product development. ABC stands for A = product appearance, B = operational behavior, and C = cultural elements. Specifically, ABC is a concept for creating cultural products. ABC attributes are involved in the six design steps, where each step incorporates the ABC attributes on different levels during-design activities. In Fig. 2, the bottom row shows the enhancement of each attribute during each design step. For instance, step 1 may focus more on the appearance and cultural content studies and less on behavior in terms of ergonomic concerns, while step 5 may focus on all three attributes. However, in reality, designers should be more open to the application of these attributes, given that creativity is not limited in any aspect.

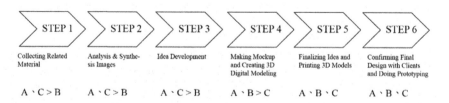

Fig. 2. Six development steps

4 An Example of a Cultural Product Development

To test the six design processes, a collaborative project was performed to create a glass teapot incorporating a Chinese cultural style. This particular project was accomplished in cooperation with a traditional glass manufacturer that is an expert on "Lazurite," an ancient Chinese colored glass style. Facing a competitive global market, the manufacturer wanted to create a new line of functional glass products rather than traditional ornaments and gifts. According to the results of marketing research, they asked designers to create a glass teapot set that would fit the east-meets-west style. To accomplish this inclusion of cultural meaning in a product, a specific approach to the six design processes were used as described below.

- Step 1. Collecting related material

We started with collecting material, including Chinese patterns, related images, and legends. For instance, we looked for objects covered with ancient Chinese decorations, teapots, vases, and vessels, anything that may be associated with teapots and that would be able to effectively invoke the appearance and cultural contents of teapots.

- Step 2. Analysis and synthesis of images

The image board was a powerful tool in this project, used for arranging images and information according to their purpose. For instance, one image board displayed information along a modern Western style–Eastern classic style axis and an abstract–concrete axis, as shown in Fig. 3. These images identify teapots with Western and Eastern styles. The other image board, shown in Fig. 4, displayed information on the two axes of ornamental–traditional vessels and abstract–concrete designs, providing a variety of images that served to enhance the shape value of a new teapot during the ideation phase.

- Step 3. Idea development

In this step, designers attempt to create as many ideas associated with cultural constructs as possible at the base of an image board, adding sketches to show a variety of visual impacts for the enhancement of ideation (see Fig. 5). Observing the visual elements on an image board, designers may be strongly inspired by the unique cultural elements and tend to integrate those elements into their ideas in order to have their design display strong cultural characteristics. At this stage, cultural visual elements show great influence over the development of cultural products. In this project, this step does not demonstrate the operational behavior much because the focus was on visual elements. But, step 5 made up for this missing part, and 3-D print modeling allowed for a usability test.

- Step 4. Making a mockup and finding potential ideas

In step 3, 2-D idea sketches focused on the development of ideas visual aspects. At step 4, a 3-D sketch-model allows designers to visualize 3-D forms to detail rough designs effectively. In other words, a sketched model can provide a sort of physical interaction, which allows designers to observe the form and check operational behaviors for its functions. However, there are some limitations in checking usability because of the rough quality of the model. For instance, in this project, it is not easy to

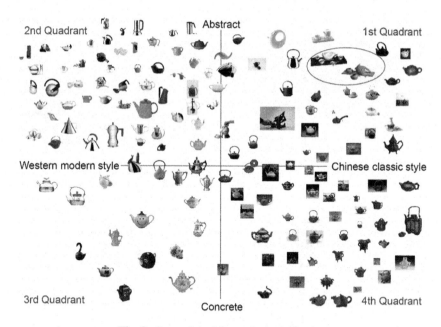

Fig. 3. Image board for style determination

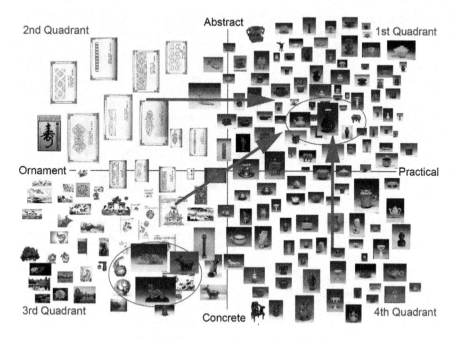

Fig. 4. Image board for inspiring ideas

Fig. 5. Examples of idea sketches

evaluate the weight balance of a glass teapot or to simulate how it feels for a user to hold the heavy glass teapot and pour tea into the cups. Technically, this problem can be solved seamlessly at the next step.

Fig. 6. 3-D digital modeling

Fig. 7. 3-D printed models for design visualization

- Step 5. Creating 3-D digital modeling and printing 3-D models

Some potential ideas were selected from among the sketch models to be built using 3-D digital modeling with computer software (see Fig. 6). In this project, designers played around with a variety of forms and cultural patterns on the computer screen. The great advantage of creating a digital model is the ability to push potential ideas one step further. By doing this, designers can have a 3-D model on hand immediately to examine its dimensions, ergonomics/usability, and physical appearance. For instance, designers can put water into the model and check the gravitational balance when holding the handle and pouring tea. In this design, we noted the problem in a 3-D model when the teapot's cap kept falling off during testing. The problem was solved by moving the dragon handle to a perfect position that stopped the cap from falling while pouring the tea (see Fig. 7). Instead of having to make a glass model, a 3-D printed model provided an actual product (see Fig. 7) to more efficiently and effectively examine the teapot's usability and functions.

- Step 6. Confirming a final design with the client and making a prototype

As mentioned, 3-D print modeling can help a designer visualize all of a product's design aspects, which enables designers to confirm a final idea with clients and assure the overall design (see Fig. 8). Furthermore, having a 3-D digital model, a manufacturer can utilize it to make a prototype for future mass production (see Fig. 9). This is more cost-efficient than traditional design processes.

Fig. 8. Printed 3-D model

Fig. 9. 3-D prototype

5 Discussion and Suggestions

The ABC attributes were utilized to support six design steps when strategizing ideas for a cultural product. At the beginning, in the idea development stage, image boards were utilized to enhance ideation activities, specifically, exploration of cultural components. To assure validation of the design steps, a collaborative project was performed to assure effective design processes. The results show that the six steps are an effective process for designing a product with cultural meaning. There are some discussions and suggestions that this project brought to light, as detailed below.

1. The image board is a very powerful and useful tool for enhancing idea development, and cultural objects rely very much on visual formation and elements to express cultural style and meaning. Thus, image boards with cultural elements were applied in the design process to inspire lateral thinking while performing ideation in search of creative ideas with cultural aspects.
2. In this way, designers can freely observe images while brainstorming with teammates to come up with as many ideas as possible. Observing the cultural contents on the image board, designers are able to more easily incorporate these cultural elements and integrate their meaning into the product. As metaphors, the cultural elements of a product should automatically stimulate users' cognitive understanding and make sense to them.
3. Sketched models can help designers visualize an idea and interact with the model. In this case, designers were able to check the overall volume in terms of 3-D shape exploration and playing with graphic and pattern layouts.
4. 3-D printing technology has changed the design process by speeding it up. Compared with traditional computer 3-D model development, 3-D printing technology enables rapid production of a model, which allows for nearly immediate checking of an actual physical model. In this case, designers can precisely check product usability and modify the design details back and forth more quickly and efficiently. 3-D printing technology has, in particular, created a breakthrough in the development process when compared to traditional glass (e.g., Lazurite) prototyping.
5. An extremely important factor is that 3-D printing is a low-cost technology that saves significant amounts of invested money compared with traditional model-making. During the prototyping stage, traditional glass design required building many prototypes by hand in order to illustrate the complex forms in a perfect condition during the form development stage.
6. On the other hand, 3-D printing technology allows the building and modification of a 3-D form in a quick and efficient manner. In other words, the 3-D printing model is an effective process for checking all aspects of an idea before processing the complicated 3-D metal tooling. However, the printing material technology is still limited by the few printing materials currently available, which include polylactic acid (PLA), acrylonitrile butadiene styrene (ABS), polyethylene terephthalate (PETT), and a few others. Although PETT material has a semi-transparent appearance, it is still unable to completely represent the clear visual sensation of glass material. Thus, the development of pure transparent materials for 3-D printing would benefit glass-related design work by more closely simulating transparent objects.

Overall, the client was satisfied with the result of this project, and designers are optimistic about the design processes developed. For the next stage, the client suggests conducting a survey to assure market acceptance of the design's quality, which includes the product's style, pricing, and cultural meaning. We expect that the product will be able to evoke consumers' pleasure in using it while observing the included cultural elements.

References

Bloch, P.H.: Seeking the ideal form: product design and consumer response. J. Mark. **59**(3), 16–29 (1995)

Creusen, M.E.H., Schoormans, J.P.L.: The different roles of product appearance in consumer choice. J. Prod. Innov. Manag. **22**(1), 63–81 (2005)

Crilly, N., Moultrie, J., Clarkson, P.J.: Seeing things: consumer response to the visual domain in product design. Des. Stud. **25**(6), 547–577 (2004)

Desmet, P.M.A.: Designing Emotions, unpublished Doctorial thesis, Delft University, NL (2002)

Desmet, P.M.A., Overbeeke, C.J., Tax, S.J.E.T.: Designing products with added emotional value: development and application of an approach for research through design. Des. J. **4**(1), 32–47 (2001)

Krippendorff, K., Butter, R.: Product semantics: exploring the symbolic qualities of form. Innov.: J. Ind. Des. Soc. Am. **3**(2), 4–9 (1984)

Leong, B.D.: Culture-based knowledge towards new design thinking and practice-A dialogue. Des. Issues **19**, 48–58 (2003)

Lin, R.T.: Transforming Taiwan aboriginal cultural features into modern product design: a case study of a cross-cultural product design model. Int. J. Des. **1**(2), 45–53 (2007)

McDonagh, D., Bruseberg, A., Haslam, C.: Visual product evaluation: exploring users' emotional relationships with products. Appl. Ergon. **33**(3), 231–240 (2002)

McDonagh, D., Storer, I.: Mood boards as a design catalyst and resource: researching an under-researched area. Des. J. **7**(3), 16–31 (2005)

Norman, D.A.: Emotional Design: Why We Love (or Hate) Everyday Things. Basic books, Cambridge (2004)

Ulrich, K.T., Eppinger, S.D.: Product Design and Development. McGraw-Hill, New York (1999)

Wu, T.-Y., Chang, W.-C.: Development of a product with pleasure: modeling the bionic design approach. Bull. JSSD **56**(2), 43–52 (2009)

Cross-Cultural Design for Social Change and Development

Study on Cultural and Creative Experience Model of Featured Towns

Wei Bi[1,2(✉)], Yang Gao[2], Li-Yu Chen[3], and Shu Hua Chang[4]

[1] School of Jewellery, West Yunnan University of Applied Sciences,
Kunming, People's Republic of China
beebvv@qq.com
[2] Graduate School of Creative Industry Design,
National Taiwan University of Arts, New Taipei City, Taiwan
lukegao1991@gmail.com
[3] Department of Interior Design, Chung Yuan Christian University,
Taoyuan City, Taiwan
chenly99@gmail.com
[4] Department of Arts and Creative Industries, National Dong Hwa University,
Hualien, Taiwan
iamcsh0222@gms.ndhu.edu.tw

Abstract. The cultivation of featured towns is an important measure taken by the country currently to promote the regional development and the construction of new-type urbanization. The construction of the experience mode centered on excursions contributes to the development of tourist industry. This article starts with the significance of the construction of cultural and creative experience mode of town and takes Heshun Town and Houqiao Town of Tengchong County as examples to analyze the construction of cultural and creative experience mode of featured town.

Keywords: Featured town · Cultural and creative · Experience mode

1 Introduction

The concept of "featured town" was originated in 2014. According to some scholars, the featured town is a system created by government departments under the supply-side institutional reform. Some scholars regard the construction of featured towns as a tool for the transformation and upgrading of regional economy. In 2016, the experience gained by Zhejiang Province in the construction of towns obtained the attention of the Central Government. The construction of featured town bears the hope of local governments to promote industrial transformation and upgrading and optimize regional industrial systems. At this stage, the construction of featured towns in China is still in its infancy. The top-level design issues, construction and operation issues, industrial development issues, functional integration issues and system and mechanism issues are still the main factors affecting the construction of featured towns. As to economy, the study on cultural and creative experience mode of featured town can provide some theoretical support for the construction and operation, industrial development and function integration of featured towns. For government, the research on the mode of cultural and creative experience in featured towns can promote the optimization of institutional mechanisms and top-level design problems in the construction of featured towns and make the government departments clarify their own responsibilities in the process of construction of featured towns. For people's livelihood, the research on the cultural and creative experience mode of featured towns can play a role of enriching people's spiritual and cultural life and maintain social stability (Fig. 1).

Fig. 1. The main factors affecting the construction of featured towns

2   The Construction Significance of Cultural and Creative Experience Mode of Towns

Featured town is a new thing produced in the development of urbanization in our country. At this stage, the research work of featured towns in our country is mainly based on empirical research and systematic analysis. Qualitative research is the main content of empirical research and the significance of the featured town, the construction process are the main content that scholars pay close attention to. The featured towns have been recognized by academic circle in the new urbanization process as the means of coordinated development of urban system. The significance of the cultural and creative experience mode related to the construction of featured towns is mainly manifested in the following aspects:

2.1   Contribute to the Development of Urbanization Process

The cultivation of characteristic towns is originated in July 2016. According to the requirements of the Notice on the Work of Cultivating Featured Towns of Ministry of Urban and Rural Construction, the National Development and Reform Commission and the Ministry of Finance, China plans to cultivate 1,000 featured towns nationwide by 2020 [1]. Judging from the status quo of national economic development, industry and employment are the key factors driving the economic development of cities and towns. Natural resources and historical and cultural resources are the key factors in the construction of featured towns at this stage. The featured town cultural and creative experience mode is based on the urban-rural integration development mode. The construction of various types of featured towns can promote the process of urbanization on the basis of building the supporting environment around the industry needs (Fig. 2).

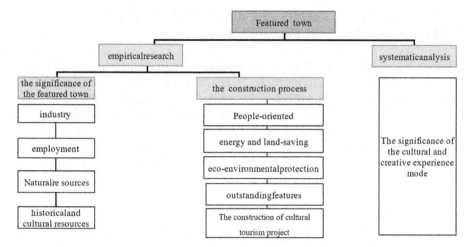

Fig. 2. The construction significance of cultural and creative experience mode of towns

2.2 Contribute to the Development of Cultural Industries in the County

The unity of renewability and non-renewability is the main feature of cultural resources. In order to promote the coordinated development of regional economy on the basis of adhering to the road of urbanization with Chinese characteristics, the state needs to actively and steadily promote urbanization in the process of building a cultural and creative experience mode of featured towns. People-oriented, energy and land-saving, eco-environmental protection and outstanding features are the concerns in cultural and creative experience mode construction process. As the main body of the allocation of cultural resources, government departments play the role of carrying forward and protecting public cultural resources. The construction of culture creative experience mode of featured town can provide a certain guarantee for the innovation and development of local cultural industry.

2.3 Contribute to the Construction of Boutique Tourist Industry

The development of tourist industry is an issue that cannot be neglected in the process of featured town construction. Relying on the tourist industry, the creation of cultural and creative products plays the role of driving regional economy. The construction of cultural tourism project can provide the town with new points of regional economic growth. From the cultural heritage, the construction of cultural and creative experience mode of featured town can provide new ways of cultural transmission based on carrying forward the local cultural function. Therefore, the development of featured town can provide certain guarantee for the development of boutique tourist industry. Cultural factors are the soul elements of the tourist industry. With the help of cultural and creative experience activities, the cultural connotation of tourism projects can be enhanced and the competitiveness and vitality of the tourist industry can be effectively strengthened.

3 The Influencing Factors of Cultural and Creative Experience Mode of Featured Town

Through the analysis of the value of tourist towns, we can find that tourist towns play the role of industrial function platform [2]. Based on the excavation of local characteristics and clear positioning of itself, the construction of cultural and creative experience mode of featured town can create supporting environment and develop creative products based on the industrial needs of cultural industries and then realize the development of urbanization through the help of human resources. Ultimately, through the linkage of cultural industry and tourism, catering industry and transportation industry, industrial upgrading is achieved.

3.1 Site Selection Issue

Site election factors can be seen as the main influencing factors in the construction of cultural and creative experience mode. During the site selection stage of the cultural and creative experience project, relevant departments need to effectively solve the contradiction between the protection of arable land and the rigid demand for land use in urban and rural areas.

3.2 The Size of the Town

The mobility of clients in the tourist industry is relatively large. The issue of floating population is one of the major issues facing the future tourist town. Reasonable control of the size of the town can make the town better cope with attracted tourists.

3.3 Industrial Layout

The impact of industrial layout on the construction of featured towns is mainly reflected in the impact on the development of tourist towns. The construction of cultural and creative experience mode of featured town requires the relevant government departments and enterprises to conduct an in-depth analysis of the internal and external conditions and local cultural resources of the town, and on this basis, to determine the long-term development strategy. In the industrial layout, relevant departments need to rely on the scientific and rationalized theme of tourism and culture to provide the town with a scientific and rational operation mechanism.

3.4 Infrastructure Construction Factors

With the increasing size of featured towns, the perfected public infrastructure has become the guarantee factor for people's needs. At this stage, some towns' public service facilities cannot meet the basic needs of tourists and local residents. From the causes of the above problems, the problems showed in the capital injection capacity and self-strength of featured town construction enterprise is the major factor causing the phenomenon from the investment and financing construction main body level. The performance of contractual capacity of the investment main body will be the major influencing factor of the quality of featured town construction.

4 Construction Measures of Cultural and Creative Experience Mode of Featured Town

The construction of cultural and creative experience mode of featured town is an important measure to innovate the existing urban tourist industry development mode. Under the background of the integration of urban and rural areas, the optimal allocation of markets and marketization of tourism public services have become an important factor in reducing the operating costs of featured towns and promoting the formation of economies of scale. Starting from the characteristics of its own cultural resources and building a themed development strategy with the characteristics of the region, we can provide tourist industry cluster [3] of sustainable development for cultural and creative experience mode of featured towns based on the uniqueness, personalization, experience and participation of tourism products (Table 1).

Table 1. The construction significance of cultural and creative experience mode of towns

National cultural values	Innovate tourism behavior patterns and tourism experience mode	Give full play to role of colleges and universities in the cultural town tourism management
Special natural landscape, rich historical resources, unique humanistic spirit and unique local materials and impressive production skills	The combination of industrial advantages, geographical features, urban development effectiveness and motivation guarantee	Tourist police teams; In the cultural town tourism management
Tengchong Houqiao Town: the traditional architectural art and national customs of Lisu people	Tengchong: the volcano group; the historical and cultural resources represented by the anti-Japanese war culture; volcanic hot spring landscape; Agricultural tourism experience activities	Tengchong: national historical and cultural towns, beautiful national towns and villages, the national 5A scenic areas and national industry demonstration base

4.1 Focus on the Development of National Cultural Values

In terms of the construction process of cultural and creative experience mode of featured towns, the government departments need to regard the tourist town as a whole scenic area. Special natural landscape, rich historical resources, unique humanistic spirit and unique local materials and impressive production skills are the necessary characteristics of featured town in the new era. The development of the value of national culture can be seen as a problem that cannot be neglected in the process of constructing cultural and creative experience mode of featured towns. Taking Yunnan Province of China as an example, the province is an important tourist province in China. It plays an important role of linkage between tourist industry and cultural industry. It is an important principle followed in the construction of featured towns in Yunnan. Through the development of tourism resources in western Yunnan, the development mode of tourism economy guided by the construction of transportation infrastructure is the main mode of development adopted by this region.

Taking Tengchong area in Yunnan Province as an example, the area has been an important transportation hub in the southwest of Yunnan since ancient times. The Ancient Bonan Road, South Silk Road and Stilwell Road played a positive role in promoting the development of our history. After turning Tengchong County into Tengchong City in 2015, from the structure of cultural resources, the realizing of economic value of cultural resources has become the feasible idea that promotes the local cultural industry development on the basis of optimal allocation. From the perspective of the development of national cultural values, the creative products related to the value of national culture mainly include the following factors: first, the humanistic spirit possessed by local ethnic minorities; second, border tourism projects with regional values; third, cultural tourism activities. Taking Tengchong Houqiao Town as an example, the traditional architectural art and national customs of Lisu people play an important role in the construction of cultural and creative products in local featured towns. The length of the border line is 72.8 km. There are national level grade I open ports such as the Houqiao port, 2,155 km from the Myitkyina of Myanmar and 31.5 km from Ledo of Indian, hence the important node of the Stilwell road in the history. In the development process of cultural and creative products, the locals can make use of Langya Mountain, Lotus Stone, Binglang River Scenery and Lisu ethnic folk style as the basis, to create tourism products. National culture has the characteristics of individualism. The construction of cultural and creative products based on tourism culture is not a simple fusion of national culture and tourism development. Rather, it starts with the tourism resources development and the problems in the process, leverages on the national cultural position to create a creative product of national culture. Starting from the actual situation in the region, innovation on the combination of national culture and other tourism resources can optimize the cultural experience mode of featured towns on the basis of highlighting characteristics, enhancing attraction and improving tourist taste.

On the basis of strengthening the overall efficiency, it will build distinctive brands and follow the principle of management in development and development in protection and require all localities to pay attention to the macro-control policies, directions, efforts and measures of town construction and development in the process of building featured towns. It is necessary to make clear the macro-control policies, directions, efforts and measures for the construction and development of various featured towns. In this regard, relevant departments also need to carry out promotion and investment attraction work on the basis of a clear definition of the size and development orientation of various types of towns so as to make the featured town system present the characteristics of consistent function and scales.

4.2   Innovate Tourism Behavior Patterns and Tourism Experience Mode

The combination of industrial advantages, geographical features, urban development effectiveness and motivation guarantee can provide guarantee for the sustainable development of featured towns. In the mode of tourism behavior, the featured town cultural and creative experience mode can help form the cultural memory through the tourism elements such as food, accommodation, transportation, shopping and traveling, and so on. Taking Tengchong in Yunnan as an example, the natural ecological resources represented by the volcano group and the historical and cultural resources represented by the anti-Japanese war culture are the basic elements of the local cultural and creative experience mode. In the field of tourism, volcanic hot spring landscape has become a famous tourist brand in the region. The project of National Martyr Cemetery and Western Yunnan War Memorial Museum has become a carrier for understanding the expeditionary force of China and understanding the role of the Kuomintang army in the anti-Japanese war. In the process of constructing the cultural and creative experience mode of featured towns, the following creative design modes can be adopted by the local people to carry out cultural and creative experience activities: First, with the help of local products such as Songhua cake, brown rice and other local specialty, build a catering culture with local characteristics; second, build a tourism accommodation service system with homestay form as the mainstay. Based on the homestay project, the local characteristic resources are effectively used, so that visitors can be familiar with the local culture in the process of living with the local residents. Thirdly, the tourism service form represented by "caravan travel" is constructed in the historic and cultural core protected area of Heshun Ancient Town. The use of such horse-riding excursions will allow local residents to increase their incomes and allow visitors to increase their knowledge of the local culture during the tour. At the level of shopping and consumption, the local area can construct some creative products such as ethnic craft making workshops and artificial paper making workshops. This measure can provide tourists with knowledge of the local traditional craft culture and experience of local craft culture and this experience can also enable local residents to better inherit the local culture [4].

Agricultural tourism experience activities at this stage have become a new mode for some regions to promote the development of tourism economy. Some cities in China have carried out a series of experience activities such as rice planting. Taking Heshun Town in Tengchong City as an example, the construction of the farming and education culture experience mode is an effective measure to innovate the local tourism experience mode. From the construction process of tourism, the locals can build a cultural and creative experience mode with ancestral temple study hall experience mode, reception-style living patterns, autonomous tourism patterns, residential construction tours, library learning patterns, park recreation patterns and wetland tourism patterns as the representative. For example, after the construction of ancestral temple study hall experience mode, the local can invite some of seniors of some surnames to carry out school education for their offspring in the hall. Some foreign visitors can also participate in teaching activities. Some local poems are compiled into a public offering to allow visitors to experience this unique traditional culture. Heshun Ancient Town Library is a historic village library in China. The construction of the experience mode based on the library learning mode allows visitors to experience the atmosphere of reading and studying of local peasants in the library. During the excursion, the local can focus on the history of the ancient town of Heshun, the development of caravan culture and jade culture and others to set quiz activities, so that visitors can take the initiative to follow the local history and culture and can be awarded with prizes of local specialties (such as rice paper and oiled paper umbrella) so as to allow tourists to form a cultural memory of Heshun. The construction of wetland tourism mode can provide visitors with ideal space for sketching. The protective development of some historical sites can also make tourists aware of the consequences of ignorance of cultural protection (Fig. 3).

Fig. 3. Tengchong traditional culture representatives

4.3 Give Full Play to Role of Colleges and Universities in the Cultural Town Tourism Management

At this stage, the state has set up tourist police teams in Yunnan, Hainan and Beijing (such as Sanya Public Security Bureau Tourism Police Detachment and Beijing Municipal Public Security Bureau Central Food and Drug Administration Security Corps). In my opinion, using the law enforcement force of the police to standardize the environment of tourism and security can provide certain protection for the normative development of the tourist industry. Tourism function is a major feature of the town. In the cultural town tourism management, the relevant departments can also give full play to the role of institutions of higher learning in tourism management [5]. Leveraging on the innovative features of colleges and universities to optimize the creative experience mode can bring visitors a unique experience of tourism consumption.

Taking Tengchong City as an example, the area has a number of honors including national historical and cultural towns, beautiful national towns and villages, the national 5A scenic areas and national industry demonstration base. The principle of economic development in towns with the core of "protecting the style, showing culture, supporting properly and developing harmoniously" is an important factor to promote the development of local tourism and cultural industries. To promote the development of local tourist industry, International Cultural and Creative Ice Town project is the creative mode that gives play to the innovation role of colleges and universities. This project includes indoor skating, skiing and other recreational projects, which can bring to the locals and surrounding region's people a unique ice and snow experience. In this creative experience mode, visitors can also learn about the unique craft such as oil paper umbrella, Dai brocade and tin foil making, and feel the traditional local culture of Tengchong such as Dongjing Ancient Music and Wa Qing Opera. Through business investment, business strategy, collection of Tsinghua University and Tus Resources, the town has introduced more than 30 units such as Tsinghua University's life science and technology, Thailand's Lanshi University Oriental Medical School, Tsinghua Internet Industry Research Institute, Tsinghua University Academy of Social Sciences, Tsinghua University Academy of Fine Arts, Central Academy of Fine Arts, Fengma Music Festival, Kang Hui Tourism, Tujia and Tsinghua University Cultural and Creative Academy. The construction of business format of three-in-one and coordinated development of "Technology park (Cao)+ Technology industry (Feng)+ Technology finance (Shi) and Tus "Park+ Industry+ Finance, Technology+ Capital+ Industry, Government+ Enterprise+ University" can effectively promote the transformation and upgrading of local industries.

5 Conclusion

The cultural and creative experience mode of featured towns has some positive effects on promoting the development of tourism economy and improving the quality of life of the masses. According to the experiences gained in Tengchong, Yunnan and other places, the construction of a sustainable tourist industry cluster plays an important role in the process of constructing the cultural and creative experience mode of featured towns. The reasonable development of the national culture value can strengthen the regional cultural characteristics of the featured town. Giving play to the role of institutions of higher learning in the construction of experience mode, allows visitors to experience a unique consumer experience. Experience mode based on historical and cultural resources can help people to deepen their understanding of the regional cultural characteristics.

References

1. Huang, J. Lu, N.: Research summary of domestic featured towns: progress and prospects [J/OL]. Contemporary Economic Management, pp. 1–6
2. Zhao, H.: Innovative development research of tourist featured town. Econ. Issues **12**, 104–107 (2017)
3. Jiang, T.: Historical memory and ethnic identity of Heshun ancient town. Ethn. Forum, (05), 58–63 (2017)
4. Yang, X.: Tengchong Heshun ancient town "Farming and Education Culture" landscape development mode exploration. Innov. Technol. **03**, 64–66 (2016)
5. Wang, J., Yin, M.: Role of optimized allocation of cultural resources in the development of cultural industries. J. Qujing Norm. Univ. **34**(05), 70–74 (2015)
6. Rongtai, L., Kreifeldt, J.G.: Do Not Touch: Dialogues between Designing Science and Humanities and Arts. Yu Chen, New Taipei City (2014)
7. Rongtai, L.: Cultural creativity, design added value. Art Apprec. **1**(7), 26–32 (2015)

Influence of Rebound Effect on Energy Saving in Smart Homes

Ko-jung Chen[1], Ziyang Li[1], Ta-Ping Lu[1(✉)], Pei-Luen Patrick Rau[1], and Dinglong Huang[2]

[1] Institute of Human Factors and Ergonomics, Department of Industrial Engineering, Tsinghua University, Beijing 100084, China
robert_tplu@163.com
[2] Shenzhen Malong Artificial Intelligence Research Center, Shenzhen, Guangdong Province, China

Abstract. The rebound effect refers to the increase in energy use resulting from reduced energy costs and improved energy efficiency. This study proves that the rebound effect exists in smart homes and measures the size of rebound effect through two experiments. Results show that when electricity bills decreased and electricity use suggestions were provided, the electricity use significantly increased. The size of rebound effect was 13.5% in both cases. When electricity use suggestions were provided, the size of rebound effect of illumination settings was highest (20.24%), while the size of rebound effect of appliance settings was lowest (6.42%). The rebound effect in future smart homes can be reduced by (1) providing real-time electricity bills information combined with electricity use feedback; (2) offering electricity use suggestions through intelligent learning.

Keywords: Smart homes · Rebound effect · Electricity use

1 Introduction

The energy efficiency of household products is enhanced by the rapid progress in science and technology. When energy efficiency is improved, the total energy consumption decreases. However, many studies in the field indicate that the reduced energy costs due to energy efficiency improvements lead to increased energy use, i.e. the so-called rebound effect [1–3]. In recent years, smart homes have attracted a substantial amount of investment in China. According to the survey by Richter (2015), in 2020, the number of smart homes will be seven times what it was in 2015, i.e. an increase from 0.3 million in 2015 to 2.1 million households in 2020. Smart homes have a significant influence on both the lifestyle of their occupants and their energy use patterns. Currently, many studies on the rebound effect have been published in energy journals. However, the existence of rebound effect in smart homes, its impact on the lifestyle of occupants, the size of such rebound effect, and measures to reduce it are still unknown.

Therefore, this study investigates the rebound effect in smart homes and measures the size of such rebound effect. This research study also explores the methods to reduce the rebound effect size, and investigates the energy-saving strategies to minimize the rebound effect.

© Springer International Publishing AG, part of Springer Nature 2018
P.-L. P. Rau (Ed.): CCD 2018, LNCS 10912, pp. 266–274, 2018.
https://doi.org/10.1007/978-3-319-92252-2_21

2 Literature Review and Research Question

2.1 Energy Saving in Smart Homes and Rebound Effect

With the rapid development of smart homes, the smart home products improved the energy efficiency of home appliances, providing a new way for energy saving. Lu et al. carried out a study in 2010, using simple sensor technology in a household to automatically sense the human positions and sleep modes. Those modes were applied to automatically turn off the air conditioning system to save energy. It was found that the adopted method saved an average of 28% of the energy with a cost of only 25-dollar for the sensor [4]. It has been reported that installing an automated system to manage the energy consumption of household appliances and other equipment could reduce the energy consumption by 18.7% [5]. Smart homes use automatic sensitivity to automatically adjust home systems, ensuring both higher comfort levels and less energy consumption. However, energy efficiency improvements offered by smart homes brings about the rebound effect. In more advanced energy-saving environments, people tend to use more energy [6, 7]. Kavousian, Rajagopal, and Fischer (2013) carried out a survey on 1628 American households with smart electric meters [8]. The study results indicate that the existence of energy-efficiency-promoting appliances (such as intelligent temperature controllers and heat insulating materials) leads to a slight increase in electricity consumptions by those households.

The size of the rebound effect is defined as the offset between the percentage of improved energy efficiency and the percentage of increased energy consumption [2]. Some studies indicate that the size of the direct rebound effect is not greater than 50% [2, 6], and that lower electricity bills are one of the main factors for the rebound effect [3]. In 2016, Wang et al. evaluated the rebound effect in seven major industries in Beijing. They found that the short-term rebound effect was 24%–37% and the long-term rebound effect was up to 46%–56%, indicating that the rebound effect on energy use should not be underestimated [9]. According to the estimates by Energy Information Administration (EIA), household electricity consumption accounts for 37% of the total electricity consumption [10]. With the growing demand for smart homes and the significance of household electricity consumption, the rebound effect in smart homes and its effect size need to be further discussed. Hence, the first research question investigates the existence and the size of smart homes rebound effect, as follows:

Research Question 1: Does the rebound effect exist in smart homes and what is the size of the rebound effect?

2.2 Energy Saving Strategies in Smart Homes

Afterward strategy, as an important energy-saving strategy, is established on key premises upon which the hypothesis that "the existences of positive and negative consequences affect behaviors" is derived [11]. The literature on afterward strategy is mostly focused on "feedback" mechanisms. Some studies indicate that real-time feedback can effectively reduce household energy consumption by 4%–9%, which can significantly enhance household energy saving [12, 13]. Smart homes use various technologies that offer effective energy consumption feedback. Such technologies enable monitoring household appliances at any time and supports real-time view. Chetty et al. (2008) pointed out that families are most likely to ignore their energy use patterns, and they hope to acquire real-time information about their energy consumption in order to save money and make their homes comfortable and environment friendly [14]. Moreover, the timing of providing feedback is crucial [15]. Some studies show that providing proper feedback and real-time information at the appropriate time can reduce the electricity consumption of each household by more than 10% on average [16, 17]. It is worth considering that whether and how users will adjust their energy use when they are informed of the existence of the rebound effect. It is also confirmed that using the proper information-providing strategy contributes to energy saving [11], and information feedback is the simplest and direct way to inform users of the rebound effect. Will providing feedback to the users and recognizing the increase in their electricity consumptions change the size of the rebound effect? Thus, the second research question will explore the strategies to reduce the rebound effect, as follows:

Research Question 2: How will the informed users adjust their electricity use in order to reduce the rebound effect in smart homes?

3 Experiment 1

Experiment 1 examined the changes of participants' electricity use when electricity bills were reduced. The aim of Experiment 1 is to investigate whether the rebound effect exists in smart homes and measure the size of the rebound effect. A within-design experiment was conducted.

3.1 Experimental Material

In order to examine the changes in the electricity use of the participants, each participant was provided with a situational simulation. There were three rooms in the situational simulation of household electricity use, i.e. living room, kitchen, and bedroom. Each room was configured with luminaires, air conditioning and three kinds of household appliances (selected by the participants). The researcher collected 19 commonly used household appliances (see Table 1), and their powers was evaluated based on existing products in the market for the reference. Participants rated the use frequency of each appliance with a 5-point scale, in which 1-point means rare use and 5-point means the appliance is in use at the time. According to calculations, participants would see monthly electricity bills of each appliance.

Monthly electricity bills of each appliance = appliance power × use frequency

$$\times \ 0.48 \,(\text{Yuan, the unit price of electricity})$$
$$\times \ 30 \,(\text{days of a month}).$$

$$(1)$$

Table 1. Calculation of the power consumed by household appliances

Area	Household Appliance	Power (W)	Average Power (W)
General	Electric luminaires	82	N/A
	Air conditioner	1200	
Living room	Air purifier	60	126.4
	Floor mopping robot	30	
	Television	100	
	Stereo system	42	
	Water dispenser	400	
Kitchen	Refrigerator	80	788
	Electric cooker	300	
	Soybean milk machine	800	
	Coffee machine	650	
	Induction cooker	2100	
	Juicer	300	
	Dish drier	250	
	Dishwasher	1100	
	Oven	1600	
	Microwave oven	700	
Bedroom	Hair drier	1000	281
	Stereo system	4	
	Humidifier	30	
	Computer	90	

3.2 Experimental Procedures

Sixteen students (seven males and nine females) were invited to participate in Experiment 1. All of them were aware of the electricity use conditions and bills at their own homes. The average age of the participants was 23.8. Participants individually took part in the experiment. The experimental procedures were shown in Fig. 1. First, the researcher introduced the experimental procedure to the participants. The experiment involved three phases of electricity use. Then, the participants selected three household appliances commonly used in the living room, kitchen, and bedroom, respectively. In the first phase of electricity use, the participants conducted electricity use (i.e., rated the use frequency of each appliance with a 5-point scale) of six appliances (two illustration devices, one temperature control device, and three household appliances) in each room. Then, the participants were informed that there was an energy-saving assistant in their smart home which can help reduce electricity bills. The energy-saving assistant could automatically adjust the brightness of lamps at home and the temperature of air conditioning system. In the second phase, the participants conducted electricity use when there was an energy-saving assistant in the home. After the second phase, the participants were shown the monthly electricity bills of each appliance. The participants were provided electricity use feedback by diagrams, which compared the difference in electricity bills between the first and second phase of the electricity use. Then, the participants conducted the third phase of electricity use. At last, the participants were interviewed about the opinions about the functions of the energy-saving assistant and the driving forces to reduce the rebound effect.

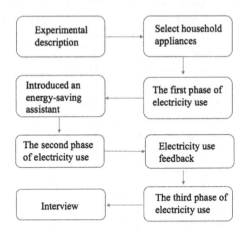

Fig. 1. Experimental procedure of Experiment 1

3.3   Results

The data of the three phases of electricity use was normally distributed. A paired t-test was conducted to analyze the data. The second phase of electricity use (M2 = 64.50, SD2 = 13.16) were significantly higher than those of the first phase (M1 = 56.81, SD1 = 10.00, t(15) = −4.14, p < .001) which confirms the existence of the rebound effect. The size of the rebound effect was 13.5%.

$$\text{Size of the rebound effect} = (\text{second phase of electricity use} - \text{first phase of electricity use}) / \text{first phase of electricity use}))$$

(2)

This indicates that the electricity use increased by about 13.5% when the electricity bills were decreased. The third phase electricity use (M3 = 58.44, SD3 = 14.35) were significantly lower than those of the second phase (M2 = 64.50, SD2 = 13.16; t(15) = 5.33, p < .000), which indicates that when the participants were provided electricity use feedback (i.e., recognized rebound effect), they significantly reduced their electricity use. The size of the rebound effect was 9.4%, i.e., the size of counter rebound effect is 9.4%. During the interview, participants were willing to reduce their electricity use when electricity use feedback was provided in the third phase of electricity use. Half of the participants thought the electricity use system should have notification function. Without the notification functions, they would not take actions to reduce their electricity consumption rates.

4 Experiment 2

The aim of Experiment 2 was to examine whether the rebound effect exists in more realistic electricity use condition of smart homes. Experiment 2 examined the changes of participants' electricity use when electricity use suggestion was provided.

4.1 Experimental Material

Two software prototypes were developed with Axure 7.0 to provide immersive situational simulations, i.e., "Electricity Use Steward" and "Intelligent Electricity Use Steward" (see Fig. 2). The software prototypes were used to remotely control environmental settings (temperature, humidity, and water temperature) and indoor appliances (in living room, kitchen, bedroom, and bathroom). Participants used software prototypes to conduct electricity use. "Intelligent Electricity Use Steward" had higher level of intelligence than "Electricity Use Steward". "Intelligent Electricity Use Steward" could provide electricity use suggestions which helps participants live more comfortable, and could also automatically help participants adjust each appliance to the recommended setting. Experiment 2 classified the electricity use into four categories: environmental setting (e.g., target temperature and air volume, target humidity), illumination setting (e.g., light in the living room, light in the kitchen), and appliance setting (e.g., speakers in the living room, washing machine in the kitchen).

4.2 Experimental Procedures

Fifty-one students (thirty males and twenty-one females) were invited in Experiment 2. All participants were aware of electricity use conditions and electricity bills at their own homes. The average age of the participants was 23.7. The experimental procedures were almost the same as the Experiment 1, whereas the electricity use of Experiment 2 was conducted by software manipulation. The experimental software presented by iPad air 2 had 9.7-inch LED screen, pixel of 2048 × 1536 and resolution of 264 ppi. In the first phase of electricity use, "Electricity Use Steward" was used to obtain the electricity consumption in common conditions. In the second phase of electricity use, "Intelligent Electricity Use Steward" was used, which could provide suggestions to adjust electricity use. Prior to the third phase of electricity use, the participants were provided with electricity use feedback by diagrams to compare their electricity use in the first two phases. Then the "Intelligent Electricity Use Steward" was used in the third phase of electricity use.

4.3 Results

The data about the four categories of electricity use settings in three phases experiment of electricity use was normally distributed. A paired t-test was used conducted to analyze the data. The electricity use in the first phase (T1) and the second phase (T2)

Electricity Use Steward   Intelligent Electricity Use Steward

Fig. 2. Homepage of the two prototype software programs

were listed in Table 2. Electricity use in the second phase was significantly higher than that in the first phase. The results indicate that when electricity use suggestions were offered, the electricity use would be reduced. Hence, a rebound effect occurred; the rebound effect size of each type of electricity use setting is listed in Table 3.

Table 2. Paired t-test of phase one and phase two

Categories of electricity use settings		Mean	Standard deviation	Degree of freedom	T value	p
Environmental setting	T1	44.92	10.36	50	4.973	.000
	T2	50.72	9.00			
Illumination setting	T1	53.70	15.28	50	7.528	.000
	T2	64.57	12.28			
Appliance setting	T1	47.19	10.52	50	3.018	.004
	T2	50.22	9.22			
Total power consumption	T1	48.60	7.94	50	7.879	.000
	T2	55.17	7.15			

Table 3. Sizes of rebound effect

Electricity consumption in the first and second phases	Size of rebound effect
Environmental setting	12.91%
Illumination setting	20.24%
Appliance setting	6.42%
Total power consumption	13.52%

There was no significant difference in electricity use between the second and third phase in aspects of the environmental setting, illumination setting, appliance setting, and total power consumption. It was found that the electricity use of the above four settings in the third phase are less than those in the second phase.

During the interview, participants demonstrated living habit is the most important reason to save energy. Most of the participants believed that they could achieve more comfortable living conditions by following offered electricity use suggestions in smart homes. This explains why participants in Experiment 2 slightly adjusted their electricity use when they found that their electric use increased in the third phase of electricity use. Many participants expressed that they would stick to their electric use habits regardless of the offered electricity use suggestions. But the statistical analysis result shows that participants are easily influenced by proposed electricity consumption rates, while they are unaware of it.

5   General Discussion

The stimulation of electricity bills and electricity use suggestions confirmed the occurrence of the rebound effect with an effect size of 12.5% in the study. According to the research by Greening et al. (2000), household rebound effects are about 0–30% [2]; thus, the rebound effect obtained in this study is within the normal range. The research by Greening et al. (2000), which involved four studies, indicates that the rebound effects in illuminating are about 5–12%, while the rebound effect reported in this study is 20%, exceeding the above range. This is possibly due to the software simulation employed in this study.

Reducing electricity bills and offering electricity use suggestions can both cause rebound effect. Even though all participants' electricity use were reduced when perceiving rebound effect, only those who were provided with immediate feedback about electricity bills had sharply reduced use. Multiple energy-saving functions can be provided for smart homes users to save energy. For example, intelligent learning is the most importation function that helps to change lifestyles. Electricity use suggestions can be offered to users in a personified manner to gradually change the users' lifestyles. Moreover, immediate personified notifications will be sent when any changes in the electricity use or any abnormality in the performance of household appliances is detected in order to optimize the users' experience.

6   Conclusion

This study verifies that the rebound effect exists in smart homes. Lower electricity bills and providing electricity use suggestions have similar rebound effect in smart homes. The size of the rebound effect is 13.5%. The rebound effect sizes vary under different electricity use patterns. Under the impact of electricity use suggestions, the reported rebound effect sizes are 6.42% upon appliance settings, 12.91% upon environment settings, and 20.24% upon illuminating settings. Hence, in order to reduce the rebound effect in future smart homes, the following recommendation can be considered: provide immediate electricity bills information combined with electricity use feedback, and provide electricity use suggestions through intelligent learning.

Acknowledgement. This research was supported by Shenzhen Malong Artificial Intelligence Research Center.

References

1. Alcott, B.: Jevons' paradox. Ecol. Econ. **54**(1), 9–21 (2005)
2. Greening, L.A., Greene, D.L., Difiglio, C.: Energy efficiency and consumption—the rebound effect—a survey. Energy Policy **28**(6–7), 389–401 (2000)
3. Small, K.A., Van Dender, K.: Fuel efficiency and motor vehicle travel: the declining rebound effect. Energy J. **28**, 25–51 (2007)
4. Lu, J., Sookoor, T., Srinivasan, V., Gao, G., Holben, B., Stankovic, J., Field, E., Whitehouse, K.: The smart thermostat: using occupancy sensors to save energy in homes. In: Proceedings of the 8th ACM Conference on Embedded Networked Sensor Systems, pp. 211–224 (2010)
5. Tejani, D., Al-Kuwari, A.M.A., Potdar, V.: Energy conservation in a smart home. In: 2011 Proceedings of the 5th IEEE International Conference on Digital Ecosystems and Technologies Conference (DEST), pp. 241–246 (2011)
6. Hong, S.H., Oreszczyn, T., Ridley, I.: Warm front study group: the impact of energy efficient refurbishment on the space heating fuel consumption in english dwellings. Energy Build. **38**(10), 1171–1181 (2006)
7. Sorrell, S., Dimitropoulos, J.: The rebound effect: microeconomic definitions, limitations and extensions. Ecol. Econ. **65**(3), 636–649 (2008)
8. Kavousian, A., Rajagopal, R., Fischer, M.: Determinants of residential electricity consumption: using smart meter data to examine the effect of climate, building characteristics, appliance stock, and occupants' behavior. Energy **55**, 184–194 (2013)
9. Wang, Z., Han, B., Lu, M.: Measurement of energy rebound effect in households: evidence from residential electricity consumption in Beijing, China. Renew. Sustain. Energy Rev. **58**, 852–861 (2016)
10. Energy Information Administration (US): Annual Energy Review 2011. Government Printing Office (2012)
11. Abrahamse, W., Steg, L., Vlek, C., Rothengatter, T.: A review of intervention studies aimed at household energy conservation. J. Environ. Psychol. **25**(3), 273–291 (2005)
12. Faruqui, A., Sergici, S., Sharif, A.: The impact of informational feedback on energy consumption—A survey of the experimental evidence. Energy **35**(4), 1598–1608 (2010)
13. Foster, B., Mazur-Stommen, S.: Results from Recent Real-Time Feedback Studies. American Council for an Energy-Efficient Economy, Washington, DC (2012)
14. Chetty, M., Tran, D., Grinter, R.E.: Getting to green: understanding resource consumption in the home. In: Proceedings of the 10th International Conference on Ubiquitous Computing, pp. 242–251 (2008)
15. Kantola, S.J., Syme, G.J., Campbell, N.A.: Cognitive dissonance and energy conservation. J. Appl. Psychol. **69**(3), 416 (1984)
16. McCalley, L.T., Midden, C.J.: Energy conservation through product-integrated feedback: the roles of goal-setting and social orientation. J. Econ. Psychol. **23**(5), 589–603 (2002)
17. Wood, G., Newborough, M.: Dynamic energy-consumption indicators for domestic appliances: environment, behaviour and design. Energy Build. **35**(8), 821–841 (2003)

Transforming a Neighborhood into a Living Laboratory for Urban Social Innovation: A Comparative Case Study of Urban Living Labs

Eun Ji Cho[1,2(✉)]

[1] College of Design and Innovation, Tongji University, Shanghai, China
ej.cho@tongji.edu.cn
[2] Shanghai Institute of Design and Innovation, Tongji University, Shanghai, China

Abstract. Cities, where more than half of the world's population resides nowadays, face a number of challenges that require innovative solutions. This paper pays attention on the emergence of Urban Living Labs that foster urban innovations by bringing various stakeholders, ranging from local governments to citizens, together to co-create innovation. Based on the concept of 'Living Labs' - "*user-driven innovation environments where users and producers co-create innovation in a trusted, open ecosystem that enables business and societal innovation*" (The European Network of Living Labs, 2015) – various types of Urban Living Labs have emerged over the recent years. This paper explores different ways Urban Living Labs operate and contribute to fostering urban social innovation. Three cases of urban living labs - Seoul Innovation Park Living Lab (Seoul, Korea), Living Lab The Neighborhood (Malmö, Sweden), and Living Lab Shanghai (Shanghai, China) – are studied. The three urban living labs are geographically, culturally, and structurally different, but have in common that they aim to foster urban sustainability, with a focus on social innovation. Main actors of each urban living lab, their motivation and roles, representative projects, and (expected) outcomes are examined. Based on the case studies and literature review, this paper highlights the distinctive nature and potential of 'design-driven' urban living labs.

Keywords: Urban living labs · Urban transformation · Design for social innovation · Design-driven living labs

1 Emergence of Urban Living Labs

In 2015, the United Nations announced an agenda for sustainable development and its 17 Sustainable Development Goals [1]. The 17 goals include 'sustainable cities and communities', as the population living in cities has already reached 50 percent of the world population, and is projected to grow up to 70 percent by 2050 [2]. Cities face a number of challenges that require 'increasingly sophisticated tools and solutions' [3].

This paper pays attention on the potential of 'Urban Living Labs' that have emerged around the world in recent years. Originally developed as a methodology to

© Springer International Publishing AG, part of Springer Nature 2018
P.-L. P. Rau (Ed.): CCD 2018, LNCS 10912, pp. 275–285, 2018.
https://doi.org/10.1007/978-3-319-92252-2_22

develop and test new technologies with end-users in real-life environments, the 'Living Lab' approach has been adopted in various contexts, including 'territorial innovation' in urban and regional settings. Based on the concept of 'Living Labs', defined as *"user-centred, open innovation ecosystems based on systematic user co-creation approach, integrating research and innovation processes in real life communities and settings"* [6], Urban Living Labs refer to a city or regional level living lab [7]. The principles of living lab approaches, such as multi-method approaches, user engagement, multi-stakeholder participation, real-life setting, and co-creation [8], are the basis of urban living labs, but there are various working definitions about Urban Living Labs. As an example, McCormick and Hartmann define urban living labs as *"sites devised to design, test, and learn from social and technical innovation in real time"* [4]. According to them, urban living labs can be considered *"both as an arena (geographically or institutionally bounded spaces), and as an approach for intentional collaborative experimentation of researchers, citizens, companies and local governments"* [ibid.]. Voytenko et al. define urban living labs as *"a form of experimental governance, whereby urban stakeholders develop and test new technologies, products, services and ways of living to produce innovative solutions to the challenges of climate change, resilience and urban sustainability"* [7]. Key characteristics of urban living labs are *geographical embeddedness, experimentation and learning, participation and user involvement, leadership and ownership, and evaluation of actions and impact* [4]. Similarly, Steen and van Bueren [5] described defining characteristics of urban living labs from four aspects: *Goal (Innovation, Knowledge development for replication, Increasing urban sustainability), Activities (Development of innovation, Co-creation, Iteration between activities), Participants (Users, private actors, public actors, and knowledge institutes), and Context (Real-life use context).*

This paper studies three cases of urban living labs - Seoul Innovation Park Living Lab (Seoul, Korea), Living Lab The Neighborhood (Malmö, Sweden), and Living Lab Shanghai (Shanghai, China) - that are geographically, culturally, and structurally different, but have in common that they aim to foster urban sustainability, with a particular emphasis on social innovation. These three cases also represent different types of urban living labs. According to McCormick and Hartmann [4], there are three types of urban living labs: strategic, civic, and grassroots. The first case Seoul Innovation Park Living Lab is an example of 'strategic' type of urban living labs that are led by government, and often *'operate in the whole city area with multiple projects under one umbrella'*. The third case Living Lab Shanghai is an example of 'civic' type of urban living labs that are led by urban actors such as universities, and focus on *'economic and sustainable urban development'*, and *'represented by either stand-alone project or city-districts'*. The second case Living Lab The Neighborhood is an example of 'grassroots' type of urban living labs that are led by urban actors in not for profit actors, and focus on a *'broad agenda of well-being and economy, often host micro-projects or single issue projects and have limited budgets'*. This study examines objectives, key stakeholders and their roles, representative projects, and (expected) outcomes of each urban living lab.

2   Case Studies

2.1   Seoul Innovation Park Living Lab, Seoul, Korea

Seoul Metropolitan Government, which has been actively promoting social innovation at a city level, established various intermediary organizations such as Seoul Community Support Center, and Share Hub, to facilitate innovation in the public sector. Seoul Innovation Park, a city-funded social innovation platform, is one of such organizations that connects and supports innovators, citizens, and various stakeholders [9]. Seoul Innovation Park Living Lab itself does not develop or experiment innovative ideas, but enables organizations that have promising ideas to experiment the ideas in real context. Every year, it announces a call for a project proposal that can address urban problems of the Seoul city through innovative solutions. Some calls target at specific issue (e.g. affordable housing) that Seoul Innovation Park Living Lab intends to address, but most calls are open to any urban problems defined by the applicants. This paper analyses the 2016's program implemented with a budget of 250 million won.

The 2016's call, titled "Changing Seoul, 100 days of experiment", aimed to solve urban problems of Seoul through citizens' ideas and involvements [10]. Any organization that has an innovative idea to address urban problems and capability to develop a concrete plan to experiment the idea in the city could apply. During one month of application period, 48 proposals were submitted. The submitted proposals were evaluated by a group of experts based on several criteria including innovativeness of the proposed solution. Six proposals, addressing different issues, ranging from lack of parking lots in the neighborhood to integrated education system for physically challenged students as well as unchallenged students, were selected. The selected proposals were financially supported up to 50 million won to experiment the ideas for 100 days in real-life contexts [10].

Making 'Happy Parking Lot' Sharing Alleys Project

One of the six proposals selected in the 2016's call was a proposal to address parking problems in residential areas. The idea proposed by the 'Happy Parking Lot Resident Committee' of Doksan 4-dong, a neighborhood located in the southwest of the city, aimed to solve the lack of parking spaces in this neighborhood by changing current 'resident priority parking' system to 'parking lot sharing' system. The idea of sharing parking spaces, which used to be allocated to individual residents in the neighborhood, was a solution proposed not only to solve parking problems, but more importantly to change the alleys in the neighborhood from a 'car-centered' one to 'people-centered' one [10]. The experiment was carried out with the support of the neighborhood administrative office and a company that provided technical support. The new system was implemented through three stages, starting with introducing the new system to the residents and inviting them to join. The implementation of the new solution was not easy especially during the first two months, as it required residents' acceptance of the new solution and collaboration, but resulted in noticeable changes beneficial to residents as well as visitors in the neighborhood. The project was highly evaluated by Seoul Innovation Park Living Lab as it led to active participation of local residents and changes in daily life, which many existing similar IT-based solutions did not succeed.

Living Lab as Innovation Incubation System

The way Seoul Innovation Park Living Lab fosters urban innovation shows characteristics similar to those of incubators. As mentioned above, unlike many Living Labs, Seoul Innovation Park Living Lab itself does not conduct any experiment or implement new solutions to address urban problems. Instead, it creates an enabling ecosystem that increases the probabilities of social entrepreneurs, NGOs, and local communities that have concrete ideas to improve urban life to emerge and survive. In this sense, what Seoul Innovation Park Living Lab produces is not only a collection of diverse ideas to address urban problems (which can be further developed into policy recommendations for the city government), but also more importantly, urban innovators nurtured through its program. In other words, it cultivates seeds of innovation in the city (Fig. 1).

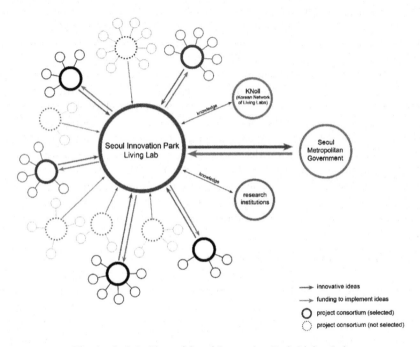

Fig. 1. Stakeholders of Seoul Innovation Park Living Lab

Furthermore, it produces a multitude of small-scale innovation ecosystems created by participating organizations for their projects. As an example, the 'Making Happy Parking Lot Sharing Alleys' project created a *"solid system for cooperation among private-public-industry-academia"* [10] which includes a neighborhood administrative office, a private company specialized in technical aspects of the proposed solution, researchers from public/private research institutions - that had a common goal to find the right solution for the problem [10]. More importantly, the project led to the formation of a local community highly motivated and engaged in the neighborhood innovation, as the project team had raised attention and participation of the local residents throughout the 100-day experiment. It did not happen automatically. It was an outcome of dedicated efforts of the project team – especially the project manager – who spent considerable amount of time in talking with the residents to get to know and persuade them to join the experiment. In the beginning of the project, the project manager spent almost everyday in the parking lots in the alleys to make observations on the use of parking spaces (e.g. number of cars parked in designated parking spaces at different moments of a day, number of cars parked illegally), and also to explain the idea of the parking lot sharing to the residents. A report by Seoul Innovation Park Living Lab [10] mentioned that the reaction of local residents was very cold in the beginning: *"Many did not want to respond to his questions but some talked to him to express their thoughts. Some requested solving the problem of illegal parking and some said that building more parking lots is more important. It was hard not to be embarrassed when some said that they understand the good purpose of this project, but they do not want this project to be done in front of their building"*. The residents started to *"open their heart"* gradually as the project manager's efforts continued everyday: *"Some gave drinks and bread encouraging him and some even brought out their portable burner and a pot to cook instant noodles for him. He was very happy, but because of this irregular unhealthy eating habits instead of regular meals, the project manager gained 13 kg in just three months."* [ibid.] The relationship, and 'solid system for cooperation' built through the 100-day experiment became a fertile ground to carry out another experiment in the following year.

2.2 Living Lab the Neighborhood, Malmö, Sweden

Living Lab The Neighborhood - one of three Malmö Living Labs (MLL) established by Medea at Malmö University, a trans-disciplinary research lab focusing on media, design and public engagement [11] - was initiated in 2007 to explore *'how a platform that could facilitate social innovation and collaborative services could be set up in the city of Malmö'*. [12] Malmö used to be an industrial city, but went through an extensive transformation over the last decade, and became a university city with an increasing number of small and medium-sized IT, media and design companies [13]. The city, now described as a 'knowledge city' and a 'regional growth engine' [14], is also characterized by a high number of immigrants who mostly live in the southeastern part of the city that has high rates of child poverty and unemployment [12].

Living Lab The Neighborhood was established in this context by a group of design researchers of Medea that have been working on social innovation (Malmö DESIS Lab) with a particular attention to immigrant communities in Malmö who are socially and geographically segregated from middle and upper class people in the city.

Living Lab as a Platform for Inclusion and Infrastructuring

The founders of Living Lab The Neighborhood - design researchers who have strong background in participatory design - aimed for an 'inclusive approach' that will allow marginalized actors to participate [12]. Particular attention was paid on identifying and collaborating with 'resourceful but less visible' actors that can be considered as 'unused assets' [15]. In this sense, Hillgren - a researcher at Medea responsible for running Living Lab The Neighborhood - once described Living Labs as enabling platforms for *"inclusion and serendipity"* [16]. One of such actors they found was an organization of immigrant women called 'Herrgård's Women's Association (HWA)'. The organization, founded in 2002 by five women *as a response to the feeling of being excluded from Swedish society* [12], consists of approximately 400 members, including children, with diverse ethnic backgrounds, ranging from Iran to Afghanistan. Although most of the members are underprivileged, lack higher education and Swedish language skills, they are active in addressing problems in their neighborhoods and have an extensive social network among immigrant women in Malmö. [12, 15] The core members of the organization meet on a regular basis for activities such as cooking, making carpets and clothing.

Living Lab The Neighborhood connected Herrgård's Women's Association to diverse stakeholders - ranging from a private ICT company, to departments of the municipality, and to other NGOs - to explore opportunities and values that can be created together. Some ideas developed through a series of meetings and co-design workshops include a catering service offered by HWA to a firm in the city by using the cooking skills of the members of HWA. Another idea was to utilize the knowledge and skills of HWA for refugee children in the city. As the city opened the door for refugee children, a number of Afghan and Iraqi orphans settled down over the recent years. The idea of offering home-made Afghan meal to the refugee children was prototyped together with a company that provides accommodation for refugee children. The positive results of the prototype led to another idea – offering a cooking class to refugee children – which was prototyped with another partner that provided its kitchen for the cooking class.

The distinctive characteristics of Living Lab The Neighborhood are represented by its strategy of 'infrastructuring' and 'prototyping', both characterized by an open nature. Living Lab The Neighborhood was focused on connecting (potential) 'actors', rather than problems to solve or new ideas to test. Although the living lab was run by a group of design experts, they did not design any solutions directly. Their main design work was what they call 'infrastructuring', a process of *"cultivating long-term working relationships with diverse actors and slowly build a designing network"* [12]. Infrastructuring is different from a project-based partnership that has clearly defined goals and partners, with a time frame, in that it is a continuous match-making process that allows *'for various constellations to develop and for different possibilities to be explored'* [17]. The rationale behind it is that new ideas do not always need to be "designed" by designers, but can be facilitated and co-designed by mobilizing the competences and creative potential of diverse actors. As the way two ideas - catering service, and cooking class for refugee children - were developed and prototyped illustrates, new ideas were emerged through interactions and collaboration among diverse actors mediated by the living lab in an open-ended way.

2.3   Living Lab Shanghai, Shanghai, China

Established by the College of Design and Innovation (D&I) at Tongji University in Shanghai, Living Lab Shanghai has focused on fostering sustainable development of a neighborhood by mobilizing knowledge and resources of the design college together with local stakeholders. A physical platform of Living Lab Shanghai officially opened in 2017, but even before the creation of a physical platform, design researchers of the college have been carrying out several projects in the neighborhood, with (sometimes implicit, sometimes explicit) support of the district government. The underpinning idea of those projects was that the whole neighborhood - where the college is located - could be a living laboratory. The neighborhood called 'Siping' is a sub-district located in Yangpu district, in northeastern part of Shanghai. Yangpu district used to be an old industrial district, but has become a knowledge-intensive district, where several top universities are located, such as Fudan university, Tongji university, University of Shanghai for Science and Technology, and Shanghai university of finance and economics. In 2010, Yangpu district has become one of the first pilot districts included in the national innovation program of China.

N-ICE 2035 Project
Contrary to the prevailing approach of place development in Shanghai that has been oriented to large-scale, top-down development, Living Lab Shanghai has promoted small-scale, community-centered design approaches. The concept of 'urban acupuncture' [18] or 'acupunctural design' [19] represents such approaches. By using an analogy with acupuncture, the acupunctural design approach intends to foster large-scale, long-term changes through a number of interconnected, small-scale projects that 'stimulate improvements and positive chain reactions' [18].

N-ICE 2035 (Neighborhood of Innovation, Creativity and Entrepreneurship towards 2035) project is one of the projects that have been carried out in the Siping neighborhood based on the acupunctural design approach. The project, officially launched in February 2018, intends to explore and prototype future urban life through several 'labs' - ranging from 'Food lab' to 'Fab lab' - built in a lane in the neighborhood. The ground floor of a residential building, which used to be occupied by small local shops selling products and services to neighborhood residents, was renovated into the labs. The labs under the N-ICE 2035 project share overall project goals, but each lab is run autonomously by different groups of experts, with their own programs and business models.

Living Labs as Diffused Platforms for Collaborative Future-Making
As N-ICE 2035 project has just kicked off at the moment this paper is written, the outcomes are unknown yet. Still, two distinctive characteristics are observable already. One is its organizational structure. As illustrated in the concept of the 'acupunctural design' approach, Living Lab Shanghai is a constellation of small labs that are spread in the neighborhood. These diffused living labs function as 'acupoints' that are inter-connected to each other, thus create synergic impacts on a larger scale. One of the strengths of such structure is its potential for expansion. As each lab runs autonomously with its own program - although all labs are framed under an overarching goal - Living Lab Shanghai is a structurally open system. New labs can be set up and added to the existing ones without causing restructuring Living Lab Shanghai. Considering that each lab focuses on different topics (e.g. food, health), this implies Living Lab Shanghai as a whole can broaden its scope by adding new labs when necessary (Fig. 2).

Another characteristic of Living Lab Shanghai lies in its (expected) role in the neighborhood and the city. The diffused labs in the Siping neighborhood are open platforms for local residents as well as potential stakeholders including companies and

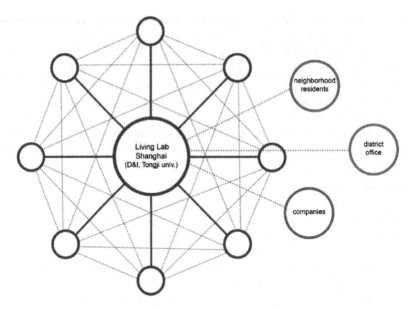

Fig. 2. Stakeholders of Living Lab Shanghai

the district office, who are invited to explore and envision possible futures together. The fact that the labs do not aim to test a new product or service with them or to design a 'solution' to address particular problems, but aim to envision possible futures characterizes Living Lab Shanghai. In this sense, they can be described as platforms for 'future-making' [20]. The year 2035 – as in the project name 'N-ICE *2035*' - serves as a point of reference for the future to be envisioned. This time frame is in line with the municipality's master plan for city development (Shanghai Master Plan 2017–2035) that aims to build the city into '*an innovative, humanistic and eco-friendly metropolis with global influence*' by 2035 [21]. While future-making practices in the tradition of participatory design have a strong emphasis in democratizing the process of planning and making 'alternative' futures with marginalized publics, often in opposition to '*centralized bureaucratic planning*' [20], the future-making activities of Living Lab Shanghai have more focus on providing inspirational models that can be in a synergic relationship with the master plan.

3   Potential of Design-Driven Urban Living Labs

This paper studied three cases of urban living labs that illustrate different forms and roles of urban living labs. The first case Seoul Innovation Park Living Lab was studied as an example of a 'strategic' type of urban living labs, funded by the city government and '*operates in the whole city area with multiple projects under one umbrella*' [4]. The second case Living Lab The Neighborhood was studied as an example of a 'grassroots' type of urban living labs, which '*focus on a broad agenda of well-being and economy, often host micro-projects or single issue projects and have limited budgets'*. Although a 'grassroots' type of urban living labs defined by McCormick and Hartmann [4] are led by urban actors in civil society or not for profit actors, this study considered Living Lab The Neighborhood as an example of a grassroots type, rather than a 'civic' type led by universities, as the grassroots organization 'Herrgård's Women's Association (HWA)' was a pillar of Living Lab The Neighborhood. Also, the activities of Living Lab The Neighborhood that focused on the needs of marginalized communities in the city, and issues of social cohesion fit to the characteristics of grassroots-type urban living labs described as being *'concerned with highly contingent and specific contextual issues that are related to the needs and priorities of particular local communities'* [22]. Lastly, the third case Living Lab Shanghai was studied as an example of a 'civic' type of urban living labs, which is led by urban actors such as universities, and focus on 'economic and sustainable urban development' [22].

Living Labs can be also differentiated by the roles of actors leading living labs [23]. The four types of actors that often appear in the literature are *enablers, utilizers, providers*, and *end-users* (e.g. [23, 24]) According to Leminen et al. [23], 'enablers' include *'various public-sector actors, non-governmental organizations, and financiers, such as towns, municipalities, or area-development organizations'*. Enabler-driven living labs are typically public sector projects that pursue societal improvements, built around a regional development body or program [23]. 'Utilizers' are companies that *'launch and promote living labs to develop their businesses'* [23]. Utilizer-driven living labs focus on developing and testing firms' products and services, and supporting the firms' business development based on data collected from users [23]. Provider-driven living labs are established by various developer organizations such as educational institutes, universities, and consultants, with aims at *'promoting research and theory development, augmenting knowledge creation, and finding solutions to specific problems'* [23]. Lastly, user-driven living labs established by user communities focus on solving users' everyday life problems, *'in a way consistent with the values and requirements of users and user communities'* [23]. Similarly, Juujärvi and Pesso [24]

Table 1. Different actor roles in an urban living lab (Juujärvi and Pesso [24])

Actors	Contribution
City representatives as *enablers*	- Creating the vision and allocating resources - Providing strategic leadership - Promoting networking
Firms and local service providers as *utilizers*	- Producing place-based knowledge - Setting small-scale objectives - Creating suitable products and services
Educational institutions as *providers*	- Engaging students as innovators - Providing innovative R&D methods - Augmenting knowledge systematically
Residents as *users*	- Producing place-based user experience - Participating in experiments - Empowering citizens through co-creation

described contributions of the four types of actor roles in an urban living lab as below (Table 1).

While these typologies provide useful knowledge to understand different types of urban living labs (for instance, Seoul Innovation Park Living Lab), this paper finds the two cases studied in this paper - Living Lab The Neighborhood, and Living Lab Shanghai - cannot be fully explained by them. In both cases, the actors who established and led the urban living labs are researchers working at universities (Malmö University and Tongji University, respectively), but their roles in the construction and operation of urban living labs are somewhat different from those of educational institutions illustrated as 'providers' in the literature.

Living Lab The Neighborhood, and Living Lab Shanghai have in common that they were established and led by researchers specialized in 'design'. Their 'design' activities are more in line with the 'new description of design' given by Manzini [25], than the traditional notion of design. Manzini pointed out what 'design' means today differs from the traditional notion of design, thus offered a new description: *Design is a culture and a practice concerning how things ought to be in order to attain desired functions and meanings. It takes place within open-ended co-design processes in which all the involved actors participate in different ways. (…) The role of design experts is to trigger and support these open-ended co-design processes, using their design knowledge to conceive and enhance clear-cut, focused design initiatives* [25]. Living Lab The Neighborhood, which started with the issue of social exclusion of immigrants in the city, focused on facilitating possible opportunities to emerge - without predefined outcomes - by connecting local immigrants communities to diverse stakeholders. New ideas were emerged and prototyped along the way, but not directly designed by the designers who led the living lab. Similarly, Living Lab Shanghai, illustrated as platforms for collaborative future-making in this paper, brings diverse stakeholders to explore and prototype future urban life together in an open-ended way. In fact, design activities of the both labs are not oriented to producing '*finished* products' [25]. Rather, they are closed to *"an exploratory process that aims to create new kinds of value relation between diverse actors within a socio-material configuration"* [26].

It is not unknown that design can play a role in living labs. Yet, this paper argues the characteristics and roles of design found in the cases of Living Lab The Neighborhood and Living Lab Shanghai are noteworthy. This study is limited in generalizability, but provides a starting point for further exploration into the potential of 'design-driven' urban living labs that can be differentiated from other types of urban living labs.

Acknowledgements. This research was conducted as part of two research projects: "Urban environmental and social innovation design research" project and "Interaction and Service design research" project (DB17010) supported by Shanghai Summit Discipline in Design.

References

1. United Nations. http://www.un.org/sustainabledevelopment/cities. Accessed 7 Feb 2018
2. United Nations: World Urbanization Prospects: The 2014 Revision (2015)

3. Eskelinen, J., Robles, A.G., Lindy, I., Marsh, J., Muente-Kunigami, A. (eds.): Citizen Driven Innovation. World Bank Publications, Washington, D.C. (2015)
4. McCormick, K., Hartmann, C. (eds.) The Emerging Landscape of Urban Living Labs: Characteristics, Practices and Examples (2017). http://lup.lub.lu.se/search/ws/files/27224 276/Urban_Living_Labs_Handbook.pdf. Accessed 17 Feb 2018
5. Steen, K., van Bueren, E.: Urban living labs: a living lab way of working. Amsterdam Institute for Advanced Metropolitan Solutions (AMS) (2017)
6. ENoLL. http://www.openlivinglabs.eu/node/1429. Accessed 7 Feb 2018
7. Voytenko, Y., McCormick, K., Evans, J., Schliwa, G.: Urban living labs for sustainability and low carbon cities in Europe: towards a research agenda. J. Clean. Product. **123**, 45–54 (2016)
8. Living Lab Methodology Handbook. https://www.scribd.com/document/366265932/U4IoT-LivingLabMethodology-Handbook. Accessed 7 Feb 2018
9. Seoul Innovation Park. https://www.innovationpark.kr. Accessed 7 Feb 2018
10. Youn, C.: The beginning of the era of "Living Labs". Internal report, Seoul Innovation Park (2016)
11. Medea. http://medea.mah.se. Accessed 7 Feb 2018
12. Emilson, A., Hillgren, P.-A., Seravalli, A.: Designing in the neighborhood: beyond (and in the shadow of) creative communities. In: Ehn, P., Nilsson, E. (eds.) Making Futures, Marginal Notes on Innovation Design and Democracy. MIT, Cambridge (2014)
13. Seravalli, A.: Making Commons (Attempts at Composing Prospects in the Opening of Production). Doctoral Dissertation in Interaction Design. School of Arts and Communication. Malmö University, Malmö (2014)
14. Hillgren, P., Seravalli, A., Eriksen, M.A.: Counter-hegemonic practices: dynamic interplay between agonism, commoning and strategic design. Strat. Des. Res. J. **9**(2), 89–99 (2016)
15. Hillgren, P.: Participatory design for social and public innovation: living labs as spaces for agonistic experiments and friendly hacking. In: Manzini, E., Staszowski, E. (eds.) Public and Collaborative: Exploring the Intersection of Design, Social Innovation and Public Policy, pp. 75–88. DESIS Network (2013)
16. Hillgren, P.: Living labs as enabling platforms for inclusion and serendipity. In: Nilsson, E. M. (eds.) Prototyping Futures. Malmö university, Malmö (2012)
17. Bjögvinsson, E., Ehn, P., Hillgren, P.A.: Design things and design thinking: contemporary participatory design challenges. Des. Issues **28**(3), 101–116 (2012)
18. Lerner, J.: Urban Acupuncture. Island Press, Washington, D.C. (2014)
19. Lou, Y., Valsecchi, F., Diaz, C.: Design harvest: an acupunctural design approach toward sustainability. Mistra Urban Futures Publication, Gothenburg, Sweden (2013)
20. Ehn, P., Nilsson, E., Topgaard, R., Watts, L.: Making futures – challenging innovation. In: Proceedings of Participatory Design Conference 2012 (2012)
21. Information Office of Shanghai Municipality. http://en.shio.gov.cn/resource/press/3104. shtml. Accessed 17 Feb 2018
22. GUST Policy Brief: Typology of Urban Living Labs (2017). https://drive.google.com/open? id=1Y5wjmLzF2YajO7Urax6t1HJwXHKNSD9w. Accessed 17 Feb 2018
23. Leminen, S., Westerlund, M., Nyström, A.G.: Living labs as open-innovation networks. Technol. Innov. Manag. Rev. **2**(9), 6–11 (2012)
24. Juujärvi, S., Pesso, K.: Actor roles in an urban living lab: what can we learn from Suurpelto, Finland? Technol. Innov. Manag. Rev. **3**(11), 22–27 (2013)
25. Manzini, E.: Design When Everybody Designs: An Introduction to Design for Social Innovation. MIT Press, Cambridge (2015)
26. Kimbell, L.: Designing for service as one way of designing services. Int. J. Des. **5**(2), 41–52 (2011)

The Co-Regulation of TV-White Spaces: The Southern Africa Development Community Approach

Salomão David[1,2(✉)], Américo Muchanga[1], and Marco Zennaro[2]

[1] Communications Regulatory Authority of Mozambique,
Praça 16 de Junho 340, Maputo, Mozambique
sdavid@incm.gov.mz
[2] International Center for Theoretical Physics,
Strada Costiera, 34151 Trieste, TS, Italy

Abstract. TV-White Spaces (TVWS) is among the promising solutions for extending internet broadband reach in the Southern Africa Development Community (SADC). White Spaces are often called the "*gold spectrum resource*", the industry, regulators and academia from SADC have been effervescently working in new ways towards flexible govern the usage of these bands by embracing standards such as IEEE 802.11af, 802.19.1 and 802.22.

This article analyses the deployment of TVWS in six SADC countries namely Botswana, Tanzania, Namibia, Malawi, Mozambique and South Africa, the study, demonstrates the steps and standards adopted to deploy trials and the adoption of co-regulation as an approach for regulating the TVWS.

Keywords: Co-regulation · TV-White Spaces · Broadband
Southern Africa Development Community

1 Introduction

The policymakers from the Southern Africa Development Community (SADC), for the last decade have been forced by community-driven service providers and academia, to harness affordable technologies to close the digital-exclusion. The absence of financial resources and land-line infrastructure in SADC brought forward the concept of leapfrogging to the information age with wireless technologies. In the region, wireless technologies became the newest cutting edge, high-speed technology for rural areas internet provision, where the world bank estimates that 65–70% of the populations currently resides.

The universal access policies and approaches are today a public issue, placing pressure on government, regulatory agencies to be more dogmatic and hands-on in ICT regulation to mitigate the digital-exclusion. Nonetheless, the scarcity of government financial and technical resources created conditions for the emergence of co-regulation.

In this study, co-regulation refers to the union of regulatory entities, research agencies, community-driven service providers and ordinary citizens cooperating to deploy, experiment and draft regulation for new technologies in SADC.

P.-L. P. Rau (Ed.): CCD 2018, LNCS 10912, pp. 286–297, 2018.
https://doi.org/10.1007/978-3-319-92252-2_23

For the International Telecommunication Union (ITU) region 1, there were changes in spectrum regulation mainly in TV broadcast bands where subsists many challenges to use TV bands segment of the spectrum efficiently. The World Radio Congress (WRC-15) established for region 1, the frequency bands 470–694 MHz to be used on a secondary basis by the land mobile service, with an understanding that secondary service should not interfere with primary or incumbent stations.

The history of TV-White Spaces (TVWS) in the SADC stands connected to Digital Migration (DM) and the tacit need to provide sustainable broadband connectivity to rural SADC. White Spaces are often called the "gold spectrum resource", the industry, regulators and academia from SADC have been effervescently working in new ways towards flexible govern the usage of these bands by embracing standards such as IEEE 802.11af, 802.19.1 and 802.22.

It is the authors understanding that TVWS was pushed forward not by the late changes in spectrum regulation possibly the most fundamental ever in the history of spectrum management (WRC-15), it was brought forward by community-driven service providers, academia and corporate giants due to the widening gap in digital inequality and the propagation capabilities of UHF/VHF spectrum.

These changes drove SADC members of the Communications Regulators Association of Southern Africa (CRASA) to opportunistically adopt TVWS as a possible solution to provide broadband in rural areas excluded from broadband coverage. CRASA is a harmonisation body of Postal and Information Communication Technologies regulatory environment in SADC.

The CRASA members perceive, regulation as an abstract concept and do take many forms from legal restrictions, contractual obligations to co-regulation. In the region, cultural aspects such as the African concept of Ubuntu and the approaches joining for an agreement have been adopted since the early days of regulation. Hence there is a link between regulation and human-centred approaches for decision making based on interaction [1]. The SADC approach of co-regulation unintentionally is infused with the Ubuntu concept, allowing the participation of experts and non-experts in the process of regulation to attain mutual understanding and adoption.

The mediation challenges to regulate the communication industry generate distributed theories such as co-regulation, which is rooted in the cultural organisation of society. However, it extends the reach of the individual to encompass interactions between different people with complete disregard for who, and what the individual is.

This study reviews the studies conducted by six distinct CRASA members, namely the Independent Communications Authority of South Africa (ICASA), the Tanzanian Communications Regulatory Authority (TCRA), the Malawian Communications Regulatory Authority (MACRA), Communications Regulatory Authority of Namibia (CRAN), the Botswana Communications Regulatory Authority (BOCRA) and the Communications Regulatory Authority of Mozambique (INCM).

The value of the article lies in providing a holistic viewpoint on the approach adopted to regulate the technology using design theories under the current technical and regulatory conditions.

The paper is organised as follows: a review of internet provision in SADC and the emergence of TVWS, the approach adopted to deploy the six TVWS trials, a short analysis and discussion of how co-regulation was used in the process of regulation and the study conclusions.

2   Methodology

Given the formative nature of both research and regulation concerning TVWS and broadband, the Authors decided it would be best to adopt case study analyses. We aimed at building upwards from the practice of each regulator and understand or frame an original understanding of each approach the steps taken to deploy the technology and regulate.

The case studies were identified iteratively: consulting CRASA to acquire successful implementations and finally consulting the regulators about the process adopted to draft regulatory framework for TVWS.

On an initial stage, the information acquired from regulators was applied a chain-referral sampling technique to identify existing studies among their acquaintances to further investigates deployments of TVWS.

On a second phase, a mix of descriptive and exploratory approach was used. The emotional component would aim to ask "what and when" about TVWS deployments and produce a design and implementation chronology. The exploratory element would be more open and seek to understand the value and outcome of each case deployment.

During the initial stage of this study were identified seven case studies, from which six have materialised in actual trials Botswana, Tanzania, Namibia, Malawi, Mozambique and South Africa. The trial in Zimbabwe until the end of our research was not conducted.

Each case was carefully analysed from the technological approach to applicability, where identified trends and similarities.

3   Co-Regulation

There exists in the SADC region a digital divide, which in recent years academia, researchers, community-driven service providers, practitioners and regulators have been experimenting opportunistic ways to allow communities to have affordable internet broadband.

Co-regulation in this study refers to the relationships among cultural, social, technological and personal sources of influence that together challenge, shape and guide the emergence of new policies. This approach for regulation emerges through participation and validation of social and cultural relationships to address a specific technological problem, typically involving both primary legislation and self-regulation where there exists involvement of bodies representing stakeholders in the regulatory decision-making process [3].

The co-regulation approach adopts an identity as the leading condiment for the personal, cultural and social influence which altogether control, challenge, shape and guide the new character of a group. A group origin and identity is situated across the cultural and heritage backgrounds of its participants.

The important aspect about co-regulation is cooperation and participation where each actor has two roles (expert and novice), in most of the cases one can be expert in the technical aspects of technology but utterly unaware about how communities perceive, the technology and regulation in place for technology usage. In co-regulation, regulatory bodies act as mediators and assemble interactions and process to produce a positive outcome for all parts involved.

Humans as social beings seek a sense of belongingness for self-realisation through participation, hence, in co-regulation cooperation is an essential mediator which enriches critical motives for involvement. In modern social cognitive theories motivated behaviour is considered the result of choices or decisions that an individual make concerning their goals, belief and values [4], while in co-regulation the motivated conduct is entangled with judgment and decision strategies where wishes and desire substitute logical processes [3].

The technologies being co-regulated are not designed or produced in the cultural setting being tested or regulated; instead, most of the cultural background is utterly unaware of the know-how and capabilities of such technical apparatus. The experts on this domain are in most cases academia, corporate giants or regulators.

This factor does not become an inhibitory factor. Instead, it does allow communities field and space for learning.

The technology embeds the cultural practice from designers; the regulators apart from technical specifications have also enhanced public participation in the draft of the regulatory framework, a mechanism to allow community participation in policy discussion.

4 SADC and TV-White Spaces

The SADC region comprises 15 countries and is home for approximately 258 million people. The Democratic Republic of Congo (DRC) is home for 28% of the population.

There has been in the past, a tendency to neglect the link between regulation and social interactions, perhaps because the process of regulating was mostly a top-bottom approach. In recent years regulators have been adopting co-regulation for policy design and implementation.

SADC with its many problems of hunger, epidemic, war, and socioeconomic issues manages to provide internet to approximately thirty-nine percent of the population mostly residing in urban areas. The Internet diffusion has mainly been confined to major cities, where a minority of the population lives although a growing number of countries have points of presence (POPs) in rural areas.

The South African Internet market, a well-consolidated market, has approximately 100 POPs and three primary Internet Service Providers (ISPs) who together have 90% of market share and other 75 small ISPs have the remainder 10%.

The remaining SADC countries started the diffusion of the internet for e-Government, e-Health, e-Banking late, mainly because it was a phenomenon driven by developed countries. Developed initiatives in the region viewed wireless communications as the financially sustainable approach to bridge the north to the south gap and to allow local governments to meet obligations to deliver, care, education, monitor

290 S. David et al.

public services, complex coordinate activities, ensure quality and foster collaboration by empowering rural communities [5–7].

The access to the Internet in the region was hindered by the lack of local expertise, resources to acquire infrastructure and a regulatory environment capable of creating policies for equity diffusion of the technology. Wireless communications for Internet depend on spectrum availability, a finite resource which has an enormous impact on the cost of infrastructure and quality of the service provided. Fiber to the Home (FTTH), Asynchronous Digital Subscriber Lines (ADSL), Very Small Aperture Terminals (VSAT) and WiMAX are the technologies widely adopted in the urban and rural SADC to provide access to the Internet [4]. With these technologies there exists a mix of realities that continues a story of inequality, unbalance and asymmetry on usage, cost and quality of the Internet service provided.

The low-cost and robust broadband connectivity in the SADC region is often unaffordable for the ordinary citizen if it is affordable is restricted to urban areas.

The Regulators from the region have been experimenting the usage of White Spaces to provide access to the Internet in areas deprived of reliable electricity. Dosch et al. suggested that the so-called white spaces are not clean bands as they result from pollution due to low-power emissions coming from Digital Television (DTV) or analogue allotments [8].

The white spaces signals are the source of interference for Cognitive Radios (CR). Nonetheless, they do not degrade the actual value of white spaces [8].

Reusing the White Spaces can reduce the cost of wireless broadband access by accessing dynamically high-quality spectrum below 1 GHz. Spectrum bellow 1 GHz is considered valuable due to the ability to cover large areas, requiring lower power signal from the transceiver to get the same output power signal at the receiver compared to other spectrum bands. Additionally, devices placed at the sub 1 GHz spectrum band can handle interference better because they operate at a lower frequency where fewer applications use spectrum, and also these bands enable transmissions to weave between buildings in an urban environment better [7].

Recently in sub 1 Ghz spectrum cognitive radios and Internet of Things (IoT), wireless applications have been experimented, turning into an exciting paradigm for wireless communication in which either a network or a wireless node changes its transmission or reception parameters to communicate efficiently, avoiding interference with licensed or unlicensed users [9]. Hence TVWS refers to segments of the TV-Spectrum in the TV operating frequencies known as VHF/UHF band, especially from 470–790 MHz when the bands are not used by licensed users in a given location [10].

The name TVWS comes from broadcast coverage maps while plotting the coverage areas, and different colours indicate different signal levels, the areas without signal are left with the white intensity [11].

Licensing protects the incumbent users of the TVWS band from interference, for that reason unlicensed white spaces devices operating in the TVWS band are not permitted to create interference with any licensed (incumbent) user.

A typical free Wi-Fi signal travels about 100 m versus TVWS signals that may extend to 400 m at the same power level, or up to as far as 10 km at high power [12]. This impressive reach has spawned the nickname "Super Wi-Fi" with frequency allocation, spectrum sensing techniques and geo-location spectrum databases being the most used techniques for spectrum allocation and protection of incumbent systems [13].

In the early days, the spectrum allocation technique is no longer used, most of the incumbent systems are allocated spectrum by sensing-only methods and geo-location databases techniques. While the sensing-only mode faces performance, design issues challenges due to the need of: first determine if an incumbent is present; second by detecting if the incumbent signals above −116 dBm and; third by reducing the transmission power downward to avoid interfering with the incumbent signal levels.

The geo-location databases gain a relative advantage in performance and design issues compared to sensing-only, as the database is already built-in knowledge regarding the bands and the exact incumbent's services presented in the location where the device is aspiring to transmit [10, 14]. The geo-location database offers a dynamic approach for spectrum allocation as different TV channels become available TVWS translates to higher network capacity, allowing a more significant number of users in a given area while protecting incumbent users [15].

The TVWS can enable a variety of use cases ranging from low-power in-building media distribution to machine-to-machine applications, but they are mainly well-suited for delivering low-cost broadband access to rural and other unserved communities. Radio signals in the TV bands, in particular, the 470 MHz to 698 MHz range of UHF frequencies travel over long distances and penetrate more obstacles than other types of radio signals, enabling non-line-of-sight wireless connectivity and requiring fewer base stations to provide ubiquitous coverage [16].

5 Technical Trials

In this section a description of the TVWS deployments in SADC will be provided with attention to the year of deployment, the location of implementation, the TVWS equipment used and the highest throughput reached.

Table 1 demonstrates the trials conducted in SADC, and it is possible to grasp that most of the deployment in SADC were performed in 2013 with the objective being the provision of Internet Broadband for Education. The 4Africa Initiative, a Microsoft project which focused on universal access and innovation was one of the key proponents of TVWS in the African continent; the project allowed the implementation of TVWS trials in Botswana, Ghana, Kenya, Tanzania, Namibia and also a second trial in South Africa (Cape Town).

Research and Development cases were led by the regulators while in 4Africa Initiative regulators were invited to participate, the Adaptrum Base transceiver station (BTS) followed by 6Harmonics were the most used type of equipment in the region.

Table 1. SADC TVWS trials.

Year	Country	Project name	Application	Throughput/Distance	Equipment
2013	South Africa, Polokwane	4Africa Initiative	Education	12 Mbps/6 km	Carlson Wireless
2013	Dar Es Salaam, Tanzania	4Africa Initiative	Education	12 Mbps/6 km	Adaptrum
2013	Zomba, Malawi	Research and Development	Health and Education	2mbps/7.5 km	Carlson Wireless
2014	Oshana, Ohangwena and Omusati, Namibia	4Africa Initiative	Education	10 Mbps/10 km	Adaptrum
2015	Francistown, Lobatse and Maun, Botswana	4Africa Initiative	Health	5Mbps/3 km	Adaptrum
2015	Maputo, Mozambique	Research and Development	Education	4 Mbps/8.5 km	6Harmonics

5.1 South Africa

The first ever technical trial conducted in the SADC region was conducted in South Africa (Polokwane), the experiment started in March 2013 with more than five partners including Google, Carlson Wireless Technologies and the Open Spectrum Alliance [13]. The Internet broadband was provided to ten schools stood supported by three BTS from Carlson Wireless Technologies [17].

The study provided, as a result, a throughput as high as 12 Mbps and latencies lower than 100 ms. To acquire such findings were used directional antennas with gains of 11 dBi to ensure good quality, and the links were of distances not higher than 6 km with line of sight to reduce interference.

It has to be noticed that later in September 2013 ICASA conducted another TVWS trial in Cape Town with the support of 4Africa Initiative, this trial lasted for six months, and is aimed at addressing spectrum field measurements to demonstrate non-interference or interference, traffic (upload and download throughput) and latency.

The study used google GLSDB; as a result, the download throughput reached 12 Mbps, and the upload throughput was 4.5 Mbps. The latency stood at 120 ms and the measurements done did not provide evidence of interference to primary stations or incumbent [18].

5.2 Tanzania

In 2013 was conducted the second trial of TVWS in the region, with Tanzania and Microsoft under the 4Africa Initiative partnering with UhuruOne a local internet service provider, the Tanzanian Commission for Science and Technology (COSTECH) deploying a network aspiring to provide affordable Internet broadband for education in Dar Es Salaam [15].

The trial was part of 4Africa Initiative, a Microsoft effort to bring connectivity, devices and technology to African entrepreneurs, developers and college graduates, in

Tanzania UhuruOne was to offer, wireless broadband connectivity, a laptop or tablet on the first phase to 50 000 students and faculty members and a later stage expand coverage to several other Universities.

The primary beneficiaries of this initiative were the Open University of Tanzania, Institute of Finance Management, College of Business Education and Dar Es Salaam School of Journalism which together they had approximately 74,000 students.

The TVWS experimenting centred on access with the lowest levels of interference using spectrum allocation to offer affordable wireless broadband. The initiative was the first ever urban TVWS deployment in SADC; the study provided understanding about the usage of such spectrum in an urban and congested location.

The download throughput reached was 8.5 Mbps, and the upload was on average 2.5 Mbps, the most extended link had a distance of 6 km.

5.3   Malawi

MACRA, the University of Malawi, the International Centre for Theoretical Physics (ICTP) and the Universal Access Fund of Malawi [9], conducted in Zomba, Malawi, on September 2013 a TVWS trial.

The trial was designed to evaluate the performance and usage of TVWS in a rural setting to support potential guidance for commercial regulation of white spaces spectrum eventually.

The trial followed research and development to provide regulators in-depth understanding of the technology coverage and performance while at the same time provide access to internet broadband to unserved rural areas and services.

The trial had as beneficiaries the Saint Mary's Girl Secondary School, the Malawi Defense Force Air-wing, and the Seismology Department.

In conclusion, the trial demonstrated to be able to provide 2.6 times better data rates given adequate weather conditions, the Internet for this trial was supplied through a dedicated 2 Mbps wireless backhaul. The download throughput registered was 400 Kbps at each beneficiary with a latency of 125 ms using Carlson Wireless Technologies (rural Connect).

5.4   Namibia

Namibia trial was denominated Citizen Connect was a 4Africa Initiative having as partners My Digital Bridge Foundation and Microsoft. The test was conducted in September 2014; it had coverage of approximately 9,424 km^2 covering the regional council of Oshana, Omusati and Ohangwena [15, 19].

The project connected 28 schools, aiming to use the TVWS technology efficiently for bridging the digital divide faced by Namibia were only 12.9% of the population in 2012 had access to the Internet. The vast network was deployed using Adaptrum (ARCS 2.0) BTS with links ranging from 8 km to 12 km providing download throughput speeds of 10 Mbps and upload throughput of 6 Mbps. In addition to the long-range non-line-of-sight links, the network relayed on extended multiple short links providing throughput of 10 Mbps allowing schools to have the voice, video, and data communications including high resolution, 3way skype video conference for remote learning.

5.5 Botswana

The Botswana Communications Regulatory Authority (BOCRA) in the first trimester of 2015, in collaboration with the Botswana Innovation Hub, Microsoft, the Botswana - Upen Partnership, USAID and BoFiNet a local ISP, partnered in the implementation of Project Kgolagano.

The project aimed at providing access to specific maternal medicine information to improve the livelihood of women located in small towns and rural areas. The network connected hospitals in Maun, Lobatse and Francistown and the system is used to combine technical studies, surveys, observational studies and focus groups to investigate the value and capabilities of TVWS for telemedicine.

The research group conducting this trial was not implicitly interested in the physical aspects of the technology, they were more interested in the applicability (benefits, challenges and perceptions) of the technology for telemedicine.

5.6 Mozambique

In 2014, the INCM conducted in Mozambique research and development having as partners the ICTP, Universal Access Fund of Mozambique, the University Eduardo Mondlane and the Network Startup Resource Centre (NSRC) aimed at providing internet broadband to one University and two vocational schools in the Boane Municipality.

The maximum throughput reached was 4 Mbps with a latency of 108 ms for a link with 8.5 km given simultaneous usage of three client stations from a TVWS BTS backhauled by a 6 Mbps internet bandwidth. The network was deployed using 6 Harmonics (GWS 3000) [16].

6 Discussion

Independently, since 2013 CRASA members conducted research on TVWS, aiming to find an alternative technology to bridge the digital divide. Results of R&D were published in journals, conferences with proceedings and also as position papers on TVWS.

The South African (ICASA) white spaces regulation approach is the product of interactive consultations between the Regulator, industry and several academic institutions such as the Meraka Institute. The process spanned several years resulting in the publication of the regulation in 2018.

In the middle 2018, Mozambique (INCM) also published the norm to govern the usage of TVWS using an approach similar to ICASA, with the difference that the norm in Mozambique being vigent for approximately 5 years.

Ubuntu "I am because you are" is the cultural idea of interconnectedness of humanity, can also be used to look at policies and regulations. Due to the inherent interdependence of CRASA members, they have influenced each other on the race for affordable internet access with the industry and communities bringing forward TVWS.

The interconnectedness provides changes in policies, which imply how communities adopt or embrace technologies.

Independently CRASA members have noticed perhaps innocently that most of the heritage value and legal heritage are getting weather-beaten by forces of the western civilisation and globalisation, the lack of Ubuntu (African group solidarity) between CRASA regulators and project stakeholders is primarily due to an inappropriate project organisational structure [1].

There is not seem to exist any universal pattern in this community participation, and it appears that the primary drive behind this approach is to acquire policy advice and public policy more directly accessible and responsive to citizens. The method does provide policymakers with a more extensive variety of ideas, perspectives and suggestions than traditional policy advice can offer. This form of community participation is in many ways entirely consonant and consistent with emerging technologies or services which aim at improving communities access to decision processes and strengthening the position of the citizen vis-a-vis the policy maker.

7 Conclusion

Our intent in this article was to clarify the nature of the approach adopted by CRASA regulators for the new TVWS technology to provide internet broadband. SADC countries have very communities' dispersal located, creating difficulties to offer comprehensive coverage, hence TVWS is one of the most wireless technologies researched for bandwidth delivered in recent years as it covers large areas at a lower cost, and reuses spectrum better compared to other wireless technologies such as WiMAX and iBurst.

The case studies here presented without creating inference to primary users of spectrum. Coexistence can be attained efficiently with the use of geolocation database.

The studies performed in Namibia, Malawi, Mozambique and South Africa, on an early stage, adopted frequency allocation, the IEEE 802.22 wireless network standard and advanced on a second stage to geo-location database (GLSD) with the IEEE8 02.11af wireless standard being an option. Moreover, for the four regulators, the initiative to integrated into the policy process participation of the state vis-à-vis private think-tanks, policy institutes, and other organisations brought conditions to harmonise the regulatory framework of TVWS in the region.

The TVWS is receiving overwhelming interest in the wireless industry and academia, with position papers composed independently and uncorrelated by regulators and academia addressing the principle of conserving resources and efficient use of spectrum [10, 20]. Since the deployment of 3G, the telecommunication sector has been experiencing fundamental changes in its regulatory treatment, most of them to safeguard the public interest. The deregulation of telecommunication sector is a consequence of the revolution in technology, hence a minuscule portion of the spectrum is open for license-free operation.

The co-regulation has been gaining momentum in recent years most case studies are performed by academia, practitioners and corporate giants having as beneficiaries of such actions communities deprived of ICT access.

The participation of external actors in the process does align with participatory approaches in our case co-regulation where the participant's identity changes from experts to non-experts of technology. The participation of this actions has different perceptions of the case and transmission protocols while methods required for regulating are exclusive to regulators and perhaps corporate giants. In most of the case studies analysed corporate giants kept a high degree of discretion in structuring and participating in trials.

While current white spaces radios use proprietary technology implementations, the various database is being developed as this area of research matures, there is an increasing need to move beyond frameworks to actual region TVWS database. One of the problems that were common to most of the case studies in the sample might be alleviated by more collaboration between CRASA members about their trials objectives and research plans.

References

1. Rwelamila, P.D., Talukhaba, A.A., Ngowi, A.B.: Tracing the African project failure syndrome: the significance of 'ubuntu'. Eng. Constr. Archit. Manag. **6**(4), 335–346 (1999)
2. Preece, J., Rombach, H.D.: A taxonomy for combining software engineering and human-computer interaction measurement approaches: towards a common framework. Int. J. Hum.-Comput. Stud. **41**(4), 553–583 (1994)
3. Kumar, R.: Why institutional partnerships matter: a regional innovation systems approach. In: ICTs for Global Development and Sustainability: Practice and Applications: Practice and Applications, p. 330 (2010)
4. McCormick, P.K.: Telecommunications reform in Southern Africa: the role of the Southern African development community. Telecommun. Policy **27**(1–2), 95–108 (2003)
5. Brewer, E., et al.: The case for technology in developing regions. Computer **38**(6), 25–38 (2005)
6. Dosch, C., Kubasik, J., Silva, C.F.M.: TVWS policies to enable efficient spectrum sharing (2011)
7. Akyildiz, I.F., Lee, W.-Y., Vuran, M.C., Mohanty, S.: NeXt generation/dynamic spectrum access/cognitive radio wireless networks: a survey. Comput. Netw. **50**(13), 2127–2159 (2006)
8. Mikeka, C., et al.: Malawi television white spaces (TVWS) pilot network performance analysis. J. Wirel. Netw. Commun. **4**(1), 26–32 (2014)
9. Baykas, T., et al.: Developing a standard for TV white space coexistence: technical challenges and solution approaches. IEEE Wirel. Commun. **19**(1), 10–22 (2012)
10. Nekovee, M.: A survey of cognitive radio access to TV white spaces, In: 2009 International Conference on Ultra Modern Telecommunications Workshops, ICUMT 2009, pp. 1–8 (2009)
11. Shi, L., Sung, K.W., Zander, J.: Controlling aggregate interference under adjacent channel interference constraint in TV white space. In: 2012 7th International ICST Conference on Cognitive Radio Oriented Wireless Networks and Communications (CROWNCOM), pp. 1–6 (2012)
12. Lysko, A.A., et al.: First large TV white spaces trial in South Africa: a brief overview. In: 2014 6th International Congress on Ultra Modern Telecommunications and Control Systems and Workshops (ICUMT), pp. 407–414 (2014)

13. Ko, H.-T., Lee, C.-H., Lin, J.-H., Chung, K., Chu, N.-S.: Television white spaces: learning from cases of recent trials. Int. J. Digit. Telev. **5**(2), 149–167 (2014)
14. Roberts, S., Garnett, P., Chandra, R.: Connecting Africa using the TV white spaces: from research to real-world deployments. In: 2015 IEEE International Workshop on Local and Metropolitan Area Networks (LANMAN), pp. 1–6 (2015)
15. David, S.C., Zennaro, M., Muchanga, A.: The Internet@ rural: why not TV-White spaces in Mozambique? In: Privilege, Information, Knowledge and Power: An Endless Dilemma, vol. 7, p. 28 (2015)
16. Ramoroka, T.: Wireless internet connection for teaching and learning in rural schools of South Africa: the University of Limpopo TV white space trial project. Mediterr. J. Soc. Sci. **5**(15), 381 (2014)
17. Lysko, A., Masonta, M., Mfupe, L.: Field measurements done on operational TVWS trial network in Tygerberg. Cape Town TVWS Trial-Technical report (2013)
18. Chavez, A., Littman-Quinn, R., Ndlovu, K., Kovarik, C.L.: Using TV white space spectrum to practise telemedicine: a promising technology to enhance broadband internet connectivity within healthcare facilities in rural regions of developing countries. J. Telemed. Telecare **22** (4), 260–263 (2016)
19. McCaslin, M.: Co-regulation of student motivation and emergent identity. Educ. Psychol. **44** (2), 137–146 (2009)
20. Eccles, J.S., Wigfield, A.: Motivational beliefs, values, and goals. Annu. Rev. Psychol. **53** (1), 109–132 (2002)
21. Sum, C.S., Harada, H., Kojima, F., Lan, Z., Funada, R.: Smart utility networks in TV white space. IEEE Commun. Mag. **49**(7), 132–139 (2011)

Experiences-Based Design for Overcoming Language Barriers in Healthcare Service: A Case Study

Ding-Hau Huang$^{(\boxtimes)}$, Chun Ming Yang, and Gia Hue On

Department of Industrial Design, Ming Chi University of Technology, New Taipei, Taiwan
hau@mail.mcut.edu.tw

Abstract. The aim of this study is to address languages barriers and cultural barriers problems through experience-based design (EBD) approach, that may occur in healthcare settings faced by the increasing numbers of foreigners in Taiwan. This study put foreigners at the center in the service of a healthcare system, applied the modified EBD approach to understand their needs and to improve the health check service process for them. The results of this study showed that EBD approach could come out appreciate solutions to solve languages barriers and improve foreigner's health check service quality. Because of the foreign patient joined the process and co-design to figure out the solution that has potential to reduce their negative feelings.

Keywords: Experiences-based design · Language barriers · Cross cultural design

1 Introduction

Taiwan is increasing the number of foreigners who come to study or work. There were 28,000 international students in Taiwan in 2016. Taiwan government has announced plans to increase the number of international student with a goal to host 58,000 foreign students in 2019 [1]. Ministry of Labor statistics showed that foreign domestic employees increased 5.77% in 2016, nearly triple 2015's growth [2]. There were 624,758 migrant workers in 2016. Most of them came from Vietnam, Thailand, Philippines, Indonesia that their native language is not Mandarin or English [2]. It is a challenge for them who cannot understand, speak, read or write Chinese in healthcare settings that lead to stressful, uncomfortable and miscommunication. In the healthcare system, miscommunication is a problem can threat to the patient's life. When using a second language in clinician and patient communication, misunderstanding errors are increasing likely. The details of a medical conversation or treatment must be conveyed accurately to patients and clinicians. "patients may fail to comply with instructions" or "elect not to have potentially life-saving treatment" is evidence occurred when clinicians and patients use a deficiently mastered second languages [3].

According to Betancourt et al. [4], cultural barrier is another main problem that "avoid miscommunication in cross-cultural situations fosters more patient-centered

© Springer International Publishing AG, part of Springer Nature 2018
P.-L. P. Rau (Ed.): CCD 2018, LNCS 10912, pp. 298–307, 2018.
https://doi.org/10.1007/978-3-319-92252-2_24

relationship". "To improve the ability of healthcare providers and the healthcare system to affected and care for patients with diverse social and cultural backgrounds" is the target of cultural competence. Depending on patients' culture, religion, or social situation can understand their feelings, behavior that improves an individual's ability to understand, follow and accept clinician's instructions. It is crucial to discern barriers of language and cultural difference for foreigners to have equitable healthcare service.

However, healthcare services are often complex, relying on interactions among multiple stakeholders. Stakeholder participation has been shown to be a beneficial component of service design, leading to innovation, a closer fit to user needs and improved service experiences [5]. Some researchers proposed the methodology for healthcare service design to understand patient experience and to ensure what is designed is related to their needs and requirements [6]. Such as experience-based design (EBD) which is kind of participatory service design approach. In many service design projects, participatory design is seen as critical to success. EBD is kind of participatory design process which is structured as a four-phase process of patients, carers and healthcare staff capturing and then understanding their lived experiences of healthcare services, working together to improve the service based on this understanding, and then measuring the effects of changes [7].

The aim of this study is to address languages barriers and cultural barriers problems through experience-based design approach, that may occur in healthcare settings faced by the increasing numbers of foreigners. This study put foreigners at the center in the service of a healthcare system, applied the modified EBD approach to understand their needs and to improve the healthcare service process for them.

2   Experience-Based Design (EBD)

EBD has four phases, capture phase, understand phase, improve phase and measure phase. In this study, we modified partial part of each phase explained as below.

In the capture phase, participants are encouraged to record their personal stories of using services, and then staff and patients participate in separate story-sharing events.

In the understand phase, participants analyse their experiences by plotting elements of their stories on customer journey maps. In this study, we used the same method. Customer Journey mapping is a diagram that illustrates the steps of customer experience products or services. It helps to conceptualize customer experience as a customer's "journey" from the first step to the final step [7] that designers understand the customer's actions, motivation, and barriers during the service process [8]. The data of processes and user experiences are provided by customer journey. Those small details can be uncovered that is a really great extent [7].

For the improve phase, EBD establishes a set of co-design teams each involving both patients and staff to explore and implement service improvements in different areas. In this study, we used service blueprint as a tool to identify and discuss the service problems. A blueprinting takes the viewpoint of the customer, specifically customer actions, interaction with products or services [9]. Blueprinting has evolved to include other aspects of service delivery, such as the distinction between frontstage and backstage and the physical evidence. People can visualize and understand an entire service process by noting details of all service actions [9].

EBD recommends evaluating improvements using both subjective measures (e.g. patients' experiences) and objective outcomes (e.g. attendance rates) but does not provide an explicit process. In this study, the exporters were invited to evaluate the improvement.

3   Foreigner Health Examination Service Case Study

The case is about general heal examination service improvement for foreigner in Taiwan. The hospital is the West Garden Hospital which is placed in a crowded area and having a lot of foreigner at Taipei City. We hosted four days' workshop and went through the modified EBD process. We tried to discover the problem and improved the service experience of foreigner doing health examination in Taiwan who can not speak and read Chinese.

3.1   Participants

There were four persons in this design team, including three graduate design students (two Vietnamese, one Taiwanese) and one Taiwanese nurse. Vietnamese participants cannot speak, read and write Mandarin; English is their second language.

3.2   Processes

Capturing Experiences. All the design team members went to real filed to experience the general health check service in West Garden Hospital. The whole exanimation procedure shows as Fig. 1. All participants do not speak Chinese in throughout the examined process. Each person was assigned a duty. Two Taiwanese participants play a role as accompany of examinee to observed and took pictures. One Vietnamese student volunteer to be an examinee. The other Vietnamese used 5W1H and AEIOU chart to observe and wrote down everything, including time, objects, feelings (Figs. 2 and 3).

Fig. 1. The process of general medical examination.

Understanding Experiences. After field experience and observation, all participants returned to the workshop. They made the customer journey map together. Participants had to make sure the time, picture and each step matched each other and stick all

Fig. 2. Team members were observing and taking note through whole serve process (registration as an example)

Fig. 3. Team members were taking photo for environment and objects

documents on the board. Then, the participant who played the patient role wrote down both negative and positive feelings, thoughts when she joined the health process. Those were divided into the negative or positive area in the customer journey map. Emotion words drawn from the stories are written on Post-it notes, which are then placed in line with the identified touch point. Positive emotional reactions appear higher on the map and negative emotions lower, thus creating a visual representation of the emotional journey (Fig. 4). Clusters of negative responses indicate problems to address. Starting from this stage there were two design professors and one nursing professor joint in to facilitating the discussion (Fig. 5).

In registration, the patients were difficult to find volunteers because of the Asian appearance that looks like a local people, Taiwanese. For example, American or Indian who has a significantly different appearance with a local people, volunteers will be easy to realize and help foreigners.

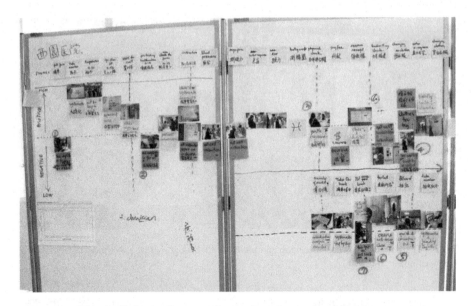

Fig. 4. Understanding experiences through customer journey map.

Fig. 5. Discussion of customer journey map.

In the X-ray section, they were asked to remove shirt and bra and to wear a gown. Next, they stand in front of the X-Ray room - public area, to waiting their turn. It was very uncomfortable and shy. Otherwise, nurse directly touch the patient back to check not bra and jewelry, without any announcements. It made the patient felt startled and resentful. One possible explanation is that the nurse rushed the patient to finish the checking and do not have time to think how to speak English with the patient. So, the nurse directly checked faster.

In the result of customer journey map showed that the patient had positive and negative feelings in each section. The patient felt extremely uncomfortable with the registration, X-ray checking, and Urine sections, especially, "do not wear a bra in public space"; "directly touch on a patient without announcement", "take urine tube into public space", and "difficult to find volunteer" (Fig. 6).

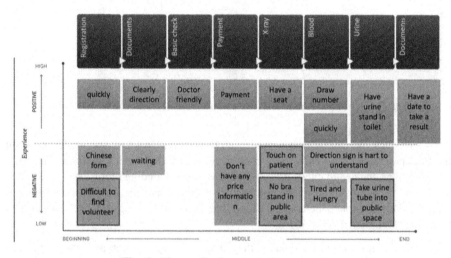

Fig. 6. The result of customer journey map.

Improving Experiences. In this step, group members define and distinction the experience between frontstage and backstage and the physical evidence. They wrote down and post notes on the Blueprinting (Fig. 7).

Base on the frontstage and backstage in the Blueprinting, they defined the elements could be changed or redesigned to find out the optimal solutions. After having solutions, they discussed with Professors to figure out one solution. The result of service blueprint showed a basic system of the healthcare process. Designers knew front-stage elements and back-stage elements of each section that they want to improve or redesign. Combining service blueprint with customer journey map, a folder idea was so provided with popular languages versions (English or Japan) that foreign patients can read by themselves. It helps to solve the problem, which the patient was difficult to find volunteers in the registration section.

The solution is a folder with many popular languages versions. When the foreigner patients go to registration, they can easily find the folder having their language in the registration area. This folder has a small pocket for placing the health insurance card in cover. Page 1 has information about price, instruction, and all steps of the process. Page

Fig. 7. Define problem to improving experiences through service blueprint.

2 has a hospital map and the case, putting all documents they had, and the QR code on the final page that let patients more convenient to search their information (Fig. 8).

Moreover, the health check process had 8 sections, spending more 2 h to finish. It is overlong for patients to do it (see Fig. 9). This studies redesigned the process having 6 sections (Registration, Documents, Blood and Urine check, Basic Check, X-ray and Payment Documents) (Fig. 10).

Measuring Improvements. Finally, they made a simple prototype with paper, and presentation to introduce the process they got this solution and received feedbacks and comments from nursing expert and professors.

4   Discussion

In its entirety, this is a great chance to have a deeper understanding of foreigner patient behavior and feeling when they joined in the healthcare setting. EBD suggests facilitating 'co-design' teams of foreigners, designers and healthcare staff to explore and implement service improvements, based on the understanding developed in earlier phases. In the capturing experience phase, all the stakeholder got together to experienced and observed the filed world could have more real story and scenario for discussion. In the understanding and improvement phase, combined customer journey map and service blue print could stronger understanding of customer experience and the customer journey in this era of increasingly complex customer behavior [10, 11]. Finally, evaluation of service improvements is shared with participants.

Limitation of this study the lack of participant groups, only Vietnamese participants. On the next program, participants should have various cultural.

The results of this study showed that EBD approach could come out appreciate solutions to solve languages barriers and foreigner's health check service quality.

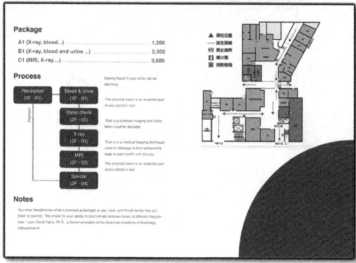

Fig. 8. The folder solution

Because of the foreign patient joining the process and also joining the workshop to figure out the solution that has potential to reduce their negative feelings. The folder solution is a simple, inexpensive that should be translated and replicated in other languages. In the future, this folder can connect to a database with QR code behind and can link to hospital's mobile app or internet to get more information.

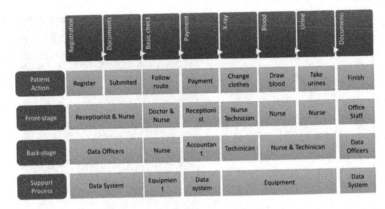

Fig. 9. The result of service blueprint

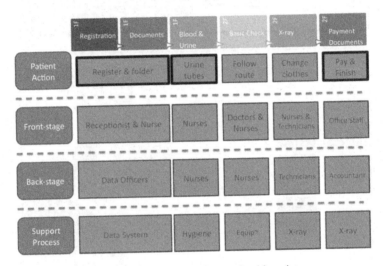

Fig. 10. The redesigned – service blueprint

References

1. Minister of Education: Taiwan aims to double international student numbers by 2019, 8 Nov 2016   http://monitor.icef.com/2016/11/taiwan-aims-double-international-student-numbers-2019/
2. Ministry of Labor: Number of foreign domestic workers surged last year, 1 Mar 2017. http://www.taipeitimes.com/News/taiwan/archives/2017/03/01/2003665919
3. Meuter, R.F., Gallois, C., Segalowitz, N.S., Ryder, A.G., Hocking, J.: Overcoming language barriers in healthcare: a protocol for investigating safe and effective communication when patients or clinicians use a second language. BMC Health Serv. Res. 15(1), 371 (2015)
4. Betancourt, J.R., Green, A.R., Carrillo, J.E., Ananeh-Firempong, O.: Defining cultural competence: a practical framework for addressing racial/ethnic disparities in health and health care. Public Health Rep. 118, 293–302 (2016)

5. Steen, M., Manschot, M., De Koning, N.: Benefits of co-design in service design projects. Int. J. Des. **5**(2), 53–60 (2011)
6. Bowen, S., McSeveny, K., Lockley, E., Wolstenholme, D., Cobb, M., Dearden, A.: How was it for you? Experiences of participatory design in the UK health service. CoDesign **9**(4), 230–246 (2013)
7. Bate, P., Robert, G.: Bringing User Experience to Healthcare Improvement: The Concepts. Methods and Practices of Experience-Based Design. Radcliffe, Oxford (2007)
8. Richardson, A.: Using customer journey maps to improve customer experience. Harv. Bus. Rev. **15**(1), 2–5 (2010)
9. Stauss, B., Weinlich, B.: Process-oriented measurement of service quality by applying the sequential incident method, Tilburg, The Netherlands (1995)
10. Hamdy, H.: Blueprinting for the assessment of health care professionals. Clin. Teach. **3**(3), 175–179 (2006)
11. Lemon, K.N., Verhoef, P.C.: Understanding customer experience throughout the customer journey. J. Market. **80**(6), 69–96 (2016)
12. Milton, S.K., Johnson, L.W.: Service blueprinting and BPMN: a comparison. Manag. Serv. Qual.: Int. J. **22**(6), 606–621 (2012)

HEDI: An Online Platform for Healthcare Engineering Design and Innovation

Long Liu[✉], Weiyu Zhang, Jinhua Li, and Hua Dong

College of Design and Innovation, Tongji University, Fuxin Road 281, Shanghai
200092, China
liulong@tongji.edu.cn

Abstract. Healthcare is a specialized sector in which products and service provision are embedded with professional requirements that are unfamiliar to most of the designers, and different stakeholders have quite different knowledge backgrounds, viewpoint of concerns, working styles, etc.. which make the communication and innovation among them complex and difficult. The Design Council in UK launched a free-to-access online EBCD (Experience Based Co-Design) toolkit to facilitate designers working closely with healthcare providers and patients in design process. In the College of Design and Innovation (D&I) of Tongji University in China, we are planning to establish an online platform based on the EBCD methodology to promote effective and efficient communication among different parties in healthcare design and innovation (healthcare providers, engineers, designers, patients, etc.) to encourage idea generating and sharing. In this paper, the functionality of the platform as well as some experience we obtained from the EBCD practice will be presented.

Keywords: Experience Based Co-design · Healthcare service system design
Online platform

1 Introduction

Healthcare is a specialized sector in which products and service provision are embedded with professional requirements, such as laws and regulations, norms and standards, technical terms, etc. which become the barrier preventing outsiders from knowing and making contribution to healthcare industry. Different parties and stakeholders in healthcare industry have obviously quite different knowledge background, viewpoint of concern, behavior and working style, habit, etc. which make the communication and innovation among them complex and difficult. Therefore, many efforts have been exerted to change such situation and to promote healthcare design and innovation.

1.1 International Researches in Healthcare Design

Many researches have shown that the concept of service design is helpful in managing huge and complicate healthcare service net, which potentially leads to break the barrier in healthcare design innovation. In 1991, professor Erlhoff in KISD firstly introduced

© Springer International Publishing AG, part of Springer Nature 2018
P.-L. P. Rau (Ed.): CCD 2018, LNCS 10912, pp. 308–319, 2018.
https://doi.org/10.1007/978-3-319-92252-2_25

the concept of service design into design domain. Carnegie Mellon University, Polytechnic University of Milan and other design school made up a service design net, which contributed to the great development in academic study and practical practice of service design. The application of service design in healthcare domain was owned to the reform of NHS (National Health Service) in Britain [1] (Department of Health 2000). In 2005, NHS proposed an experience-based work model of healthcare service design-EBCD (Experience Based Co-Design) [2].

1.2 EBCD in Healthcare Design

NHS conducted more in-depth research on the EBCD methodology, made usage guides and toolkits freely available to interested designers via website. Therefore, EBCD has been well promoted. Freire and Sangiorgi found that involving service acceptors in the process of service design promoted patient's experience, but it also influenced the stability of service. After studied up to 80 healthcare service design projects which used Experience Based Co-design as a method, Donetto and other researchers [3] found that 50% interviewers believe it is a time-consuming program, and only 50% of them plan to apply EBCD to their work in the future, even out of 90% agree the biggest benefit of it lies in the involvement of patients indeed. This report demonstrated that study in EBCD should go further as far as in healthcare service design domain.

1.3 Healthcare Situation in China

Mention hospitals, people will always think of many bad experiences, such as a long line of waiting, bad smell of corridors, complex healthcare inspection items and so on. In recent years, frequent disputes between doctors and patients in our country have occurred, and some of them have become extremely polarized issues. Patient experience and healthcare staff experience were ignored by us.

Patients' experience was glaringly absent from the whole process of medical for a very long term, what's more, hospitals and doctors, not patients, are seen as the center in the whole process of healthcare service, but now, thing goes differently. In 2006, Medical Center in Cleveland, the top hospital in American, built "Patient Experience Office". In 2014, Shanghai First Maternity and Infant Hospital set up the "Patient Committee". In 2016, Dr. Smile Medical Group set a job position called "patient experience officer", who is in charge of examining the treatment process and getting feedback from patients. It indicates that the mounting public attention has been launched into EBCD in healthcare industry.

China has entered the age of aging. It is estimated that by 2023, the elderly population will exceed 300 million. The aging population will inevitably bring about more medical needs and further increase the medical burden on our country. High-quality medical service requirements and strong medical demand will inevitably bring more opportunities and challenges to China's medical industry.

2   Experience-Based Co-design (EBCD) in Healthcare Domain

2.1   Introduction of EBCD

EBCD is a form of participatory action research [4] that seeks to capture and understand how people actually experience a process or service. EBCD improves users' experience by deliberately involve service providers, users and stuff in the service activities, collect their subjective, personal feelings to identify touchpoints—key elements that influence a user's overall experience [5].

Drawing upon participatory design principles, the co-design element in EBCD aims at opening up the boundaries of designing in healthcare services in order to include new stakeholders and forms of expertise; patients are called to share their specialist form of expertise (knowledge) and participate in the design process from the idea generation stage [3].

Given the increasingly influential notion of co-designing public services ('service development driven by the equally respected voices of users, providers and professionals') [6, 7], EBCD represents one approach to reposition (largely) passive recipients of a service as more active consumers and citizens in a coalition, or partnership, with staff [8].

2.2   Practices in EBCD

Study in service design for healthcare in China is just beginning, only a few researches involved general introduction and case study about it, without any practical program. For example, the introduction about the principles, methodologies and system components of applying service design in abroad made by Changfu [9], the concept of healthcare service design in the digital era imposed by Miaosen [10]. There are more and more researches focusing on quality improvement in healthcare service from the perspective of process management and optimization (Xiansong) [11], but it lacks systematic study and application for medical service design in general design domain. EBCD provides an effective mentoring and methodological model for the healthcare industry to improve service quality and enhance service experience. However, no case of EBCD used in healthcare practice in China has been found yet, and there is a lack of research on EBCD and the characteristics of medical environment in China. In the meantime, domestic research on service design is still in its infancy, and there are few systematic design processes or methodologies targeted at enhancing healthcare service experience.

2.3   Analysis of EBCD

EBCD methodology seeks to equip users, providers and designers to work together on service and quality improvement to let designers who lack enough professional knowledge in healthcare domain get a much stronger support in such special design that will explicitly strive to improve users' experiences. Five main points of it are discussed here:

Multi-model Method of Design Process. The design process of EBCD combined both linear process and cyclic iteration process and four steps are included, see Fig. 1:

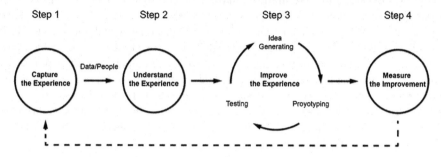

Fig. 1. Main process of EBCD methodology.

The First Step. Gaining users' experience and shooting videos correspondingly.

The Second Step. Defining the thing need to be improved and setting priorities. Since the videos made previously and patients, carers, and staff involved in the first step are brought into the second step to analyze, we can supplement and improve experience without returning to the first step, which is different from most of the cyclic iteration process in service method.

The Third Step. Design improvement, EBCD shared the similar process with other design method, by generating concept, making prototype, testing and getting feedback, to ensure designs meet real needs and promote design with more details.

The Fourth Step. Measuring the improvement, it links the end of this design process and the beginning of the next one to facilitate the improvement work in healthcare service design using EBCD become a sustainable and circular process.

Narrative-Based User Experience. What EBCD focused on is users' emotional experience which can indirectly reflect their demands and usability of service during that time, analyzing the reasons behind emotion can help to find out some potential demands. The primary way to collect users' emotion in EBCD is storytelling, that lead users to tell the real story when they accept service. Then we analyze the emotion involved in the story to explore the things need to be improved in service.

Make Patients, Carers and Staff Become Design Participators. Patients, carers and staff in EBCD methodology are not only seen as objects of study, but also the design participators, involved in every part of design process, who make active contribution to service improvement. It brings two benefits:

From the Short-term Design Process. It ensures improved service meet users' needs indeed, moreover, users' experience supply a gap that designers are unfamiliar with that service.

From the Long-term Design Process. It offers patients and stuff an opportunity to communicate and understand each other, which has the power to change their behavior and attitude gradually, as a result, the quality of healthcare service will get improved with far-reaching influence.

Open Framework and Systematic Toolkit. EBCD provides methods and tools can be used in every step of design process, to be specific, poster design, conference agenda, etc. allowing people without getting trained can operate and implement EBCD according to the guidance. For designers, EBCD is an open methodology which provide inclusive framework of thinking to guide goals and outputs in each step, not just restricted to the application of some method or tool. In some practical projects, designers adjusted and adopted design tools in other field according to actual requirement like brainstorming, business canvas, etc. NHS and scholars in other institutions are keep going deeper in exploring and enriching theory system of EBCD, like introducing evidence-based design.

Online-Based Open Resource Pool. NHS provides free instructor of EBCD methodology and toolkit on its official website to people who are interested in to understand and use it, which contributed to the great accumulation of practical projects rapid development in theory in recent years. In order to promote the development in healthcare service design efficiently, NHS call on building user experience video library to collect user experience data to support relevant projects in the future. Video library is proved to reduce the working time and difficulty level effectively.

These innovation points of EBCD provide a strong back and reference for the online platform we want to build.

2.4   Limits of EBCD in China

Some experience we obtained from EBCD by analyzing its main features include: (1) EBCD was a direct response to observing how early projects – which includes extensive work to understand patient experience (much of it innovative at the time) - were paying insufficient attention to the co-design phase. Staff involved were relying on traditional, narrower approaches to making improvements to services. (2) Since the requirements on designers are much higher than before, online EBCD toolkit is not effective enough in current situation, however the approach to entering healthcare service design domain is still limited. We need a tool for designers to get better involvement, training, and communication in healthcare design. (3) Study of service design in China is just beginning, lacking methods and tools of design process. EBCD is not used in any practical projects in China so far, and there is lack of studies combining the features of healthcare environment in China with that in abroad. Localize EBCD to adapt to Chinese environment is the first step.

Healthcare industry in China is undergoing a series of changes: from product design to service design, from medical centered to healthcare centered, from offline hospital to online platform, from high-end hospital to primary hospital. China's healthcare industry is already at the critical point of innovation and reform. But the development of healthcare technology and the assignment of healthcare resource are different in the country. EBCD method can point a new direction of the development of Chinese healthcare industry. Based on EBCD, we need a more efficient tool for promoting healthcare design and innovation, with an accessible way to use.

3   HEDI (Healthcare Engineering Design and Innovation Platform)

In the College of Design and Innovation (D&I) of Tongji University in China, we are planning to establish an online platform based on the EBCD methodology to combine different fields (research, technology and practice) and promote effective and efficient communication among different parties in healthcare design and innovation (healthcare providers, engineers, designers, patients, etc.). HEDI (an online platform for healthcare engineering design and innovation) offers an opportunity for knowledge learning, information sharing, ideas generating and data collecting. It bridges the professional gap between multi-parties in healthcare design and lowers the collaboration obstacles between different parties and involves healthcare users in this process, see Fig. 2.

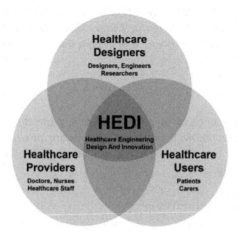

Fig. 2. Role of HEDI.

3.1   Importance of Building HEDI

By now, many efforts have been exerted to promote healthcare design and innovation. More and more designers and design organizations are engaged in design projects aiming at improving healthcare efficacy and quality. It raises the urgent need of a tool which enables the co-design be accepted and used in healthcare field.

Professionalism Knowledge Gap. It appears that the co-design discussions in which patients, staff and designers worked together to agree priorities were a crucial aspect of EBCD intervention and it focus on patient-centered care [12]. But there is still a huge gap caused by professionalism between healthcare providers and designers, designers need to be involved in the EBCD method to make their contributions more useful and practical. In order to bridge the gap, it is essential to build an EBCD based platform which enables designers have access to healthcare knowledge.

Multi-party Collaboration. Now more than ever, we need healthcare professionals working in the design field. Professional disciplines are bringing their expertise to the same table, yet these approaches still require a significant amount of translation. In this role, front line clinicians and other professionals need to translate healthcare to the designer in design field where significant improvement of user experience could be made [13]. *To meet these demands, we need a resource sharing platform which can make the communication among different parties (researchers, engineers, healthcare providers, quality managers, patients and relatives, designers, etc.) more convenient and efficient.*

Following Design Opportunities. The range of ideation tools within EBCD have been reviewed as limited, since they do not support participants to go beyond suggesting simple solutions to immediate issues [14]. *It raises concern that more radical solutions as well as systematic possibilities for new service innovations are not explored following this participatory approach. It indicates a demand for individualized tools used within these activities to assist design activities. Therefore, some other improvements can be made following EBCD process such as data analysis, case study and personnel assignment.*

3.2 Users of HEDI

Users of this platform can be divided into two parts: professional one who worked in healthcare industry and know it very well (healthcare providers, engineers, senior designers) and amateur one who want to know more about this domain (new designers, patients, carers), see Fig. 3.

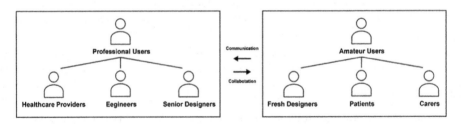

Fig. 3. Classification of users on this platform.

Patients and carers are the main users of healthcare service, they are also a huge missed group of people with true needs of healthcare service. It is essential to get patients and carers involved, they are encouraged to express their true feelings and comments about the service or processes they experienced in HEDI. Connections are built between them and healthcare service providers and designers.

EBCD projects typically take between 6–12 months to complete [15]. The relationship between each parties need to be maintained during this long process in order to make the experience consistent and fluent. By HEDI, they have access to discuss their project and share ideas. In this way, patients, as healthcare service users, gain a sufficient attention from others. Designers have access to know more professional knowledge about healthcare and bring design methods into it. Healthcare providers have opportunities to know the real needs of users, existing problems and ways to deal with it.

3.3   Functionality of HEDI

EBCD is not only a part of the content, but also the structure of HEDI. We learn from EBCD process to build the framework of HEDI. Each functions, tools and materials are arranged according to a logical way (from capture experience, understand experience, improve experience, measure improvement to data analysis). Components of HEDI covered each main steps of EBCD, which completes the functions and highlights the logic in using it, see Fig. 4.

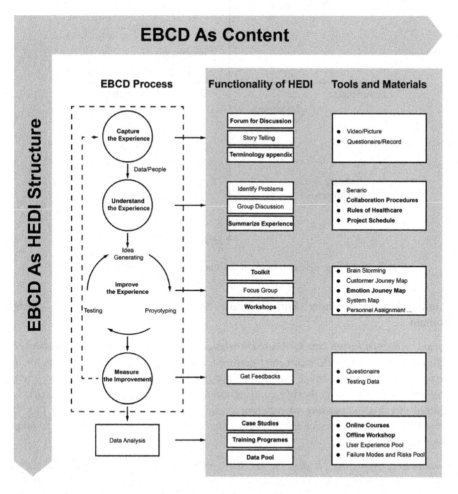

Fig. 4. Applying EBCD process in building framework of HEDI platform.

Considering different groups of users have different knowledge backgrounds, needs and potential contributions, this platform is designed as having two main function modules: communicating module and learning module. In terms of healthcare, designers who have little knowledge and experiences about it have access to professional people, target users and design methods. Patients who have direct experience on healthcare service have right channel to express and be involved in practical programs, see Fig. 5.

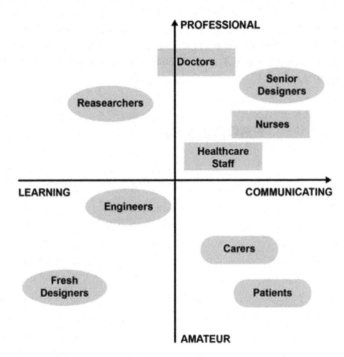

Fig. 5. Applying EBCD process in building framework of HEDI platform.

Communicating Module: For Different Stakeholders in Healthcare Design Domain

Forum. An open forum can facilitate knowledge sharing and idea expression between different parties. Every user can start new topics and post replies on the forum, for the purpose of discussing service quality, asking questions about service process, giving professional suggestions, sharing good experiences, etc. All information is classified in different sections according to different groups of people who engaged in (service providers, designers, service users, etc.), which enables information attaches to target people easily.

Terminology Appendix. It also makes the communication between different parties easier by translating the complex technical nature of their language into plain language, for the purpose of making unprofessional people understand. Terminology appendix section can be built by users of HEDI, each of them have access to edit or create terminology appendix, especially in their own professional field. Some tables and objective questions are used for user testing, it helps healthcare users express their feelings and give suggestions. Set credit mechanism, building trust and finding a common ground between participants to stimulate information sharing in designers and service providers, and feedback from patients and carers, see Fig. 6.

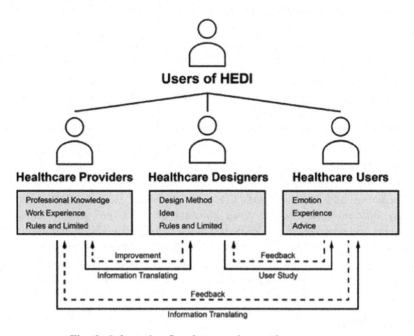

Fig. 6. Information flow between three main user groups.

Toolkits. Provide a suite of toolkits to facilitate communication between different parties, it includes useful models and tools like collaboration procedures, personnel assignment in focus group, questionnaire model, etc. which are managed according to design phases. These toolkits are generated from the experience of previous designers in healthcare service design, then exposed to fresh designers to work in a efficient way. It includes not only the rules need to be obeyed and skills designers have to command in healthcare design, but also the experience and advices about how to enter healthcare industry as quick as possible.

Workshops. Offline EBCD based workshops help to transfer knowledge and skills into concrete service outputs. Multi-parties can communicate and interact with each other in a direct way during workshops. Since users of HEDI have better acquaintance about how it works than people outside this field, it is convenient to recruit volunteers from HEDI to participate in focus group.

Learning Module: For Fresh Designers Who Want to Work in Healthcare Domain

Case Studies. Providing case studies and best practice examples to indicate the practical application of EBCD in healthcare, for new designers, is a good way to avoid unnecessary effort in exploiting principles and also a guidance. These cases, ranging from idea generation to implement phase, were uploaded by senior designers or experienced staff in the hospital by different ways like photos or videos, so that the authority of it could be confirmed.

Training Programs. Approximately 50% of those who have led EBCD projects did not receive any formal training in the approach [15]. It is necessary to provide training program like online courses for designers who plan to work at healthcare service design. Training programs are charge for a little fee for making videos and hiring teachers who can be senior designers and experienced professors. Offline workshops could also be reached in some fixed time in order to gather people who shared the same interests together to get trained and promote mutual learning.

Data Pool. The relevant data we collect from HEDI platform could be divided into different groups according to keywords, stages and stakeholders for later use. These data including subjective outcomes like user experience data, service quality, and objective outcomes like waiting time, numbers of users, etc. which indicate the touchpoints and problems in service system that will be quite useful in analyzing design trend and users' needs. These data, after manipulated and analyzed by statistical tools, could be an evidence base for building user experience pool, failure modes and risks pool. All of these are important for designers to do their work in a radical way.

4   Conclusion

HEDI provides designers an opportunity to enter the healthcare design industry to integrate their perspective and expertise into the real design and healthcare facilities with the strong support of users and healthcare professionals. On the implement of HEDI, several key questions are mentioned and solutions are provided accordingly. But some problems still need to be considered carefully in future, like the security of personal information, the facilitating mechanization of encouraging people to express their ideas, and statistics and analysis of big data we collected. Based on these general design guides, in consideration of different parties has different needs for engaging in HEDI, a design concept with large potential to develop really promising online learning, sharing and co-working platform are proposed in this study.

References

1. Department of Health: The NHS plan: a plan for investment, a plan for reform. My Publications (2000)
2. Freire, K., Sangiorgi, D.: Service design & healthcare innovation: from consumption to co-production and co-creation. In: Nordic Service Design Conference (2010)

3. Donetto, S., Pierri, P., Tsianakas, V., Robert, G.: Experience-based co-design and healthcare improvement: realizing participatory design in the public sector. Des. J. **18**(2), 227–248 (2015)
4. Cain, T.: The Sage handbook of action research: participative inquiry and practice. Eur. J. Inf. Syst. **10**(3), 176–177 (2014)
5. Dewar, B., Mackay, R., Smith, S., Pullin, S., Tocher, R.: Use of emotional touchpoints as a method of tapping into the experience of receiving compassionate care in a hospital setting. J. Res. Nurs. **15**(15), 29–41 (2010)
6. Sato, M., Shimomura, K.: Making the most of collaboration an international survey of public service co-design. J. Ind. Manag. Ind. Manag. Inst. **35**, 243–302 (2003)
7. Wolstenholme, D., Cobb, M., Bowen, S., Dearden, A., Wright, P.: Design-led service improvement for older people. Australas. Med. J. **3**(8), 465–470 (2010)
8. Abma, T.A.: Patient participation in health research: research with and for people with spinal cord injuries. Qual. Health Res. **15**(10), 1310–1328 (2005)
9. Changfu, L.: Application of service design in medical service management. Industrial Design Research (2015)
10. Miaosen, G., Xueliang, L., Dongjuan, X.: Innovative medical and health service design for digital society. Packag. Eng. **12**, 24–28 (2015)
11. Xiansong, M.: The construction of hospital patient centered service system. Chin. Health Serv. Manag. **1**, 15–17 (2000)
12. Iedema, R., Merrick, E., Piper, D., Britton, K., Gray, J., Verma, R.: Codesigning as a discursive practice in emergency health services: the architecture of deliberation. J. Appl. Behav. Sci.: Publ. NTL Inst. **46**(1), 73–91 (2010)
13. Evans, J.: Evolving leadership in healthcare design. Herd **7**(4), 9–12 (2014)
14. Bowen, S., Mceveny, K., Lockley, E., Wolstenholme, D., Cobb, M., Dearden, A.: How was it for you? Experiences of participatory design in the UK health service. CoDesign **9**(4), 230–246 (2013)
15. Donetto, S., Tsianakas, V., Robert, G.: Using Experience-based Co-design (EBCD) to improve the quality of healthcare: mapping where we are now and establishing future directions. King's College London, London (2014)

Growing a Community-Supported Ecosystem of Future Living: The Case of NICE2035 Living Line

Yongqi Lou[✉] and Jin Ma

Tongji University College of Design and Innovation, 281 Fuxin Road, Shanghai, China
louyongqi@tongji.edu.cn, majin.poly@gmail.com

Abstract. This paper reports a design-driven social innovation initiative titled "NICE2035 Living Line" that Tongji University College of Design and Innovation recently launched in collaboration with the local administrative authorities in Siping community (Shanghai, China). While there is great demand for social and economic innovations that can address the challenges the city faces today, urban communities, especially the old ones, lack the vitality needed to support the city to achieve its goal. The urban community has long been seen as merely a place for living and leisure, and therefore a place where innovation outcomes are consumed not generated. The NICE2035 Living Line project challenges this dominant view of communities and adopts a design-driven approach to building an ecosystem of innovation and entrepreneurship on a small street within an old residential community where the college resides. Within this ecosystem, labs and start-ups produce diverse prototypes of alternative future ways of living. This paper examines the purpose and function of the ecosystem (why it exists), the system elements (what is systematized), and the process by which the elements interact with each other (how the system operates). This preliminary study of the project provides a basic framework for further studies on the mechanisms of such complex sociotechnical systems.

Keywords: Social innovation · Urban community · Ecosystem
Design-driven innovation · Future living · NICE2035

1 Introduction

Today, few would doubt that innovation thrives in cities [1–4]. When imagining the most innovative places in a city, one would likely think of innovation companies, high-tech parks, downtown areas, the CBD, university campuses, and research institutions, etc. An urban community, however, often lies outside the scope of that vibrant image. This misconception has its roots in the developments of contemporary architecture and urban planning.

Ever since the influential *Athens Charter* [5, 6], a city has been defined as a functional site for four basic types of human activities: dwelling, working, leisure (recreation), and transportation (circulation) [7]; and to plan and organize the first three functions in a city was to separate them from one another [8]. Our understanding of

© Springer International Publishing AG, part of Springer Nature 2018
P.-L. P. Rau (Ed.): CCD 2018, LNCS 10912, pp. 320–333, 2018.
https://doi.org/10.1007/978-3-319-92252-2_26

cities has evolved since the 1930s. The *Charter of Machu Picchu* [9] in 1977 recognized the limitations of the notion of a "functional city" in its fragmentation of a living organism into a set of separated functional sectors. It proposed to reintegrate the divided components and restore lost interdependence and interrelationships and emphasized the value of culture, life, and humanity—especially ordinary citizens—in urban development. However, in the years after the *Charter*, dominant urban planning and architecture design still favors the disposition and management of the built environment over people and pays less attention to human activities (urban contents) and urban stewardship.

Following this tradition, the urban community[1] has long been regarded merely as the set and setting for daily life and leisure. Communal urban environments were and are designed as places where people can live and relax while consuming and enjoying products produced by other parts of the city. In a typical innovation chain—from invention, engineering, design, production, and distribution, to use and enjoyment—the community sits at the consumption end (back end) and is isolated from the innovation production occurring in other parts of the city.

If cities were vigorous and innovative enough to be able to maintain these communities purely as areas for life and leisure, there would be no problem. Unfortunately, most cities in the world now face the acute stressors of social, economic, environmental, and cultural deterioration [10]. Trapped in predicaments caused by natural disasters, social changes due to deindustrialization, weak economic recovery, or failing infrastructure, cities across the globe are seeking powerful drivers to innovate and address these challenges. To do so, a city must creatively integrate its diverse components and resources. Should urban communities be seen as inherent parts of the city organism? How communities might participate in the innovation process is a timely inquiry for researchers, administrators, practitioners, and—most importantly—the people who live in them.

Although the phenomenal "garage culture" in Silicon Valley that began in the 1930s and has flourished since the 1970s is a legendary example of the connection between community and innovation, the potential that urban communities have to drive innovation has not received sufficient attention. Our inquiry begins with a fundamental hypothesis: if there are appropriate conditions, an urban community will lead the innovation chain rather than become its tail, and community members will become creators rather than merely consumers. A new paradigm of innovation will occur through shifting the community from the back end to the front end.

This paper presents a case of a social innovation initiative entitled "NICE 2035 Living Line" that Tongji University College of Design and Innovation recently launched in collaboration with the sub-district "Siping community" in Shanghai, China. "The Living Line" is the first project under the umbrella title of "NICE2035." We see the NICE2035 Living Line project as an ecosystem of urban community-supported social innovation. We approach the Siping ecosystem three ways: its purpose and function (why the system exists), the system elements (what is systematized), and the

---

[1] The notion of "community" used in this paper denotes a residential area. In the Chinese context, residential neighborhoods, areas, and districts are all called "communities" (社区).

processes through which these elements interact with each other (how the system operates). This preliminary examination provides a basic framework for further studies on the mechanism of such complex sociotechnical systems.

2 Project Set-up, Paradigm, and Approach

On February 4, 2018, the Tongji University College of Design and Innovation and the Siping sub-district office (Yangpu District, Shanghai) announced the launch of the "NICE2035 Living Line" project. "NICE 2035" stands for "Neighborhood of Innovation, Creativity, and Entrepreneurship toward 2035," a program put forward by the College of Design and Innovation. It is an umbrella title for a collection of social innovation initiatives grounded in the Siping community—the neighborhood where the College is located. The Living Line project is the first prototype cluster that kicked off.

The Living Line—Lane 1028 of Siping Road—houses a series of research labs and innovation enterprises. Each explores future living with distinct focuses ranging from food and dining, entertainment, new materials applications, mobility, and new ways of working, to co-creation incubation, robotics, and advanced manufacturing. The first group of units that settled on the Living Line include the Tongji-Dadawa Sound*Lab, Tom's BaoBao Food Lab, NoCC Fashion Lab, Neuni Material Lab, Design Harvests Rural Lab, Aroma Art Fragrance Lab, Timemore Coffee Lab, Hiwork Working-Space Lab, Xuberance 3D Printing Lab, Fablab O Maker Workshop, 021-NICE Incubator, NICE Crowd-funding Platform, and DomiBox 24 h Unattended Shop.

The Living Line is a co-creation hub where rich interactions occur between ideas, people, labs, resources, and capital. It intimately connects Tongji to its neighborhood: the wider Siping community. The university brings in its global knowledge community and talents to Siping to establish labs and start-ups that produce prototypes of alternative futures of living; the community accommodates this group and interacts with it on Lane 1028—a small street now simply called "the prototype street" by participants. The prototype street functions as a living lab—an open-innovation ecosystem operating in a real urban setting and providing for the innovation needs of tangible and intangible environments. This small street has become a complex place that integrates product research and development labs, an innovative education unit, prototype stores, co-creation spaces, as well as an incubator into an urban social system. The participants become new community members. The products of the Living Line are a variety of prototypes for future living scenarios. However, these are not the "end-products" by any means. These prototypes are directly connected to venture capital, private equity, and industries. Cultivated within this ecosystem, innovations will have a greater chance of adoption and translation into the real businesses that feed new industries, new models, new economies, and new technologies. In doing so, the initiative will be able to contribute to enhancing the competitiveness of Shanghai regarding service, manufacturing, consumption, and unique culture. Figure 1 summarizes the innovation paradigm of NICE20135 Living Line.

The conventional innovation model is linear. It begins with technological inventions firstly developed by engineering and industrial design, then distributed through commercial marketing, and finally consumed by end users. This is a technology-pushed

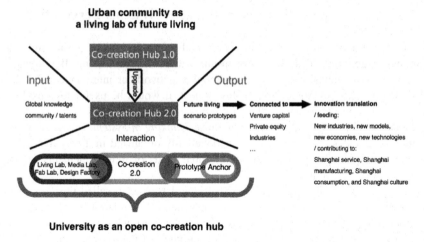

Fig. 1. The paradigm of NICE2035 Living Line. Copyright © Yongqi Lou, 2017.

and market-pulled innovation model [11]. The Living Line overturns this model by shifting the role of the urban residential community in the innovation process from the passive consumption end to the active innovation source. In vivid contrast to the conventional model, the initiative adopts the approach of design-driven innovation, which creates new meanings for application of technology and creation of new markets.

From the conventional perspective of urban planning and governance, "residents"—the community's members—are seen as the objects that need to be looked after. The old model is: people create fortunes for society, family, and individual during working hours in their working places; once back in the community, their activities shift to living, leisure, and social communication. We challenge this dichotomy and ask whether the community resident can also play the role of the urban innovator in the place where he/she lives.

Our choice to use a community as the focus for this initiative has several reasons. First, the community is close to all kinds of problems that people encounter in the city and therefore is a natural setting for experimenting solutions. This explains the key idea of developing the community as a living lab for future living. Second, the urban community is close to consumers, and thus is close to potential human needs for alternative futures. Their in-depth understanding of their needs as users will allow inhabitants to creatively invent, choose, or apply technology and translate innovations into appropriate businesses. Third, the urban community has greater diversity regarding its cultures, education levels, professions and disciplines, ages, and social relationships in comparison to general institutions and enterprises. Fourth, the community has a higher tolerance for failure thanks to its informal organization, which is a great advantage of community-supported innovation [12].

3   The Case Exploration Framework: A Systems Perspective

As introduced above, the Living Line is a social innovation initiative that cultivates a community-supported ecosystem of open-innovation for future living. By calling it an ecosystem, we emphasize that it is "a complex network or interconnected systems. [13]" Before taking a closer look at this project, it would be useful to consider two fundamental concepts: *system* and *social innovation*.

Meadows [14] began her renowned treatise *Thinking in Systems* with: "A **system** is an interconnected set of elements that is coherently organized in a way that achieves something.... [A] system must consist of three kinds of things: elements, interconnections, and a function or purpose."

This is a powerful starting point [15]. Richard Buchanan called this "a commonplace definition," a definition that rests upon variables—a relationship among "X" in the process of "Y" that achieves "Z." [16] To further grasp what a system is—if it does exist—Buchanan suggests that one must ask him/herself the following questions [16]:

1. What is systematized? (What are the components?)
2. How does the system operate? (What are the interactions among the components?)
3. Why does the system exist? (What are the purposes/goals/values?)

We adopt these three themes as a framework to examine the NICE2035 Living Line project: (1) the purpose of the Living Line; (2) the components (i.e., the contents) of the Living Line system; and (3) the interactions occurring within the system.

Given the complexity of the Living Line system, its contents are highly heterogeneous. Building on Richard McKeon's work, Buchanan [17, 18] identifies four kinds of interactions: "thing-to-thing interaction, person-to-person interaction, person-to-environment interaction, and person-to-idea interaction." Borrowing this schema as a clue to grasping the interacting units of the system, we look into the contents of the Living Line system from four aspects: things (objects), people, environments, and ideas. In other words, one might regard the Living Line system as a system of things or objects, a system of people, a system of environments, or a system of ideas. These are four different areas the system's materials cover. To comprehend the process or mechanism of how the system operates, we must explore the interactions among these contents.

The Living Line's social innovation characteristic echoes nicely with the system framework of purpose, content, and interaction. The common characteristic of social innovation initiatives, identified by Ezio Manzini, is that "they emerge from the creative recombination of existing assets (from social capital to historical heritage, from traditional craftsmanship to accessible advanced technology), which aim to achieve socially recognized goals in a new way. [19]" In essence, social innovation creatively integrates existing resources in an innovative way to achieve social purposes. Previously dormant and irrelevant things now become valuable resources and constitute the contents of the social innovation system or network. The purpose of every social innovation system has a salient emphasis on the well being of society. And, among the interactions in such systems, people play a key role. We will bear these considerations in mind when studying the case.

4 Designing for the Ecosystem of the NICE2035 Living Line

4.1 Revitalizing the Community by Innovating Future Living

The purpose of the NICE2035 Living Line project is to revitalize the community in ways that create a new economy; the project's focus on innovating on future ways of life paves the way toward this goal. We will analyze the purpose on two levels: the city of Shanghai, and the Siping Community.

Like cities all over the world that are confronted with new development challenges, Shanghai is now under great pressure caused by industrial transformation, an aging population, and environmental concerns, to name but a few issues. Inspired by the national policy for mass innovation and entrepreneurship, Chinese cities in general are paying increasing attention to their innovation capacity to compete against each other for social and economic advantage. Shanghai is trying to build up its unique identity to advance the city's competitiveness in a race that involves big cities in the Yangtze River Delta and the Pearl River Delta, including Shenzhen. Various nationwide innovative city ranking surveys show that Shanghai and Shenzhen are battling for second place while Beijing sits squarely at the top [20, 21]. While Shenzhen is rising rapidly thanks to its energetic high-tech enterprise environment, Shanghai is a city known for its great tolerance, diversity, individuality, and entrepreneurship. In addition, Shanghai has a unique cultural heritage—its people's profound appreciation for exquisite quality of life. Therefore, instead of competing against other cities on the level of high-tech or hardware innovation, the city of Shanghai's opportunity lies in innovation on future ways of living by exploring human needs. The path for Shanghai to achieve leadership in innovation should be grounded on insights into high-quality future living and the ability to choose, invent, apply, and distribute technologies that support such living.

In the recently released *Shanghai Master Plan 2017–2035* (also known as "Shanghai 2035") [22], the municipal government recognized that communities (urban residential areas) should be playing a more important role in developing Shanghai into a more attractive, humane city. Although living and leisure are still regarded as the main functions of urban communities, there is a growing awareness that communities may have the potential to create an environment for innovation and entrepreneurship. However, the focus is still limited to individual personal development, rather than the possibility that the community can be one of the major arenas for innovation and entrepreneurship. To reboot community vitality, the government is calling on young people to go to these communities. Herein lies a paradox: if the community fails to offer attractive contents to engage young people in meaningful activities, how can the community develop into a place aimed at young people?

Yangpu district was the locality for Shanghai's heavy industry for over a century. To shift from "industry Yangpu" to "knowledge Yangpu," the district government began to work with Tongji University to develop the "knowledge economy circle around Tongji" a decade ago. Siping community is a sub-district of 2.75 square kilometers, with a population of over 100,000, sitting at the core of the circle. It is a combination of old residential quarters and excellent educational resources—including Tongji University—embedded within. However, the Siping community tends to be monotonic in its function, environment, business, and demographic structure. It consists of the earliest and largest workers' residential quarters in China built in the 1950s; over two-thirds of its residential quarters were built in the 1970–'80 s. Portions of this community are suffering from long-term social and economic stagnation and the problems associated with an aging population. Many residential areas look worn out due to the poor building, facilities, and public space quality. Few shops and business in the streets and lanes of this community address the lifestyles attractive to young people, and even fewer are culturally relevant—despite being next to the university. Among numerous faceless, cheap restaurants and hardware shops, some officially prohibited business also exists. Lane 1028 of Siping Road is a typical small street within this community. The lane is about 200 m long and 7 m wide, once occupied by hardware stores and building materials shops, remotely connected to the everyday life of residents living in that area.

The justification for the NICE2035 Living Line was obvious: the city of Shanghai provides an ideal test bed for innovation of future living, and the Siping community is eager to improve quality of life across all aspects and upgrade its economic impact. Yongqi Lou, the Living Line's initiator, sees this as a great opportunity for the university to contribute its knowledge spillover towards enabling the community to generate the new economy. He phrased the purpose of the Living Line in this way: "In the global knowledge era, the knowledge community is becoming the subject of innovation. We must unleash the university's resources and creativity and establish a suitable platform for more entrepreneurs to create new future ways of living. By doing so, the consumption end will be the driver for industrial transformation [23]".

4.2   Things, People, Environments, and Ideas

The conditions at both the city and community levels require the Living Line project to consider unique contents that can be produced by this particular community. What are the resources? What could be the contents? Who will be the players? What are the ideas or values that drive the contents? We will approach the contents that the Living Line system integrates from four aspects.

Things

When viewed from the perspective of things and physical objects, the most significant elements in the Living Line system are labs, an incubator, start-ups, and other stakeholder entities. Among the labs installed in the Living Line, there are several anchor projects that were chosen for their potential to set the tone for the rest of the prototype street. For example, Tongji-Dadawa Sound*Lab initiated by Musician Zheqin Zhu in collaboration with Yongqi Lou is a sound-based lab that explores the possibilities for integrating music, algorithms, media design, interaction design, and AI and data design into social and public applications. Artists work closely with leading researchers and designers worldwide to redefine music as the impetus to stimulate cross-boundary, cross-disciplinary, and cross-cultural frontier explorations. Tom's BaoBao Food Lab is another example. The Founding CEO of Baobao, Qihua Tong, is passionate for the art of making the highest quality steamed buns (also called baozi in Chinese)—a delicious street food that has over one thousand years of history in China—with the finest local ingredients [24]. The first overseas branch of Baobao was opened in Boston in 2016. The food lab on Lane 1028 nonetheless takes a more future-oriented turn. It aims to redefine the idea of dining and related experience through combining Chinese traditional food culture with product, service, process, and environmental design to forge a well-respected Asian food brand that faces toward the future rather than the past. Around such anchor projects, more labs have converged. The Living Line is turning into an environment where researchers, designers, and scientists explore how we will eat, live, dress, work, move, and consume entertainment, and how technologies such as AI, big data, and robotics can become enablers. The Living Line community is interdisciplinary by nature.

People

The Living Line initiative is, for all intents and purposes, a system of people. It is a network between the grassroots leader Yongqi Lou, the participating entrepreneurs, venture capitalists, government officers, old and new residents in the Siping community, and the networks that participants bring into this initiative—for example, talent clustered around the College of Design and Innovation. Among people who have landed on the Living Line, the heads of anchor projects share some common characteristics. First, they appreciate the vision of NICE 2035 and are willing to work together toward the same goal. Second, they have had successful entrepreneurship experiences before and are now open to taking risks in a new entrepreneurship experience with a goal that they value. They can afford to fail in this experiment. Third, they are motivated because their labs on the Living Line have the potential to reshape their existing business and bring them to a new level. Therefore, instead of waiting for investments, they invest in the labs with their own money, their own ideas and core technology, and their own teams, paying market rates to rent shops facing the street.

Environments

As an ecosystem, the environments that constitute the Living Line initiative deserve a closer look. There are two kinds of environments: tangible environments such as the spaces on Lane 1028 and intangible environments that provide resources to feed the project, such as the group of participating organizations and networks. Preparing the project took several years, including space renovation, interaction augmentation, talent convergence, and ecosystem improvement. During the entire process, Tongji's College of Design and Innovation promoted and helped develop each participating unit. Whenever a new lab was inaugurated, the bond between the College and the community was strengthened and consolidated further. These projects together formed a small network of interconnected activities, adding to the overall environment. In addition to these two major organizations, the cluster of labs, start-ups, and the incubator together form a small intimate environment for individual units on the Living Line. The interaction between the labs allows ideas conceived in one lab to be advanced by integrating input from other labs. Each lab contributes to the innovative environment and each benefits from it.

Ideas

The Living Line system consists of rich and diverse ideas and values, too. Ideas produced by labs as the first fruits of the Living Line are the most understandable components in this system. However, this is also a system made up of stakeholders' visions, values, and interests. To address the Living Line system, we need to understand its inherent diversity and heterogeneity on that level. To sustain itself, the system must create the conditions for harmonious and orderly interactions among the ideas [16]. The most important thing is not seeking to avoid conflict—conflict is inevitable for complex systems such as the Living Line. Instead, creating mutually beneficial conditions serves to unify the conflicting ideas into a larger whole—the system continues to work without falling apart.

4.3   Interconnection and Interaction of Things, People, Environments, and Ideas

Viewing the NICE2035 Living Line system based on these four kinds of contents—things, people, environments, and ideas—clarifies the key components of this system and their distinct focuses. However, the system is more than the sum of its components, because it is the process of mutual influence, reciprocal action, and dynamic exchange between the components that allows the system to operate [16]. Examining the interconnections and interactions reveals the mechanism of the system. Although it is not the purpose of this paper to comprehensively study the mechanism of the Living Line system, we have seen many interesting patterns emerge from the project that intensively reflect the dynamic interactions and interconnections between the system components within and across various contents. They overturn the old models in the community building and design industries and point to the underlying mechanism of the complex sociotechnical system that is the Living Line. In the following section, we will introduce some of these.

A New Business Model

The typical business model of traditional design is that the designer is paid for the service he/she provides: the designer offers a plan for the final design product and in turn is paid by the client at a rate according to the professional standard. For example, the payment for an architecture design, interior design, landscape design, etc. is normally 1–10% of the construction cost. In this model, the designer is engaged in one tiny portion of the entire industrial chain. However, the prototype start-ups on the Living Line take a distinct business model. The designer is more than a service provider: he/she is the (co-)founder of a new enterprise, one who invests in the enterprise and participates in implementing its ideas. In this case, the designer's reward is calculated based on the enterprise's value assessment or market value. Design-driven entrepreneurship is an opportunity for design to create a new economy of unprecedented scale.

The business model is an example of interconnections between the system components in the "things" aspect. The economic factor integrates start-ups, capital, industry, and the innovation chain as a whole.

The Cluster Effect

A clustering phenomenon occurred during the preparation and launch phases. The NICE2035 Living Line attracted about one hundred participants acting as partners (lab/start-up/incubator leaders), coordinators, sponsors, or volunteers. Although their domains are diverse, they are working on like-minded enterprise entities and share a common vision for design-driven innovation in the next economy. By clustering together in the community, they make meaningful connections with capital, new resources, and other companies. Such connections may be translated into the real business and the business may lead to the realization of products, revenue growth, and even scaling-up [25]. The cluster effect is obvious when the prototype street was coming into being, when the first group of entities joined in and the spaces were made available. How did such an effect happen when there was nothing but a vision and ideas?

We observed two types of connections that led to the cluster effect at different stages: personal relationships among individuals and social ties between person and network. The former played a more crucial role when the initiator Yongqi Lou first activated and promoted the project; the latter was more salient when the project was becoming visible.

As Manzini observes [26], grassroots initiative leaders play a crucial role in a social innovation on both a personal level and an institutional level. First, the activation and promotion of the initiative "cannot be separated from the personalities, energy, and charisma of their promoters." Second, a social innovation relies on the initiator's "capacity to create around [himself/herself] a group of capable enthusiasts, to create an organization." The developing trajectory of the Living Line supports such an observation. The first group of Living Line partners joined because they had either long-term or unforgettable experiences of working with Lou. Lou personally worked together with invited partners on the anchor projects from the big picture to details such as the content for the opening show. His partners were impressed by the vision and approach proposed by Lou and excited about the prospect of the community. The preliminary cluster took shape mainly based on personal relationships with a leader they trust. Having created around him "a group of capable enthusiasts," Lou and the key partners began to establish an internal executive committee that will make decisions for key issues of managing and promoting the Living Line. In this phase, person-to-person interaction is the dominant kind of interaction.

Once the anchor project participants were on board, they, along with their networks, formed a magnetic field that kept drawing new partners closer. Here, social ties now act more significantly in expanding the cluster. When new partners contact, communicate with, and become an ally of a network, they are interacting with an environment. After becoming members of this community, these partners and their resources become part of the environment for other partners and newcomers. In this way, the cluster grows.

The cluster effect also occurs in the interaction between ideas, people, and the environment. For example, when the Sound Lab Director Zheqin Zhu proudly presented the first artwork "Sound Glaze" at the Living Line launch ceremony, she could barely contain her delight, "just a couple of days after I posted this work on my social networks, guess what: I received four major invitations asking for collaboration. People from genetic engineering asked if I could turn genetic information into sounds. And there are invitations from a real estate business, a train transportation firm, and a huge computer company." Director of the Timemore Coffee Lab shared a similar experience, saying that it was during the process of getting to know other Living Line partners that he met a traditional arts and crafts master and was inspired to collaborate on a new series of coffee products. The idea-to-idea interaction and person-to-idea interactions enrich the environment of the Living Line and create more meaningful encounters among people and ideas.

The cluster effect helps to shape a mutually beneficial environment. The more allies that join, the more resources and opportunities each partner may enjoy.

Community by Choice

Unlike the conventional residential community configurations, which were not chosen by their own members, the Living Line is a community by choice. The previous principle of building a community is content follows container: the physical space and environment (the container) of a community is pre-determined by the real estate developer, and then people move there and have all kinds of activities (the content)—in doing so, a community comes into being. A typical problem that troubles the modern city is that the urban community lacks meaningful encounters between residents and therefore becomes stagnant. This is not surprising, considering that people often become members of a community mainly thanks to their economic status.

The community that the Living Line aims to foster is a community by choice, whose principle is container follows content. The initiator planned the "products" to be realized and built up the alliances between partners, capital, and local government first, and then he managed to locate a possible place to host the whole project. This pattern will also apply when the Living Line is ready to be scaled up. When the Lane becomes saturated, and the business of the labs and start-ups continues to expand, the future living prototypes will spill over and need a new container (space) to accommodate them. Then, the core members of the Living Line will reach out to capital and government to secure to a new location: it could be a once prosperous, now abandoned department store building, or a factory, or even another street. In addition to entrepreneurship activity, this pattern also applies to housing projects. If there is a group of people with shared needs for living, leisure, and work, and they wish to live in the same area, the NICE2035 program can help them to get connected with designers, developers, and other stakeholders to build their homes based on their choice. Healthcare and care service for the elderly provide vast potential scenarios in this case.

The community by choice embodies a significant strand of interactions between people and their environment. People's activities lead to the new environment, and the new environment facilitates and nurtures the desired activities.

Technology Tie-ins

Although a community-in-place sits at the heart of the Living Line system, people, tangible and intangible resources, and ideas are not confined to the physical spaces on Lane 1028. People move around with other obligations running in parallel to the Living Line enterprise; their networks are intangible and are diffused around the city or even the world. More importantly, the open innovation happening in the Living Line welcomes talents and resources from everywhere. Outside Lane 1028, the Living Line project is also a diffused innovation organization—small and connected. Technology, especially digital media, has promising applications to integrate different components of the Living Line system, and stimulate and maintain connections required for the system to sustain and grow.

The NICE2035 program is developing a location-based crowd-funding platform that aims to weave people, ideas, resources (both tangible and intangible), and physical places together. This platform will support any Living Line member—be it a unit or an individual—to start a co-creation, crowd-funding, or crowd-sourcing project. Once the project is completed, co-creators or co-funders will be able to redeem their points through either the online platform or offline encounters. This digital platform will provide an online-offline holistic service to start-ups and innovations.

Digital media is characterized by its openness, effectiveness, and flexibility, and it is easier to make information related to needs and solutions more accessible to a broader body of community members. Ideas encounter the available resources that otherwise may not be known. The peer-to-peer connection offered by the platform brings members closer to each other and creates a virtual environment to spark off new activities. Technology may serve as a special tie that triggers and sustains interactions across all kinds of components in the Living Line system.

5 Concluding Remarks

The Living Line project is the first prototype cluster of the greater NICE2035 program. It embodies the key feature of the program and has demonstrated a promising approach to stimulating creativity and innovation in the city. The NICE2035 Living Line project is a bottom-up initiative that intentionally creates the conditions for creative forces in university and community to meet, collide, fuse, and collaborate. It converts an old urban residential community into a living lab of possible future ways of living. All experiments are carried out based on the hypothesis that an urban community can move beyond its role at the consumption end (back end) and become a source (front end) of the innovation chain and industrial chain; the community members, instead of merely being end-product consumers, are also creators.

While cities are facing the challenges presented by industrial transformation and communities lack vitality due to the homogeneity of social activities, universities contain extra creativity and innovation capacity that has yet to be fully utilized. Unleashing the university's overflowing creativity into the community reenergizes the community and triggers future living oriented innovations. To allow such innovations to further develop into businesses and contribute to the new economy, the Living Line cultivates a community-supported ecosystem for entrepreneurship. In the process, the university college activated various dormant resources and creatively integrated them into an ecosystem.

The practice of design-driven, community-supported social innovation is emerging. The body of literature that studies the mechanism and process of such practices remains scarce. We report and analyze this case from a systems perspective, approaching it from its purpose and function (why the system exists), its components (what is systematized), and the process these components interact with each other (how the system operates). When analyzing the components (the contents) of the Living Line system, four systems perspectives emerge: a system of things, a system of people, a system of environments, and a system of ideas. A sociotechnical system as complex as the Living Line comprises all these areas. These four areas serve as four places to discuss distinct elements of the system most relevant to that angle. To grasp the system as a unified whole, not merely a sum of its contents, we use several themes to illustrate important segments of "the process of mutual influence, reciprocal action, and dynamic exchange between the components." The interconnections and interactions in the business model, cluster effect, forming a community by choice, and technology tie are part of the mechanism of how the Living Line system operates. We hope that this case study will offer some insights into a possible perspective and framework for further, more comprehensive study of the mechanism of such complex sociotechnical systems.

The Living Line project is still in its infancy and has a long way to go. It will continue to produce materials for people to further study the key issues in a grassroots design-driven social innovation initiative. For example, which organizational structure can most effectively steward the operation of the initiative? What impact will interactions between old and new community members bring to the initiative? Will the ecosystem change as different participating units develop at different speeds? Each milestone of the Living Line will open a new window enabling us to further see how the process and mechanism adapts, changes, and evolves.

References

1. Shearmur, R.: Are cities the front of innovation? A critical review of the literature on cities and innovation. Cities **29**(SI2), 9–18 (2012)
2. Hardesty, L.: Why innovation thrives in cities. MIT News. http://news.mit.edu/2013/why-innovation-thrives-in-cities-0604. Accessed 14 Feb 2018
3. Florid, R.: The historic links between cities and innovation. CityLab. https://www.citylab.com/design/2015/12/the-historic-link-between-cities-and-innovation/422226/. Accessed 14 Feb 2018
4. Greg Satell, G.: Why cities are our most important innovation platform. Forbes. https://www.forbes.com/sites/gregsatell/2013/11/09/why-cities-are-our-most-important-innovation-platform/#7aadf3b47169. Accessed 14 Feb 2018
5. The fourth international congress for modern architecture: charter of athens (1933). http://orcp.hustoj.com/2015/10/10/charter-of-athens-1933/. Accessed 14 Feb 2018
6. Mumford, E.: The CIAM Discourse on Urbanism, 1928–1960. The MIT Press, Cambridge (2000)
7. Curtis, W.: Modern Architecture Since 1900. Phaidon Press, London (1986)
8. Le Normand, B.: Introduction to Designing Tito's Capital: Urban Planning, Modernism, and Socialism in Belgrade, pp. 96–97. University of Pittsburgh Press, Pittsburgh (2014)
9. Universidad Nacional Federico Villarreal: The Charter of Machu Picchu. J. Arch. Res. 7(2), 5–9 (1979)
10. Rockefeller Foundation: 100 Resilient Cities. https://www.rockefellerfoundation.org/our-work/initiatives/100-resilient-cities/. Accessed 14 Feb 2018
11. Verganti, R.: Design Driven Innovation: Changing the Rules of Competition by Radically Innovating What Things Mean. Harvard Business Press, Boston (2009)
12. Florida, R.: The Rise of the Creative Class—Revisited. Basic Books, New York (2014)
13. Oxford Online Dictionary: S.V. "ecosystem". https://en.oxforddictionaries.com/definition/ecosystem. Accessed 14 Feb 2018
14. Meadows, D.H.: Thinking in Systems: A Primer. Chelsea Green Publishing, White River Junction (2008)

15. Ma, J.: What is a system? A lesson learned from the emerging practice of DesignX. In: Rau, P.-L.P. (ed.) CCD 2017. LNCS, vol. 10281, pp. 59–75. Springer, Cham (2017). https://doi.org/10.1007/978-3-319-57931-3_6

16. Buchanan, R.: Systems and the pathways of human experience: an emerging challenge for design. (Keynote speech presented at the Emerging Practices Conference on Design Research and Education. Tongji University, Shanghai) (2016)

17. Buchanan, R.: The Structure of inquiry (Lecture, Tongji University, China) (2016)

18. Kim, M.: Design for participation: an inquiry into the nature of service, Ph.D. Dissertation, Carnegie Mellon University (2015)

19. Manzini, E.: Design, When Everybody Designs, p. 11. MIT Press, Cambridge (2015)

20. Zhu, L.: Top 10 Chinese cities for entrepreneurship and innovation in 2017. China Daily, 21 September 2017. http://www.chinadaily.com.cn/a/201709/21/WS5a0baa27a31061a738 4041e4.html. Accessed 14 Feb 2018

21. The rising lab: which cities in China are the most innovative? Yicai Global, 18 May 2017. https://www.yicaiglobal.com/news/which-cities-china-are-most-innovative. Accessed 14 Feb 2018

22. Shanghai Urban Planning and Land Resource Administration Bureau. Shanghai Master Plan 2017–2035 (2018). http://www.shanghai.gov.cn/nw2/nw2314/nw32419/nw42806/index.html. Accessed 14 Feb 2018

23. Lou, Y.: NICE2035—The paradigm of design driven community-supported social innovation (speech at the launch ceremony of the NICE2035 living line) (2018)

24. Tom's Baobao. http://www.tomsbaobao.com/#about. Accessed 14 Feb 2018

25. Bagley, R.O.: The cluster effect. Forbes, 9 February 2012. https://www.forbes.com/sites/rebeccabagley/2012/02/09/the-cluster-effect/#1ac9700731ff. Accessed 14 Feb 2018

26. Manzini, E.: Design, When Everybody Designs, p. 61. MIT Press, Cambridge (2015)

Facilitating Gerontechnology Adoption: Observational Learning with Live Models

Lu Peng[1], Qi Ma[1], Rita W. L. Yu[1], Alan H. S. Chan[1(✉)],
Pei Lee Teh[2], and Ka Kit So[1]

[1] Department of Systems Engineering and Engineering Management,
City University of Hong Kong, Kowloon, Hong Kong
{lupeng2-c,qima22-c,winglamyu7-c,
kakitso2-c}@my.cityu.edu.hk, alan.chan@cityu.edu.hk
[2] School of Business, Monash University, Selangor, Malaysia
teh.pei.lee@monash.edu

Abstract. This study aims to investigate the effectiveness of observational learning with live models in facilitating technology adoption for older people. A between-groups observational training with a video-taped demonstration was developed. Model generation (child, young adult, and old adult) was set as factor that may affect training outcomes. Sixty Hong Kong Chinese people aged 60 or above were divided into three groups. Results confirm that the self-efficacy and behavioral intention of older people significantly improved after the training. The greatest improvement of self-efficacy and behavioral intention was found in the old adult and child model groups, respectively.

Keywords: Aging population · Gerontechnology adoption
Observational learning · Model generation

1 Introduction

Decreasing fertility rates and extending life expectancy at birth have made aging population a serious issue in the world. Compared with that in 2017, the number of persons aged 60 or above is expected to more than double by 2050 and to more than triple by 2100, that is, rising from 962 million globally in 2017 to 2.1 billion in 2050 and 3.1 billion in 2100 [1]. Population aging is projected to have a profound effect on societies where many countries are likely to face increasing fiscal and political pressures from health care, old-age pension, and social protection systems [1].

Gerontechnology aims to apply technology to assist in dealing with problems and difficulties arising from aging to give older people the chance to lead healthy, independent, and socially engaging lives on a continual basis [2]. Many previous studies corroborated that the use of gerontechnology by seniors has the potential to alleviate aging-related problems [3–8]. However, older people do not show as considerable enthusiasm for adopting new technologies as young people [9, 10]. For instance, they do not use smart phones and tablets as frequently as young people do. In mainland China, elderly people aged 60 or above accounted for only 4.8% of Chinese Internet users compared with 42.9% of adults aged 30 to 59 and 52.2% of young adults aged 29

P.-L. P. Rau (Ed.): CCD 2018, LNCS 10912, pp. 334–345, 2018.
https://doi.org/10.1007/978-3-319-92252-2_27

or below [11]. Thus, the low adoption rate of technology limited the benefits of technology for older people. In addition, as technology becomes highly integrated in everyday life, not being able to use technology may put older adults at a disadvantage in terms of their ability to live and function independently and successfully perform daily tasks [12].

Acceptability is the key factor to integrate new technologies at home, particularly when the users are elderly or low information communication technology (ICT)-educated persons [13]. Technology acceptance means "the approval, favorable reception and ongoing use of newly introduced device and system" [14]. Fishbein and Ajzen [15] verified that a person's behavior is driven by his or her intention to perform the behavior. Hence, behavioral intention is an immediate antecedent of behavior. Self-efficacy is a perceived capability to perform or learn behaviors at specific levels [16]. The achievement, self-regulation, and motivation of individuals can be powerfully influenced by self-efficacy [16]. People with high self-efficacy would have substantial interest and motivation in performing a certain behavior. Information technology acceptance is a behavior of an ongoing use of a newly introduced information device or system; hence, this behavior is closely correlated with behavioral intention and self-efficacy of using information technology.

A study of gerontechnology acceptance was done by Chen and Chan [17] with 1,012 seniors aged 55 or above in Hong Kong. They validated that individual attributes, such as age, gender, education, gerontechnology, self-efficacy and anxiety, health and ability characteristics, and facilitating conditions, are explicit and direct predictors of technology acceptance. Chen and Chan [17] also confirmed the importance of environmental supports (e.g., financial support and training opportunities) in helping Hong Kong elders overcome barriers to technology. A study of acceptance of smart phone technology by older Chinese adults was done by Ma et al. [18] with 120 Chinese older adults aged 55 or above. Evidently, facilitating conditions are important factors influencing the perceived ease of use, and the opportunity of getting external help is highly important for smartphone acceptance. Few other studies stressed the importance of attending training programs or workshops for older individuals to build self-confidence, elicit positive attitudes, and increase the intention of using technology [19, 20].

Social cognitive theory (SCT) has been widely used in understanding the process of knowledge acquisition and information technology training in psychology and education studies [21–23]. This theory states that people acquire knowledge from observing others performing a behavior and its consequences. The subjects to be observed and imitated are termed role models. Gupta et al. [24] confirmed that observational learning leads to better performance compared with traditional lecture with passive learning. In addition, observational learning is associated with positive reported evaluation, less negative effect, and great satisfaction during training. Conducting observational learning through a video-taped demonstration with a human model is popular and cost-effective [22, 25]. Research on technology training for older adults have investigated the self-reported experiences of older people and their training preferences [26, 27], but how observational training influence older adults' information technology acceptance has not been studied yet.

Given that training environments are critical for examining expected training outcomes [27], the impact of human elements, such as models, instructors, and learning peers, are worth considering. Studies affirm that older adults experience difficulty when receiving technical support from young people and that they profoundly learn when helped by their peers. This scenario is probable when their peers have similar problems and considerable understanding of the difficulties faced by older adults when using technology [28, 29]. However, certain studies recommend facilitations from younger generations, such as children and grandchildren. For instance, Fausset et al. [30] suggested letting the older adults' children play a major role in influencing technology adoption and use. Lin et al. [31] corroborated that older adults chose younger children and friends with skills they admired as their role models in learning to use the Internet. According to the aforementioned statements, an investigation of the effects of model generation on facilitating the older adults' information technology acceptance is needed.

In this study, behavioral intention and self-efficacy were taken as the measurements of information technology acceptance. Model generation was set as a factor that may influence training outcomes. The current study aimed to investigate the impact of observational learning with live models on enhancing older adults' information technology acceptance and to study the effects of model generation on training outcomes.

2 Methodology

2.1 Experimental Design and Hypotheses

An experiment of observational learning with a video-taped demonstration in between-groups design was developed. Three training groups (child, young adult, and old adult) were included in this experiment. Model generations consisted of the child model with demonstrators aged 6–14, the young adult model with demonstrators aged 18–25, and the old adult model with demonstrators aged 60–70. One female and one male demonstrators were involved in each generation model group. Sixty participants were randomly assigned to the three training groups with twenty participants in each generation group. Other than different model generations, each participant in the three groups received the same training content and procedure.

The following hypotheses were tested in this experiment:

H1: Observational training with a video-taped demonstration is effective in improving the self-efficacy of older adults toward using information technology.

H2: Observational training with a video-taped demonstration is effective in improving the behavioral intention of older adults toward using information technology.

H3: Observational training outcomes, including self-efficacy and behavioral intention, are significantly influenced by model generation

2.2   Participants

A total of 60 participants, including 33 females and 27 males, were recruited. All were aged 60–80 (M = 68.4, SD = 5.17) without severe cognitive impairments. Cognitive function was measured by the Mini-Mental State Examination (MMSE), and older participants with scores of 18 or above were involved in the experiment, as suggested by Tombaugh and McIntyre [32]. The participants have little (less than 1 week) or no experience in using tablets and apps. They signed an informed consent before joining the study.

2.3   Apparatus and Training Materials

The apparatus used in the experiment included a notebook computer, tablets (Samsung Galaxy Note 10.1 N8000, size of 10.1 in. with 62.7% screen-to-body ratio), and pre-observational and post-observational learning questionnaires. The participants took observational learning by watching a video on the notebook computer. The video was about the daily use of three different apps [YouTube (video-sharing app), WhatsApp (social app), and Mass Transit Railway (mobile app)]. The tablets were used as plat-forms for information technology operation. The videos were recorded by three types of generation models. All models had at least one year of experience using tablets and the three apps to maintain homogeneity. In addition, models were required to perform actions by following a given script to ensure that the video content was standardized. Questionnaires were used to measure the participants' self-efficacy and behavioral intention before and after the observational learning. Eleven and five statements using a 7-point Likert scale were included in the self-efficacy and behavioral intention assessment part. A 7 point refers to "extremely agree" with the statement, and a 0 point refers to "extremely disagree" with the statement. For instance, one of the statements for self-efficacy measurement was "I am confident in using a tablet by myself." If the participants extremely agreed with the statement, they could give a score of 7. How-ever, if they extremely disagreed with the statement, they could give a score of 0. The questionnaires for pre-observational learning and post-observational learning were the same.

2.4   Procedures

Before the observational learning, the participants were asked to fill the pre-observational learning questionnaire. Thereafter, they were required to learn how to use the three apps by watching the video displayed on the notebook computer. After watching, they imitated the steps without the video showing. After they finished their observational learning, they were requested to complete the post-training questionnaire. The testing procedure took approximately 20 min.

2.5 Data Analysis

Factor analyses, evaluations of descriptive statistics, and analyses of variance (ANOVA) for scores of self-efficacy and behavioral intention were performed with the use of the SPSS 22.0 software.

3 Results

3.1 Reliability and Validity of Measurements

Before data analyses, the reliability and validity of measurements for self-efficacy and behavioral intention were evaluated. The Kaiser-Meyer-Olkin measure of sampling adequacy (MSA) was 0.65, which was higher than the criterion value of 0.5 for being acceptable for factor-analytic purpose [33]. The communalities were all above 0.3, and the Bartlett test was significant. These scenarios verified that the sampling satisfied the conducting of factor analysis. Principal component analysis was used to calculate factor loadings of the retained factors (self-efficacy and behavioral intention), and the results showed that they were higher than the satisfied criteria value of 0.5. The composite reliability was examined to test the internal consistency and reliability of measurements. The values of the two constructs were higher than a value criterion of 0.6 [34]. All the results satisfied the requirements of convergent validity and reliability.

3.2 Demographic Information

Demographic data, including gender, age, marital status, education, working arrangement, self-assessed economic status, living arrangement, and tablet experience, were collected from the participants. Majority were married (68.3%), received primary education (31.7%), retired (88.3%), with general economic status (75%), and lived with household members (68.3%). Table 1 exhibits the detailed demographic information.

3.3 Effectiveness of Observational Learning

Effectiveness of Observational Learning for the Entire Sample
The effectiveness of observational learning on facilitating technology adoption was measured with a paired t-test by comparing self-efficacy and behavioral intention before and after the training. Significant enhancements for self-efficacy (t(59) = −6.69, $p < 0.05$) and behavioral intention (t(59) = −4.39, $p < 0.05$) emerged after the training. The average score of self-efficacy after the training was 19.1% higher than that during the pre-training. In addition, the average score of behavioral intention after learning was 9.9% higher than that in pre-learning. Figure 1 illustrates the differences of self-efficacy and behavioral intention between pre-training and post-training.

Effectiveness of Observational Learning for Three Generation Model Groups
All the three model groups of different generations significantly increased in self-efficacy after learning ($p < 0.05$). Specifically, the self-efficacy in post-training was 16.4%, 15.7%, and 26.1% higher than that in pre-training for the children, young adult,

Table 1. Demographic information and tablet use experience (N = 60)

Categories (M ± SD)	Frequency	Percentage (%)
Gender		
Male	27	45.0
Female	33	55.0
Age (68.4 ± 5.17)		
60–65	23	38.3
66–70	14	23.3
71–75	17	28.3
75–80	6	10.0
Marital status		
Single	1	1.7
Married	41	68.3
Widowed	5	8.3
Divorced/separated	13	21.7
Education		
No schooling/pre-primary	6	10.0
Primary	19	31.7
Lower secondary	17	28.3
Upper secondary	8	13.3
Tertiary	10	16.7
Working arrangement		
Full-time worker	0	0.0
Part-time worker	7	11.7
Retired	53	88.3
Self-assessed economic status		
Profoundly poor	1	1.7
Poor	7	11.7
General	45	75.0
Rich	7	11.7
Profoundly rich	0	0.0
Living arrangement		
With household members	41	68.3
Living alone	11	18.3
In nursing home	7	11.7
With others	1	1.7
Tablet experience		
Yes (less than a week)	33	55.0
No	27	45.0

and old adult model groups (Fig. 2). Regarding behavioral intention, a significant increase of 14.6% occurred in the children model group ($p < 0.05$). No significant differences for the young adult and old adult model groups emerged between

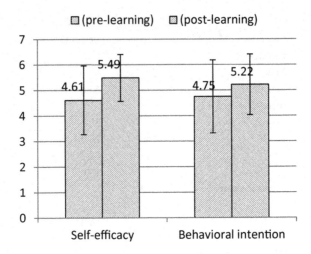

Fig. 1. Differences of self-efficacy and behavioral intention between pre-learning and post-learning

pre-training and post-training (Fig. 3) with corresponding increase rates of 7.0% and 2.5%, respectively.

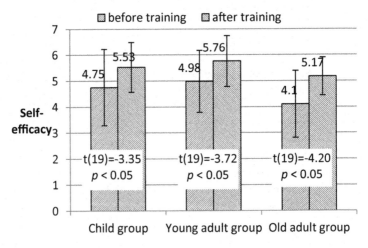

Fig. 2. Differences of self-efficacy between pre-learning and post-learning for three generation model groups

3.4   Effects of Model Generation

Before the observational training, the sixty participants were randomly divided into three generation model groups, with no significant differences in self-efficacy ($F(2, 57) = 2.38$, $p = .102$) and behavioral intention ($F(2, 57) = 1.55$, $p = .221$). The effects

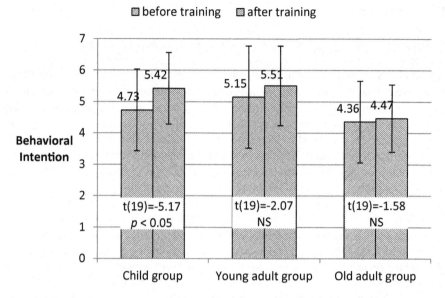

Fig. 3. Differences of behavioral intention between pre-learning and post-learning for three generation model groups

of model generation on training outcomes were tested with ANOVA by comparing the mean values of self-efficacy and behavioral intention in post-training among the three generation model groups. The results confirmed the absence of statistically significant differences in self-efficacy ($F(2,57) = 2.18$, $p = .122$) or behavioral intention in post-training ($F(2, 57) = 2.62$, $p = .081$) among the groups.

3.5 Moderating Role of Demographics

The moderating effects of the participant demographics (gender, age, tablet experience, and living arrangement) on self-efficacy and behavioral intention after the training were tested. The effects of gender were tested with the t-test by comparing the mean values of self-efficacy and behavioral intention in post-training between the male and female participants. Linear regression was done for self-efficacy and age to detect whether self-efficacy linear dependence on age occurred. Similarly, linear regression was done for behavioral intention and age. The moderating effects of tablet experience and living arrangement on training outcomes were tested with the t-test and ANOVA. The results indicated that all the demographics of participants in gender, age, tablet experience and living arrangement had non-significant effects on self-efficacy and behavioral intention after the training.

4 Discussions

Technology training has been recommended as a facilitating condition to improve technology adoption for older people [17, 18]. Observational training with a video-taped demonstration is popular and cost-effective. In this study, the self-efficacy of the entire sample significantly improved after the training. In addition, a statistically significant improvement of self-efficacy occurred in all the three generation model groups. The result supported the research [25, 35] that observational learning with modeling provides a method of strengthening self-efficacy. H1 was supported.

Given that significant differences in behavioral intention between pre-training and post-training for the entire sample were observed, H2 was supported. Evidently, older adults had a higher intention of adopting information technology in post-learning than that in pre-training. A significant increase in behavioral intention was observed in the child model group ($p < 0.05$), but no significant increases in behavioral intention for the young adult or the old adult model group were observed. The results supported the statement of Luijkx et al. [36], which confirmed that allowing grandchildren to educate older adults on using information technology is worthwhile because older adults easily adopt their enthusiasm and may be persuaded to use technology.

No significant differences in self-efficacy or behavioral intention of post-training among the three generation model groups were observed. H3 was not supported. However, differences in increase rate of self-efficacy and behavioral intention among the three groups were evident. The greatest improvement of self-efficacy occurred in the old adult model group, which indicated that they had the best performance on improving self-efficacy for old technology learners. Schunk [37] corroborated that success of instructors with similar characteristics can raise the observers' self-efficacy because they believe that they have a similar ability to be as successful as the performers. In the elderly model group, the video demonstrators and the learners were of similar age, and their successful operation of technology devices can highly enhance the learners' confidence. Although the old adult model group made the greatest self-efficacy improvement with observation learning, behavioral intention did not consistently improve. The greatest improvement of behavioral intention was found in the child model group. According to planned behavior theory, human action is guided by the following three kinds of consideration: (1) beliefs about the likely outcomes of the behavior and evaluations of these outcomes (behavioral beliefs), (2) beliefs about the normative expectations of others and motivation to comply with these expectations (normative beliefs), and (3) beliefs about the presence of factors that may facilitate or impede the performance of the behavior and perceived power of these factors (control beliefs) [38]. Model generation may have an impact on normative belief to influence the behavioral intention of older learners. Children generally have high enthusiasm for and interest in information technology and their passions may impose high normative expectations on learners. Furthermore, older people tend to be motivated by children the most as child demonstrators are just like their grandsons/granddaughters. Thus, older learners had a significant improvement in behavioral intention with a child model.

The results of this study provide certain guidelines in technology training for older adults: (1) observational training with a video-taped demonstration is an effective method to improve technology adoption by older people, (2) old demonstrators can make the greatest improvement in an aging learner's self-efficacy toward information technology use, and (3) child demonstrators can make the greatest improvement in an aging learner's behavioral intention toward information technology use. In addition, the following limitations of this study should be considered: (1) the participants were recruited mainly from the elderly care centers of Tung Chung, Hong Kong due to limited resources and time efficiency consideration, which may have resulted in some selection bias of the sample, and (2) a tablet was chosen as the only platform to operate apps during the training because this devise is widely used and suitable for older people with vision impairments. However, mobile phones may be the most widely used devices for older people in practice. Other devices can be tested in the future.

5   Conclusions

The effectiveness of observational learning with live models in enhancing older people's technology adoption was tested in this study. Self-efficacy and behavioral intention were the measurements of information technology acceptance. With observational training, the self-efficacy and behavioral intention of older people significantly improved. Statistically significant differences of self-efficacy between pre-training and post-training were observed in all the three generation model groups, but significant differences of behavioral intention were only found in the child model group. Observational learning with the old adult model had the best performance on improving self-efficacy for aging learners. However, observational learning with the old adult model produced the least effect on improving older people's behavioral intention, where the greatest effect was found in the child model group. Demographic variables, including gender, age, tablet experience, and living arrangement of the participants, had no significant moderating effects on training outcomes. In conclusion, observational training with live models can increase technology adoption for older people, and a combination of child and old adult models is recommended.

Acknowledgments. The work described in this paper was fully supported by a grant from City University of Hong Kong (SRG7004906).

References

1. United Nations: World population prospects: the 2017 revision. United Nations, New York. http://esa.un.org/unpd/wpp. Accessed 23 June 2017
2. Lesnoff-Caravaglia, G.: Gerontechnology: Growing Old in a Technological Society. Charles C Thomas, Springfield (2007)
3. Adler, R.: Older adults and computers (1996). http://www.seniornet.org/php/default.php?PageID=5476&Version=0&Font=0
4. Cody, M., Dunn, D., Hoppin, S., Wendt, P.: Silver surfers: training and evaluating Internet use among older adult learners. Commun. Educ. **48**, 269–286 (1999)

5. White, H., McConnell, E., Clipp, E., Bynum, L., Teague, C., Navas, L., Craven, S., Halbrecht, H.: Surfing the net in later life: a review of the literature and pilot study of computer use and quality of life. J. Appl. Gerontol. **18**(3), 358–378 (1999)
6. White, J., Weatherall, A.: A grounded theory analysis of older adults and information technology. Educ. Gerontol. **26**(4), 371–386 (2000)
7. Loges, W., Jung, J.: Exploring the digital divide: Internet connectedness and age. Commun. Res. **28**(4), 536–562 (2001)
8. Pressler, K.A., Ferraro, K.F.: Assistive device use as a dynamic acquisition process in later life. Gerontologist **50**(3), 371–381 (2010)
9. Fisk, A., Rogers, W.A., Charness, N., Czaja, S.J., Sharit, J.: Designing for Older Adults: Principles and Creative Human Factors Approaches, 2nd edn. CRC Press, New York (2009). ISBN 978-1420080551
10. Kuo, H.M., Chen, C.W., Hsu, C.H.: A study of a B2C supporting interface design system for the elderly. Hum. Factors Ergon. Manuf. Serv. Ind. **22**(6), 528–540 (2012)
11. China Internet Network Information Center: The 40th statistical report on internet development in China (Report, July 2017). http://www.cnnic.org.cn/. Accessed 15 Aug 2017
12. Czaja, S.J., Charness, N., Fisk, A.D., Hertzog, C., Nair, S.N., Rogers, W.A., Sharit, J.: Factors predicting the use of technology: findings from the center for research and education on aging and technology enhancement (CREATE). Psychol. Aging **27**, 333–352 (2006)
13. Portet, F., Vacher, M., Golanski, C., Roux, C., Meillon, B.: Design and evaluation of a smart home voice interface for the elderly: acceptability and objection aspects. Pers. Ubiquit. Comput. **17**(1), 27–144 (2013)
14. Arning, K., Ziefle, M.: Understanding age differences in PDA acceptance and performance. Comput. Hum. Behav. **23**(6), 2904–2927 (2007). https://doi.org/10.1016/j.chb.2006.06.005
15. Fishbein, M., Ajzen, I.: Belief, Attitude, Intention, and Behavior: An Introduction to Theory and Research. Addison-Wesley Series in Social Psychology. Addison-Wesley, Reading (1975)
16. Bandura, A.: Self-efficacy: the exercise of control. J. Cogn. Psychother. **604**(2), 158–166 (1997)
17. Chen, K., Chan, A.H.S.: Gerontechnology acceptance by elderly Hong Kong Chinese: a senior technology acceptance model (STAM). Ergonomics **57**(5), 635 (2014)
18. Ma, Q., Chan, A.H.S., Chen, K.: Personal and other factors affecting acceptance of smartphone technology by older Chinese adults. Appl. Ergon. **54**, 62–71 (2016)
19. Lam, J.C., Lee, M.K.: Digital inclusiveness–longitudinal study of Internet adoption by older adults. J. Manag. Inf. Syst. **22**(4), 177–206 (2006)
20. Lagana, L.: Enhancing the attitudes and self-efficacy of older adults toward computers and the internet: results of a pilot study. Educ. Gerontol. **34**(9), 831–843 (2008)
21. Compeau, D.R., Higgins, C.A.: Application of social cognitive theory to training for computer skills. Inf. Syst. Res. **6**(2), 118–143 (1995)
22. Gupta, S., Bostrom, R.: Research note-an investigation of the appropriation of technology-mediated training methods incorporating enactive and collaborative learning. Inf. Syst. Res. **24**(2), 454–469 (2013)
23. Tsai, H.Y.S., Shillair, R., Cotton, S.R.: Social support and "playing around" an examination of how older adults acquire digital literacy with tablet computers. J. Appl. Gerontol. **36**(1), 29–55 (2015)
24. Gupta, S., Bostrom, R.P., Huber, M.: End-user training methods: what we know, need to know. ACM SIGMIS Database **41**(4), 9–39 (2010)
25. Gist, M.E., Schwoerer, C., Rosen, B.: Effects of alternative training methods on self-efficacy and performance in computer software training. J. Appl. Psychol. **74**(6), 884–891 (1989)

26. Mitzner, T.L., Fausset, C.B., Boron, J.B., Adams, A.E., Dijkstra, K., Lee, C.C., Rogers, W. A., Fisk, A.D.: Older adults' training preferences for learning to use technology. In: Proceedings of the Human Factors and Ergonomics Society Annual Meeting. vol. 52, no. 26, pp. 2047–2051. Sage Publications, Los Angeles (2008)
27. Czaja, S.J., Sharit, J.: Designing Training and Instructional Programs for Older Adults. CRC Press, Boca Raton (2012)
28. Xie, B.: Information technology education for older adults as a continuing peer-learning process: a Chinese case study. Educ. Gerontol. 33(5), 429–450 (2007)
29. Woodward, A.T., Freddolino, P.P., Wishart, D.J., Bakk, L., Kobayashi, R., Tupper, C., Panci, J., Blaschke-Thompson, C.M.: Outcomes from a peer tutor model for teaching technology to older adults. Ageing Soc. 33(08), 1315–1338 (2013)
30. Fausset, C.B., Harley, L., Farmer, S., Fain, B.: Older adults' perceptions and use of technology: a novel approach. In: Stephanidis, C., Antona M. (eds.) UAHCI 2013. LNCS, vol. 8010, pp. 51–58. Springer, Heidelberg (2013). https://doi.org/10.1007/978-3-642-39191-0_6
31. Lin, Y.C., Liang, J.C., Yang, C.J., Tsai, C.C.: Exploring middle-aged and older adults' sources of Internet self-efficacy: a case study. Comput. Hum. Behav. 29(6), 2733–2743 (2013)
32. Tombaugh, T.N., McIntyre, N.J.: The mini-mental state examination: a comprehensive review. J. Am. Geriatr. Soc. 40(9), 922–935 (1992)
33. Kaiser, H.F., Rice, J., Mark, I.V.: Educ. Psychol. Measur. 34, 111–117 (1974)
34. Hair, J.F., Anderson, R.E., Babin, B.J., Black, W.C.: Multivariate Data Analysis: A Global Perspective, vol. 7. Pearson, Upper Saddle River (2010)
35. Wood, R.E., Bandura, A.: Social cognitive theory of organizational management. Acad. Manag. Rev. 14, 361–384 (1989)
36. Luijkx, K., Peek, S., Wouters, E.: "Grandma, you should do it-it's cool" older adults and the role of family members in their acceptance of technology. Int. J. Environ. Res. Pub. Health 12(12), 15470–15485 (2015)
37. Schunk, D.H.: Social origins of self-regulatory competence: the role of observational learning through peer modeling. Paper presented at the Biennial Meeting of the Society for Research in Child Development, 61st Indianapolis, IN, March–April, p. 27 (1995)
38. Ajzen, I.: Nature and operation of attitudes. Ann. Rev. Psychol. 52, 27–58 (2001)

Modern Service Design Thinking on Traditional Culture-Based Services: A Case Study of the Service Businesses in Suzhou Old Town Areas

Xin Shen and Cheng-Hung Lo[(✉)]

Department of Industrial Design, Xi'an Jiaotong-Liverpool University, Suzhou,
Jiangsu Province, People's Republic of China
ch.lo@xjtlu.edu.cn

Abstract. This paper presents a case study that utilizes modern service design thinking techniques to investigate culture-based service businesses. The study is carried out in two heritage sites in Suzhou, which itself is a historical city located in the south of Yangtze River in China. Ethnographic methods are used to explore and collect the data. Service design thinking principles and methods are then applied to analyze the observed service businesses and identify common thematic issues and design opportunities. Service prototyping techniques are also used to review and rearrange a customer's journeys in the services. The result shows that modern design thinking concepts such as the user-centered approach can provide fundamental transformations to those services. It also illustrates a more cross-cultural development with the cross-cultural encounter between the modern design techniques and the traditional culture-based services.

Keywords: Service design thinking · Cultural consumption · Heritage sites

1 Introduction

Historical geography is concerned with the geographies of the past and with the influence of the past in shaping the geographies of the present and the future (Gregory et al. 2009). The historical areas and streets discussed in this study refer to those built in the historical period and still in use by contemporary citizens with the streets' original traits well kept. Along with the development of urban space, these areas and streets have become a combination of landscape space, tourism space, cultural space, leisure space, and business space.

Based on the geographic and historical characteristics of the space, the businesses running within the area provide a platform for cultural consumption. In this study, the historical streets of Pingjiang Road and Shantang Street in Suzhou, China are selected as representative examples to explore and analyze the service activities. Specifically, the research focuses more on the service businesses that have Suzhou local culture or Chinese culture in general as part of their value propositions.

© Springer International Publishing AG, part of Springer Nature 2018
P.-L. P. Rau (Ed.): CCD 2018, LNCS 10912, pp. 346–357, 2018.
https://doi.org/10.1007/978-3-319-92252-2_28

1.1 Cultural Consumption

Historical districts with modern lifestyle are urban spaces revived for enticing activities of consuming not only material goods but also the imputed historical and cultural meanings in these sites (Yu 2017). It's the development of "symbolic economy" (Zukin 1995) that makes the business services in these districts special. A "display culture" (Dicks 2012) is usually being created in this type of areas with historical architecture and cultural relics on display. And entrepreneurs are invited to invest in renovating the buildings in the area, turning them into places for consuming publics to experience the traditional local culture (Yu 2017). For the customers, purchasing commodities is not just a consumption activity, but also the behavior of engaging the local history and culture. The customers' experiences are largely "framed" by the branding of the space (Goffman 1974).

1.2 Service Design Thinking Principles

The basic thinking patterns in this study are based on the five principles of service design thinking proposed by Stickdorn (2011), which are User-centered, Co-creative, Sequencing, Evidencing, and Holistic. They are described as follows.

User-Centered

According to Stickdorn (2011), a certain degree of customer participation is necessary to deliver services in that the inherent intention of which is to meet the customer's needs. Beyond the thinking, a user-centered approach will bring together a set of focused methods and tools for the service designer to gain a comprehensive understanding of an individual's experiences, habits, motivations and the wider context on a cultural and social term.

Co-Creative

Generally speaking, there is usually more than one type of customer groups involved in designing a service. Besides, other types of stakeholders involved such as suppliers and employees may also possess various expectations and requirements. In order to gain insights from different perspectives, an environment of co-creation that facilitates the generation of ideas within heterogeneous stakeholder groups can be created. By including different parties in a design process, efficient communications and interactions between the stakeholders could be evoked, which may also result in long-term engagement.

Sequencing

One of the most significant differences between designing a product and designing a service is that a service is a dynamic process that takes place over a certain period of time. To control the rhythm of a service, service design thinking deconstructs the design process into discrete touchpoints, which represent the contact points between a customer and the service provider. The sequence of these touchpoints needs to be choreographed to achieve an integrated act. The systematic communication between the service and the customer will ensure a climactic progress of the customer's emotions.

Evidencing

During the service process, intangible experience takes place inconspicuously. To make customers aware of intangible services and prolong service experiences into the post-service period, physical evidence such as souvenirs can be used to trigger the memory of the service and establish emotional associations.

Holistic

Furthermore, the design of touchpoints should not be put into account without considering the physical environment and the wider context where the service takes place. As Stickdorn (2011) claimed, service design thinking supports the co-operation of different disciplines towards the goal of corporate success through enhanced customer experiences, employee satisfaction, and integration of sophisticated technological processes in pursuing corporate objectives.

2   Methodology

2.1   Field Study

Pingjiang Road and Shantang Street (Fig. 1) are located in the eastern-central and northwest parts of Suzhou historical district (Fig. 2). Both areas were included in the list of the first 30 historic and cultural streets and districts of China. The recognizing bodies include the State Administration of Cultural Heritage and the Ministry of Housing and Urban-Rural Development of the People's Republic of China. In addition to the landscapes and architectures, the areas are now commercial districts and popular tourist sites after years of restoration and renovation. The streets are lined with local businesses selling products and providing services that speak of the local culture, including teahouses, opera theaters, shops, bookstores... etc. Pingjiang Road and Shantang Street are the typical fields with various elements including landscape, tourism, culture and modern business. Studying the background of the sites help the service designers to gain a boarder understanding of the services, potential users, and other stakeholders.

Fig. 1. Typical sceneries of Pingjiang Road (left) and Shantang Street (right)

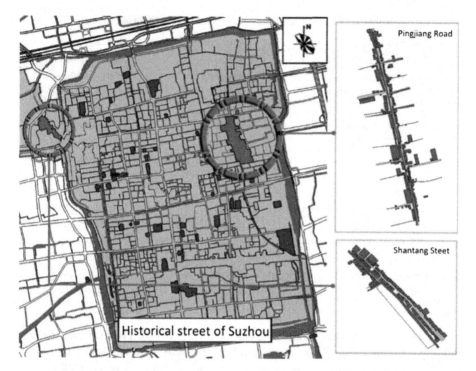

Fig. 2. The locations of Pingjiang Road and Shantang Street (Wang et al. 2015)

2.2   Selected Service Cases

To investigate into the services in the chosen sites, 15 service businesses on Pingjiang Road and Shantang Street were selected as the representativel cases. The basic information of these cases are listed in Table 1. As Flick (2009) and Mason (2002) stated, the emphasis in data collection for within-case and across-case analyses, is on interviews, archives, and (participant) observation. In this study, the method of participatory observation has contributed significantly to the understanding of the chosen cases.

2.3   Tools

This part introduces the main service design tools used in conducting this research study. A case example will be demonstrated for the use of each tool. Some of the tools might be particularly useful at one specific stage and others are utilized throughout the study.

Stakeholder Maps

As shown in Fig. 3, a stakeholder map was drawn at the exploration stage as a visual representation of the various groups involved in studying the case of Ting Yun Agilawood, a retail store selling tea and agilawood. A comprehensive list of stakeholders and their relationships are visualized, including the staff, customers, competitors, government...etc. By representing the stakeholders in this way, the interplay (indicated

Table 1. Explored service businesses on the two heritage streets

Name of service	Type of business	Location
Shantang Kunqu Club	Theater	*Shantang Street*
Hua Wu Que	Flower shop	*Pingjiang Road*
Suzhou Fan Museum	Museum	*Pingjiang Road*
Qing Yu Tang	Theater	*Pingjiang Road*
Higher Tea House	Tea house	*Pingjiang Road*
Yi De Cheng Snuff	Snuff shop	*Pingjiang Road*
Zhen Cai Tang	Chinese silk tapestry studio	*Pingjiang Road*
Liu Ru	Homestay hotel	*Pingjiang Road*
Xin Zhen Yuan	Restaurant	*Shantang Street*
Xian Feng Traditional Restaurant	Restaurant	*Shantang Street*
Ting Yun Agilawood	Tea and agilawood shop	*Pingjiang Road*
Old Silver Workshop	Silver accessories retail	*Shantang Street*
Xi Yang Jing	Peep show	*Shantang Street*
Taizhou Traditional Handcraft Art	Paper cutting store	*Shantang Street*
Yue Chan	Hotel	*Pingjiang Road*

by the red arrows) between various groups can be revealed. For example, the relationship between the suppliers and the government needs to be considered in terms of providing tea and agilawood-related supplies and setting the price range. Further, these groups can be clustered together by their shared interests or importance and influence on the service, allowing the service provider to deploy the resources effectively. In this case, the stakeholders are divided into internal groups and external groups.

STAKEHOLDER MAPS

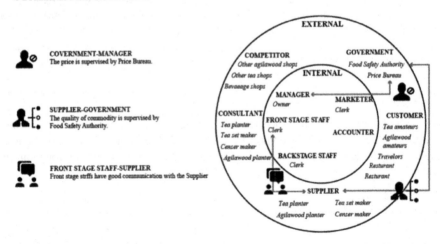

Fig. 3. The stakeholder map of Ting Yun Agilawood (Color figure online)

Customer Journey Maps

A customer journey map provides a structured visualization of a user's experience. In the case of observing Higher Tea House (Fig. 4), a time-based customer journey map (pre-order – order – eating and watching – pay – leave) is constructed to show all the touchpoints that allow the customers interact with the service. Centered around the customer's perspective, the user insights and the factors influencing the user experience are clearly shown with this method. For example, a customer may be inspired by the elegant environment when entering the tea house but feel down when kept waiting for the dishes. Besides, breaking the experience into segments based on specific touchpoints helps identify both the problematic areas potentials for future improvement.

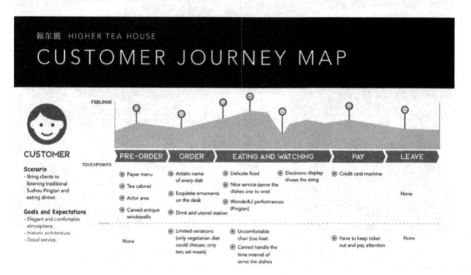

Fig. 4. The customer journey map of Higher Tea House

Mobile Ethnography

The functions of smart phones have become really versatile. They serve as a great ethnographic tool for collecting user-centered information. For example, the images taken in Higher Tea House (Fig. 5) provides snapshots of how the service operation of the tea house is perceived by the customer. The images also provide good cues for identifying the touchpoints in the eyes of the customers, which may be different from those originally designated by the service provider.

Storyboards

Figure 6 shows a series of drawings indicating the hypothetical implementation of the new service design for Xian Feng Traditional Restaurant. Through directly visualizing a sequence of events, the contextual details and touchpoints of dining in the restaurant are revealed and reviewed at ease. The analysis and discussions regarding the potential opportunities and problems can then be facilitated by the detailed simulation of actual scenarios.

Fig. 5. The photo records of Higher Tea House

Desktop Walkthrough

A small-scale mock-up of Higher Tea House service environment is made, as shown in Fig. 7. A desktop walkthrough is a highly flexible and engaging manner for iterative refinements. New situations and touchpoints are easily provoked simply by moving the characters around.

Service Blueprints

A service blueprint for the snuff shop is demonstrated in Fig. 8. In this blueprint, each individual aspect of the service is specified, incorporating the perspectives of the customer, the service provider and other stakeholders that may get involved. The blueprint also specifies the details of the whole process from the very initial touchpoint to behind-the-scenes, as well as the interplays between different stakeholders.

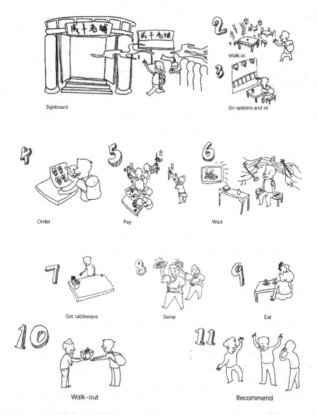

Fig. 6. The storyboards for the possible service scenarios in Xian Feng Traditional Restaurant

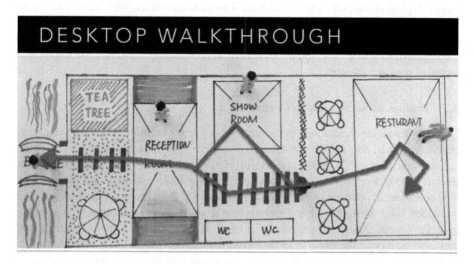

Fig. 7. Desktop walkthrough technique for developing service sequences in Higher Tea House

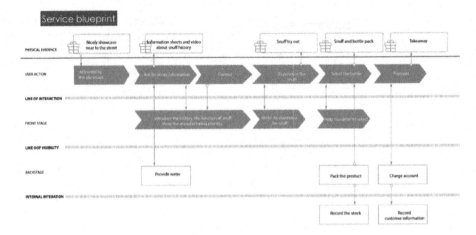

Fig. 8. The service blueprint for Yi De Cheng Snuff

3   Empirical Analysis

3.1   Business Services on Pingjiang Road and Shantang Street

Based on the historical and cultural appealing of Pingjiang Road and Shantang Street, the business services in these districts not only sell commodities, they also invite the visitors to enjoy the landscape, appreciating the traditional artefacts, and indulge in the atmosphere. The commercial activities vary from retail stores selling traditional handicrafts to teahouses for experiencing the traditional way of sipping tea and listening to appreciating Chinese musical performances such as Pingtan, a storytelling and ballad singing in Suzhou dialect. There are also museums of traditional arts such as the local opera known as Kunqu. As the tourist sites for inheriting the historical culture over 1000 years old, both Pingjiang Road and Shantang Street have been shouldering the responsibility to accommodate tourists from all over the world and exhibit the rich forms of regional cultures.

3.2   Profiles of Service Users/Customers

Different from the traditional consumers whose consumption behaviors center on everyday goods, the tourist consumers of modern age display a much more active attitude that focuses on satisfying certain lifestyles they wish to pursue (Lewis and Bridger 2000). For the tourists who visit Pingjiang Road and Shantang Street, what they consume, in addition to the material needs gained from the goods and services, are the added value from the cultural significance attached to them. Normally, the tourists look for unique intangible experience as well as tangible goods with exquisite aesthetics to memorize the trip. Besides, the fact that tourists constitute a major part of the target consumers suggests that the target consumers may have planned and fixed time slots for staying in the area.

3.3   Thematic Issues

The visualization tools such as the customer journey map provide the common frames of references to compare the included service cases. Upon reviewing the visualization data generated for the cases, we can easily identify and aggregate common issues among them. They are discussed as follows.

Lack of User-Centered Practices

With only one or two staff members working in some stores, the customers can be easily overlooked. The long waiting time would influence the service sequences that are constructed with different touchpoints. For example, Yi De Cheng Snuff, which is known for its unique snuff making techniques based on natural raw materials. When analyzing its customer journey map, we found different customers could stay at different stages in the service process. While some might be reading the background knowledge of the snuff displayed on the walls, some might be trying out the snuff, and some might be selecting the snuff bottles. With only one staff member assisting the customers in their diverse activities, it is inevitable that some customers would be neglected.

Lack of Attractive Touchpoint

As mentioned, tourists usually have a somewhat optimized schedule and it is often not possible for them to visit every shop during the tours. Thus, establishing an salient first touchpoint would gain competitive strength in attracting the customers. Take Ting Yun Agilawood as an example. The front gate is rather small and decorated in a plain style, which does not help the business much in diverting the flow of people into its service.

Lack of Tangible Evidence

As the principle of evidencing states, physical evidences such as souvenirs can help trigger the memory of the service and establish emotional associations. But for most of the service cases in the study, many intangible aspects of the services remain abstract and difficult to be registered as service memories. In the case of Xi Yang Jing located on Shantang Street, the customers are paying for experiencing the traditional peep show. While the core value of the service is building up a memorable experience, the customers are left with no tangible evidences after the performance.

Lack of Cross-Culture Practices

As observed on site, foreign visitors are particularly intrigued by different forms of cultural experience in the district. However, almost all of the service cases have not provided multi-language introductions and instructions. Cultural appreciation relies on the understanding of background context, which is often conveyed through the language used in the region. And how to remove this barrier for foreign visitors is always a challenging issue. For example, Qing Yu Tang is a theater for customers to drink tea and experience Suzhou Pingtan, which is a traditional stage performance combining story-telling, singing, and playing music instruments. Though it could be an in-depth cultural experience for the foreigners, there is no multilingual signage or translation service available to explain what Pingtan is or the tea culture in Suzhou.

4   Conclusions

We have carried out an empirical investigation on the two famous heritage sites in Suzhou, an ancient city with over 1000-year-old historical culture. We position the work as a cross-cultural enquiry based on the encounter between modern design thinking and traditional service models employed in the selected service businesses. We have used various methods and techniques, at both principle and practical levels, to analyze the cases and identify their thematic issues. The work is by all means exploratory and an initial attempt to apply modern design methods to culture-based services in this historical region. Repeated visits to the sites and the deeper collaborations with the service businesses are surely the next step to pursue. Nevertheless, we suggest some potential improvements below based on the initial findings.

Multiple Platforms
Before physically enjoying the service, customers nowadays usually encounter the first touchpoint with the service on the internet. Online platforms such as Dianping, Wechat and Weibo build up a virtual space for people to share their experiences and opinions on a service. Specifically, anyone can visit the site to search for a teahouse on Pingjiang Road, read the reviews from other customers, and learn about the recommended services. Through the series of commenting and searching activities, the user of the platform is connected with the teahouse service in the virtual space. For the service providers, it is an opportunity to establish their media impression for engaging regular visitors and reaching potential customers. Online media play an important role in introducing, shaping, and sharing the services.

Richer Content and Form
To adapt to the modern context, the content of the cultural experience could be adjusted. For example, the themes of peep shows could include foreign culture or new technologies to be more educational and inspiring. Besides, computers and other automated mechanisms can be used to replace human labor force on iterative service functions, including introducing the background and basic knowledge of a certain type of culture. For example, setting up digital screens showcasing the background of Kunqu or explaining the local way of sipping tea could save a considerable amount of time and energy.

Acknowledgement. This work is partially supported by the Service Design module delivered in the Industrial Design program in Xi'an Jiaotong-Liverpool University. We thank the participating students for their collected effort, which enriches and enables the work to have a broader access and inclusion of the service cases.

References

Dicks, B.: Culture on Display: The Production of Contemporary Visibility. Peking University Press, Beijing (2012). (Chinese ed., Feng, Y. Trans.)
Flick, U.: An Introduction to Qualitative Research, 4th edn. SAGE, London (2009)

Goffman, E.: Frame Analysis: An Essay on the Organization of Experience. Harvard University Press, Cambridge (1974)

Gregory, D., Johnston, R., Pratt, G., Watts, M., Whatmore, S.: The Dictionary of Human Geography. Blackwell Publishing, Oxford (2009)

Lewis, D., Bridger, D.: The Soul of the New Consumer: Authenticity What We Buy and Why in the New Economy. China Machines Press, Beijing (2000). (Chinese ed., Jiang, L., Liu, W. Trans.)

Mason, J.: Qualitative Researching, 2nd edn. Sage Publications, London/Thousand Oaks (2002)

Stickdorn, M., Schneider, J.: This is Service Design Thinking. Wiley, Hoboken (2011)

Wang, D., Niu, Y., Lu, L., Qian, J.: Tourism spatial organization of historical streets-a postmodern perspective: the examples of Pingjiang road and Shantang street, Suzhou, China. Tour. Manag. **48**, 370–385 (2015)

Yu, H.: The publicness of an urban space for cultural consumption: the case of Pingjiang road in Suzhou. Commun. Public **2**(I), 84–101 (2017)

Zukin, S.: The Cultures of Cities. Blackwell Publishers, Cambridge (1995)

Driverless Vehicle-Based Urban Slow Transportation Service Platform

Jintian Shi[1] and Xiaohua Sun[2(✉)]

[1] Tongji University, Siping 1239, Shanghai, China
shijintian1017@126.com
[2] Tongji University, Fuxin 281, Shanghai, China
xsun@tongji.edu.cn

Abstract. Driverless vehicles have brought dramatic changes in many aspects of transportation, as an irresistible trend. And there was also abundant research on transportation service design based on driverless vehicles. However, specific to slow transportation, studies on driverless vehicle-based service design are few. In this paper, we selected four typical using contexts of low-speed environments: campus, airport, communities far from city center, and industrial park. And then we discovered the pain points and common demands of urban low-speed environments, as well as the characteristics of driverless vehicles, it was found that, in the guidance of service system design, driverless vehicle can address these problems of slow transportation. We used the logic of service system design as important approach to develop driverless vehicle-based slow transportation service system. This slow transportation service platform took an in-vehicle smart system as the control system. Based on this smart system, mobile phone app and in-vehicle AR screen, this platform could satisfy the pain points and demands of urban slow transportation. Moreover, this driverless vehicle-based urban slow transportation service platform could integrate people, environment and vehicles coherently, to meet users' needs, improve service process efficiency and make sustainable influence on environment.

Keywords: Driverless vehicle · Slow transportation · Service platform design

1 Introduction

The development of driverless vehicles will fundamentally change the current vehicle's driving style, using mode, riding experience, etc. And it will change driving into a complicated system. In this system, people, environment and vehicles are closely integrated together to create a higher-efficient transportation service system., which transforms the previous "vehicle-road-driver" closed-loop system. Based on levels of automation for on-road vehicles from SAE, the current development of driverless vehicle is in Level 3 (conditional automation) [1]. Level 3 and Level 5 require vehicles to drive and interact with people highly relying on the driving environment. While among a variety of circumstances, it is urban slow transportation environments that have the most frequent and deepest interactions with people.

Meanwhile the methods for constructing a slow transportation service platform based on driverless vehicles are different in various using contexts [2]. Typical using contexts contain metro stations, parking lots, outdoor gyms, campuses, airports, parks and so on. In this paper, based on driverless vehicle, four typical using contexts in urban low-speed environment are discussed as the research objects. We summarize corresponding characteristics of different contexts, with service system design approaches as methods, aiming to design a driverless vehicle-based service platform to solve the pain points of urban slow transportation environments, and satisfy people's needs in low-speed environments.

Nowadays, the research and development of driverless vehicles primarily focus on three directions: urban slow-transportation environment, special conditions and urban expressways. Since the driving environment under these three conditions is relatively simple and suitable for the operation of driverless vehicles at this stage, there are many studies on these three environments [3]. Urban slow transportation environment is the most related to peoples' lives, but there are few studies on it based on driverless vehicle. In urban slow transportation environments, campuses, airports, communities far from city center, and industrial parks are the four typical using contexts. They have some common problems and demands. The following section will be elaborated on these.

2 Four Typical Using Contexts of Urban Slow Transportation

Slow transportation, also called non-motorized transportation, refers to non-motorized transportation systems that are mainly bicycles and pedestrians and supplemented by environment-friendly motor-assisted vehicles, it primarily lies in urban low-speed environments [4]. The using contexts of urban slow transportation are diverse, while campuses, airports, communities far from city center, and industrial parks are the most representative of today's slow transportation circumstances. As an important component of transportation system, slow transportation deeply penetrates our lives, however it is always not valued and remains many burning issues.

2.1 Pain Points of Urban Slow Transportation

The Contradiction Between the Narrow Space and the Needs for Transportation with Flexibility and Rich Forms. For the slow transportation environment, it is generally in the range of 3 km, and the space is relatively small. In this short-distance transportation map, the main part is the scattered-spot user: individuals. Most of their demands for transportation is related to "the last kilometer" or "the first kilometer", namely the transportation path is more about "multiple points-to-single point" route. Therefore, large-volume transportation tools cannot be a good way to flexibly connect the distributed demand subject in the limited space. This situation is especially common in airports. Such as in this always crowded environment, how to transport many passengers to check-in desk in the departure hall, how to transport passengers from security checkpoint to boarding terminals and how to deliver luggage to the parking lot at the arrival place. But large vehicles cannot flexibly connect the scattered demand entities in a limited space, it requires a smart and precise dispatching system to meet the needs of users who are dispersed and with different time urgencies.

Moreover, how to dispatch transportation resources based on the current conditions of environment to the maximum efficiency, and how to save parking and driving space and release more slow transportation space for people are two important issues that need to be solved [5].

Lack of Continuity Among Service Phases. Taking campus as an example, nowadays many campuses own shared bicycles, which are the important means of transportation for teachers and students in campus life. But due to the regularity of campus activities and the large number of users, there always no bicycles near the starting point when using, or need to walk a while to search for available bicycles. These problems are highly time-consuming, which prolongs the utilization time of transportation services. How to closely link the pre-stage, in-stage and after-stage of the slow transportation service and ultimately improve the overall efficiency is the key to improving the utilization rate of slow transportation service.

Lack of Communication Between the Transportation Tools and Users. As mentioned above, slow transportation is the most basic transportation tool compared with motor vehicles, which penetrate every aspect of people's life and exposed to the widest group of users. Between the slow transportation with people, a mutually beneficial relationship could be established with proper human-robot interactions. If designed well, transportation tools can access data from the user, and then based on these data transportation tools can provide some information for interested people, which works like a local information hub. However, the relationship between slow transportation vehicles and users is remained to be established. And the current transportation vehicles don't have the function of local info platform, which is not conducive to interpret users, understand the users and entertain users.

Nowadays, the industrial parks are bigger and bigger. The development of landscape construction and enterprise culture are flourishing. Many industrial parks have become an important tourist attraction for cities, such as Google and Apple, so they need to receive many foreign visitors or business partners every day. However, under the existed slow transportation environment of many parks, there is no effective transportation tool as a bridge to connect passengers to the external environment well. So, it lacks a bridge to let users understand the environment better and make the environment serve users better.

2.2 Common Demands of Urban Slow Transportation

Slow Transportation Requires a Flexible Transportation Service System. Slow transportation vehicles should occupy less parking space as much as possible, and at the same time, improve the flexibility of driving in a short distance. Set reasonable "point" such as stop and scheduling point. Set reasonable "line": In view of the current situation of high path repetition rate in the slow transportation environment, design the most efficient driving path. Set reasonable "face": Maximum the degree of connection to the scattered users, thus expanding the use of vehicle range and user group distribution.

There Needs More Interactions Between Slow Transportation Tools and Users. Interactions between slow transportation with people aims at constructing a positive relationship, creating values mutually. In the digital network time, digital information can help to strengthen the relationship between people and objects, people and people, people and the world, and in this situation, even reconstruct the interactive relationship between people and transportation system. As discussed above, slow transportation environment connected to all aspects of people's lives to more deeply than other types of transportation, so if constructing an effective information transmission mechanism in slow transportation service system, it will make the platform and people have deeper interactions. This kind of information transmission could be by texts, voice, visions, movements, environments and so on. Once people use the offerings, the interaction get started: the service platform could understand and learn from people through collecting data, imported data or various kinds of communications. People also get learned the features of the platform based on some feedbacks.

Slow Transportation Services Should Satisfy Diverse Demands Through Comprehensive Functions. In the same scenario, different users may have different needs. For example, the same user will have different requests of service time under different time periods, or under the same urgency of time, there will be different service routes and service forms under different using scenarios. Taking the community which far away from the city center as an example, this environment needs a slow transportation service system, which includes rush commuting to the downtown area, daily transportation in the district, patrolling of security personnel, and sightseeing in the leisure time. Therefore, the demand for the comprehensiveness of functions on this slow transportation service platform is also very high.

And many characteristics of slow transportation environment determine that driverless slow transportation vehicles can well promote the development of slow transportation. After our research, it was found that driverless vehicle could effectively improve slow transportation system efficiency and user experience.

3   Advantages of Using Driverless Vehicle in Slow Transportation Environments

Driverless Vehicle (also known as an autonomous car, self-driving car, robotic car [6]) and unmanned ground vehicle is a vehicle that is capable of sensing its environment and navigating without human input [7]. [8] Driverless vehicle can provide people with transportation function and entertain value, also be helpful to shape a positive relationship among people, vehicle and environment.

3.1   Driverless Vehicle Functions Well in Short-Distance Environment

Short-distance transportation environment has many characteristics, such as strong flexibility, high transfer frequency, short driving time and many participants. Moreover, under slow-transportation environment, people are more closely related to surrounding environment. In such a low-speed and relatively narrow environment, driverless slow transportation vehicles can set up automatic docking and connection, calculate and arrange reasonable paths, also flexibly connect people and environment to the maximum. Because driverless vehicle is manipulated by the in-vehicle controlling system, cloud platform and the service platform itself, it could be more sensitive to be deployed and managed in limited space.

Driverless vehicle defaults to be in continuous operation on the road, except the recharging time. This continuous operation can maximize the use of and liberate transportation resources to some extent: On one hand, this continuous operation can improve vehicle utilization, realize the real sharing of resources of public vehicles. On the other hand, it can greatly save parking spaces, which is more meaningful than the past when the slow transportation spaces were being occupied, eventually enlarging capacity of area for transportation. This also provides advantages of external environments for good operation of driverless vehicles.

3.2   Driverless Vehicle Is Suitable for Environments with High-Path Repetition Rate and Simple-Driving Conditions

In urban slow transportation environments, campus, airports, communities far from the city center and industrial parks are the typical ones. The driving path repetition is high and driving environment is relatively simple in these typical using contexts. In campuses and industrial parks, the driving path has a certain regularity and repeatability in different periods. Walking is the main way of transportation in the airport and some residential communities where cars and people are separated. These environments are closed, which does not involve in urban transportation regulations, and the driving environment is relatively simple. Driverless slow transportation vehicle can improve the efficiency of vehicle utilization and serve more people in this environment.

3.3   Driverless Vehicle Can Contribute to the Interaction Between Vehicle and People

The current slow transportation tools are only the carrier of transportation services. Both the vehicles and the users do not understand each other, and the interaction between the two is passive. Transportation tools do not collect user data, do not learn user data, do not optimize services and benefit other users. Users can't feedback their experience, personal data and schedules to vehicles timely, which can't help transportation vehicles to know more about users' information and surrounding environment. However, the slow transportation vehicle and a driverless service platform should be a university's local information hub. Therefore, in this driverless vehicle, an in-vehicle smart system was embedded. This smart system functioned like a virtual character, to enable the vehicle to interact with people more naturally. Through this interaction, users can input their own data or information, help transportation vehicles penetrate real needs and optimize it services in a very natural way. And this service platform can provide relevant information to help other users based on recorded data. Active interactions between vehicle and users will be helpful for the platform to provide on-demand services satisfying diverse needs.

3.4 Driverless Vehicle Can Support Better Function Integration

Nowadays, many environments are becoming more and more functional-compound, especially for different users. For example, the campus is not only a daily workplace for teachers and students but also the collection and distribution of environmental information around the campus. At the same time, it also bears certain social functions, such as holding some public exams or lectures, and being visitors' tourist destination on holidays. Therefore, taking the campus transportation service as an example, we need to meet routine, way-finding, information guidance and campus visiting. Driverless slow transportation vehicle can provide corresponding services to these different needs, through integration of functions. The driverless vehicle is directly controlled by in-vehicle smart system and service platform, not by people. Therefore, for driverless vehicles it is easier to be integrated into the whole system, easier to be dispatched, and easier to compound functions. This advantage helps driverless vehicle, based on different users and needs, to provide personalized routes of slow transportation.

3.5 Driverless Vehicle Can Enhance Transportation Comfort

Slow-transportation environment is always the last stop away from the user's destination, acting a role of transmitter. Improving riding comfort can greatly help users faster access to new environment and switch to new state. Because of the smooth-running speed, the use of clean energy, and the small transportation noise, driverless vehicles can greatly improve the driving comfort.

4 Driverless Vehicle-Based Urban Slow Transportation Service Platform Design

Campuses, airports, communities far away from city centers, and industrial parks are representative using contexts in slow transportation system. In response to their common demands, we propose a driverless vehicle-based urban Slow Transportation Service Platform (STS Platform) made up of with several function modules, under the designing approach of service system. And each of them have unique features in different urban low-speed using contexts.

Besides the offerings, on driverless vehicle-based STS Platform, an in-vehicle smart system was embedded to control the vehicle, together with various techniques in vehicle to detect the surroundings. This smart system can not only make driverless vehicles easier to be controlled, make driverless vehicles collect people's input, also be helpful for the STS Platform to provide multiple services.

4.1   The Working Principles of Driverless Vehicle-Based Urban Slow Transportation Service Platform

As the above discussed, urban low-speed environments, representative of campuses, airports, communities far from city centers and industrial parks, have some common demands, like requiring a flexible control system, building interactive relationship with people, providing multiple services meeting diverse needs. So, building STS Platform to satisfy so many integration of demands, which kind of designing methods is the proper one?

Service system design, as an effective designing logic, is good at dealing with varieties of relationships in complicated systems. On STS Platform, both the relationship among "people-environment-vehicle" with its inner relationship are important components. Any components will make effects on the whole transportation system, service system design can use some approaches to call on this complexity. The designing approach of stakeholders and task analysis grid can make an overall consideration of participants, combing them up into different categories, firstly to expand the service coverage, and then to filter or optimize core services based on the importance level of stakeholders (primary ones/secondary ones/others) [9].

In slow-transportation, there are many transportation transfers, high-frequencies of get on/get off, frequent passenger change, and large amount of traffic of passenger in this system. This requires systematic design thinking to arrange these multiple using contexts and touch points into a coherent using experience. Experience prototype in service system design is a simulation of the service experience that foresees some of its performances using the specific physical touchpoints involved [10, 11].

Under the designing approaches of service system, STS Platform can build proactive relationship between vehicles with people through smart interactions. Firstly, experience prototype can evaluate the whole service experience, help STS Platform make people interact with driverless vehicle more naturally; secondly, the approach of stakeholders can help driverless vehicle take a full consideration of diverse users, which contribute driverless vehicle to acquire more information from uses in a proper way, eventually to make STS Platform provide more accurate services for users. Under such a highly interactive relationship, it can help both people and STS Platform to establish the cognitive model of each other, for people to simplify the use of services and optimize the experience of services, for STS Platform enrich the types of services (see Fig. 1).

4.2   The Modular Functions of Driverless Vehicle-Based Urban Slow Transportation Service Platform

After discussing the methods of driverless vehicle-based slow transportation service system design, how to address the pain points and common demands of slow transportation will be elaborated in the following as a form of four modular functions?

STS Platform could base on the cloud information, such as personal schedule, campus timetable, local guidance information, to supply people with diverse functions: summon and book, parcel delivery, route customization and information hub service.

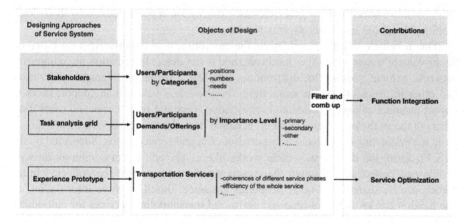

Fig. 1. Designing approaches of STS platform

Based on the in-vehicle smart system, STS Platform is armed with four modular functions:

Time-Based Sharing Mobility Service. This platform supports booking or summoning driverless vehicle based on conditions of people (personal schedule, time urgency, students class timetable, etc.) For example, in campus, teachers could book the vehicle through App at a certain time, and they just wait for being picked up at the nearest boarding point; Meanwhile, the platform could base on the class time and dormitory information to arrange some hitchhiking for relevant students or staffs.

Route Optimization Sharing Mobility Service. Based on the environment conditions of campus (transportation status, roads, navigation signage, buildings and so on) and requirements of users, driverless vehicle-based slow transportation service platform can provide different people with different on-demand services. In airports, transportation service demands could be sorted by various categories: sorted by user type, services could be classified to single user demands, group user demands, and family demands, different type of users have different requirements of vehicle type and capacity. Sorted by time urgency, activities in airports could be classified to emergency, rush for boarding, normal boarding, and casual airport shopping. Once users' boarding card scanned by the vehicle, it will provide customized route for users based on their own time urgency. Sorted by luggage, service demands could sort into with carry-on luggage and no hand luggage. In this situation, the system will allocate driverless vehicle with proper capacity or turn on the function of luggage storage for single passengers while they away temporarily. There is a variety of transportation needs, and after permutation and combination of these specifications, this driverless vehicle-based slow transportation service system could give customized routes for them.

Local Information Sharing. People could import to or connect their personal data with this platform, and the in-vehicle smart control system could also base on the sensory data and cloud data, not only helpful to understand users more, for providing customized slow transportation services; but also, the driverless vehicle works as a moving information hub, to give relevant information recommendations about local mobility, local life and other aspects to visitors.

The in-vehicle smart system detects the environment of the driverless car based on the in-vehicle sensors and other hardware, and it can detect information including road network, vehicle, parking lot distribution, building distribution, signage, pedestrians and other information. At the same time, the driverless vehicle can support users to import personal calendar, residential information, personal preferences and other data. Through the analysis of multiple users' personal data, the driverless vehicle will have a basic understanding of the local transportation, life and service status. Supported by the STS Platform, the driverless vehicle works like a "driver": it can communicate with people and collect data through the communication, meanwhile the collected information can be shared with other people as guidance. Based on these information, on one hand, it can provide real-time and optimized transportation services for individuals in need. On the other hand, the driverless vehicle can also serve as a mobile local info hub, providing public information to people in need [12].

For example, the community far away from the downtown area, because the land price is relatively low, often covers a large area. There are often some commercial facilities such as supermarkets, gyms, which forms a relatively independent living ecosystem. So, the daily commuting within the community is also an important problem. In such an urban low-speed environment, STS Platform can do the most reasonable and efficient route planning, and do not take up too much capacity. At the same time, in the basis of different user's travel schedule, reasonable distribution of multiple users with vehicles, can reduce the waiting time, the repetition rate of paths and vacancy rate, thus to improve flexibility in slow transportation effectively.

Parcel Delivery Service. This driverless vehicle cannot only carry people but also help deliver the parcel. People can make reservations through cell phone app, or directly use the available driverless vehicle, set the destination and arrival time to deliver goods, and view the running path of the current driverless vehicle at the mobile phone side. This service can help students carry luggage during the start of the school season or the end of the school season. Or for residents living in large communities, when they come back home after shopping, they can use the driverless vehicle directly to help them carry their goods to their home. For items that are not able to pass the airport security check, people can also use this service through the mobile phone app and transport them to the airport mailing place with the driverless car, then mail or deposit their items (see Fig. 2).

4.3   A Use Case of Driverless Vehicle-Based Urban Slow Transportation Service Platform on Campus

Slow Transportation Demands on Campus. Currently, as more and more Chinese universities are expanding, the number of students and teachers is increasing. So, the campus is becoming more and more functional to meet the daily needs of many students and teachers. At the same time, campus daily activities have certain regularity in time distribution and spatial distribution, which can help unmanned cars plan more

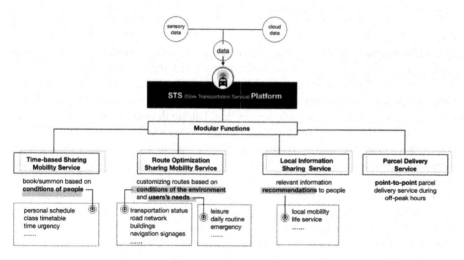

Fig. 2. Functional modules of STS platform

efficiently and serve daily commuting time and line between teachers and students (see Fig. 3). Based on their purposes of using the vehicle, the campus transportation service users could be mainly divided into four categories: students (for going for class), teachers (for going for work), visitors (for navigation), and visitors (for sightseeing).

Fig. 3. Functions for campus slow transportation service system

Functions for Campus Slow Transportation Service System. Driverless vehicles can provide customized routes and services based on different needs. For example, when the teachers and students are running for the class, driverless vehicles will run the nearest line, and at the same time, the in-vehicle screen will provide the news or life service voice information of the campus today. When an external visitor comes, the in-vehicle screen will show a campus map with detailed campus information, and support text input, touch input and voice input. Even for external visitors who only have little information of destination, driverless vehicles can also help them reach their destinations fast. When carrying with leisure visitors, driverless vehicles will choose the route which is the most suitable for viewing. During the tour, passengers can see the introduction of the site and the traveling mood of other tourists through mobile phone AR or in-vehicle AR screen. They could also upload texts, travelling notes, photos, videos or share music on cloud through mobile phone to leave digital travelling footprints. This service can help visitors get to know this environment better.

Through the detection of the campus environment and the connection of cloud data, the driverless vehicle can also be used as the campus life information point, it can provide information of transportation, catering, leisure, people flow and other information near the campus to students, teachers, and visitors. The parcel delivery function of the driverless vehicle can not only serve the teachers and students but also assist the logistics transportation department of the campus in the non-peak period.

User Journey. The above are some typical functions for campus slow transportation service system, and a user journey on campus, taking a period from 8:50 a.m.–10:00 p.m. as example, will be elaborated in the following part, which can help readers to have a better comprehension of the services:

This morning, Patrick made an appointment with his friend Sonia to take a tour at his campus, and they agreed to meet at campus gate at 9:00. He booked a driverless vehicle for two seats through mobile phone app in advance of 10 min, and waited at his dormitory for picking up. Sonia arrived at Patrick's campus gate, got learned some campus food recommendations through a driverless vehicle. At 9:58, Patrick is taking a driverless vehicle to pick her up. After boarding, the driverless vehicle customized a campus touring route based on their demands. At the campus cafe during the tour, Sonia noticed some travelling notes from other visitors about the café on in-vehicle AR screen, saying that "the coffee here is great" and "I like the interior design style of this café." These notes reminded Sonia that she also viewed some hot recommendations about this café through a driverless vehicle at the campus gate, so she decided to go for a cup of coffee. One hour later, their campus tour finished. After the driverless vehicle sending Patrick and Sonia to campus gate, Sonia gave a big toy to Patrick as present. Patrick request the same driverless vehicle to deliver the parcel to his dormitory, and sent Sonia to the nearest metro station (see Fig. 4).

5   Conclusions

Driverless vehicle-based urban slow transportation service is a new also valuable research direction. The features and advantages of driverless vehicle determine it could serve people well, in urban slow transportation environments. In this paper, we designed a driverless vehicle-based slow transportation platform (STS Platform) to provide people with multiple services adapted do diverse using contexts. Besides the

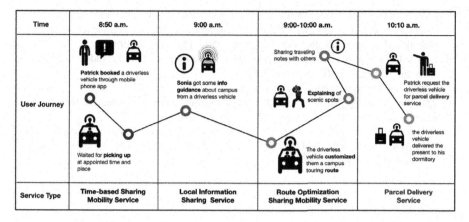

Time	8:50 a.m.	9:00 a.m.	9:00-10:00 a.m.	10:10 a.m.
User Journey	Patrick booked a driverless vehicle through mobile phone app / Waited for picking up at appointed time and place	Sonia got some info guidance about campus from a driverless vehicle	Sharing traveling notes with others / Explaining of scenic spots / The driverless vehicle customized them a campus touring route	Patrick request the driverless vehicle for parcel delivery service / the driverless vehicle delivered the present to his dormitory
Service Type	Time-based Sharing Mobility Service	Local Information Sharing Service	Route Optimization Sharing Mobility Service	Parcel Delivery Service

Fig. 4. A user journey of campus slow transportation service system

multiple services at in-front stage, at the back stage, driverless vehicle as a mobile carrier of sensors, the collected information can also support the platform to make some real-time visualizations of evaluations for the transportation, population traffic, the validity, population distribution status and other indicators of the region. The simulation and analysis of the development and potential of a certain region, could play a role in a broader area. And we will continue to research on this area in the next research plan.

Acknowledgments. This paper was supported by the Funds Project of Shanghai High Peak IV Program (Grant DA17003).

References

1. Ibañez-Guzmán, J., Laugier, C., Yoder, J.D., et al.: Autonomous driving: context and state-of-the-art. In: Eskandarian, A. (ed.) Handbook of Intelligent Vehicles. Springer, London (2012). https://doi.org/10.1007/978-0-85729-085-4_50
2. Parent, M., Gallais, G.: Driverless transportation in cities with CTS. In: 2002 Proceedings of the IEEE, International Conference on Driverless Transportation Systems, pp. 826–830. IEEE (2002)
3. Feng, W.: Research on intelligent vehicle driverless technology in low-speed environment. Zhejiang University (2015)
4. Japan Cabinet Office: White paper on traffic safety in Japan (1993+) (1971)
5. Shi, J., Sun, X.: Service system-based urban mobility system design for chinese metropolis. In: Karwowski, W., Ahram, T. (eds.) IHSI 2018. AISC, vol. 722, pp. 693–699. Springer, Cham (2018). https://doi.org/10.1007/978-3-319-73888-8_107
6. Breazeal, C.: Social interactions in HRI: the robot view. IEEE Trans. Syst. Man Cybern. Part C **34**(2), 181–186 (2004)
7. Thrun, S.: Toward robotic cars. Commun. ACM **53**, 99–106 (2010)

8. Gehrig, S.K., Stein, F.J.: Dead reckoning and cartography using stereo vision for an autonomous car. In: 1999 Proceedings of IEEE/RSJ International Conference on Driverless Robots and Systems. IROS 1999, vol. 3, pp. 1507–1512. IEEE (1999)
9. Self, D.R., Schraeder, M.: Potential benefits of engaging primary stakeholders in developing a vision. Strateg. Dir. **26**(3), 3–5 (2010)
10. http://www.servicedesigntools.org/tools/21
11. Zhu, W., Miao, J., Hu, J., et al.: Vehicle detection in driving simulation using extreme learning machine. Neurocomputing **128**(5), 160–165 (2014)
12. Shi, J., Ma, K.: Digital touchpoints in campus slow traffic service system. In: Stanton, N.A. (ed.) AHFE 2017. AISC, vol. 597, pp. 349–361. Springer, Cham (2018). https://doi.org/10.1007/978-3-319-60441-1_35

Cities as Sustainable Service Platforms

A Framework for Institutional Service Delivery in the Urban Context

Jarmo Suominen[1,2(✉)]

[1] Aalto University, Espoo, Finland
jarmo.suominen@aalto.fi
[2] Tongji University, Shanghai, China

Abstract. Cities are complex systems of infrastructures and entities, which are usually developed independently, focusing on their efficiency. Cities deliver various services, such as health care, education and transportation. These services are delivered through urban entities such as hospitals, schools, universities and care homes, each built and managed independently. As a consequence, even though there might be enough resources in the built environment, there might be a lack of access in terms of actual service delivery. This is due to the trend that many times urban innovation happens by building new instead of using existing resources in more sustainable ways. Recently, new digital technologies and platforms have emerged to enable the sharing of various resources. However, since resource sharing has emerged on the customer side, institutions are still largely controlling their own independent resources. This article analyzes opportunities for institutional resource sharing and the role of service operations and platform applications. The research reveals new opportunities for operating environments and proposes a new service-oriented model for organizing institutional service delivery and using cities as sustainable service platforms.

Keywords: City · Service platform · Sustainability

1 Introduction

Cities are complex networks of various resources and infrastructures. They have systems for housing, transportation, sanitation, utilities, land use and communication. Their density facilitates interaction between people, government organizations and businesses. Urban resources are being developed through independent projects, driven by their own purposes and efficiency. This approach has been relevant in the past, enabled by land use strategies and driven by city planning and real-estate models of operation. As a consequence, cities could be illustrated as archipelagoes, environments of independent islands, each island creating its own isolated entity. This has caused cities to expand in order to enable new needs and demands to be fulfilled. However, due to the development of digitalization and new postindustrial value-creating processes, there is a shift of needs for physical resources. Now, many urban environments are facing the paradox of having too much space but not enough access.

© Springer International Publishing AG, part of Springer Nature 2018
P.-L. P. Rau (Ed.): CCD 2018, LNCS 10912, pp. 371–390, 2018.
https://doi.org/10.1007/978-3-319-92252-2_30

While the processes of creating value are changing, many of the needs that in the past required controlled and managed physical environments are changing as well. Workplaces and environments for education and health care, administration and accommodation will face dramatic changes with regard to the need for space and control. Office hotels and co-working solutions have been evolving partially to solve this challenge. Customer-oriented services such as Airbnb and Uber have also been enabling the use of resources owned and managed by individuals. This has opened new opportunities in new markets and application areas. However, most of the current applications are still focusing on the customer side of resource sharing, while institutional sharing remains underdeveloped.

Urban environments have numerous resources that are managed and used by various institutions. As an example, even a small urban entity might have public resources such as schools, day care centers, libraries and police and fire stations, which could be used as a more integrated platform for public service delivery. The focus in this article is on how to use combinations of public and private resources as a service platform for institutional service delivery. If cities could overcome traditional borders between organizational silos and procurement, a new approach could take place. The hypothesis of this research is that by utilizing urban assets as a platform for public service delivery, cities will become more accessible and sustainable.

2 Objectives

The objective of this research is to analyze urban structures as environments for institutional service delivery. Currently, each service provider manages, controls and even owns its own entities, causing competition over the supply of similar resources. This is partially due to the nature of institutional procurement and management processes of the past, but the situation also arises because of the symbolic and operational values of a service provider owning its own entities. This type of thinking could be rooted in *goods-dominant logic*.

> *Goods-Dominant Logic: The purpose of an activity is to make and distribute units of output, preferably tangible. Goods are embedded with utility (value) during manufacturing. The goal is to maximize benefits through the efficient production and distribution of goods.* [1]

This logic has been influenced in many ways by how cities are today – environments of independent "products" connected by enabling infrastructures. As a consequence, cities have oversupplies of certain resources, at certain locations, and a lack of resources in other locations. City-planning processes are in place to balance supply and demand, but needs will change over time. Some locations and resources may lose, while others will increase their relevance over time. In order to be able to deliver services in sustainable ways, a new logic is needed.

> *Service-Dominant Logic: Goods are a distribution mechanism for service provision. Goods derive their value through use – the service they provide. The customer is always a co-creator of value. This implies value creation is interactional. Value is always determined by the beneficiary. Value is idiosyncratic, experiential, contextual and meaning laden.* [1]

Based on service-dominant logic, the "products" of cities, such as buildings, could be seen as platforms for value creation. Buildings are evaluated through their instrumental rather than absolute value. This difference affects how the built environment could be developed, what interactions cities are for and what technologies they will use. By separating activities from environments, the built environment could be analyzed from a service-platform point of view. The analysis should cover all the levels of the environment, starting from spatial and building layers and reaching up to areal and city layers.

3 Methods

Service-dominant logic identifies two main elements for service delivery: *operant resources* and *operand resources.* Operant resources are primarily knowledge and skills – competencies. In general, these are resources that produce effects. Operand resources are primarily physical resources – goods. These are resources upon which an operation or act is performed to produce an effect [1]. In their article "A Spatial Model of Effectiveness Criteria: Towards a Competing Values Approach to Organizational Analysis," Quinn and Rohrbaugh   proposed a framework for organizational analysis for operant resources [2]. The model suggested that dimensions of control-flexibility and internal-external focus underlie conceptualizations of organizational effectiveness (Fig. 1).

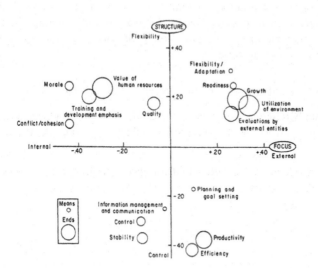

Fig. 1. Quinn Rohrbaugh framework

The main parameters of the framework are focus and structure: focus shifting from internal efficiency to external effectiveness, and structure shifting from a control-driven static model to a flexible, adaptable model. These parameters have been used to analyze the operant resources of institutions to evaluate their objectives. An adaptation of this framework is then developed to analyze operand resources as physical environments for service delivery (Fig. 2).

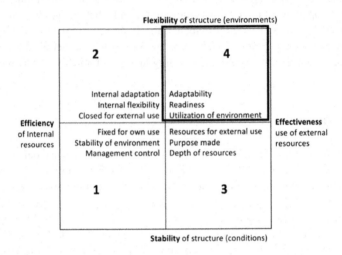

Fig. 2. Quinn Rohrbaugh framework adaptation by Suominen

As a result of this research, a comparative analysis has been made to evaluate the suitability of the service platform (operand resource) for the objectives of the activity (operant resource). In the case studies, the focus is on understanding the environments of given institutional operations. In this framework, environments are evaluated through the following categories.

3.1   Evaluation Categories for Characteristics of Service Platforms

On the case study references, service platforms are evaluated and categorized, based on the adapted framework, within categories defined by core parameters, focus and structure.

Static Model: Efficiency of Internal Resources/Stability of Structure. The static model is fixed for internal usage, without internal flexibility. This is typical for many solutions of the past, which are based on a predefined brief and built for that purpose only. This drives static and predictable solutions and enables traditional processes of management and control of the facility. Typically, the solution is not adaptable for any internal or external change and therefore has high investment and planning risk.

Internal Model: Efficiency of Internal Resources/Flexibility of Structure. The focus is on internal issues, while the structure is flexible. Internal flexibility allows internal adaptation to needs. This has consequences to internal development potential and the role of human resources in it. This is typical for many quite recent solutions. By increasing internal flexibility and adaptation, the quality of outcomes could be higher. The internal focus may lead to very deep network structures that are not easily accessible for external stakeholders. Flexibility of conditions is typically achieved by transformable or multipurpose solutions in the physical environment.

External Model: Effectiveness of External Resources/Stability of Structure. The focus is on effectiveness and external resources. Solutions are open to external stakeholders, however, while the structure is static and based on control. This requires external stakeholders to learn and understand the characteristics of a given solution. It is open and available for external use, but with internal control. The benefits of this concept are that it utilizes its own available resources and thus increases the usage rate of those resources. That itself could be seen as a sustainable approach in urban development. Entities are no longer isolated, standalone institutions but are shared with other stakeholders as well. This is also an example of a sharing economy application in a built environment.

Dynamic Model: Effectiveness of External Resources/Flexibility of Structure. The focus is on external effectiveness, and the structure is flexible. The solution is adaptable, flexible and capable of utilization of the resources available in its environment. This type of solution is capable of creating value with the environment and flexible to adapt to changes. The resolution of the solution is higher: Instead of defining the solution as a building or independent entities, it could be defined as a network of resources. When organizing the solution as a network, a new type of network management and service operations are needed. Instead of operating one entity at a time, new opportunities will emerge when approaching the solution with a resource operations point of view.

3.2   Network Structure

In order to evaluate the capabilities of the various network structures, analyses of physical environments have been conducted. In spatial analyses, "space syntax" tools have been used. Space syntax encompasses a set of theories and techniques for the analysis of spatial configurations developed by Hillier et al. at The Bartlett, University College London [3]. The general idea is that spaces can be broken down into components, analyzed as networks of choices and then represented as maps and graphs that describe the relative connectivity and integration of those spaces – especially integration, which measures how many turns have to be made from a spatial segment to reach all other street segments in the network, when the shortest paths are used. This has been used to represent the depth of the spatial network structure.

The network structure of physical environments was chosen to be analyzed because of implications of given structure to actual behavior. Deep structures with disconnected resources don't support interaction in the same way than shallower and more connected structures. Deep structures also indicate internal focus, environments supporting strong internal ties. While shallow structures are enabling weak ties to be included in value creation to increase external effectiveness. In the article, The Strength of Weak Ties [4] the degree of overlap of individuals' personal networks is discussed from the point of view of how it varies as a consequence of the strength of one individual tie to one another. Strong ties are links between us and people we know well and work closely with. Weak ties are those which we don't interact often with. They are people we see or communicate with only on occasion. The advantage of communicating with weak ties is that they are links to other groups who know different things, from different networks than we do bring us new ideas and connections. Author Mark Granovetter suggested an application of the argument on weak ties to the study of innovation diffusion. This argument applies not only to the diffusion of innovations but to the diffusion of any ideas or information. The impact of this principle on the diffusion of influence and information, mobility opportunity, and community organization is explored. Stress is laid on the cohesive power of weak ties. While most network models deal with strong ties, Emphasis on weak ties lends itself to the discussion of relations between groups [4].

4   Case Studies: Tangible Service Platforms

When analyzing physical environments from the platform point of view, the hypotheses is that the architecture of the solutions should be open and flexible, utilizing the resources of the environment and enabling flexible adaptation for changing conditions. As an assumption, solutions that focus on the effectiveness of external resources within flexible structures are most suitable for the elements of urban service platforms. This requires that a particular type of service architecture and network structure is taken into consideration in all levels of city planning and architectures (Fig. 3).

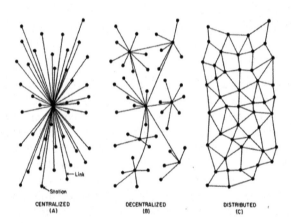

Fig. 3. Network typologies for centralized controlled, decentralized efficient and distributed effective structures.

In city planning, it would be beneficial to develop already existing service-intensive environments further, creating access and proximity for diverse service entities. In mobility and transportation planning, the location of service hubs would be most relevant when they support developed service environments. On the building level, the accessibility of resources requires open architectures and shallow network structures. Case studies have been made on various layers of urban environments, on the levels of spatial, building, areal and city scale. Solutions have been evaluated from the point of view of both the network structure and the internal efficiency/external effectivity orientation (based on the proposed framework). Condensed summaries of each research area follow.

4.1 Space as a Service (Spatial Level)/Case: MIT Buildings on Campus

This section of the case study deals with the building issues of accessibility and affordances of existing resources. In the article Methods and tools for evaluation of usability in buildings [5] authors are presenting various tools for analyzing the usability and manageability of buildings. However, in order to understand the building as a service platform, new methods are needed. For this research, the network structures of a total of 12 buildings on the campus of the Massachusetts Institute of Technology (MIT), Cambridge, were analyzed. Solutions were categorized based on the network structures, which were compared to the operational objectives of each environment. The buildings were analyzed by using a space syntax program with the floorplans. The aim was to identify the main elements of the solutions in terms of structure and focus. Structures were categorized based on the parameter of control/static–flexibility/dynamic and the axis of focus on internal efficiency–external effectiveness.

It is evident that these two analyzed case examples had different goals; however, the aim of the study was to understand the capabilities of any particular network structure in terms of accessibility and suitability for value co-creation. This approach favors the open and connected structure of MIT's Media Lab over the clustered and more closed structure of MIT's Picower Center. From the point of view of orientation to internal efficiency/external effectiveness, it seems that the focus of MIT's Picower Center is more on internal efficiency, while MIT's Media Lab focuses on external effectiveness (Fig. 4).

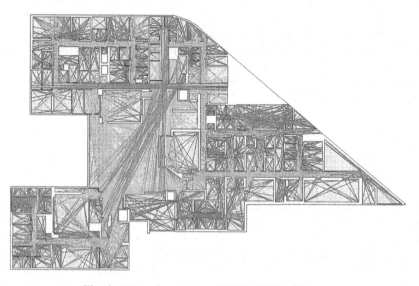

Fig. 4. Network structure of MIT's Picower Center.

Solution is decentralized and focused on internal efficiency. Resources are deep in the network structure. Accessibility for external use is low. At Picower, the floorplan analyzed was the main floor for interaction. It contains a main lobby, entrances to three auditoriums and sub-entrances to three main departments, which are isolated from one another (Fig. 5).

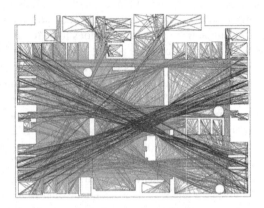

Fig. 5. Network structure of MIT's Media Lab

Network structure is distributed; focus is on external effectiveness. Resources are accessible due to the network structure and shallow depth. Resources are perceived easily by external stakeholders. As a result, this study illustrates how the focus on internal efficiency or external effectiveness has its implications for physical environments. In decentralized but clustered structure of Picower center, each cluster could function efficiently and independently. However, in terms of human interaction and social learning, this type of network structure doesn't typically support interaction between internal clusters of external stakeholders. On the other hand, more open and connected structure of Media laboratory offers opportunities for internal and external interaction. The solution of Media Laboratory also offers more opportunities to share competencies and histories of mutual activities. This type of open structure also is more open to external activities.

4.2   Building as a Service (Building Level)/Case: Entity of High School

This section of the case study deals with a value co-creation platform between a high school and learning communities at Aalto University, Otaniemi. School as a Service (SaaS) is a concept that defines a school as a network of resources rather than a standalone building. The SaaS solution is to develop the service architecture of a school based on principles of service-dominant logic [1], and it is enabled by applications of the platform economy. School as a Service is an new concept utilizing a service platform both for institutional demand and to deliver education. In this particular case, the service architecture defines the conditions for value co-creation (learning). While the brief for the school has stayed almost the same, the deployment is different. The planning process includes mapping of local assets, identification of available resources, designing the "home base" and planning campus-wide resource usage. SaaS is a joint project with the City of Espoo to create a new concept for the use of teaching facilities and resources.

SaaS case was looking at how to organize one institutional service delivery – in this case, teaching – based on a flexible structure and external efficiency. Traditional school solutions learning is mostly decoupled from the community and delivered in a standalone platform by teachers to students. This type of solution is characterized as a product, which could be innovative and flexible, but it is based on the logic where value is embedded in the product itself. A school is usually run in isolation from the environment, and the focus is on delivery of teaching, while students are subjects of this activity. The school is operated as a standalone facility, and the structure is static, enabling control of the environment (Fig. 6).

Fig. 6. School as a product

Characteristics of product-logic at a typical school include a focus on internal efficiency and a static structure, enabling control and delivery of planned activities. The focus of product innovation is on product-specific standalone solutions with isolated operations and facility management. This type of solution requires extensive planning. Most of the investments are up front, and the investment risk and planning risk are high due to the time span of the production and the potentially turbulent environment of the solution. It is based on the idea of controlling all required resources and creating the conditions for pre-planned service delivery. In this case study, however, the focus was on a flexible structure and external effectiveness.

Organization of education and delivery of teaching is currently resource consuming and static, it is based on a stand-alone solution with independent entities of education. The focus of SaaS project was on utilization of existing resources and communities of learning to enable more connected learning environments and to create value together with other stakeholders in the learning community, school is defined as a service, based on the network of resources around its home base. In practice, the study was identifying various resources of learning in close proximity of the "home base" for the school and was studying a model for resource operator, in order to enable dynamic optimization of given school institution. This defines new "service architecture" for the school. The aim of the study was to test this new solution by proposing interventions based on the goal of the solution and to evaluate them with, for example, an action research methodology. School operations were proposed to be executed in a network of resources rather than in a traditional standalone entity. While the traditional model could be described within the product-based logic, this new hypothesis is based on service-dominant logic [1] (Fig. 7).

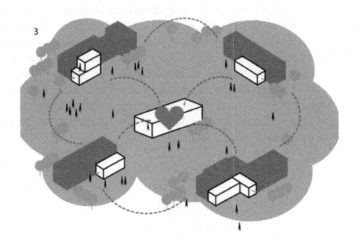

Fig. 7. School as a Service

In prototyped SaaS concept, a new service architecture defines a school as a set of resources for supporting learning. SaaS is sustainable by optimizing and recycling the use of spaces and equipment and by increasing social diversity and sharing resources with the surrounding society. The school uses available shared resources within the community (Fig. 8).

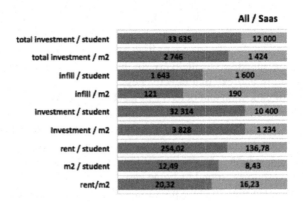

Fig. 8. Financial analysis between product and service models (source: ACRE).

Aspects of social learning are important elements of flexible and scalable school embedded in the community. This is a systemic solution, where the focus is on external effectiveness and the structure is flexible. Pedagogy is focused on problem-based learning, emphasizing 21st-century skills, critical thinking, creativity and communication and collaboration. This type of solution could be characterized as service innovation enabled by a resource operator. The focus is on value co-creation, and the structure is flexible. This enables new types of learning communities to emerge and increases opportunities for social learning (Fig. 9).

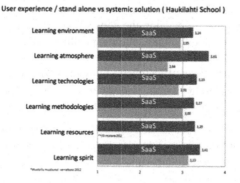

Fig. 9. Comparison between product and service model experiences (source: IRO)

As a result, School as a service solution enables more adaptable and flexible solution for the delivery of education. It fosters social learning, by extending learning community beyond traditional environments and by utilizing accessible resources at Aalto university campus. The solution was decreasing planning and investment risk, based on the adaptability of the network. It also has the impact on the increase of social density, interaction inside and between various groups and optimization of the use of local resources, enabling more sustainable development of urban communities. SaaS has received five innovation awards: The Mayors Award for Innovation, 2016; National Award for Innovation, 2016; Espoo Medal for Innovation, 2016; International Innovation Award, 2017; and Best Learning Community, Espoo, 2017. It has been recognized as a sustainable model for future learning environments by the Finnish government.

4.3   Campus as a Service (Areal Level)/Case: Campus of Otaniemi

This section of the case study deals with the structure and elements of an open service platform for innovation ecosystems in local level, at the Aalto University Campus. The relationship between innovation and design, urban systems, policies and real estate development is poorly understood. With vast investments committed to the creation of new cities, urban expansion, and "innovation districts," it is imperative to move beyond traditional, formal, and static modes of urban planning and towards an evidence-based process focused on learning, creative human interaction and innovation – the human interaction scale.

The Otaniemi campus has emerged from a set of fixed standalone entities controlled by individual organizations and departments towards more open and accessible environment. The main design driver of the past, in terms of user orientation, has been the internal efficiency of each solution. Solutions were static and network structures deep. The core of the campus was designed by the recognized Finnish architect Alvar Aalto, and those buildings are protected and allow minimal changes in their physical appearance. However, working practices have changed dramatically since its original planning, resulting in large amounts of unused spaces. At the same time, there is a need for new environments to meet changing demands. In order to develop environments which are fostering value co-creation the concept and elements of social learning has been used as a framework for innovation capabilities of the given environment. It means that learning is the practices of communities as an issue of refining their practice and ensuring new generations of members. In the article, Social theory of learning [6] Etienne Wenger has identified concepts of belonging, becoming, sharing purpose and activities together as essential elements of human interaction as social learning.

1. *Learning as belonging, focus on community: a way of talking about the social configurations in which our enterprises are defined as worth pursuing and our participation is recognizable as competence.*
2. *Learning as becoming, focus on identity: a way of talking about how learning changes who we are and creates personal histories of becoming in the context of our communities.*
3. *Learning as experience, focus on meaning: a way of talking about our (changing) ability – individually and collectively – to experience our life and the world as meaningful.*
4. *Learning as doing, focus on practice: a way of talking about the shared historical and social resources, frameworks, and perspectives that can sustain mutual engagement in action [6].*

At the campus, learning becomes an issue of sustaining the interconnected communities of practice. [6] However, the utilization rate of most of the campus buildings has been low, on average around 30% of work hours. Thus, traditional real-estate models are best on control of given area very little sharing of resources were happening (Fig. 10).

The occupancy rate of typical campus buildings shows that most of the time, most of the spaces are underutilized and empty. In order to increase occupancy and utilization rates, a new logic was proposed and research projects established to support the development. Campus development has used SaaS as a case example of how to utilize its existing resources. A first SaaS solution was established in 2016, and a second one followed in 2017. These will be followed by additional establishments in 2019 and 2020 (Fig. 11).

By analyzing the existing network structures and the orientations of current resources at the campus, it was possible to develop a new, open and accessible campus strategy. Operand elements of the Campus as a Service platform case include institutional demand by the City of Espoo. Demand for resources to provide services for residents in Espoo, services like education, health care and sports. Aalto University is providing activities and processes for teaching and learning; teachers, professors,

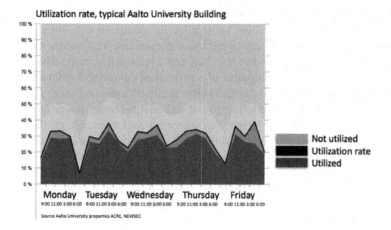

Fig. 10. The typical occupancy rate of one building at Aalto campus (TUAS building)

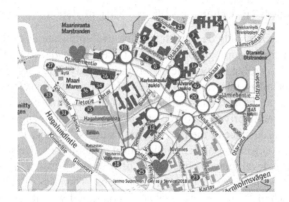

Fig. 11. Map of the resources that the first two schools use at the Otaniemi campus.

workshops connected to its innovation ecosystem. Operant resources provided by ACRE include university properties, with the university as the owner (or operator) of the resources. It typically has resources that are underutilized but accessible. By introducing the SaaS concept, where, in this particular case, a high school is creating value with a university, a new development strategy was also defined. By using the outcomes of research at the spatial and building levels and by identifying relevant stakeholders and operators, the Campus as a Service thinking starts to emerge.

The topic of this case study has been on the design of distributed systemic networks in the regeneration of local communities – a research on functionally and culturally diversified spatial design based on shared services and agent-based development. Instead of the normative planning scale approach to physical spaces, this research studies the presently acute emergent processes and interplay stemming from plot-, block- and building-level interaction to the community scale. The resolution of the study is higher, from building and areas to spaces and proximities. The research explores the ways in which the formal environment of institutional activities responds to the needs of its users and how to improve the competitive abilities of locations, encounters, innovations and employment in communities. This means not only mapping present needs and spaces but also building a responsible, responsive, sustainable long-term model for the development of a networked culture and environment. It also studies the dynamics between the short-term needs of users and other participants in design processes and the long-term cultural and environmental possibilities and turns this into a design tool. The study has increased understanding of the networked interaction between places, and the authors will create design tools for modelling this interaction toward innovating locations.

As a result, Campus as a service study has revealed the actual rate of accessibilities of resources at Aalto Campus. Traditional deep structures are difficult to utilize on service systems, in comparison to open and accessible resources in more shallow network structures. The Study also points out issues of social learning and importance of enabling environments for local innovation ecosystems.

4.4   City as a Service (Urban Level)/Case: City of Espoo

This section of the case study deals with the city level implications of utilizing city as a service platform for various public services. Cases of spatial, building and campus design were used to design a city-wide opportunities study. The City of Espoo has been a "living lab" for many interventions in the fields of education, care and well-being. Based on the Campus as a Service model, the City of Espoo has also started the process of establishing a public/private resource-operator function, utilizing a service platform developed as a consequence of the previous case studies. The city level case study also looked at the new expansion of the public transit system in the Helsinki metropolitan area. It tested the development opportunity of a school network at Espoo designed strategically around new metro transportation hubs. This was enabled by a service model where a school is defined as a network, connected with its environment, rather than an isolated production plant for teaching. Currently, institutions for education and health care have strategies for being more flexible, adaptable and effective. However, their operational environments are static, based on control and traditional management. There is a contradiction between the objectives of the operations and their environments. On a city scale, this seems to be the case, especially because of procurement and management models supporting standalone solutions that focus on internal efficiency.

The focus of the study was on procurement, management and service delivery, as well as organizing methods for public services. The procurement process itself is different in a service-based model in comparison to a product-based model, in terms of management, budget structure and service structures. Studies have been carried out mainly through comparative analyses between traditional and new models. While traditional city development processes are focused on proactive "pre-production" phase of cities, the service-based model is utilizing the "post-production" phase because of its adaptability and flexibility. In traditional model user preferences and demand are in focus preferably before the actual planning process is starting. Participatory design is an approach to design attempting to actively involve all stakeholders in the design process to help ensure the result meets their needs and is usable. The term is used a way of creating environments that meet better stakeholder needs. The difference on the service-oriented solution, that users could participate also after the initial design. This approach is defined as "post production" of cities (Fig. 12).

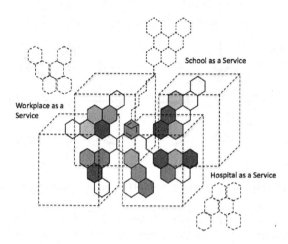

Fig. 12. City as a Service

As a result, analyses of City as a service model have pointed out the paradox between underutilized resources and existing demand for institutional service delivery. There are plenty of empty resources, but lack of accessibility and control over them. The current solution is to build more resources, instead of enabling more access to existing resources.

5 Conclusions

The traditional model for designing environments for service delivery is based on product-dominant logic, placing the main focus on operand resources, as physical resources operated by the actual organizations delivering services for users. In this approach, the focus is on tangible outcomes where value is embedded in the products. The approach is transactional, focusing on delivery of added value for users as subjects of service delivery. This common approach will lead to the consumption of resources and will cause cities to expand in order to obtain new resources. This model increases both investment and planning risk, relying mainly on the predictability of operational environments and on the needs of the institutions and users. This model, which could be called the product model, will also decrease areal prosperity by focusing on internal efficiency and the independence of resources, which will increase only the existence of resources rather than their use. The service-based "new" model focuses on value co-creation, where the approach is both relational and systemic and the focus is on processes and operant resources. This will create conditions where value is co-created with users and will encourage the effective utilization of the environment. The service-based approach will focus on environments as platforms for service delivery and the effective use of existing resources. This will allow innovations in the use of environments in more sustainable ways, utilizing already existing resources by changing the resolution of development from isolated entities to connected environments (Fig. 13).

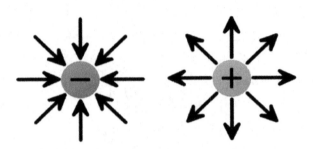

Fig. 13. Decreasing and increasing areal prosperity

An increase of areal prosperity means that service-oriented solutions could potentially optimize utilization and occupancy in close proximity to such a solution. It could enable more sustainable solutions for urban development. Eventually, within this paradigm shift, cities will be using more of what they already have, with denser usages, rather than expanding geographically and decreasing the utilization of existing resources.

As a summary, when analyzed physical environments as a service platforms certain characteristics are important. On the spatial level the openness of the solution, shallow network structure and perceivable resources will increase external effectiveness and utilization of resources. On building level solutions that are capable of utilizing also external resources, will enable more adaptable and flexible solutions. On campus (local) level, it is evident that traditional deep structures are difficult to utilize on service systems, in comparison to open and accessible resources in more shallow network structures. On city level the paradox between underutilized resources and existing demand could be addressed by innovation on usage patterns and increased accessibility to resources, rather than building new independent and isolated resources.

5.1   Service Platform Model for Institutional Service Delivery

The service platform model matches institutional demand and the accessible supply of resources. The platform model has already been utilized in various fields for commercial resource sharing. Institutional applications have not emerged so readily, seemingly because there are different issues of predictability, control and management in comparison to customer applications. Institutional service platforms should be based on the capabilities of translating demand from various operating systems to the supply side and vice versa. Such a system will benefit from machine learning capabilities, utilizing the potential of artificial intelligence for dynamic matching, leading to more optimized use of resources.

Service platform will be utilizing defined solution space which is based on availability of accessible resources with relevant choice architecture and analytics based on choices and solutions. It will eventually have an impact to the dynamics of local markets as well as to the planning processes and practices of cities.

5.2 Resource Operator Model for Service Oriented Urban Solutions

In the case of service delivery, new resource operations driven markets will potentially evolve. As the SaaS case example revealed, new competencies are needed. The existing model of school operations requires, in principle, operations for facility management, the delivery of teaching, human resources management and management to enable technologies and tools. The service-oriented model will potentially enable new markets to emerge for resource operations. Such an activity could be established as a public municipality owned organization, or as a private service company. Resource operations will allow more dynamic and flexible optimization and utilization of the environment's resources.

Resource operator model will potentially enable long-term planning by revealing a more predictable picture of available resources. On the organizational analyses framework, it will enable control of flexible resource utilization. A current example of a resource operator is existing in commercial malls, where the operator is managing the content, retailers, restaurants and other resources. The physical environment is equivalent to the service platform where the operator is balancing relevant mix of resources.

5.3 Procurement Model for Service Oriented Urban Solutions

While current models of procurement are, in many cases, optimized for management and investments of standalone entities, new models of procurement for service platforms are needed. With service-based models for platforms for institutional service delivery, the focus is on the network of resources rather than a predefined entity. Procurement will benefit from new methods and tools for analyzing various platform scenarios and their consequences in more sustainable city development socially, ecologically, financially and operationally.

The cost structure of service-oriented solution is usually different than in traditional independent "product" based model. This due to changing model of ownership and control. In the service-oriented model, institutions will need to redefine the core functions and assets they need to deliver the service. That requires the process of "asset mapping" and operational analyses, to evaluate what institutions already have and how they could be used. Eventually, this will lead to a new development for the requirements of the new procurement process.

5.4 Design Methodologies for Service Oriented Urban Solutions

Value co-creation is a focal point of service-based models. Current design and planning models are based on predictive methods for analyzing particular needs and demands. Participatory design tools are used to define design drivers for a specific project.

Understanding user needs beforehand is elementary in the purpose-driven process of producing independent environments based on product logic for service delivery. A new environmental design model is based on value co-creation and driven by the "customer journey." This approach enables the complementary processes of service design and service architecture. Service design focuses on activities and processes of interaction, identifying relevant touchpoints of interactions. Service architecture focuses on the conditions of value co-creation, enabling activities to be executed in flexible ways, not necessarily tied to one specific building or project.

Service design is representing the solution by illustrating all the essential components of the service, including physical elements, interactions, logical links and temporal sequences. It identifies sequences of actions and actors' roles in order to define the requirements for the service and its logical and organizational structure. Service architecture therefore is focusing on environments of value creation and is representing the solution by means of planning documents for actual interventions and constructions on the physical environment (Fig. 14).

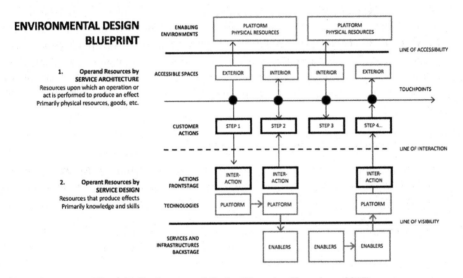

Fig. 14. Environmental design blueprint (Suominen 2017)

The environmental design blueprint combines aspects of service design and – architecture and focuses on value co-creation, enabling the use of service-oriented solutions and the utilization of more sustainable ways of using environments. The blueprint model combines activities and their environments into one framework and enables matchmaking between an organization's aims and its environments as operating systems. A focus on value co-creation should be seen in all layers of society and the urban environment. Value is created among individuals, organizations and networks in a given environment.

5.5   City as a Sustainable Service Platform

Currently, a definition of a "smart city" is that it uses different types of data collection sensors to supply information that is used to manage assets and resources efficiently. This includes data collected from citizens, devices and assets that is processed and analyzed to monitor and manage traffic and transportation and information systems, schools, libraries, hospitals and other community services. These "smart" technologies will enable smarter usages of a city. However, for smarter and more sustainable cities in the future, the innovation lies in usages. It is as important how cities are used as how they are being built. Cities are facing similar challenges in changing the logic of institutional service delivery than industrial organizations are facing by changing focus, cultures and processes, like illustrated in the article the transition from product to service in business markets [7].

Service model will enable cities utilizing existing resources in more sustainable ways increasing local prosperity and social cohesion by creating value together. This paper has presented a synthesis of ongoing research for a new model of service architecture for physical environments. This development has already had an impact in opening new markets, economic opportunities and technological innovations for urban service platform tools and operations. This study illustrates how the focus on internal efficiency or external effectiveness has its implications for physical environments and open structure is more open to external activities and effectiveness. Systemic solutions are decreasing planning and investment risk, enabling more sustainable development by utilization of available resources. Traditional deep network structures are difficult to utilize on service systems, in comparison to open and accessible resources in more shallow network structures. The city as a service model aims to solve the paradox between underutilized resources and existing demand by institutional service-oriented delivery solutions.

5.6   Next Steps

A new explanatory theory for empowering communities, crucially based not on areas or buildings but on dynamic relationships between people and the built environment, is needed. People utilize their environment not according to its physical characteristics but by recognizing familiar patterns – relationships. These relationships are based on space and use. There is a need for a usable theory of relationships and their controllable dynamics in spaces and communities. There is a need for the development of new spatial concepts and typologies that can accurately describe and positively guide the value creation of urban design for its users, and a need for new design methods and concepts to support the planning and design of more efficient, sustainable and valuable networked and innovation-producing places and communities for the future. As a consequence of case studies presented here a model of a campus where accessible indoor spaces are included in the community sphere are being developed. This requires more extensive and cross disciplinary research of service and operational models. New service platform for sustainable resource sharing for institutions is also being developed to enable city to become a service platform.

References

1. Lusch, R.F., Vargo, S.L.: Service-dominant logic as a foundation for building a general theory. In: The Service-Dominant Logic of Marketing: Dialog, Debate, and Directions (2006)
2. Quinn, R.E., Rohrbaugh, J.: A spatial model of effectiveness criteria: towards a competing values approach to organizational analysis. Manag. Sci. **29**(3), 363–377 (1983)
3. Hillier, B., Hanson, J.: The Social Logic of Space. Cambridge University Press, Cambridge (1984). ISBN 0521367840
4. Granovetter, M.: The strength of weak ties: a network theory revisited. Sociol. Theory **1**, 201–233 (1983). https://doi.org/10.2307/202051. JSTOR 202051
5. Blakstad, S., Hansen, G., Knudsen, W.: Methods and tools for evaluation of usability in buildings. CIB W111 Usability of Workplaces. Phase 2. CIB Report, Publication 316 International Council for Research and Innovation in Building and Construction CIB General Secretariat, The Netherlands (2008)
6. Wenger, E.: Communities of Practice: Learning, Meaning, and Identity. Cambridge University Press, Cambridge (1998). ISBN 978-0-521-66363-2
7. Jacob, F., Ulaga, W.: The transition from product to service in business markets: an agenda for academic inquiry. Ind. Mark. Manag. **37**(3), 247–253 (2008)

The Transition to a New University Campus as an Opportunity for the Urban Regeneration of the Former Milan Expo 2015 Areas

Paola Trapani[1(✉)], Luisa Collina[1], Barbara Camocini[1], Laura Daglio[2], and Martina Mazzarello[1]

[1] Design Department, Politecnico di Milano, Milan, Italy
{paola.trapani, luisa.collina, barbara.camocini,
martina.mazzarello}@polimi.it
[2] Department of Architecture, Built Environment and Construction Engineering,
Politecnico di Milano, Milan, Italy
laura.daglio@polimi.it

Abstract. In Milan, in the 1990s, the Ministry of Education and Research inaugurated the policy of opening new decentralised university campuses with a twofold aim: to relieve pressure on the central headquarters and, at the same time, restore functionality and liveliness to the suburban neighbourhoods, which have been affected in the last two decades by the decentralisation of industry. The paper presents a research work still in progress, carried out by a group of the Politecnico di Milano on behalf of the Università degli Studi di Milano, concerning the definition of the meta-project briefing for a new campus to be located on the ex EXPO 2015 area. Although the event was a formidable territorial marketing tool for the city, a new destination for the space occupied by the pavilions must be implemented for the future. The company that owns the area, Arexpo, decides to build a scientific and technological park in which public and private institutions must be housed, including the new campus for the science faculties of the university. The project appears as an opportunity to make a transition to a more environmentally, socially and economically sustainable educational and research site. The Politecnico di Milano research group uses methods at the crossroads between Strategic, Service and Spatial Design to immediately involve the various primary stakeholders in a collaborative project to create the guidelines that will be given to the architects in charge of planning the new site.

Keywords: Transition to sustainable futures · Case studies
Cross-cultural product and service design · Design for social development
Localization · Participatory design · Community engagement · Co-design
Capability development · Human experience sense-making
Multidisciplinary research · Learning & teaching environments
Higher education facilities · Meta-design

© Springer International Publishing AG, part of Springer Nature 2018
P.-L. P. Rau (Ed.): CCD 2018, LNCS 10912, pp. 391–408, 2018.
https://doi.org/10.1007/978-3-319-92252-2_31

1   Background

In Milan, a policy supported in the '90s by the Ministry of Universities and Research has favored the expansion of new university campuses towards the outskirts of the city. This has not only relieved the central headquarters congestion but has also saved some peripheral areas from an assured decline, triggering processes of urban regeneration for the benefit of the city as a whole. Examples include the transfer of the IULM to Romolo, the opening of the Bovisa Politecnico campus, a new Bocconi's campus at the former milk plant in Milan, and Unimi Bicocca (see Fig. 1).

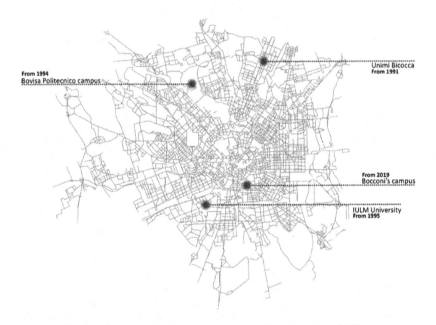

Fig. 1. Transferred university campuses within the city of Milan.

The paper presents the report of research work, currently in progress, carried out by a team of the Politecnico di Milano on behalf of the Università degli Studi di Milano with the aim of defining the meta-functional requirements of a new campus to be located in the area occupied by Expo 2015.

In 2015, Milan hosted the Universal Exposition with over 21 million visitors, 141 participating countries and about 5,000 events in 184 days [1]. Although Universal Expositions are a formidable tool of territorial marketing, once the curtain has fallen, often the areas occupied by the exhibition pavilions have not found new uses, taking the path of decline and abandonment, with consequent urban degradation [2].

To avoid the recurrence of this downward spiral, in 2011 the Lombardy Region had already established the company Arexpo to transfer the ownership of the areas of the universal exhibition. After the closing of the event, a first attempt to sell the space for public tender fails, creating a climate of distrust for the future.

Arexpo thus establishes that the area should host a Science and Technology Park based on similar sites around the world. There should be placed several facilities including Human Technopole, the most significant medical and biomedical research center in Italy, the Galeazzi hospital that also has a vocation for research and training, and the new campus for the scientific Faculties of the Università degli Studi di Milano.

The first step requires Arexpo to select a player in the international arena who can fulfill a double role: they not only should develop a feasible and robust master plan but should also be in charge of implementing it as the areas concessionaire for 99 years. Lendlease Italia wins the tender thanks to the proposition of a long-term vision rather than merely speculative which has been presented publicly in Milan in November 2017.

Established in 2000 as an Italian branch of the Australian corporate company, Lendlease Italia has already built in Milan CityLife (2007), the Armani hotel (2011), along with the hospitals of Brescia in Lombardy (2016). The master plan for Arexpo provides for the construction of a 440,000 square meters park whose environmental value increases the real estate value. Lendlease aims to design, finance, implement, and manage in the long term a complex urban regeneration project that has at its core an active and lively community. Therefore, public and private functions are integrated thanks to the requirement to assign a public use to the ground floor of all the private buildings in the area.

For Carlo Ratti, principal of the design studio that authored the master plan, it addresses five main design challenges:

- How to solve the link with the historic center of Milan?
- How to transform the "decumanum" that is the linear park that formed the backbone of Expo, into something new?
- How to create a shared ground capable of facilitating serendipitous encounters, which are a vital component of the contemporary way of working?
- How to transform the master plan into an open and flexible design platform?
- How to respect the DNA of Milan that is a living laboratory in Italy, whose mobility has historically developed around a network of canals and waterways?

Ratti claims that the master plan aspires to transcend the vision of the zoned city dear to Le Corbusier, indeed ordered and functional but arid, proposing mixed uses developments that rely on a digital infrastructure as a backbone of integration.

According to Andreas Kipar from Land, the studio in charge of the landscape design, the park has a vocation to food production, sport, health, and biodiversity. The *cardo* and the "*decumanum*" axes become the backbone of a system of squares disseminated through the park and the botanical gardens. Not only are the existing trees preserved, but also 3,000 new trees are planted to build pollination strips. Phyto-treatment plants purify the water canals. No fence is foreseen, to allow the around-the-clock fruition of the green area.

2 Diagnosing the Problem

In this context, about 150,000 square meters of the space should be used for the new campus to host the science faculties of the Università degli Studi di Milano. The plan is an opportunity to question the future ways of teaching, learning, conducting research and multidisciplinary collaboration. From the very beginning, the Università degli Studi di Milano involves the Politecnico di Milano as the consultant responsible of drafting a first version of the meta-design[1] briefing with the functional requirements, both qualitative and quantitative, addressed to the participants to the tender launched by Arexpo. The second version of the document, currently under development, contains more precise quantitative data to allow the winner of the tender, Lendlease, to estimate a realistic financing project.

After a first stage of data collection, including co-design workshops with representatives from different departments and students, site visits and interviews carried out at the current campus, benchmarking activities with recent international case studies, the present state of the art emerges clearly: most of the scientific branches of the Università degli Studi di Milano, at the moment scattered in existing structures, are no longer up to standard and need urgent redesign to modernize research laboratories and annexed facilities.

The core of the campus called "Città Studi" where most of the scientific disciplines are located was founded before the 1930s (See Fig. 2).

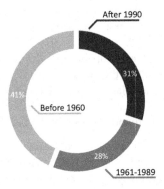

Fig. 2. Spaces classification by year of construction.

Moreover, it is clear that the zoning of the space, rigidly organized by the fields of scientific knowledge, has favored over the decades the consolidation of disciplinary silos and has hindered the collaboration and the sharing of equipment with serious repercussions also on the economic sustainability of the institution.

---

[1] In the section on methodology (see para. 6), we explain in greater detail what is meant by meta-design and participatory processes.

3 Identifying the Specific Opportunities

For the project team, the problem can be turned into the opportunity to progressively refine the needs expressed by different stakeholders (such as Departments and Programs' Committees) in relation to issues as diverse as prospect enrolments, recruitment of personnel, acquisition of new devices and instruments, activation of innovative teaching and research methods and collaborations, implementation of advanced organizational and management methods, services, ways of smart working, etc.

In any case, the underlying purpose of the Politecnico research group is not to enforce at this stage the most cutting-edge solutions for immediate adoption, but rather to create the conditions so that these innovations, if supported by the community affected, at any time could find implementation within the new structure.

The transition to a new location is seen as an ambitious opportunity to reorganize the complex system in a more sustainable way improving the lives of thousands of people. However, "transition" is not only meant literally as a move to a different location but it is also defined here as "a continuous process of societal change, where the character of society (or of one of its complex subsystem such as education) undergoes structural changes" [3]. In this second meaning, transitions usually impact the entire socio-technical system at hand[2] because they impact the whole set of required elements and their mutual relationships: institutional policies and regulations, infrastructures, technology, cultural meanings, customs and habits, markets, maintenance networks and supply chains. Adopting a perspective at the socio-technical system level invites to sit at the same table a vast range of stakeholders: in this case, university's managers, staff and students, private investors, suppliers, citizens' groups and associations, etc. Systemic innovation is therefore inherently multi-actor, multi-factor, multi-level, highly uncertain, and long-term [3].

In this perspective, education can be considered as a societal function that requires a cluster of services and products for its implementation. According to UNEP (2002), "Product Service Systems (PSS from now on) are a particular type of value proposition that shifts the business focus from the proposition of (physical) products alone, to the offer of a bundle of products and services that are jointly capable of satisfying a particular customer demand" [3]. Of course, we must broaden our idea of campus not only as a physical compound scattered through buildings and facilities but also as the sum of all daily functions it accommodates. The starting assumption is that the campus is essentially a network in a continuous evolution of nodes that aggregate and dissolve in response to opportunities for collaboration and interaction [4], which should be supported by the flexible and efficient physical arrangement.

Applying this concept to our transitioning demographic group with impelling and always changing education and research needs, we could envisage alternative education and research production and consumption models, which shift the concept of 'equipment' or 'space unit' from something privately owned by a given department to a complex PSS that should be combined with social interactions experiments and

---

[2] We refer to education as an example of a complex socio-technical system, but the same could apply to housing, healthcare, mobility, etc.

distributed economies. For instance, it should be possible to access the tools sterilization service without having to take charge and manage a sterilization room for the exclusive use of the department.

A PSS framework is the only promising of steering toward the campus sustainability which is always environmental, social, and financial at the same time [5], and can do so at the required scale and pace.

The starting assumption is that the campus should be considered as a common good [6] organized on a model of "functional economy" [7]: most of its functions are accessible without the burden of managing privately owned devices. This model regulates the availability of space and equipment, organized in intelligent product/service systems with different access rights according to user profiles. Booking workstations, equipment, books, rooms, thinking-pods is possible on a variable time basis (per hour, day, week, month, semester, etc.) and in different ways: free of charge (for students, teachers, and university staff), on-demand or on contract for external stakeholders.

Digital platforms make the access to assets transparent and independent of their management and provide real-time data on the operating conditions of the systems.

4   Research Aim

The objective of the research is to investigate how interactive tools borrowed from spatial, service, and strategic design can contribute not only to the collection of data and requirements, but also to actively involve stakeholders at an early stage of the meta-design brief of a contemporary integrated campus.

5   Research Objectives

The research aim looks more attainable when broken down as follows:

- Reviewing recent literature on design methods and tools within three areas:
  - "Strategic Design": the intention is to cross methods and tools of spatial and service design to trace a third path suitable to capture the most relevant interactions, whether already in place or desired, to inform the set of spatial guidelines.
  - "Participatory Design": a co-design framework is required to gain experiential insights and highlight critical issues about daily practices and behavioral patterns on campus;
  - "Spatial Analysis": methods and tools in this field can afford an in-depth understanding of the settlement's physical requirements to improve its rationalization and efficiency;
- Conceiving and implementing bespoke design tools for co-design workshops addressed to primary users and stakeholders.
- Running the workshops.
- Understanding and assessing the attendants' experience of co-designing as non-professional designers.

The adopted hybrid service/spatial design approach looks promising to dissolve the present physical separation between faculties and researchers, which has generated over the years rigid disciplinary silos and self-referential, narrow-minded attitudes to the detriment of innovation and research advancements.

6   Research Methodology

The research team adopted a "constructivist" methodology, involving a continuous interaction with the Executive Team and the different demographic groups of the campus community. According to this worldview, the reality is a social construction, and it's meaning is the product of the endless negotiation between participants' understanding and sense. Shading light on judgments and believes is crucial when shaping a complex artifact like "an integrated campus," which is not a given object of the natural world.

From the constructivist methodology derive the "user-centered methods" employed to address a wide range of participants categories that use the campus facilities on a daily basis. The research team trusts that these methods can help accompanying the community during the delicate transition to the new settlement, seizing the opportunity to question the current situation and to envisage new synergies, working methods, and spaces organization.

The next paragraphs describe the data collection procedures and methods used in this investigation to acquire information from the different demographic categories. Generally speaking, we can conclude that the participants become aware of the fragmented nature and continuously changing layout of the present campus, which has proliferated out of control and rational planning over the years also due to the need for maximum exploitation of the historical assets.

The information is complemented with the analysis of case studies from "desk research," undertaken with the aim of keeping an open view on the most cutting-edge research and best practices at the international level.

The whole process is based on a practical and productive "communication system," which allows at each stage the research team to share with participants the information processed, to write the meta-design brief and at the same time build a shared mental model of it.

The research team is leading a process of "knowledge transfer" aiming at transforming users into "experts of their experiences" [8]. On the other side, designers donning the hat of facilitators are transformed into co-designers.

A cross-disciplinary approach is valued for its ability to foster participation, empowerment, transparency, and accountability [9], either by improving the efficiency of public services and public policies or promoting critical social goals such as citizen participation and democracy [10].

6.1   Interviews with the Executive Team

In the initial phase of the research, a series of interviews to the Executive Team of the Università degli Studi consisting of the General Manager, the Rector, and the Property

Manager, was carried out to define three main categories of spaces and to identify a hierarchy between them. "Core spaces" have been established as those that host the main functions, namely didactic spaces (e.g., classrooms and educational laboratories), departmental spaces (e.g., research laboratories and offices/studios), the library, research spaces, and offices. "Essential Ancillary Spaces" are those that accommodate functions not necessary but of important support to the good functionality of the campus. Finally, "Supplementary Ancillary Spaces" spaces complete the main infrastructure, whose development depends on the generated induced activity.

Moreover, the interview with the Property Manager provided the initial set of qualitative and quantitative data on those categories.

The relationships that emerged between those categories of spaces inform the Arexpo master plan, both at the campus and the urban scale. They are represented in a diagram (see Fig. 3) included in an illustrative report, which has been presented to the Departments representatives and, in a second step, to the Academic Senate. This first report has been published on the Università degli Studi website and forwarded to Arexpo before the tender.

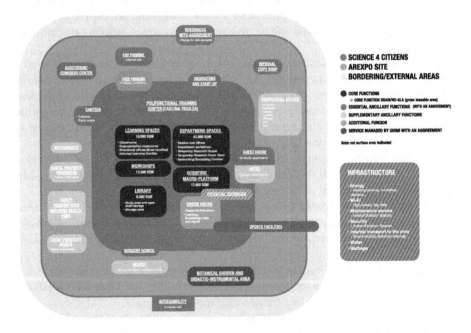

Fig. 3. The diagram of the different functions.

6.2   Students Focus Groups

Data are also collected from students. The first meeting takes place at the beginning of July 2017 (see Fig. 4).

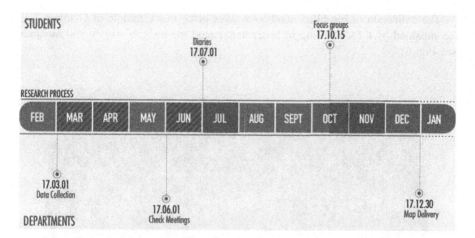

Fig. 4. Research activities timeline.

The research team and the General Manager introduce the state of the art and the objectives of the data survey to twelve faculties representatives, proposing the use of a couple of tools: a "diary" (see Fig. 5) is distributed to each of them to record activities and the relative space-use during the day, along with interviews with other students.

Fig. 5. Students' diaries.

The collection of the filled notebooks takes place in the middle of October 2017, accompanied by a focus group to better understand the insights weight and hierarchy (see Fig. 6).

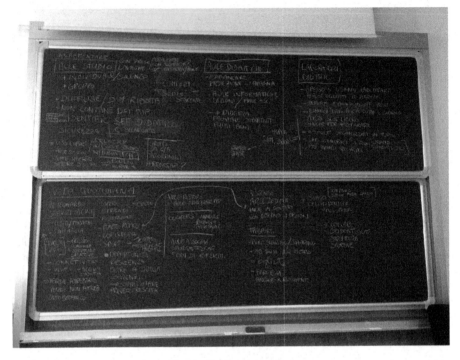

Fig. 6. Students' insights.

The second tool is a password-protected *Pinterest page* to document issues such as the lack of services or space or, on the contrary, to propose case studies or best practices. Being online, this tool has the potential of reaching out a more extensive range of students, including those who are currently studying abroad. Unfortunately, despite the expectations, this tool fails to be successful perhaps due to the requirement to sign up or the unfamiliarity of students in scientific disciplines.

6.3   Co-design Workshops with the Research Departments

The research team acts as the facilitator to stimulate a participatory process of rationalization of activities and spaces within the research laboratories in each department. The proposed design challenge at this stage is to spot any opportunity for micro-aggregations, namely the organization of shared areas and activities between related departments, or their arrangement within the macro-platform of shared infrastructures.

In March 2017 starts the data collection to design the deck of cards. Charts for quantitative data collection are at first presented to the participants during a public meeting and then forwarded by Property Management to each department delegate. After finalizing the deck of cards, the method for their use is explained to departmental directors during a meeting chaired by the Executive Team. Subsequently, a calendar of appointments is organized with working bees consisting of two or three departments with similar themes or research methods. The result of this first round of workshops is the creation of an initial draft of functions and aggregations diagram. In a second round, the departments' representatives finalize it autonomously, this time with the collaboration of colleagues from very different specializations. The purpose is to conceive a robust map of spaces and functions (see Fig. 7) more consistent with reality.

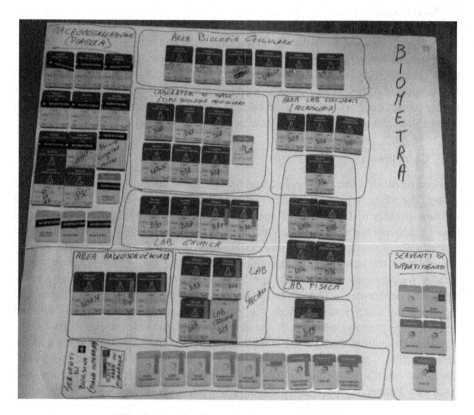

Fig. 7. Sample of a map of spaces and functions.

On this occasion, forms to collect and combine quantitative and qualitative data on surfaces, equipment, and requirements about the spaces indicated on the maps are also distributed. The overall process requires seven meetings with 14 departments throughout June 2017.

The deadline for the delivery of the refined maps is set up in September 2017. Each department forwards to the Property Management team a photo of their map, along with the related quantitative data sheets. The research team then begins processing the visualization graphs, indicating the shared spaces or services between departments and envisaging the infrastructure macro-platform. The contents of these revised maps are verified through a new calendar of meetings with each department in November/December 2017. During a joint meeting, the general outline is eventually presented without quantitative data to highlight the qualitative value of the suggested micro and macro-aggregations.

We recall here that the original aim is to guide the campus community in a delicate process of questioning the current status and imagining collaboratively viable and desirable configurations for the future.

7   Deliverables

According to the consecutive steps of the research, and the related goals, different typologies of deliverables were produced including graphics, reports, and presentations. The primary challenge has been that of finding a trade-off between the abstractions of a meta-design brief that should leave a certain degree of freedom for further project developments, and the need to accurately define, describe and visualize the qualitative and quantitative requirements of the new campus.

7.1   Guidelines 1.0

The first report was part of a more comprehensive set of documents for the master plan tender. Therefore, its purpose is merely that of determining the main characteristics of the new campus and its surroundings. The guidelines convey data and information through different methods including texts, graphics, drawings, and pictures. The report adopts a performance-based approach and includes a general statement of the primary objectives of the new complex regarding activities and infrastructures along with a detailed requirements description at the urban and campus scale. The overall draft of the future settlement is the result of both bottom-up participatory processes and top-down decisions resulting from the present situation. The document lists and describes the primary functions of the campus and their dimensioning according to standards developed through the comparison between the current facilities and the benchmarking with similar complexes at an international scale. "Core Functions" which are strictly part of the campus (directly managed by the state university) and "Ancillary Functions" (outsourced or externally offered) distinguished in "Essential" or "Supplementary" are singled out also to highlight the diverse management frameworks and ownership.

A large number of case studies collected are classified and inserted as images to synthetically illustrate the characteristics of the different internal and external typologies of spaces required.

Moreover, being the final positioning of the campus a topic of the tender, the guidelines include the morpho-typological exploration of three different arrangements within the Expo site (see Fig. 8) to evaluate the related planning indexes and the core functions areas. This section of the document is delivered with the aid of an external architectural firm as a consultant.

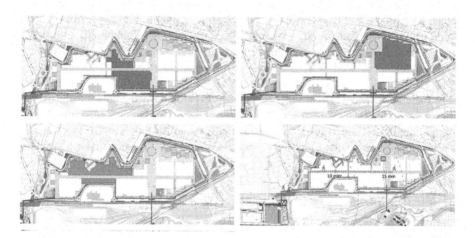

Fig. 8. The morpho-typological exploration of three different arrangements within the Expo site

As a result of the participatory process, a more thorough description of specific research facilities is added as attachments to the report, edited by the staff representatives.

Finally, a diagram (see Fig. 3) shows the different levels of correlation between the campus and the urban context regarding accessibility, integration, and proximity.

Concentric areas around a central polarity with the Core Functions of the campus hub appear distinctly in the chart. Proceeding outwardly, the Essential Ancillary Functions are not directly related to the campus' mission but are of great importance to the functionality and sustainability of the project. Finally, Supplementary Ancillary Functions allow the completion of the primary infrastructure, whose development depends on the generated benefit and the neighborhood dynamism. The diagram is integrated with quantitative information about spaces and users, retrieved from sector-specific studies and survey data on existing and required size. Essential Ancillary Functions (e.g. dining, residences, etc.) and Supplementary Ancillary Functions (e.g. catering, shopping malls, etc.) can be located either within the campus buildings, or within the EXPO 2015 area or in the neighbourhood, favouring the concept of an urban integrated campus that guarantees the site permeability and the multi-functionality of the complex.

7.2   Guidelines 2.0

The second report contains the breakdown and analysis of the Core Functions, to be used for the concept design of the complex, once the contract will be awarded and the campus site defined. The guidelines, still under development, include information on the spaces for education and research, particularly stressing on the primary goal of flexibility required from a rapidly changing environment. In particular, the research facilities are extensively addressed through the gathering and organization of the results of the participatory process.

The main challenge of the document is to link and translate the language, activities, behaviors, and even idiosyncrasies of the scientific community into a synthetic architectural brief addressed to the architects. Diagrams provide a communication device understandable both by the participants particularly eager to check their desiderata and by the architects in need of synthesis and an information selection.

Single diagrams (see Fig. 9), one for each Department, show the lists of labs and related ancillary spaces. Highlighted are the shared facilities used simultaneously with other departments. Hatched areas signal the possible positioning on underground levels with neither direct natural light nor ventilation. Colored dots identify the typologies of spaces according to structural and services requirements. Finally, the department's activities located in the shared research facility, which hosts cutting-edge equipment and instruments, are detailed.

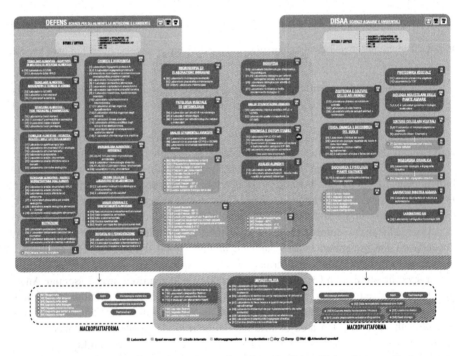

Fig. 9. Sample of two departments that share facilities (Color figure online)

A summary diagram shows the proximity relationships between departments suitable for sharing space. A different set of charts has also been developed for the breakdown and analysis of an advanced research platform, which includes completely different areas and facilities.

Finally, the guidelines include tables to classify and quantify the different research spaces according to construction characteristics. No subdivision among the departments is shown to allow for the maximum flexibility considering the time gap between the construction phase and possible future changes. Consequently, the approach pinpoints the goal of a "loose-fit" architecture [11], able to accommodate future reorganization of the layout with a reduced amount of work, energy, and resources, thus pursuing environmental and economic sustainability objectives.

8   Research Impact and Recommendations

To measure the effect of the transition to a new campus, we provide some figures about the demographics affected.

On average, about 12,000–13,000 people per day are present on campus, with a reduction during the summer break, particularly evident in August. The group includes teaching staff, administrative, technical staff, students, research fellows and doctoral candidates, maintenance staff, and external visitors (researchers, teachers from other universities, attendants of conferences, meetings, recruitment procedures, etc.).

The current average number of students per month is 11,000 (excluding August), and the average number of staff from Monday to Friday is 80% of the total number of employees (July - 40%, August - 80%).

A trends analysis of enrolments, associated with the placement data of the various disciplinary areas, suggests an increase of between 10 and 15% in the number of enrolments due to the higher attractiveness of a new campus. Therefore, the estimated student population can rise to 20,000.

Given the massive impact of the campus move, we include some recommendations to the primary stakeholders of the new campus project based on the insights that the Politecnico team has gained over these months of data collection, analysis, and development of the meta-design briefing.

The new campus can be an opportunity to conceive a new urban organism [12] local and global, physical and virtual, able to use resources efficiently and regenerate the surroundings thanks to some essential characteristics.

The Flexibility of Spaces (Short, Medium and Long-Term). Current innovation trends in teaching, research and work organization in general, as well as the always changing needs of the university, make it necessary to adopt design criteria that are highly flexible from several points of view:

- "Structure." It should be considered choosing and setting up a structural grid suitable for different uses (e.g. for vast educational spaces, laboratories, and studios).
- "Construction." Technical equipment must be inspectable, easily expandable and integrable through advanced initial predispositions and scalable spaces. Mobile walls and staircases, demountable and modular counter-walls and false-ceilings, mobile lighting systems, etc. should make space always reconfigurable.
- "Distribution and space." The adoption of suitable plots shapes and depths should allow the variation of spatial configurations, both as departments' extensions and as

a functional destination. The different types of spaces should be reversible both in the short term (e.g., switching from a dining space to a study space at certain times of the day) and in the long term (e.g., from workshops to studios or vice versa in different months or semesters). Over time, volumetric expansions should be feasible to accommodate future needs.

Hybridization of Functions. The styles of production and access to knowledge are constantly evolving under the influence of technological innovation and the possibility of creating "intelligent" assets thanks to the Internet of Things [13]. The campus is no longer only a place of production and access to knowledge, but also a place for meeting, individual and group study, participation in continuous training courses, cultural and sporting events, exhibitions, etc. For some out-of-home students and teachers is even the place of residence. This hybridization is reflected in the space organization and the composition of a varied schedule of around-the-clock activities, which minimize the under-use of assets.

Accessibility. If the management model is that of a functional economy, then it is necessary to map all campus functions and assign a rating relative to the degree of accessibility according to different user profiles, different activity calendars, and forms of payment.

Sustainability. Maintaining a common over time requires the adoption of a sustainable management model, which is by definition complex and multifactorial. A robust framework is not limited to ensuring the economic and technological sustainability of the campus but also includes the environmental and social sustainability. The window of opportunity is already limited, as the restoration of natural resources of the planet occurs at a much slower rate than their current consumption [14].

A Place of Collective Design. A campus is by definition the place of multidisciplinary knowledge. If the future of research and teaching is oriented towards interdisciplinary interaction increasingly precocious and pervasive, then the campus can be an excellent collaborative platform complemented by the proper infrastructure: the scientific macro-platform, the library, gardens, and greenhouses, etc. The management model of the collaborative platform aims to leverage the different competencies within the university to respond to the opportunities of research as they arise.

Recommendation #2 Addressed to the Management Team. New PSS models are always radical innovations, which generally fail if exposed unprotected to the main-stream dynamics. Therefore, it is crucial to let those experiments develop and mature inside intentional niche that can function as 'incubation pods' providing the required environmental condition: e.g., the presence of dedicated strategic investments, etc. The pod is a ring-fenced environment where all relevant stakeholders can participate to a process of social learning not limited to the technical aspects but also including new practices and culture, innovative policies and regulations, financial instruments, and legal bodies.

The scaling up process happens according to a constant pattern: at the early stage this social learning effort is erratic and scattered in many directions: trial-and-error attempts are subject to a great deal of uncertainty about design, and this often leads to dead-end paths. Repeated experimentation and interactions between the niche actors, often under the tutoring of experienced 'social heroes' [15], may result into the establishment of a broader community of actors who exchange experience and failures, methods, tools, and best practices.

Gradually, radical innovations percolate into a dominant design gaining momentum and taking advantage of unique opportunity windows. Once the change breaks through into the mainstream ways of doing, the existing regime is seriously threatened, and the new scheme may lead to broader landscape developments [3].

Recommendation #3 Addressed to Teachers, Researchers, and Students. The demographic population directly involved in the transition to the new campus is ultimately the collective subject that can determine its outcome.

The decision to participate in co-design activities, initially perceived by some attendants as a childish game, and the following collaborative development of the meta-requisites of the new campus has paved the way for a new attitude and posture to research and collaboration.

Considering that the participants did not have a background in Design, being all academic from scientific disciplines, it is remarkable the prompt adoption of the proposed methods and tools to make the conversation meaningful, clear of misunderstandings, possible hidden agendas, and even rivalries.

The open discussion and rethinking of the research methods and practices led to the establishment of new partnerships and activities that can take advantage of the equipment's concentration in a macro-platform characterized by highly specialized areas.

It is recommended that this new mindset be maintained in the future, not only during the construction phase of the new campus but also during the relocation and final settlement.

"Living in and through transitional times calls for self-reflection and new ways of 'being' in the world. Fundamental change is often the result of a shift in mindset or worldview that leads to different ways of interacting with others. Our individual and collective mindsets represent the beliefs, values, assumptions, and expectations formed by our individual experiences, cultural norms, religious and spiritual beliefs and the socioeconomic and political paradigms to which we subscribe [16].

References

1. Expo (2015). http://www.expo2015.org/rivivi-expo/. Accessed 20 Feb 2018
2. Ordine degli architetti, pianificatori, paesaggisti e conservatori della città di Milano, http://www.ordinearchitetti.mi.it/en/notizie/dettaglio/862. Accessed 20 Feb 2018
3. Ceschin, F.: Sustainable Product-Service Systems: Between Strategic Design and Transition Studies, Kindle edn. Springer International Publishing, Heidelberg (2014). https://doi.org/10.1007/978-3-319-03795-0
4. Amelar, S.: Taking down the walls. Dialogue n.30 (2016). https://www.gensler.com/research-insight/publications/dialogue/30/taking-down-the-walls. Accessed 20 Feb 2018
5. United Nations General Assembly, Resolution adopted by the General Assembly, 2005 World Summit Outcome, 60th edn, 38 p. United Nations Millennium Declaration (2005)

6. Ostrom, E.: Governing the Commons: The Evolution of Institutions for Collective Action. Cambridge University Press, Cambridge (1990)
7. Stahel, W.R.: The functional economy: cultural and organizational change. In: Richards, D. J. (ed.) The Industrial Green Game. National Academy Press, Washington DC (1997)
8. Visser, F.S., Stappers, P.J., van der Lugt, R., Sanders, E.B.-N.: Contextmapping: experiences from practice. In: CoDesign, vol. 1, no. 2, pp. 119–149 (2005)
9. Bason, C.: Leading Public Sector Innovation: Co-creating for a Better Society. Policy Press, Bristol (2010)
10. Pestoff, V.: Innovations in public services: co-production and new public governance in Europe. In: Towards Peer Production in Public Services: Cases from Finland, pp. 13–33. School of Art, Design and Architecture, Aalto University, Helsinki (2012)
11. Marmot, A.: Educational Innovation through Building Adaptation. Archit. Des. **87**, 96–105 (2017)
12. Ferri, G.: New Urban Body, Exhibition, Triennale di Milano, Milano (2017). http://www.newurbanbody.it/. Accessed 20 Feb 2018
13. Ellen MacArthur Foundation: Toward the Circular Economy: Opportunities for the Consumer Goods Sector (2013). http://www.ellenmacarthurfoundation.org/business/reports/ce2013. Accessed 20 Jan 2018
14. Evans, S., Bergendahl, M.N., Gregory, M., Ryan, C.: Towards a Sustainable Industrial System. With Recommendations for Educations, Research. Industry and Policy. University of Cambridge, Cambridge (2008)
15. Manzini, E.: Design, When Everybody Design. MIT Press, Cambridge (2015)
16. Irwin, T., Kossof, G., Tonkinwise, C., Scupelli, P.: Transition Design. Carnegie Mellon University, Pittsburgh (2015)

Bridge the Physical and Virtual Design for Hutongs - Creative Design Supports Hutongs Community Participation

Huan Wang and Zhiyong Fu$^{(\boxtimes)}$

Tsinghua University, Beijing 100084, China
huanwangre@gmail.com, fuzhiyong@tsinghua.edu.cn

Abstract. In the context of the urban renovation process, hutong community has become the focus of creative design in Beijing, and there have been practical cases of hutongs that can improve public participation and accessibility for the city. By collecting the performance of hutong renovated instances in physical space, virtual network, and participating public reflection, this paper analyses the influence of creative design factors on public participation. The result shows that the combination of the physical and virtual design, primarily working on the facade of the street-facing buildings, and the integrated use of the community platform, are most conducive to incremental public participation. The research combed the mode of creative design support hutong involvement and updating, rising that bridge the innovative design in physical and virtual dimensions is a potential promotion to the sustainable renewal of hutong in the urban renovation.

Keywords: Creative design · Hutong · Community participation
Physical space · Virtual network platform

1 Introduction

As a precious heritage of Beijing's traditional neighborhoods, hutong (or called alley) developed in the Yuan Dynasty of the early capital. At the end of the feudal period ended in the Qing Dynasty, Beijing had 2076 alleyways, of which 978 ones directly nominated as Hutongs. Hutong is the dispensable east-west direction street next to the main road, direct access to every household, as the end of the urban space practice, forming an integrated capital transportation system and be preserved so far [1]. Hutong brings together diversiform aspects of civic life and opens to the public in the city directly. It has been transformed into a community in the context of urban development to better adapt to urban life [2].

Hutong is the traditional urban space with such features as brief structure, flexible transformation, various design perspectives and the public participating in the characteristics. Based on having apparent advantages of culture demonstration, entirely a few renovated hutongs have been redesigned new appearance with the creative surfaces, which inspired multiple public activities (Fig. 1). At the same time, the general social networking platform supported by information technologies in recent years has

© Springer International Publishing AG, part of Springer Nature 2018
P.-L. P. Rau (Ed.): CCD 2018, LNCS 10912, pp. 409–420, 2018.
https://doi.org/10.1007/978-3-319-92252-2_32

creatively enabled information transfer across boundaries of entities and has also played a significant role in stimulating more possibilities of hutongs. It is this creative design works of physical and virtual from two dimensions' perspective that transforms the hutong from the negative isolated space into an actively motivated area.

Fig. 1. Photos of physical design and virtual design for Yangmeizhu Xiejie (Hutong) in Beijing. (Public participating activities (left), renovated street appearance (middle), a street-facing building is being rebuilt (right).

"Creative City" has become one of the vital evaluation in current international metropolis development, so does creative design also have a better practice platform in a variety of cities [3]. During more than 20 years of innovative exploration, the original design of hutong in Beijing has developed from the space of physical dimension such as hutong streets and buildings to the complex integrating physical architecture space and virtual network community space under the residential community, carrying abundant, diverse public activities to support community development [4]. At this point, it is necessary to understand and explain interactions and supportive effectiveness, through these three dimensions, physical space, virtual network and community public participation, to provide a concrete guideline approach to creative design for hutong.

2   Background

"I do not know who opened the first head; the street wall has dug a hole and used as a shop. Later, more and more people dig holes, or simply remove the entire gable." [5]

———*Mr. Zhang, a deller in Nanluogu Xiang*

The community renovation of Nanluogu Xiang (or Nanluogu Lane) is a well-known case of the Hutong street innovation and reuse practice. As one of the oldest hutongs in Beijing, Nanluogu Xiang was initially formed in the Yuan dynasty more than 700 years ago. Hutong extends from north to south about one-kilometer-long to both sides of the main street, symmetrically distributing eight hutongs and retaining the original structure [6]. Having been preserved entirely for hundreds of year, Nanluogu Xiang began to expose the signs of a commercial with the tendency of Shichahai Bars Street development. Due to its rich culture and distinctive geographical advantages, Nanluogu Xiang quickly became a fashionable business district. Over commercial development led to confusion in the status of "pastel-style," even though locals seldom stayed in hutongs, let alone participate in community activities. The shops form the new surface of hutongs, but they have lost the humanistic perspective of Beijing's unique civic culture.

However, we see another scene from Yangmeizhu Xiejie:

> *"Citizen-centered, organic renewal, multiple subjects, joint participation ...... Yangmeizhu Xiejie is gentle and rational explored, has been widely recognized by the world, as one of the landmark areas in Dashilar. So that Dashilar also was named the 18 promising designs community in the world." [7]*

——www.gov.cn

Compared with Nanluogu Xiang, Yangmeizhu Xiejie represents a constructive reflection of the creative design supporting hutong renovation. Since 2013, Yangmeizhu Xiejie has been the earliest to start retreating in the Dashilar area, with 529 relocated out of 1700 residents. The remaining 1,171 residents are scattered in various large residential complexes to maintain the living atmosphere of local life. Following many creative designs for community life and activities, such as the transformation of the old courtyard house called "Courtyard House Plugin en Masse II", the implantation of miniature gallery and library named "Micro-Yuan'er" experiment, and also the annual "International Design Week" to display the latest creative design. On the one hand, Yangmeizhu Xiejie Organic Renew project planned a transformation of the retreated space into public community activities area and encouraged the creative cultural industries to use and redesign the traditional street space. On the other hand, the project provides an online platform for innovative information dissemination and promotion of public recognition and participation in community activities. To date, Yangmeizhu Xiejie has practiced six creative courtyard designs, launched five online community platforms and regularly released various public participation activities such as films, hand-made works, and exhibitions. This exploration of organic renewal mode, linking the physical space and virtual space of hutong, promoting the communication of residents and visitors, demonstrating Beijing culture [8]. It has become a model for the participatory community, and as the leading event area of Beijing International Design Week for many years, has been regarded as Beijing's trendiest hutong.

In fact, not only are Beijing's hutongs such as Yangmeizhu Xiejie, Beiluogu Xiang, Yandai Xiejie, Qianliang Hutong and Fangjia Hutong etc, quite a few cases have creatively designed in communities based on street-based architecture and online platform under the premise of essential hutong remodeling to support community public participation, which could be sufficient experience for further design. It can reach an argument that creative design for hutong aims to not only the street-facing space, including buildings, streets, and facilities but also to extending the benefits from virtual network space under digital media technology because of its active unlimited communication of specific people, area, and activities [9]. Furthermore, it is suggested that the creative design for hutong rebuilding can practically improve the public participation, transform old communities into ongoing vitality units.

On this basis, this paper aims to analyze how creative design support hutongs community public participation through physical and virtual dimensions in the context of urban renovation. By capturing the data indicating the way of hutong creative design and reflection of public participating from practical cases investigation, this research explains the dominant design factors and design approach. Combined with the participating reflection to analyze the relationship between the design factors and influence, to derive the mode of creative design of the participatory community.

3   Challenges and Approaches

For the single pattern and flexible adjustment methods, hutong has formed a complex community synthesis through spontaneous or planned renovation process in response to the needs of contemporary open space [10]. The challenges of this paper come from reasonable quantification of design factors, as while the analysis the participation brought by the creative design of hutong and carry out the overlay analysis with the related factors as the link:

How to Define Creative Design? How to Distinguish it from the Primary Renovation of Hutongs?
Most hutongs have undergone rebuilding streets, facilities, and walls, no doubt presenting a neat appearance. From the view of creative design, it is common that design works focus on creating new functional possibilities and visual feelings to attract the public to enter or contact with each other and thereby stimulate the vitality of this space. Therefore, there is a general visual and functional breakthrough. In the face of urban renovation program of hutongs, which tends to be shabby and outdated, the creative design of this study mainly determined by three conditions: firstly, whether the original residential functions transformed into the tasks required by the new contemporary urban life or the introduction of the new format. Secondly, for the cases whether the original constructive form is expressed by using new materials and technologies, whether the space enclosed by the supposed courtyard is broken up and reorganized. Finally, whether we can find the combination of contemporary virtual online resources effectively enhances community engagement.

How to Analysis Physical and Virtual Space Design Factors? How to Distinguish it from the Necessary Renovation of Hutongs?
This paper capture, screen and sort the data from a human perspective and summarize it as a spatial-based data analysis system, including data on the physical construction, virtual network data and related participatory activities reflection.

Among them, the physical space data from the hutongs street surface and street-facing buildings covering hutong community's public space. Construction obtains the data for the street-facing buildings because of the variability between scale, function and aesthetic: Street-facing Facades, which are primarily enclosing, Front-yard, which is the front-facing semi-open part and Building Signboard, which is attached on the front surface [12] (Fig. 4). Virtual data includes hutong space-based network platform, such as Douban [18], WeChat [19] and Sina Weibo [20]. Subjects should consist of both physical and virtual data, while the virtual community data situation is entirely out understanding, shows the distinguished contribution of creative design.

How to Quantify the Influence of Creative Design to Participation from Community Physical and Virtual Dimension?
Beijing Hutong renovation cases have a higher starting point for the renovation and have conducted creative design and increased community participation in the case of the work experience at various times, while they into activities have social effects vary considerably, the universality of the platform is also different. As varies social and environmental factors could become the resource, cultural conservation is a very complicated system, as well as cultural engagement [15]. Therefore, taking the total amount from the beginning of the creative design work until now, then quantified as the annual average, the number of reviewers and the number of participants as the community participation reflection data, besides researching community social platforms combined with the score. That can be the more realistic description of the overall vitality.

The trend of urban renewal construction has been unstoppable. The development is both an opportunity and a challenge [14]. This research tries to analyze the effect of creative design on the hutong renovation and reformation by investigation of practical project cases, to define and explain creative design factors of physical and virtual public space and how they work, to discuss the mode of the creative design supporting hutong community participation.

4 Data Characteristics

According to the above description, the cases selection assessments are:

(a) The projects should be hutong-centered creative design in the context of urban renovation for public space, involving multi-dimensional creative design work from the architectural space, street facilities, and digital media network platform.

(b) The projects are located in the Dongcheng and Xicheng District of Beijing inner city, maintaining the traditional scale and spatial characteristics. Following the rules of the hutong when it first set up, which is the width of street is six steps (about 9.3 m), and named after three symbols including Hutong, Xeijie and Xiang.

(c) The projects should be conducted in Douban Tongcheng [18], Sina Weibo [19], WeChat Official Accounts (app) [20], Dianping [21] and the internationally accepted TripAdvisor [17], where ratings and activity rankings and the number of independent entities are substantial.

(d) These projects have undergone the creative design work. Those are accepted as examples of hutong practices that provide right space for innovative design, such as Ju'er hutong [11].

The cases researched in this paper include Yangmeizhu Xiejie, Ju'er Hutong, Nanluogu Xiang, Beiluogu Xiang, Yandai Xeijie, Wudaoying Hutong, Qianliang Hutong, Shijia Hutong, Fangjia Hutong, Dongmianhua Hutong (Fig. 2).

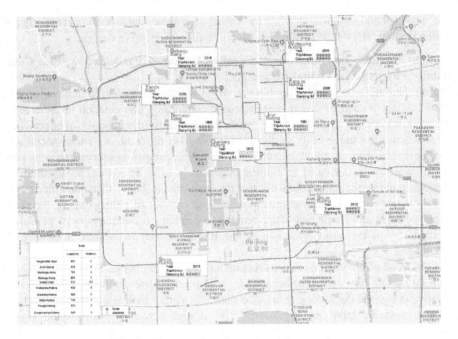

Fig. 2. The cases location and activity mapping.

5 Results

5.1 Description of Creative Design

According to the research approach, the two aspects of the physical and the virtual community space of hutongs are surveyed respectively. The dimensions and design of the streets included in the hutong street entity spatial data that is street-surface, facilities, and facing-street buildings enclosing street spaces. For the virtual public community space, the usage frequency of the open platform and the release of the participatory activities in the virtual community have been collected as primary data.

These cases of hutongs with creative designs have completed the infrastructural work of street-centered rectification and management before the creative design of public space quality. In the past, the dirty and messy areas were all improved to a certain degree. However, the design carried out from the perspective of creative design took into account both the physical and the virtual dimensions of public space, and the cases showed a particular gap. The characteristics are as follows: The creative design of hutong physical space is based on street-facing buildings as the leading carrier, all the hutong have been redesigned along the street. However, the design of facilities and street surfaces is unconsidered, which shows 70% and 40% relatively (Fig. 3).

The following is to analyze the creative design and research data of the street-facing buildings, trying to find out the distinct characteristic of design factors from the perspective of architectural design, that are street-facing facades, front-yard, and building signboard.

	Amount	Yangmeizhu Xiejie	Ju'er Hutong	Nanluogu Xiang	Beiluogu Xiang	Yandai Xiejie	Wudaoying Hutong	Qianliang Hutong	Shijia Hutong	Fangjia Hutong	Dongmianhua Hutong
Street Surface	4	0		0		0	0				
Facilities	7	0	0	0	0	0	0	0			
Facing-street Buildings	10	0	0	0	0	0	0	0	0	0	0

Fig. 3. The creative designs for physical space in hutongs.

The pie chart illustrates the preference of creative design for street-facing buildings (Fig. 4). Creative design is the most common in facades, while signboard and front-yard involve less. The buildings in Qianliang Hutong and Shijia Hutong all renovated facades and Yangmeizhu Xiejie, the least remodeled building, also maintained a 74%. In contrast, front-yard is the type of creative design with the least working, only in Beiluogu Xiang appears only a maximum of 45%, while Doufuchi Hutong does not involve the design of the front-yard space. Signboard design work has fluctuated from 8% to 33%, which is closely related to the hutong's limited scale and complicated space tenure.

Fig. 4. The description and comparison of street-facing facades, building signboards and front-yards for the street-facing building.

Fundamental descriptive data also includes the posting of creative displays, sales, or other public activities by the virtual social networking platform. Overall, WeChat Offical Accounts was the most widely used, Douban Group Accounts only dominated Beiluogu Xiang, and Weibo Verified Accounts performed modestly. On the individual, the number of subjects in the virtual network community obviously shows low, medium and high category. The low level of participation shows that there are no more than 15 principal bodies in the three platforms, such as Ju'er Hutong only 5 and Nnaluogu Xiang of 13. Of the moderate participation, Wudaoying Hutong appeared 90. Beiluogu Xiang showed unusually high engagement in social platforms, with more than ten significant accounts in a single platform and 37 in WeChat Official Accounts, bringing the total to 235 (Fig. 5).

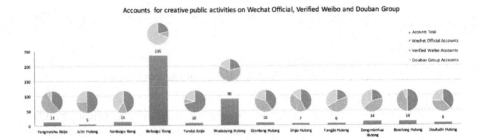

Fig. 5. Social network platform for community participating activities in hutongs.

5.2 Public Participating Reflection

Concerning public reflection, the user ratings of the two most trusted community life sites, TripAdvisor and Douban, were surveyed, in the light of the extent of public participation. TripAdvisor is an international public platform where Wudaoying Hutong and Nanluogu Xiang show very high annual average reviewers and maintain high scores of 4.5 and 4.0, followed by Shijia Hutong, Yandai Xiejie, and Ju'er Hutong. Douban, as a highly trusted online community in China, with the Tongcheng section devoted to urban activities, shows that Beiluogu Xiang's Activities and participants are at their highest level. Following is Yandai Xiejie, the number of community events posted on the community platform, and participants, there is a clear positive relationship between the number of the visible community platform for the promotion of participation has a significant role (Fig. 6).

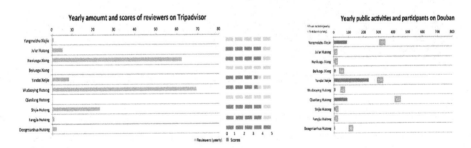

Fig. 6. Reviewers, activities, and participants in TripAdvisor and Douban Tongcheng

This paper aims to figure out how the three dimensions of creative design, which are physical community space, network community space and public participatory activities, coordinated with each other to promote public participation in the community and activate the traditional hutong space. Bridge physical and virtual design for hutongs regarding a bright open public area [16]. Therefore, based on primary data, this paper further analyzes and deduce the practical mode that creative design supports community participation.

5.3   Creative Design for Physical Hutong Space

First, analyze the relationship between creative design and the spatial scale of the hutong physical space. The results show no significant relationship between design and length of the alley, but with a little bit of width. The most active objects appeared when the average width of the hutong was 5.5 m and 6 m in the context of building's average width of 3 m, while most of the hutong with creative designs floated more in the design proportion of 2%–29% The average trend of 5–7 m average interval is the most common trend is apparent, the prevalence of creative design has been 17.5%. It can be summarized that the hutong width of 5–7 m leading to the most conducive to the creative design work for the physical space (Fig. 7).

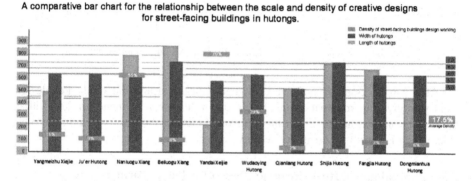

Fig. 7. A comparative bar chart for the relationship between the scale and density of creative designs for street-facing buildings in hutongs.

According to the actual situation, this result corresponds to the stellar reputation of the creative hutongs in Beijing. The two high-performing hutongs are Beijing's prestigious commercial street, which is Nanluogu Xiang and Yandai Xiejie, mainly offers business activities instead of non-community participation activities. The rest of the cases are renovated design from 1% to 30%. Conclusions can also include that the hutong does not exceed 30% of the architectural design work, no matter how long the hutong is on a 5–7 m broad scale.

5.4   The Impact of Creative Design Factors on Participation Reflection

Next, whether these three dominating elements of creative designs street-facing buildings, facades, front-yard, and signboard, could have an impact on the public participation of the hutong? This paper aligns the participatory data from the virtual community platform across three design types for buildings. Then the correlation turns up:

Those hutongs involving physical designs in a large percentage shows a high level of reflection from network community platforms. Among them, the Douban Participants and TripAdvisor Reviewers, which are most relevant to actual participation in the community, show the highest similarities with the trends of Street-facing buildings' facades and signboards, such as the highest amount in both Nanluogu Xiang and Wudaoying Hutong. Lower street hutong design work carried out a few, but also the case of small participation. It can be concluded that the design of the exterior design of the street-facing buildings is not only the foundational work but also efficiently indicates the involvement of the hutongs, especially street-facing facades and building signboards (Fig. 8).

	Street-facing facades	Building signboards	Front-yards	Network Accounts	Douban Public Activitie	Douban Participants	Tripadvisor Reviewers	Tripadvisor Reviewers Scores
Yangmeizhu Xiejie	14	7	3	13	89	1238	3	0
Ju'er Hutong	13	11	4	5	1	6	156	4
Nanluogu Xiang	158	124	3	13	5	47	1122	4
Beiluogu Xiang	17	19	10	235	13	34	0	0
Yandai Xejie	53	47	8	10	235	4017	140	4.5
Wudaoying Hutong	60	62	11	90	10	41	69	4.5
Qianliang Hutong	4	3	1	10	90	3321	0	0
Shijia Hutong	3	1	1	7	10	27	115	4
Fangjia Hutong	13	12	1	6	4	26	8	4
Dongmianhua Hutong	7	7	2	14	6	48	1	4.5

Fig. 8. A comparison of physical and virtual design factors for hutongs

Also, it is necessary to add that compared with the façade and signboards design, front-yard gives the minimal extent. That is due to the severe influence of the width of the hutong on the one hand, and the unfavorable use of the open space on the other side, which is driven by creativity activity content.

5.5 Physical and Virtual Creativity Design for Public Participation

Finally, based on the understanding of the influence of the material and virtual design factors on the engagement, this paper analyzes creative design enhances the public's evaluation of the hutong. Associated with creative design and public participation and reflection, it is evident that quite a lot of hutongs with a high public participation score of 4–4.5 have done considerable design work on both physical construction and virtual networks (Fig. 8). At the same time, there are only a few hutongs that only achieve high participation in the online community construction, and relying on the physical space to reach individuals who enhance their cooperation and evaluation, such as Nanluogu Xiang and Fangjia Hutong.

Besides, the Hutong cases have the choices of which online social platform to go to launch out. These examples, which have done a lot of work on Douban and TripAdvisor, all show a significant amount of physical design work and gain more than 4 points of reflection. And even though there is a high number of reviewers, fewer public events, and fewer participants, the scores show only 4 points accordingly. Both Nanluogu Xiang and Ju'er Hutong demonstrate this feature, indicating that reviewers' reflections are objective. So far no case can get better participation only by doing community network platform.

During the research process, a regularity reached unexpectedly. The hutong increased the exposure of the public after the creative renovated work, which provided the public access to the community space and the feasibility of participating in the activity and given not less than 4 points of reflection. A conclusion that the creative design of hutong as a medium for increasing public participation in cities and perception in urban renewal is worthy of sustainable development, which could be a structure improve to open public space.

6 Conclusion

In this regard, this paper focuses on creative design to support hutong public participation in the context of urban renovation. The research found that joint design of physical construction and the virtual network can effectively increase the participation of the community, and the most feasible is to design facades of street-side buildings in the physical space. Hutong innovation can be constructively supported by the comprehensive redesign of creative design in three dimensions: street-facing building designs providing the basic space situation, virtual community networking platform convey timely information and informative reflection, which promotes information design.

In this way, the practical mode of inducing the relationship between the various elements, combining the traditional hutong space and the urban development background, and combing out the creative design support based on Beijing's Hutong pattern in the context of urban renovation to enhance community participation is as follows (Fig. 9):

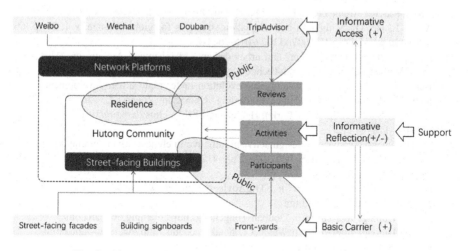

Fig. 9. The general mode of supportive creative design for hutong

The research also found that urban spaces such as hutong have the high potential for function and style transformation. The creative design of street-facing buildings plays a more significant role in their openness to the public. The network community holds a supporting role in transmitting information and complements such alley Physical space is more closed space deficiencies.

References

1. Hou, R.Z.: Beijing Historical Atlas. Beijing Publishing House, Beijing (1998)
2. Feng, J.G.: The Last Hutong. China Central Compilation and Translation Press, Beijing (2008)
3. Tang, Y., Klaus, R., Kunmann, K.R.: Culture, Creative Industries and Urban Regeneration. Tsinghua University Press, Beijing (2016)
4. Zhu, W.Y., Hou, X.Q.: Let's Talk About Community Revitalization I. Social Sciences Academic Press, Beijing (2015)
5. Liu, Z.H.: Neighborhood News. Beijing Daily (2016). http://www.bjd.com.cn/zc/sbs/201605/11/t20160511_11021219.html
6. Li, T.S., Zhang, E.D.: The History of Nangluogu Xiang. Beijing Press, Beijing (2010)
7. Li, B., Zhang, M.Z., Kong, X.X.: Inheritance and Innovation of 496m - Samples of Yangmeizhu Xiejie in the Protection and Renovation of Historic Cultural District. The State Council of People's Republic of China (2017) http://www.gov.cn/xinwen/2017-03/28/content_5181376.htm
8. Yangmeizhu Xiejie Organic Renovation Program referenced in Beijing Design Week. http://www.bjdw.org/
9. Taner, O., Steve, T., Tim, H.: Revitalizing Historic Urban Quarters. China Architecture & Building Press, Beijing (2016)
10. Clare, C.M., Carolyn, F.: People Places: Design Guidelines for Urban Open Space. China Architecture & Building Press, Beijing (2010). Yu, K.J., Sun, P. (Translators)
11. Wu, L.Y.: The Old City of Beijing and its Ju'er Hutong Neighbourhood. China Architecture & Building Press, Beijing (1994)
12. Ching, F.D.K.: Architecture: Form, Space, and Order, 1st edn. Wiley, Hoboken (2014)
13. Wang, J., He, D.: Mitigation and adaptation strategies for global change, vol. 20, p. 665 (2015). https://doi.org/10.1007/s11027-015-9644-1
14. Wang, J.: "Urban regeneration" and urban design. Urbanism and Architecture (Urb Arch), no. 2. Heilongjiang Science and Technology Press (2009)
15. Tang, M., Chen, T.: Cultural landscape evolution under rapid urban development: a case study of Shichahai historical area in Beijing, China. In: Zhang, Z., Zhang, R., Zhang, J. (eds.) LISS 2012. Springer, Berlin, Heidelberg (2013). https://doi.org/10.1007/978-3-642-32054-5_178
16. Ni, M.: Open your space: a design activism initiative in chinese urban community. In: Rau, P.L. (ed.) CCD 2017. LNCS, vol. 10281, pp. 412–431. Springer, Cham (2017). https://doi.org/10.1007/978-3-319-57931-3_33
17. Beijing Hutongs referenced in TripAdvisor. https://www.tripadvisor.com/Attractions-g294212-Activities-Beijing.html
18. Beijing Hutongs referenced in Douban Tongcheng. https://beijing.douban.com/
19. Beijing Hutongs referenced in WeChat Official Accounts. http://weixin.sogou.com/
20. Beijing Hutongs referenced in Sina Weibo. https://www.weibo.com/
21. Beijing Hutongs referenced in Dianping. http://www.dianping.com/beijing

Case Studies of Designing for Ecology: Branding EVEN

I-Wen Wu$^{(\boxtimes)}$, Hsien-Fu Lo, and I-Ting Wang

Graduate School of Creative Industry Design,
National Taiwan University of Arts, New Taipei City, Taiwan
service@even.tw, hsienfulo@gmail.com,
etinw@ms43.hinet.net

Abstract. Ecodesign is an approach of product design with materials and decision-making of process in special consideration for environmental impacts. However, during a design process, as for demands on eco-friendliness, there are many uncertainties and multiple contradictions due to the advancing technology and industry. Therefore, in this paper, a systematic analysis was proposed in order to extend the traditional framework of process design to a green brand that treats environment friendly and makes a sustainable development come true. This study aims to provide a framework of ecological design for traditional process that seeks for a sustainable development or transformation into green design. With research on ecological literature and case study, the study reveals the prospects and difficulties between design and ecology, as well as ecology and industry.

Keywords: Ecological design · Green design · Sustainable design

1 Instruction

Ecodesign is an approach to designing products with special consideration for environmental impacts of product throughout its whole lifecycle. Along with the developing industrialization and global economy, issues such as deficiency in biodiversity, intensifying pollutions and fierce climate change have emerged. Over the past twenty years, technologies and theories in ecodesign have been progressing and shown the urgent needs from society in it. Aiming at fields such as arts and processes, this research carries out case study through ideation, design, development and survey on product innovators, in an attempt to analyze process framework and each ecodesign products made by innovators under this research framework.

Although the cases of designers/innovators in this study are small studios run by individuals, the researcher focus on such process of conceiving and developing ecodesign from owners in order to create more models of ecodesign innovation as reference for more designers and innovations.

© Springer International Publishing AG, part of Springer Nature 2018
P.-L. P. Rau (Ed.): CCD 2018, LNCS 10912, pp. 421–430, 2018.
https://doi.org/10.1007/978-3-319-92252-2_33

2 Literature Review

2.1 Ecodesign

Before fossil fuel started a bright chapter of industrialization in the 19th century, people had been manufacturing things in biological patterns and getting along with Mother Nature in a harmony. Most resources in the past were naturally regenerated with few harmful side effects and safely degraded after discard. Less demand for resources means less damage to the planet, where used to gradually repair itself in natural processes. However today, the earth can no longer afford what have been added onto it; progress and growth are driven by gradually increasing consumptions that result in more and more wastes.

Berman indicates that, for example, as for a dirty factory powered by fossil fuels, manufacturing each kilogram of products would also produce averagely 28 kilograms of wastes. [1] We have thrown out things not because they are worn out or broken, but because they no longer look glamorous. Most consumables turn into wastes in six weeks. Once upon a time, the relationship between mankind and environment tended to be naturally harmonious, but will not come again. The harder we work to improve our lives, the more severe we hurt this world to advance. More products means more damages to environments. In order to solve this imbalance, we have to improve from aspects such as materials and processes in a wish to achieve "sustainability and harmony". Proctor pointed that, more and more designers have realized that designing products not only requires a sense of beauty, but also an ethic to the environment currently. [2] Thus, such design that emphasizes on environment and nature has gradually become a trend, and that is "sustainable design".

In addition to caring environment by sustainable design, Tu also put forward that a sustainable design should innovate to reduce material use and waste in order to bring down operating costs and apply green marketing to building a green image for enterprise which enhances its market competitiveness. This also meets the goal and purpose "cleaner, cheaper, smarter" in sustainable development. [3] This visions matches and benefits management and promotion of green designs and brands.

Since every home appliance has an impact on our environment and lives, it is so crucial to have greener, cheaper and smarter designs. Therefore, the "sustainable design" has risen and received more and more attention. But how to choose and tell whether a product is sustainable? Proctor mentioned few simple elements that can help us identify a green design product: biodegradable, fair traded, locally sourced, low energy consumption, less waste in production, non-toxic, recyclable, recycled material, and proper management of material sources. As long as the product meets one or two of above items, it can be called a "product of sustainable design". [2]

The researcher categorized above nine elements into three aspects: material, process and management, as shown in Fig. 1. The case in this paper will be in exploration of degree in "sustainable design" through the three aspects (see Fig. 1).

Material: biodegradable, non-toxic, recycled.
Process: low energy consumption, less waste, recyclable.
Management: fair traded, proper management of material sources, locally sourced.

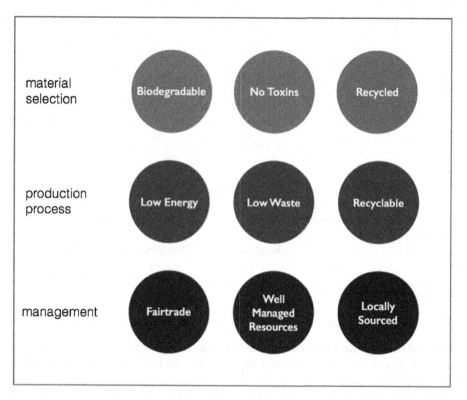

Fig. 1. Classification of ecodesign elements.

2.2   Conceptual Model of Furniture Design

The researcher presents a creation in the form of furniture. In a long history of furniture design, art works in forms of chairs are the most representative subjects. Gier and Buur suggested: "We have chosen to narrow down the wide field of furniture design in order to exclusively on a furniture (chair) must starts from the aspects, form, material and technique". "This project understands tectonics as the manner in which chairs are joined together and as will be made apparent, along with an understanding of the term tectonics, what must also be considered are materials, form and technique, insofar as these constitute prerequisites for the formation of the architectonic totality". Moreover, they even suggested that: "Technique prepares and works up the materials and gives form to them and to the joinings, partly through the techniques of adapting and finishing them, but also through modes of joining the constituent elements that have been adapted to the chosen material". [4]

The three elements constitute the concept model of furniture design in below triangle scale "Tectonics". This study also adopts this model in developing its creation structure (see Fig. 2).

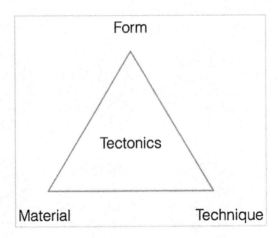

Fig. 2. Concept model of furniture design.

3   Research Method

3.1   Analysis on Conceptual Model of Ecodesign and Furniture Design

This study carries out a self-interpretation by analyzing researcher's own creation. The study has drawn its materials through applying ideas on text analysis aiming at media, techniques, forms, and ideas of work for in-depth self-analysis and interpretation. In order to comply with the idea of ecodesign, as on drawing materials, I adopted the natural and biodegradable material, woods, removed from local old houses or recycled pieces from scrapped furniture in Taiwan. In the process of manufacturing, a mass of handwork consumes less energy, and the use of traditional mortise and tenon techniques makes the structure strong and durable.

In the stage of painting after the work is completed, due to the stable quality of wood that is hard to deform, it does not need recoat it again. Therefore, regular furniture has removed the secondary undercoat that contains organic agent and adopts natural coating from wood preservation oil that is eco-friendly and nontoxic. It is natural and nontoxic, so you can feel the mild texture and quality of natural wood.

Moreover, since I adopted natural wood, if the work has broken after many years, it can be naturally decomposed after discard, so the creation will not create impact to environments. Above mentioned ecodesign elements are summarized in below:

(A). Material: biodegradable, non-toxic, recycled
(B). Process: consume low energy, waste reduction, recyclable
(C). Management: locally sourced

In the conceptual model of furniture design aforementioned, "Tectonics" is constituted by techniques, forms, and materials. As on material, I put the concept of ecodesign into it and started the creation with the point of recycling wood. This is also the core idea of ecodesign, so I used "Tectonics" triangle framework as the basic model and extended the material as creation concept to construct a design model of techniques, forms, and concepts.

3.2   Creation Framework

Ideation
Each piece of art or creation contains creator's inspiration and creativity, so does mine. Because I was born in an environment that was more in needs compared with other same-aged children, under a restrictive father, my childhood was full of regret and imagination, so I always attempt to use childlike creation to fill up the fear and emptiness in my heart in the past. Therefore, a lot of inspiration of creation came from my childhood memories. As for every piece of wood collected from different places, they are bonded with their own histories to be told. There are many factors to inspire a creation work, including childhood memories, recycled wood, cultural reflection and the focus onto environment; all of them are sources of my creation.

Creation Model
Integrating the ecodesign elements and design connotation constructed by techniques, forms and concepts, the follows illustrate my creation model:

(A) Techniques: the process of integrating ecological elements.
(B) Forms: Furniture designed in creative shapes.
(C) Concepts: EVEN (Empathy Value, Eco Nature)

Because my name is "I-Wen", so I gave myself a harmonic English name "Even". It means smooth, uniform, reciprocity, even, equal, balance and steady, so I determined to put the idea of "even" into my creation. I hope I can extend such concept of "even" as smooth, equal and balance into a ecodesign idea of "an equality among all creatures", so in addition to the reflection of care in environment during aforementioned manufacturing process, I hope to do more for the environment. My materials were all sourced from Mother Earth, and I sensed a responsibility to pay back to earth for what I borrowed from it. Therefore after I complete each piece of work, I will plant a tree to reflect my idea of ecodesign in contribution to the environment.

From ideation, ecological process, to reflection of the "even" concept, I completed the following ecodesign creation framework: (see Fig. 3)

4   Case Study

In this chapter, the researcher picked one piece of work for each of the four approaches in drawing materials for inspiration. Although the source of inspiration for each work might not be the same, I chose the work that has higher proportion of such inspiration approach as an example.

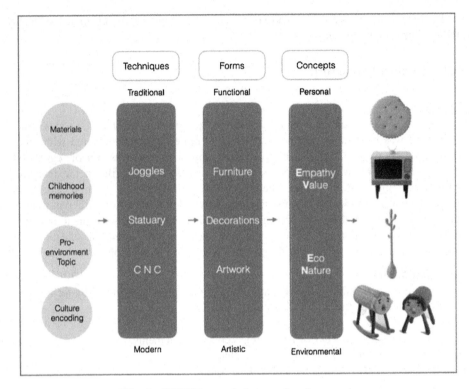

Fig. 3. "EVEN" - ecodesign creation framework

4.1   Materials, Shapes, and Colors: Cookie Stool

Inspired by the colors, textures, traces, appearances and other features of material itself as the design ideation, cookie stool was thus born (see Fig. 4).

Recycled old wood is very different from ordinary wood; their surfaces are often full of dirt that covers the original colors. When I first came into picking recycled wood, I could not tell the type of wood quickly from appearance, and I had to shave it with a blade to clean it. On one occasion, I brought back an old board full of grime and dirt, but after I shaved it, it was a great contrast of colors and textures, showing an orange and yellow luster just like a crisp cookie oily baked! At that time, I started using woods that have similar colors to cookie and built my cookie stools. These stools in cookie shape recall my memory of tasty milk cookies at elementary school.

4.2   Childhood Memories: Kid's TV

Kids fed up by TV shows
In my childhood, I was often beaten by my father, not because I did something wrong, but just because my father was not happy. My dad was a taxi driver who does not work in regular hours, so he often gambles and drinks when he was free. When he returned

Fig. 4. Taste in memory – Cookie Stool

home, he was often not on a good mood, and a little disobedience might have caused an abuse from him. However, I put myself in TV shows, although I grew up in such a restrict family that if I did not catch my father's call, I will be beaten. Living in under such intense and terrifying pressure, I could only be bombarded with messages from TV whenever I got a chance to immerse myself in TV and feel no interference from outside (see Fig. 5).

Fig. 5. Kid's TV – a locker

Therefore, this work is the object I intent to convert messages I received; I created a locker in TV shape: antenna is a piece of chalk, screen is the blackboard; after opening the screen panel, there are two drawers inside that you can place things in. When you use it, you can write, paint, and place things that are all actions of sending out messages and the TV is one to receive them.

4.3   Pro-environment Topic: Clothing Tree

This work is a round shaped tree baby wrapped in a diaper (see Fig. 6), giving a personification to a coat and hat hanger. It gives life imagination onto the work in order to express the idea that a tree will be planted after completing a piece of work.

Fig. 6. Clothing Tree (shaped tree baby wrapped in a diaper)

4.4   Culture Encoding: Cattle & Horse for Kids' Ride

Kids are not riding on cattle or horse, but their parents. The work plays a humor on a Chinese idiom through literal translation into three-dimensional images. Generally, in the market, you only see Trojan toys made in animal shapes, but I replace the symbol with parents in the shape of toys, wishing to create a sarcastic connotation on cultural implication, in a hilarious way (see Fig. 7).

Fig. 7. Cattle & Horse for Kids' Ride

I planted a tree for each of above works when they were completed.

5 Conclusion

Through case analysis, this paper establishes an ecodesign model and finally spreads the core concept through operating brands (see Fig. 8).

Fig. 8. "EVEN"s brand concept

Even = all are equal
Respect the natural environment
Use recycled wood
No mass production
Only callous hands
Here are only art works

And furniture in design
It's kind of humorous
You can use it for a long time
In the end,
Each work is finished, a tree will be planted.

Keeping an ecological balance has always been a contradiction and conflict in the development of human history. "Design" seems to only serve for the industry, so can we save the world by design? Perhaps ecodesign is would be a solution, but at best it only slows down the ecological impact and destruction. Therefore, I hope to share my ecodesign and creation mode, attempting to not only slow down the ecological impact and destruction, but also contribute to the environment as reference for traditional process to create sustainable developments in the future.

References

1. Alan, B.: Green Design: A Healthy Home Handbook. Frances Lincoln, London (2008)
2. Rebecca, P.: 1000 New Eco Designs and Where to Found Them. Laurence King Publishing, London (2009)
3. Jui-Che, T.: Product Sustainable Design. Ya-Tai Tu-Shu, Taipei (2002)
4. de Nicolai, G., Stine Liv, B.: Chairs' Tectonics. The Royal Danish Academy of Fine Arts school of Architecture Publishers, Copenhagen (2009)

A Study for the Elderly-Oriented Public Rest Facility Design Based on User's Demands and Perceptual Cognition

Hao Yang[1](✉) and Yueran Wang[2]

[1] North China University of Technology, Beijing, China
hao-yang12@ncut.edu.cn
[2] Tsinghua University, Beijing, China

Abstract. The study focuses on improving senior people's using experience on public rest facilities. By means of field observation, Chinese senior people's rest behaviors are analyzed and three kinds of rest postures are underlined. Analytic Hierarchy Process is used to clarify the merits and drawbacks of the three postures from different evaluation dimensions and discover the posture most suitable for senior people. On the premise of this result, questionaires are sent out to collect senior people's demands for rest facilities and the subjects are asked to assess the demands perceptually to quantify the problems. Using factor analysis and regression model to mine the factors that influence the use of rest facilities significantly, which are postures, exterior and danger. Based on the results, design is proposed targetedly. The design proposal takes Chinese senior people's body size and application circumstances into consideration so that senior people's using experience can be optimized.

Keywords: Rest facilities · Senior people · Product design · Postures
Factor analysis · Regression analysis

1 Introduction

The aging process in China is accelerating faster and faster. It is the whole society's responsibility to create a reasonable and livable social environment and make the senior people have an ideal senectitude. For a person, at any age, one of the important influential factors that reflect his degree of independence and social participation is personal travelling behaviors [1]. Rest facilities are major components for any outdoor public space. With the increasement of age, functions of senior people's joints and muscles will fade away which may result in a negative using experience for these facilities. Design in this field is of significance for senior citizens' travelling as well as using spaces effectively and participating in social events. For senior people who always have plenty of leisure time, public rest facilities are more meaningful and valuable.

Scientific Research Foundation of North China University of Technology (NCUT11201601).
Research Program on Education and Teaching Reformation and Curriculum Construction of North China University of Technology (NCUT2018JGM15).
Yuyou Talent Support Program of North China University of Technology (107051360018X N012/018).

P.-L. P. Rau (Ed.): CCD 2018, LNCS 10912, pp. 431–443, 2018.
https://doi.org/10.1007/978-3-319-92252-2_34

There is a great difference among cities distributed in various regions of China in the level of development. And China has a vast and increasing population which is distinct from many advanced Western countries. Thus it is not appropriate to follow western design results directly. Current studies about Chinese public facilities are always surveys rather than design researches. Based on the characteristics of physical, psychological and resting behaviors of the elderly in China, this study collected data from elder subjects and factor analysis is used to find out the common factors behind their needs. Targeted design can be proposed according to the implication of these factors which have a significant influence on the use of rest facilities. The application of Chinese senior people's body dimension is also meaningful in this study.

2   Background

2.1   Physical Characteristics and Rest Postures of the Elderly

When a man begins the veteran stage of his life, a rapid decline in various physiological parameters will appear. Among them, muscular flaccidity and osteoporosis can induce a decrease in maximum force of bones and torque of joints. For the elderly, it is difficult to force again if the body is kept in a stationary state for a period of time. Thus it is not suitable to have a sedentary behavior. Domestic research has demonstrated that compared with the lower limbs, the level of the attenuation and atrophy of the number of muscle fibers in the upper limbs is lower, and older people always show a physical movement disorder in their legs first [2]. Diseases which are common in the elderly group, such as arthritis and rheumatism, may also reduce their ability to move the lower limbs. Therefore, it is common that old people are not able to stand up easily after sitting down and a more suitable rest posture is essential.

On the aspect of joint activity degree, there is little difference between the male and the female old people. But compared with the middle-aged, the degree of the elderly's narrows [3]. Leaning is a reasonable rest posture. With the body leaning against something such as rest facilities rather than sitting down deeply, the lower limbs' forcing difficulty to stand up can be avoided and the limitation of joint activity can be alleviated, while the elderly's rest demands can be satisfied. Thus it is rational to take leaning posture into consideration in the design of public rest facilities.

2.2   Chinese Senior People's Rest Behaviors in Public Space

Hypothesis—from Behaviors to Postures
Traditional Chinese senior people are always family-oriented. After retiring, they prefer helping their sons or daughters take care of their offsprings to having a long journey or working out for a long time. Chinese senior people are used to have regular activities in a particular public space which is always home-centered. In this way they can carry on the housework after finishing outdoor activities. The main rest-behavior-characteristics in public space include: watching others, communicating with each other, relaxing and meditating, and resting in the course of a walk [4]. Different behaviors represent their unique psychological and behavioral characteristics, with corresponding postures such as deeply seating, shallowly seating and leaning. The four kinds of behaviors are not

seperated from each other but overlapping. The elderly's demands for rest facilities can be decomposed by clarifying these characteristics and analyzing the common postures.

Behavior A–Watching others' behaviors. For the sakes of aging, leaving from work and a narrowed social circle, compensatory psychology prominently functions in senior people. Watching others' behaviors can bring about an experience that cannot be obtained by themselves directly and achieve some kind of emotional compensation. When such a behavior happens, senior people always choose a chair with a backrest and present a posture of sitting deeply. But a part of them also sit shallowly to interact with the observed objects conveniently.

Behavior B–Communicating with each other. Senior people without working stress are inclined to sit together encircledly and communicate with each other when they rest in public space. The main rest posture in this situation is sitting shallowly with raising their heads. Such a posture can show some kind of inclusiveness and help them integrate into the others.

Behavior C–Relaxing and meditating. It can be seen frequently that senior people resting on the public seat, thinking by themselves and enjoying the surrounding environment. At such a moment, the seats always distribute along a hollow space with a strong privacy, such as an area with a lot of plants. A posture of sitting deeply is common in this context so that the senior people can get a space for meditating.

Behavior D–Resting in the course of a walk. Compared with the youth, the majority of senior people hold a living-oriented travelling purpose rather than a survival-oriented one. Without a necessity to work, walking accounts for a high proportion in the way of travelling. Nevertheless senior people generally have a poor physical function. Although willing to walk, it is difficult to continue for a long time. In the break of a walk, a short rest is necessary for the elderly group. This situation is of some kind of temporary nature, so the most common posture is sitting shallowly while sometimes leaning behaviors can be seen. For this behavior, supporting frames or tiny brackets are always used by senior people for a transient rest.

By means of field observation, it can be seen that the posture of sitting deeply rarely appears in outdoor public space. And it does not conform to the physiological characteristics of the elderly.

Outdoor rest facilities include chairs, benches, stools, lean brackets etc. On some common public facilities, posture related problems such as unsuitable depth of seat (the buttock-popliteal length), too many bars on the interactive parts or uncomfortable backrest angle may impose many obstacles on senior people (Fig. 1). In order to assess the rationality of the rest postures mentioned above, evaluation system needs to be set up from the perspective of the user's cognition to produce a perceptual evaluation.

Fig. 1. Typical rest facilities with serious problems

Assessment of Suitable Postures

In this part, Analytic Hierarchy Process (AHP) is used to assess the three postures which are deeply seating, shallowly seating and leaning. The data comes from senior people's perceptual evaluation. From the point of users, this part tries to judge which posture is most suited for senior people.

AHP is a method combining qualitative judgment and quantitative analysis and is suitable for assessing design proposals which are always of fuzziness and nondeterminacy. In domestic field of industrial design research, some researchers have assessed designs of product appearance or interactive space such as aircraft cabin by this method, and obtained persuasive conclusions [5, 6]. The evaluation system includes three levels which are target layer, standard layer and object layer. In order to obtain the evaluation results, a higher level of elements will be used as the standard to make a comparison between elements of a lower level. And an evaluation matrix is set up. On the selection of evaluation indicators, the Technology Acceptance Model offers two key points: perceived usefulness and perceived ease of use [7]. Besides, as a public product, design for the rest facilities needs to take compatibility and perceived danger into account, which mean whether the new product is in conformity with the user's inherent experience and whether they may feel dangerous. Therefore, four evaluation indicators are proposed which are perceived usefulness, perceived ease of use, compatibility and perceived danger. The specific connotation of the four indicators was explained to the subjects during the data collection. The target of this evaluation system is "A Comfort Degree Assessment of the Elderly-oriented Public Resting Facility", and the assessed objects are the three rest postures. The final AHP mdel is shown in Fig. 2.

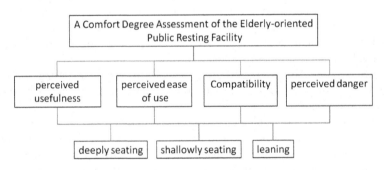

Fig. 2. AHP model for assessment of the elderly's rest postures

30 raters are invited to make an assessment to the three postures. Every rater's judgment matrix is calculated to seek an ordering weight. All the raters' ordering weight values are dealt with to get a geometric mean and produce the group decision. Using the software yaahp 10.3, total order weight values of every rater's judgment matrix are generated. C.I. Values of all the raters' judgment matrices are less than 0.1, passing the consistency test. The group-decision results are listed as Table 1:

From the results it can be seen that leaning is the most recognised posture for older users (W = 0.3556). And it is in the first rank in the sense of perceived usefulness and perceived ease of use.

Table 1. Results of AHP model

	Perceived usefulness	Perceived ease of use	Compatibility	Perceived danger	Total order weight (W_i)	Total ordering
	0.4133	0.1078	0.1867	0.2922		
Deeply seating	0.1634	0.1220	0.3874	0.5278	0.3073	3
Shallowly seating	0.2970	0.3196	0.4434	0.3325	0.3371	2
Leaning	0.5396	0.5584	0.1692	0.1396	0.3556	1

The second one is shallowly seating and not much less than the lean posture (W = 0.3371). Among all the indicators, shallowly seating gets a highest weight value on compatibility, which conforms to common sense.

On the aspect of perceived danger, there is still a shortage of leaning posture. Users generally feel that leaning is of the highest risk while deeply sitting is the safest one among the three postures. Although this result is reasonable, it also exposes the opportunities of future designs.

The main reason why users consider leaning as useful and easy to use but feel dangerous is that leaning is an unstable posture. Existing leaning frames are always with only two contact points, which are buttocks and feet, as interaction parts. Weight of the torso will cause the body to slip down from the supporting surface. So compared with sitting position which makes the body almost impossible to slide, the whole body is in a moving state in the leaning status and such a posture imposes an unstable experience in perception on the users.

Although deeply sitting is stable, it does not conform to the physiological characteristics of the lower limbs of the elderly. A reasonable solution for designers to work out is to set up a support under users' knee and make the two contact points of the leaning position into three and forming a stable triangular structure.

In order to achieve such a design, it is pivotal to clarify the significance level of the postures' influence on usability of public resting facilities. And whether there are other influencial factors is also necessary to identify for putting forward a design proposal. The next part focuses on the two pieces of information.

3   Method

3.1   Survey Design

Design of rest facilities belongs to the domain of humanistic care rather than a high-tech or a new skill keeping pace with the times. From the point of the elderly, problems of public rest facilities always exist on aspects such as distribution of the facilities, interval distance, scale and size of the product, users' perceptual factors and so on. Rosemary's study for the environment and health of different regions of Glasgow, Scotland had pointed out that there are not enough seats for the elderly to rest on their way of walking [8]. Study of Maria from Switzerland also showed that senior people hold the view that height of public seats should not be too low [9]. According to the early research, such kind of problems exist on contemporary Chinese urban public rest facilities in the same way. These problems are less involved in the development of technology and belongs to the perceptual level of people to a larger extent. To solve these problems, there are not many obstacles on the technical level. This part of research aims at clarifying the depth of the sensibility of certain group of users by quantifying their perceptual demands.

3.2   Data Collection

The research focuses on senior people's psychological feelings and needs. By means of random visits, 48 senior people from three typical districts in Beijing, which are Haidian District, Shijingshan District and Shunyi District, are interviewed. The subjects are asked to speak out what they care about on public rest facilities and the everyday times of using this kind of facilities are recorded. By corpus analysis, frequency of problems that is cared by the elderly is accumulated and it can be found that 17 problems appear frequently. The result and key words of the problems are listed as Fig. 3.

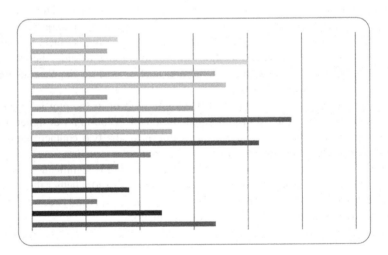

Fig. 3. Frequency accumulation of problems cared by senior people (times)

Likert 7-level scale is used to compile a questionaire. And 200 elder users were invited to score the 17 problems. Score 1 means the user does not care the problem at all and the value 7 means the subject pays an extreme attention to it. Score 1–7 show the level of concern of the elderly about the issue. A total of 186 valid questionnaires were collected.

4   Result

4.1   Factor Analysis for Users' Demands

The Cronbach's α of this questionaire is $\alpha = 0.907$ and shows a high level of internal consistency reliability. Due to the large number of variables, factor analysis is used to analyze the data (n = 186). The aim is to extract commonalities from variable groups and classify problems with a same essential into one factor to simplify variable information and find core issues.

Kaiser-Meyer-Olkin Test shows a KMO value of 0.820. And Bartlett Test of Sphericity unfolds a result which is very significant ($p < 0.001$). It means the 17 variables of this research is suitable for factor analysis.

The factors with an eigenvalue greater than 1 are reserved and we can get 4 common factors. The cumulative percentage of variance reaches 78.432%. After varimax rotation, the results are listed as Table 2:

After analyzing the information from the variables contained in the four common factors in Table 1 and extracting the inherent concepts, the four factors can be named. F1 can summarize information of eight variables. It can be found that all these variables reflect problems about postures and physical unconvenience. F2 summarizes four variables which all illustrate shortcomings about form and appearance, such as problems of surface hardness, materials, style and colors. As is described above, senior people pay attention to practicability as well as appearance of products. F3 summarizes information of three variables showing difficulties or dangers that such facilities may cause. F4 summarizes two variables which are about using experience, such as communication and vision at night. Thus the four factors can be named as POSTURE, EXTERIOR, DANGER and EXPERIENCE. These four aspects of problems are what users care about most.

4.2   Effect of the Factors

Frequency of use of certain product reflects whether users have enough recognition for it. The more times a product is used everyday, the more trust and recognition the users have. On the contrary, for the facility which is seldom used by citizens, it shows that people have a certain degree of skepticism about it. Thus the frequency of use of rest facilities is considered as a dependent variable. The four common factors have some effects on the variation of the frequency of use of rest facilities or not is a key point for the product design. And whether the effects are positive or negative as well as how is the significance level of the effects need to be confirmed.

Calculate the scores of the four common factors and take the scores as independent variables. As is mentioned above, the everyday frequency of use of rest facilities is considered as the dependent variable. In this way a regression model can be set up. Replacing the original variables by factor scores can retain the main initial information as well as avoiding multicollinearity problems caused by variables reflecting people's subjective opinions. The results are listed as Table 3.

The coefficient of determination of this model is $R2 = 0.702$. It means the variation of independent variables can explain more than 70% of the dependent variable's

Table 2. Results of factor analysis

	Existing problems	Factor 1	Factor 2	Factor 3	Factor 4
F1	1. The interactive surface is too small to get a rest (common on little chairs in shopping malls)	**0.879**	0.189	0.194	0.039
	2. The interactive surface is too low to sit down comfortably (common on stone benches under landscape trees)	**0.800**	0.309	0.019	0.100
	3. Waist ache caused by an inappropriate backrest angle	**0.791**	0.315	0.104	−0.044
	4. Cervical vertebra pain caused by a lackage of head support	**0.789**	0.098	0.412	−0.096
	5. The chair surface tilts downward and makes the body slip out	**0.713**	−0.030	0.270	0.172
	6. Pain on knee joints makes it hard to curve the legs and unable to sit down	**0.710**	0.270	0.181	−0.049
	7. Waist ache caused by a lackage of waist support	**0.629**	−0.034	0.417	0.175
	8. Hard to stand up after sitting down	**0.595**	−0.450	0.235	−0.105
F2	9. The surface is too stiff to offer a comfortable sitting experience	0.109	**0.900**	0.169	0.105
	10. The surface is hard to clean up. The worry about staining clothes makes people disinclined to use public rest facilities (such as wooden or stone benches)	0.286	**0.870**	−0.082	0.179
	11. The shape is too traditional and not artistic	0.090	**0.713**	0.364	−0.439
	12. Colors are conservative	0.410	**0.711**	0.083	0.405
F3	13. The facilities are always out of reach of children	0.205	0.067	**0.920**	0.152
	14. With the growth of age, limbs are not flexible and the handrails always trip the elderly	0.354	0.024	**0.835**	0.230
	15. The corners will make people stumble	0.330	0.211	**0.826**	0.165
F4	16. Sitting next to each other is inconvenient for communicating	0.148	0.011	0.241	**0.890**
	17. Unable to see around at night	−0.120	0.277	0.223	**0.806**
	Eigenvalues	7.235	2.613	2.140	1.345
	% of variance	42.560	15.370	12.589	7.913
	Cumulative % of variance	42.560	57.930	70.519	78.432

variation. The goodness of fit is relatively ideal. The Durbin-Watson value is 2.913, which shows a weak relevance between the residuals. They are independent from each other. From the results it can be seen that three common factors have a significant influence on the frequency of use ($p < 0.01$), which are F1, F2 and F3. They are not incidental random occurrences. Designing based on the three factors is justified. F4 is

Table 3. Results of regression analysis

	Standardized coefficients	t	Sig.
(constant)		96.513	0.000
F1	0.768	18.927	0.000
F2	0.309	7.623	0.000
F3	0.108	2.671	0.008
F4	−0.067	−1.650	0.101

not significant ($p > 0.05$) so the experience of communication or vision at night is not a critical problem in public rest facilities design.

From users' demand analysis it can be known that factors of POSTURE, EXTERIOR and DANGER have seriously affected the frequency of use of rest facilities for the elderly. In order to satisfy senior people's needs for rest facilities by design, it is necessary to propose solutions corresponding to these factors. And users' experience may be improved.

5 Discussion

5.1 A Design Proposal of Leaning Facility

It can be known from Table 3 that POSTURE influences the frequency of use most. And this fully exposes the poture problems in existing products. Optimizing the rest postures by design is a rational way to make the facility meet senior people's needs. Besides, the main problems reflected in Fig. 3 show a fact that in view of exterior, the surface should be rich in morphological changes with a smooth transition in shapes and avoiding a feeling of hard texture. The surface should be glossy and easy to clean. The shape should present a sense of design which is elaborate and delicate. And the colors ought to be bright and novel. Compared with boxy lines and shapes common in traditional seats, a glossy and smooth shape should be the first choice of designers.

In view of DANGER, the handrails should be canceled and make the line-change of the edges mellow. Acute angles and branches must be refrained from the shaping work. The product design is achieved based on demands analysis. The proposal is as Fig. 4.

The transition of different parts of this design is rounded and mellow. Its shape comes from the form of pistils growing from petals of a bud, with a feeling of ascending and stretching to represent senior people's standing up gracefully and the gap between the products and users can be perceptually narrowing to some extent. The signifier and signified of the exterior semantic meanings can be combined together effectively in this way.

According to the results listed in Table 1, the posture applied in this design is leaning by which senior people do not have to sit down utterly when using and thus it can be more convenient and easier for them to stand up. The facility ensures that the angle between the user's torso and thighs is about 130° under the leaning posture. Such an leaning attitude is comfortable and can save a lot of labour when standing up. In order to prevent the seating body from declining, a knee-support frame is added on the

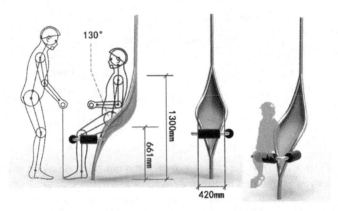

Fig. 4. A design proposal

position of legs. The outer layer of the frame is wrapped in soft material which can reduce muscle stress. This angle can make the spine of the elderly be kept under a natural posture and reduce the force of lumbar vertebra. Even without a waist cushion, the elderly will not feel tired.

5.2   Positioning

Volume of public rest facilities depends on the locus in which it is located. And the locus selection depends on people's needs. Hieronymus's study showed that setting up seats in places such as parks, squares or game fields can attract the elderly to take a walk here. The appropriate walking distance for the elderly is 150 m and rest facilities ought to be set every 150 m at least, along the edges of their action fields and on both sides of roads where the frequency of use is high [10]. This requires that volume of the facility should not be too large or take up a lot of space. It must be exquisite enough and easy to dismantle.

Besides, diversified psychological and behavioral characteristics of the elderly require the design to be provided with a variety of modes in assembling and arranging under the premise of conforming to human-machine relationship. Therefore, designers should take the spacial size of a regional system into account, which needs the design can be presented either in a combination of a group of products or by a single unit.

Chinese senior people always hold various recreational activities in parks. Rest facilities ought to help to build a site for senior people's exchange and interaction. This is important for enhancing their sense of existence in the society and relieving their negative emotions in life [11]. Thus in the aspect of modular combination, the design proposal adopts a smaller volume and ensures the facility conforms to a sense of aesthetics either it is placed in a circle or in a straight row (Fig. 5).

Fig. 5. Application scene of the proposal

5.3   Scale and Size

From the age group 40–44, people's height begins to decrease significantly with age and the trend will last for the latter half of life. Sitting height and extensional range of limbs hold the same downward trend [12, 13]. Such reduction demands the facility design to take Chinese senior people's body dimension into consideration. Domestic researches have given out relative conclusions [3, 14].

Based on Chinese elderly's body dimension data, using the large percentile size of male senior people to set the height and width of leaning surface and backrest so that the big and tall senior people can lean on it. The sitting hip breadth of 90th percentile of Chinese male elderly is 399 mm [3]. Considering the thickness of clothes in winter, the widest part of the surface is set as about 420 mm.

Using medium percentile size of female senior people to design the knee supporting frame and preventing males' legs from being unable to be put in which is brought about by small size, or females' knee from reaching the frame which is caused by a large size. The method to obtain the size is subtracting buttock-popliteal length from buttock-knee length to get the thickness of shin. Considering the thickness of trousers in winter and basic leg movements, the distance between the knee supporting frame and leaning surface bracket is ascertained.

The distance from the top of the leaning surface to the ground is about 1300 mm which is determined by male elderly's large percentile size. The volume is small and suitable to be put in a variety of indoor and outdoor occasions.

6 Conclusion

In the aging society, attention to the using experience of the disadvantaged senior people represents the degree of social civilization. Product design should not focus on the appearance and economical efficiency only. Under such a principle, the research analyzes the leaning posture's merits and dismerits. Physical functions of senior people's lower limbs declines and sitting down completely is not a good way to rest. Leaning is useful and easy to use but makes elder users feel dangerous. By comparison of three postures, an improved rest posture is proposed.

By means of factor analysis and regression analysis, significant effective results are obtained to guide design works. From aspects of posture, exterior, danger and experience, users' perceptual cognition and physical characteristics are taken into consideration and well-directed design points are put forward.

Relative research about elder users' behaviors and experience are still keeping on. Based on the results of this study, more design proposals can be made and it is appropriate to select an optimized one as the solution to problems of public rest facilities.

Finally, a limitation of the current study is that the analysis relies on the use of perceptual judgement which limits to a certain extent the validity of the analysis. In next phase of research therefore, a 1:1 model would be made for subjects to lean on and to evaluate their experience by variation of physical signals such as information from EEG. Additional insights into senior people's demands would be brought about.

References

1. McGee, M.A., et al.: The description of activities of daily living in five centers in England and Wales: the medical research council cognitive function and aging study. Age Aging **27**, 605–613 (1998)
2. Meng, Y.: Design of Tools Assisting Elders in Traveling Based on Ergonomics. Shaanxi University of Science & Technology, Xi' an (2012)
3. Sun, S.: Study on Chair Comfort of the Elderly. China University of Mining and Technology, Jiangsu (2015)
4. Gao, W., Fang, T.: Users' psychology-based research on aged-oriented public chairs. J. Anhui Univ. Sci. Technol. (Soc. Sci.), **5**(16), 42–44 (2014)
5. Wang, L., Cao, Q., Mo, X., et al.: Study of users' Kansei on commercial aircraft cockpit interior design. J. Mech. Eng. **22**, 122–126 (2014)
6. Chen, M., Jin, M., Wang, K., et al.: Evaluation of coal mine machinery industrial design based on fuzzy AHP. J. Taiyuan Univ. Sci. Technol. **03**, 223–227 (2015)
7. Davis, F.: User acceptance of information technology: system characteristics, user perceptions and behavioral impacts. Int. J. Man-Mach. Stud. **38**, 475–487 (1993)
8. Day, R.: Local environments and older people's health: dimensions from a comparative qualitative study in Scotland. Health Place **14**(2), 299–312 (2008)
9. Valdemarsson, M., Jernryd, E., Iwarsson, S.: Preferences and frequencies of visits to public facilities in old age–a pilot study in a Swedish town center. Arch. Gerontol. Geriat. **40**(1), 15–28 (2005)

10. Borst, H.C., Miedema, H.M.E., de Vries, S.I., et al.: Relationships between street characteristics and perceived attractiveness for walking reported by elderly people. J. Environ. Psychol. **28**(4), 353–361 (2008)
11. Zhang, X.: Study on Recreation Behavior of Old People in the Black Bamboo Park in Beijing. Beijing Forestry University, Beijing (2007)
12. Mick, D.J., Ackerman, M.H.: Critical care nursing for older adults: pathophysiological and functional considerations. Nurse Clin. North Am. **39**(3), 473–493 (2004)
13. Perrig-Chiello, P., Perrig, W.J., Uebelbacher, A., et al.: Impact of physical and psychological resources on functional autonomy in old age. Psychol. Health Med. **11**(4), 470–482 (2006)
14. Hu, H.: Anthropometric measurement of the elderly. Tsinghua University, Beijing (2005)

The Research and Co-creation Model for Urban Interaction Design and Practices

Yuyao Zhou$^{(\boxtimes)}$ and Nan Jiang

Department of Information Art and Design, Tsinghua University,
Beijing 100084, People's Republic of China
{zhouyy17,jiangn17}@mails.tsinghua.edu.cn

Abstract. The city is the basis of people's life, carrying the behavior and interaction of residents every day. With the rapid development of information interaction technology, the city is paying more and more attention to Human-oriented and Human-Computer Interaction (HCI). The Smart City is a new city form developed in such a new technology environment. This paper focuses on applying the methods of HCI to the construction of smart city. We analyze related cases and create an element model of Urban IxD, and then get the operation framework of urban innovation. After that, the operation framework is applied to co-creation workshop. Finally, based on stakeholder discussion, the models of city co-creation are built. These models and frameworks are intended as a common design model to help builders to discover design opportunities and create appropriate solutions for urban innovation.

Keywords: Urban IxD · Smart city · HCI · Urban innovation
Co-creation

1 Introduction

Needs and functions of development of cities are constantly evolving with the development of social economy and information technology. City information has experienced three stages: network, digitization and intelligence. The smart city is regarded as the stage of advanced urban development that matches the knowledge economy. This is the inevitable rule of urban developed to a certain stage, people-oriented, innovative, interactive and sustainable development is important concept.

In November 2008, IBM's Chairman, CEO and President Sam Palmisano, during a speech at the Council on Foreign Relations, outlined a new agenda for building a "Smarter Planet" [1]. In this background, the global boom of "Smart City" started to emerge. The smart city concept integrates information and communication technology (ICT), and various physical devices connected to the network (the Internet of things or IOT) to optimize the efficiency of city operations and services and connect to citizens [2]. The whole city will be a multi-dimensional interactive place where people and objects interact with each other, the interaction between people and the environment, and the transmission of objects and data are sent in a tangible and intangible space. At present, there is a great effort to build smart cities in China and abroad, and many countries have formulated and implemented many strategies, and also emphasized the

© Springer International Publishing AG, part of Springer Nature 2018
P.-L. P. Rau (Ed.): CCD 2018, LNCS 10912, pp. 444–454, 2018.
https://doi.org/10.1007/978-3-319-92252-2_35

concept of co-creation. Organizations such as MindLab in Denmark and Nesta in the UK, for instance, emphasized the need to implement co-production processes as the only viable solution to the growing complexity and wicked nature of issues tackled by public authorities [3].

The traditional HCI solves the relationship between human, machine and interface. In the context of the city began to expand to space. Terry Winograd said that "inter-active design is about building an interactive space for people's lives, not just an interface that people interact with". This paper takes the concept of Urban Interaction Design (Urban IxD) as the research direction, which is about the interaction between people and the urban environment. Urban IxD is not only about the coming together of various disciplines in addressing urban developments, but also about finding new relations between professional designers, academics, policy makers and citizens [4].

At present, in the background of smart city, HCI and Service design are new concepts for exploring the development of the human-oriented city, which lacks unified understanding and overall guidance framework. This paper focuses on how to make use of various organizations and methods in the HCI field to create urban innovation schemes. We collected different characteristics of urban innovation cases, analyzed the relevant elements of each case, and then used the territory map to summarize the Urban IxD's factor model and analyze the operational model. In recent years, we have been organizing workshops on urban co-creation, and we have used the operation mode to get the validity of the model. Finally, we summarize the co-creation model of stakeholders.

2   Related Work

2.1   Theoretical Research

The initial concept of a smart city started with cities utilizing communication technologies to deliver services to their citizens and evolved to using information technology to be smarter and more efficient about the utilization of their resources. Initially, resources were limited to fields that were tangible, mainly energy and mobility systems. In recent years, however, not only what can be done with information technology has changed significantly, but also the resources and areas addressable by a smart city have broadened significantly [5].

Among the most important standards, ITU has recently published the Smart-Sustainable Cities Focus-Group (SSC FG) results, which demonstrate among others the 10 types of smart services that a smart city can deliver: Smart Water, Smart Energy, Smart Transportation, Smart Healthcare, Safety/Emergency, Education and Tourism, Smart Waste Management, Smart Buildings, e-government and e-business [6]. Many new research projects around the world are beginning to rise. It started with the IBM Smarter Planet Initiative [7], quickly followed by the MIT City Science program [8] and Trinity's Smart & Sustainable Cities initiative [9], all addressing vital aspects of this vibrant field. The form of co-creation is also very popular in urban innovation. Urban Living Labs (ULLs), in fact, have become a trend in cities all over the world. The term is used to refer to a wide variety of local experimental projects of a participatory nature. The aim is to develop, try out and test innovative urban solutions in a real-life context [10]. Brazil has set up Network of Smart and Human Cities (RBCIH) to put together members from academy, private initiative and local government [11]. At the same time various data platforms are the foundation for building smart cities. Smart city uses different types of electronic data collection sensors to supply information which is used to manage assets and resources efficiently [12]. Like online collaborative sensor data management platforms are on-line database services that allow sensor owners to register and connect their devices to feed data into an on-line database for storage and allow developers to connect to the database and build their own applications based on that data [13]. The city of Santander in Cantabria, northern Spain, has 20,000 sensors connecting buildings, infrastructure, transport, networks and utilities, offers a physical space for experimentation and validation of the IOT functions [14].

2.2   Case Study

Our research method starts from the case, summarizing the characteristics of existing projects, form a regular research framework and model. We selected four different characteristics of the case (Product, Open source, Service, Participation). The overall two categories, the first two obtain data from products, the latter two is to guide you how to city innovation.

Case1: Copenhagen Wheel

The "Copenhagen Wheel" is designed by the MIT Senseable City Lab of the Massachusetts Institute of Technology [15]. The wheel of Copenhagen transformed the traditional bicycle into electric bicycle, and installed mobile sensors on the bicycle to collect all kinds of data in user's travel process. As you ride, the sensing unit in the Copenhagen Wheel is capturing information about your personal riding habits as well as information about your surroundings. Access this data through your phone or the web and use it to plan healthier bike routes and to achieve your exercise goals. You can also share your data with friends, or with your city. Thereby it contributes to a fine-grained database of environmental information from which citizen can all benefit. The project focuses on how people travel, including products, hardware and Apps, which further improves urban traffic and environment by collecting user data.

Case2: Smart Citizen Kit

Citizen Kit is an Arduino based sensor kit that provides sophisticated sensor network tools to citizens, enabling the measurement of levels of air pollution, noise pollution or air humidity [16]. The project was originally developed within the Fab Lab Barcelona at the Institute for Advanced Architecture of Catalonia and crowdfunded via the Goteo and Kickstarter crowdfunding platforms. With its relatively low-cost model the Smart Citizen Kit sees itself as acting as a bridge between more typically technical and non-technical citizens, both seeking to solve environmental challenges in unconventional ways through better monitoring. The kit exists of an open source hardware device, a website where the data is being collected, an API and a mobile app. It connects people with their environment and their city to create more effective and optimized relationships between resources, technology, communities, services and events in the urban environment.

Case3: Civic Service Design

Civic Service Design (Tools + Tactics) was produced by the Service Design Studio at the NYC Mayor's Office for Economic Opportunity [17]. It refers to the practice of creating, better understanding, and improving upon programs at any stage; it uses "civic service design" to mean applying the tools and methods of service design to government-run or funded programs. The goal for service design is to make public services as effective and accessible as possible for all New Yorkers. The project emphasizes the use of design methods to promote the government's thinking on project goals. The use of design methods for government decisions is rare, which is more conducive to the government's strategy to meet the needs of citizens.

Case4: App MyCity

App MyCity is a contest for the world's best urban app [18]. Awarded every year at the NewCities Summit, it rewards new mobile applications that improve the urban experience, connect people, and make cities more fun, fair, vibrant, and sustainable places. The project is hosted by an international non-profit organization called NewCities. The format of the competition is novel, and it is a low-cost way for the organization to obtain high value solutions. The participated citizens can also show their own ideas through the competition. If the scheme is adopted, the mutual win can be achieved.

We get the real and effective data from the four actual cases and organize it, and based on this we can get the following characteristics of the factors. The specific methods, forms and outputs of urban innovation were found out, as shown in Fig. 1.

	Copenhagen Wheel	Smart Citizen Kit	Civic Service Design	AppMyCity
Stakeholders	Government+Citizen +Organization	Citizen+Community +Organization	Government+Citizen +Organization	Citizen+ Organization
Organization	Copenhagen government+MIT Senseable City Lab	Fab lab+Institute for Architecture of Catalonia	NYC+Citi Community	New Cities Foundation
Technology	Product manufacturing, Software, ICT, Data	Arduino, Software, ICT, Data	Open data, Design thinking	Data, Code, Organizational strategy
Approach	Co-creation	Crowdfunding	Hackathon	Competition
Output	Data	Open source data Participatory tools	APP, Website, Service	APP
Field	Mobility	Environment	Public service	Lifestyle

Fig. 1. The elements of four typical cases

By extracting the important elements in the case, we can draw the following territory map. The main focus of this model is on how to represent the elements of Urban IxD in the three dimensions of HCI.

3   Core Elements of Urban IxD

3.1   Territory Map

One of the ways we analyze the project is by having them create "territory map" of the project space because it mediates interaction between all elements.

As shown in Fig. 2, the HCI domain consists of three main dimensions: Design, Computer Science and Cognitive Psychology. The design includes concepts such as interaction design, user experience, participatory design and visualization. Design can inspire more creative urbanization programs and more ways to lead people step by step. Computer science includes the technology needed to build a smart city. Technology plays a key role in building a smart city and technology makes more efficient use of physical infrastructure (roads, built environment and other physical assets) through artificial intelligence and data analytics to support a strong and healthy economic, social, cultural development [19]. Sustained technological innovation is an inexhaustible motive force for the development of a smart city, but technology is only the realization means of smart city, not the ultimate goal. Cognitive psychology is mainly concerned with the user requirements, user experiences and user feelings in the city. Seligman defines the well-being theory [20] as a theme of positive psychology. He defines five factors needed for humans to flourish: positive emotion, engagement, meaning, relationships and achievement. Focusing on user psychology can further promote the effectiveness of urban innovation.

The combination of design and technology will produce output, and the output of urban innovation will be widely ranging from policy formulation and strategic planning to products and data in life. Both design and cognitive psychology are concerned with stakeholders. There are many different types of groups in the city, and it is because of the co-creation that we can produce smart cities which are in the interest of the group. Computer science and cognitive psychology together lead to the approach. There are various approaches of urban innovation, in order to create common motivation and goals for everyone. Deakin defines the smart city as one that utilizes ICT to meet the demands of the market (the citizens of the city), and that community involvement in the process is necessary for a smart city [21]. This shows the importance of technology, user needs and co-creation.

3.2   Operation Framework of Urban IxD

After studying the factors of HCI and urban innovation, the paper analyzes the operational framework of urban innovation. The interactive design method is combined with the elements of urban innovation to obtain the following five steps, as shown in Fig. 3.

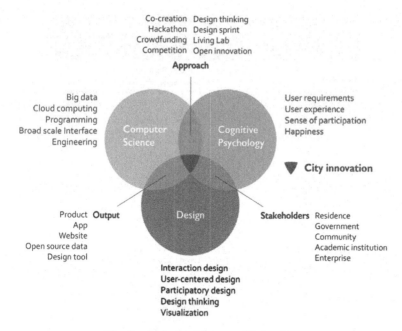

Fig. 2. Analysis of factors of Urban IxD

Citizens' participation is the foundation for urban innovation. Citizens have a stronger sense of presence, more participation and autonomy, and innovative services from enterprises and governments have been continuously stimulated. Data is the foundation of information, and now residents can also be one of the data sources. The whole process includes five steps. The first step is to determine the background of the project, explore the functional features of different scenarios using space, or explore the needs and emotions of different users based on people. The second step is to identify the specific fields of the project, and we summarize 6 fields that cover different aspects of life: Mobility, Live and Play, Production, Consumption, Management and Infrastructure, Community and Health. Every field has its own system and interoperability with each other, which constitutes a huge network system of smart city. The third step is to start thinking about ways to achieve urban innovation. Such as living lab to provide specific scenarios for everyone to create, and design thinking provides a mode of thinking to guide people to think about innovation. The fourth step is the specific form of output. The final result of smart city is varied. It can be a macro policy plan, or a specific product innovation. From the design level, product or service design are two main forms to change people's life. Either a large product or small one involves the technology and the popularization of the public. From the citizen's own mobile phone to get the living data or release a small cost kit, which is an instance of getting a data in a wide range from a micro view. The final step is to achieve two goals from the project: improving the lifestyle and behavior or improving the feelings between the residents and the residents, residents and the city.

		Foundation: Citizen& Data		

		Time / Space / People
First step (Setting up the project background)	Background	**time / space:**Exploring the connection between the smart city and the creation space from the perspective of urban planning **people:** Exploring the development of smart city from the life needs and emotional needs of urban residents
Second step (Identify the areas of problem solving)	Fields	1.Mobility 2.Live and Play 3.Production 4.Consumption 5.Management and Infrastructure 6.Community and Health
Third step (Approach we need)	Approach	Design thinking, Design sprint Living Lab, Open innovation
Fourth step (Forms of project output)	Output	Strategic planning, Product, App, Open source data, Tool
Fifth step (The purpose of the project)	Emotional	1. lifestyle and behaviour 2 .Improving the feelings between the residents and the residents, residents and the city

Fig. 3. Operation framework of Urban IxD

4   Co-creation Workshop

Through the workshop, we practice the above operating framework. In 2014–2018, three typical cases were selected to illustrate. The cases focused on community, space and city respectively.

4.1   Creative Community

In 2014, we organized the first workshop about the creative community, it had attracted more than 40 people from government agencies, social organizations, business circles, IT experts and design professional teachers and students to participate. The design of the six teams are based on Internet communication technology such as Internet of things, sensor network and so on, so as to form a new management form community based on large-scale information intelligent processing.

Each team presents a different design object: the design of electronic waste recycling platform, the prototype design of community old-age self-help, the design of remote control robot, Babel Tower breaker Bracelet design, the design of the joint office, commercial exhibition and creative communication space design and the design of city pet dog intelligence community.

From the outputs of the workshop, the proposal of the creative community is a transformation from emphasizing technology as the core to emphasizing the service of technology as the core. From the outputs of six groups, there were three groups aimed to strengthen the emotional connection between residents and residents. The other three groups aimed to improve the relationship between the residents and the city. These outputs are based on community resident demands, solving the problems of people's livelihood as the theme, optimizing the life style of the people for the direction, exploring the establishment of model of social construction innovation, optimizing existing resource allocation, mobilizing more people to participate in social construction. There are two main forms of output: online + offline platform and product as a medium.

4.2 Co-creation Space

In 2015, we organized a co-creation space workshop. With the theme of "Co-working Space", we explored the community building rules and creation models in co-working. This workshop is divided into seven groups using the same format as the creative community workshop we made before. According to the community needs, each group eventually explored different styles of co-working spaces based on their occupations or hobbies, including "Beautiful Village" Co-working Space, "DIY Jewelry" Co-working Space, Crowdfunding Platform, Designer "No. 3" community, Integration of Innovation Investment Space, Financial Services Space and Youth Space.

Unlike the previous urban design workshop, this workshop took space and time as the starting points, explored the relationship between smart city and co-working space from a more macroscopical perspective of urban planning. Seven groups are no longer focused on products to create communities, but for specific space design. Design involves factors such as economy, management, culture, technology, capital and function. There are many forms of space, which are dominated by people, dominated by regions and dominated by function.

4.3 Future City Innovation Workshop

We recently organized the 2018 Future Cities Workshop in collaboration with MIT. This workshop adopts the methods and tools of Design Thinking to co-create in the form of teamwork. The workshop summarizes the key issues of eight member companies and regroups the questions of each company. From the user perspective, the workshop summarizes Mobility, Living and Health, Working and Production, Commercial, Management and Infrastructure, Culture and Play six cities innovation direction, and participating in the workshop member companies together to derive and summarize the innovation implementation paths in all fields. The six topics correspond to the results of the mobile business scene for the business scene, smart cultural town, smart park one-stop service, new business scenarios, infrastructure staff office, cultural town real-time service information.

The special feature of urban innovation lies in the complexity and spatial attributes of the urban system. It is understood from two dimensions: the first is the dimension of human beings, including those who live in cities, the managers of cities, the construction and operation of communities, and the organizations that work in cities, cities, providers, and governments. The second is the spatial scene dimensions: from big to small, city and city clusters, area (including the new area and characteristic town), plot/single building.

From the results of these urban workshops, we can see that they are based on the time, space and people backgrounds, aimed to improve the relationship between urban residents and residents, or between urban residents and the city. Urban residents are people who often live in the city and have a sense of identity and belonging to the city. The participation of residents in urban planning refers to the urban residents' attempts to influence and promote urban planning decisions and to share the process of urban planning. In view of the elements of the concept, the subject of participation refers to all non-governmental organizations, residents, and government. Participation object refers to the process of participating in urban planning related activities; the way of participation can be either organizational participation or spontaneous participation.

Nowadays, the city is no longer simply a physical city that only exists for survival. The development of information technology brings all kinds of possibilities to all of you. Every discipline and every dimension is added to the urban construction. The interaction between the Internet and people constitutes a very important foundation for a smart city or a future urban development. Through organizing the city's co-working workshop, we hope to gather people from different professions to design the idea of smart city. The workshop is more conducive to the stimulation and collision of your mind, and also can help a single field of thinking transformed to a comprehensive view of the system.

5   Discussion and Future Work

Urban IxD is to apply the research and practice of HCI to the background of smart city. An important feature of this is that it brings together working groups that are already different from each other, cooperate with interdisciplinary and institutional partners, and emphasize the importance of citizens.

Figure 4 based on the relationship between the three important stakeholders in the city, we analyze the creation model of urban innovation. The key to creating collective wisdom is that under the guidance of the urban development strategy, the government and enterprises pay attention to the needs of citizens and social innovation, and the citizens participate actively as data sources. This operating system must be simultaneously top-down and bottom-up.

Citizens at the bottom, is the main body to build smart cities. The city not only provides residents with the physical space of their dwelling, but also the spiritual space attribution of residents' feelings. At the highest level, the government is the co-ordinator of a smart city. It is the government's responsibility to choose a combination of long-term planning and current conditions in line with the local model of construction path. Enterprises are in the middle, and as a professional company, their

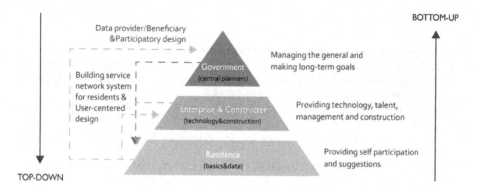

Fig. 4. Co-creation model between stakeholders

involvement in promoting smart city development not only opens up new businesses and markets for the company, but it also makes up for the government's lack of technical and professional knowledge. The three help each other and work together to promote the development of smart city.

After this, we still have other valuable things to do:

- We have done a lot of city workshops, then we can consider doing more city innovation practice projects. Getting more data and information from the project to refine the model to make it even more instructive.
- Although smart city is a very broad concept, urban interaction is a good point for us to get involved in. Then we can put forward our own concept to improve the application of design at all levels.

6 Conclusion

In order to apply HCI to smart city, this paper starts from the concept of Urban IxD, summarizes the factor model of urban interaction through case studies, develops the application framework of urban interaction in urban environment, and applies it to urban workshops. Finally, from the point of view of stakeholders, we discussed the value of co-creation. We practice and confirm the relevant method, so that we believe the conclusion have the guiding significance. We will continue perfecting and verifying our conclusion and pay attention to development and promotion of creativity of innovation participant. Also, we will develop more distinctive products and services for urban innovation.

Acknowledgments. These cases are from MIT Senseable City Lab, Fab lab, NYC, New Cities. Sincerely thanks to Tsinghua University Institute of Service Design.

References

1. Smart Planet. https://en.wikipedia.org/wiki/Smarter_Planet
2. Peris-Ortiz, M., Bennett, D.R., Pérez-Bustamant Yábar, D.: Sustainable Smart Cities: Creating Spaces for Technological Social and Business Development. Springer, Cham (2016). https://doi.org/10.1007/978-3-319-40895-8
3. Bason, C., Mygind, J., Sabroe, R.: Co-production Towards A New Welfare Model. MindLab, Copenhagen (2013)
4. Brynskov, M., Bermudez, C., Fernandez, M., Korsgaard, H.: Urban Interaction Design: Towards City Making (2014)
5. Schleicher, J.M., Vögler, M., Inzinger, C., Dustdar, S.: Towards the internet of cities: a research roadmap for next-generation smart cities, pp. 3–6 (2015)
6. Anthopoulos, L., Janssen, M., Weerakkody, V.: Smart service portfolios: do the cities follow standards? pp. 357–362 (2016)
7. IBM Smart Planet. http://www.ibm.com/smarterplanet/us/en/
8. MIT media lab. http://cities.media.mit.edu/about/initiative
9. Smart & Sustainable Cities. https://www.tcd.ie/research/themes/smart-sustainable-cities/
10. Steen, K., Van Bueren, E.: Urban living labs: a living lab way of working (2017)
11. Pereira, G.V., Bernardes, M.B., Bernardini, F.: Building a reference model and an evaluation method for cities of the Brazilian network of smart and human cities, pp. 580–581 (2017)
12. Hamblen, M.: Just what is a smart city? 1 October 2015. computerworld.com
13. Boyle, D., Yates, D., Yeatman, E.: Urban sensor data streams: London 2013. IEEE Internet Comput. 17(6), 1 (2013)
14. Schaffers, H., Komninos, N., Pallot, M., Trousse, B., Nilsson, M., Oliveira, A.: Smart cities and the future internet: towards cooperation frameworks for open innovation. In: Domingue, J., Galis, A., Gavras, A., Zahariadis, T., Lambert, D., Cleary, F., Daras, P., Krco, S., Müller, H., Li, M.-S., Schaffers, H., Lotz, V., Alvarez, F., Stiller, B., Karnouskos, S., Avessta, S., Nilsson, M. (eds.) FIA 2011. LNCS, vol. 6656, pp. 431–446. Springer, Heidelberg (2011). https://doi.org/10.1007/978-3-642-20898-0_31
15. Copenhagen Wheel. http://senseable.mit.edu/copenhagenwheel/
16. Smart citizen kit. http://waag.org/en/project/smart-citizen-kit
17. Civic service design. www.nyc.gov/servicedesign
18. Smartcityhub. https://medium.com/smartcityhub/what-is-the-city-of-the-future-what-means-smart-5ebbab137967
19. App mycity. https://newcities.org/appmycity/
20. Seligman, M.E.P.: Flourish: A Visionary New Understanding of Happiness and Well-being. Free Press, New York (2011)
21. Deakin, M.: From intelligent to smart cities. In: Deakin, M. (ed.) Smart Cities: Governing, Modelling and Analysing the Transition, p. 15. Taylor and Francis, Abingdon (2013)

Innovation Design of Rural Tourism Based on Service Design Methods—A Case Study of Beijing Lingshui Village

Yanfei Zhu[1], Zhisheng Zhang[1(✉)], Chengqi Xue[1], Tianyang Zhu[2], and Jie Shen[1]

[1] College of Mechanical Engineering, Southeast University,
Nanjing 211189, China
409647204@qq.com
[2] College of Mechanical and Electrical Engineering,
Beijing University of Chemical Technology, Beijing 100029, China

Abstract. This paper takes service design methods and tools to improve the rural tourism service design in China. Choosing the existing tourist country Lingshui Village which is located in Mentougou district, Beijing, China as the research object. Using the methods and tools of service design to solve problems in the process of tourism industry service innovation. At last, build the Lingshui Village tourism industry service system and design new products, realize the innovation of Lingshui Village tourism service design.

Keywords: Service design · Rural tourism · Innovative design

1 Introduction

Rural tourism plays an important part in rural development, and it's also a new growth point of economic development. It has become a popular choice for modern urbanite tourists thanks to its short distance and original experience. However, a rapid homogeneity-oriented process of the rural tourism competition caused a waste of resources and a decline in tourist satisfaction and the quality of the service. Therefore, the improvement of tourist travel experience and the development of rural economy has become a burning issue in the rural tourism nowadays.

2 Background Work

2.1 Service Design

Service is a process in which service providers transmit service content to service recipients through certain service channels and cause service recipients to change their state. The term "service design" first appeared in the design management book 《Total Design》 by the Bill Hollions and his wife [1]. The Board of International Research in Design define as: "A service is set up from a customer's point of view, and its purpose is to ensure a service interface" [1]. In today's era of service economy, service design is a systematic solution that includes service models, business models, product platforms and interactive interfaces. The goal is to focus on the users, improve the quality of service and improve the experience of consumers. It can be tangible or intangible.

2.2   Literature Review

For Rural Tourism, Foreign Scholars Have Carried Out Related Research
Lo et al. through a study of 516 tourism stakeholders from 34 Malaysian rural tourist attractions, a scenic spot information management system has been established. The present situation of scenic spots can be displayed by data and information, which has a great impact on the development of rural tourism [2]. Bodoc Tefania argues that digitization is affecting rural tourism, and tourism blogs have an irreplaceable advantage in improving their awareness of tourism destinations [3]. Jeroscenkova et al. discussed the application of cultural heritage in the development of tourism and established the fund for cultural heritage protection of the European Union [4]. Paiu et al. indicate that Rural Tourism has become a new mode to replace traditional tourism [5].

For Rural Tourism, Chinese Scholars Have Carried Out Related Research
Chen takes advantage of renewable energy technology in the development of low-carbon rural tourism. Taking Changsha as an example, the study applied local biomass energy, solar energy and wind energy to the development of low-carbon rural tourism and how to use these renewable energy methods [6]. Gao and He from the perspective of urban-rural integration, green rural tourism in the underdeveloped areas of western China needs local culture and character to realize urban-rural integration, adhere to the principle of sustainable development the principle of measures to local conditions and the principle of characteristic development [7]. Zheng in view of the current situation and existing problems of rural tourism brand management, some suggestions are put forward [8]. Hong analyzes the development of rural tourism resources based on ecotourism, and points out that rural ecotourism can improve the income of rural residents, provide new potential for rural consumption market, and provide new growth point for agricultural development [9].

In the Research of Rural Tourism Service Design in China
Hu in order to meet the needs of rural tourism development in Zhejiang province, takes Baisha Village as a typical case, carries on the product innovation, the management and the service innovation. The marketing innovation has carried on the thorough research [10]. Wang et al. use service design tools to make travel, leisure, culture, food and other node element for redesign, highlight the local characteristics and protect the environment of Laiyuan, Huangtuling [11]. Li and He through the service design to explore and define the rural social innovation problem. The service design method participates in the social innovation of Nihegou Village, find the local rural social innovation solution and construct the sustainable rural community [12]. Zhang summarizes the basic principles and paths of the rural tourism service system based on the technology embedding, through the analysis of the application secretary of the rural tourism service

system based on the embedded data, thinks that the technology embedding can improve the rural tourism service system [13].

2.3 Research Technique

The main purpose of this study is to apply the theory, tools and methods of service design to the operation, service and strategy of rural tourism under the background of the imbalance between the development of modern rural tourism and social demand in China and to establish a perfect service system for rural tourism in China. Taking Lingshui Village of Mentougou in Beijing as an example, this paper explores the feasibility of combining rural tourism with service design, takes the regional historical and cultural resources as a breakthrough point, and devotes to the construction of tourist experience oriented. The rural tourism innovation service system is realized with the goal of sustainable economic cycle development villages. The research methods used in this paper mainly include:

Literature Research Method. Referring to the historical and cultural literature of Lingshui Village, analyzing, combing, summing up and deeply digging out the selling points of cultural resources that can be used for service design fusion.

Qualitative Analysis Method. Through in-depth interviews with tourists, villagers, staff and other target groups, the paper explores the demand of tourists and the existing problems of rural tourism from a more comprehensive perspective, and summarizes the problems of tourists' satisfaction and dissatisfaction, as well as the rural tourism service design has not been met the new needs.

Quantitative Analysis Method. Through the questionnaire investigation on the tourist demand, to find the data support for the qualitative analysis result, enhance the reliability of the qualitative analysis result.

The Methodology of Service Design. According to the characteristics of this study, based on the theory of service design, a rural tourism service system is constructed by using appropriate service tools.

3 Investigation

In order to obtain and understand the operating status of Lingshui Village and tourists' demand, this research can be divided into the following three stages:

3.1 Investigation of Natural and Human Resources

Lingshui Village, which located in the town of Zhaitang, Mentougou district, western Beijing, gathered into a village as early as about 2000, it is one of the three famous villages of Chinese history and culture in the western Beijing [14]. In 2005, it was listed as "famous Village of Chinese History and Culture" by the State Administration of Cultural relics. In 2016, Beijing Tourism Development Committee named "the most beautiful village in Beijing" [15]. There are many scholars in Lingshui Village in history and the village is famous for its many achievements and fame since the Ming and Qing dynasties [14]. About the middle of the Qing Dynasty, they decided on eight scenes in the village: "Donglingshiren", "Xishansongcui", "Nanlingyuantiao", "Beita yuantiao", "Wenxinggaozhao", "Songtiyuer", "Gubaicantian" to show love for their hometown [16]. Today's "Lingshui eight scenery", which is composed of natural scenery, cultural relics and historic sites, forms high-quality tourist resources. However, due to the serious lack of service planning in the tourism system, Lingshui Village tourism has not been developed organically, nor has it formed due economic benefits.

3.2   Interview and Research in the Village

Research Methods. In this section, in-depth interview is the main method. In-depth interview is a qualitative research method, which requires to draw up the interview outline through previous research, and then to communicate with stakeholders face to face deeply. The interview interacted with the interviewees in a semi-structured way to fully understand the pain points of interest of the target people and finally explained the deep needs of various groups of people.

Research Implementation. The author first identified the three main types of tourists, villagers and managers, wrote different interview scripts according to the different characteristics of the three kinds of people, so as to obtain the deep needs of all parties in a short time and increase the value and credibility of the interview. This section was conducted in Lingshui Village, Beijing. A total of 15 target groups were interviewed, including 7 tourists, 4 villagers and 4 managers, covering all the key stakeholders. All of them were interviewed face to face and took notes on spot. All the raw materials were analyzed and the output was summarized after collected, and the time was 2017.

Research Result

(1)   **The Main Problems Based on the Interview with the Tourists**

- The village should be more convenient in transportation, more cultural features are needed, and use the internet for unified publicity. Eat and live well are very important during the vacation.
- The village must have its own cultural features to avoid stereotyped, and focus on differentiated management to have its own memory points to avoid cliche and commercialize.
- Overcharing customers such as in "Snow Town" in Heilongjiang Province should be avoid, which makes people have poor impression in catering, lodging and sanitary condition in rural tourism.
- It is hoped that rural tourism can establish norms and standards and provide diversified services. Tourism content and service level need to be improved.
- It is hoped that rural tourism can be popularized and mature and become more ecological.

(2) **The Main Problems Based on the Interview with the Villagers**

- The distribution of the eight scenic spots in the village is irregular and have many detours, which makes the number of tourists asking for directions is particularly large.
- Most villagers make a living by catering and lodging, but the contents of the service are very similar and failed to design and develop in depth according to their own characteristics, and cannot obtain tourist resources effectively.
- The tourism resources in the village have non overall planning, are obsolete and scattered, and the entertainment items in the rural homes are not effectively supervised.
- Part of the village's agricultural and sideline products are self-sufficient, part are provided to the village's restaurants, and part are purchased by tourists in the retail stalls, but there is no fixed distribution channel for the sale of specialty products.

(3) **The Main Problems Based on the Interview with the Managers**

- The managers in the village are generally senior aged. Due to the number of personnel, the content of supervision and the limited level, the system management model has not been formed.
- The service form in the village is single, not systemized and lack of external publicity window.
- Most of the young generation have left the villages to work in cities, they have not paid much attention to the inheritance of traditional culture and service inheritance in the villages.

3.3   Survey on Tourist Demand

Research Methods. In this part, the questionnaire is mainly used. As a quantitative research technique, questionnaire can use statistical tools to process the survey results, locate users and describe and explain the wide range of characteristics of users accurately, and present their views in a structured way. This questionnaire is presented through a progressive way, including four sections: personal information, preference, service requirements and reference. There are 22 questions altogether, including single choice, multiple choice and divergent topics.

Research Platform. This part of the survey selected China's largest online questionnaire survey and voting platform —— WJX.CN, through WeChat, web pages and other channels. The questionnaire covers as many people as possible, including people from Jiangsu, Beijing, Zhejiang, Shanghai and so on. The results of the investigation are of general suitability.

Research Result. In this part, 406 valid questionnaires were collected by WJX.CN, and the effective rate was 100%.

(1) The Basic Situation of Tourists

The results of the questionnaire showed that the distribution of tourists was evenly distributed between men and women, and there was no difference in preferences of the genders (Fig. 1). The age is mainly concentrated between 20–30 years old, and most have college or higher degree, covering all walks of life (Fig. 2).

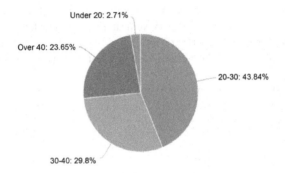

Fig. 1. Gender distribution

Fig. 2. The age distribution

(2) Analysis of Tourists' Preference for Rural Tourism

This part mainly investigates the views of tourists on rural tourism, the understanding level and their preference. Statistics show that most tourists have heard of rural tourism but have not participated in it. Some people have participated in rural tourism but only once or twice (Fig. 3).

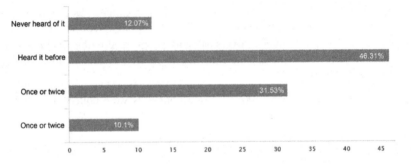

Fig. 3. Frequency of participation

Most tourists would like to participate in the rural tourism once six months to two years, a small number of people choose more than two years. Because of the short-distance of rural tourism, more than half of the tourists usually choose 2–3 days of weekend or small vacation to visit, and a considerable number of tourists choose to use one day to visit (Fig. 4). Compared with long-distance tourism, the rural tourism time is shorter and the consumption is lower. The relatively acceptable price range of rural tourism consumption is 500–1000 yuan, which belongs to the popular relatively low price. Tourists pay more attention to eating and living during the visit (Fig. 5).

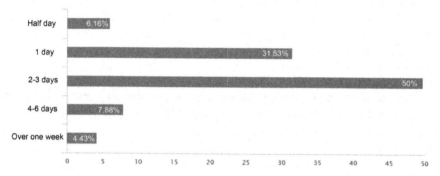

Fig. 4. Travel time

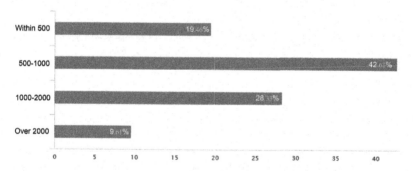

Fig. 5. Expected cost

As the chart shows, self-driving travel is obviously superior to other way of travelling, followed by group charter, indicating that tourists take short trips in the form of family, friends and units. Due to the rapid pace and high pressure of urban life, the main purpose of tourist travel is to relax and decompress. Seasonal natural beauty is more attractive to tourists (Fig. 6).

(3) **The Analysis of Tourists' Demand for Rural Tourism Service**

This part mainly investigates the specific needs of tourists for rural tourism services. It can be seen from the data that most people get to know the rural tourism through the

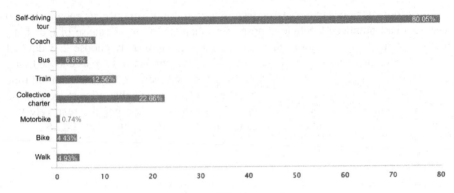

Fig. 6. Way to travel

internet and electronic media, followed by relatives and friends (Fig. 7). The brand reputation of rural tourism has an important impact on attracting repeat visitors and new tourists. Travel photos are usually displayed via WeChat and Weibo (Fig. 8).

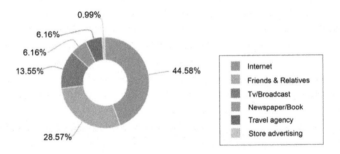

Fig. 7. Understand channels

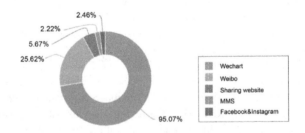

Fig. 8. The way to share

The hotel with distinctive theme has strong attraction for tourists, and they expect that the characteristic accommodation and board can be compared through the platform and can be booked in real time, which shows that tourists have a reverence for individualization, interesting and convenience (Fig. 9).

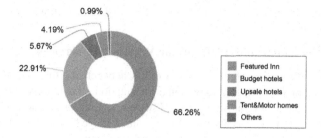

Fig. 9. Accommodation preference

The tourists are willing to choose the organic health farm and sideline products and the cultural and handmade souvenirs to share with their relatives and friends, and the vast majority of tourists will be willing to buy healthy agricultural products through the network platform again (Fig. 10).

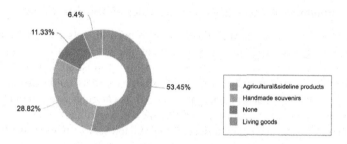

Fig. 10. Shopping inclination

(4) The Analysis of Tourists' Views on the Improvement of Rural Tourism

The investigation shows that tourists have a high expectation for rural catering, the improvement of the quality of accommodation brand, the highlight of the local characteristics of villages and the excavation of cultural connotations, as well as the traffic and information communication inside and outside the villages. They have a positive and optimistic attitude for future rural development in general (Fig. 11).

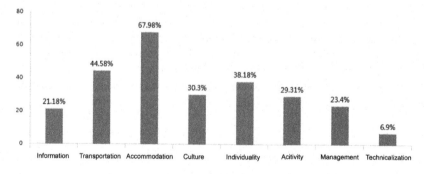

Fig. 11. Improvement requirement

Through the investigation of the three stages of Lingshui Village, we can find that there are three main service gaps:

1. Lack of Communication Platform for Visitors and Services

The need for information communication exists between the tourist and the service. With the development of technology, some information channels have already served the information exchange on both sides. However, the research results show that the service platform of professional service in Lingshui Village has not been formed, which has led to a series of problems, such as insufficient publicity of tourism resources in the village, long time to book rooms and communication, unreasonable tour routes of tourists in the village, and so on. The interactive platform of information really causes the service side to not get the feedback and follow-up service from the tourist side in time, and the tourist side and the service side can't exchange information and share the experience, resulting in the poor interaction between the tourist side and the service side.

2. The Combination of Regional Characteristics of Tourism Resources is Weak

The natural scenery of Lingshui village is very beautiful, its rich in historical and cultural resources. It is conducive to the regional characteristics of elements extracted by mining village, currently has eight attractions as a tourist attraction. According to the results of the survey, the brand image of the service has not been integrated and unified design planning, lack of recognition, such as catering, accommodation within the same industry homogenization is serious, the service still stays in the basic experience level, did not form a characteristic, differentiated service market. In addition, the service side, such as lack of brand shaping power, marketing concept is relatively outdated, product marketing failed to inject cultural connotation and brand spirit. The lack of design impede tourists to understand and choose Lingshui village as tourist destination.

3. Imbalance Between Supply and Demand of Services in and out of the Village

As far as the service of the village is concerned, on the one hand, the number of current managers is limited, the age level is relatively high, on the other hand, the young people in the village all go out to work, and the policy of introducing talents is not adopted in the village, short of subsequent talent training. As a result, the village service management has not yet connected the various industry service links from the source. Within and outside the village, if the tourists choose the countryside as a tourist destination because of advocating the original ecological organic and healthy life, it is unable to understand the village effectively before traveling, and can't carry out follow-up information feedback and product purchase again after traveling. Therefore, it is imminent to make use of the existing resources to adjust the structure and establish an effective ecological service system.

4 Service

4.1 Thoughts on Service Design into Rural Tourism

Nowadays, rural tourism has become a complex integrated service system. Rural tourism development needs begin to shift to more service, involving multiple stakeholders. In this service system, the tourism experience is closely related to the operation service, the diversification of services has become an important profit point for the development of the village. Therefore, the application of service design theory and tools to the development of rural tourism is helpful to the optimization and promotion of rural tourism quality.

4.2 User Portraits

According to the previous investigation, using user portraits to create virtual character files for tourists, villagers and managers, analyze the virtual characters of different types of characters, in order to truly reflect the needs, wishes and behavior expectations of users (Fig. 12).

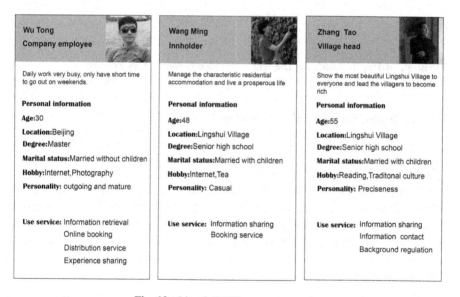

Fig. 12. Lingshui Village user portraits

4.3 Tourists Journey Map

Using tourists journey map to visitors'behavior before, during and after travel and how to use service to define service contacts. Through the analysis of tourist experience, discover the pain points that tourists encounter in the service acceptance process, to open up service gaps, develop solutions, and identify business opportunities. From the map we can see the earlier stage, middle stage, later stage service contact points and service pain points (Fig. 13).

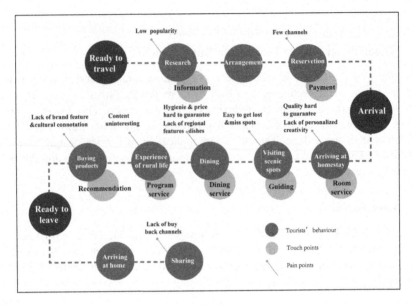

Fig. 13. Tourists journey map

Through in-Depth Analysis, the Main Service Gaps are as Follows

(1) Information channel gap (2) Brand image gap (3) Organic supply and demand gap.

4.4   Ecological Circulatory System Map

Using the Internet as the medium, from the three dimensions of information channel gap, brand image gap and organic supply and demand gap, the ecological circulatory system of Lingshui Village is constructed. Through the consolidation of the service supply chain integration between the information flow and the material flow in the whole tourism industry, the service closed loop can be formed. The relationship between the various organizations of the service system, purposeful behavior through the legend of the form of expression (Fig. 14).

4.5   Blueprint

The service blueprint depicts the design of Lingshui Village Service system, which describes the contacts through which visitors come into contact with Lingshui Village tourism, what products and services can be provided by in-village tourism projects, as well as activities on and off the side of the service side and the tourist side (Fig. 15).

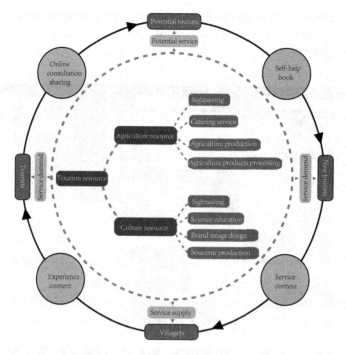

Fig. 14. Ecological circulatory system map

Entity scence	Download APP	Recommend information	Scenic spot	Merchant	Trading system	Take delivery	Sharing
User task	Click push	Confirm an order	Inquire	Communite	Confirm an order	Wait	Evaluate
Interaction line							
Front desk touch point	Information browsing	Payment Inform	Guide	Communication Experience	Payment Inform	Information updating	Data collection
Visibility line							
Back desk task	Edit content	Design Maintenance support	Maintenance support	Personal training	Infomatization management	Company cooperation	Data analysis
Support processes			Establish association	Supervise	Maintain		Reward points

Fig. 15. The service blueprint

5 Outcome

5.1 Official Account Design

The application program of Lingshui Village tourism mobile terminal is developed by using the Internet platform. The service items are integrated into the network platform, the interactive channels between the tourist side and the service side are established. Therefore, to enhance the nature of the information available and the interactive nature of the service. The Application can provide Lingshui Village information guide, travel strategy, event introduction, appreciation of specialty purchases and information sharing platform services (Fig. 16).

Fig. 16. Lingshui Village APP

5.2 Guide Design

The guiding system of Lingshui Village is redesigned to combine regional traditional culture with new materials to create the rustic flavor and classical meaning in order to highlight the regional characteristics of Lingshui Village. At the same time, QR code is set in the guide, the tourist side can get the background information of the scenic spot through the mobile phone QR code scan, and carry on the real time tour of the village line (Fig. 17).

Fig. 17. Lingshui Village guide

5.3 Design of Tourist Souvenirs

The pine tree, one of the elements of the scenic spot in the eight scenic spots of Lingshui, is extracted as a visual cultural symbol, combining with the historical and cultural background of the talented people in Lingshui Village, it is used in the bookself design, which is simple and easy to carry for tourists' own use or gift (Fig. 18).

Fig. 18. Lingshui Village tourist souvenirs

5.4 Package Design of Agricultural and Sideline Products

Through the package design of the special product of the Mentougou district, the package of e-commerce and local picking demand are satisfied, the product brand of the local agricultural and sideline products is also reflected. Besides, the uniform environmental protection package visual effect is realized (Fig. 19).

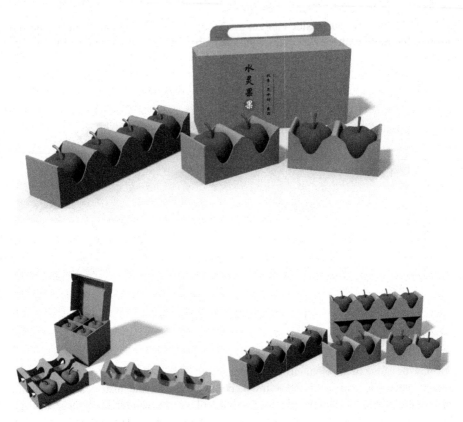

Fig. 19. Lingshui Village package design of agricultural and sideline products

6 Conclusion

In the Internet era, the original rural tourism service model is going out of fashion. In this paper, taking the typical tourist village Beijing Lingshui village as an example, the service design application innovation is realized and a win-win situation through the tools and methods of service design is achived. The application innovation realizes the structure of Lingshui village service system and design and practice present online and offline, by taking the Lingshui village historical and cultural appreciation experience as a principal and combining the Internet platform. This study has injected new vitality into the development of rural tourism, provided reference to the design of rural tourism services.

References

1. Luo, S.J., Zhu, S.S.: Service Design. China Machine Press, Beijing (2011)
2. Lo, M.C., Wang, Y.C., Songan, P., Yeo, A.W.: Tourscape: a systematic approach towards a sustainable rural tourism management. In: Proceedings of 8th International Symposium of the Digital Earth, Sarawak (2015)

3. Bodoc Tefania, L.: Digital world and its impact on tourists and rural tourism. In: Proceedings of the 25th International Business Information Management Association Conference - Innovation Vision 2020: From Regional Development Sustainability to Global Economic Growth, Amsterdam, pp. 2498–2504 (2015)
4. Jeroscenkova, L., Rivza, B., Rivza, P.: Decision making on the use of cultural heritage in rural tourism development in Latvia. In: Proceedings of 22nd Annual International Scientific Conference Research for Rural Development, Jelgava, pp. 233–237 (2016)
5. Paiu, M.C., Rahoveanu, A.T.: Rural tourism-alternative for development rural areas. In: Proceedings of the 29th International Business Information Management Association Conference - Education Excellence and Innovation Management through Vision 2020: From Regional Development Sustainability to Global Economic Growth. Vienna, pp. 958–962 (2017)
6. Chen, C.Q.: Researches on application of the renewable energy technologies in the development of low-carbon rural tourism. In: Proceedings of 2010 International Conference on Energy, Environment and Development, Kuala Lumpur, pp. 1722–1726 (2011)
7. Gao, N., He, J.: Study on green rural-tourism in undeveloped western region of China under the perspective of urban-rural integration. In: Advanced Materials Research, vol. 518–523, pp. 6075–6078 (2012)
8. Zheng, H.Y.: Rural tourism brand management. WIT Trans. Inf. Commun. Technol. **46**(3), 2303–2307 (2013)
9. Hong, T.: Study on the development of rural tourism resources based on ecotourism. Revista de la Facultad de Ingenieria **32**, 455–462 (2017)
10. Hu, J.Q.: Technical innovation of rural tourism in zhejiang: a case study of Baisha village, Hangzhou city. In: Advanced Materials Research, vol. 807–809, pp. 1721–1724 (2013)
11. Wang, J.C., Wang, N.: Rural tourism and rural development under the integrated planning background - Huangtuling village tourist plans in Laiyuan, Baoding. In: Advanced Materials Research, vol. 1044–1045, pp. 1533–1537 (2014)
12. Li, T.T., He, S.F.: Research on the participation of service design in rural social innovation, taking the social innovation of Nihegou Village as an example. Design **24**, 125–127 (2017)
13. Zhang, W.L.: Study on the rural tourism service system based on the technology embedding. Agro Food Ind. Hi-Tech **28**, 339–342 (2017)
14. Liu, D.C.: Lingshui Village treasures of traditional villages. Beijing Obs. **4**, 30–31 (2015)
15. Zhang, X.F.: Study on customer experience of family hotel in Lingshui Village, Beijing. Doctorial dissertation, Central South University of Forestry and Technology, Changsha, China (2016)
16. Kang, J.: Lingshuijuren Village in western Beijing. Beijing Arch. **10**, 41–44 (2016)

Well-Being Design for an Aging Society

Ming-Ming Zong[1](✉) and Chen Li[2]

[1] School of Design and Art, Beijing Institute of Technology,
Zhuhai, People's Republic of China
zmm77800@126.com
[2] Graduate School of Design,
National Yunlin University of Science and Technology,
Douliu, People's Republic of China
fionaleel125@qq.com

Abstract. While population aging is an irreversible global challenge, this demo-graphic shift also brings a great opportunity to design innovation. For assisting older adults' healthy and active aging, products and services should be adapted to their social identities and diverse well-being needs in their daily activities. This study addressed the question of how the integration of Science, Arts and Design (SAD) can contribute to design for older adults' overall well-being. A case study of programs in Qiqihar University, Ming-Lab and Zhuhai of BIT was used to show how to transform design for older adults from SAD in design education to CHEER in design practices. Firstly, a review of the status of SAD was conducted. As multiple technology advances, many of aging problems can utilize SAD to cope with older adults' daily problems and promote their quality of lives. The analysis of SAD enables us to identify the strengths and weaknesses of the current education systems in China as well as to discover further design trends. Then, the "CHEER" framework for well-being design is introduced that includes five main components: Collaboration, Humanity, Empathy, Ecology and Renaissance (CHEER). Each component give insight into what students could do to realize older adults' well-being through their design proposals. Furthermore, this study presented several design proposals to outlines design features, merits and challenges of the "CHEER" framework. Together with the "CHEER" framework, this study is indented to offer inspiration for de-sign researchers and educationists to join forces in their endeavors to de-sign for older adults' well-being.

Keywords: Aging society · Older adults · Well-being design
Design framework · Product and service design

1 Introduction

Population aging is one of the major challenges facing the present-day world. Taking active measures to tackle this problem is not only the responsibility of the government, but has also provided opportunities for researchers and practitioners in the design field to make service innovations and assume their social duties. In the initial stage of design for older adults, many developed countries had successfully adopted some design paradigms such as "Universal Design", "Inclusive Design", "Accessible Design" to

P.-L. P. Rau (Ed.): CCD 2018, LNCS 10912, pp. 472–483, 2018.
https://doi.org/10.1007/978-3-319-92252-2_37

enable older adults with physical and mental handicaps to maintain their independent living skills and integrate into the mainstream society [1–3]. In view of the physical, cognitive and behavioral decay that elderly users experience during their aging process, researchers and practitioners in the field of design for older adults have proposed a lot of effective solutions and displayed the humanistic concern of the design discipline itself [4].

The interesting thing about the product and service design for older adults is that it both needs to be closely linked to older adults' everyday life and culture, and needs to vary with the changes of the times and society, and this second part demonstrates its characteristic to keep up with the times. Hence, it's a challenging and constantly changing topic. In recent years, as the connection of Science, Art and Design (SAD) has become increasingly deepened, the service of and study on design for older adults in China's design education have continuously yielded good results. The products and services for older adults have become increasingly rich, but meanwhile, under the influence of SAD, the study on design for older adults on different levels has also encountered many problems. As some practical experience has shown, the design paradigms such as "Universal Design", "Inclusive Design" and so on have their limits when dealing with design for older adults' well-being, as they fail to assist designs to satisfy older adults' comprehensive needs for well-being in life. This calls for researchers and practitioners to rethink the problems that might exist in the current research framework of design for older adults. Therefore, this study mainly focuses on the research perspective and methodology in design for older adults' well-being, for they are the two core points in this filed. In view of these two points, the study takes creating well-being in life as the ultimate goal of design for older adults, and attempts to re-examine the merits and demerits that China's design education possesses in carrying out the SAD integration. Furthermore, based on the author's teaching experience over the past years, the study proposes the "CHEER" framework for well-being design and explores, by combing the author's teaching experience, whether the core concepts in the design framework could bring about crucial changes to the process of design for older adults.

2 Status of SAD in Chinese Design Education for Coping with Well-Being in Aging Society

Since the 1980s, design education has been developing for more than three decades in China, and has achieved numerous accomplishments in different aspects. In view of its overall teaching model, the integration among science, art and design has become the principal approach most colleges and universities adopt to educate and cultivate students to make design innovation. The aim of SAD integration is to break education's one-dimensionality, and nurture design students' comprehensive and integrative knowledge of science and art. In today's age of big data and artificial intelligence in particular, design education, under the guidance of SAD, will focus more on cultivating the "coordinating" and "integrating" ability of design students, and mobilize social resources for design innovation through interdisciplinary research, exchanges and cooperation. As to the issue of design for older adults, the SAD teaching model has brought about plenty of benefits to aging industry and the related service design. For example, for those problems such as poor mobility, memory loss, digital divide and so on, which are inevitably brought about by aging and which older adults often meet in daily life, SAD integration will encourage design students to conduct an interdisciplinary integration of resources, find out proper solutions to design problems, and promote the quality of life of the aged. And these are the positive effects that the SAD teaching model has brought to and will continue exerting on design for older adults.

From 2005 to 2016, we had been attempting to conduct an in-depth integration be-tween the SAD teaching model and design project on the older adults' well-being in three different universities, which are Academy of Fine Arts and Artistic Design at Qiqihar University, the Ming-lab at Beijing Institute of Technology (BIT Ming-lab), and Beijing Institute of Technology, Zhuhai (BIT, Zhuhai). During this process, we have published more than 50 studies on the well-being culture, among which 36 studies are related to aging industry. These studies cover multiple research areas of the aging society, such as life and mobility aids to the older adults with disability, garment design, household goods, interactive interfaces and the Internet service platforms, etc. In addition, BIT Zhuhai has also signed a strategic cooperation agreement with Industrial Culture Development Center of China's Ministry of Industry and Information Technology on jointly promoting the development of "the Study on Well-being Culture and Industry Services" in China.

The rise of older adults' well-being design lies in the fact that, with the gradual improvement of people's living conditions, older adults' various needs for well-being have gradually emerged. Aside from their physical and spiritual needs, they have attached greater importance to building their social connections and realizing their personal value. The notion of well-being finally leads to the "FU (福)" concept, which is frequently mentioned in Chinese culture. In traditional Chinese culture, Confucianism considers that "FU" is "being active in forging ahead, and enthusiastic in pressing on", Buddhism deems that "one's fate (FU) is in one' own hands and one should do charitable deeds and accumulate virtue to improve one's lot", and Taoism holds that "FU" is to let things take their own course and comply with nature. When the notion of "FU" is reflected in older adults' well-being design, it stands for close attention to four "Jing" states from outside to inside in older adult's daily life: the first "Jing" state refers to Environment (环境) - the social environment older adults live in; the second "Jing" state refers to Context (情景) - the context that product and service design is in; the third "Jing" state refers to State of Mind (心境) - the relaxed and pleasant user experience and atmosphere that a product or service could provide for its users; the fourth "Jing" state refers to Purity of Heart (心净) - older adults' spiritual resonance with the designer which makes them achieve an ideal state. Older adults' well-being design thinks that the value of products and services not only lies in the satisfaction of elderly users' demands for functionality, but is more about the emotional injection in the products and services, and this has elevated the design from merely satisfying the practical functions to showing humanistic care on the spiritual level. Thus, I hope that I could rethink the value of design for older adults from the perspective of well-being design, so that product and service design for older adults could better assist them to pursue their ideals in life.

Our years of project teaching experience has proved that the SAD integration is the only way towards the development of design projects for older adults' well-being. Design students should, according to the specific requirements of design projects, strive to integrate new knowledge in different disciplines, including art, medicine, psychology, mechanics, ergonomics and so on, to form their design thinking. During this process, SAD will be able to provide many new perspectives and solutions. The greater value of SAD lies in the fact that it has put forward many demands and challenges for the study of design for older adults. In common design projects, the basic demand is to find out a common problem encountered by many older adults and then manage to solve it. While in an older adults' well-being design project, SAD will guide the project towards an in-depth exploration of the notion of "FU" and offer a vague space for design students to probe in. Several questions, for example, "what are the key issues of well-being for older adults?", "what is the most effective solution at present?", are the greatest concerns of design students in projects, as well as the key factors in the intensive study of projects.

Based on the feedback of the student teams who had participated in the design project, this study will rethink the problems and challenges confronted by the application of SAD in older adults' well-being design. First are about the research perspective of well-being design and the value judgement of the well-being issue. In social gerontology, aging is not just a biological process, but a process that will bring about plural changes, including changes in one's social participation and social behavior realization, and even changes in one's social duties [5]. Hence, the perspective of older adults' well-being design should not be confined to addressing the common problems brought by physiological changes and decay of body functions, which is exactly the limitation of universal design, inclusive design, and many other many current general design paradigms. It's also necessary for older adults' well-being design to actively create the sense of happiness, reconstruct the value of life for older adults, and bring forward better solutions to satisfy older adults' individual needs. Second is about the research methodology of well-being design, and about how to weigh up the related information and transform older adults' demands for well-being into soluble issues in design. At present, the cur-rent research methods in the field of older adults' well-being design are not flexible enough, with research methods related to "ergonomics" and "human factors" being the dominant methods. Both undergraduate and graduate design education haven't carried out a systematical instruction of those new research methods such as emotional design, user experience and service design, thus these methods haven't been widely applied in the field of design for older adults. This has led to severe homogenization among the practical design projects for older adults, and "functionality" has become the only connection between the design and older adults. For those who have been through the vicissitudes of life, although such function-oriented products could bring them convenience in life, the products can hardly satisfy their high-level demands and expectations, thus they might be easily rejected. What's more, long-term focus on the negative effects of aging will also exert some influence on design students' cognitive patterns of design for older adults, and may also hinder their positive and systematical design thinking when design for older adults.

3   CHEER Design Framework for Older Adults' Well-Being

Based on reflections upon the in-depth SAD integration in older adults' well-being design, this study proposes that design in this filed should expand its research vision, update its research methodology, and re-judge its design framework in accordance with the related professional principles and the current national conditions, in order to explore how to apply SAD integration to making rational older adults' well-being design. Through summarizing the teaching cases in older adults' well-being education in Academy of Fine Arts and Artistic Design at Qiqihar University, BIT Ming-lab, and BIT, Zhuhai in recent years, this study believes that a systematical framework that can discover and solve problems is needed in student teams' learning of older adults' well-being design. In design, to simplify problems casually or to take some issues for granted is inadvisable, just as merely paying attention to solutions that can lead to actual production is wrong.

After conducting a careful literature review regarding the practical process of a series of completed older adults' well-being design projects, this study has found that student teams frequently encounter difficulties in the following five steps: "demand analysis", "concept generation", "experience design", "solution selection" and "prototype test". Thus, in view of the specific requirements of each step, the researcher of this paper has put forward five ingredients, namely, "collaboration", "humanity", "empathy", "ecology", and "renaissance", and they together form the "CHEER" design framework for older adults' well-being (see Fig. 1). The aim of this design framework is to guide the design for older adult to base itself on the concept of well-being, attach adequate importance to the inner connection between design and older adults, and strive to improve the well-being of the elderly through design. And this framework helps design students to figure out what older adults' well-being is truly about before they start working on it, assist them to seek out the critical factors in tackling related problems, and provide them with meaningful insights in their efforts to realize well-being for the elderly.

4   Five Ingredients for Older Adults' Well-Being Design

The core of the "CHEER" design framework includes five ingredients: Collaboration, Humanity, Empathy, Ecology, and Renaissance, and they together demonstrate the connotations and requirements of older adults' well-being design in each step under the guidance of the SAD. The five ingredients can be applied to many a research project, for example, projects of the products, environment and interactive interfaces related to older adults' lives. Although these five ingredients are common to many different design cases, they can help students to learn how to make their proposals come true, and how to effectively respond to users' individualized demands which are based on their own life experience. Next, the study will introduce these five ingredients one by one, and use some cases to illustrate how these ingredients can exert a positive impact on design students' proposals.

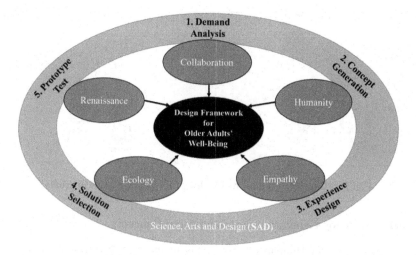

Fig. 1. "CHEER" design framework for older adults' well-being.

4.1 Collaboration for Analyzing Older Adults' Everyday Needs

Collaboration constitutes the first ingredient in the framework, and it relates to how design student teams analyze older adults' everyday needs in older adults' well-being design projects. The goal of well-being design is to stimulate students' divergent thinking, create ample flexibility in the design projects, and make design students experience difficulty in demand analysis. Thus, the concept of Collaboration has been put forward to guide design teams, in their exploring the life of older adults, to collaborate with elderly users as well as experts in other disciplines so as to draw on others' diverse experience and make proper analysis of older adults' well-being needs at different levels.

In well-being design case of the diet of older adults carried out by BIT Ming-lab, the student team hoped to use their design to assist older adults to make nutritious breakfast easily, but they had no idea how to make proper demand analysis. Then, the teacher encouraged them to conduct multiple negotiations with the enterprise so as to determine which kinds of resources could finally be integrated. At last, under the jointly efforts of the enterprise and the students, the team set urban empty-nesters as their target customers, and conducted further investigation and analysis of the empty-nesters' demands for breakfast. In the end, the team found that older adults attach great importance to nutritionally balanced breakfast and have relatively fixed eating habit. The match of porridge and eggs, or the match of yogurt and fruit juice, is the most common breakfast match among the empty-nest elderly, and "warmth", "convenience", "multi-functionality" and "being easy to clean" constitute the greatest concern of older adults. Thus, the team ultimately devised the "Double" breakfast machine to elevate older adults' sense of happiness when eating breakfast, and the product has gained recognition from both elderly users and the enterprise (see Fig. 2).

478   M.-M. Zong and C. Li

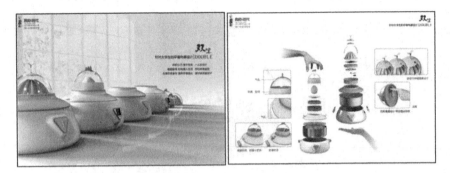

Fig. 2. "Double" breakfast maker design for empty-nest older adults.

4.2 Humanity for Generating Suitable Design Concepts

The second ingredient Humanity corresponds to the step "Concept Generation" in design. To solve the social problems related to the aging of the population calls for a re-examination of the living state of older adults. The concept generation in older adults' well-being projects should abide by the fundamental concept of Humanity, and integrate science and art with older adults' life, culture, and aesthetic values. Only in this way can the well-being value of design concept be improved.

In a well-being design case of older adults' clothing conducted by Academy of Fine Arts and Artistic Design at Qiqihar University, the design team took "humanized design" of older adults' clothing as the standard for its concept generation, and divided older adults into three types according to their physical conditions, namely, the healthy type, the sedentary type, and the recumbent type. Then, the team conducted a thorough and systematical analysis of the relationship between the physical and mental features of these three types of older adults and the humanized design of clothing, and analyzed the application of the humanized design of clothing. Specifically, based on the physical and mental features of older adults, the team carefully examined the characteristics and causes of the style, structure, fabric, color and decoration of older adults' clothes made under the principle of humanized design. Guided by the Humanity concept, the design team has finally put forward a design proposal which both guarantees an elegant clothing style for all the three types of older adults and ensures that all clothes are easy to wear in daily life. Besides, their design proposal has also taken into account older adults' self-esteem and their wish to be fashionable, so it has successfully enhanced older adults' sense of happiness through improving their clothing (see Fig. 3).

4.3 Empathy for Understanding Deep User Experience

The third ingredient Empathy corresponds to design students' in-depth understanding of user experience after the step of "Experience Design". When it's necessary for a design team without any elderly member to conduct experience design for older adults, the team should depend on empathy to make the right decision [7]. Therefore, to assist student design teams to understand older adults and their experience is an essential task in promoting the experience design for older adults' well-being. The concept of

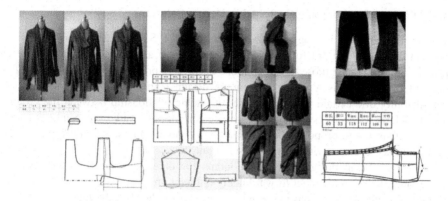

Fig. 3. Garment design for older adults with different physical conditions.

"empathy" in the "CHEER" design framework is aimed to help designers develop their empathy and get increasingly closer to older adults' life and experience, and to increase the possibility that a certain product or service design can satisfy the needs of elderly users.

In a well-being design case about the community fitness facilities for older adults carried out by BIT Ming-lab, the design team has conducted a one-month investigation in communities to observe the exercise environment for older adults, and interviewed many older adults there, trying to figure out how to create better exercise experience for older adults living in cities. The students managed to learn more about the interpersonal interaction and man-machine interaction during older adults' fitness process. This has helped them to properly understand the authentic exercise experience of older adults and find out the problems in their exercise process. At last, the design team found four typical exercise models among older adults, and has successfully developed a fitness program "Elder-Fitness", which better meets the fitness requirements of older adults in communities (see Fig. 4).

Fig. 4. Fitness apparatus design for older adults in urban community.

4.4   Ecology for Choosing Sustainable Design Solutions

The fourth ingredient Ecology corresponds to the step "Solution Selection" in design. Student teams usually put forward several solutions to a project, so how to select a proper solution among those many solutions becomes a problem to be considered. The concept of Ecology is aimed to encourage design teams to take into account the sustainability of a certain proposal so that the stable relationship between the product and its elderly users can be enhanced, resource consumption and waste can be reduced, and excellent design proposals both promoting economic and social development and protecting ecological environment can stand out [8].

In a well-being design case about lamps for older adults carried out by BIT Ming-lab, the design team put forward many different proposals with a view to the fact that older adults often get up in the night to use the toilet. But the team got stuck in choosing an ultimate proposal to carry the design forward. Thus, the teacher enlightened the students and asked them to think which design proposals conform to the concept of Ecology and possess sustainable value. In the end, the team chose the proposal using the natural material loofah to design lamps (see Fig. 5). This design concept highlights the power of dim light and brings warm lighting to older adults at night. Also, its design thinking featured by anti-functionality has made the design attach importance to the transmission of emotions. What's more, the natural material loofah makes the product economical, durable, environmentally friendly, heat-insulated, and can be easily replaced if damaged. Thus, this design has given consideration to the overall interests of the product's developers and users, and it also conforms to the target of well-being design.

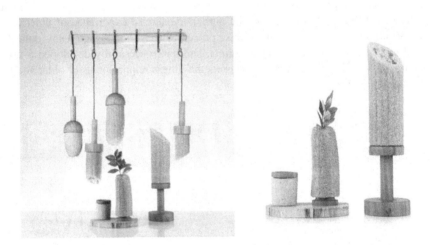

Fig. 5. Loofah night lighting design for older adults' bedroom.

4.5   Renaissance for Promoting Older Adults' Flourishing

The last ingredient Renaissance in the design framework is aimed at the problems in the prototype test of products and services. Renaissance means to promote the flourishing of the user and help the user regain the vigor and vitality of life. For design for older adults centered on well-being, a good prototype test should be able to find out whether the design could promote the flourishing of older adults [9]. Renaissance can remind design student teams who conduct prototype tests to pay attention to whether a prototype could stimulate older adults' sanguine attitude and actively bring into full play their personal potential, and whether a prototype could assist older adults to become what they want to become or become their best selves.

In a well-being design about older adults' wheelchairs carried out by BIT Ming-lab, the design team found that there is no or no obvious difference between the older adults having difficulty getting about and other ordinary older adults in terms of both groups' cognitive processes, such as perception, attention, memory, thinking. And the design team also found that the older adults having difficulty getting about are not very much hindered in their general life and work. The team hoped that their design could stimulate the enthusiasm of the older adults having difficulty getting about to move around and complete the necessary actions in life without the help of nursing staff, and hoped that their design could boost the vitality and sense of achievement of these elderly users. Therefore, the design team took whether older adults are willing to independently use this wheelchair both indoors and outdoors as the criterion for their prototype test, and received positive feedback from most older adults having difficulty getting about. Then, they settled on this following design proposal (see Fig. 6).

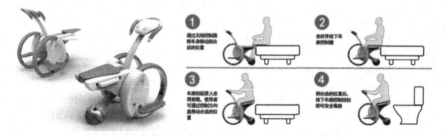

Fig. 6. Wheelchair design for older adults' with low-mobility.

5 Challenges and Suggestion in Realizing Older Adults' Well-Being in Design Practices

The project of older adults' well-being design has been conducted for many years in the Academy of Fine Arts and Artistic Design at Qiqihar University and the Ming-lab at Beijing Institute of Technology, and it's still in its initial stage in Beijing Institute of Technology, Zhuhai. Thanks to the endeavors of teachers and students in different universities, the older adults' well-being design framework based on SAD has been put forward and testified. The design framework includes five ingredients corresponding to each of the five steps in design projects, as problems may easily arise in these five steps. Under the guidance of the five ingredients, a group of good designs for the well-being of older adults have been made, covering many fields closely linked to older adults' lives, such as products, environmental improvement, clothing design and so on, and these designs have received positive feedback from both students and older adults. Such experience has made the researcher of this study more convinced that because older adults differ from one another in many aspects, such as the decay of body function, life experience, behavioral motives, means to ameliorate the situation and so on, it's very difficult to study this user group as a subject with common character. On the contrary, older adults' well-being design should not only tackle the common problems on the surface, but should also try to find out solutions to those individualized problems by going deep into older adults' lives, so as to build up an effective link between the education of design for older adults and China's manufacturing industry. This is a principal challenge for older adults' well-being design, as well as the only way to its further development.

In addition, through detailed analyses of the living state of older adults, and by exploring the features of the sense of happiness aroused by products, the project of older adults' well-being design has found that products and services often play multiple roles in the life of older adults. For instance, instead of merely making up for the physical deficiency brought about by aging, the use of products and services can promote the communication among family members, friends and relatives, and can also help individuals to enhance their personal abilities. Therefore, products and services would appear in varied life situations, and serve as the medium for the sense of happiness. Based on the many cases of older adults' well-being design, the study continues to propose three suggestions on the development of older adults' well-being design. First, pay attention to how products and services exist in older adults' everyday life, so that these products and services could better satisfy the everyday needs of older adults and get integrated into their daily activities. Second, manage to help older adults experience happiness in using products and services. A certain design can not only bring about practical products and services to older adults, but can also encourage them to develop positive attitudes and habits in life and help them to re-construct their connections with society after they retired. Third, try to increase the attractiveness of products and services, as well as the customer loyalty, so that older adults can discover, experience and construct the true happiness in their lives, and lead a healthier, fuller and vigorous life under the guidance of the products.

6   Conclusion

Adopting the perspective of well-being design, this study has analyzed the development process of products and services for older adults, made the attempt to re-examine the merits and demerits that China's design education possesses in implementing SAD integration, and has put forward the "CHEER" framework for well-being design based on the researcher's teaching experience over the past years. The study has summarized the author's years of teaching experience at the Academy of Fine Arts and Artistic Design at Qiqihar University, the Ming-lab at Beijing Institute of Technology, and Beijing Institute of Technology, Zhuhai, and explored how the key concepts in the design framework can help to solve the difficulties and problems during the process of design for older adults. Employing the research method of case study, this study has found that the "CHEER" design framework can assist design student teams to gain a thorough understanding of older adults' everyday needs and then satisfy these needs, so that student teams can have the opportunity to make their designs powerful enough to touch every aspect in older adults' well-being culture, such as the environment for one's old-age life, life services, the development of well-being products and so on. With the aid of the older adults' well-being design project, which is a design exploration and attempt full of humanistic care, this study is aimed to promote the more systematic and maturer development of older adults' well-being design under the joint endeavors of designers and researchers. The follow-up research of this project will expand its scope from Chinese culture to the global aging culture so as to seek more international cooperation opportunities in the field of older adults' well-being design, and bring well-being to older adults all over the world.

References

1. Mace, R.: What is universal design. The Center for Universal Design at North Carolina State University, USA (1997)
2. Clarkson, P.J., et al.: Inclusive Design: Design for the Whole Population. Springer Science & Business Media, USA (2013). https://doi.org/10.1007/978-1-4471-0001-0
3. Erlandson, R.F.: Universal and Accessible Design for Products, Services, and Processes. CRC Press, Boca Raton (2007)
4. Fisk, A.D., et al.: Designing for Older Adults: Principles and Creative Human Factors Approaches. CRC Press, Boca Raton (2009)
5. Hooyman, N.R., Kiyak, H.A.: Social Gerontology: A Multidisciplinary Perspective. Pearson Education, London (2008)
6. Righi, V., Sayago, S., Blat, J.: When we talk about older people in HCI, who are we talking about? Towards a 'turn to community'in the design of technologies for a growing ageing population. Int. J. Hum.-Comput. Stud. **108**, 15–31 (2017)
7. Kouprie, M., Visser, F.S.: A framework for empathy in design: stepping into and out of the user's life. J. Eng. Des. **20**(5), 437–448 (2009)
8. Williams, D.E.: Sustainable Design: Ecology, Architecture, and Planning. Wiley, Hoboken (2007)
9. Desmet, P.M., Pohlmeyer, A.E.: Positive design: an introduction to design for subjective well-being. Int. J. Des. **7**(3), 5–19 (2013)

Author Index

Printed in the United States
By Bookmasters